D1429478

This second volume of the history of Cambridge University Press deals with a period of fundamental changes in printing, publishing and bookselling. The purpose of this book is not only to chronicle the history of the Press, but also to set it in this context of change: to examine how the forces of commerce collided with the hopes or demands of scholarship and education, and how, in the end, one was made to exploit the other.

The volume opens with the new arrangements made by the University for printing in Cambridge in the 1690s, and closes on the eve of the opening of new premises in London. In the first years, the leading figure was Richard Bentley, whose controversial part in the activities of the Press was critical to its fortunes. As always, the success of the Press depended on London and the London book trade. This book explores the changing nature of this relationship, and the extent to which the University Press also became an international publisher. Drawing on hitherto unused documents, and setting them alongside the books that were printed by the University Press, Dr McKitterick has frequently revised its received history, and has set it in a new light.

A HISTORY OF

CAMBRIDGE UNIVERSITY PRESS

VOLUME 2

Richard Bentley, by Sir James Thornhill, 1710.

A HISTORY OF

CAMBRIDGE UNIVERSITY PRESS

VOLUME 2

SCHOLARSHIP AND
COMMERCE
1698–1872

DAVID McKITTERICK

Fellow and Librarian
Trinity College, Cambridge

PUBLISHED BY THE PRESS SYNDICATE OF THE UNIVERSITY OF CAMBRIDGE
The Pitt Building, Trumpington Street, Cambridge CB2 1RP, United Kingdom

CAMBRIDGE UNIVERSITY PRESS
The Edinburgh Building, Cambridge CB2 2RU, United Kingdom
40 West 20th Street, New York, NY 10011-4211, USA
10 Stamford Road, Oakleigh, Melbourne 3166, Australia

First published 1998

Printed in the United Kingdom at the University Press, Cambridge

Typeset in 11/13 pt Fournier   [SE]

A catalogue record for this book is available from the British Library

ISBN 0 521 30802 x hardback

CONTENTS

ILLUSTRATIONS

The device on the title-page was originally engraved by Simon Gribelin in 1711.

Sources

Illustrations are reproduced by permission of the following: the Syndics of Cambridge University Library (figs. 3, 10, 13, 14, 16, 17); the Keeper, Cambridge University Archives (fig. 29); the Master and Fellows, Trinity College, Cambridge (frontispiece, figs. 1, 4, 5, 6, 7, 8, 9, 11, 18, 19, 24, 25, 26; the President and Fellows, Queens' College, Cambridge (fig. 2); Cambridge University Press (figs. 23, 28); Birmingham Museums and Art Gallery (fig. 12); the British and Foreign Bible Society (figs. 27, 31); the Trustees of the Chevening Estate (fig. 22); private collection (figs. 15, 20, 21, 30). All photographs of materials in Cambridge have been taken by the staff of the Photography Department of the University Library, to whom I am especially grateful for dealing cheerfully and skilfully with some unusual challenges.

PREFACE

The first volume in this history of university printing and publishing at Cambridge began with the licence granted by Henry VIII in 1534 to the University to print 'omnimodos libros', all manner of books. It considered the output of the several University Printers between the appointment of Thomas Thomas in 1583 and the later years of John Hayes in the 1690s. For most of this period, the University was responsible for licensing what was printed, and for appointing University Printers, in accordance with the provisions of 1534 and subsequent legislation. Most importantly, the authority of the University permitted its Printers to print the privileged books, the Bible and the Book of Common Prayer, besides the metrical psalms. For those Printers who chose to print these books, they provided a financial bedrock.

In other words, while individual University Printers were answerable to the University, their everyday business was their own: they were private businessmen, without finance other than what they could themselves raise. They owned their own equipment – presses, type and other accessories – and they owned or rented property in which to work. In practice, it became the custom for such essentials to pass on from one generation to another. Although to some extent the same became true of the rights to print individual books, most business was arranged between individuals or their estates. Such rights were part of a corporate inheritance. The University was a customer, and a vital one; it was not the owner.

The 1690s brought a crisis, and fundamental change. The crisis was the result of agreements reached between the University Printer, John Hayes, and the oldest and most serious rival to the prosperity of printing at Cambridge, the Stationers' Company. By concentrating, as a consequence, on the more profitable parts of the trade at the expense of learning and scholarship, Hayes exposed his position to criticism from those by whose licence he worked. Hayes was permitted to work out his career as University Printer; but meanwhile in 1696 the University took up the reins as an institution, with the creation of a committee whose duty it was to oversee a newly founded Press. A printing house, new presses and new type were all vested in the University corporately, with money raised on its behalf from private benefaction. Henceforth, the private activities of University Printers were circumscribed by the interests of the University more generally.

Much of the present book is concerned with the ways in which, generation by generation, tensions varied between private and corporate interests, between University Printers and the University that employed them. It is also concerned with the extent to which it was possible to run a printing house according to the ideals expressed in the 1690s: ideals having little regard for publishing or distribution, or therefore for cash-flow. As a study of a printing house, it is much concerned with materials – type and paper, and the means of printing – and with those responsible for their choice and exploitation. As books were sent out into the world, so comments returned, requiring adjustment or justification. Behind these activities lay the authors and the booksellers, mostly but by no means entirely in Cambridge. For a university press, those responsible in the 1690s assumed that the constituency of reading was international. At that time the focus was principally on north-west Europe. By the 1860s it was world-wide.

Such questions impose a complicated agenda. On the one hand, the everyday working of the Press, as printer and to varying extent as publisher, dictates this book's central concern. McKenzie's authoritative study of the early years, between 1696 (when the new arrangements were conceived) and 1712, remains unrivalled as a study of an early printing house at work. Given its existence, it is unnecessary to repeat much of what can be read there, although I have tried to convey sufficient for those without access to his two volumes or who wish to follow the course of the Press's history simply between these two covers. Instead, the focus of these early years has been shifted towards the political and intellectual background to its foundation, and to a fuller consideration than has appeared anywhere hitherto of the extent to which, almost for the first time, the Press achieved a European presence.

As in the previous volume, the following pages follow a broadly chronological pattern. To a very great extent they are constructed on the periods of time during which individual University Printers held office. But three principal considerations override this pattern: first, the changes in the manufacture of books; second, events and tendencies in the world of printing and publishing outside Cambridge; and third, the recurrent interests and preoccupations of successive generations of printers, regardless of the means employed to meet them.

While to a great extent mechanical and other technical changes took place in the printing and allied industries within an unusually short space of time – shorter than for many other manufacturing industries – the most dramatic of them, including the introduction of iron and then machine presses, the development of stereotyping and the mechanisation of paper-making, occurred in the midst of a prolonged series of smaller changes and attempts at change. The ordinary divide adopted by historians between a hand-press period and a machine press period, often dated conventionally if overapproximately at about 1800, conceals the nature of this process. Since this book covers a period that comfortably spans this date, the theme of changes in the various processes in the manufacture of books is a constant one. My purpose is to emphasise the gradual course of change, in an industry encompassing both printing and publishing, manufacture and distribution, and to explore something of the state of continuous change that characterises, to greater or lesser degree, at least some parts of these activities throughout their history – if most dramatically in the nineteenth century and since. Within this, I have also sought to explore the consequences for those who worked in these activities, as changes in technology and in the circulation of books (and hence money or credit) imposed their own programme and requirements.

The second principal theme is the relationship between printing and publishing, including financing and distribution. It was misunderstood and under-estimated in the 1690s, and it was only partially resolved by 1870. For the whole of this volume, the University Press was a printer; its publishing activities were intermittent, and frequently marked by failure. It therefore depended directly on booksellers or authors, apart from the University itself, as customers for its skills; for long periods there was little sign of initiative even when others were making profits that it might have reaped for itself.

At the core of this was the privilege to print the English Bible and prayer book. As a consequence, these books figure repeatedly, and to an extent that might appear disproportionate in a study of almost any other press. In the history of the manufacture of these books, which required constant attention to costs, quality and materials, in a context of editions vastly larger than those of any other books printed at Cambridge, is some of the most fruitful evidence for the nature of changes in printing over the period of almost two centuries covered by this book. From the consequences of the tension between the money to be gained from printing the privileged books, and the much more difficult proposition that an academic press existed to print for the convenience of those by whom it was established (essentially the position taken by Richard Bentley in the 1690s), come the words in my title, commerce and scholarship. But these words apply not only to the tensions surrounding the manufacture of the privileged books. Further tensions always existed between printing and publishing, and between scholarly ideals and the ordinary everyday reality born of dullness, laziness or neglect. Commerce and scholarship were by no means always comfortable bedfellows, and at some periods they were in conflict.

This volume ends on the eve of the Press's opening a branch in London. In retrospect, the establishment of a London office, rather than continuing the tradition of an agency, appears to have been an arrangement made with astonishing speed after the briefest of discussions in Cambridge. But it also signified a sea-change in purpose and attitude on the part of the Syndics. In so far as there was any immediate pressure for so profound a reform, it was the knowledge that within a short time the two University Presses of Oxford and Cambridge would be publishing a revised version of the English Bible, the first major translation into English since the Authorized or King James version of 1611. The move also brought the Press, as an organisation, into the world of London publishers, and thus made it possible to compete on more equal terms in the new worlds of school texts. In a manner of speaking, the country had come to London. The London office expanded rapidly, and with it a London warehouse. By the twentieth century it had grown so much that there was considerable tension between those in London, who considered themselves publishers but who had no direct control over what they published, and those in Cambridge, who were charged with the

University Press as a whole, including decisions both as to what was published, and how it should be printed, but who had little or no direct knowledge of London publishing. The inevitable rivalries and jealousies that were the result were not laid to rest until the London office was finally closed. The Press maintained its presence in London until the Edinburgh Building was completed at Cambridge in 1981, next to the new printing house completed in 1963, and the whole of its activities could at last again be brought together on one site for the first time since the mid-nineteenth century. The opening in London is thus an appropriate terminus for the present volume, and preparation for the next and last.

As in the sixteenth and seventeenth centuries, the dominant theme in the eighteenth and most of the nineteenth is therefore, again, one of tensions: between Cambridge and London; between printer and publisher, whether in Cambridge itself or elsewhere; between production, distribution and (thus) finance; between decisions as to what should be printed, and the means whereby the world should learn of the resulting books. Even in Cambridge these were not easy matters. For many, if they thought about it, the University Press existed more as a necessary adjunct to education, preaching or administration than as a learned printer or publisher whose books were addressed to a market that was ultimately international. Others in the first years of the nineteenth century questioned the very basis of its prosperity, when they argued that a university founded on the established church should not print Bibles for nonconformists. Through all this there ran a common theme: whether, or how, the Press should acknowledge that in order to survive it should seek out markets for its works, and how much it should be permitted to exist simply as a vehicle for some activities of the University. As the promoters of the new University Press in the 1690s, and those responsible for it in the 1870s, both discovered, it was a stark choice between *succès d'estime* and the realities of a publishing world in which London always dominated. In other words, and from a very different perspective, the University Press sought success in ways that had much in common with those printers who took advantage of the lapsing of the Licensing Acts in 1695, and established themselves independently of London authority.

Thus this volume is defined both by events in the University, and by events in the Press's own history, of printing and publishing. It is impossible to understand the history of the University Press without also constantly recalling the preoccupations, tendencies, personal skills, animosities and energies of those to whom it was responsible, and on whose behalf it was operated: members of the University themselves. I have, therefore, placed considerable stress on the nature and development of the University during this period: on its own internal affairs, on the powers of the colleges as they affected, or were exploited by, their members, on changes in teaching and in scholarship or research, and, crucially, on changes in the University's relationship with the world at large, both academically and politically. I read Peter Searby's recent history of the University between 1750 and 1870 only after I had finished writing this book. Until its publication, students of the subject have largely relied – as for some aspects they will always rely – on monographs now of considerable age. The two accounts by Christopher Wordsworth of the studies of the University in the eighteenth century, and of life at Oxford and Cambridge more generally during this time, are more than a century old. D. A. Winstanley's volumes on eighteenth- and nineteenth-century Cambridge are highly selective in their dealings, though essential accompaniments to anyone venturing in this territory.

In view of these several considerations, and so that the history of the Press may be understood in its proper local as well as its larger context, I have in the following pages referred continually to matters that some may regard as being beyond the ordinary bounds of the history of a printing and publishing house. Only by considering the intellectual and social context of the University Press may some understanding be gained of its ability to survive where others would have perished. To understand that also requires some appreciation of the history of printing and the book trade more generally. Conversely, it is also my hope that in treating the history of a single institution, I have cast light on wider questions, particularly on the history of the book in this country.

ACKNOWLEDGEMENTS

To write a second volume on a subject, and as a consequence frequently to call on the same people again, is to incur a double debt. I am therefore the more grateful to the many people who have been ready with help, knowledge or advice. Once again, and most of all, this volume owes more to Don McKenzie than he may immediately wish to realise. To him, my debts are part bibliographical, part historical and part personal. To everyone familiar with his account of Cambridge University Press between 1696 and 1712, it will be evident how much I have drawn on his work, though I have introduced further aspects of the history of the University Press at this time. Some of this was used in a lecture delivered in his honour at Oxford in 1996. Although the selective nature of the surviving documents for subsequent years makes it impossible to consider the everyday working of the Press in quite such illuminating detail, this book is built on his foundations.

The papers on which he drew are mostly in the University Archives, which house the larger part of the documents used in this volume. In 1973 Messrs Chadwyck-Healey, as part of a major programme to publish the archives of the book trade, issued many of the Press's archives on microfilm, thereby much easing my task. However, the great quantity of records deposited since then by the Press in the University Archives has added considerably to the demands I have made there, especially of Elisabeth Leedham-Green. Without her having set a complicated archive in order, and then facing my innumerable everyday enquiries, this volume could not have been written.

Most of the work for this volume has been done in the University Library and in the library of Trinity College. To the staff of one, and to my colleagues in the other, I offer my thanks, here as always. Elsewhere in Cambridge, I have called freely on college libraries and archives, and have invariably been met with generosity. In the British Library, I am particularly grateful to the staffs of the Reading Room, the North Library and the Students' Room in the Department of Manuscripts, as well as to others hidden behind the scenes – the more so as they faced an exceedingly difficult period in the Library's history. The Guildhall Library and the St Bride Printing Library have both been essential, as has the National Register of Archives. The late Dr Gordon Huelin made me welcome among the archives of the SPCK. When I began this volume, the archives of the Bible Society were still in London, and had not moved to Cambridge. I am grateful to both societies for allowing me to use their collections. At Oxford, and as usual, much of the history of Cambridge is to be found in the Bodleian Library, while at Oxford University Press Peter Foden has been of great help. Reading University Library houses the publishers' archives of J. W. Parker and part of those of Macmillan; and at Didcot I have had the advantage of using the archives of W. H. Smith, where Mr T. W. Baker-Jones made my task a pleasant one. In the United States, I have received especial help in the Houghton and the Widener Libraries at Harvard. Other matters became better focused as a result of visits to the Netherlands and Australia. Many other obligations have arisen piecemeal; I record especially the contributions of Hugh and Judy Amory, Giles Barber, Alan Bell, Michael Black, Anne Dickson, Don Eddy, Simon Eliot, Bernhard Fabian, Peter Filby, the Ven. D. N. Griffiths, Edith Hazen, Theodore Hofmann, Arnold Hunt, Ian Kidman, Wallace Kirsop, Richard Landon, John Lane, John Morris, Mike Petty, Nicholas Pickwoad, Mary Pollard, David Riley, Marvin Spevack, Frank Stubbings, Jonathan Topham, Ian Willison and Michael Winship. No-one working on eighteenth-century printing in Britain can neglect Keith Maslen and John Lancaster's edition of the Bowyer ledgers, and I would like to record here my particular thanks to these two old friends. I must also once again thank the many antiquarian and second-hand booksellers, in several countries, who have tolerated prolonged searches on their shelves and on their stalls. By providing perspectives utterly different from the more systematic collections of libraries, they have often forced me to take a different view – I trust to the benefit of the reader.

For various reasons, this book has been long in the making. The University Press has been generously patient. But one result has been that my wife and daughter have shared a correspondingly long gestation. In their different ways, their help, encouragement and wisdom have been crucial.

ABBREVIATIONS

In the following list of abbreviations and in the notes all books are published in London unless otherwise stated.

Baker-Mayor   Thomas Baker, *History of the College of St. John the Evangelist, Cambridge*, ed. J. E. B. Mayor, 2 vols. (Cambridge, 1869)

Bentley, *Correspondence*   Richard Bentley, *Correspondence*, ed. Christopher Wordsworth, 2 vols. (1842)

Bennet and Clements, *Notebooks*   Norma Hodgson and Cyprian Blagden (eds.), *The notebook of Thomas Bennet and Henry Clements (1686–1719); with some aspects of book trade practice* (Oxford Bibliographical Soc., 1956)

Black, *Cambridge University Press*   M. H. Black, *Cambridge University Press, 1584–1984* (Cambridge, 1984)

Boase, *Modern English biography*   Frederic Boase, *Modern English biography*, 6 vols. (1892–1921)

Bowes, *Catalogue*   Robert Bowes, *A catalogue of books printed at or relating to the University and town of Cambridge from 1521 to 1893* (Cambridge, 1894)

Bowyer ledgers   Keith Maslen and John Lancaster (eds.), *The Bowyer ledgers; the printing accounts of William Bowyer father and son, with a checklist of Bowyer printing 1699–1777* (Bibliographical Soc. and Bibliographical Soc. of America, 1991)

Cambridge under Queen Anne   J. E. B. Mayor (ed.), *Cambridge under Queen Anne, illustrated by memoir of Ambrose Bonwicke and diaries of Francis Burman and Zacharias Conrad von Uffenbach* (Cambridge Antiquarian Soc., 1911)

Carter, *Oxford University Press*   Harry Carter, *A history of the Oxford University Press. 1. To the year 1780* (Oxford, 1975)

Clark, *Endowments*   J. W. Clark (ed.), *Endowments of the University of Cambridge* (Cambridge, 1904)

Cole, *Correspondence*   *Horace Walpole's correspondence with the Rev. William Cole*, ed. W. S. Lewis and A. Dayle Wallace, 2 vols. (New Haven, 1937) (Yale edition of Horace Walpole's correspondence)

Coleman, *British paper industry*   D. C. Coleman, *The British paper industry, 1495–1860; a study in industrial growth* (Oxford, 1958)

Cooper, *Annals*   C. H. Cooper, *Annals of Cambridge*, 5 vols. (Cambridge, 1842–1908)

Darlow and Moule   T. H. Darlow and H. F. Moule, *Historical catalogue of the printed editions of holy scripture in the library of the British and Foreign Bible Society*, 2 vols. (1903–11)

DNB   *Dictionary of national biography*

Dyer, *Privileges*   George Dyer, *The privileges of the University of Cambridge*, 2 vols. (1824)

Enschedé, *Typefoundries*   Charles Enschedé, *Typefoundries in the Netherlands from the fifteenth to the nineteenth century*, trans. and revised by Harry Carter and Netty Hoeflake, ed. Lotte Hellinga (Haarlem, 1978)

ESTC   Eighteenth century short title catalogue

Foxon   D. F. Foxon, *English verse 1701–1750; a catalogue of separately printed poems with notes on contemporary collected editions*, 2 vols. (Cambridge, 1975)

Gaskell, *New introduction*   Philip Gaskell, *A new introduction to bibliography*, repr. with corrections (Oxford, 1974)

Gray, *Correspondence*   Thomas Gray, *Correspondence*, ed. Paget Toynbee and Leonard Whibley, with corrections and additions by H. W. Starr, 3 vols. (Oxford, 1971)

Gunning, *Reminiscences*   Henry Gunning, *Reminiscences of the University, town and country of Cambridge*, 2 vols. (Cambridge, 1854)

Hansard, *Typographia*   T. C. Hansard, *Typographia: an historical sketch of the origin and progress of the art of printing* (1825)

Hearne, *Remarks and collections*   Thomas Hearne, *Remarks and collections*, ed. C. E. Doble etc., 11 vols. (Oxford Historical Soc., 1885–1921)

Herbert, *Historical catalogue*   A. S. Herbert, *Historical catalogue of printed editions of the English Bible, 1525–1961, revised and expanded from the edition of T. H. Darlow and H. F. Moule* (1968)

Historical MSS Commn   Royal Commission on Historical Manuscripts

Historical register   J. R. Tanner, *The historical register of the University of Cambridge ... to the year 1910* (Cambridge, 1910)

Howe, *London compositor*   Ellic Howe, *The London compositor, 1785–1900* (Bibliographical Soc., 1947)

Johnson, *Letters*   Samuel Johnson, *Letters*, ed. Bruce Redford, 5 vols. (Princeton, 1992–4)

JPHS   Journal of the Printing Historical Society

JWCI   Journal of the Warburg and Cortauld Institutes

Locke, *Correspondence*   John Locke, *Correspondence*, ed. E. S. de Beer, 8 vols. (Oxford, 1976–89)

McKenzie, *Apprentices 1701–1800*   D. F. McKenzie, *Stationers' Company apprentices, 1701–1800* (Oxford Bibliographical Soc., 1978)

McKenzie, *Cambridge University Press*   D. F. McKenzie, *The Cambridge University Press, 1696–1712; a bibliographical study*, 2 vols. (Cambridge, 1966)

McKitterick, *Cambridge University Library*   David McKitterick, *Cambridge University Library; a history. The eighteenth and nineteenth centuries* (Cambridge, 1986)

McKitterick, *Cambridge University Press*, 1   David McKitterick, *A history of Cambridge University Press. 1. Printing and the book trade in Cambridge, 1534–1698* (Cambridge, 1992)

McKitterick, *Four hundred years*   David McKitterick, *Four hundred years of university printing and publishing in Cambridge, 1584–1984* (Cambridge, 1984)

Maxted, *London book trades*   Ian Maxted, *The London book trades, 1775–1800; a preliminary checklist of members* (Folkestone, 1977)

Monk, *Bentley*   J. H. Monk, *The life of Richard Bentley, D.D.*, 2nd edn, 2 vols. (1833)

Moxon, *Mechanick exercises*   Joseph Moxon, *Mechanick exercies on the whole art of printing (1683–4)*, ed. Herbert Davis and Harry Carter, 2nd edn (Oxford, 1962)

NCBEL   The new Cambridge bibliography of English literature, ed. George Watson and Ian Willison, 5 vols. (Cambridge, 1969–77)

Newton, *Correspondence* Sir Isaac Newton, *Correspondence*, ed. H. W. Turnbull *et al.*, 7 vols. (Cambridge, 1959–77)

Nichols, *Illustrations* J. and J. B. Nichols, *Illustrations of the literary history of the eighteenth century*, 8 vols. (1817–58)

Nichols, *Literary anecdotes* J. Nichols, *Literary anecdotes of the eighteenth century*, 9 vols. (1812–16)

Oates, *Cambridge University Library* J. C. T. Oates, *Cambridge University Library; a history. From the beginnings to the Copyright Act of Queen Anne* (Cambridge, 1986)

PBSA *Papers of the Bibliographical Society of America*

Philip, *Blackstone* I. G. Philip, *William Blackstone and the reform of the Oxford University Press in the eighteenth century* (Oxford Bibliographical Soc., 1957)

Plomer, *Dictionary 1668–1725* H. R. Plomer, *A dictionary of the printers and booksellers who were at work in England, Scotland and Ireland from 1668 to 1725* (Bibliographical Soc., 1922)

Plomer, *Dictionary 1726–1775* H. R. Plomer, G. H. Bushnell and E. R. McC. Dix, *A dictionary of the printers and booksellers who were at work in England, Scotland and Ireland from 1726 to 1775* (Bibliographical Soc., 1932)

RCHM Royal Commission on Historical Monuments

Roberts, *Evolution* S. C. Roberts, *The evolution of Cambridge publishing* (Cambridge, 1956)

Roberts, *History* S. C. Roberts, *A history of the Cambridge University Press, 1521–1921* (Cambridge, 1921)

Rothschild *The Rothschild library; a catalogue of the collection of eighteenth-century printed books and manuscripts formed by Lord Rothschild*, 2 vols. (Cambridge, 1954)

SB *Studies in Bibliography*

Scrivener, *Authorized edition* F. H. A. Scrivener, *The authorized edition of the English Bible (1611), its subsequent reprints and modern representatives* (Cambridge, 1884)

Shadwell, *Enactments in Parliament* *Enactments in Parliament specially concerning the Universities of Oxford and Cambridge ...* ed. L. L. Shadwell, 4 vols. (Oxford Historical Soc., 1912)

Shorter, *Paper mills* A. H. Shorter, *Paper mills in England, 1495–1800* (Paper Publications Soc., 1957)

Sutcliffe, *Oxford University Press* Peter Sutcliffe, *The Oxford University Press; an informal history* (Oxford, 1978)

TCBS *Transactions of the Cambridge Bibliographical Society*

Term catalogues *The term catalogues*, ed. Edward Arber, 3 vols. (1903)

UA Cambridge University Archives, Cambridge University Library

VCH *Victoria history of the counties of England*

Van Eeghen, *De Amsterdamse boekhandel* I. van Eeghen, *De Amsterdamse boekhandel, 1680–1725*, 5 vols. in 6 (Amsterdam, 1960–78)

Venn J. and J. A. Venn, *Alumni Cantabrigienses; a biographical list of all known students, graduates and holders of office in the University of Cambridge to 1900*, 10 vols. (Cambridge, 1922–54)

Wellesley index *The Wellesley index to Victorian periodicals, 1824–1900*, ed. Walter E. Houghton, 5 vols. (Toronto, 1966–89)

Willis and Clark R. Willis and J. W. Clark, *The architectural history of the University of Cambridge and of the colleges of Cambridge and Eton*, 4 vols. (Cambridge, 1886)

Winstanley, *Early Victorian Cambridge*   D. A. Winstanley, *Early Victorian Cambridge* (Cambridge, 1940)

Winstanley, *Eighteenth century*   D. A. Winstanley, *The University of Cambridge in the eighteenth century* (Cambridge, 1922)

Winstanley, *Later Victorian Cambridge*   D. A. Winstanley, *Later Victorian Cambridge* (Cambridge, 1947)

Winstanley, *Unreformed Cambridge*   D. A. Winstanley, *Unreformed Cambridge* (Cambridge, 1935)

NOTE ON CURRENCY

The following may be useful to those unfamiliar with English currency
before the Decimal Currency Act, 1971, when the pound was newly divided
into 100 pence.

4 farthings = 1 penny (1d.)
2 halfpence = 1 penny (1d.)
12 pence = 1 shilling (1s.)
20 shillings = 1 pound (£1)
1 guinea = £1.1s.0d.

Sums of money are conventionally written, for example, as £5.13s.4d.

〜 I 〜

A world for books

At first sight, there seems to be little connection between two dates, separated by less than three years, one of them relating to the business of Parliament and the other to a decision by the University of Cambridge. Firstly, in May 1695 the last of the Licensing Acts lapsed; and with it there came to an end legislation that had controlled printing in England and Wales since 1662.[1] For the first time since the sixteenth century, save for the exceptional circumstances of the Civil War in the 1640s, printers were free to establish businesses outside London, York (excluded from the geographical restrictions in the 1662 Act) and outside the authority of the universities of Oxford and Cambridge. Secondly, and three years later, on 21 January 1697/8, the University of Cambridge voted to appoint the first *curatores*, or, in modern terms, Syndics, for a University Press, and thus founded the Press on the footing as we know it today.

There was no legal connection between these two events. Yet their results were to be intertwined over the next centuries. An unrestricted printing trade, operating both in London and outside the traditional confines, and the newly established Cambridge University Press, each faced challenges that had much in common. In ways much more complex than the old relationship between Cambridge and London, they gradually also became competitors, rivals and occasional allies. The following pages are concerned with a period of fundamental changes in printing, publishing, paper-making, book-binding and bookselling: in technology, finance, skills and communications. They are also concerned with one of equally fundamental changes in the organisation, appearance and composition of the University of Cambridge and its constituent colleges. But they are concerned no less with the contexts of these changes, and in particular with their inherent tensions, both within Cambridge and between the fluctuating preoccupations of the University and a known world whose geographic, linguistic, scientific and scholarly boundaries had extended so vastly by the middle of the nineteenth century.

In 1695, the lapse of restrictive legislation initially had the result that might have been expected, as printers sought out careers and fortunes away from London.[2] Of those who took advantage of the events of that year, the first was William Bonny, who moved from London to Bristol and there issued a book dated November 1695, 'Printed by W. Bonny for the author and are to be sold in London': the arrangements for sale were a reminder of the inadequacy of the local market in itself. In 1696 presses were set up in

1

Shrewsbury and Plymouth.[3] But in the second largest town in the country, Norwich, there was no press at this period until 1701, when Francis Burges established one for the first time since the sixteenth century, and began to publish the first newspaper to be printed outside London other than in time of war or plague.[4]

Most of these presses, and others like them, lasted a relatively short time. For the book trade as a whole, the period between 1695 and the passing of the Copyright Act of Queen Anne in 1709 was one of uncertainty and muddle, in which booksellers' and authors' rights were ill-defined. As many a printer had discovered ever since the fifteenth century, it was more straightforward to print books than to distribute and sell them. Early enthusiasm was as much liable to defeat by the realities of competition as by government intervention. Communications, the population structure and the centres of money in most of the country were dominated by London.

In approximate terms, the population of England increased from probably just under 5 million in 1696 to just over 21.5 million in 1871, roughly 4.3 times. Between 1851 and 1871, the increase in population was almost as great as the entire population of England in the 1690s. The increase did not follow a smooth upward curve. Between 1726 and 1731, it actually declined by 3.42 per cent, and the rate of increase was at its greatest (8 per cent) between 1821 and 1826.[5] London always preponderated. In the 1690s, the population of the capital was perhaps 585,000, or about 12 per cent of a total for the country at large of perhaps 4.95 million. The next largest city, Norwich, had perhaps 30,000 in about 1690, though Bristol, York and Newcastle upon Tyne were not far behind.[6] In 1728, one calculation suggested that Cambridge contained 7,778 people in all, including 1,499 members of the University.[7] The first national census, in 1801, recorded 10,087; and only in 1871 did the figure for Cambridge as a whole exceed that estimated for Norwich in the 1690s.[8]

For the book trades, population figures mean very little by themselves.[9] Outside these conurbations, towns and villages might contract as well as expand. Populations changed at different rates, at different periods. This variety in population shifts – geographical and numerical – carried with it the inseparable onus of shifts in demand for housing, foodstuffs and clothing. But it did not necessarily coincide with shifts in demand for books, pamphlets or newspapers, and still less with changes in demand for particular kinds of books. More important than the overall shifts in population was the pattern and number of households. Between 1801 and 1851 the number of inhabited houses in Great Britain increased almost 1.95 times, to 3.65 million, a slightly faster rate of increase than the heads of population. By 1851, census returns suggested that there were 5.7 people to each house.[10] Since books are in practice bought for households, rather than just for individuals, this provides a more accurate idea than overall population figures of the largest possible market – irrespective, that is, of reading ability. Books may be passed among children, shared among adults, or passed from generation to generation. Customers may appear as individuals, but the books that they buy are characterised partly by their subsequent shared or successive reading.

The degree to which this shared experience occurs varies with different kinds of books. A family Bible (one of the staples of the University Press for long periods in the eighteenth and nineteenth centuries), or a dictionary, may last many years. In the case of the Bible it is intended to last, for generations. Likewise, standard works of literature tend to pass from one generation to the next. But on the other hand, children's books, for example, may be read to pieces within a generation, among fewer than half a dozen people. Other books, such as legal manuals, or works on the faster-moving sciences, contemporary politics, or the more transient ecclesiastical disputes, may be of interest to only one person in a household, and again only for a single generation at most.

Thus, the crude expression of books per head of population is no guide to books in use. Questions of literacy pose yet greater questions, with which the present study of an academic press need have no immediate concern: for books from the University Press, a reasonably competent level may be assumed. But the following pages are very much concerned, if only by implication, with questions respecting the use of books.

The market for books involved and depended on numerous other factors, including age, education, wealth, distribution of population, locality and topography. The expansion of the book trade in the eighteenth and nineteenth centuries may be examined in several ways, none by itself satisfactory because none of the resources is complete and because the bases of comparison at different periods are themselves differently founded. Most obviously, the publications recorded in the *Eighteenth century short title catalogue* offer the fullest basis. It records much more single-sheet material than does the *Nineteenth century short title catalogue,* which emphasises books and pamphlets. Neither includes much of the kind of ephemeral publications which the short-title catalogues to 1640 and to a lesser extent for 1641–1700 sought out. Even if comparisons are restricted to books and pamphlets, useful figures still prove elusive. The *ESTC* has made very considerable efforts to record provincial printing, a field where, so far, the nineteenth-century record has made fewer inroads.[11] The restriction by the *NSTC* to (in the British Isles) the holdings of five copyright libraries and one further university library means that much of the country has been so far omitted: the holdings of provincial printing in these libraries are often weak and unrepresentative.[12] But while quantitative surveys are uneven, and trustworthy comparative figures have yet to be gathered, there are clear overall trends which may be addressed with more confidence. First, from the 1770s onwards there was a clear and noticeable increase in the numbers of new publications, a trend emphasised by the many political and economic pamphlets of the 1790s but also a result of the many fresh editions of older works brought out following the demise of indefinite copyright. In the nineteenth century, a gradual rise in the first four decades became much steeper in the 1840s and early 1850s (partly due to a flood of cheap literature and reprints), slackening again over the next two decades or so before another substantial increase in the 1870s.[13] In all of these trends, wartime, political crises, or (as in 1831, for example) agitation over reform were all liable to prompt irregular patterns.

While bibliographical entries of the kind employed by the short-title catalogues have the merit of offering discrete numerical identifiers, they do not in themselves distinguish how many books were simply reissues or alternative issues of other works, having no difference other than in the imprints, be they of date or of bookseller. Nor do the numbers by themselves indicate the difference between larger and smaller publications, a pamphlet or a heavy volume. In other words, we may learn something of the bookselling and publishing trade, but not much about the printing trade. For the latter, we would require a breakdown of production, of sheets contained in each edition and of the numbers of copies printed, from as few as a dozen to the many thousand copies printed of popular chapbooks or broadside ballads.[14] To understand the expansion of the printing trade comprehensively, we would need to seek how much was printed, measured in reams of paper.

Such details are irrecoverable. But we may also look at the personnel of the trade: at the numbers of master printers and others involved in printing, or at the numbers of booksellers. For these there is not even the internal, if ultimately unsatisfactory, consistency of the *ESTC*. Several contemporary surveys of the London trades survive from the eighteenth and nineteenth centuries, startlingly different in their standards of efficiency and usefulness. In London alone, Samuel Negus recorded seventy-five master printers in 1724. By 1785, Pendred recorded 124. In 1808, Caleb Stower reported 216. In 1824, John Johnson reported 306. In 1855, Hodson's *Directory* recorded 368.[15] The only national effort to record printing houses in this period was under the authority of the Seditious Societies Act, 1799, by which returns were to be made to the Secretary of State of printers and of allied trades such as typefounders and press-makers. In 1799, the first (incomplete) year of operation, some 105 printers or premises were recorded in London, and 109 in Middlesex. Others were added in subsequent years, though duplication of registration, and disagreement over the efficacy of the legislation, again make detailed comparisons impossible.[16] These figures, erratic and irreconcilable, suggest that the number of printers multiplied by five between the 1720s (when the trade had not been shackled by the Licensing Act for more than two decades) and the 1850s. Hodson's list is unlikely to be complete even for London, while the much smaller numbers of the 1720s made a survey more feasible. But all figures subsumed a variety of activities, from the large book-printing houses such as Bowyer or Strahan in the eighteenth century, or Clay in the nineteenth, to the many small run-down businesses with only two or three men and a single worn press. The Bowyers and the Clays were not representative of their generations. In the sixteenth and early seventeenth centuries, the Stationers' Company had laboured to maintain control by limiting all but a small coterie of printers to one press each. It was not always effective; but with the ending of such restrictions the task of determining the manufacturing capacity of the printing trade becomes impossible.

In most respects, this is to speak virtually to the exclusion of Britain outside London and some of the suburbs. It is a commonplace (and one repeated in this book) that in the eighteenth century, printing houses were established in the larger towns across the country; that such printers often depended on the regular incomes to be derived from newspaper printing; and that they required a local body of customer support. Even in the special case of Cambridge, there is much to support these tenets, to which others might be added. The non-university printers that established themselves from the mid-eighteenth century usually supplemented, rather than competed with, the University

Press. But the notion of an expanding printing trade is more complicated than is implied in the rehearsal of such events. Various factors complicate the issue. First, and not infrequently (it seems almost to have been the norm), printers and booksellers relied for their livelihood on more than the single activity or manufacture that their occupational labels suggest. Secondly, a printer may enjoy a large or a small business or clientèle – some requiring books or pamphlets, others little more than notices. For small businesses in particular, printing could often be only part-time. Thirdly, and more complicatedly, since it was a principle that was established only over a comparatively long period, demand for printing changed not only in volume, but also in its nature. The application first of written and then of printed documents to commercial activities, including those in primarily agricultural areas, increased the need for modestly equipped printers able to provide short runs of receipts, forms, letter-heads, bill-heads, toll-gate tickets, labels and other everyday needs.

In this manner, the size of the local population became a less critical element in the equation between numbers of printers and numbers of customers. Hodson's directory of the book trade, 1855, recorded printers in many places boasting populations of under two thousand. In a world where, by the early nineteenth century, printing was perceived throughout the country as a necessity for a range of activities extending far beyond reading books, pamphlets and newspapers, the printing industry was a complex one. The present volume is concerned with a press whose work in printing ephemera extended no further than the circle of a university, and whose principal business was always in the printing (and sometimes publishing) of books and pamphlets. But the context of these publications – in the output of the book trade as a whole, among other miscellaneous or slighter printed matter, on the tables of those who read them amongst other things, printed or manuscript, often imported from abroad – was also itself the way by which the University Press was defined: by what was held in common, the materials of paper, ink, glue, thread and bindings, and the visible words or figures, requiring verbal or numerical literacy. These definitions existed alongside the more commonly recognised ones such as the choice of texts and the broadly similar educational, religious and social characteristics of most of its authors.

Whatever the sizes of the various local populations, local presses – elsewhere as in Cambridge – survived only by the existence of a sufficient market, varying according to the nature and needs of any particular community, and by the presence of suitable communications with elsewhere. Printing thrived only where it could reach a substantial literate and committed body of readers. In the seventeenth century, Norwich had depended for its occasional printing needs either on Cambridge or on London. But even Cambridge, with easier access to the capital, a greater number of local stationers, and the needs and demands of the University, supported a press for most of the seventeenth century only by the fact that much of what was printed there was sold to stationers in London. Printing was a means of supporting a retail book trade, both directly by what was sold in Cambridge and indirectly as a means of creating goods that could be exchanged for credit.[17] In other words, neither in Norfolk nor in

Cambridgeshire was there sufficient local need for printing in itself to justify a press on more than the smallest scale. The lapsing of the Licensing Acts in 1695 made printing legally possible in Norwich; but it was to be sustained by a local population, in the city and county, far larger than that of Cambridge, its surrounding countryside and villages. In early eighteenth-century England, a local printer might print for local needs, be they political or social; and he might print a regular local newspaper, thus ensuring a regular income as well as a readership held together by common interests and by advertising. Nationally, the many local newspapers that were to be established across the country in the following decades depended partly on communications with London, as a source for news; but they also depended, far more, on an efficient and regular arrangement for the distribution of what was printed.[18]

Moreover, while the number of newspapers thus expanded overall, it was not an even progression. Newspapers were also closed, or were amalgamated with their rivals, as ventures failed or proprietors died. There were local newspapers in Bury St Edmunds by 1716, Northampton by 1720 and Stamford by 1710. No less than three had been founded in St Ives by 1720, a reflection of its geographical position at the head of navigation on the River Ouse.[19] But by the time the *Cambridge Journal* was established in 1744, all but the *Northampton Mercury* had ceased publication. The reasons for the collapse of local newspapers were many; but those that survived did so because they were able to organise a regular network of news, customers and readership.

Cambridge University Press did not print newspapers, and the first periodicals to emerge from its presses were founded only in the 1820s: the annual volumes recording observations at the University Observatory, and the *Transactions* of the Cambridge Philosophical Society. But its readers, and most of the county, had by then depended for generations on a newspaper and periodical press. At less than a day's ride from London, Cambridge fell comfortably within the outer London orbit of news. By contrast, Norwich supported a newspaper from 1701, and as further printers established themselves there, so they too began further newspapers, as a part of competition.[20] Cambridge, a much smaller town, with little demand for printed matter from its hinterland, supported one only from 1744, and a second from 1762. Both the *Cambridge Journal and Weekly Flying Post* and the later *Cambridge Chronicle* circulated widely, especially to the west and across the fens; the latter in particular, by its especial attention to news from the University, demonstrated that it had identified what would now be called a niche. In 1766, the two newspapers merged. Each depended on improved communications, and not simply on the local populace. The history of these two local Cambridge newspapers demonstrated that, while on the one hand they complemented the work of the University Press, and even promoted it by including occasional advertisements or other notices, on the other they found their principal business in parts of the market that were far removed from that Press. Their needs were at the same time both more modest than those of the University Press, in that the local population could support a newspaper but not a regular programme of publications from a learned press; and yet greater, in that they required regular commitment, week by week, from their subscribers and readers.[21]

The closeness of London was emphasised when in 1793 Benjamin Flower established the *Cambridge Intelligencer*, and used Cambridge as a base from which to attack the French wars and to urge constitutional reform. Like other newspapers, those in Cambridge were eager to emphasise the geographical spread of their circulation, and hence customers, a feature which had a direct bearing on all-important advertising revenue.[22] Flower, with national political interests, was able to claim by 1801 that he had agents or interests as far away as Edinburgh, Glasgow and Aberdeen, and that most of the 1,800 copies printed weekly were sent outside Cambridge.

By the 1840s, Cambridge depended on the long-established and conservative *Cambridge Chronicle*, on the *Cambridge Independent Press* (generally liberal, with strong nonconformist interests, and the principal newspaper of the Fens) and the *Cambridge General Advertiser*, founded in 1839, politically independent and widely read in Norfolk as well as in Cambridgeshire. The nearest other towns having weekly papers were Bury St Edmunds (the *Bury Post*, founded 1782, and the *Bury and Suffolk Herald*, founded 1821[23]), King's Lynn (the *Lynn Advertiser*, founded 1842), Bedford (the *Bedford Mercury*, founded 1837, and *Bedford Times*, founded 1845) and Hertford (the *County Herald* (1792), the *Herts County Press* (1830) and the *Hertford Mercury* (1834)).[24] By 1871, King's Lynn, Wisbech, Bedford and Bury St Edmunds each had three weekly papers, and St Ives and St Neots one apiece. Besides London titles, twenty-nine local papers circulated in the diocese of Ely, which reached into Bedfordshire, Huntingdonshire and Suffolk.[25]

Booksellers too depended on centres of population and local trade. In the early eighteenth century, 46 per cent of townspeople, or about 14 per cent of the national population, lived in towns of less than five thousand inhabitants. Shopkeepers combined bookselling with other goods, not only the ubiquitous patent medicines but also anything from groceries to textiles to hardware. In Cambridge in the mid-eighteenth century, the newspaper printers also kept shop. Walker and James used their journal to advertise their stocks of books, patent medicines, stationery, shoe polish and sticking plaster. Fletcher and Hodson advertised at various times Bibles, prayer books and (in 1763) books printed by Baskerville, as well as schoolbooks, 'a large Collection of Mr. Newbery's Entertaining Books for the Amusement and Instruction of Little Masters and Misses, neatly bound and gilt', besides an assortment of medicines.[26] A few months later, the firm advertised paper hangings 'of the most beautiful patterns, and newest Taste', as well as an assortment of prints and drawing books.[27] Shopkeepers expected to deal in what opportunity might offer. In 1765, John Jenkinson, bookseller in Huntingdon, took in the stock of Ann and Susannah Cawthorne, haberdashers of hats, so as to sell it off and make space for books.[28] In 1768, the *Cambridge Chronicle and Journal* contained an advertisement for Caleb Preston, of Boston in Lincolnshire, giving notice that he had established a printing business to join his other interests in stationery, magazines, medicines and musical instruments.[29] In King's Lynn, Thomas Hollingworth advertised old and new books, stationery, musical instruments, fishing tackle, domestic equipment including chocolate mills, nutmeg graters and shaving brushes, besides medicines, paper hangings and tide-tables. 'He likewise Gilds, Letters and Methodizes Gentlemen's Libraries at reasonable Rates.'[30]

Further such examples might be found in other parts of the country. While few merchants were able to boast of the extraordinary array of household necessities offered by John Malcolm of Aberdeen in the 1770s (his verse advertisement listed over three hundred different kinds of goods, including 'Gimblets, Iron Wire and Books, Catechisms, proverbs and Stay-Hooks'[31]) conjunctions of merchandise and services frequently depended on a mixture of the accidents of opportunity and of means of supply.[32] In early nineteenth-century Cheltenham, Bettison's circulating library offered the usual bookselling, printing and binding, set beside perfumes, medicines and supplies of coal.[33] In practice, retail businesses, and perhaps especially those away from London and the university or cathedral towns, depended for their existence on a range of activities among which bookselling might be only a minor one. For many in the country, shops had taken the place of fairs, whether for books or for other necessities. A writer in the 1760s, noting the decline of Stourbridge fair, the annual event that had once brought to Cambridge traders from all over the country, blamed the changes on increasingly easy communication by road or by canal, on the numbers of travelling salesmen who took orders direct from individual localities, and on increasingly well-supplied shops across the country.

> Now instead of buying their Goods from the third and fourth Hand, the little Shopkeepers even of obscure Villages have them from the first. When the Fair comes, which formerly supplied the County of Cambridge with all the Commodities, and the Articles of Luxury fit for Sale, the Tradesmen are overstocked, and the Majority of them, obliged to keep their Money to pay at fixed Terms their Correspondents, have none to spare, even in Case of an advantageous Purchase; as for foreign Commodities, several Tradesmen of the very inland Counties procure them from the Source. Thus the Fairs are become useless, and excepted some Gentlemen, Farmers, and Labourers, who buy at these places a few Trinkets, and useful Goods, few capital Tradesmen deal with those who keep Fairs . . .[34]

Booksellers in London and Cambridge figure repeatedly in the following pages; but in the context of the national book trade they were unusual: unusual in the proportion of space they gave to selling books, and unusual in that most of the businesses mentioned concentrated on a market that may be broadly defined as academic, ecclesiastical and not of the cheapest. Both in character and in their stock, they were always in a minority nationally among retail shops offering books.

In such circumstances, stocks of books were inevitably limited, selected for shops where a reasonable turnover overall was critical to commercial survival and where this was sought by diversifying goods offered for sale. The development of circulating libraries, viewed with suspicion by some booksellers, was turned to the trade's advantage. Quite apart from the specialist commercial lending libraries that became a feature of recreational reading, booksellers too established their own collections, smaller or larger, of books that could be borrowed, in the same premises where stock was also offered for sale. The advantages were obvious: for the customer, there was convenience; for the bookseller it was possible, given reasonable custom, to recoup a more predictable, faster and regular return than could be obtained by holding only retail stock. The London bookseller James Lackington praised circulating libraries as places that encouraged reading, and therefore book-buying; he refrained from explaining the details of his own financial interest.[35] It was partly as a result of this new source of income that booksellers were increasingly able to become independent of other goods. Meanwhile, and to an extent not always matched in continental Europe, the cognate paper trades in stationery and in prints[36] retained their presence.

Whatever their stock, communication and distribution became of ever more importance as the population grew, as expectations were encouraged through advertisements, and different parts of the country became increasingly interdependent.

Apart from the University, the local economy depended on agriculture. The market for printed matter was limited. The nearest towns, Ely to the north, Huntingdon and St Ives to the west, and Newmarket to the east, made comparatively little difference in this respect, especially for much of the eighteenth century. To the north were the fens, much of the area flooded in winter and viewed by strangers as an unwholesome place to inhabit. In 1724, Daniel Defoe wrote of viewing them from the Gogmagog hills, just to the south of Cambridge:

> One could hardly see this [the view over the fens, north towards Ely cathedral] from the hills and not pity the many thousands of families that were bound to or confin'd in those foggs, and had no other breath to draw than what must be mix'd with those vapours, and that steam which so universally overspread the country.

As for the rest of the county, to the south, Defoe reported that it was 'almost wholly a corn country; and of that corn five parts in six of all they sow, is barly, which is generally sold to Ware and Royston, and other great malting-towns in Hertfordshire . . . As Essex, Suffolk, and Norfolk, are taken up in manufacturing, and fam'd for industry, this county has no manufacture at all; nor are the poor, except the husbandmen, fam'd for any thing so much as idleness and sloth, to their scandal be it spoken; what the reason of it is, I know not.'[37] Norfolk, by contrast, he found populous, and thriving with the weaving industry. In the country between Norwich and the Suffolk borders there were, by his calculation, no less than a dozen market towns.[38]

Travel in Cambridgeshire could be hazardous. In February 1757 James Bentham, historian of Ely cathedral and brother of the University Printer, complained that he could not get to Cambridge by water because of the frost.[39] Both the *Cambridge Journal* and the *Cambridge Chronicle* repeatedly contained reports of snow that disrupted road travel. Bentham was a vigorous advocate of turnpikes, and campaigned successfully for a road from Cambridge to Ely. Funded largely by private money, the route through Stretham was finally opened in the mid-1760s, and quickly replaced the old ones either to the west across the fens via Haddenham or via Fordham and Soham to the east.[40] Gradually the roads to the south were also improved. A further bequest by William Worts provided for a causeway to link Cambridge with the Gogmagog hills.[41] The road between Cambridge and Stump Cross, on the border of Essex, was turnpiked in

1724–5; that to Godmanchester (and hence to the north, and of particular importance because of the weight of traffic generated each year by Stourbridge Fair) in the mid-1740s;[42] that to Royston and Baldock following legislation in 1769; and that west to St Neots following similar legislation in 1772.[43] While these undoubtedly led to improvements, the new arrangements – in Cambridgeshire as in many other places elsewhere in the country – were not always welcomed wholeheartedly.[44] In 1729/30 Parliament found itself considering complaints over the details of the road between Cambridge and Trumpington.[45] North of the town, the much-resented toll gate at the east end of Chesterton Lane was removed only in 1852[46] – seven years after the opening of the railway line between Cambridge and Norwich via Ely. In the second half of the eighteenth century milestones and signposts were gradually added by the main roads as further guidance.[47]

Such changes affected the immediate country round Cambridge, and its everyday supplies of food and other essentials. But the same was also true of the rest of the country, as, with varying degrees of success, and depending variously on private as well as corporate interests, a web of communications was established that not only improved connections between centres of population, but also brought different patterns of communication, by routes never dreamt of by earlier generations. Speed and new avenues for trade, news or personal travel became matters for advertisement, as the country was drawn more tightly together both socially and economically. The first number of the first newspaper in Cambridge, the *Cambridge Journal and Weekly Flying Post*, emphasised its superiority over its established rivals elsewhere by using the vocabulary of speed, and appealing to readers' anxiety to learn what was new:

> By means of the great Expedition used in this Undertaking, we are two Days before the Northampton Mercury, with the same Post; and all Sunday's Post before the Ipswich Paper.[48]

Compared with many other southern parts of England, Cambridgeshire and the neighbouring portions of Huntingdonshire, Norfolk, Suffolk and Essex were thinly populated throughout the period with which this volume is concerned. In the seventeenth and eighteenth century, Cambridge was remote from the ordinary through routes of England. Compared with Oxford, few foreign visitors bothered with the town or the university unless they had a particular person whom they wished to see, or some other precise reason for their visit. For tourists, this remained true to a noticeable extent even after the railways had been established and made travel more straightforward. It was not on a road route to any major town.

But while newspaper printers looked to a network of connections based on more or less local towns, the University Press looked always primarily to London. In the eighteenth century, the road to London was greatly improved, albeit somewhat unsystematically, and not invariably to general advantage under the several turnpike trusts.[49] In 1763, the local guidebook, *Cantabrigia depicta*, gave details not only of the frequent posts from Cambridge to London, to the north, and to Norfolk, but also of three different services to London by stage waggon, a waggon to Birmingham and Coventry once a fortnight, and local carrier services linking Cambridge to East Anglian towns. At a more local level there were the newsmen, employed to distribute newspapers and collect subscriptions and advertisements but also willing to take packets. One set out for north Essex and Hertfordshire from the bookshop of Thurlbourn and Woodyer every Saturday, to visit Chesterford, Saffron Walden, Newport, Quendon Hockerill, Much Hadham, Widford and Ware. The publishers of both the local newspapers likewise employed men who would deliver parcels to towns and villages over a wide area.[50] By river, there was a regular boat to King's Lynn every Tuesday, to Downham every Saturday, and to Wisbech every Monday.[51] Fifty years later, these services had been increased, and now included not only more waggons to London but also twice-weekly waggon services to Norwich, Yarmouth and King's Lynn as well as weekly services to Birmingham, to Stamford and to Suffolk and Essex. There were boats to King's Lynn twice a week.[52] By 1830 the amount of traffic between Cambridge and the rest of the country had increased so much that every Monday six waggons set out from Cambridge to London, and the number of services each week between London and Cambridge had doubled in less than twenty years.[53] By the late 1820s, the stage-coach took only five and a half hours between London and Cambridge, making it easy to be in Cambridge in time for breakfast.[54]

The road from London to Norwich passed Cambridge to the south; that to York to the west. The details of local transport arrangements provided in the various guidebooks may not all be reliable or complete, and the condition of the roads remained variable with the weather and time of year. But the pattern of investment in transport is clear enough.

For bulky materials, including books and paper, the cheapest method of transport until the railways were properly established was by water. In this, Cambridge was at an immediate disadvantage, since the only such route to London was via King's Lynn. The Thames, serving London and Oxford, tended to make Oxford more attractive to London publishers, especially when there were great quantities of materials to be shipped between warehouse and printer, and printer and publisher. In 1703, Henry James, President of Queens' College, noted that the cost of carriage for paper from London to Cambridge, and back again, was five shillings per hundredweight, compared with two shillings for the similar distance between London and Oxford.[55] Any paper used in Cambridge for books that were to be published or distributed through London had to be moved for fifty or more miles twice over, along the uneven roads between the Press, its usual source of supply and its market.

Hence the cost of transport was critical in the development of the University Press, which in the last years of the eighteenth century sought out sources nearer to Cambridge, including the mills at Sawston.[56] For much of the eighteenth century, at least on the principal routes, there seems to have been a general decline in the cost of carriage by road. In 1752 it was even claimed that it had dropped by 30 per cent since the advent of turnpikes.[57] But apart from the general improvement in the quality of the roads, which permitted heavier loads as well as faster travel, legislation in the 1750s and the early 1760s favoured larger loads. Thereafter costs remained generally stable, until they rose in the 1790s, to fall again, briefly, in the first years of the nineteenth century and then to rise again after the European wars.[58] Inevitably there were many regional and seasonal variations, for costs were incurred not only by the constants of turnpike dues, but also by the more variable state of the roads and by the varying cost of feed for horses. While to a great, and perhaps controlling, degree, the development at Cambridge in the 1750s of an extensive business in the printing of Bibles and prayer books was the creation of a small group of men with Joseph Bentham, the University Printer, at their centre, it must be remarked that this coincided with a general lowering of transport costs. To claim that the cost of transport was the controlling feature in the developments at the Cambridge press during the 1750s and 1760s would be to overstate its influence. These developments would not have taken place without the determination of London customers and Cambridge printers. But they could hardly have prospered without transport charges that still left the cost of printing, as delivered to the customer, comparable with, or less than, those that were achievable in London from printers unhindered by long-distance bulk haulage.

Though the town authorities waged many a campaign on the subject of rivers and trade, their attention was concentrated on the waterways to the north and to the north-west: to the sea at King's Lynn and to Huntingdon and the hinterland of the River Ouse.[59] Repeated consideration was given from the early 1780s onwards to build a canal that would connect the River Stort (and hence the Thames) with the River Cam, but none was ever constructed, even after parliamentary permission had finally been obtained in 1812.[60] Instead, and within ten years, attention had been transferred to projecting a railway that would have linked the Stortford navigation with the River Cam at Clayhithe.[61] It seems unlikely that many people expected a canal to pay its way.

The real change came with the railways. Cambridge was linked to London by rail from 1845, initially only by the Eastern Counties Railway from Shoreditch and Stratford. The time needed for travel between Cambridge and London was reduced to two hours or less, and Cambridge came within easy reach for a day's excursion – to the dismay of members of the University, who saw their accustomed peace in ruins.[62] To G. E. Corrie, Vice-Chancellor at the time that Sunday excursion trains were introduced, and a determined conservative, the offence seemed a double one 'as distasteful to the authorities of the University as they must be offensive to Almighty God and to all right-minded Christians'.[63] But the railways helped to increase public awareness of Cambridge, both as a town to visit and also as a place of learning and publishing: among the visitors that the University Registrary, Joseph Romilly, encountered on Easter Monday 1846 were three ladies and a girl in search of the Pitt Press.[64] More importantly for the University Press, the new railways could also carry bulky and heavy materials, and in particular paper.

Though the University succeeded in arranging that the station should not be so close to the centre of the town as to encourage undergraduates to make off to London for the day, the railway companies were generally free to build new lines independent of such interference. When in the late 1820s and early 1830s hopes were raised of a railway from London to York, the preferred route to be surveyed was via Cambridge rather than along the line of the great north road.[65] Had this come about, Cambridge might have been transformed still further. Instead, Cambridge found itself (for a while) on the main route to Norwich and East Anglia rather than to the north. What was to have been the line from London to Norwich, sanctioned by Parliament in 1836, was initially built only to Colchester,[66] and thus when the London (Shoreditch), Cambridge, Ely and Norwich line was finally opened in 1845, Cambridge found itself in an unaccustomed role as an important centre of transport. By 1851, there were connections and branch lines to St Ives, March and Peterborough via Ely, and Newmarket.[67]

The opening of the railway between London and Cambridge in 1845 made it possible, for the first time, to move bulky and heavy goods easily. The Cambridge presses were brought within easy range of London publishers. The arrival of Daniel and Alexander Macmillan in Cambridge in 1843, and their subsequent foundation of a publishing house that maintained its links with the printing house in Cambridge even after the firm had removed its publishing to London in 1863, exploited this new-found convenience. These new developments dominate the last part of this volume.

The period of this volume also saw the University changing in ways that exposed its Elizabethan statutes as increasingly irrelevant.[68] By the early 1870s, the University was set, not always wholeheartedly, on a path of reform. The changes in the University that brought about a reformed press of a quite different kind, more broadly based than hitherto, in the 1860s and, especially, in the 1870s, were not all prompted directly by outside pressures and comparisons. They were more tangled than this; and to some degree they reflected the weakening power of the individual colleges in the face of a university organisation that grew rapidly in the mid-century. At the most obvious level, the development of new triposes (commencing with moral sciences and natural sciences in 1851) was visible confirmation of compromise with the older disciplines. Under the statutes of 1882 the University was to appoint the first University Readers and Lecturers, where previously virtually all university teaching appointments (as distinct from those in colleges) had been of professors only. The establishment in 1870 of a university journal designed to gather together official notices that had previously been posted piecemeal, emphasised a new central organisation as well as providing an obvious practical improvement. In buildings, as so often a reflection of priorities, college laboratory space, never great, gradually gave way to new university facilities – most celebrated in the Cavendish Laboratory, completed in 1874, but proposed in a comprehensive report addressed to the University in 1853.[69] The emphasis here was on the sciences: the case for improved provision for 'Literary professors' (including those for divinity, who in the early 1850s could expect audiences of 350) was pressed less. Meanwhile, the passing of the old Caput[70] and the creation in its place of a body more broadly representative of current opinion marked a generally recognised change in the University's outlook as well as its internal organisation. It also consolidated the power of the University.

To this day, colleges in Cambridge remain independent one of another, with separate governing bodies, separate endowments, separate accounting arrangements, and separate provision not only for accommodation, libraries and chapels, but also, to a great extent, for teaching. The University, for its part, to which every student and senior member belongs just as much as each is normally a member of a particular college, has grown in influence and power since the mid-nineteenth century. It is responsible for other teaching including the provision of lectures, for both the main university library and the many faculty libraries in the various subjects, for providing and maintaining scientific laboratories, and (as it has been since the University's very beginning) for the conferring of degrees. But the growth of its relative importance is such that it can obscure the interests, influence and contributions of individual colleges two or three hundred years ago.

In the eighteenth century, and for most of the nineteenth, the centres of power in the university lay not with the University, but with the colleges. In itself, the University possessed little wealth. Many of its decisions, and even sometimes apparently quite minor administrative ones, were determined by Graces proposed to the Senate; but the most powerful body was the Caput. The only specialist standing committees that existed were two: for the University Press and for the University Library. For some purposes, the Masters of Arts in the University had rights to vote: these included elections to a few posts (including the Chancellor of the University and the University Librarian). This body could, *in extremis*, also challenge the Caput. In practice, the colleges held far more power. Since in university politics colleges often voted more or less in blocks, and particular colleges became associated with particular shades of political or religious opinion, the power of the largest colleges was considerable, and even dominating.

The two largest, by a considerable margin, were St John's and Trinity. The large size of their fellowships meant that these two colleges dominated the University as well. As a whole, the colleges held the wealth of the university. They controlled the advowsons of virtually all the livings that were intended (at least in theory: there were many scandalous exceptions) to ensure that space would always be made for younger generations by the natural progression of more senior fellows to marriage and to parishes around the country. Day by day, and night by night, fellows gathered each in their colleges to combine in the groups that influenced the daily life of the university. Committees, or in Cambridge parlance Syndicates, composed of members of different colleges, were created only exceptionally, to meet particular needs.

Thus, though the Press was the University's, the University in its turn was defined by its constituent colleges, and so was dominated by separate groups of people of very different interests, frequently divided by jealousy, enjoying very different standards of wealth, and varying very greatly in numbers. The young Thomas Gray, just arrived at Peterhouse, summed up his impressions of Cambridge in 1734:

> I warrant, you imagine that People in one College, know the Customs of others; but you mistake, they are quite little Societies by themselves: yᵉ Dresses, Language, Customs &c are different in different Colledges: what passes for Wit in one, would not be understood if it were carried to another: thus the men of Peter-house, Pembroke & Clare-hall of

course must be Tories; those of Trinity, Rakes; of King's, Scholars; of Sidney, Wigs; of S[t] Johns, Worthy men & so on.

Gray then turned to the more general picture, first to the town and then to the colleges again:

It is a great old Town, shaped like a Spider, with a nasty lump in the middle of it, & half a dozen scambling long legs: it has 14 Parishes, 12 Colledges, & 4 Halls, these Halls only entertain Students . . . there are 5 ranks in the University, subordinate to the Vice-chancellour, who is chose annually: these are Masters, Fellows, Fellow-Commoners, Pensioners, & Sizers; the Masters of Colledges are twelve grey-hair'd Gentlefolks, who are all mad with pride; the Fellows are sleepy, drunken, dull, illiterate Things . . .[71]

Dominated numerically by the numbers of fellows and undergraduates in St John's and Trinity, the University's fortunes were in one fundamental sense measured by those of the sixteen (later, with Downing, seventeen) colleges. The numbers of students matriculating at Cambridge declined after the 1660s, and by the 1760s were less than a third of what they had been during the 1570s and 1580s. Gradually they recovered through the latter part of the eighteenth century; but it was only after the Napoleonic wars that they began to rise at a pace which obliged colleges to take serious steps to contain them, in new buildings. Between the 1690s (that is, the beginning of this volume) and the 1820s–30s matriculations more than doubled. By the 1870s they more than trebled.[72] With the exception of Downing, founded in 1800, no new college was founded at Cambridge during the period of this volume.[73] In large measure, the size of the colleges depended on the size of endowments, though their fortunes in attracting undergraduates also fluctuated over shorter periods in keeping with the reputations and personalities of individuals. Queens' College, for example, enjoyed a renaissance in the early nineteenth century thanks to its President, the evangelical Isaac Milner. But it remained that the two largest colleges exercised continuing and dominating power. By the early 1860s, Trinity contained about one-third of the entire undergraduate population, more than twice the number of its old rival St John's. The great expansion in undergraduate numbers in the nineteenth century was supported by major building projects, in which there was a strong element of competition; but it was also encouraged by the establishment of the practice of allowing undergraduates to live 'out', in lodgings.[74] In the 1820s, St John's erected New Court (Rickman, 1827–31), Trinity erected King's (later New) Court (Wilkins, 1823–5), King's sold off its historic court, now the western part of the Old Schools, and erected the Wilkins Building (1824–8), Corpus erected a new court at the front of the College, also by Wilkins (1823–7) and Jesus built the east side of Pump Court (1822). Gisburne Court, in Peterhouse, was built in 1825–6. In another spate of expansion, William Whewell, Master of Trinity, used his private wealth to buy the site for the courts named after him on the east side of Trinity Street (the first was built in 1860); and, both to designs by Waterhouse, Gonville and Caius built New Court in 1868, and Jesus the north side of Pump Court in 1869–70.[75]

Gradually during the eighteenth and nineteenth centuries, the colleges' mutual iso-

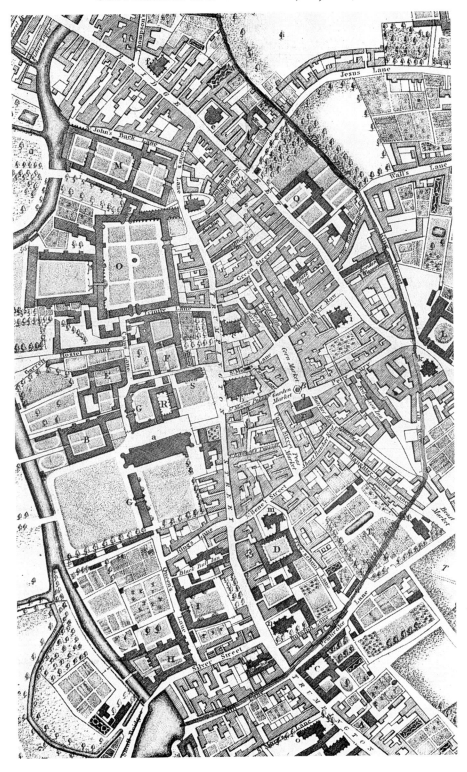

lation was worn away, as the affairs and needs of the University became more centrally defined. Thanks to private enthusiasms, the University acquired a botanical garden in the middle of the eighteenth century. There were no university (rather than college) laboratories,[76] no university lecture rooms, no departmental libraries. Loyalties and alliances generated by the examination system did not form effectively until classics was challenged by mathematics in the early nineteenth century.

The nineteenth century was an age of societies. Of those whose affairs impinged on the affairs of the Cambridge University Press, some were inevitably local – just as the Press drew most of its business, other than the printing of the privileged books, from local authors. Links were not always obvious between such societies, the fortunes of the Press and the activities of the University on which it depended directly or indirectly. As Charles Babbage was amused to acknowledge, it was the existence of the Bible Society, and opposition to it, that gave him the idea of the Analytical Society, from which sprang some of the most effective reforms in Cambridge mathematics.[77] The foundation of the Cambridge Philosophical Society in 1819, of the Cambridge Camden Society in 1839, and of the Cambridge Antiquarian Society in 1840 each provided a platform of potential corporate strength and influence. Likewise, alliances were forged in journals, in the classics, in mathematics, in philology, in the sciences. They helped to make reform possible. The isolated voices of the mid- and late eighteenth century had in the end been ineffective because they had no organised support, and no

Fig. 1 Cambridge in 1798. Detail from William Custance, *A new plan of the University and town of Cambridge to the present year 1798*.
The old Press buildings lay on Queens' Lane and Silver Street, until the site south of Silver Street (in the centre at the foot of the map) was gradually developed and the Pitt Press was built in the 1820s.
Some of the principal buildings include:

    a King's College chapel
    b Great St Mary's church
    e The round church
    i Holy Trinity church
    n St Botolph's church

    B Clare College
    C Pembroke College
    D Corpus Christi College
    E Trinity Hall
    F Gonville and Caius College
    G King's College
    H Queens' College
    I St Catharine's College
    L Christ's College
    M St John's College
    O Trinity College
    Q Sidney Sussex College
    R The Schools
    S The Senate House

Modern Trinity Street and King's Parade are both labelled Trumpington Street.

means of prolonging their work; nor, in the context of academia, did they have any means of pressing their case with the strength of others. Though many in eighteenth-century Cambridge were involved in the Society of Antiquaries, and some in the affairs of the Royal Society, the identification of these London bodies with interests and views that were not only metropolitan, but also often quite deliberately removed from the concerns or ideas of the University, ensured that eighteenth-century Cambridge would remain weak. In a university community that was prone to self-regard, the result was yet further debilitating.

Few people read more than one or two newspapers; but many of those familiar with the books printed or published by the University Press read several periodicals. The *Gentleman's Magazine* and the *Critical Review* took a close and frequently well-informed interest in the life and publications of the University in the eighteenth century; and in the nineteenth century the quarterly journals – the *Edinburgh*, the *Quarterly*, *Blackwood's* and others – were as much read in the university as they were elsewhere. Besides these there were the specialist journals, in classics and theology especially; and nineteenth-century Cambridge witnessed the foundation of a series of titles designed for particular interests: the 1830s–1840s, when the need for such links seems to have been particularly felt, saw the establishment of the Cambridge Antiquarian Society's publications, the *Ecclesiologist* from the Cambridge Camden Society, the *Cambridge* (later *Cambridge and Dublin*) *Mathematical Journal*, as well as some that enjoyed only brief lives. As the signed journal article became more familiar, so emphasis shifted to the importance of periodical articles in their own right. *Macmillan's Magazine*, like its rival the *Cornhill*, built much of its reputation on the names figuring in its contents lists. The leading Cambridge journals founded in the 1860s included the *Messenger of Mathematics* and the *Journal of Philology*. All these existed besides more light-hearted ones, frequently written by undergraduates or recent graduates, printed by the growing number of smaller presses in Cambridge and on the whole of short duration.

In developing most of their readership by requiring subscriptions, such journals had a social as well as a publishing function. They were a more convenient form for dispersing opinion and knowledge to overseas, by subscription. Pamphlet publication, for many people the preferred brief means of sharing opinion in the eighteenth and nineteenth centuries, by no means disappeared; but publication of an article in a journal became a surer and more systematic way of finding an audience, one that was supported by the increasing custom (established for some journals in the eighteenth century) of distributing offprints among friends, acquaintances or those whose opinion an author might wish to court. In other words, changes in the style and means of publication, brought about by publishers and authors, became in themselves the further means to change and manipulate interests within the educational community.

The new societies and new journals, and the bonds of common interest that they represented, sidestepped college interests; their membership and readership did not rely solely on social standing in a university where professors and heads of houses had unique advantage; and they were not restricted by the University's own administrative structure, whether the powers of the Caput, the delegated powers of the permanent syndicates or the composition of the many temporary syndicates charged with making recommendations for consideration on particular issues. As each of these ventures depended on the printing press, so the place of the University Press was both active and passive: to enable new alliances and to be itself re-examined.

'Cambridge is very ugly, she is very dirty, & very dull.' By no means everyone, local or distant, agreed with Gray's analysis in spring 1738.[78] Its style was certainly distinctive, architecturally, socially and educationally. It was unlike other eighteenth-century towns. The powers of the University and of the colleges determined local organisation, whether in employment, building, shopping, entertainment or legislation. Jealousies between town and gown abounded, and there was little evidence to suggest that the non-university inhabitants possessed very much spare wealth, or desire for ostentation. Even at the beginning of the nineteenth century, the local guide book was uncompromising: 'Cambridge can boast fewer public amusements, than perhaps any town of its size and consequence in the kingdom.'[79] Certainly there was nothing like the assembly room at Bury St Edmunds. For centuries, the University insisted that there should be no theatre at Cambridge, though plays formed a regular part of college entertainment at least until 1747.[80] Instead, for a few weeks each year, plays were permitted at the time of Stourbridge Fair – licensed by the University.[81] By the first years of the nineteenth century, this had taken the form of an annual visit of the company from Norwich, whose performances were presented in an ambitious temporary structure. Compromise was eventually reached, and in the geographical no-man's land between the fair and the University in 1814 the Barnwell theatre in the Newmarket road was replaced by the Theatre Royal. This became one of a chain of theatres linked to Norwich, Bury, Ipswich, Yarmouth and Colchester.[82] The organisation and funding of popular entertainment of this kind depended, like the printing and publishing of books, on networks of communication and on outlets in centres of population.

Almost as recompense, there were concerts in plenty – in the town hall, in Great St Mary's church, in the colleges and in the Senate House, as well as winter series of subscription concerts in the Black Bear inn.[83]

The presence of the University also ensured a provision of teachers of linguistic, musical and artistic skills, whether for the more adventurous fellows of colleges, the better-off undergraduates, or members of the town's non-university population. In 1804, the *New Cambridge guide* noted several teachers of French (many of whom resided only during term-time), of the violin, the pianoforte, the flute, and of drawing.[84] A few years earlier, such a list would have included Italian and copper engraving and etching.[85]

By the early nineteenth century, too, there were several book societies, of which the oldest was that which met on Wednesday evenings in the society's own room at the Bull inn. It owned not only a library, but also globes, maps and mathematical instruments. Both here and at Nicholson's circulating library, town and gown could mingle on neutral ground, though Nicholson's principal purpose was to let out mathematical and classical books to undergraduates. For those who wished, it was also possible, on payment of a fee, to attend professorial lectures.[86] The book clubs appealed to different tastes; and none was more serious than that attended by George Pryme, J. H. Monk and other senior members of the University:

> This Master of Arts' reading room was a kind of Club, which was holden at a private house in Green Street, where tea and coffee might be had, and newspapers and pamphlets were taken in. Members were elected by ballot. The institution of the Philosophical Society, which may be said to have been formed upon it, occasioned it gradually to die a natural death. Previously to its being in Green Street, it was held at a house in Sidney Street, opposite to Sidney College; it was called familiarly "the Drum."[87]

Such activities offer us some clues as to the interests of the people among whom the books printed or published by the University Press and the other local printers and booksellers were offered. They were by no means solely devoted to the concerns of the University's teaching and examination system. Many undergraduates came to Cambridge not to read for a degree, but in order to acquire the accoutrements of civilised behaviour before they gained adulthood and independence. To this end, in 1709 William Worts left money to encourage recent graduates to travel, intending that his benefaction should permit an absence abroad of as much as three years.[88] Nineteenth-century slang distinguished between 'fast' and 'reading' men, and spoke of books for 'lounging' rather than study. This book is concerned with the more overtly serious end of this spectrum, and therefore with only a tiny minority among the increasing numbers of books that were published. First, it is necessary to understand something of the changes to books, their printing and selling in just over one and a half centuries. This forms the substance of the next chapter.

2

Changes to books and the book trade

The history of the University Press in the eighteenth and some of the nineteenth century is cyclical to a degree that suggests far more than the ordinary forces of a market economy. Instead, the abrupt reforms and associated recoveries were thanks to small groups of individuals who at various times imposed their wills on situations that had become so intolerable for a sufficient number of resident members of the University to approve actions attacking the placidity that marked so much of this period. Richard Bentley and his associates in the 1690s; William Richardson and his associates in the 1740s; Isaac Milner and his associates in the first years of the nineteenth century; all introduced overdue reforms, and for a few years each recreated a Press that was innovative, busy and of international importance.

By experience, the Press learned how to manage the relationship between printing and publishing. It did so even as publishing itself was changing. The continuous trend towards specialisation; the gradual disappearance of the bookseller who also published books, and his replacement by the publisher who also sold books; the establishment of the London publishing congers, and their subsequent collapse; the habit of sharing publication costs, profits and agencies even for quite small works; the gradual move of the London publishers to a dominant and exclusive national position; dramatic changes in publishing dynasties, in the mid-eighteenth century, the 1820s and the 1860s; the changing importance and nature of agencies; the growing powers of individual publishers with adequate independent capital or the means to raise it; changing price structures between manufacturer, publishing bookseller, agent and retailer; the constant experiments to discover capital in the under-capitalised business of publishing, whether by taking long credit from printers or by manipulating retail booksellers and their customers; the power exercised by the major publishing societies with whom the University Press dealt, especially the Society for Promoting Christian Knowledge and the Bible Society, who did not hesitate to use their purchasing strength when negotiating lower prices or better quality paper and work for their printed Bibles or (for the SPCK) prayer books; and the emergent strengths of organised labour, which obliged the Syndics to monitor wage rates in London. These were some of the contexts among which books were manufactured at and sold from the Press's successive premises.

Much more than just local rearrangements, the present volume is concerned with a period of greater change in the manufacture and distribution of books than at any period hitherto since the fifteenth century. During the years of this volume the centre of printing was moved several times. The cramped conditions of converted premises, adapted in the 1690s, gave way after a few months to a spacious purpose-built printing house. This in turn became inadequate, and from the mid-eighteenth century the Press acquired buildings on the other side of the street leading down to the River Cam, until in the nineteenth century it was able to build the Pitt Building and then gradually acquire further adjacent plots, in a process of constant expansion.[1]

Between the end of the seventeenth century and the mid-nineteenth century, the business of printing itself became increasingly complicated. Though the printing revolution, a series of changes in methods, materials and equipment that might be roughly dated 1800–20, was in large part responsible for this, there were many other features that in themselves were of independent origin. They had as much to do with the organisation of printing, and the demands of authors on publishers.

Successive changes in taste for different kinds and qualities of paper dominated the production of books. Baskerville made his reputation by the smoothness of the paper in his books, initially with the newly invented wove paper developed by Whatman. For some years, wove paper remained unusual in the trade, until at the end of the eighteenth century it became a feature of bibliophile taste. Then, with the advent of machine-made wove paper, it lost this cachet and became the most common kind of paper.[2] But the wove, rather than laid, mould was only one aspect of the subject. Hot-pressing imparted a widely admired glaze, and (since pressing reduced the bulk of sheets) could also aid the binding process.[3] Regardless of the mould or of finish, the raw materials of paper affected colour, bulk, printing quality and the way in which a sheet might change (and thus a book look) over a period. Shortages of rag were endemic in the paper trade, but by the early nineteenth century demand for paper was such that alternative materials were required urgently. Even before the adoption of chemical wood pulp in the 1850s, the quality of much paper had deteriorated markedly. The bleaching agents introduced in the early nineteenth century to combat poor whiteness were disastrous for the life of paper. Successive University Printers gave considerable attention to obtaining paper that was of sufficient quality, in an environment where it could no longer be assumed that paper stocks would be of even a minimum quality. In other words, while the mechanical revolution in paper, the introduction of the paper-making machine, was important, the much more immediate question for book printers was one of quality.

In type design, and hence in the most fundamental (though by no means the only) aspect of the appearance of books, this volume spans a period long enough to witness the creation, decline and then a revival of a fashion. The type obtained by Crownfield from the Netherlands was that which was most currently fashionable in England, praised by Moxon and by non-specialists alike.[4] But with the advent of William Caslon's designs in the late 1720s and 1730s, tastes changed abruptly. Chambers's widely read and much republished *Cyclopaedia* was emphatic, and by its endorsement probably did more to influence eighteenth-century taste than any other publication. Caslon, it explained, though not bred to the art of letter-founding, has, by dint of genius, arrived at an excellency in it unknown hitherto in England, and which even surpasses any thing of the kind done in Holland, or elsewhere.

The lesson was emphasised by a full-sheet specimen of the different sizes of Caslon's types, roman and italic, Greek and exotic.[5] For a while, Caslon's designs and their imitators dominated the market, until tastes changed again, thanks partly to Baskerville but probably more to his imitators. A fashion for letters having much more abrupt contrasts between thick and thin strokes coloured the output of British typefounders in the last part of the eighteenth century, in a taste fed and taken to extremes by Didot and others on the Continent.[6] In practice, some compromise was necessary, because type with extremely thin walls will easily break under pressure, and because of the requirements for a fairly robust type for stereotyping. By the 1830s, taste for Caslon's faces was reasserting itself. In the late 1850s the typefounders Miller and Richard issued their old-style type, a compromise with a clear acknowledgement to Caslon that became one of the most widely used of all type-faces.[7] Meanwhile, in a search not only for novelty, but also for a means to economy of space on the printed sheet, modern-face types were developed by all the major typefounders, and it was these which dominated book printing for two-thirds of the nineteenth century.

Both of these most basic ingredients of printing, paper and type, were developed in tandem with changes in printing presses. Baskerville's books were printed not only on specially chosen or specially treated paper, but also on presses that had been modified so as to produce a more accurate impression.[8] Stereotyping, in which the University Press played a leading part,[9] was likewise aided by the further accuracy obtainable with Stanhope's iron press. The advent of the printing machine introduced still further demands on type, as well as on paper. Changes in materials and changes in technology were rarely in time one with the other. The late eighteenth century onwards witnessed not only change, but also experiment as an integral part of an intricate series of processes that had, somehow, to be integrated.

For authors most obviously, changes in methods of illustration were of critical importance for several reasons. Books printed by the University Press are not, in the eighteenth and most of the nineteenth centuries, notable for their wealth of pictures; but some were necessary, especially in the sciences and in mathematics. Although instructions were given soon after the reorganisation of the University Press for the purchase of a rolling-press, on which to print copper plates, there is no conclusive evidence that one was ever bought. Several of the early books, from the quarto Horace of 1699 onwards, required copper engravings. However, details of payment for them are inconsistent. It seems more probable that when such plates were required the sheets affected were either shipped to London, to a specialist printer; or a rolling-press printer was engaged to come to Cambridge temporarily; or (especially once the print trade was established in the town in the second half of the century) plates were perhaps printed elsewhere in Cambridge itself.[10] Certainly the engraving of a comet in the 1713 edition of Newton's *Principia* was printed off not in Cambridge, but in London.[11] A small rolling-press could be transported quite easily, and the trade in local prints, whether of local scenes or of local worthies, depended on skills possessed by people who were often itinerant. The most celebrated engraver known to have worked in Cambridge for a prolonged period was also a native of the town, Peter Spendelowe Lamborn, whose plates for Bentham's history of Ely cathedral (1771) and large plates of Cambridge architecture (1767–9) are masterpieces of their kind. Lamborn worked in the town from 1757 until his death in 1774, and the largest of his plates would have required a press bigger than could be moved easily. But while he may have installed such a press at Cambridge, others did not. It is probable that the large engravings by Thomas Jefferys to illustrate John Taylor's account of the *Marmor Sandvicense* (1743) were printed in London.[12] This constant dependence on London skills for printing illustrations other than woodcuts was modified with the arrival of engravers seeking out other work in the town; but it ended only with the advent of lithography, and the establishment in Cambridge of specialist lithographic printers, some of whom became highly skilled, in the early nineteenth century.

Cost was always to the fore, whether for engraved decoration in the eighteenth century or for photography in the mid-nineteenth.[13] Different methods of illustration could both limit and transform authors' presentation of their work. In the eighteenth century, the choice at Cambridge was straightforward: between engraving (or, occasionally, etching) and woodcut; and the better work, whether of illustration or of diagrams, tended to be intaglio. In 1706, Rudolph Wetstein, the Amsterdam bookseller, wrote to Bentley concerning the ornamental title-page for his forthcoming edition of Horace. Bentley could, he explained, have one either engraved or etched, but he recommended engraving. An etched plate would provide no more than seven or eight hundred copies, and could not be reworked ('neque rescalpi potest'), whereas an engraved one would permit two thousand copies, and could be re-engraved at little cost.[14] The limitation on the number of impressions that could be pulled not only affected the choice of how copper-plates were to be executed, but also the appearance of books. In those requiring long print-runs, and low cost, plates were frequently used until much detail had been lost, and the advantages of fine engraving, and rich tonal effects, had been destroyed. This affected few of the books printed at Cambridge, where in the eighteenth century print-runs of books containing such illustrations were usually comparatively short, and where such books as required them had little need of detail. Maps were of the simplest, and scientific or mathematical diagrams were less complicated to print. The successive mid-century editions of the University's public verses, decorated with the same engraved ornament, formed one of the few series that required much reworking on the copper printing plate.[15]

Woodcuts were more robust, and for ordinary work such as the figures in Newton's *Principia* had the great advantage that they could be printed letterpress with the printing type. Since the University Press itself does not seem to have possessed a rolling-press of its own, there were further practical advantages, in that there was no need to liaise with another party. Yet, as Newton like others well realised, mistakes were equally possible in both media. Woodcuts, cut across the grain, were more difficult to execute than engravings, because, as Robert Dossie explained in his *Handmaid to the arts*,

In cutting it, and picking out the separated pieces, the grain of the wood, when it is crossed, renders the remaining parts so extremely fragile, that they are apt to break and fly out to the destruction of the effect: and this has occasioned the rise of copper-plates to supersede the other, in all cases except for very ordinary purposes.[16]

Other intaglio processes, principally mezzotint developed in the seventeenth century, and aquatint developed in the second half of the eighteenth, had no effect on book printing at Cambridge University Press, though the popularisation of the latter, especially by Ackermann, in the first years of the nineteenth century brought fresh possibilities, well exploited in the London trade. For Cambridge University Press, more mundanely, the development of wood-engraving (for which the wood is sawn across the grain, rather than with the plank) by Bewick and others had its own influence on illustrations and especially on more finely detailed diagrams.

Colour printing in eighteenth-century Cambridge was unknown; and when in the 1790s Busick Harwood offered hand-coloured copies of his *Comparative anatomy and physiology*, he was careful to promise that they would be copied from the artists's original, so as to preserve veraciousness.[17] The advent of lithography made colour possible at relatively little cost, and it was quickly introduced into the pages of the *Transactions* of the Cambridge Philosophical Society.[18] William Metcalfe founded much of his livelihood on the lithographic press he installed in Cambridge alongside his ordinary letterpress equipment. The University Press, having no lithographic press of its own, relied either on Metcalfe or on London lithographic printers for the illustrations inserted into its books. In doing so, the Press remained set in a long tradition that had separated letterpress from the printing of engraved or other intaglio illustrations and diagrams. Lithographic printing remained a separate skill, often executed in specialist printing houses, and with a quite separate organisation of labour. Even by the mid-nineteenth century, when London could offer many establishments providing printing in both kinds, the University Press remained dependent on others.[19]

Thus, and like most other printing houses, the University Press had only one regular means of printing its own illustrations: by letterpress. Woodcut and wood-engraved decorations, diagrams or vignettes, printed from wood blocks at the same time as type, saved press time and (since loose sheets did not have to be folded, sewn or glued in) saved time at the binders. By the end of this volume, such cuts were frequently printed not from the wood, but from stereotypes or electrotypes, processes that among other possible advantages preserved the cuts themselves from accidental damage at press. Photographically prepared process, or line, blocks were not developed until the 1870s, and half-tones a little later still.[20] They were to transform the appearance of books, the livelihood of artists and the economics of printing. For authors, they brought entirely new ways in which their work could be presented.

New printing methods – and, most of all, the introduction of photography and then its mechanical application to printing – brought changes to how scientific phenomena might be presented, how manuscripts might be studied with a new confidence and frequently in better detail, and how scenes, real or imagined, might be conveyed to the reader, as the photographer and process engraver took the place of artist and wood-engraver.

This process of change, as revolutionary for the depiction of illustrations as Gutenberg's invention of movable type and the means to print it, was a gradual one. The many early photographic processes, and most of the contemporary attempts at other means for printing illustrations, had in the end little effect on commercial printing. H. Fox Talbot's *Pencil of nature*, generally regarded as the first photographically illustrated book, was published in parts in 1844–6; but photography was not applied to printing on a commercial scale until photozincography was introduced in the late 1850s, and made popular in Britain in the 1860s. Though Fox Talbot suggested the principle of half-tone printing in 1852, it was not introduced commercially on a large scale until the 1880s.[21] The application of photomechanical processes to printing, the replacement of hand or autographic ones, and the eventual dividing of the ways between these two entirely different methods of reproduction, was no sudden revolution; and it was worked out over a multitude of experimental processes by the way.[22]

At no other time in its history so far had the book undergone so rapid alterations in its appearance as between the dates of the beginning and the end of this volume. Paper, type, illustration and bindings were all changed fundamentally, in a series of events of which the gradual abandonment of the hand-press in favour of the machine, the adoption of machines for paper-making, and the introduction of cloth as the normal covering for a book, were but part.

By the end of the eighteenth century even the Cambridge trade was offering to bind books in a style of lavishness that was, for some, merely extravagant. John, or 'Maps', Nicholson, perhaps today the most widely known of all booksellers in eighteenth-century Cambridge thanks to James Caldwall's engraving of his portrait by Philip Reinagle, made some of his living modestly enough, by selling or lending textbooks to undergraduates.[23] But his advertisement portrayed a more exalted side to his business, where fashion and style were at least as important as contents, and where bindings could be

> performed at his Shop in the most elegant and fashionable Style, in Green and Blue Turkey, Red Morocco, Russia, Calf and all other kinds of inferior Bindings; having lately purchased a fine Collection of superb Tools executed by the most eminent Artists. Gentlemen's Libraries may be polished up in a neat Manner, and books that are decayed, if the Leather be whole, may be refreshed and preserved to a degree that will not only surely render tham ornamental, but more durable by several Years.[24]

In what seems to have been a new departure in salesmanship, books were displayed on the counter.[25] Even the local bookseller W. H. Lunn, who sought in his shop opposite the Senate House to sell books as cheaply as possible, was under the necessity of acknowledging widespread expectation, in the vocabulary with which he puffed his stock:

> The public will please to observe, that Books in this Catalogue, said to be new and neat, are bound in calf, and those said to be elegantly bound, are likewise all new, unless otherwise expressed; and most of them executed by the first workmen in England.[26]

It is easy to over-emphasise such aspirations. In the 1780s and 1790s, John Bowtell made his reputation in Cambridge for the fineness of his bindings in Russia or morocco, amongst other work repairing some of the most valuable of the manuscripts and early printed books in the University Library. But in 1798 he was obliged to give notice in the *Cambridge Chronicle* that thanks to a prevailing shortage of calf-skins it was timely to remind potential customers that he was also able to bind in a style of paper imitating leather.[27] Appearances might be thereby preserved; quality was compromised. Much of the history of bookbinding for ordinary books, as well as of more expensive work, is of compromises between materials, cost and workmanship.

For the trade in academic books with which this book is largely concerned, changes in the outward appearance of books in the following fifty years were gradual. Leather, stretched and pared down, remained popular. But increasingly inadequate supplies, and the need to reduce the cost of binding still further, both favoured the introduction of cloth bindings. Though a coarse cloth had been familiar since the mid-eighteenth century on cheap books subject to considerable wear, especially schoolbooks and some practical manuals, the finer calico and others were introduced only in the 1820s. Such bindings could provide a more robust covering than the paper, or paper and boards, hitherto familiar, though the comparative strengths of books bound in any of these materials depended more on the sewing than the covering. It has become common to speak of edition bindings by this period, but in practice this is a misnomer. Though publishers might take advantage of cloth to make large quantities of cased bindings simultaneously, it remained that for many books only a part of an impression was bound up for sale immediately: the rest remained stored in sheets, as had been the practice for centuries. Accordingly, books in this period of transition, though still in their 'publishers'' bindings, are frequently bound in different styles or materials. This remained so for the rest of the century, and beyond. Within these variations, the appearance of academic books made its gradual transition, quarter cloth with paper sides being common in the 1830s, but gradually giving place to full cloth. No less noticeably, the weight of these full cloth cased bindings was gradually increased, the cloth becoming more substantial and the boards tending to be thicker.[28] Such changes were acknowledgement of the lasting qualities to be expected of cloth bindings, which would never be replaced by leather. In this, as in so much else, the University Press was conservative in the presentation of its books. The sober black cloth, blocked with the arms of the University, which are such a feature of its publishing in the 1850s and 1860s, was in marked contrast to the garish colours, liberal designs in gilt and inventive use of materials that characterised the more ordinary trade publishers.[29] Scholarship was to be sold by understatement.

Bindings on Bibles and prayer books, publications with which the University Press was crucially concerned, did not follow the ordinary trends of the trade. The great publishing societies, the SPCK and the British and Foreign Bible Society, were instrumental in popularising the concept of the publishers' binding, for they required books that could by their appearance be readily identified with their work. Binding for their books was contracted out by the societies themselves, who kept close watch on costs and standards. Leather remained common for long after it had been replaced by other materials on secular books, and blind-stamped covers gave information of publisher and price (if any). These were books intended to be sold cheaply or to be given away. At the other extreme, bindings of Bibles and prayer books had always been appropriate not just for better quality of materials, but for extravagance. In between lay all the variety that customers could desire.

Whether on the privileged books, or on others, the trends were the same: towards savings in materials and costs, including the costs of labour. Though the binding trades proved much less susceptible to mechanization than those in printing or paper-making, the trend was also – and much more obviously to most people – towards standardization.[30] The choices that had been those of the bookseller or of the customer became those of the publisher, whose prominence was thereby increased.

The changes in the European book trade in the latter part of the seventeenth century, cementing the leading role of the Low Countries as a centre for publication and for distribution, were built not least on trade by catalogues printed in quantities far larger than hitherto.[31] Circulated across Europe, they offered up-to-date information on what was available, and, no less critically, they offered a means of maintaining intellectual control of the increased numbers of printed books. The dominance of the Netherlands in this trade is to some extent reflected in the comparative lack of general printed catalogues of new books from individual members of the contemporary British book trade: the term catalogues, valuable as they were, were always very selective. In printing, the technical superiority of the Dutch was generally acknowledged, both in academe by John Fell and his associates and in the trade by Joseph Moxon.[32] But travellers who took an interest in such matters also noted the disparity of prices between bookshops in London and in Amsterdam. 'Latin books may be bought far cheaper in Holland than here', remarked the German bibliophile Uffenbach in 1712, noting at the same time how few English-language books were (so far as he knew) exported to the continent.[33] Britain depended on foreign-printed books, as she had since the fifteenth century, and booksellers were proud to boast of their latest imports.

A reformed press at Cambridge could not reverse the process, but its context would be inevitably an international one. The decision to found an organisation more directly answerable to the University, and controlled by a senior group of its officers, was not solely a response to an intolerable local situation. The University Printer in the 1690s, John Hayes, had become entirely independent of the body by whose appointment he held office, the University itself. No doubt for some this was reason enough to wish for change. More importantly, it seemed that change was possible in a European context. Bentley, Newton and their circle, in a court headed by a Dutch monarch, looked overseas as much as to Britain.

The appointment of a Dutchman, Cornelius Crownfield, not only brought to Cambridge Dutch printing skills and connections with the Dutch typefounding trade. It also provided a crucial link with the Dutch, and therefore European, book trade. Some associated with the new University Press saw the appointment as a means to promote their own interests. For Richard Bentley at least (in 1696 working still from London, as Royal Librarian, and not yet Master of Trinity College), the case for reform was an international one. In the scholars he encouraged at Cambridge from 1700 onwards, notably Kuster and Sike from Germany, he confirmed this outlook.

For most of the period covered by this volume, the University Press produced, broadly speaking, two kinds of books. By the end it was returning to a third.

First, as a learned press founded in a university, its list was dominated by the church, sermons, books of controversy, ecclesiastical history, and biblical or religious exegesis; by Latin and, somewhat intermittently, Greek classical literature, history and philosophy; by oriental studies (in effect the Arab and Jewish Middle East); by mathematics; and by the natural sciences. There was little poetry other than the occasional verses written to mark national events; there was little in modern languages; little modern (as distinct from ecclesiastical) history; no imaginative prose; scarcely anything on painting, sculpture, music or other arts; no practical manuals; and, overall, comparatively few books carrying illustrations beyond the diagrams essential to, for example, mathematics or astronomy.

Second, the Press from time to time exercised its privilege to print not only the Bible and Book of Common Prayer, but also law books. For the first decades of the eighteenth century no attempt was made to print the privileged books – the Bible and prayer book; but from the 1740s onwards strenuous efforts were made to re-establish the Press as one of the country's principal suppliers of these books both in small formats for private use and in larger sizes more suitable for family ownership or for the lectern in church or chapel. In the early nineteenth century, stimulated by the new British and Foreign Bible Society, the Press briefly dominated the market for Bibles that was more usually led by the King's Printers and by the Oxford University Press. The sale of the Bible and prayer book, based on pricing and retailing assumptions utterly different from those obtaining for most books, took the Press not only into societies organised for the distribution of Bibles, but also to retail outlets having no interest in other books from the Press, and into specialist religious suppliers for whom the Bible and prayer book were objects to be dressed up in varieties of materials and colours so as to suit a multitude of individual requirements or tastes.

Third, and last, there were schoolbooks. In the seventeenth century, some of the University Printers, notably Buck and Daniel in the 1630s, and Hayes in the 1680s and 1690s, had been among the country's leading suppliers. But in the eighteenth century and for more than half of the nineteenth, the University Press played virtually no part in this trade. No reasons are recorded for this reticence; and in the 1870s this situation was to be finally, if tardily, reversed. The Press's educational printing (in the early nineteenth century most books of this kind printed in Cambridge were published by Deighton in Cambridge or Parker in London) was aimed primarily at the university market or, very occasionally, at the uppermost forms of schools.

Requirements for schoolbooks followed a course, again, that was only partially related to raw population totals. Most obviously, changes in the numbers of children of school age, coupled with interest in educational provision, encouraged an industry led in the eighteenth century by publishers or authors with outlooks varying from John Newbery to Joseph Johnson or Mrs Hannah More.[34] Other established publishers such as Longmans and Rivingtons quickly found their own niche in this market. The demise of the stranglehold exercised in the seventeenth century by the Stationers' Company and the Cambridge press over elementary Latin texts and other books for schools brought a new freedom for other publishers to exploit the educational market, often in conjunction with authors, societies or schools that came to exercise influence considerably beyond their original intention.

For Cambridge University Press, the market for undergraduate teaching became much more important. The revolution in the eighteenth- and early nineteenth-century curriculum, whereby mathematics, classics and theology came to preside over university studies, not only required a succession of explanatory books, but also provoked a fresh spirit of rivalry among authors and colleges.[35] The introduction of written examinations (the Senate House exams) common to all undergraduates wishing to take an honours degree inevitably moderated some aspects of the spirit of intercollegiate rivalry, and encouraged others. Beyond Cambridge, and of much greater long-term importance for the University Press, the development from the 1850s onwards of national public examinations, under the aegis of the universities, brought change on a yet greater scale – for education and for publishers alike.[36]

Yet for much of the nineteenth century the University Press took part in these changes not as a publisher, but more often as a printer. Deighton in Cambridge, J. W. Parker in London, and Macmillan first in Cambridge and then in London, leaders in educational publishing, created their success thanks to printing obtained from the University Press. The Syndics of the Press, as publishers, showed little interest in one of the fastest-growing parts of the nineteenth-century book trade.

Indeed, so far as concerned the list of books that they published, the Syndics proved themselves extraordinarily resistant to the changes in the kinds of books that were published in the eighteenth and nineteenth centuries. In keeping with the conservatism of most parts of the University, the list of books published by the Syndics was cautious in the extreme. This was only partly the result of limited financial resources. The programme of publication envisaged by Richard Bentley and his allies in the late 1690s and early 1700s foundered for lack of co-operation among the booksellers. The three-volume edition of the Greek lexicon known as *Suidas*, published by the Syndics, became a millstone round their necks and was finally remaindered after Bentley's death. Bentley himself published two of the most notable of all books printed at the eighteenth-century University Press, the second edition of Newton's *Principia* (1713) and his own edition of Horace (1711). The advent of government subsidy in the 1780s, as compensation for the loss of the almanac privilege,[37] brought a new spirit of adventure not so much in a newly inspired Syndicate, as amongst a smaller group outside their number. This smaller group successfully seized the opportunity to promote their own interests in classical literature, though the initiative was damaged by some of its progenitors' tendency to self-importance.

The Press was more important as a printer. In the seventeenth century this had been its great strength: the authority and the ability to present an alternative to the monopolies of the London trade. The University's right to print 'omnimodos libros' (in the words of Henry VIII's charter of 1534) gave it a continuing advantage in the Bible trade. By it, Baskerville was enabled to print his great Bible of 1763, as well as a series of editions of the prayer book. But following the expiry of the Licensing Acts in 1695, and the subsequent expansion – nationally as well as in London – of the number of printing houses, the University Press no longer had a protected existence as a more general printer. It became, in effect, one printer among many: one with advantages for certain kinds of books, and with the essential advantage of being the most convenient premises for a sizeable body of active authors, the resident members of the University. But for London booksellers it had all the disadvantages of distance. Few London authors, published by London booksellers, could relish seeing their work printed at Cambridge, beyond proper supervision, when there were others equally or better equipped in London itself. Changes in this attitude only came – and then slowly – with the introduction of the penny post, the development of an efficient railway system (Parker, Macmillan and Clay were indefatigable travellers between London and Cambridge) and, some years after the end of this volume, the advent of the telephone.

Printing for authors meant, for the University Press, much more than the term seems at first to suggest. Certainly it included privately commissioned work, whether from Bentley or, in the mid-eighteenth century, from John Taylor. It also encompassed work for booksellers and publishers, most frequently the more substantial ones in Cambridge, from Jeffery in the 1690s to Thurlbourn in the mid-eighteenth century to Deighton by 1800 to Macmillan by the 1850s. In the overwhelming number of books emanating from the University Press, the Syndics had no interest other than as printers: and since much of this work was by private arrangement between the University Printer and the bookseller or author in question, they had no effective interest at all. The truth was that Henry VIII's premise, that the University might print what it would, provided it took responsibility for it (expressed as licensing by the Vice-Chancellor and his assistants), had become neglected. Long before the mid-nineteenth century, the University was taking no formal responsibility for all that it printed, save in the most indirect way. It appointed a University Printer; it required him to print certain books agreed by the Syndics and such administrative papers as were necessary each year for the smooth running of an increasingly paper-dependent organisation; but it left him free to use the University's equipment as he would, for most of his time. Such an arrangement, folly at best but actually the result of culpable neglect, potentially left University Printers in personally very profitable positions. Much more importantly, it permitted an active, imaginative and well-informed publisher, Macmillan, to profit at the University's expense, and to lay the foundations of a list that became ever stronger as the University Press's own meagre list became ever more disabled.

As a publishing enterprise, the Press was weak in many ways. As printer, it was more robust. First, as has just been indicated, it was in the personal interest of each

University Printer that the equipment available to him should be adequate. Less ambitious Printers paid less attention to this, just as the declining energies of illness or old age were reflected in neglect of equipment (in the case of Crownfield in the 1730s to the point of scandal). Second, the appointment of a new University Printer regularly prompted new investment, in presses or type. Third, the competitive nature of the Bible trade, enabling the major customers to play one printer off against another, in a context of restricted competition (Cambridge, Oxford, the King's Printers), meant that the Syndics were obliged to ensure that type, in particular, was in sufficiently good order, and not too worn. Fourth, most spectacularly, it was increasing demand in the Bible trade at the beginning of the nineteenth century that encouraged the Syndics to embark on a programme of experiment and development intended to apply a new process, of stereotyping, to the mass production of cheap books.

In the national context, the foundation of the Bible Society in 1804 was the saving of the Press, in that it brought business without which the Press could not have continued except perhaps in a very truncated form. But in turn the gradual reduction in Cambridge's share of the Bible trade threatened a further crisis, especially following the introduction of printing machines, that was only removed by the arrival of large orders from the Parker Society in the 1840s and 1850s. In other words, it was not the interests of London (on this occasion London publishers) which saved the Press, but of an organisation that, like the Bible Society, existed independently of the ordinary trade. The Press, like the local Cambridge societies, existed independently of the colleges save in so far as their members chose to cabal or encourage particular interests; it also existed, like those societies, alongside the ordinary book trade: part of it, yet defined by a different set of references and values.

By the nineteenth century, the presence in the town of two major publishers, first Deighton and then Macmillan, was an advantage to many members of the University, authors and customers alike. Conversely, these publishers were also an ever-present reminder of what the University itself had for generations neglected and was still neglecting in the portfolio it presented to the outside world: to a world that included parliamentary enquiries, religious and theological judgement, revolutions in the education of children, and, by no means least, fundamental changes both in the assumptions and definitions of science and in the ways by which scientific enquiry was to be pursued, shared and published. These topics are all addressed later in the present volume.

At the end of the seventeenth century, at the very time that the new University Press was being brought together, John Edwards, of St John's College, wrote vividly of the pains and miseries to which authors were subject: not only in gathering and ordering their materials, but in their publication and in their readers. Like others before him, he wrote of books that were intended more for show than for learning; but he added a modern gloss to this topic:

> Those that take them down to dust them, handle them more than the Owners: their main Study is to have them well bound, gilt and letter'd on the Back. This modern way of Scholars placing their Books hath something remarkable in it; for whereas heretofore they

set their Books with the *Front* forward, it hath been the late Practice to place them with their *Backs* towards them, presaging thereby that they would not trouble themselves to look into them: This then is mere Shew and Pageantry.[38]

For most members of the University and for most of the time between the beginning of the eighteenth century and the middle of the nineteenth, the University Press was the most obvious means of multiplying their work. By no means all chose to use the University Printer, and still fewer were in a position to persuade the Syndics that they should publish their offerings. Though many found themselves in the hands of the Press as a result of applying to a local bookseller as publisher, whether Thurlbourn or Merrill in the eighteenth century, or Macmillan in the nineteenth, for others the University Press was the obvious first resort – and hence, for some authors, to be consciously rejected. For many purposes, the Press was not equipped. It had no means of printing music; its facilities for illustrated books were always limited; and it either lacked entirely or possessed very little stock of many specialist – including oriental – type-faces. In some respects it eventually became invaluable, able to print a pamphlet in two days if necessary and thus (for example) contribute to the pace of the many semi-public debates that occupied the energies of those who sought to reform the University in the nineteenth century.

In this age of print, it still remained that assumptions might be questioned. This was especially true in a university environment that depended so much on the lecture, the spoken word, on notes prepared for such lectures, and on notes that might be taken at them. In the early 1830s it was the practice at St John's College for students to copy out in manuscript notes on the first three sections of Newton's *Principia* – until they were printed in 1834 'with a view of saving to the Student the time and trouble, which it has hitherto been necessary to bestow in copying them'.[39] Sir James Stephen, Regius Professor of Modern History from 1849, decided to print his lectures on the history of France not simply so as to avoid repetition, but because he believed it was undesirable to teach such a subject by lectures:

> It has, indeed, been suggested to me, that an annual recitation of my lectures would supersede the necessity of sending them to the press. My answer is, that, after once making the experiment, I have renounced the hope of being ever able to repeat the same discourses year after year. I must venture to add, that I am extremely sceptical as to the real value of public oral teaching on such a subject as mine. If Abélard himself were living now, I believe that he would address his instructions, not to the ears of thousands crowding round his chair, but to the eyes of myriads reading them in studious seclusion.[40]

But not everything had to be printed, nor was it desirable that everything that was printed should be seen to be so. Most lectures remained in manuscript – if indeed they were written out before being delivered. Most, likewise, remained in single copies. The lectures of the Lucasian Professor of Mathematics were required either to be printed or to be deposited in manuscript in the University Library. Barrow's had been printed; Newton's remained in manuscript.[41] William Whiston's *Lectiones astronomicae de eclipsibus*, delivered between February 1708/9 and summer 1710, are likewise in the

Library.[42] A few acquired a circulation that depended on the pen rather than the press. Of these, apart from Newton's on optics, the most celebrated became the lectures of Roger Cotes, Plumian Professor of Astronomy, whose lectures on hydrostatics and pneumatics were not printed until 1738 – twenty-two years after his premature death. In the years following his death, his lectures and demonstrations were repeated, and the written version of the lectures themselves was 'frequently' lent out to be transcribed. Robert Smith's edition of 1738 was prompted by the need for a correct text, from Cotes's own manuscript.[43]

John Nicholson, or 'Maps' as he was universally known, has already been mentioned. He was a bookseller in Cambridge for half a century.[44] His circulating library was relished; he was active in publishing especially books that would be of help to undergraduates; he maintained a substantial stock of books suitable as accompaniments to lectures in mathematics and classics; and his assiduous pursuit of business took him regularly into the colleges. Reinagle's portrait, given a place of honour on the stairs of the old University Library, depicts him walking across Great Court in Trinity, a pile of worn books grasped in his arms. Besides his business with the printed word, he was also able to supply (for a suitable fee) exercises and compositions in manuscript for undergraduates. According to hearsay, he could supply sermons in like manner, though this necessarily discreet aspect of his business has left little trace.[45] In some of this he was not alone. In 1766 the *Cambridge Chronicle* included an advertisement by George Knapp, bookseller and stationer on Market Hill, for 'Manuscript Sermons, the genuine Works of several Pious and learned Divines, deceased, wrote in a very fair hand, and believed to be originals', to be sold at prices between one and three guineas a dozen.[46] In 1789, John Bowtell advertised that 'Gentlemen of the University'

> may have MSS. or printed books transcribed correctly, in a neat manner and on moderate terms, by applying to Mr. Bowtell, bookseller, at whose shop a specimen of writing may be seen.[47]

In another vein, and rather more celebrated (partly no doubt because he was a good self-publicist, but partly also, and ironically so, because his goods were printed rather than handwritten) the Revd John Trusler offered sermons printed in a type-face designed to look, from a distance and to a casual observer, like handwriting. A discreetly worded advertisement inserted in the *Cambridge Chronicle and Journal* in 1771 alerted the clergy to his scheme: copies of his address were available from the Cambridge booksellers,[48] and the project seems to have been a success in so far as Trusler himself claimed to have printed over two hundred such sermons by 1790. After the initial advertising, Trusler preferred to avoid the ordinary routes of the book trade, so as to prevent embarrassment for his customers, who meanwhile paid 1s. each for their sermons.[49] But the appearance of newspaper advertisements suggests that the existence of such aids can scarcely have been a secret. In 1785 the *Cambridge Chronicle and Journal* included one for 'Two sermons, in a type imitative of manuscript' on 'The policy of integrity' and 'Mutual love the characteristic duty of Christianity': copies could be had from the Cambridge printer Francis Hodson, from Jackson at Oxford, or from James Dixwell in St Martin's Lane, London.[50] Trusler was not alone. In 1794, John Deighton's catalogue offered fifty-two sermons by the pseudonymous Revd Theophilus J. St John, LL. B., also printed in imitation of manuscript and at the same price. Two years later, W. H. Lunn, bookseller in Cambridge a little along the road from Deighton, announced that he had bought the entire remaining stock of the similar sermons of Daniel Pape.[51] The practice of using sermons printed in imitation of manuscript continued into the nineteenth century. In 1807 the *Cambridge Chronicle and Journal* contained advertisements for a collection of sixty by a dignitary of the Church of England, 'done up separately for the pulpit' and published by Ostell, in London. At first the advertisements were inserted in Latin, though this was soon dropped in favour of English.[52] Trusler's, St John's, Pape's and others' sermons, printed yet claiming the visual attributes of manuscripts, published yet restricted in their circulation, part of the book trade yet advertised in terms that made plain their difference, hovered between manuscript and print. With the other kinds of literature that were offered within the trade, whether sermons in manuscript (in 1794 Deighton was also offering 'a quantity of original manuscript sermons to be sold cheap'), notes of lectures, or student exercises, they are reminders of the ill-defined and sometimes anarchic boundary between manuscript and print, the world of the written word and the world of printers' ink, printer and publisher. With the advent of lithography and its application in the nineteenth century to work prepared from the reproduction of handwriting, for private publication, the boundary became obscured still further.[53]

The Cambridge University Press stayed firmly within one camp, as printer and, increasingly, as publisher conventional in that its books were readily identifiable within a tradition that looked unwaveringly back to Gutenberg. At the same time, many of the people who were most influential in its affairs within the University came to regard it with peculiarly personal feelings of proprietorship. For Richard Bentley, to whom the Press owed its existence in its modern corporate form, it was almost a fiefdom, in which editors were to be organised, authors (including Sir Isaac Newton) were to be cajoled, and printers were to be paid out of his own purse as he took on the task of publisher. Indeed, in the sense that he commissioned, paid for printing and also arranged distribution, he was acting the part of the more familiar modern publisher. That this was done under the name of the University, since some (but by no means all) of his actions in this process required the sanction of the Press syndicate, obscures still more the exact relationship between author, press and public.

Further kinds of obscurities are to be seen at the beginning of the nineteenth century, in the relationship between Richard Porson (d.1808) and the Press. For all his slovenly personal habits, Porson brought bibliophily to his scholarship, whether in the Greek types that he designed for the Press's use, introduced in 1809, or in the expectations shared by many in his generation that his work should be issued on larger as well as small (i.e. adequate) paper, and that the paper qualities should be commensurate. In employing a Greek type based on the hand of one of its authors, the Press again drew attention to the fragile distinction between manuscript and print in one aspect of the printing process.[54] Again, in other words, personal taste and influence became a fundamental part of a process that was in its essence ordinary, the publication of a book.

The Press's existence as a printer and publisher was thus defined by varying degrees of private interest, whether in a context of ambiguities between manuscript and print, or in the individual choices, self-proclaimed responsibilities, and determinations of authors. In this way the place of a learned press was formulated within the contexts both of an expectant university and of the national and international book trade. Public policy and interest might ordain, either through legislation (usually, in the case of the University Press, by Grace of the Senate, but also by Act of Parliament); but this public process always remained to be defined by the actions, assumptions and expectations of private individuals, both in its execution and in its interpretation at the hands of printers and readers alike. Officially the context of the Press was the University, and through the University the wider world of learning. This definition had its roots in the assumptions and provisions of the licence granted to the University by Henry VIII in 1534. But, like any other printing house and like many another publisher, the Press's fortunes and its everyday existence depended on the ambiguities, opinions, ambitions and interpretations brought by each author, printer, bookseller and reader individually.

In the eighteenth century, despite nationally advertised prices, prices for new books might vary across the country. In 1751, a brave attempt was made to list books currently available, in a sixpenny pamphlet of fifty-two pages, *A catalogue of the most esteemed modern books that have been published for fifty years past, to this present time, with prices affixed*. At the end, reflecting the separate parts of the book trade, was a catalogue of Bibles and prayer books, and a list of almost eighty chapmen's books.[55] Manifestly incomplete, even to a casual glance, it gave the appearance of a more rigid price structure than was in fact the case. The claim in 1750 by a bookseller in King's Lynn that he sold 'as cheap as in London' was reminder enough of this everyday fact.[56]

Prices might also vary according to what credit arrangements a bookseller was prepared to offer. In London, at the end of the century, James Lackington made his fortune and his fame by insisting on selling books at fixed prices for ready money only.[57] Despite his claims, he was not the first to do so.[58] W. H. Lunn, trained in London, attempted the same at Cambridge, like Lackington boasting of the cheapness of his books. But information on available books remained spasmodic, in the absence of organised trade lists. In 1805, the *Monthly Literary Advertiser* was launched to overcome this disability, though its coverage always remained incomplete – for London but also, and increasingly noticeably, for the growing provincial publishing trade. The larger booksellers found their own means of assembling information: William Pickering, for example, employed an interleaved and annotated copy of the *London catalogue of books, with their sizes and prices. Continued to August MDCCCXI* (1811), with extra catalogues and cuttings inserted.[59]

These were not only matters for the trade. In the view of J. E. B. Mayor, an outspoken and ferociously industrious fellow of St John's College, the lack of a list of books in print contributed to the modern (and damaging) emphasis on books of the season, on the safety of familiarity that was the basis of book clubs and circulating libraries. For him, it was a moral issue as much as a commercial one; and he drew attention to the very different position in Germany, where Hinrichs' *Allgemeine Bibliographie für Deutschland* was cumulated at regular intervals, where the Leipzig bookseller Avenarius issued a *Bibliographisches Jahrbuch*, and where Kayser's *Vollständiges Bücher-Lexikon* provided a guide to past publications.

> Surely our publishers might learn a lesson from their German brothers; let them select some competent bibliographer, and make it known that he is willing to catalogue all new books sent to him; authors and publishers will certainly spare for him one of the copies which they now waste on incompetent critics, and the puffing system, degrading to all who are mixed up with it, will receive its deathblow.[60]

Until the 1870s, booksellers and readers therefore had little overall and shared information on what was available in print. Instead, they relied not least on the advertisements bound in at the ends of volumes, sometimes printed on spare leaves and sometimes inserted as separate catalogues.[61] The practice of inserting these catalogues remained commonplace long into the twentieth century. Such lists, produced by the individual publishers, were also frequently to be found bound into books issued by other firms.[62]

No satisfactory national lists of books 'in print' were published until Joseph Whittaker conceived his *Reference catalogue of current literature*, and in 1874 (that is, after the close of this volume) issued a collection of publishers' catalogues bound up within a single pair of covers: the index to the whole, from which modern compendia of books in print are derived, was an afterthought.[63] By the 1870s, Whittaker could also advertise the prices at which books might (subject to discounting) be obtained of all booksellers: there was no distinction, as there had been in the eighteenth century, between prices obtaining in London and those in the country, depending on the number of agents, wholesalers and other intermediaries through which a book might have had to pass from printer to retail customer.

From the time of Thomas Thomas, the University's printers had been subject to public scrutiny. With privileges that enabled them to reap the benefits of some of the most lucrative parts of the publishing trade, including the printing of Bibles, the prayer book, schoolbooks and almanacs, the Cambridge press was both a part of the ordinary book trade, and yet distinct; operating in London (albeit intermittently, and usually via agents) and yet in the country. The periodic re-examinations of Henry VIII's patent of 1534 and of Charles I's confirmation of the University's position in 1628, were born of the inevitable clash between private interest and legal protection of a seeming monopoly (admittedly one shared with Oxford). But the series of accommodations reached with the Stationers' Company and its members in the seventeenth and early eighteenth centuries were in essence private settlements, between various interests within a single trade.[64] Their origins lay in national political and ecclesiastical discipline; and this remained the formal position until the end of the seventeenth century. But they also, and for many people primarily, concerned the management of the book trade. In practice, they rarely (though it was liable to be called as relevant by one side or the other) affected the public weal.

With the demise of the Licensing Acts in 1695, the requirement that books printed at Cambridge should be licensed by the Vice-Chancellor and his assistants lapsed also. Instead, the University approval assumed a different significance, at once more limited and yet possessing further intention. The old process had been a legal one, and therefore not necessarily implying any approval on academic or scholarly grounds: in practice, however, the University's licence was assumed also to bear this further weight. There was no financial element, since the commercial risk was with the individual University Printer or his commissioning bookseller. With the re-establishment of the University Press under the direct aegis of the University, soon after 1695, the old framework and assumptions were discarded. The consent of the Syndics to print a book became a financial and commercial decision. Their decision to publish became partly one that was also, inescapably, financial, yet carrying with it a weight of corporate recommendation.

The distinction between the different burdens of the University's imprimatur before and after 1695 was dramatically illustrated in the argument over the benefits and faults of university education conducted in the 1690s between John Locke and John Edwards, former fellow of St John's College. In 1697, Edwards issued an attack on Locke, *A brief vindication of the fundamental articles of the Christian faith*, and had it printed and published in London. Innocently or by design, he arranged for the University's (legally unnecessary) approval to be printed in the form of a letter from the author to the bookseller:

> Sir,
>
> You know Books Printed at Cambridge are commonly Licensed by the University, and acordingly when I designed the following Papers for the Press there, I requested Mr. *Vice-Chancellor* and the *Regius* Professor of Divinity to peruse them, which they did, and then returned them to me with an *Imprimatur*: and two other Heads of Colleges (for I applied myself to no more) were pleased to sign the same. The Form was thus:
>
> *April* 17. 1697.
>   Imprimatur,
>   *Hen. James Procan.*
>   *Jo. Beaumont Reg. Theol Prof.*
>   *Jo. Covell S.T.P.*
>   *Jo. Balderston S.T.P.*
>
> But since I found it necessary to be printed in *London*, and that I might not seem neglectful of the Favour and Kindness of the worthy Persons before mentioned; And that you and the Reader may see that the Ensuing Undertaking was so far approved of by those Learned Gentlemen, that they licensed the printing of it: I have thought it fit for their satisfaction and yours to set down their Names.[65]

Cambridge booksellers, perhaps sensing the impropriety, arranged for the page to be cancelled by covering it with a blank sheet.[66] But Covel was immediately attacked by

Locke, and escaped only by claiming that he had not read the book even though he had signed the *imprimatur*: 'Till it was printed I assure you I never so much as saw it or knew the least syllable of its Contents.'[67] His crime, he believed, was 'too much Credulity and Easinesse', a defence that Locke was obliged to accept as he turned his spleen on Henry James, the Vice-Chancellor, who could scarcely escape by the same route. Cross-questioned by the Archbishop of Canterbury, James alleged that he had required 'a blotting out of divers passages'. He also added the detail that Edwards had been (very properly) forbidden to print the *imprimatur* in London, and in doing so had displeased the Duke of Somerset, Chancellor of the University.[68]

These various tales and subterfuges, unsatisfactory in themselves, were least of all satisfying to Locke, who reasonably pointed out that the damage to him was a fact:

> The booke is gon and goes abroad into the world with those Reverend licencers names to the imprimatur. The vice Chancellor the professor of divinity and other eminent Doctors of divinity and heads of houses in the University of Cambridg are publishd by Mr Edwards as approvers of his booke. Tis alledgd that they and others are displeased with him for it But the world sees not any marke of the least displeasure. And the booke carrys up and down with it the appearance of being the favorite of the University and is not with standing what has been said to your Grace by Dr James like to doe soe to posterity . . . For as for that maske of white paper pasted of late over the imprimatur on those of the books that are sold in Cambridg, all that hear of it laugh at it as a pretty invention.[69]

Like a plaster, the cancelling white paper could be – and was – removed by those who wished to pry. But the more important, and more enduring, point was that the University's *imprimatur* had been exposed as no more than a convenient fiction, to be exploited as authors saw fit, with no risk of legal obstacle. In the personal drama between Locke and Edwards, with a supporting cast of Masters of colleges, the Vice-Chancellor, the Chancellor of the University and the Archbishop of Canterbury, the University saw out the legislation that had been a major justification for its authority to print for over a hundred and fifty years.

In the eighteenth century the book trade figured in a series of legal decisions respecting copyright, decisions that gradually defined the author and the nature of literary property. An industry that had hitherto been essentially a private one, permitted to be largely self-regulating through the Stationers' Company, became a matter of public debate.[70] In similar vein, the universities themselves became objects of more frequent public gaze. The numbers of their members dwindled, but interest in them increased. Between 1701 and 1799 well over a hundred pieces of parliamentary legislation were passed affecting the affairs of Cambridge and Oxford.[71] In the early nineteenth century this course ran to a further stage, with calls for a parliamentary commission of enquiry into Cambridge. The first such calls were unsuccessful. But those of a few years later could no longer be put off, and in 1850–2 and 1870–4 Cambridge was subjected to extended public investigations of its organisation and finances.

In 1781, under the terms of the Almanac Duty Act the universities of Oxford and Cambridge accepted money raised by Parliament specifically for them.[72] It was the first time they had accepted public money on a regular basis, for an indefinite period; and modest though the sums were (£500 per annum for each university) a principle had been established: that the universities were public, not private, concerns. In introducing the legislation, Lord North spoke of these payments as compensation, replacement from the public purse of what the universities had hitherto enjoyed by private arrangement with the Stationers' Company. But for one Member of Parliament at least, it smacked more of private patronage than of public well-being. George Byng, MP for Middlesex, opposed the proposal. 'It was a job, and of the same nature with those favours which the noble lord so profusely bestowed, at the public expence, in order to strengthen his own interest.' It remained for James Mansfield, as Solicitor General, to put such an allegation to rest; and he put the distinction starkly. 'The proposed grant could not be deemed a private one; for nothing could be more eminently a public interest than the prosperity of the two universities.'[73] Others, too, saw the question in extreme terms, but arrived at a different conclusion. In answer to Lord North's plea for encouragement of the universities, Charles Turner, MP for York, and a member of Trinity College, protested that 'he did not believe a tittle of this assertion'. 'On the contrary, he verily believed that the two universities were a public evil, and not a public benefit.'[74] Turner's views were apparently founded on his contempt for civil law, which for him had figured largely in his time as an undergraduate: the universities could not always look to their own for support.

Public interest, public obligations and public responsibilities not only brought the universities nearer to the centre of public attention. They also brought their activities, including printing and publishing, under public scrutiny. The presses were commercial businesses in ways that (for example) the teaching activities of the colleges and universities were not. But they were not permitted by their governing bodies to behave like other commercial publishers, taking on cheap and reliable work, with rapid sales, so as to support more ambitious and longer-running projects.[75] Their status as scholarly presses, as well as their privilege, permitted them to print the Bible and prayer book; and in the second half of the eighteenth century these two books became the economic rocks on which it was possible to build a structure of publications many of which required subsidy such as this assured income could provide. It was a way of running a business that flouted all the usual practices of a printing and publishing house, and ignored the usual requirements of a publisher that books should sell reasonably quickly. With a poor turnover on virtually every activity apart from Bible and prayer-book printing, the University Press was bound to remain modest in the context of a book trade that grew beyond all recognition in the late eighteenth century. Parliament might legislate for its support; but the receipts from the almanac duty had little practical effect on everyday work in Cambridge. It proved easier to increase the printing side than the publishing; but even that was not achieved lastingly until changes occurred outside the University's control.

The definition of a learned press adopted by Stanley Morison disregarded any context wider than the institution which supported it:

An Institutional Learned Press must be directed by an uninterrupted succession of printers, whose purpose of producing works of learning . . . is guaranteed by the objects of its
owners and controllers whose productions require, by the constitution of the Press, the
sanction of academic standards.[76]

The organisation and prosecution of such a press – any press – depend on, and are
therefore defined by, the materials and personnel available; the means of distribution
and sale; and the nature of the customer base. The University Press exists in this
material and social synthesis of printing and publication, controlled further by the
established authority of the university. Thus the defining contexts are simultaneously
local (the university and its sphere of influence; the town of Cambridge), national and
international (usually via London); and they are those of the book trade: of suppliers,
manufacturers, customers and readers. Distinctions in the second are as important as
those implied in the first.

In the late 1690s, with a new printer appointed from the Netherlands, Bentley and
his contemporaries looked for their readers as much on the Continent as in the British
Isles: primarily in the Netherlands itself, in Germany, and in France. A common language, Latin, both made more precise the potential audience for books printed at
Cambridge, and also enlarged it so as to encompass much of educated Europe. The
Leipzig *Acta Eruditorum*, founded in 1682, was published in Latin for just such
reasons.[77] Like other learned presses, the University Press was to be defined, silently
and informally, by the republic of letters, *respublica litterarum*, the network of shared
assumptions and beliefs which provided the means and the circumstances of learning
and which transcended the boundaries of country or native language.[78]

These were not new ideas. They had determined much of the behaviour of the
learned world at least since the fifteenth century, and their origins may be traced many
centuries earlier. But the context in which these exchanges took place changed generation by generation, the means of communication inevitably varying according to political or military, as well as technical, limitations. Even by the early eighteenth century
they also expressed an ideal in which national values played a part that could forestall
the international linguistic appeal of Latin. In Germany, Kuster's work was the more
admired because it was that of a person born in Germany. In the Netherlands, attention was drawn to the scholarly and scientific achievements of England, as a country.
The republic of letters drew its strength from seeking to ignore boundaries; but there
were many unconscious lapses from such an ideal.

The strains to such relationships and ideals by the end of the eighteenth century
were manifest. To the generation of the Napoleonic wars, the decline of Latin as a
common idiom stressed divisions not so much between France and her enemies, as
between the peoples of northern and southern Europe:

Let me be permitted now to explain, in a few words, what are the local circumstances, and
predominant ideas, which fix, as it were, the bent of the German Literati. In fact, so long
as science spoke the same language throughout Europe, so long as the Latin was the
common idiom with the learned in this part if the world; the same spirit was preserved
among them, and their labors had nearly the same tendency. But since the general

prevalence of the custom of writing in the vulgar language of the country, the European Literati have nearly ceased to form so strict a Cast by themselves. Those of each country are insulated, in some measure, from the rest, and are constrained to act upon their national character, the taste and impulse of which they must necessarily follow.

Nature, in placing an immense barrier between the people of the Continent of Europe, seems to have divided them into two distinct races, whose temperament and character are entirely different.[79]

Thus the republic of letters retained its reputation as one that could ignore war. The fault lay with nature, not with man. Although intentions at Cambridge proved unsustainable in their original form, the republic of letters remained a phenomenon to which the University Press was eventually to return, albeit in modified form. Meanwhile in some parts of continental Europe the concept retained its ability to redefine political or social groupings. As an American observer put it in 1816:

When you talk with a man in civil life of his country, you will find that he means that peculiar and independent district in which he was born, as Prussia, or Hesse, etc.; and you will find, too, that his patriotic attachment to this spot is often as exclusive and vehement as that of John Bull or a true American. But talk with a man of letters, and you will instantly perceive that when he speaks of his country he is really thinking of all that portion of Germany, and the neighbouring territories, through which Protestant learning and a philosophical mode of thinking are diffused. Nay, further, take a Prussian, or Hanoverian, or Hessian politician or soldier, and he will talk with as much horror of expatriation from Prussia, Hanover, or Hesse as Bonaparte ever did of 'denationalizing' a flag; but a professor or a rector of a gymnasium moves as willingly from one of these countries into another, and feels himself as much at home after his removal, as if it were only from Cassel to Marburg, or from Berlin to Halle.

My second proof is, that they not only feel themselves to belong to an independent body of men, but are really considered to be so by the several governments under which they happen to live. I do not now refer to the unlimited freedom of the universities, and the modes of instruction there, which make each professor independent; I refer merely to the mode in which professors are removed from one country to another. The king of Prussia would not appoint to any military or civil service, or even to any clerical office in his dominions, any but a Prussian; the king of Hanover, any but a Hanoverian, etc.; but if a man of letters is wanted, all such distinctions are not even thought of; nor is it the least reproach to the person appointed, or the least offence to his government, that he is seduced from his native country, though it certainly would be the highest in the other cases. Thus Eichhorn was brought from Weimar; Boeckh, now so famous in Berlin, was a Hanoverian; Heyne was a Saxon; Buhle, the editor of Aristotle, is in Prussia, etc.; and new instances of this sort are occurring every day through the whole of Germany.[80]

The context was part of German-speaking Europe. Beyond, affairs were less admirably ordered. Such a view, of the interchangeability of scholarship, could not be maintained in practice. Personal jealousies, national loyalties not only to scholarly abilities but also to technical capabilities combined to threaten and frequently dislodge the very foundations of this redeveloped intellectual republic. Britain remained off-shore, notwithstanding the few voices raised in appeal for a place integrated in European intellectual affairs. In the 1690s the University Press's ambitions were to contribute to the *respublica litterarum*. As is stressed repeatedly in the following pages, the intentions were scholarly before they were commercial. By the 1730s the mood had changed, as the list of books issuing from Cambridge aimed increasingly at a more domestic audience. For learned works, this changed again only in the 1780s and 1790s, as classical scholarship in particular looked to Europe and to European learning – with distrust, contempt, longing or admiration. The wars with revolutionary and Napoleonic Europe served only to obscure relationships, on a scale not experienced hitherto.

The Bible trade was different. It looked to an audience defined not by scholarship, but by religion, and by the English language; and it looked further afield. For much of the eighteenth century, following the resumption of Bible printing in the 1740s, it was here that the Press made advances overseas. Throughout the eighteenth century, sales to North America seem to have been negligible. Demand from elsewhere came gradually, usually according to the fortunes of the British flag. Missionary activity in India in the mid-century resulted in the provision by the Society for Promoting Christian Knowledge of supplies of Cambridge-printed Bibles, though this does not appear to have been sustained. In the early nineteenth century, the British and Foreign Bible Society ensured that Cambridge Bibles reached Australia.

For all books, agents and booksellers made their own selections. But from the end of the 1830s, books were also sent to institutions as gifts from the University – to other libraries in Britain, in continental Europe, in the United States, in the colonies and, occasionally, elsewhere. This was prompted by a mixture of motives. In one sense it was simply an extension of an old principle in a new form, of one academy acknowledging and supporting another. Other gifts denoted particular occasions. So, singly or in groups, books from Cambridge were sent to Jamaica, Canada and Corfu in the 1840s; to Adelaide, Toronto, Grahamstown, Melbourne and Montreal in the 1850s; to Ontario in the 1860s; to Melbourne, Sydney, Manitoba, Chicago (following the fire of 1871) and Natal and Strasbourg in the early 1870s.[81] University and publishing interests were thus fused, as each supported the other.

For a learned press, the view was beyond Britain, overseas to northern and western Europe and, with colonial expansion, to North America, to India, Australia and New Zealand. By the 1860s, Cambridge University Press, like its neighbours Macmillans, looked to regular trade across the English-speaking world. But as will be seen in the penultimate chapter, it was only with the establishment of this new firm in Cambridge that the overseas book trade and that in Cambridge became finally interdependent on a major scale, across a wide spectrum of subjects. Macmillans made determined and successful efforts to exploit personal connections between Cambridge and America or the colonies. The growth of the American and colonial book trade in the nineteenth century came only gradually to rely on the kinds of books that formed the staple of the University Press's own list, depending until the early 1870s on the development of major libraries and of higher education. The University Press's own eventual change in direction, after the end of this volume, brought in turn changes in the patterns of trade.

The usually learned and distinct interests of the Press had a strictly limited appeal in the context of most bookshops. Its books were specialist, and they tended towards specialist markets. The clergy, educated gentry, and the professions looked to book-shops in the cathedral cities, rather than to modest market towns. For Morison, Cambridge University Press epitomised the learned press. In fact, its books existed not merely side by side with those of commercial presses such as the businesses of Jacob Tonson in the 1690s, or of Deighton in the early nineteenth century, or of Macmillan in the mid-nineteenth century. As the following chapters show, the Press was also dependent on them, while at the same time exploiting its most valuable of all privileges, to print the Bible and the Book of Common Prayer. The Press occupied a privileged position, from which it was able to reap sales on a scale achieved by few other printers. But as was realised, slowly and painfully, it depended for the rest of its scholarly pro-gramme on the support that only commercial booksellers or publishers could provide. The Syndics of the Press launched themselves as publishers in the London trade only after the end of this volume.

❧ 3 ❧

Founding a new press

The 1690s mark a fundamental change in the history of the University's printing at Cambridge. Whereas before then University Printers were in effect their own masters, their work always to be licensed by the University but their business otherwise wholly independent of it, from the 1690s the University took command. The appointment of the first Syndicate for the management of the University Press, in premises rented by the University rather than by a private individual, and using equipment owned by the University, marks a re-foundation. It was inspired by two factors: the lapsing of the old legislation that had ensured the University's authority in what was printed, and the disquieting activities of the then University Printer, John Hayes, in his privately agreed accommodation with the Stationers' Company.

This chapter explores the foundation of the new press, the part played in this by Richard Bentley and others, and its first years under a Dutch immigrant printer, Cornelius Crownfield, as materials and men were assembled, and the first books were printed.

In 1696, the University of Cambridge possessed no Press. It had had active University Printers, sometimes more than one at the same time, ever since it had appointed Thomas Thomas, former fellow of King's College, in 1583. Thomas married the widow of a wealthy local bookbinder and equipped himself as a printer near Great St Mary's church, with the express aim of improving provision for teaching. Though he was the first actually to print, the University had had the right to do so ever since 1534. So long as the number of printers in the country was controlled (more effectively at some times than at others), and so long as the number of presses outside London was firmly limited, the University of Cambridge, like Oxford, offered a privileged position of considerable attraction. But whereas in the 1670s John Fell and Thomas Yate combined to set the Oxford press firmly within the tradition of learned presses that could be traced back to the fifteenth century,[1] in Cambridge at this time there were no such figures. Nor, despite occasional criticisms, do there seem to have been such ambitions.[2] Instead, the University Printer of the day, John Hayes, was manipulated (whether willingly or not is far from clear) into a position whereby he printed to the profit of those who invested in him – notably the Stationers' Company and its long-serving treasurer, George Sawbridge – but brought little glory to the University other than as a printer of almanacs and schoolbooks of the most traditional kind. His masters were the Stationers' Company, who owned his press and equipment, and who referred to his business as the Company's press, a part of the Company's publishing business known internally as the English Stock.

For some in Cambridge, it was hardly a satisfactory situation. The age-old rivalry between the two universities was as familiar in the late seventeenth century as to other generations before and since. In 1675, Isaac Barrow, Master of Trinity College, sought to persuade Cambridge to build a new senate house by reminding his audience that Oxford had just completed the Sheldonian, and that Cambridge should do even better.[3] The University refused, and Barrow instead brought his energy to bear on a new library for his own college – a library so magnificent that when in 1697 Celia Fiennes viewed the recently finished building, and commented that it 'farre exceeds that of Oxford', that is, the Bodleian Library, she seems to have been under the impression that she was in the University Library itself.[4]

Thus, between the 1670s and the 1690s, Cambridge saw erected a library of which it could be proud – albeit one built by a college rather than the University. But its printers were not to be boasted of. There seems now to be no record of who it was that first put forward the firm suggestion that Cambridge should follow the example of Oxford, and establish its press on a new footing. In Oxford, Fell and his partners had shown the way, leasing the right to print from the University in 1672. Four years after Fell's death, the equipment in which they had invested was made over to the University, and delegates were appointed in 1691. Today, Oxford University Press dates its continuous history as a learned press, administered by a delegacy, from 1690.[5]

Since 1689, the Chancellor of the University of Cambridge had been the Duke of Somerset, whose early willingness to contribute to the needs of the University can be measured partly by his generosity in enabling Trinity, his own college, to complete its library at a time when lack of money had brought the project virtually to a standstill.[6] Later on, he was to give generously for the building of the Senate House.[7] But he has been principally commemorated in the University for his work in connection with the University Press.[8]

Whether Somerset himself took the lead in establishing a new University Press, or someone else encouraged him to use his position to do so, the earliest detailed document that survives concerning the new arrangements is one by Richard Bentley, written probably in 1696. It is curious, in that at this date Bentley had no standing in the University other than that to which he was entitled by his degrees. He had graduated BA, aged eighteen, from St John's College in 1680, and between 1682 and the beginning of 1696 had been attached to the household of Edward Stillingfleet, first as tutor to his son and then as chaplain to Stillingfleet himself. In 1694, by now firmly established as a classical scholar, he had been appointed Royal Librarian. But he was not to return to Cambridge, as Master of Trinity College, until 1700. In so far as he had had any opportunity to consider the work of a learned press at first hand, rather than by his correspondence with scholars on the Continent, it was at Oxford, where he had attended Stillingfleet's son at Wadham College, and had taken his MA by incorporation (having taken it in Cambridge six years previously) in 1689. In particular Bentley had become acquainted with John Mill, protégé of Fell, advisor to Fell's executors after his death in 1686, and a Delegate of the Oxford press; with Edward Bernard, Savilian Professor of Astronomy and Delegate from 1691; and with Humphrey Hody, of Wadham, who had edited pseudo-Aristeas for the Oxford press in 1684 and had at that time also demonstrated it to be spurious.[9] For Bentley, the interests encompassed by such men, including Greek, the Bible and questions of authenticity, formed the background not only of his reading in the Bodleian Library but also in due course of his own work on like subjects, including his part in the Phalaris controversy, his advocacy of a press able to print Greek at Cambridge, and his ambition to edit the Bible. In 1691, his 'Epistola ad Millium' was included in the edition of Malalas's *Historia chronica*, printed at Oxford. In this manner he broke into print not at his own university, but at that of John Fell.

Bentley has, rightly, been given most of the credit for the successful establishment of the new press at Cambridge, and for its succesful prosecution during its first years. But quite apart from the contributions of others either in Cambridge itself, or having some connection with the Press as authors, the new arrangements had their origins firmly in London and the current debate on the future of press control. As Royal Librarian, Bentley interpreted his position as having a wider responsibility than simply to guard the books. In 1694–5, the debate in and out of Parliament concerning the Licensing Acts, the future of the Stationers' Company, the nature of copyright and literary property, the interests of the universities, and the interests of the royal and university libraries alike in receiving newly published books, all formed an agenda that could not be ignored by one having custody of the royal library.

How far Bentley was privy to John Locke's detailed criticism of the 1662 legislation[10] has not so far been established; but as members of the same circle of friends the two men must have had some knowledge of each others' opinions: perhaps (there is no real evidence) they even pooled their knowledge. Locke's view of the 1662 Act was disparaging, especially on account of the evident interest – working, in his view, against that of the country – of 'a lazy ignorant company of Stationers' in particular.[11]

Among his several criticisms of the 1662 Act, Locke offered details of the damage wrought on British scholarship and the British book trade by restrictions on editions of classical authors:

> The Company of Stationers have a Monopoly of all the Clasick Authers and scholers cannot but at excessive rates have the fair and correct editions of these books and the comments on them printed beyond seas. For the company of stationers have obteined from the crown a patent to print all or at least the greatest part of the clasick authers, upon pretence, as I hear, that they should be well and truly printed where as they are by them scandalously ill printed both for letter paper and correctnesse and scarse one tolerable edition made by them of any one of them: whenever any of these books of better editions are imported from beyond seas, the company seize them and make the importer pay 6s 8d for each booke soe imported or else they confiscate them, unless they are soe bountifull as to let the importer compound with them at a lower rate. There are dayly examples of this I

shall mention one which I had from the sufferers owne mouth. Mr Sam Smith two or three years since imported from Holland Tullis works of a very fine edition with new corrections made by Gronovius who had taken the pains to compare that which was thought the best edition before, with several ancient MSS and to correct his by them. These Tullis works upon pretence of their patent for their alone printing Tullis works or any part thereof and by virtue of this clause of this act the company of Stationers seized and kept a good while in their custody demanding 6s.8d per book, how at last he compounded with them I know not. But by this act Scholers are subjected to the power of these dull wretches who doe not soe much as understand Latin whether they shall have any true or good copys of the best ancient Latin authers, unless they will pay them 6s. 8d a book for that leave.[12]

There was, in Locke's view, no justification in the Stationers' possessing the sole right to print authors so long dead. Instead, their publication should be governed by ordinary competition – as in the Netherlands:

This liberty to any one of printing them is certainly the way to have them the cheaper and the better and tis this which in Holland has produced soe many fair and excellent editions of them whilst the printers all strive to out doe one an other which has also brought in great sums to the trade of Holland. Whilst our Company of Stationers haveing the monopoly here by this act and their patents slubber them over as they can cheapest, soe that there is not a book of them vended beyond seas both for their badnesse and dearnesse nor will the Schollers beyond seas look upon a book of them now printed at London soe ill and false are they besides it would be hard to finde how a restraint of printing the Classick Authors does any way prevent printing Seditious and Treasonable pamphlets which is the Title and pretence of this Act.[13]

Repeatedly, Locke turned to the example of the Netherlands, 'the sole manifacture of printing bringing into the low Countrys great sums every year', where thanks to unrestrained trade booksellers could sell London-printed books more cheaply in Amsterdam than in St Paul's churchyard. Thanks, also, to restrictions on taking apprentices and employing foreigners, English printing was of dismally low quality – again to the loss of the country.

The nation looses by this act for our books are soe dear and ill printed that they have very litle vent amongst forainers unless now and then by truck for theirs which yet shews how much those who buy here books printed here are imposed on.

There was ample reason for the University to resent the intrusive and sometimes controlling hand of the Stationers' Company in its affairs. The arguments advanced by Locke pertaining to the book trade in general had much in common with the specific interests of the University. Cambridge depended on foreign interchange, whether personally or in print. It had a vested interest in the price and quality of books. Locke wrote of the need for editions of classical texts. It was just this area to which attention was to be first applied at Cambridge – and, moreover, with the help of a Dutchman. Locke may have been summarising his own opinions and those of his friends. But it was Bentley who applied them to practical effect.

Ever alert to the materials of printing, Richard Bentley had by the mid-1690s already faced difficulties in his search for satisfactory means of publishing his work. 'I had then prepar'd a *Manilius* for the Press, which had been publish'd already, had not the dearness of paper, and the want of good Types, and some other occasions hinder'd.' The words were written in 1699; but he was referring to the years between his sojourn in Oxford and the establishment of the press at Cambridge.[14] Despairing of English printing, he had also been disappointed by Leipzig, where he had turned for a printer of his work on Philostratus.[15]

It is not clear what status the surviving proposals put forward by Bentley had in the context of discussions during 1695–6 about the possibility of a new press at Cambridge. Somerset appeared uncharacteristically casual in the letter he addressed to the Senate on 29 June 1696, speaking of 'a short & imperfecte scheame . . . by way of a foundation'. The 'scheame' as Somerset proposed it has not survived, and its relationship to the proposals put forward by Bentley cannot therefore be determined. But it is remarkable that in consulting Bentley, those that did so chose to go outside the immediate purlieus of the University, to a scholar who, however distinguished, was not a resident member. Those with whom he is known to have kept up friendships in Cambridge do not seem to have been among the most obviously influential in the daily workings of the University itself. In July 1696 Bentley returned to Cambridge to take the degree of DD. He was keeping his old contacts with his university, and it may be that this suggested an opportunity – either to Bentley himself, or to those with whom he fell into conversation on the current topic of interest that summer. The fact that the document recording his proposals was described at both the beginning and end as 'by Dr Bentley' further suggests, but does not prove, that his ideas followed, and were perhaps therefore a development of, those put forward by Somerset.

Bentley's proposals were as follows:

1 That ye Chancellor, ye Vice-Chancellor, ye Regius and Margarett Professors of Divinity, ye Law Professor, ye Physick Professor, ye Mathematick Professor, ye Professor of Hebrew & Arabick, ye Greek Professor, & Dr Bentley ye present Library keeper to His Majesty, be constantly of ye number of Curators to govern ye Press. & if any other Persons shall be thought necessary, they may be added to those aboue mention.

2 All Books that are printed with ye new Types may be licenced by three or more of ye Curators, who are to be very carefull in determining what Books shall be printed.

3 That under ye Curators, & by them should be appointed an Architypographus, who may be ye Publick Library keeper for ye time being, or whom else they shall judge best qualify'd for that Office, which may be held, quamdiu se bene gesserit: his Employment to be ye constant inspection of ye Press, & ye immediate direction of ye Printer, Corrector, & all inferior Officers; as alsoe ye Care of Matrices & Punchions, which are to be preserved carefully in a Publick Chest for that purpose; All Books to be printed with ye new Types, may be offer'd to Him by ye Undertakers, & by Him to ye Curators, before they are sent to ye Press.

4 The Architypographus may agree with ye Undertaker in ye name, & by ye Direction of ye Curators, for ye use of ye new Types; & by their Order may receiue & expend

such summs as they shall judge necessary for the service of yᵉ Press, for which he may be accountable to them at their meeting

5 The Curators may determine yᵉ Price of yᵉ Copy between yᵉ Publisher & yᵉ Bookseller, if yᵉ former be employ'd by them in yᵉ Publication of any Book.

6 Those persons that are willing to put forth such Books as shall be approved by yᵉ Curators, may receiue by their appointment, an Encouragement suitable to yᵉ Merit of their Undertaking, out of yᵉ University Chest (besides what they haue from yᵉ Bookseller for their Copy) & out of the same Fund such an Annual Establishment as yᵉ University shall think fitt, may be allowed to ye Architypographus.

7 Nothing to be printed off, after yᵉ second review of any Book by yᵉ Publisher, till it be again examin'd by yᵉ Architypographus.

8 That yᵉ Curators aboue mentioned, or any Fiue of them (whereof yᵉ Vice-Chancelor to be one) may meet two or three times every year (besides their usual Meetings upon ordinary Occasions) particularly to view yᵉ condition of yᵉ Press; to pass all accounts of Receipts & Disbursments relating to yᵉ new Types; to enquire whether yᵉ respectiue Officers perform their Duty, & whether proper Materials & able Workmen are employ'd; & to add alter, or retrench what they shall find conuenient, as may be most for yᵉ Honour & Interest of yᵉ University.[16]

While Bentley was keen to provide for proper supervision – the Undertaker to be supervised by the Architypographus, who was himself to be a senior and experienced scholar, and the whole to be managed by a body of curators, headed by the Vice-Chancellor – he showed no inkling of the realities of publishing. To him, it was an arrangement between scholarship, printers and the University. Authors were to be properly rewarded and their texts were to be meticulously proof-read. Booksellers were an afterthought. We may recall Fell's remark to Isaac Vossius in 1670/1, when he was considering a future press at Oxford: 'a press freed from mercenary artifices, which will serve not so much to make profits for the booksellers as to further the interests and convenience of scholars'.[17] In view of his time in Oxford, when he had had an opportunity to hear of the realities of running a press, it was a remarkably innocent document, coloured perhaps by the commonly held scholarly suspicion and dislike of publishing booksellers.[18] For he made no suggestions as to whence the new press might be financed other than out of the University Chest and such as booksellers might pay for copies. He showed no knowledge of how long it took to sell books, particularly in an academic market, where books might remain unsold and therefore in print for decades. And as a result he did not consider how money was to be generated year by year, whether by the usual means of running some fast-selling books with those that would inevitably take longer, or by some advantageous arrangement with a regular London stationer or group of stationers.

The difficulty of regular finance by regular income from sales was to prove too much for the press as Bentley envisaged it. Cambridge was not the first to discover the difficulty; and Cambridge was in a weaker position than Oxford when the question could no longer be avoided. Cambridge produced no contemporary figure such as Arthur Charlett, Master of University College, Oxford, whose energies as a correspondent were put to a host of learned causes at the end of the seventeenth century and beginning of the eighteenth, and not least to the promotion and publicising of the university press. But in the end even Charlett had to conclude, 'The vending of books we never could compasse.'[19]

There was a further difficulty that Bentley did not foresee, in that quite apart from the sale of books, the book trade survives best if it is underpinned by a steady income from assured sales of well-established titles: what the modern publisher knows as the back-list. For Cambridge, for much of the seventeenth century, this had been assured sale of repeated printings of the Bible. The heyday for Cambridge-printed Bibles had been the mid-century. But between a quarto edition printed by Hayes in 1683, and a series of duodecimo editions printed by Joseph Bentham in the 1740s and 1750s, no Bible was printed at Cambridge. Instead, the country was supplied from London, the Netherlands and (especially under John Baskett) from Oxford under a succession of agreements beginning with one with the Stationers' Company in 1692. Baskett became Queen's Printer in 1712.[20] Thus this steady financial support was spurned by Cambridge. In secular books, too, Oxford was in an apparently more fortunate position, thanks to the overwhelming success of Clarendon's *History of the rebellion*, of which the first edition, in three noble volumes, was published by the University in 1702–4. Again, it was Baskett, as publisher also of successive subsequent editions of Clarendon in 1707–28, who thus consolidated his position as, in effect, the principal financier of the Oxford press for more than two decades.[21]

In 1696, most of this lay in the future, though for the present there was no question of Cambridge's seeking to print the Bible, prayer book or law books. News of the University's preparations spread quickly among those who might have an interest. Bentley, for one, was eager to push forward. 'Our University press goes on; we expect Letter from abroad by y[e] next Convoy: Presses and all tackling are allready provided at home',[22] he wrote to Evelyn in January 1696/7. Early in February, Nathaniel Hough, a young graduate of Jesus College, appeared to believe that matters were proceeding faster than in practice was to be the case. 'The University has lately built a new printing house, and have sent for choice letters into Holland, designing to hire a printer, buy paper, and manage the whole business with their own stock; so that now we shall have good editions, and a clean character.'[23] He may have been misinformed as to the timetable for repair and rebuilding of the old Queens' stage-house; but his remarks on good editions and clean type, drawn from the gossip of common rooms, perhaps express as clearly as any the irritation felt in the University at Hayes's usual unambitious standards, and the specific hopes that the new arrangements promised to fulfil.

John Hayes, University Printer at Cambridge since 1669, was not his own master, and not the owner of the equipment that he used. By an agreement with the Treasurer of the English Stock of the Stationers' Company, that is, the publishing arm of the Company, he both had handed over his press, type and other equipment, and had become the Treasurer's hired servant. The English Stock, managed by a powerful coterie within the Company, whose history could be traced back to the late sixteenth century and who had become increasingly wealthy (and therefore powerful) through the seventeenth century, controlled some of the most lucrative of all publications, including almanacs and a range mainly of educational books and classical authors. For the English Stock, Hayes was in an advantageous position, in that his appointment as University Printer enabled him to print whatsoever books he chose: 'omnimodos libros', in the words of the charter granted to the University by King Henry VIII in 1534. By coming to an arrangement with him, the Stock not only gained a malleable employee; it also ensured that a potential threat to its virtual monopoly was neutralised. This arrangement had not been arrived at without some argument in the Stationers' Company itself, in that until 1690 Hayes had, in fact, been employed not by the Company or by the Stock as a whole, but by the London bookseller George Sawbridge, who had kept the real nature of his relations with Hayes from the Company whose interests he was supposed to promote. In that year, for 100 guineas, the Company had bought out the interest of Sawbridge's successor Edward Brewster, who was then serving as its Master; it had bought the equipment at Cambridge at the same time. By an agreement which suggests that the University itself set little value by the potential offered in the 1534 charter, at the end of the year the Company and the University concluded an agreement by which the University's privileges were made over to the Company for £100 per annum. In September 1691, the management of the printing house at Cambridge was put into the hands of a committee of the Stationers' Company.[24]

Accordingly, when on 7 September 1696 the Court of the Stationers' Company heard formally that the University was considering setting up a printing house 'at their owne Charge', and that it was acquiring type and other necessaries, the news cannot have been altogether welcome. Only in the past few years had the Company first dealt with an internal scandal, and then successfully established itself in the very premises, and with the very man, who posed a threat comparable only with the difficulties even at the same time exercising it from Oxford. For its part, the University felt the situation delicate enough for the Vice-Chancellor of the day, John Eachard, Master of St Catharine's College, to journey to London and explain its intentions to the Master of the Stationers' Company in person.[25] Thus the London trade was officially acquainted with Cambridge's abrupt change of mind.

In a great measure, the University's announcement was reassuring. There was 'no intention to print anything in prejudice to the Company in any wise but only to print some Classick Authors, and such Bookes of Learning as they shall find to be wanted, and that their desire was to rent the Companyes Printing house to carry on this their designe, or to give such a summe of money as the University and the Company shall agree on'.[26]

These unexpected developments came at a time when the Company was repeatedly exercised by attacks on its interests. Less than five years previously, its schoolbooks had been pirated in York. Its almanacs were pirated in Chester and elsewhere.[27] Unauthorised imports challenged its monopolies from overseas. Even in London, printers who rushed too precipitately to print the Company's books had to be punished, albeit usually with lenient fines. And the difficult, increasingly tangled, matter of relations with

Oxford exercised the Court of the Company far more frequently than the comparatively simple questions respecting Cambridge. As was usual in matters where the Court of the Company required expert reflection, a Cambridge committee was appointed, which in September 1696 visited the University.[28] The vice-cancellarial preliminaries bore fruit, in that it was now agreed that the University should have the Company's printing house, for a sum to be settled; the University was to repair and improve a building on the same site; and was to meet the cost of moving into these new improved premises the equipment used by Hayes as soon as building work permitted. These were either costs and measures that the University would have expected to face even without agreement, or so slight as not to matter. In other words, the Company seems to have capitulated as readily as could possibly have been hoped. Perhaps it realised the weakness of its position. Hayes was no longer a young man; and the parties in the agreement of 1690 had included Hayes personally. In face of the University's new interest in printing, the Company could not expect to renew its agreement with another principal.

In comparison with the difficulties that imbued relations between the Stationers' Company and the University of Oxford, relations between Cambridge and the Company seemed amicability itself.[29] In fact they were complicated by collegiate, financial and personal interests. As landlords both of the old printing house occupied by Hayes, and of the site proposed for the new venture (fig. 2), Queens' College had an interest in ensuring a continuing return if not from the Stationers' Company, then from the University. In 1696, Eachard was succeeded as Vice-Chancellor by Henry James, President of Queens' College, who remained in office until the autumn of 1698; thus, both in his college and in the University, the same man was able in great measure to regulate the well-being of the new press.[30] Hayes himself seems not to have wished to move. He had been in his house, and occupied the printing house, since 1669, when he had succeeded John Field. Alterations to the premises proposed for him, in the old stage-house belonging to Queens' College and adjoining his existing ones on a site just to the north in Queens' Lane, were begun in October 1696. They took longer than some might have hoped, and were completed only in autumn 1698. But it was not until spring that year that it was finally decided to leave Hayes where he was. Accordingly the University took over what it had once thought adequate to refit for Hayes, and it was in this much smaller building that the new University Press was born.

The Queens' College stage-house remained the Press's premises until after Hayes's death in November 1705. By then it had proved to be inadequate. More importantly, it was cheaper to rent, at £1.10s. compared with the rent of £25 paid by the Stationers' Company for Hayes's premises. By the time that Hayes's affairs had been wound up, and the books in train at the time of his death had been completed, almost another two years had passed. So, it was to be the summer of 1707 before the press described to the Stationers' Company in September 1696 was finally moved into the premises that had been too easily assumed. The rent for Hayes's old premises was agreed at £22, a slight reduction for the College; and the former stage-house was let out to another tenant, until a few years later it was established as the first regular University facilities for the teaching of Chemistry and Anatomy.[31] It was still in use as an anatomy theatre in the

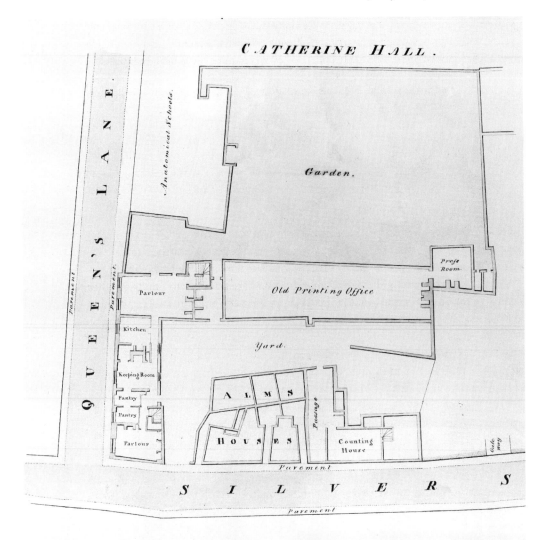

Fig. 2 Plan of the Press's premises at the corner of Silver Street and Queens' Lane, drawn by Alexander Watford in the early nineteenth century. The old printer's house is on the corner, and the stage-house (for a while the home of the University Press under Cornelius Crownfield) is marked to the north as Anatomical Schools.

nineteenth century. Field's printing house remained in use for its original purpose until 1804, when it became warehouse accommodation. Meanwhile, in the 1760s the Press began to establish itself on the south side of Silver Street, in the beginning of a process that was eventually to colonise the entire site bounded by Silver Street, Laundress Lane, Mill Lane and Trumpington Street. But the old premises on the corner of Queens' Lane were not given up until 1835.[32]

To one outsider at least, the Cambridge plans in the 1690s seemed to presage another bout between university interest and the Stationers' Company. As early as September 1695, a year before the Company heard formally of Cambridge's intention, report already spoke of the planned press. The likely course of events required little imagination:

> I would have booksellers live in a dependence upon scholars, by whose labour and industry they gaine their wealth, and act in subserviency under them, and not presume to dictate and give lawes, as they have done of late too much. The Theater presse [at Oxford] has mortifyed them sufficiently; and I doubt not, but that they wil open as fiercely against the University of Cambridge when they have established a peculiar press of their owne, to bee managed by Delegates, and have furnished it with variety of types, and Greeke especially, upon wch at present they are so worthily and carefully intent, as they have done formerly against Bp Fell.[33]

Thomas Smith, who took this pessimistic view, was well placed, as librarian of the Cotton Library, to know Bentley's opinions and, perhaps, fears. As Royal Librarian, Bentley had been resident at St James's Palace for several months, and most of the earliest discussions concerning the new Cambridge press are traceable to London, rather than to Cambridge. In August 1696, John Evelyn was unequivocal in speaking of 'that noble presse which my worthy & most learned friend Dr Bentley . . . is with great charge & industry erecting now at Cambridge'.[34] By that time Bentley was in formal charge of the project which all available evidence suggests that he had himself instigated. For on 6 July 1696 the University approved a Grace giving him authority to buy types for the press. In this way, the new foundation figured for the first time in the official decisions of the University. The decision was necessary because money was to be spent. As for administration, there was no need for a declaration of intent any more specific than that. It is no wonder that Evelyn was still writing in January 1696/7 of 'Dr. Bentley's new Imprimerie'.[35]

Evelyn was in no doubt. But in using the word 'Imprimerie' in the course of a letter to Bentley himself he was perhaps also taking up another part of the conversations of the previous few months. Although the word was indeed widely used in the late seventeenth century simply to mean 'printing house', it had also a particular resonance. For those who had dealings with the learned press, it referred directly to the French Imprimerie Royale, established by Richelieu in 1640 and with which Evelyn had become acquainted during his sojourn at Paris in 1643–4.[36]

Expectations for the new press at Cambridge varied according to individuals' own hopes for scholarship or publication. Bentley himself, with an eye even in 1695 to what might be printed, enquired unsuccessfully as to the possibilities of a survey of Roman inscriptions based on the collection of Marquard Gude, who had died in 1689.[37] Evelyn pondered the possibility of an English edition of d'Aviler on architecture, a project that would have required a great many engraved plates.[38] His thoughts also turned to the press (still not at work) in January 1696/7 when booksellers pressed him for a revised fourth edition of his Sylva. Neither project was taken up. Bentley found John Place, the bookseller interested in d'Aviler, not yet ready:[39] the book remained unpublished in an English translation in Evelyn's lifetime;[40] and the new edition of Sylva did not appear until 1706, in London. As for Bentley himself, if he had any personal hopes that he might put the Cambridge press to use for his own books, there was no sign of this for the present. But it is clear that one of the earliest priorities was the acquisition of Greek type, and here we may see Bentley's personal interests at work. Observers in 1695 and 1696 remarked on the particular importance attached to Greek in the new enterprise.[41] In 1697, Bentley contributed to the edition of Callimachus left unfinished by the untimely death of Graevius's son: the work was published at Utrecht. He was also in contact with Graevius respecting a proposal to meet a long-felt want, for a fresh edition of Hesychius, now planned for publication at Cambridge.[42] It was a project that may have been born in London, stimulated by Thomas Gale's work on the subject. But in 1697 Gale was appointed Dean of Durham, and moved out of everyday contact with his old circles in London and Cambridge. In the end the new edition of Hesychius developed, under Bentley's protégé and Graevius's 'juvenis eruditissimus' Ludolph Kuster, into a yet greater project, for a new edition of *Suidas*.[43]

In all this, the figure of Bentley dominates the surviving correspondence. It was he to whom the University delegated the power to buy type for the new press; it was he who seems to have been especially active in eliciting possible publications; it was he whose proposals were in very large measure taken up. And yet, he was still in London, as Keeper of the Royal Library. He had no immediate prospects of return to Cambridge. Of those for whose chairs he might have considered himself a candidate, Joseph Beaumont, of Peterhouse, had been Regius Professor of Divinity since 1674; and Joshua Barnes, of Emmanuel College, had been Regius Professor of Greek since only 1695. Of other crown appointments, John Montagu had been Master of Trinity College since 1683; but in the mid-1690s there can have been no inkling that he would in 1699 be appointed to the Deanery of Durham. If Bentley had entertained any hopes of the chair in Greek they were disappointed in the very year in which the first mention seems to have been made of a University Press on a fresh footing. Barnes, born in 1654, and the editor of a major edition of Euripides, appeared to some a stronger candidate than Bentley, who in 1695 was embroiled in the Phalaris controversy, and had not yet published his damning proof of the letters' inauthenticity. Bentley's opinion of Barnes was guarded, most celebrated in the often quoted remark that he knew as much Greek as an Athenian blacksmith;[44] but his criticism in 1697 of the spurious epistles that Barnes had attached to his edition of Euripides in 1694 was, in the words of his biographer, J. H. Monk, phrased 'in terms not of displeasure but of compliment'.[45] If he had been thwarted in his hopes, he did not show it publicly.

Thus, while Bentley had a personal and a scholarly interest in promoting the new press, he was not in complete command. In 1712 he wrote of the Cambridge University Press as having been 'projected and founded solely by myself, and purchased and endowed solely by my friends'.[46] This was to ignore the fact that despite talk of it, there is today no evidence that money had been forthcoming from his London friends.

In fact, all the evidence of Bentley's part in the affair derives directly from Bentley himself, or from his circle of friends in and around St James's. Financial support, as well as encouragement, came most bountifully from the Chancellor of the University,

the Duke of Somerset, who in 1697 gave £200, and loaned as much again.[47] In practice, Bentley could have done nothing without Somerset's encouragement. It is difficult
now to elicit the nature of the collaboration between the various promoters of the press
in 1695–8, for it has been obscured partly by some of the many jealousies to which
Bentley's activities and opinions gave rise; and partly by the lack of surviving correspondence by the several interested parties. Neither Somerset nor Bentley prompted
unbiased opinion, and personal politics may have coloured some of the opinions
expressed at the time. In 1703, for example, William Piers, Fellow of Emmanuel
College (that is, the college of Barnes) was unequivocal in attributing the Press's
condition not to Bentley, but to Somerset: 'Si Typorum elegantiam mireris, gratias
merito ingentes habeto Illustrissimo Principi Carolo Duci Somersetensium,
Munificentissimo nostrae Academiae Cancellario, cui Cordi est nostrum, imo suum
denuo revixisse Typographeum.'[48] The changes in plans for publication as the Press
was gradually assembled, and its premises made ready, betwen 1696 and 1698, offer
further evidence that the project was not so much the labour solely of Bentley, strenuous and ultimately successful as that was, as a collaboration.

Whatever the extent of this collaboration, or of its varying mutual impetus, one
crucial link between the University and its Chancellor was through James Talbot, chaplain to the Duke of Somerset. Talbot, three years younger than Bentley, had been a
fellow of Trinity College since 1689, and had a minor reputation as an author. His youthful translation of Seneca's *Troas* (it was composed while he was an undergraduate), dedicated to the Earl of Shrewsbury, had appeared in 1686, published by the London
bookseller Jacob Tonson; and in 1695 his poem occasioned by the death of Queen Mary,
Instructions to a painter, upon the death and funeral of Her late Majesty, Queen Mary had
been one of several published also by Tonson.[49] This poem, unlike most that commemorated the late Queen, was not only published somewhat after the rest, but was also
framed quite differently. From its title onwards, it reminded its readers also of Dryden's
translation of du Fresnoy's *De arte graphica*, published by William Rogers in the same
year. Talbot had been a contemporary, both at Westminster school and as an undergraduate, with Dryden's son. It may have been this connection that brought his first
introduction to Tonson in 1686, for by that date Tonson had become Dryden's principal
publisher. By the mid-1690s, with his further interests in editions of Shakespeare,
Congreve, Shadwell and Etherege, Tonson's reputation as a publisher with an especial
concern for literature was firmly established. In 1695, Dryden himself was contracted to
him to supply a translation of Virgil, and the two men's successful collaboration as translator and publisher was to be triumphantly proven on its publication in 1697.[50]

The connections were as much political as literary, and dated from the revolution of
1688. Tonson and the Duke of Somerset were united in their Whig interests. Both
became members of the Kit-Cat Club, for whom Tonson served as the social focus, and
where in 1703 Somerset was to set an example by presenting his portrait by Kneller –
the first of what was to become the series now mostly in the National Portrait Gallery.[51]
These connections likewise now bore fruit for the new press.

The publication of Dryden's translation of Virgil in 1697 was unusual for its time, in that it was financed principally by subscriptions. This was a proceeding that was to become common in the eighteenth century, especially for expensive books (such as the Virgil) or for books that might be expected to have only a limited, or mostly local, readership. Those wishing or obliged to publish their work privately found it especially attractive, not least because the cost of paper could be met from advance payments. It avoided the grasp of booksellers, though booksellers frequently viewed its operation with disfavour and even met it with hostility. Tonson and Dryden were by no means innovators in this respect; but their method of proceeding was in part to cover the considerable costs not only of meeting Dryden's charges as translator, but also the costs of the many copper plates. The increasing taste in England for books in lavish formats, ornamented with copper plates, required extra capital in publishing to meet these new, and heavy, production costs. Tonson himself had already proved its worth in his edition of *Paradise lost* in 1688, with its illustrations engraved by Michael Burghers and others after Medina. Publication by subscription, which brought in new money, well before publication, to pay for paper, copper-plates and printing, was a convenient means to meet the demands of the new fashions, while for the subscribers, or customers, it offered a considerable saving.

For the new Cambridge press, little was possible without booksellers to finance what was to be printed there. The University showed no sign of wishing to invest in publishing, as distinct from establishing a printing house; and even for a printing house little would have been possible without private benefactions. If any thought was given in 1695–7 as to which booksellers might be expected to support the new press, almost no clues have now survived. In Bentley's correspondence, the only London stationer named was John Place. As for the Cambridge booksellers, two of the wealthiest and most active had both died recently: Henry Dickinson had died in the winter of 1694–5, leaving behind a large stock of books, and William Graves died just over a year later.[52] The principal stationer in Cambridge from the 1690s was Edmund Jeffery. But though he was to be a frequent customer and supporter of the Press, he was in no position to maintain it alone. Some support from London was therefore essential.

In London, the wealthiest was already ruled out as a candidate, in that the Stationers' Company was not only already committed to supporting Hayes, but was also embarrassed by unsaleable works of scholarship from Oxford. More used to the rapid sales of schoolbooks, the Company discovered only difficulties following its agreement to take stock from Oxford as part of an agreement with the University.[53]

Of all the London booksellers, none was more experienced in subscription publishing than Tonson. It is not clear who other than he might have conceived the series of fine quarto editions of the principal Latin poets that, after so many dreams, formed the flagship of the new Cambridge press. The first to be published was James Talbot's edition of Horace. It is tempting to suppose that the interests of his patron and the University's Chancellor, the Duke of Somerset, were made to combine with his personal interests to see his book published in as grand a manner as possible. Certainly Tonson had been his previous publisher; and Tonson, with his knowledge of subscription publishing, and his strong interest in books that were typographically dis-

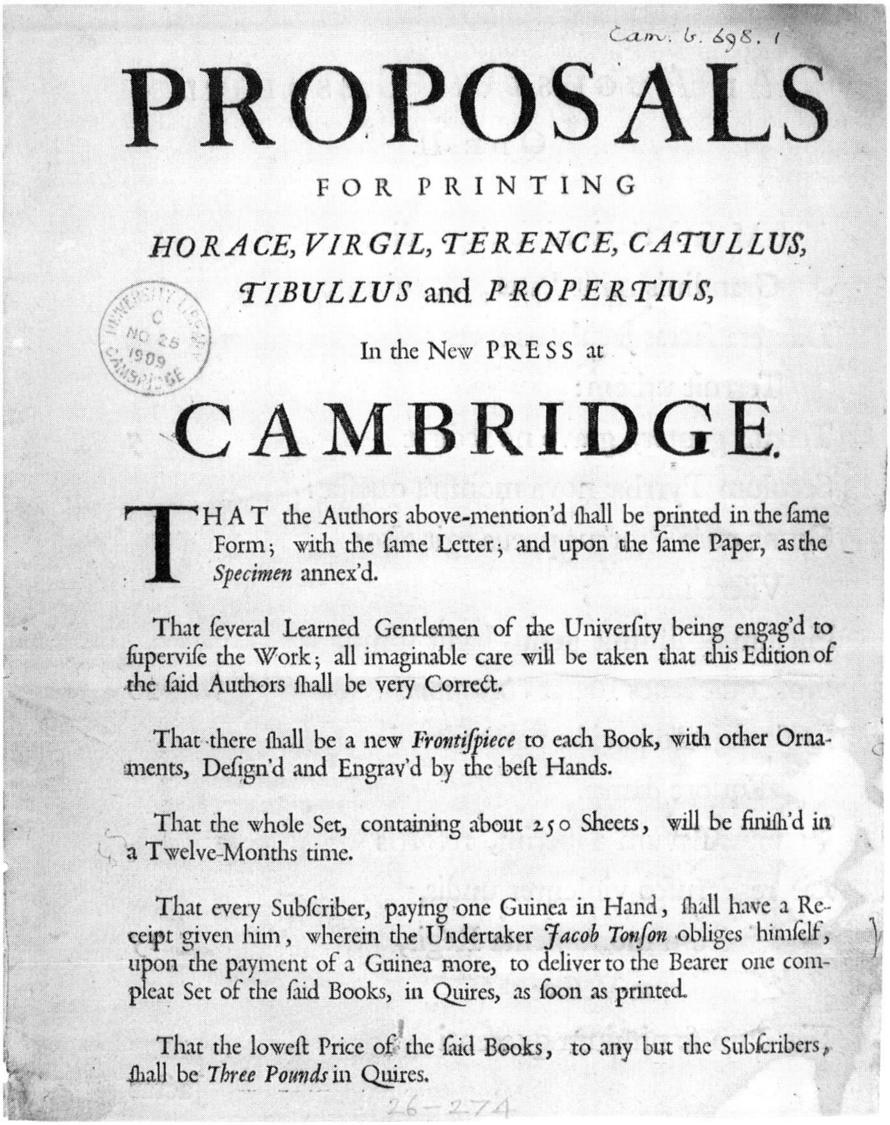

PROPOSALS

FOR PRINTING

HORACE, VIRGIL, TERENCE, CATULLUS, TIBULLUS and *PROPERTIUS,*

In the New PRESS at

CAMBRIDGE.

THAT the Authors above-mention'd ſhall be printed in the ſame Form; with the ſame Letter; and upon the ſame Paper, as the *Specimen* annex'd.

That ſeveral Learned Gentlemen of the Univerſity being engag'd to ſuperviſe the Work; all imaginable care will be taken that this Edition of the ſaid Authors ſhall be very Correct.

That there ſhall be a new ***Frontiſpiece*** to each Book, with other Ornaments, Deſign'd and Engrav'd by the beſt Hands.

That the whole Set, containing about 250 Sheets, will be finiſh'd in a Twelve-Months time.

That every Subſcriber, paying one Guinea in Hand, ſhall have a Receipt given him, wherein the Undertaker *Jacob Tonſon* obliges himſelf, upon the payment of a Guinea more, to deliver to the Bearer one compleat Set of the ſaid Books, in Quires, as ſoon as printed.

That the loweſt Price of the ſaid Books, to any but the Subſcribers, ſhall be *Three Pounds* in Quires.

Fig. 3 Jacob Tonson, *Proposals for printing Horace, Virgil etc. in the new press at Cambridge* (1698).

tinguished, was now brought in to help launch the new press. Printed proposals were issued (fig. 3), perhaps in the middle of 1698, with the assurance 'That several Learned Gentlemen of the University being engag'd to supervise the Work; all imaginable care will be taken that this Edition of the said Authors shall be very Correct.' The whole series, of Horace, Virgil, Terence, Catullus, Tibullus and Propertius, was promised to be completed within twelve months, and would take up about 250 sheets. The price to subscribers was two guineas; for others it was three pounds.[54]

Printing of the Horace (fig. 4) began in mid-November 1698, and took just over a

Fig. 4 Frontispiece to Horace, edited by James Talbot (Cambridge, 1699).

year. In the event, after this had been published in January 1699/1700 there was a pause. Production of the Virgil was put in hand in February 1698/9; of Terence the following June; and of the joint Catullus, Tibullus and Propertius (delayed by the death of its intended editor, William Bancks of Pembroke College, in 1699) in March 1700.[55] But none of these further volumes was to be completed until the summer of

60

1702. Talbot dedicated his book to the ten-year-old Duke of Gloucester, son of the future Queen Anne and thus heir to the throne. The list of subscribers who invested in an undertaking that depended on an untried press was headed by Prince George of Denmark, husband of Princess Anne, followed by Thomas Tenison, Archbishop of Canterbury, Lord Somers, Lord High Chancellor, and the Earl of Pembroke, the Lord Privy Seal. Like the Duke of Somerset, they were among several who subscribed for three sets each. Sir Godfrey Kneller, Martin Lister, William Congreve and John Locke[56] were among those reserving single sets. In Cambridge itself, both the Provost of King's and the Master of Trinity took two sets each; and as a college King's proved notably forthcoming – subscribing no less than thirty-three sets in all.

The University Press was established as a printing house, not as a publisher, and most historians of it have, not unnaturally, allowed its course as printer in the eighteenth century to order their own manner of proceeding. As printers from the fifteenth century onwards have learned, the production of books also requires a means to disperse and sell them. The lessons of distribution, of advertisement, and of competitive markets proved in the fifteenth century more difficult to assimilate than the techniques of printing itself. Each generation since has produced printers who have not understood these necessities. At both Oxford and Cambridge, the printers became in the end also their own publishers for some books. At Cambridge, there was soon a clear division drawn between Syndics' books (which later in the century might also attract a subsidy), work for the University, and those printed for others – including the University Printer in his private capacity.

Accordingly, while the Grace passed by the University on 21 January 1697/8 appointed *Curatores proeli vestri Typographici*,[57] the first meeting of these *Curatores*, on 23 August following, was concerned first with arrangements with those who would pay for and disperse their work (Tonson and Jeffery), and only then with commissioning a printer to begin to assemble the necessary type with which to print Tonson's Latin poets. The Minutes were precise, as befitted a body of people not yet familiar with their tasks:

1 Agreed then at a meeting of ye Curators of ye University-Press, y^t Mr Jacob Tonson have leave to print an Edition of Virgil, Horace, Terence, Catullus, Tibullus & Propertius in 4to with ye double Pica Letter: he paying to such persons as shall be appointed by ye said Curators 12^s per sheet for ye impression of 500 Copies: 14^s for 750; & so in proportion for a greater Number: & y^t Dr Mountague, Dr Covell, Mr Leng, Mr Laughton & Mr Talbot shall sign ye Articles of ye agreement above mentioned, on ye part of ye University.

2 Agreed at ye same time, y^t Mr Edmund Jefferies have leave to print an Edition of Tully's Works in 12mo with ye Brevier Letter: he paying 1^l.10^s. per sheet for 1000 Copies.

3 That Cornelius Crownfield have leave to send to Roterdam for 300^l weight of ye double Pica letter in order to ye printing of Virgil, Horace &c., in ye Manner above mention'd.[58]

This is the first appearance of Crownfield in the University's records of its meetings and decisions. He was at first an employee, and not, like his predecessors, a University Printer appointed by Grace of the University. Only after Hayes died, in 1705, was an election held for this post, and Crownfield elected to it. Little is known of his early career, save that he was a Dutchman. By 1695 he was in London, lodging in Shoemaker Row, one of the main thoroughfares in the crowded parish of St Anne, Blackfriars, the westernmost parish of the City.[59] The area's connections with the book trade were long established, and the King's Printing House lay between his lodgings and the river; but it is not so far known whether he had any connections with the London book trade before coming to Cambridge. Although he rapidly anglicised his name to Crownfield, he seems to have kept his native accent for many years afterwards. In 1724, one of his customers still spelled his name more phonetically as 'Cornvelt'.[60] William Cole, one of the greatest of all gossips in eighteenth-century Cambridge, claimed to have been told by him repeatedly that his name was 'Groenfelt'.[61] These various clues to pronunciation, as well as the anglicised form of name that he employed, suggest that he may have been connected with a family of printers and stationers in Delft, named Krooneveld, or Kronevelt. It is possible that he had come over to England originally with the army of William III.[62] It is probable that when he was discovered by Bentley, and considered to be suitable for the new press at Cambridge, he was not only a journeyman printer in London, but also had opportunity to demonstrate that his links with Holland, and in particular with the printing trade there, were sufficient to meet Cambridge's needs.

As Oxford had two decades earlier, Cambridge likewise looked to Holland for type and for printing skills. Dutch printing was universally admired, while the type-faces developed by Christoffel van Dijck in the mid-century had successfully established themselves as a new taste, to be set beside older designs by Granjon, Garamond and others still also available from the Dutch typefounders.[63] In 1676, Joseph Moxon had summarised what became a common view:

> How much printing has improved the Regularity and Beauty of these Letters is visible by comparing Printing with Written Letters; but especially the curious printing of Holland, which does indeed of all others merit the greatest Applause.[64]

His further analysis led him to more precise enthusiasm, as he renewed his attempts to encourage the adoption of van Dijck's designs in England:

> Since the late made *Dutch-Letters* are so generally, and indeed most deservedly accounted the best, as for their Shape, consisting so exactly of Mathematical regular Figures as aforesaid, And for the commodious Fatness they have beyond other *Letters*, which easing the Eyes in Reading, renders them more Legible.[65]

Apart from type, the first two presses were acquired at the end of 1697, though only one seems to have been put immediately to full use. A third, obtained in February 1698/9, was not in use until March 1699/1700, and a fourth, the property of John Owen, was installed in January 1701/2.[66] No more were acquired until 1740. Even in the heyday of the first years of the century, not all the presses were employed at one time. Delays were caused partly by the tardy arrival of essential parts; but more persistently, they required frequent repair. This remained a general problem with wooden presses, and remained a daily fact of life until they were replaced by iron ones in the early nineteenth century. As in many printing houses, at least one seems to have served as a proofing press. Crownfield usually had no more than two at work simultaneously, and one of those at half-press – that is, worked by one man rather than two.

Crownfield had begun work in Cambridge in November 1697, 'fitting up yᵉ Universities Printing House, and disposing yᵉ Letters in their several Cases'.[67] The first pressman to figure in the accounts, Robert Ponder, who was at work by November 1698, remained until 1705, and then returned briefly in 1709. In general, however, the pressmen remained for only short periods – for reasons that are not clear. Though Campbell, writing over forty years later,[68] claimed that a good pressman might earn a guinea a week, piecework earnings at Cambridge were generally much less. But there is no evidence that pressmen left because work (or wages) were any more plentiful in London. More appositely, at least some of both the pressmen and the compositors had other sources of income, not always in the book trade. 'Many of them play great Part of their time', wrote Campbell, his remarks apparently equally applicable to London or elsewhere. Work came piecemeal, and there was no guaranteed weekly wage. The pattern of employment for compositors was broadly similar to that of a pressman, for though each group tended to keep itself and its skills distinct, they depended on each other for their daily routines of work. Campbell again, writing in the 1740s, not only emphasised the distinction between the compositors' and pressmen's callings, but also perhaps indicated something of the reason for the comparative mobility of pressmen.

> The Hands employed by the Printer are the Compositor and the Pressman, which are two distinct Branches, the one knowing little of the other's Business. The Compositor is he who ranges the Letters and makes up the Forms; the Pressman only works at the Press, takes off the Impression, and requires no other Qualification than Strength and a little Practice.[69]

In great measure, Campbell's distinction between the skills of the compositor, and the brute strength of the pressman, was repeated implicitly by successive writers of printers' manuals from Moxon onwards. Moxon himself was scathing of the carelessness of pressmen.[70] This attitude accounts in part for some of the weaknesses in much eighteenth-century printing in Britain, and for the attention that Baskerville gave not only to his type, paper and ink, but also to his presswork. But one printer, in 1713, was more thoughtful about the 'ill Custom' that had crept into British printing houses:

> Another Cause is, The little Esteem we have for Press-Men, and the narrow Prices given them. 'Tis from them the Work receives its Beauty and finishing Strokes. The Dutch, who, it must be acknowledged, are the neatest Printers in the World, have different Thoughts of them: They give larger Wages to good Press-Men than to Compositors: they will not allow a Press-Man to work above Eight or Nine Hours in a day, lest by working much he work not well. But here [i.e. Edinburgh] and in England, he that works Seventeen or Eighteen Hours, is reckon'd a choise Workman: And indeed there is a Necessity for

working much, their Wages are so small; but then it is not possible to do so much and well too. For my Part, I'd rather give a Crown a Day to a good Press-Man, who brings Reputation to my Work and preserves my Letter, than Eighteen Pence to one who must certainly destroy it by careless and base Working. And therefore, I recommend it earnestly to you to get Home good Press-Men from Holland (as I have done with no small Charge,) till we bring ours selves into a fair and comely Way of Working at the Press. 'Twas from thence our Forefathers learn'd that Part of the Art; and until that Method be practis'd by all of us, I cannot see how we can revive Printing here; since the best Letter in the World, and tho' set up by the most skilful Compositors, will make but very pitiful Work, if the Press-Men are not good Workmen.[71]

With one possible exception, Crownfield seems to have engaged none of his countrymen as pressmen, and to have recruited in England.[72] For his compositors, he recruited more largely among foreigners: the high proportion of work in Latin may have helped in this respect, or even obliged him to take this course.

Following Crownfield's appointment to the Press, there was a period of transition, in which John Hayes continued in effect as the only local printer, on occasion using the new equipment. It was to be a year before Crownfield submitted his first bill for printing the first sheet of the Horace.

In other words, once the decision was taken in August 1698 to print Tonson's series of quarto poets, matters moved quite rapidly. Composition for the first sheet was charged the following November. But even allowing for a prolonged period in which to set up the press, and assemble and sort the necessary type, it seems that the University had no clear formal idea of what should be printed. The delay may have been to allow editorial work, though there is no evidence of this in the University's deliberations. In the intervening months of 1696–8, Bentley, based in London, had become a less prominent figure. His ideas for publications all came to nothing, while James Talbot, Fellow of Trinity and having as his patron the Duke of Somerset, moved into the foreground. Money was raised, Somerset giving £200 and lending as much again, and the Senate added to the gifts of private individuals by authorising expenditure of £500 on the new press.[73] Although there was talk of contributions among Bentley's circles, in practice they came from Cambridge; and some at least of that initiative came from Talbot, who thus saw the Press established not only with ideas, but also with money and with work.

If those who had promoted the Press expected a well-printed book in the first of all to appear, the new edition of Horace, there must have been some disappointment.[74] While the several engravings – headpieces, tailpieces and a frontispiece, all engraved by Simon Gribelin[75] – added visual distinction to the edition, the presswork of the text was less satisfactory. Irregular inking, unaligned back-up of one page of type to another, crooked placing of the sheets in the press, slurred impressions of the type and stray ink smears vitiated the competent setting of the type, and the intrinsic beauty of van Dijck's freshly cast double pica type. The compositor was Crownfield himself; but the presswork was by Robert Ponder, who had arrived at the Press by November 1698. Ponder was from London, son of the bookseller Nathaniel Ponder and former apprentice of the printer Thomas Braddyll. When he arrived at Cambridge he had been out of his apprenticeship for about four and a half years.[76]

Ponder remained the only pressman until in June or July 1699 he was joined from London by Jonathan Cotton, a man still not out of his apprenticeship on account of the poverty of his master, John Redmaine.[77] As for compositors, while Crownfield himself continued to work on the quarto Latin poets, two others had arrived by the end of 1699: William Bertram and Christian Michaelis. John Delié joined in January 1699/1700, and Clement Knell in February. For a while in 1701–2 there were seven, though five or six were more usual and the figure later dropped back to four. Not surprisingly, Crownfield recruited several either direct from the Netherlands or from among the immigrant community: Delié may have come from Oxford, and Michaelis came from Germany. Johannes Muckeus, who like Michaelis had especial skill in setting Greek, and was to be crucial to the successful – and speedy – completion of the three-volume *Suidas* in 1701–5, arrived in summer 1701 and became one of Crownfield's longest-serving employees. In general, compositors, amongst the most skilled of all journeymen, tended to stay longer than pressmen – provided, that is, there was work for them to do.[78]

Organisation in these first years was piecemeal. Orders for type were not always exactly correlated with commitments or need, and Crownfield had constantly to make up inadequate supplies. With respect to engravings, the curators' handling of the printing of their first major project, Tonson's quarto Horace, was singular. The finished volume, like others in the series, contains various engravings – a frontispiece cut by Gribelin depicting the *Alma mater* device against a landscape introducing some of Cambridge's major buildings, and a number of ornamental head- and tailpieces, also engraved by Gribelin. All this was in keeping with Tonson's intentions for a series of Latin classics of markedly superior elegance not just in a British but in a European forum. It may be presumed that Tonson, as publisher, paid for the engravings. But their printing was done at Cambridge. The first sheets that were to feature engravings (at the head of A1r and on G3v) were set and printed in November–December 1698; but the curators only agreed to order a rolling-press in January following, on condition that Talbot – to whom the task was entrusted – should raise money for it in London.[79] The press was finally installed in September,[80] but once there it seems to have posed a difficulty. Accounts for its use are incomplete.[81] James Child, who was brought up from London to operate it, found only intermittent employment; and though he may perhaps have found some casual work such as printing bookplates for colleges, he soon left Cambridge. Even by the end of 1699, a special *douceur* had to be paid to another pressman, John Ebrall (or Eborat) to ensure that he remained in Cambridge: 'five shillings for his encouragem^t to stay wth us till ye whole Horace were finished'.[82] By 1705, Crownfield found it more convenient to ship parcels of paper to James Child in London so that plates could be printed there.[83] In other words, though there was a rolling-press at Cambridge for a while, it is not certain that the University ever owned it. Within a short time it had either fallen out of use or, more probably, been removed. As in London, intaglio and letterpress printing remained divorced, two separate skills requiring different equipment (a rolling-press and a common press) but also, no less importantly, working to quite different rhythms in the context of book printing.

Bentley, following the example not only of Oxford but also of other learned presses, had thought once of Greek as an early desideratum. In practice, the first type that he saw acquired for the new Cambridge press seems to have included very little Greek, and perhaps only in one size, long primer. It is a further measure of the extent to which he had either distanced himself, or been distanced, that the question of further Greek type was not raised again until the spring of 1699. As to which particular type-face was desirable, the choice lay between Amsterdam and Paris. In Paris, the *Grecs du Roi* had been celebrated ever since they had been cut by Claude Garamond in the mid-sixteenth century; but they remained privileged types, restricted for the use of the Imprimerie Royale. In Amsterdam, though there was no such historic connection, the Voskens type-foundry offered to meet, in a Greek context, the kind of typographical aspirations that the Cambridge Press had already shown in embarking on the Latin quarto poets. The type offered by the widow of Dirck Voskens, cut originally by Robert Granjon and modelled on the *Grecs du Roi*, offered no restrictions such as applied in Paris; and on the basis of seeing a specimen, four hundred pounds of paragon were ordered for Cambridge in May 1699.[84] The type was delivered in August, and thus, for the first time, the Press was equipped to print Greek in books of the same scale as the Latin classics. In fact, it did not use the new paragon Greek at once, and instead embarked within a few weeks on a duodecimo Greek New Testament. The new type was not used extensively until the volume of University verses on the death of the Duke of Gloucester, in the late summer of 1700.

Meanwhile there were those who had not forgotten the French *Grecs du Roi*. By May 1699, the very month in which the order was given for Greek types from the Voskens foundry in Amsterdam, James Talbot was in touch with Matthew Prior, in Paris, and through Prior with Nicolas Clément, *sous-bibliothécaire du Roi*, and the Abbé de Louvois.[85] The French authorities were willing in principle, but only at a price, as Prior explained:

> The conditions they reciprocally desire from us are, that in the preface of some volume which we shall first print we shall own the obligation with some encomium of gratitude, that we shall give them in books from England what we propose to pay them in money for these types, and keep up a kind of communication with them *propter bonum ac commodum reipublicae literariae*, and that we shall give them the way of making that ink in which the essays upon Horace and Virgil which you sent me are printed.

As we have seen, Talbot was of the Somerset circle; and a year later Somerset himself had been drawn into the negotiations. 'I do believe they are a little ashamed of their proposal to oblige us to insert in the title-page of every book *Cantabrigiae Typis Academicis, Caracteribus Graecis Regis Christianissimi*', wrote Somerset to Prior in May 1700.[86] In time this royal title, inevitably unacceptable to a University that owed its loyalty to the Head of the Church of England, was modified to the simpler

Typographeio Regio Parisiensi; but even though Somerset thought he saw room for compromise the Cambridge press never acquired any of this celebrated type.[87]

This was, however, only one aspect of a matter in which it is possible to suspect, if not to see in great detail, continuing tensions between Bentley and Talbot that now began to affect the appearance as well as the selection of books printed at the Press. On 1 February 1699/1700, Bentley was installed as Master of Trinity College. Thus, for the first time, he was at last able to attend meetings of the Curators of the Press, as head of a house. By that time the duodecimo edition of the Greek New Testament was well advanced, using the long primer Greek that had formed a part of the original consignment of type to the Press organised by Bentley in 1697. In the early spring of 1700 the Press was still also in negotiation with the French Imprimerie Royale, in the hope of obtaining the *Grecs du Roi*, presumably in all three sizes: double pica, great primer and pica. As we have seen, discussions had been proceeding for some months; and it may have been these delays that led the curators on 20 March 1699/1700 (the first meeting that Bentley could have attended) to order four hundred pounds weight of English Greek, to be procured via the London booksellers Smith and Walford. This order was cancelled on 8 June, apparently because of the intervention of none other than the Chancellor himself, the Duke of Somerset. By then the negotiations with Paris had failed; and the order instead was placed for type from the van Dijck foundry in Amsterdam. Once this alternative type arrived, it was used extensively for the edition of *Suidas*, begun in September 1701 and discussed further below.[88]

The sequence of events is important, since it dictated the appearance of the Press's books. Unfortunately, we do not know exactly when this new English Greek was received at Cambridge; but it seems to have been in place by August 1701.[89] There was no point, then or at any other time, in buying type that would not be needed in the foreseeable future, and it is not necessary to search far for the purpose that may have been in their minds, and Bentley's mind in particular. In July 1700, the month after the order for Greek type in English size had been countermanded, work began on a new edition of Edward Stillingfleet's *Origines sacrae*, a folio with its main text set in English. Stillingfleet, it will be remembered, had been Bentley's employer and patron. He had died in 1699, and this was the first edition to be published after his death. It was printed for Henry Mortlock, a London stationer whose other publications included not only various further works by Stillingfleet, but also Bentley's *Dissertation upon the Epistles of Phalaris* and his commencement sermon preached in Great St Mary's church in Cambridge in 1696. Although Bentley's name does not appear on the new edition of *Origines sacrae*, all the evidence points to his being responsible for introducing it to the Press. And yet, by the time that work on it was begun, the Press still did not have Greek type in the correct size. So the few words that were necessary were set in the only type that could be made to fit, namely long primer. It seems to have been achieved by careful leading, rather than casting on a larger body (for which the Press, in any case, was not equipped), and the resulting contrast in sizes, within a single line, was not visually happy. All this may have been merely unfortunate; but once again the interests and activities of Bentley seem to have been at variance with those of Talbot and his patron the Duke of Somerset.

Talbot, Fellow of Trinity and perhaps disappointed of the mastership of his college, seems to have retired from Cambridge in 1702. In 1704 he resigned the chair of Hebrew; and he spent the few remaining years of his life (he died in 1708) at Spofforth, in Yorkshire, a valuable living to which he had been presented by the Duke of Somerset. Thus Bentley was in effect left as victor, able not only to see his protégé Henry Sike installed as Professor of Hebrew,[90] but also to promote the well-being of the Press as he saw it, to introduce authors and editors, to act as patron, and to continue to build links between the Press and those – such as Sike – who could support it. Not all his suggestions and projects were successes. Nothing ever came, for example, of his hope that a catalogue might be published of Stillingfleet's library, for which he offered the services of Crownfield: 'Our letter and work is neater; & what is ye principal thing, you will have it finished twice as soon here', he wrote in 1703 to Narcissus Marsh, who bought the collection and eventually established it as a public library in Dublin.[91] With others, such as Ludolph Kuster, from Westfalia, or John Davies, of Queens' College, he was more fortunate; and it was Bentley more than anyone else who finally persuaded Sir Isaac Newton to revise his *Principia* for a second edition. Then Bentley in effect acted as his publisher.[92] The memory of Talbot remained, and does much to explain Bentley's decision to transfer his attention from Greek to the text of Horace: his edition, finally published in 1711, was in some measure a refutation of Talbot's edition published a dozen years previously.[93] He came to Trinity with a reputation for arrogance, and the fellows of the College quickly found that report did not exaggerate. Of the Press, he was wont to claim more as his own than can be justified; 'projected and founded solely by myself, and purchased and endowed solely by my friends'.[94] But just as arguments between Master and fellows tended to obscure his real achievements for the good of Trinity College, so his tendentious claims for his role in the Press are a distraction from the true nature of his achievement there.

The search for suitable types, both Roman and Greek, had taken the agents of the University not only to London, but also over the Channel and the North Sea, to Paris and to the Netherlands. In part this was as a result of a wish for types that were of a particular quality or historical significance; and in part, no doubt, it was as a result of the advice and knowledge of the printer, Cornelius Crownfield. It was also an acknowledgement that if the Press was to succeed it must do so in an international context; and thus with materials that would bear comparison with those overseas. Book trade meant not only international traffic in books and money, but also products of international standard. Without always acknowledging the fact, the Cambridge press was seeking a place in the *Respublica literaria*, as those associated with the Imprimerie Royale assumed in their suggestion that Cambridge should trade books, rather than money, for the *Grecs du Roi*. Such a place was to be defined both by individuals and their projects and by the materials – type – by which their work was to be propagated. Tonson's own connections, as publisher of the first books to be printed at the new press, were both in England and with the continent.[95] When in the autumn of 1700 Talbot faced the need to sell his smaller, duodecimo, edition of Horace, he turned to the London booksellers R. Clavell, Samuel Smith and Benjamin Walford,[96] and to the booksellers at the centre of the international trade, in the Low Countries:

> I wish you would order my friend and your humble servant, old Elzevir, to recommend this impression in his namesake's types to Leers of Rotterdam, so that he may take off a number of copies, which shall be afforded at reasonable price. The book will not be published these ten days. I am my own bookseller, and without Jacob Tonson's assistance have already six hundred copies bespoken by the schoolmasters and tutors.[97]

After the four volumes of Latin poetry in quarto, published in 1699–1702, 'chartâ nitidâ & charactere largiori',[98] Tonson moved away from the Cambridge press, to other printers. For an equivalent edition of Livy (which would have taken up three volumes), he turned to Amsterdam. For Lucretius, published in 1712 and avowedly modelled on the Cambridge quartos, he employed a London printer. For his folio edition of Caesar, 1712, most celebrated of all, and the culmination of his efforts to produce books visually comparable with the grandest and most elaborate from the best presses overseas, he also remained in London. For at least part of his market, Tonson looked abroad, just as he depended on the Netherlands and Germany for help with some of his classical texts. There was little point in his continuing to print at Cambridge.

The Cambridge bookseller, Edmund Jeffery, had fewer ambitions, and less sense of possibilities overseas. Much less well established than Tonson, he was also unable to exploit the trade in the same way, and his proposed multi-volume duodecimo edition of Cicero proved abortive.[99] Instead, he turned originally to the new press as the obvious local connection, and he remained with it even as he also developed his connections with London. Between 1699 and 1717, over fifty works printed at the Press appeared over his name either alone or as a shareholder, the number falling off only as Crownfield's own position as a bookseller and publisher in his own right became stronger. Other Cambridge booksellers proved much less supportive, the names of Edward Hall (d. 1703) and Thomas Dawson (d. 1708) appearing on the title-pages of only three books apiece. Though it appears that a few authors such as Thomas Bennet and William Whiston made efforts to persuade their London publishers to use Crownfield's presses, less than 10 per cent of the books printed by him between 1698 and 1712 were for London booksellers alone.[100]

While the contract with Tonson was crucial in providing an assured return for the University's investment in the new Press during its infant years, it was one that was strictly limited. In the longer term, a regular supply of work had somehow to be generated where none had been for several decades while Hayes had occupied the printing premises. Authors in Cambridge had to be found, or cajoled; to be launched on the world with their first books, or to be persuaded to have their work printed in Cambridge rather than London. Religion, sermons and classical literature were the staple. In bringing together a group of scholars who would labour to provide the editions and other works that would be both the life-blood and the most obvious manifestation of a learned press, none was more active than Bentley. The edition of

Stillingfleet's *Origines sacrae* (1702) was due almost certainly to him. Encouraged by Bentley, Ludolph Kuster settled in Cambridge while working on his edition of *Suidas*. Bentley's own edition of Horace, long in the press, and not least a rebuke to Talbot, appeared finally in 1711. Newton's *Principia* followed two years later. Both were in effect published by Bentley privately, thus guaranteeing Crownfield work for his presses. If he had his occasional disappointments, for example in failing to persuade John Evelyn to look favourably on the Cambridge press for a new edition of his *Sylva*, there were many more successes, some of them turning into long-term steady sellers.

Bentley was also of the circle who made regular use of the library of John Moore, Bishop of Norwich and then, from 1707, of Ely. It is inconceivable that Bentley and Moore, both in London, and closely acquainted, had not discussed the proposed press in the late 1690s; it is also not unreasonable to suppose that the two may have hoped that a new press might be a vehicle for the publication of work inspired or enabled by Moore's growing library. Though no mention was made of his collection – or of any other resource – in Bentley's scheme for the Press, the evidence of the following few years suggests that not a little of the justification, as well as the expectations, of a new press lay in the existence of a library belonging not to the University or to any college, but to a private individual. Moore, a member of Clare College, whose circle also included Newton, Richard Laughton, William Whiston, Charles Morgan and Samuel Clarke, made a practice of drawing round him promising scholars, especially in history, theology and the classics, encouraging them to use the manuscripts and early printed books in his exceptional library. From the first, he was a firm supporter of the new press, contributing on two separate occasions to the costs of its establishment, and providing Tonson with some of the necessary texts to be used by the editors of the Latin poets.[101] Among those using his library whose work was now brought forward to be printed at Cambridge were his chaplain William Whiston of Clare College, who dedicated to Moore his *Short view of the chronology of the Old Testament* (1702); Peter Needham of St John's, whose edition of the *Geoponica* (1704) was both based on materials in Moore's library and dedicated to their owner; Joseph Wasse of Queens', who borrowed early editions of Sallust for his own edition completed by Crownfield in 1710; and John Davies, also of Queens'. Davies used a late manuscript from Moore's library for his edition of Julius Caesar, published in 1706; and in 1709 he acknowledged Moore's help by dedicating to him his edition of Cicero's *Tusculanae disputationes*. In Bentley's addenda to Davies's work the three men met as collaborators, Bentley addressing his contribution to his 'Amicissimo juveni' and paying tribute to Moore, a Maecenas in his generosity in sharing his library with others, whether for Cicero or for other projects.

The riches of Moore's library, and his readiness to share it with those who would make known its contents, were celebrated internationally. This was a library cast on a European scale. Most spectacularly of all, in 1701 Moore obtained from France the early eighth-century manuscript of Bede's *Historia ecclesiastica*, written at Wearmouth-Jarrow and subsequently in the library at the court of Charlemagne. It was at the time (as it remained for 180 years) the earliest copy known in western Europe of the Latin text, one unknown to Abraham Whelock whose edition had been printed at Cambridge in 1644. An edition based on Moore's manuscript was put in hand by John Smith, prebendary of Durham and rector of Bishop Wearmouth, whose work towards a fresh edition of Bede had thereby to be fundamentally altered.[102] It may be that Bentley, who had been an undergraduate at St John's at the same time as Smith, already intended that the new edition should be printed at Cambridge when in summer 1702 (that is, soon after Moore had acquired the manuscript) he contacted the Oxford typefounder Peter de Walpergen with a view to commissioning a newly drawn Anglo-Saxon alphabet based on designs by Humfrey Wanley.[103] But de Walpergen died in 1703, and nothing came of the project. Instead, only in 1713/14 the Curators at Cambridge agreed to buy '300 Weight of English Saxon Letters', and so obtained the type that was ultimately used for the new edition of Bede.[104] Moore died in 1714, and Smith in 1715. So neither lived to see the eventual publication (under the auspices of Smith's son) in 1722 of the greatest treasure in Moore's library, a library that had itself by then, thanks to George I, become the dominant part of the University Library.

As the Curators realised from the beginning in engaging with Tonson, the new press could not survive without some arrangement for financing the books that were to be printed: a printing business had been established, but there was no capital beyond that necessary to buy the initial equipment; and the University certainly had no intention of becoming a publisher.

Following Tonson, the search lit on John Owen as one who would take the risks of publication, arrange funding, and also arrange with booksellers both in London and overseas. Apart from his being thought to be a Dutchman,[105] nothing is known of Owen's career before he came to the attention of the Delegates of the Oxford University Press in 1698, and was charged with taking a remainder stock of Oxford publications over to Holland to exchange for other books. In the course of this mission he claimed substantial sums for expenses, but the project was an abject failure. On his return some books were acquired by the Bodleian, while others were sold at auction in Oxford itself. Not only were the books sold so cheaply that the University made a substantial loss on the whole proceeding; Owen was also criticised for having allowed the books to be sold at prices that damaged the ordinary import trade of the London stationers.[106]

Meanwhile, Owen was further trying to establish his own business as a bookseller, and in 1700 he announced a number of works of which some were printed at the Oxford press.[107] His ambitions as a learned publisher were reflected both in an interest in Greek texts, and in his republishing an engraved sheet (originally printed at Oxford in 1689) by Edward Bernard depicting ancient alphabets.[108] Perhaps the Cambridge authorities, persuaded of his interests, merely considered Owen's speculations in the Dutch trade unfortunate, though it is difficult to justify the very considerable trust that they were quickly to put in him. His prospectus of 1700 had announced an edition of the tenth-century *Suidas*, to be edited by Ludolfus

Neocorus, that is, Ludolph Kuster. But agreement on this major project (it finally was to take up three massive volumes) was reached between Owen and the Cambridge press (not that in Oxford) only in October 1701. By it, Crownfield was to print 1,500 copies, in three volumes folio, at a price of £1.10s.6d. per sheet; in return, payment was to be spread over the course of production, Owen paying for a hundred sheets once two hundred had been printed, two hundred once three hundred had been printed, etc. Once work was completed, the University was to be entitled to withhold three hundred copies until full payment had been received, not later than six months after completion.[109]

Of all the early projects of the new Press, it was by far the most ambitious, and it was published in 1705. Printing began more or less simultaneously on the first two volumes, and the first payments to the compositors were made on 1 November 1701: an advertisement in the *London Gazette* suggested work had begun about a month previously.[110] But the first proposals had been dated 1 April; and they had set out both the ambitions of Kuster, as editor, and also the proposed publication details. Kuster had been especially excited by three manuscripts in the Royal Library at Paris. As so often with the major projects of the Cambridge press under Bentley, there was a local source that was also of importance – in this case the notes made by Bishop John Pearson, former Master of Trinity College, of readings in the Vatican manuscript: Pearson's notes at that time resided conveniently in the library of his own (and Bentley's) college. The first announcement was sanguine. The whole would consist of about 550 sheets (this had been revised down from 600 in the draft of the notice), and would be delivered to subscribers by Christmas 1702 – twenty months after the date of the prospectus. The price was fixed, with a discount offered for early payment.[111] A further, similar, prospectus followed in October. Not surprisingly, predictions both of the timetable and of the size of the volumes proved to be serious miscalculations.

Owen's career at this time, when he still owed money to the University of Oxford (it was never to be repaid), was aggressive. In November he organised another auction of imported books, this time in Cambridge, and a further auction seems to have taken place the following spring.[112] During the next few months he worked more and more closely with Crownfield, providing a printing press, and suggesting that it was a gift to the University. Paper was obtained from Sir Theodore Janssen and from John Baskett in London, as well as from Oxford.[113] But his financial position was weak. In October 1703, the Curators agreed 'in Consideration of his present Circumstances' not only to treat the gift of the press as a purchase (11 guineas was allowed for it), but also to come to as amicable an arrangement as possible to terminate his account.[114]

In the same month he also surrendered his rights in *Suidas*.[115] By doing so, he gave up a project to which he had given considerable energy, not least in seeking out subscribers in London and Oxford. Contacts in Oxford included William Worth of All Souls College, editor of an edition of Tatian in which Owen had shared in 1700, and who by 1703 had obtained six subscribers, three of them in Worcester.[116] A further five came through Edmund Brickenden of Oriel College, who used his county of

Somerset connections to rouse interest in *Suidas* in Wells. But in the absence of others willing to search out subscribers in other parts of the country, the list by October 1703 was mainly confined to the two university towns and, overwhelmingly, to Cambridge. Two London booksellers, Messrs Smith and Walford and Thomas Bennet, accounted for twelve copies on ordinary paper and six on large: in view of the booksellers concerned, they were almost certainly intended for the overseas market.[117] In all, Owen calculated that he and Crownfield had each acquired a similar number of subscriptions, Crownfield's share being almost entirely of libraries or individuals in Cambridge.[118] Now, instead of Owen, the project was to be undertaken jointly by the University and by the London merchant Sir Theodore Janssen, whose wealth was no doubt some comfort as the costs of this project accumulated. Since Janssen, a member of a family from Angoulême settled partly in Amsterdam, was familiar both with the paper trade (and hence with by far the largest element in the costs) and with the exiled Protestant booksellers of Amsterdam, he was a prudent choice.[119] No doubt he saw the matter at the time as an investment. The work was not completed until April 1705, and the project took over 13 per cent more paper than had been allowed for in setting the price.

For Owen, the *Suidas* débâcle, which removed him from a project to which he had lent his name and given his energies either in Oxford or in Cambridge for the last four years, occasioned little more than a pause. Less than a year later, the Curators agreed to extend him credit to print an edition of Caesar's commentaries, edited by John Davies.[120] By 1705 he was still further engaged to Crownfield, as compositor and corrector of this edition. Since he both expected to be the publisher of this book, and was paid by Crownfield for any work he contributed to its production, the effect of this unusual arrangement was that he was both receiving ready money at the earliest possible time, and also putting himself in a position to pay for the work when it was completed.[121] Also in 1705, he undertook both an introduction to oriental languages by Simon Ockley (for which he used Hayes's oriental types) and an edition of Sallust, eventually to be published in 1710 by the University, following the collapse of Owen's business. In June 1706 work further began on the last of Owen's projects with the Press, an edition by John Davies of the sure-selling Minucius Felix: had he wished to ensure that his investment would be soon returned, he could not have chosen more prudently. The only other book from Cambridge bearing Owen's name was an edition of Cellarius, *Notitia orbis antiqui*, of 1703. But this was printed in Amsterdam,[122] where the second volume was published by Caspar Fritsch, after Owen's collapse, in 1706.

How much money, as distinct from credit, Owen was ever able to command is not clear. The pattern of his work at Cambridge, including auctions of books, working as a compositor, and his choice of a straightforward work rather than a risk when his creditors would soon have to be faced, all suggest that there was little margin to cushion his ambitions. His edifice, built on an inadequate cash flow, collapsed in the autumn of 1706, with money owing both to the University and to Sir Theodore Janssen, who had supplied paper for the *Suidas*, Caesar and Sallust.[123] Owen's business had never been much more than a bubble, and the Curators of the Press, anxious for business, had chosen to believe that it was something more. As a consequence, the University was left with unpaid bills, and stocks of books that, in the case of Caesar and the *Suidas*, it found it could not sell. The praise offered by the *Acta Eruditorum*, by the *Journal des Sçavans* and by Le Clerc in the *Bibliothèque Choisie*, to the University for having supported the venture came in the same year as affairs with Owen reached a crisis;[124] it was deserved, but it was of little practical help. Even after some attempt had been made to salvage matters from the disaster, the annual accounts for 1707–8 recorded debts by 'ye Late John Owen' of £155.0s.6d., or more than a quarter of all monies owing to the Press at the end of the year. At the conclusion of the same accounting year, the local bookseller Edmund Jeffery owed £123.9s.3d.; but though the sum was almost as great, the risk to the Press was very much smaller. The following year recorded a bill against Owen of £135.0s.6d. for Caesar's commentaries, and this remained a regular feature for several years further.

In all this, the puzzle is not whether Owen is to be pitied or excoriated, but how the Cambridge curators chose on two quite separate occasions to ignore past events, and grant him yet further opportunity: first on his being engaged when the Oxford project had already foundered at the expense of that university; and second when he was allowed to proceed with Caesar and further schemes so soon after he had been separated from the *Suidas* and other projects. It is hard in this train of events not to see the figure of Bentley, the man whom Owen attacked after his final separation from the Cambridge Press:

> a Person of an high Character, and a Pretending Encourager of Arts and Sciences, and Printing in particular, (by the Encouragement of whose specious Promises I was induced to leave Oxford) [who had been] Sedulous and Industrious to ruine and destroy me, by such Injustice and Cruelties, which if I should particularize, would gain Credit with few but those of the University of Cambridge.[125]

Bentley was Vice-Chancellor when Owen was first contracted to publish *Suidas*, a work that was itself the product of one of his protégés. Of the books to which Owen put his name, the Caesar and the Minucius Felix were both edited by Davies, one of Bentley's closest associates in the Press. Indeed, it seems that, following the *Suidas* crisis, Bentley was principally responsible for arranging the terms by which Owen was to engage for the Caesar.[126] It would have been natural for a deeply and repeatedly disappointed man such as Owen thus to turn on the one person who had continually supported him in Cambridge, even to the embarrassment of the University. None of this amounts to proof; but as Bentley demonstrated time and again in other parts of his career, he was more energetic than any of his contemporaries in seeking and arranging often very necessary improvements. The principle of an arrangement such as the University undertook with Owen was correct. But the details, and the individual, were flawed by poor judgement on the part of men who had no commercial experience.

In the absence of realistic professional advice on the book trade and its dangers, the

Syndics could only learn by experience. They employed an overseer of their printing. Crownfield was employed initially as inspector of the press, at an annual salary of £26.[127] Only in December 1705 was he appointed University Printer, despite the fact that it was within the University's power to appoint a second man (next to Hayes) had it so wished.[128] But unlike John Hayes, and unlike most of his predecessors, Crownfield gradually widened his interests to become a bookseller in his own right – not only of books that he printed himself, but also of more general stock. To a considerable degree, this was forced on him, as will be explored in the following chapter.

4

Crownfield, authors and the book trade

As has been emphasised, in founding the new University Press little thought was given to the manner whereby any books that were printed might be sold. Tonson offered an immediate alliance, assured sales by his prosecution of the series of quarto Latin poets. The Press itself did not expect to publish, in the sense of finance, many books. Nor was any provision made for the slow returns on investment that are the accompaniment to almost all new books that are not sold outright.[1] In most respects, Hayes, the other Cambridge printer, was protected from such considerations, assured of sales through the Stationers' Company and likewise assured of its investment. But the University Press had no such support. It came into the world with no inheritance other than a scholarly one; and it was to learn by experience. Crownfield himself was employed as a printer, not as a bookseller, though within a few years he was to begin a bookselling career that lasted until his death.

In Cambridge, the local bookseller Edmund Jeffery was by far the most prominent investor in the new press. Before the end of 1698 he had issued *Proposals* for printing Cicero, ten volumes in duodecimo, the whole to be issued at a subscription price of £1.7s.6d. In the event, nothing came of this project, which was overtaken first by proposals in Oxford for an edition in twelve volumes, in octavo, and then by the authoritative series of separate octavo texts printed in Cambridge and published by Jeffery.[2] The first, the *Tusculanae disputationes*, edited by John Davies and Richard Bentley, appeared in 1708–9.

Jeffery had in 1698 been only recently established in Cambridge, having succeeded to the business of the most prominent of the local booksellers, Henry Dickinson, who had died in the winter of 1694/5.[3] He welcomed the arrival of new investment in printing, and began to establish himself as a figure of some national, not simply local, importance. Even while the University's newly acquired type was still in the hands of John Hayes, Jeffery arranged for it to be used to print a sermon preached at the public commencement on 3 July 1698.[4] Within the space of three years, his name had appeared not only on many sermons by university figures, but also on a pocket edition of the Greek New Testament (1700) and the beginning of a succession of works of theological controversy by Thomas Bennet, Rector of St James's church, Colchester and Fellow of St John's College. In 1705 he undertook an edition of Anacreon by Joshua Barnes, unusual in that Barnes was more accustomed to publishing his own works, and indeed was to do so for his edition of Homer in 1710–11. Other local booksellers appeared less frequently. For most books, however, some co-operation with a London bookseller was essential. In 1698, one of the books printed by Hayes with the new type acquired for the University Press was a sermon by Peter Nourse, Fellow of St John's College. Its title-page recorded that it was printed for Edward Hall, bookseller in Cambridge, and was to be sold by Luke Meredith, bookseller in St Paul's Churchyard. Two years later, Meredith died, leaving an estate including an out-standing account with Hall of £139, more than any other bookseller among over twenty spread across the country in Oxford, Cambridge, Exeter, Lichfield, Ludlow, Newcastle, Market Harborough, Bristol, Coventry. His Cambridge dealing had also included Jeffery, Samuel Simpson, Robert Nicholson, Richard Green and Thomas Dawson.[5] Jeffery established regular links with James Knapton, in St Paul's Churchyard, in a relationship recorded both in title-page imprints and (on several occasions when the title-page was silent in this respect) in advertisements in the Term Catalogues. Of others in which Cambridge booksellers had an interest, a book on two much-respected Cambridge figures, Laurence Chaderton and James Usher (1700) was shared between Thomas Dawson in Cambridge and Samuel Smith and Benjamin Walford in London. Perhaps the common tendency to omit full details of publication where more than one bookseller was involved reflected only modest purchases on the part of the London agent; but nonetheless, Puffendorf's *De officio hominis et civis* (1701), printed 'impensis Edvardi Hall', the Cambridge bookseller, included an advertisement for recent books printed for Timothy Child, of St Paul's Churchyard, and was advertised as Child's book in the Term catalogue. A sermon preached at Loughborough by John Alleyne, formerly Fellow of Emmanuel College, appeared with no name of any bookseller on its title-page in 1701, and only contemporary advertisements in the Term Catalogue and in the *Bibliotheca Annua* record the name of those with an interest: Thomas Dawson in Cambridge and Smith and Walford in London.

To a new stationer, the Press presented an obvious means of producing a publica-tion. In the first years of the century, Richard Thurlbourn established his business in Cambridge. His surname was to become familiar to several succeeding generations as that of one of the most active of all the local booksellers.[6] His first publications in 1707 seem to have been two sermons, and an anonymous work by Robert Jenkin, Fellow of St John's College, *Defensio S. Augustini adversus Joannis Phereponi . . . animadversiones*, of which Knaplock took copies for sale in London. Knaplock also took copies of another of Thurlbourn's books two years later.

To some London booksellers, the Press was attractive in its own right. Alexander Bosvile, of Fleet Street, memorialised by John Dunton as a 'very genteel person',[7] pub-lished Ambrose Philips's *Life* of John Williams, benefactor of St John's College (1700) as well as, like Knapton, the work of the industrious Thomas Bennet. Other London booksellers were drawn in by more specialist interests in figures associated with Cambridge: Henry Mortlock, for example, was already established as publisher of Stillingfleet, and Benjamin Tooke had an established interest in William Whiston, whose *Short view of the chronology of the Old Testament*, printed at the University Press, he published in 1702. For convenience' sake, the Cambridge press had much to recommend it, not only for sermons preached in the University Church, but also for authors further afield, who returned to it. Thomas Rud, or Rudd, who graduated from Trinity College in 1687–8 and became master of the school at Newcastle upon Tyne in 1699, arranged for Crownfield to print his Latin *Syntaxis et prosodia*, written primarily for his pupils and published by a Durham bookseller.[8]

So, in these ways, the vision of the press of the mid-1690s, intent on producing scholarly research and standard editions, was gradually changed into one whose accompanying function was to serve the needs of everyday education. William Stukeley, who came up to Cambridge in 1703, later recalled his reading with some of his teachers at Corpus Christi College:

> Mr. Fawcett read to us in Tullys offices, the Greek Testament, Maximus Tyrius by Davis, Clerk's Logics, Metaphysics, Grotius de jure Belli & Pacis, Pufendorf de Officio Nominis & Civis, Wilkins Natural Religion, Lock of human Understanding, Tullys Orations. Mr. Danny read to us in Wells Arithmetica numerosa & speciosa, Pardies Geometry, Tacquets Geometry by Whiston, Harris's use of the Globes, Rohaults Physics by Clark. He read to us Clarks 2 Volumes of Sermons at Boyles Lectures, Varenius Geography put out by S[r]. Isaac Newton, & many other occasional peices of Philosophy, & the Sciences subservient thereto . . .[9]

Maximus Tyrius, Le Clerc, Grotius, Puffendorf, Tacquet and the Greek New Testament were all available to him in editions recently printed by the University Press.

Crownfield himself soon ventured into speculating on his own account as a publishing bookseller. It is not clear whence came the impetus for him to do so; but the course of events, in a trade that depended so much on credit, is fairly clear. In 1700, Tonson seems to have decided against publishing a duodecimo version of Talbot's edition of Horace that he had already published in quarto in 1699, and Talbot thereupon took on the task himself. 'I am my own bookseller, and without Jacob Tonson's assistance have already six hundred copies bespoken by the schoolmasters and tutors.'[10] In practice, Clavell, Smith and Walford took copies in London, and the book was advertised in the Term Catalogue.[11] Tonson's withdrawal from the Cambridge press left it in a situation bereft of any regular major London publishing bookseller. By 1700, Tonson's decision not to proceed further than his initial quartet of Latin poets cannot have come as a surprise (the final volume was not to appear until 1702); but it resulted in a period of some confusion that saw Crownfield emerge as his own publisher.

The first books for which Crownfield bore most of the costs were a duodecimo version of John Laughton's Virgil, in 1702, and Whiston's edition of Tacquet's Euclid, in 1703. The Virgil was designed to accompany the earlier Horace, with the same typographical layout and published at the same price, 2s. Like Tonson, Crownfield realised the value of similarity of appearance in books intended for similar customers. But he also had his eye, necessarily, on London, and he shared Whiston's Tacquet with Jeffrey Wale, a bookseller in St Paul's Churchyard, though Wale's name did not appear on the title-page: the book was advertised, naming Wale, in the *London Gazette* and in the Term Catalogue.

Thus he had already established his position both as printer and bookseller well before he became involved in the much larger question of the publication of *Suidas* in 1705. Crownfield turned likewise to Wale in 1706, for an edition of a sermon by Andrew Snape, Chaplain to the Duke of Somerset, preached at Hanover when Snape was overseas to represent the University in celebrating the anniversary of the foundation of the University of Frankfurt; and Wale, again, was prevailed on to take copies of a further anniversary sermon, this time preached in King's College chapel, at the end of 1707. Wale was an unfortunate choice for Crownfield, for he was gazetted as a bankrupt in the same month that the Syndics agreed to print Snape's Cambridge sermon.[12] When in 1710 a second edition of Whiston's Tacquet was needed, Crownfield found allies instead in two local booksellers, Richard Thurlbourn and William Dickinson. But by the end of the same year Crownfield had already embarked on printing a larger and more ambitious book, illustrated with engraved maps, that he was to publish on his own; and in the winter of 1711–12 there appeared his edition of Varenius' *Geographia generalis* prepared by James Jurin, Fellow of Trinity College. It was one of a trio to appear over Crownfield's name within a year, the others being Peter Needham's edition of Theophrastus (incorporating the earlier unpublished work of James Duport) and John Davies's of Minucius Felix. These three books, dedicated respectively to Bentley, to John Moore, Bishop of Ely, and to Henry James, President of Queens' College and Regius Professor of Divinity, were in the learned tradition for which the Press had been established.

Crownfield's catalogue, printed at the end of the Varenius, revealed something of his investment in the books that he had printed over the last several years. The list was headed by the *Suidas*, still available on both ordinary and large paper, and published in 1705. Davies's quarto edition of Julius Caesar, 1706, was likewise available in both forms, as was Wasse's quarto edition of Sallust, 1710. Whiston's lectures on Newtonian mathematics, prepared *in usum juventutis academicae* and his edition of Tacquet, both 1710, were followed, finally, by Davies's revised edition of Minucius Felix, whose printing was completed in the same month as the Varenius itself. Crownfield had obtained copies of these books for sale, but he had not figured on every title-page: the *Suidas* had been a project principally of John Owen, on behalf of the Syndics; the Caesar had been Owen's own (though copies had, from the start, been taken also by Knapton in London and John Hall in Oxford[13]); and the Sallust was to have been his also, save that the Syndics had eventually to take up the stock on Owen's failure to pay his debts. Whiston's lectures, intended presumably for more students than simply those in Cambridge, had been published not in Cambridge, but by the London bookseller Benjamin Tooke, next to the gate to the Middle Temple in Fleet Street.

In other words, apart from his own publications Crownfield had begun to acquire stock from other booksellers, and in the case of Owen's publications had perhaps acquired the whole of the stock available. His business could no longer be said to be primarily in printing; he was also a bookseller on a substantial scale. Drawn into the

London trade, he became involved even with the unscrupulous Edmund Curll, with whom he collaborated to publish in rapid succession four editions of Bentley's *Remarks upon the late discourse of free-thinking*.[14] Crownfield remained a bookseller – more than a printer – with an ever expanding list of titles, until his retirement in 1740. The catalogues that he periodically included on spare pages at the end of his books provide some clues as to his preoccupations, and to the speed with which his investments sold. The *Suidas* (of which Crownfield personally never held more than a very few copies) has become notorious in the history of the University Press, in that it remained in stock, a financial and seemingly unsaleable embarrassment, until 1752.[15] In fact, there was to be little unusual in a work's remaining in print for half a century: the particular difficulty on this occasion was that it was the Syndics who were holding the copies, rather than a bookseller, and rather even than Crownfield, who was in a position to obtain copies at whatever pace he wished. Meanwhile, in 1720 he continued to advertise the quarto Caesar of 1706, as well as the *Suidas*;[16] in 1730 he could still offer copies of the 1710 edition of Sallust, and of the 1712 edition of Minucius Felix.[17]

For whom were these books intended? Occasionally there is internal evidence from the stationers, as well as from the authors. Both in the edition of 1703, and again in that of 1710, the directions to the binder in Whiston's edition of Tacquet on geometry were printed in English, Latin and French; but Whiston himself intended his book 'for the use of young students in the university'[18] – not, necessarily, for an overseas market. In this multi-lingual instruction, we may probably perceive the hand of Crownfield rather than Whiston: the hand of a member of the book trade well aware of a market where English was not the first language of those who would be responsible for handling and selling his books. But in the case of Barnes's edition of Anacreon (1705), which contained not only portraits of Anacreon and of the editor himself, but also of the dedicatee, the Duke of Marlborough, the unusual decision to include an illustration of the dedicatee can only have been the editor's. The timeliness of thus celebrating Marlborough, 'heros invictissimus' in the southern Low Countries, was not lost on at least one reviewer overseas.[19]

As Oxford had learned to its cost, in trusting John Owen to promote sales in the Netherlands, and as Cambridge also learned by experience, the overseas trade was not easy. In April 1703, Henry James, President of Queens', believed that Owen had arranged for Dutch booksellers to take 300 copies of *Suidas*; but since nothing of this appears in the accounts reconciling Owen's position later that year, it seems that he had been misled. Had Owen's claim been better founded, the University would have found itself in a better position.[20] Though both the principal exporting London booksellers, Messrs Smith and Walford, and Thomas Bennet, subscribed for multiple copies of *Suidas*,[21] Sir Theodore Janssen well realised the need to find more customers for these expensive volumes overseas. Probably rightly, he considered the University to be mistaken in refusing an offer made shortly before publication – by either the London bookseller David Mortier, or more probably his brother Pieter Mortier in Amsterdam:

Dr Bentley had told me you [i.e. Crownfield] would write to some booksellers in holld. since we refused Mr Mortier's offers, it might perhaps be of service but j think we could not pitch on a fitter person for disposing of a good quantity of Suidas beyond sea than sd. Mr Mortier, whose offer j think was very reasonable.[22]

A few days later he returned to the subject: 'j believe we stood in our own light in not accepting of Mr Mortier's proposal who is a brisk man and might have helpt us to ye Sale of a good Number.'[23]

From the first, Bentley and his allies had looked to overseas, not just to London and the market in mainland Britain. The period of the founding of the new Cambridge press coincided with an extended visit to England in 1698–9 by Johann Burchard Mencke, son of the editor of the most powerful of all the overseas journals, the Leipzig *Acta Eruditorum*, a journal whose reviews were by no means restricted to the sciences. In England, the young Mencke was on friendly terms with Bentley, during the very months that he was in a position to encourage the young man to keep his father apprised of what was afoot in Cambridge.[24] Certainly the elder Mencke proved to be amicably disposed towards many of the Press's publications. More generally, the treaty of Ryswick in September 1697 seemed to offer stability in Europe, and with it the chance of uninterrupted intercourse. At least one new journal, *The History of the Works of the Learned*, was launched on just such a hope. 'We doubt not, seeing Learning revives beyond Sea upon the settling of the Peace, but it will encrease proportionately here.'[25]

But less than four years after the treaty of Ryswick, Europe was again at war, over the Spanish succession; and the southern parts of the Low Countries became a theatre for Marlborough's campaigns. These were not conditions to encourage trade. Yet in practice many parts of the book trade continued with remarkably little disruption. In Leipzig, Otto Mencke continued to publish the *Acta Eruditorum*, which enjoyed a circulation across much of northern, central and western Europe and had links even as far south as Naples.[26] From soon after Crownfield's press was established, its books were regularly reviewed in Leipzig. In Amsterdam, Jean Le Clerc, while more than willing to engage in arguments as to the merits of individual texts and editors, praised not only the new press at Cambridge, but also the concerted campaign by scholars in London, Cambridge and Oxford to provide reliable editions of classical texts. He welcomed Tonson's quarto Latin poets more as a tribute to Cambridge than to their publisher:

> Il n'y a personne, qui ne louë les Directeurs de l'Academie de Cambrige, du dessein qu'ils ont fait de publier en beaux caracteres, & le plus correctement, qu'il sera possible, divers Auteurs Latins. Quoi que l'on en ait plusieurs Editions, en plus petits caracteres, & avec des Notes plus étendues; on ne peut voir qu'avec plaisir les belles Editions qu'ils ont déja données, & il y a beaucoup de profit à lire les Remarques Critiques, que l'on a ajoutées à la fin. Il semble que l'on entend mieux les Auteurs, qui sont si bien imprimez, & que l'on a plus de satisfaction à les lire, quand on n'y voit rien, qui ne plaise à la vuë. La grosse Lettre, qu'on y a employée, est si belle & si nette, & le papier si bon, qu'on ne peut pas douter, quand il n'y auroit que cela, que ceux qui le peuvent, & qui se piquent du choix des livres, ne les achettent à quelque prix que ce soit.[27]

France was forbidden to English traders; and instead books found their way into that country via the Netherlands, whose booksellers, placed also on the direct route to much of Germany, thus controlled a large part of the overseas market.[28] The Netherlands were not simply England's major trading partner in books; they were dominant. Setting aside Ireland, in the second half of the 1690s and in the first years of the eighteenth century the country regularly accounted for more than 85 per cent, and sometimes more than 95 per cent, of all imports from the Continent – followed at a great distance by Germany and (in time of peace) France. For exports, the Netherlands also dominated, though not in such overwhelming proportion. In the late 1690s, they accounted for over 40 per cent of all England's book exports to continental Europe, and in the first years of the eighteenth century this figure increased, even to 74 per cent in 1703–4. Germany (including eastern Germany) and France were predictable other substantial markets.[29]

Tonson, seeking sales as well as editorial help, was a regular visitor overseas. He was in the Netherlands in 1700, 1703, 1707 and again in 1710.[30] Part of his purpose was to prepare for his folio Caesar; but he also had his Cambridge quarto Latin poets to sell. Like books from other English presses, several of those from Cambridge were to be found in the catalogues of the Dutch booksellers. Pieter van der Aa, of Leiden, dealt partly with Thomas Bennet, bookseller in St Paul's Churchyard, his orders in summer 1705 including the recently published *Suidas*, to be supplied on credit against orders that Bennet in turn placed with van der Aa.[31] In Rotterdam, Reinier Leers had been trading in books printed by Hayes for several years, and a selection of Crownfield's work now began to appear in his catalogues.[32] The quarto Terence and Virgil (but not the Horace) were advertised, for example, in the catalogue for 1702, Stillingfleet's *Origines sacrae* and Needham's edition of the *Geoponica* in 1705, *Suidas* in 1706. As one of the most prominent of the international booksellers in the Low Countries, for some authors Leers came first to mind when foreign circulation was hoped for. 'I wish', wrote James Talbot to Matthew Prior of his duodecimo Horace, 'you would order my friend and your humble servant, old Elzevir, to recommend this impression in his namesake's types to Leers of Rotterdam, so that he may take off a number of copies, which shall be afforded at a reasonable price.'[33] The duodecimo Horace was reviewed briefly in the *Acta Eruditorum*, in Leipzig, and was made the occasion to laud the new press at Cambridge.[34] If Leers took the edition of Horace of which Talbot wrote, it did not feature in his catalogues; but there were plenty of other English-printed books that did. Via Leers, books from Cambridge were acquired for the Royal Library in Paris, as part of a vigorous campaign by the library keeper Nicolas Clément to improve holdings of modern foreign books. In a substantial operation, Leers became one of the principal suppliers to the French royal library, in exchange for engravings from the royal collection:[35] the arrangement avoided a charge on the royal purse, and as a consequence, many of Leers's catalogues featured arrays of recent French work of this kind. By these channels, the Bibliothèque du Roi acquired Stillingfleet's *Origines sacrae* (1702), Arthur Annesley's edition of Catullus, Tibullus and Propertius (1702), the Cambridge *Suidas* (1705), and Whiston's edition of Sir Isaac Newton's *Arithmetica uni-*

versalis (1707). Cellarius' *Notitia orbis antiqui* (1703), published in Cambridge by John Owen, travelled by the same route.[36]

With the help of reviewing journals to promote their stocks, and relying on journalists such as Le Clerc and Basnage de Beauval, the Dutch booksellers at the end of the seventeenth and the beginning of the eighteenth centuries created and to a great extent manipulated the international market.[37] Intellectual and commercial ambitions were married in the foundation in 1684 of the *Nouvelles de la République des Lettres*, edited by Pierre Bayle and published in Amsterdam by Henry Desbordes.[38] In Rotterdam, Henri Basnage de Beauval linked with the bookseller Reinier Leers to launch the *Histoire des Ouvrages des Sçavans* in 1687.[39] In The Hague, Thomas Johnson founded the *Journal Littéraire* in 1713.[40] The indefatigable Jean Le Clerc, having learned much of the trade as well as of the demands of a regular reviewing journal with the *Bibliothèque Universelle et Historique*, published by a group of booksellers in Amsterdam between 1686 and 1693, extended his frame of reference in the *Bibliothèque Choisie* (1703–13), published by Hendrik Schelte in Amsterdam, and followed it after Schelte's death in 1714 with the *Bibliothèque Ancienne et Moderne*, published initially by David Mortier and then by the firm of Wetstein. After Le Clerc withdrew from his long career in editing this series of journals, the firm of Wetstein in 1728 established the *Bibliothèque Raisonnée des Ouvrages des Savans de l'Europe* (1728–53), a journal which broke with tradition by being deliberately anonymous. Each of these was circulated in England; but with the *Bibliothèque Angloise*, founded in 1717, Michel de la Roche and his publisher, the widow of Paul Marret, concentrated for the first time on the British trade, aiming opinion and trade towards the Continent not from London, as he had with the *Memoirs of Literature* (1710–14), but from Amsterdam.

Le Clerc made no attempt to disguise his Anglophile bias. In the course of its history, the *Bibliothèque Choisie*[41] devoted no less than 22 per cent of its reviews to books published in England – more than for any other country save for the Dutch Republic itself. Le Clerc knew England at first hand, having lived briefly in London in the 1680s, and counting Locke among his most long-standing correspondents. Unlike, for example, Jacques Bernard, his successor as editor of the *Bibliothèque Universelle et Historique*,[42] Le Clerc had the advantage of understanding English. Cambridge University Press benefited; but so did the learned press in Oxford and London. By 1718, Le Clerc could write with benefit of hindsight, and thus justify the editorial policy that had dominated his journal through its eleven years' existence:

> Combien peu de Gens y a-t-il deçà la mer, qui sachent l'Anglois? Cependant il y a une infinité de bons Livres dans cette Langue, qu'on n'a point, traduits, & qui ne le seront apparemment jamais; dont il est néanmoins très-avantageux au Public d'avoir au moins quelque connoissance.[43]

Whatever his interest in promoting literature in English, Le Clerc also devoted much of his considerable energy to promoting English scholarship. In 1707, he reviewed Davies's edition of Caesar, printed at Cambridge the previous year. Amongst his various sources, Davies had made use of manuscripts and of the Rome edition of 1472 owned by John Moore. For Le Clerc, this seems to have been an even more arresting example than usual of what he perceived as a renaissance in classical scholarship in England, where editors (and by no means Davies only) were able to use the resources of large private libraries in the pursuit of scholarship.

> Elle n'a pas été jusqu'à present fort à la mode en Angleterre, où les Savans se sont appliquez plûtôt aux Sciences plus relevées, comme à la Philosophie, qu'à ce qu'on nomme proprement *la Critique* & les *Belles Lettres*. Mais depuis quelques années, on a commencé à les goûter & à les cultiver, plus qu'on n'avoit fait, dans les deux Academies, & particulierement dans celle de Cambrige. On ne sauroit s'empêcher de féliciter l'Angleterre, à cause de cela, puis qu'elle reçoit chez elle une espece d'Erudition, qui commence beaucoup à s'éteindre deçà la mer. Ceux qui connoissent le génie appliqué & pénetrant de la Nation Angloise, & la noble envie qu'elle a toûjours euë d'eceller, en tout ce qu'elle a entrepris de cultiver, augurent toutes sortes d'avantages pour la République des Lettres; en voyant ce que cette Ile fameuse a commencé à produire, depuis quelque tems, en cette espece de Litterature. Aussi y a-t-on communément, dans les Academies, des moyens de travailler que l'on n'a pas ailleurs; soit par la facilité d'y subsister tranquillement, & sans être trop distrait, soit par les belles Bibliothèques qu'il y a. On en retirera des fruits d'autant plus grands, qu'en ce païs-là on joint le soin de cultiver son jugement avec l'étude des Belles-Lettres, plus qu'on ne fait en aucun autre lieu; où ces deux choses sont presque devenues incompatibles, par la faute de ceux qui en font profession, qui ont séparé ce qui devoit être uni pour toûjours, & devenir entierement inséparable. Il est ridicule de s'appliquer à entendre de bons Auteurs & à imiter leur style, sans se rendre capable de penser aussi bien qu'eux, & même de les surpasser en cela; puis que l'on demeure, toûjours beaucoup au desous d'eux, à l'égard du stile.[44]

Quite apart from his activities as a journalist in the Low Countries, activities that in themselves were complementary to his position as a clergyman and religious controversialist, Le Clerc was also among the earliest authors at the new University Press. In February 1699/1700, the Curators agreed to print, for the London bookseller Timothy Child, a fresh edition of his *Physica, sive de rebus corporeis libri quinque*:[45] the book, in duodecimo, was finished the following July. Further editions followed in 1705 and 1708. An edition of his *Logica* appeared in 1704, again for London booksellers.

Davies, a key figure in the work of the University Press, became one of Le Clerc's most loyal correspondents, even through the difficult years of arguments with Bentley. Like many of his contemporaries among the journalists who helped most to define the so-called republic of letters, Le Clerc was especially alert to the appearance of the books before him for review. Remarks on the size of type were a regular feature of notices both in the *Bibliothèque Choisie* and in Bernard's *Nouvelles de la République des Lettres*. Of an edition of Maximus Tyrius printed by Hayes in 1703, the youthful work of Davies and published only two years after he had been elected a Fellow of Queens' College, Le Clerc thought that those responsible had 'un peu épargné le papier', and that the type was noticeably 'serrée' or cramped.[46] The contrast between Hayes's work and that of the new University Press was highlighted by the position of the notice of Davies's work in the *Bibliothèque Choisie*, in the midst of a group of books printed by Crownfield. By

contrast, Piers's edition of Euripides, published in the winter of 1702–3 was a noticeably better exercise in typography. 'Les caractères sont neufs, & on les a fait venir de
Hollande', remarked Le Clerc, before commenting on the Duke of Somerset's lead in
reviving the press at Cambridge: 'Ce Seigneur mérite que non seulement les Gens de
Lettres de Cambrige, mais encore tous les autres, qui se servent des Editions faites avec
ces caracteres, lui sâchent gré de sa génerosité.'[47] It was partly a matter of type and page
size. But it was also a matter of the new *goût hollandois*, as the eighteenth-century French
punchcutter P. S. Fournier was later to describe it – a taste that Moxon had noted in the
early 1680s and that has affected type design ever since. This was for type-faces so
devised that they appear large on their bodies, and so look large even while the type
itself takes up a very similar amount of space to type of the same size, but smaller face.
'All the accomplishments that can render *Letter* regular and beautiful, do more visibly
appear in them than in any *Letters* cut by any other People.'[48] The taste was associated
with the Netherlands (and perhaps with Amsterdam in particular, as the centre of Dutch
type-founding); but it was not a solely Dutch phenomenon.[49]

The decision to invest in Dutch type at Cambridge thus began to pay dividends in
the international market. As Le Clerc remarked in 1704, noticing the Tonson edition of
the Latin poets,

> Il semble que l'on entend mieux les Auteurs, qui sont si bien imprimez, & que l'on a plus
> de satisfaction à les lire, quand on n'y voit rien, qui ne plaise à la vuë. La grosse Lettre
> qu'on y a employée, est si belle & si nette, & le papier si bon, qu'on ne peut pas douter,
> quand il n'y auroit que cela, que ceux qui le peuvent, & qui se piquent du choix des livres,
> ne les achettent à quelque prix que ce soit.[50]

Crownfield's Dutch type met with approval in Amsterdam. But so, too, did the lay-out
of some of his books. Of Davies's new edition of Minucius Felix, published in 1712,
Le Clerc remarked in particular the felicitous way in which the notes were organised:

> Les Notes sont très-bien disposées sous le texte, en sorte qu'elles sont toûjours partagées
> également sous les deux pages, qui se regardent; ce qui fait un agreable effet à l'œuil & qui
> ne donne aucune peine au Lecteur, pour les trouver.[51]

In fact, apart from the edition's being printed on a larger sheet of paper (and hence
being slightly larger in form) than its predecessor printed by Crownfield for Owen in
1707, there was little difference in the overall design of the page. Le Clerc's opinion
may have been coloured by his recalling the page design of Gronovius' edition printed
at Leiden in 1709, almost identical to that of the Cambridge edition that he now praised:
even the disposition of the decorative engraving on the title-page was identical. In
casting about for comparisons, he found himself repeatedly obliged to recall the
Estiennes, whose combination of classical texts, outstanding type and sensitive lay-out
marked them as Crownfield's most obvious peers. But there were criticisms as well: in
praising the Minucius Felix, Le Clerc also criticised others by implication. He was not
alone in remarking that the Amsterdam edition of Bentley's Horace, published by
Rudolph and Gerard Wetstein in 1713,[52] was an improvement on the Cambridge edition

of 1711 because it placed the notes at the foot of the page rather than at the end – a feature to which Bentley himself seems to have been reconciled only with some reluctance.[53] Le Clerc also considered the larger paper of the Amsterdam copies superior to that from Cambridge.[54] As for presswork, rather than typography, Samuel Clarke's magnificent folio Caesar, published by Tonson in 1712, showed what might be achieved compared with what Crownfield's team had managed for the poets. 'Les Caracteres sont aussi gros, que ceux des Poëtes, que l'on a déja vus; mais le tirage, pour parler en termes d'imprimerie, me paroît meilleur dans cette Edition.'[55]

The Amsterdam edition of Bentley's Horace had the benefit of coming after the difficult progress of the 1711 edition through the press. Bentley watched its production anxious that standards should be at least as good, and disapproving of the proposed index.[56] The same title by Jan Goeree, engraved by Bernard, was used for both, slightly reworked for the edition of 1713. But it was also noticeable that, unlike the 1711 edition, the Amsterdam edition matched in height (and hence on scholars' and collectors' shelves) the edition which Bentley's was designed to supersede – that prepared by Talbot for Tonson in 1699. As a book, the Amsterdam edition was superior in several ways.

Notwithstanding the enthusiasm shown by some reviewing editors, it remained that books printed in England could be difficult to obtain in the Low Countries; and that even if they were obtainable, they could be expensive. In September 1705, Le Clerc complained to Lord Shaftesbury of his particular difficulties at that moment with editions from Oxford of Xenophon (1703) and of Dionysius Halicarnassus, edited by John Hudson (1704), as well as with the Cambridge *Suidas*, edited by Kuster. They were too expensive for him to buy, and he was therefore unable to say anything to encourage their reception until he could find someone from whom to borrow them – 'ce qui n'arrivera que tard, parce que peu de gens achettent ces livres ici'. On this occasion, Shaftesbury obliged, and a review duly appeared in the *Bibliothèque Choisie* the following year.[57]

But in addition to this, there seems to have been a shortage of people in Cambridge willing to correspond regularly with such journals, English or foreign. Promises of further information to follow did not materialise;[58] journals depended in practice on a very few correspondents who inevitably could not deal evenly with the output of the British press;[59] and instead space was absorbed with details, even to the printing of proposals *in extenso*, from Oxford, London, Paris and Italy. The press at Cambridge was at last producing worthwhile books for the international scholarly community; and there were readers overseas who wished to hear of them; but communication between the two, via the book trade, was irregular and often mediocre.

Understandably, the foreign trade concentrated its attention on comparatively few books – from the Cambridge press as from others. Bentley was a household name, and the slow progress through the press of his edition of Horace was a repeated matter for report. Interest in Ludolph Kuster's edition of *Suidas*, the largest, most difficult and most hazardous of the projects at Cambridge in the first years of the century, was the more acute in that Kuster was himself a foreigner, already known for his earlier work, and in particular his contributions to the short-lived *Bibliotheca librorum novorum*, published at Utrecht. The *Suidas* was agreed by the Curators in October 1701, and Bentley's Horace in September 1703;[60] but though Kuster's much longer work was to be published in 1705, nothing of Bentley's appeared until 1711. Each in its way brought headaches; but difficulties with the intended bookseller, John Owen, and with the unusually heavy investment in paper for so large a project, made Kuster's project especially burdensome.[61]

The difficulties with Owen have been discussed in the last chapter. Outside Cambridge, the learned world thirsted for news. Kuster himself had whetted appetites with a pamphlet on his proposed work in February 1701, before the Cambridge press had even agreed to publish the edition.[62] The promise that it would not only be an improvement on the *editio princeps* printed by Chalcondylas in Milan in 1499 and on the other early editions, but would also include consideration of manuscripts in Paris and (perhaps) Florence was all designed to attract attention. The pamphlet succeeded in this purpose admirably. In October, apart from an advertisement in the *London Gazette*, the *Nouvelles de la République des Lettres* reported the project, and in April 1703 further reported that printing of the edition was half complete.[63] On publication, reviews appeared in, among other places, the *Nouvelles de la République des Lettres* – extremely briefly – in August 1705, and at more length in the *Acta Eruditorum* in January 1706, the *Bibliothèque Choisie* in 1706[64] and the *Journal des Sçavans* in October 1707. Critical interest was aroused, and was generally enthusiastic; but it was quite another matter to sell the book. Of 1,500 copies printed (including 150 on large paper) a now unknown number had already been sold by subscription.[65] The subscription price for ordinary paper copies had been set in 1701 at £2.15s., but the volumes proved to be almost a quarter as big again as had been anticipated, and the Press was therefore already in danger of making a serious loss. In May 1705 the subscription prices were revised, to £2.17s.9¼d. for ordinary paper, and £4.0s.11¼d. for large paper. Prices to new purchasers were to be £3 and £4.10s. In London, the bookseller Christopher Bateman was to be allowed a discount of 5 per cent.[66]

The overseas market, so far little exploited, was critical. When agreement was reached in the summer of 1706 (no doubt with a little relief) with two overseas booksellers, Rudolph Wetstein in the Netherlands and Caspar Fritsch of Leipzig, there was little room for manoeuvre. As the Minutes of the Curators reveal, this was not as much as had once been hoped. The various memoranda are worth quoting in full, since they show not only the Press in negotiation with both Wetstein in the Netherlands and Fritsch in Leipzig, but also how payments were to be paced. Since the project had been funded by Sir Theodore Janssen (the original bookseller, John Owen, having failed), his interests remained central to the proceedings at successive meetings of the Curators in July–August 1706:

> Wetstein to send 200 Suidas's in Commission at 33 Gulders per booke; what they dispose of, they are to pay for every 3 months, one half in mony, the other half in such bookes as we shall send 'em a Catalogue of; and they shall procure what they have not themselves, at such prises as they are sold for in the shops for ready mony in Holland. We are to deliver

our Bookes on board at London, & to send 'em an Account in what ship, & as soone as they receive advice thereof, they are at their charge & account. They are to deliver our bookes o'board at Roterdam at their Charge, & to send us advice, & as soone as we receive advice, we are upon yᵉ same account as they are wth theirs.

Agreed to this by yᵉ Vicechancellʳ & Curatʳˢ, Sʳ.

Theodore Janssen approving of it,

Bardsey Fisher Vicechancellʳ

July 25th. 1706. Agreed then by Mʳ Vicechancellr deput: Dʳ Ashton, wth yᵉ Curators then present that yᵉ University deal wᵗʰ Mʳ Fritch of Leipsic for one hundred & three Suidas; a hundred pound to be payd down to yᵉ University or Sʳ Theodore Janssen, & yᵉ rest in bookes such as yᵉ University have approv'd of, to yᵉ value of two hundred pounds more (mem: yᵉ 3 odd Suidas are allowd in stead of Rebate)

C. Ashton V. Chanc. Deput.

At a meeting of yᵉ Curatʳˢ Aug. 12th. Dr Balderson vicechancellʳ deput: as by letter from Mr Wetstein, he saies he'l pay for each Suidas 32 Gulders for 50 bookes, half in 6 & yᵉ other half in 12 months, after yᵉ delivery of yᵉ bookes into his hands, & to allow him yᵉ usual allowance, one booke in 7.

As to 'tother 50 bookes, viz. by exchange of bookes, (still at yᵉ rate of 32 Gilders) he desires no allowance of one in 7. but as follows in yᵉ first article at top of yᵉ page.

Jo: Balderston. P.V.

Thus Crownfield extended his duties to business as a bookseller. In 1698, the Curators had assumed that all the Press's affairs could be reduced to payment in cash; but now, faced not with a single publishing bookseller, or a pair of them, but with the need to disperse copies of an expensive work that they had been obliged to publish themselves, they were obliged to accept books in exchange. So, partly by exchange and partly in money, Crownfield acquired some of the recent standard works from the presses of the Low Countries and of Germany. From Wetstein, among a list of twenty-five titles he received a dozen sets of Vossius' *Opera* in folio, editions of Cicero, Callimachus, Juvenal, Ovid and Quintilian, five copies of Grotius' *Epistolae* and three sets of Commelin's catalogue of the Hortus medicus in Amsterdam. From Fritsch in Leipzig his purchases included multiple copies of Cellarius' *Geographia antiqua*, Pausanias, Fabricius' *Bibliotheca graeca* and Thomas Reinesius' *Syntagma inscriptionum antiquarum*.[67]

These were not dead stock from overseas booksellers seeking to unload slow-selling titles. They were just the kind of books of which Cambridge stood in need, and they had been chosen with care. The odd numbers of the books bought from Wetstein in particular suggest that Crownfield made some enquiries for orders amongst his customers before placing his order. Stock superfluous to Cambridge could be traded with other booksellers in London. By no means all college libraries had funds to take advantage of the sudden presence in Cambridge of books that would usually be expensive to stock. In 1701, Queens' College subscribed to him for *Suidas* on large paper – one of several college libraries to have done so by autumn 1703.[68] By 1705, Queens' was employing him as a more general supplier, and over the next few years it steadily increased its business with him. The copies of Hofmann's *Lexicon* and of Julius Pollux bought by the College in December 1706 were almost certainly part of the consignment, mostly of books published in Holland, obtained from Wetstein earlier that autumn in exchange for 100 copies of *Suidas*.[69] Other books, from the same consignment, were sold to the University Library in January.[70] Trinity College was buying from him by 1702 and regularly by 1709.[71] Though Crownfield thus became established as a principal supplier in the Cambridge retail trade, his stock was for the present almost entirely (other than his own publications) of foreign books. By 1714–15 he was supplying English books as well, besides stationery goods.[72] Until then, English books were usually to be bought from other local booksellers, such as Jeffery or Thurlbourn.

The difficulties were not only in England. In the Low Countries, Kuster, with a wide knowledge of the book trade and now with his own interests as author to encourage him, kept in close touch with Bentley. At the end of a long letter that ranged over the business and characters of various booksellers, as well as over his own and others' editorial projects, including suggestions for the Cambridge press, he added a postscript:

> Out of love, which I have for Suidas, I must add an article about it. I see, Sir, that the others booksellers here, and chiefli the company, are jealous, that the Wetsteins (who, for to tell the truth, are not much beloved amongst the others booksellers) have Suidas alone, et commands the price therof. Therefore they have resolved amongst them, not to take any of them from Wetstein; which hindereth the sale of it migthely. I know that the others want it; but, as I have told, out of jealousie, they will not take them of Wetstein, but will treat rather with the University, if they can agree. Therefore one of them, whoes name is Wolters, hath given me this present note in Dutch, which Dr. Sike can interpret to you. I think, Sir, there can be no better way to sell the book queek, then to treat with the company, who hath a great treade and correspondence. They are willing to treat for some honders, upon reasonable terms: that is to say, they expect, I believe, that, if they shall pay the whole in monney, they may have every copy for about 45 schilling, Englisch monney, and a certain time allowed to pay. I wischd the University might agree, that the book might be once sold. Therefore, if you pleaseth to let me know, what the University is resolved to do in this case, and what conditions they please to propose, I shal make it known to the others. I do not suppose, that the Univers. hath made such a bargain with the Wetsteins, that they cannot send them to any other abroad, which would not be profitable tho the Universty: because, as long as the Wetsteins have Suidas alone, it will sell very sloly. I do but desire you, Sir, to conceal my name in this matter. For if the Wetsteins should hear of it, they should think, as if I would join with the other booksellers against them; wch is not my dessein. For they are my friends. Al the matter is, that I think myself obliged to promote the interest of the University, and the reputation of my own book.[73]

Apart from stock from Rotterdam and Leipzig, Crownfield also found himself dealing with a further bookseller, Paul Vaillant of The Hague. Again, it was on a basis of exchange for Vaillant's stock, not of payment in cash. Copies of *Suidas* were charged at £3 each, and in addition Vaillant took copies of other Press books: Davies's Caesar, Barnes's Anacreon, Maximus Tyrius, and Peter Needham's *Geoponica*. As a result, further books went to Queens' and other colleges; and, in exchange for four further copies of *Suidas*, a set of Erasmus was obtained for the University Library.[74]

The edition of *Suidas* was not cleared from the warehouse until 1752, when the Cambridge bookseller Thomas Merrill bought seventy-five sets, the price having now dropped to a guinea a set. It was just over half a century since, in October 1701, the Curators had first calculated the charge to John Owen and then reached agreement with him for the project. Many other books have stayed in print for longer. In his Sandars Lectures in 1954, and thinking as a publisher in the mid-twentieth century, S. C. Roberts looked back on the saga as a 'sad story' and suggested that it contributed materially to the severe shortage of cash that the Press experienced in much of the first third of the eighteenth century.[75] Indeed it did. But the story is more interesting than that. Quite apart from the false hopes that had been raised initially by Owen, the Curators had mis-estimated the true costs not of printing (as usual, they had allowed a profit, or overheads, of one-third in their quotation to Owen in 1701) but of publishing. They had set themselves successfully at the overseas market, and had found willing buyers. But the money represented by the stocks of books acquired by Crownfield did not pass directly into the hands of the Curators. Instead, Crownfield acquired stock for which he was obliged to pay only gradually. The annual accounts for 1705–6 and 1706–7 are missing. But those for the following year record his repayment of £20.10s., and in 1708–9 he paid £80.10s. In this way, by means of extended credit, Crownfield was enabled to establish himself as a bookseller and publisher in his own right, using money laid out by the University for a quite different purpose.

From the first, while the Curators agreed to print for London booksellers, such as Tonson, they could also look to Cambridge booksellers. With the *Suidas* they embarked on a major publication project of their own. There was room also for private work.[76] In the late seventeenth century this had become increasingly common. In Cambridge, Thomas Mace had published his *Musick's monument* in this way in 1676, and Joshua Barnes had published his own history of Edward III in 1688. Barnes's more important, and more celebrated, edition of Euripides, published in 1694, had been issued over the name of a local bookseller, Richard Green. Independent by nature, learned in an unconventional way, and ill at ease with the book trade, he resorted once again to seeking out subscriptions when his edition of Homer was ready for the press. By now he was well versed in the dangers, as well as in the advantages, of such a course. He counted his history of Edward III a success, though he claimed to have lost £300 in providing bound copies. The Euripides, published by the trade, had been a disappointment partly because the Chancellor of the University (the Duke of Somerset), to whom the book was dedicated, had not contributed as much as had been hoped or anticipated. His edition of Anacreon, published by Edmund Jeffery, had profited him (he claimed) only £10, and for this book he had had to meet the cost of the three engravings himself.[77]

Ever anxious, Barnes found himself beset both by his colleagues and by the book trade. His colleagues (apparently led by his old adversary Bentley, ever a stickler in others' obligations when it suited him) criticised the attention he was giving to Homer at the expense of his duties as a teacher and lecturer; and the book trade was not prepared to help publish these authors as they deserved.

I have been all yᵉ year engaged on Homers Iliad (yᵉ Odyssey being ready before) yᵉ Conscience of which work gave me yᵉ Courage to dispence with yᵉ other business of my Place, of which I wrote timely to Dʳ. Bentley & Mr Vice-Chancellor. And surely if my conceit is not wide of all true reason, I need not doubt but all men of Learning would gladly allow of yᵉ change, since by yᵉ Labour I make lectures for all Countrys & for all Ages. Why should I doubt of an Equal Interpretation from men of Learning, thô of my own Country? Who if they disdain to speak against their own Conscience, must allow that I have equall'd yᵉ very best of my Predecessors in Diligence about yᵉ Business of my Place, which if any pretend not yet to know I am able to prove? Sʳ. it is my confort you are one of my witnesses *how* I read, thô perhaps not, *how often*; & yet if it might please yᵉ University to enlarge my Auditory, I'll engage to be more frequent tho to take more pains, 'tis not possible.

Sʳ. now, as I said, I am upon *Homer* & being such an *Officer* of such a Body, and a *Curator* of yᵉ press, and *Homer* such an Author who cannot have too much respect shewn him, from yᵉ greatest Body of Learning in yᵉ World, what due encouragement may I not hope for? Booksellers will cramp & spoyl by their baser spirits yᵉ best designd Author, as *Anacreon* being confind to so small a Volume, was necessarily deprivd of yᵉ noble Indexes I had prepard. I therefore intend to print *this* myself in Curious paper and Letter, in *Folio*, if I may find reasonable encouragement from oʳ. press, only to bring in Mʳ. Crownfield for so much of yᵉ Share, as yᵉ Paper and yᵉ Work of yᵉ Press shall amount to, the University, as an Honourary to *Homer* & his *Editor* (who pretends by far to outdoe all that went before him and to equal yᵉ. Edition with yᵉ best of yᵉ Antients) *freely lending me their Letters* & what else they think fit, in return to which Favour yᵉ *Book to be dedicated* to yᵉᵐ. yᵉ *kindness to be acknowledg'd* in yᵉ best manner, with a Repetition of their *Liberality* before shewn on *Euripides'* Account. Whether this will not redound to yᵉ honour of the University as such, as to my particular Benefit, any unprejudic'd Person may see; and God forbid, that yᵉ Affairs of yᵉ University should not be managd with all Impartiality, Humanity, and Regard to Learning . . .[78]

He had, as he pointed out to Thomas Hearne, little choice in practice but to use the University Press. He had strong connections with Oxford; but as Regius Professor of Greek in Cambridge these were not connections that he felt well able to allow to develop. He was already known to have contributed the descriptions from Emmanuel College to Edward Bernard's union catalogue of manuscripts in 1697, and to have provided John Mill with readings of a manuscript Greek New Testament in Emmanuel for his edition published at Oxford in 1707.[79] Hearne's siren songs were already vain by the time that Barnes wrote this. In August 1707, the fundamental work on the *Iliad* was completed. Barnes determined not only to have it printed himself (and find a bookseller to take in copies as well, if he could), but also to take advantage of the Greek type at the University Press: he described this type to Hearne as 'new', though it had in fact been in case at Cambridge for several years, and had been used in the *Suidas*.[80]

When the Curators agreed terms – rather less generous than he had once hoped – with Barnes in June 1708 there were several recent precedents, if none for so large a project. In November 1707 they had agreed with Thomas Rudd, then a schoolmaster at Newcastle upon Tyne, for the printing of a second edition of his Latin Syntax; with Robert Cannon, of King's, for his sermon preached the previous month before the

Queen at Newmarket; and with J. F. Vigani for his pharmaceutical notes.[81] The principal consideration for a larger project, and perhaps especially when it concerned a private individual rather than an established member of the book trade, was the organisation of the several payments during printing, since initially the Press would have to pay both for labour and time: for booksellers, as for Barnes, the undertaker (or, in Barnes's case, the editor) was responsible for the cost of paper. An agreed timetable for payment, linked to production, would also ensure that should any delay occur in delivery of copy it would be at the expense of the undertaker (Barnes) rather than the Press. Thus, if Barnes collected his subscriptions efficiently, capital outlay would be at a minimum for each party – printer, undertaker and customer. As usual, the Curators included a charge of (approximately) a standard 50 per cent of the total of composition, correction and presswork.

So, on 15 June 1708, it was

Agreed that the Greek Professour do proceed in Printing his Homer, upon the following Conditions viz.

That wn. an 100 Sheets are wrought off (viz. 50 of each Vol. Iliad & Odyssea) he shall within 6. Weeks pay for 50. & so on, to the finishing the Book in the same Proportion; except the last hundred sheets, for wch he is to have six Moneths credit, if he desires it.

That if he shall neglect, or refuse to pay for fifty sheets six Weeks after an hundred are finishd, & so on, as above directed; upon every such failure the University shall have power to seize upon what is finish'd for their own Use.

That wn. all are finish'd, he shall have ffive hundred Books only & upon paying the Whole, that is due upon these Articles, he shall have the remainder deliver'd to him.

Homer's Odyssea for Mr Barnes.

	£	s	
Composing a sheet.	00	16	00
Correcting a sheet.	00	2	08
Working at Press 1250 Copies.	00	06	00
One 3d. to the University	00	12	04
	01	17	00

Homer's Ilias for Ditto.

Composing a sheet	00	16	00
Correcting a sheet.	00	02	08
Working at Press 1500. Copies	00	07	04
One 3d. to the University.	00	13	00
	01	19	00

I do agree & stand to ye Conditions, expressed in ye Articles above written. Winess my Hand,

Joshua Barnes.[82]

The first sheets of the *Odyssey* and the *Iliad* had already been printed, perhaps partly as a specimen, when Barnes's agreement with the Curators was thus formalised. Work at the Press began in earnest the following October, and the accounts submitted by the compositors and pressmen suggest that apart from the usual pauses in production because of the weather,[83] production proceeded without undue delay until the last sheets were printed off in November 1710.[84] The *Iliad*, though it proved slightly more complicated, was finished at about the same time – both volumes being dated 1711.

Meanwhile, for Barnes, all was by no means straightforward. Even before the first sheets had been printed, he had had two sets of specimens printed off in 1706 and 1707. The second served also as proposals, of which he sent 100 copies to Oxford in December that year. A further set of proposals was prepared in the late summer of 1708.[85] Gradually, the extent of Barnes's personal investment in his work became clear even to outsiders. In January 1707/8 he told Hearne that the project would cost him almost £1,000,[86] but while his supporters wished him well, they could not see how he could find more than three hundred subscribers – '& Booksellers will, of course, obstruct what you intend'.[87] By June he was more sanguine. The paper from Genoa, much delayed, had arrived at Cambridge, and the world could look to a production such as it had never seen before.[88] 'None would imagine what service you and I have done Homer', he wrote to Hearne, in high spirits shortly after Crownfield had returned from Holland with an engraved frontispiece, 'rarely designd' by Goeree, the same person who had been responsible for the equivalent in Bentley's Horace the previous year.[89]

The price initially advertised to subscribers had been 30s., 10s. as down payment and the rest to be paid on delivery. But Barnes had calculated wrongly; and as the cost of paper and printing increased while the edition made its way slowly through the Press, he faced growing embarrassment. With the work near completion, he considered that an ordinary retail price of 40s. would be appropriate. By the end of 1710, with publication upon him, he had to be content with booksellers who would charge no more than 35s. The anxieties and arguments over price were straightforwardly commercial; and as a privately printed book the University did not necessarily have any authority in the price to be charged. Nonetheless, the Vice-Chancellor (Charles Roderick, of King's) ordained that the retail price for the two volumes should be 20s. and 15s. in sheets for the *Iliad* and *Odyssey* respectively. His action in establishing the price seems to have been intended not as a prelude to publication, but an attempt to defend Barnes from booksellers who subsequently sought to undermine the price on which his private purse depended.[90]

With the work finally finished, Barnes had to begin the laborious task of delivering copies and settling accounts – tasks that would for ordinary books have fallen to the bookseller. The first copies were distributed in London in December 1710, those who were not among the first to receive them inevitably causing difficulties. From Oxford, John Hudson suggested that he should trade copies of other books for his Homer; but such a course would not bring him the money that he so needed to pay off his debts to the printer. Others 'shuffled' with their bills. Most importantly, Barnes found it impossible to sell copies at more than the subscription price. In the end, he feared that he would have little option but to trade books for books, once he had sold as many as he could for ready money.[91] By the following summer, with laggardly sales, he was begging that Hudson should not only press the Oxford booksellers, but should also seek out pupil-mongers, and persuade them to take multiple copies – at a discount if they would take half a dozen.[92] Now, too, it seemed to him that Crownfield had played him false, and had printed more than had been contracted.[93] The records of work at the Press show no sign that this was the case; but Barnes's suspicions were marks of how far relations between him and his printer had deteriorated since he had lodged with Crownfield in the printing house in the autumn of 1708 and again in February 1709/10.[94]

The source of this further dispute lay, not surprisingly, in how copies of Barnes's work were to be sold overseas. The subscription price in England for the two volumes was 30s., the price advertised in the *London Gazette* as recently as February 1709/10.[95] But now Crownfield, with whom Barnes was obliged to share stock, was said to be selling copies so cheaply that copies were to be had in Holland at 26s.6d.[96]

Reviews overseas were generally favourable, if offering little financial reward and even threatening sales in London. Le Clerc's *Bibliothèque Choisie* drew attention, as so frequently in its reviews, not only to the scholarship, but also to the presentation. The criticisms of production were perhaps meant as a compliment in the company that was proffered, but they showed only cautious appreciation of the care that Barnes had taken to obtain suitable paper. The type, Greek and English, was from Holland; but even so it did not find complete favour. Despite the care to use materials of an international standard, Crownfield's press still did not compare as well as it might with even Schrevelius' edition of Homer printed at Leiden in the 1650s – let alone with Estienne himself.

> S'il y a eu quelques Editions d'*Homere*, qui aient été plus belles que celle-ci, pour les car-actères, le papier, ou l'impression, comme celle d'*Henri Estienne*, in folio, & celle de *Corneille Schrevelius* in 4. il faut avouër néanmoins qu'elle est fort belle à tous ces égards, & qu'elle surpasse de beaucoup toutes les autres, pour l'exactitude du Texte, & des Scholies; comme on le verra, pour peu qu'on la feuillete. Pour celle de *Schrevelius*, on sait qu'il n'y a rien de loüable, que le papier et l'impression; mais on sera surpris de voir que les meilleures Editions fussent si fautives . . .[97]

The tale of Barnes's failure to find a publisher had reached even the ears of the *Bibliothèque Choisie*, which was careful also to emphasise his earlier achievements, notably his editions of Euripides and Anacreon. This was deserved praise; but as the purpose of Hendrik Schelte, publisher of the *Bibliothèque Choisie*, was partly to promote his own stock (some of it, including the Homer, from England) it was hardly an impartial court.[98]

The *Journal des Sçavans* complimented Barnes the following June: 'la plus riche, la plus correcte, & en même tems la plus belle de toutes les Editions d'Homere'.[99] But with one notable exception, Barnes found few financial rewards in his Homer. When Prince Eugene of Savoy visited England in spring 1712, an effort was made to interest him in some of the more notable recent books. Clarke's edition of Caesar, published by Tonson and dedicated to Marlborough, was an obvious choice, and the prince rewarded the gift with 30 guineas. Seizing the opportunity, Barnes presented his Homer, and received 20.[100] It was among the last public events of his life, for on 3 August following he died, suffering from what Hearne described as a 'consumptive cough'. Hearne, like Barnes a far from easy man, felt the loss particularly. 'He was my great Friend and Acquaintance, and I look upon him to have been the best Grecian (especially for Poëtical Greek) in the World. He was withal a man of singular good nature, and never spoke ill of any Man, unless provoked in the highest Degree.' Barnes left unfinished the sales of his Homer, and Hearne for one could not discover how many copies had been sent to Hudson for sale among the Oxford colleges.[101] From the beginning, Hearne had disapproved of offering copies below the subscription price – an act that both cheapened Barnes's achievement and seemed an injustice to subscribers. Now he sought to help Barnes's widow, as the booksellers scented prey:

> I am still of the same Mind, that the Books ought not to be sold for less Price yⁿ Subscribers paid. Yet our Booksellers here talk of no more than fifteen Shillings. And perhaps those at Cambridge may bid as low. I suppose Dr. Hudson hath written to you again, and told you the Result of his Inquiries in this Affair. For my part, if I were to advise them (as I am resolv'd I will not) to be sold for under Subscription Price, I should think it more prudent to let some Forreign Booksellers have them, that so, by that means, our own narrow spirited Booksellers might see their Folly in offering so mean and scandalous a Price.[102]

Her husband had died with the cost of printing Homer still not paid off; and though Mrs Barnes told Hearne that his debts could be met without selling his books at less than their true value (instead, she sold off stock from their farm at Hemingford[103]), she was keen that the remaining copies of Homer should be dispersed: if Oxford failed, then the residue could be sent to the London booksellers.[104] Though both Hearne and Mrs Barnes believed that the volumes should not be sold under their subscription price, there was little option if they were to be sold in a reasonable time. The booksellers were in an impregnable position, and could afford to wait on events. So, less than two years after their publication, the two quarto volumes faced remaindering. It was an ignominious end, and by ordinary standards a premature one. But the affair demonstrated yet again that there was more to publishing than printing. The Cambridge press had printed Barnes's work, and Crownfield had retained some copies from what had not been subscribed, to sell on his own behalf. But it is noticeable that if he ever made any offer for further copies neither Barnes nor his widow saw fit to relay this to their Oxford confidant, Thomas Hearne.

Barnes found only partial answer to his hopes in publishing his Homer. Richard Bentley enjoyed better success in engaging Crownfield first to print his own edition of Horace and then a revised edition of Newton's *Principia*.

On 9 September 1703, five months after the University had given its formal approval to an agreement with Sir Theodore Janssen for the printing of *Suidas*, the Curators noted 'the charge for printing Dr Bentley's Horace for himselfe'. The cost of composition (in great primer) was set at 5s. a sheet, of printing off an edition of 1,025 at 4s.8d. a sheet, and of a third extra to the University Press, 4s.10d. a sheet: total 14s.6d. per sheet. No reason was given in the Curators' Minutes for the decision to allow Bentley's work to take this course; indeed, he may have preferred it from the beginning. But the expenses associated with the printing of the *Suidas* were already heavy, and the Curators' financial year ended with a much increased debt to the University.

The Curators' decision was only reached after some negotiation, and the surviving estimates by Crownfield indicate not only Bentley's preliminary deliberations on the physical form of the edition, but also something of the final compromise on price.

The Charges for Printing Horace in 4to

46 sheets, a 1000 number takes up 108 Ream of paper, at 8^{s}: 6^{d}: per R is	45:18:0
for printing 34 sheets with Great Primer Letter at 16^{s}: per sheet —	27:4:0
for printing 12 sheets with Long Prim er letter, at 1^{l}: 8^{s}: 0^{d}: per sheet —	16:16:0
for carriage of Paper, and extra expence	3:0:0:
	———
every Book in 4to will cost 22^{d} wanting half a farthing	92:18:0

The Charge for printing Horace in 8vo

30 sheets, a 1000 number takes up 70 R of paper, at 8^{s}: 6^{d}: a Ream is —	29:15:0
for printing 18 sheets with Pica letter at 1^{l}: 0^{s}: 1:½d per sheet —	18:2:3
for Printing 12 sheets with Long prim mer letter, at 1^{l}: 8^{s}: per sheet —	16:16:0
for Carriage of paper &c. —	2:10:0
	———
	67:3:3:

every Book in 8vo will cost at ye Rates set down here 16^{d}: per Book and about half a farthing[105]

Crownfield's estimate not only suggests that Bentley at one stage considered an edition in octavo. It also reveals a difference between the charges accepted by the Curators and those quoted to Bentley. For the former, and for a quarto, composition and printing of sheets of text were agreed at 14s.6d., and of sheets of notes 25s.; and for the latter

Crownfield quoted 16s. and 28s. respectively. As Bentley was eventually charged the figures agreed by the Curators, it may be presumed that this estimate, made before the Curators agreed the proposal, was cause of some dispute. Paper, however, cost more than anticipated, since in 1703 Crownfield estimated it at 8s.6d. a ream, and Bentley was eventually charged 11s. The reasons for Bentley's decision to embark on a quarto rather than an octavo are now lost. To print in octavo would have meant a very considerable saving; but Bentley knew from the beginning that his edition would be compared with that of Talbot, published in quarto in 1699. In the event, there was a compromise, Bentley's being printed in quarto, though on a smaller size of paper.[106]

Bentley's own plans changed greatly in the course of his work, as he sought to improve both its presentation (by better paper) and its content. In 1703, twelve sheets were deemed sufficient for the notes and preliminaries, in bulk a little more than a third of the book. But by 1711 these had grown to almost a quarter as much again as the sheets bearing the text.

Whether he sought independence or no, Bentley embarked on the publication of his own work, with money from his own pocket. Work had, in fact, begun on the Horace a little while before the Curators' meeting; but this early start did not presage an equally timely finish. Interest in Bentley's project was immediate. Printing began in April 1703; and that very month, with Tonson's series of quarto poets still fresh in people's minds, the *Nouvelles de la République des Lettres* reported that the new edition would appear in two or three years. This was over-optimistic, and once the text had been completed there was a year's gap in production before work began on setting and printing the notes. In March 1705, the *Nouvelles* announced that the Horace would appear 'bientôt'.[107] But progress was still slower than anticipated, proceeding in fits and starts, and the book was completed only in November 1711. The engraved frontispiece, from Holland, by Goeree, is dated 1708: the records of the University Press at this time suggest that printing had otherwise reached a complete halt. Meanwhile the learned world waited with the best patience it could. For some of that world, the prospect was one of controversy; and the prospect was clearly relished. Bentley had been provoked by Talbot's edition, and the quarrel between the two men became common gossip, as Hearne noted:

> This Afternoon I saw M[r]. Pawle, Fellow of Jesus Col. in Cambridge, at ye Publick Library, who told me y[t] D[r]. Bentley had suspended the Publication of Horace, as I had also been inform'd before, & y[t] he had most egregiously abus'd D[r]. Talbot y[e] former Editor, not w[th]standing his being highly serviceable in some things to him relating particularly to this work, w[ch] however D[r]. Bentley had not y[e] civility to acknowledge.[108]

Though Talbot was soon forgotten, Bentley's own reputation, quite apart from rumours of what he was about, ensured continuing interest. 'The Waggs of Cambridge, where hee is not loved, make sport with this long designed & long exspected edition', wrote Thomas Smith to Hearne in April 1709. 'Whenever the edition is made public, Gronovius will fall upon it, who is a fit match for him: & it is a question, not easily to be decided, w[ch] of the two is the more insolent & haughty Critic.'[109]

Many of the details of publication, as well as of production, were placed in Crownfield's hands, and so Bentley incurred further charges: for brown wrapping paper, cords, packing cloth and carriage for ten bales of finished sheets to be sent to London; for correspondence with Wetstein in the Netherlands and with other booksellers; and £1.12s. to Mathias Hoppe, one of the Press's principal correctors.[110]

From here, Bentley and Crownfield moved to the sale of the book. Printing was completed in the late autumn of 1711, and by the following April Crownfield could report a satisfactory first few months: 660 copies sent to London, 143 delivered to other customers by Crownfield himself, 20 sent to John Laughton, 10 copies sent to the binders to be put into pasteboards, and 1 copy to a Mr Sittwell, to be paid for by Henry Mortlock. There were 119 copies remaining in Crownfield's hands, and he believed that Bentley had 76. As so often the arithmetic is inexact: the total, of 1,029 copies, does not tally with that for which Crownfield had charged: 1,050 copies.

The response was predictably mixed, as some scoffed at so much labour. Even before seeing it, Hearne was quick to pass judgement yet again: 'I cannot forbear thinking that the Dr. would have done more real service to the Publick, and have deriv'd more credit and reputation uppon himself, by publishing some sacred Author that was never yet printed or else is grown very scarce.' But even Hearne had to acknowledge 'I shall be extreme glad to see the Edition; because he is certainly an excellent Critick, and I am highly sensible that he will have a great Number of curious & learned Remarks and Observations upon other Authors.'[111] For his part, Roger Gale marvelled like others at the rumour that Bentley had spent no less than £800 in what would now be called research expenses.[112]

Bentley dedicated his work to Lord Harley; another copy, bound in red turkey leather and elaborately decorated by Richard Balley, one of the finest of London bookbinders, went to John Moore.[113] Others who received copies in plainer copies, in calf but still with gilt edges to the leaves, included Newton and Trinity College.[114] Bentley was always careful to place presentation copies where they would be most effective.

His part in persuading Newton to publish a revised edition of his *Principia mathematica* is well known. But the book was not published by the University Press. As was quickly pointed out,[115] and as Newton found to his cost, Bentley also acted as its financier and, in effect, its publisher.

In April 1708, a specimen sheet was prepared, principally to induce Newton to take up the work systematically. He had been encouraged to publish a second edition from very soon after the appearance of the first, and had seriously considered it at least by 1694.[116] But it was not until 1708 that he bowed to pressure from Bentley. Without fully appreciating the task on which he was embarking, in April Bentley arranged for a specimen to be set up and printed for Newton's inspection.[117] His subsequent letter to Newton reveals him immersed in the details of the press, dealing with choice of paper, the design of the page, and the importance of emulating the best overseas models.

> I bought this week a hundred Ream of this Paper you see; it being impossible to have got so good in a year or two (for it comes from Genoa) if I had not taken this opportunity with

my friend Sr Theodore Jansen, ye great Paper merchant of Britain. I hope you will like it & ye Letter too. wch upon trials we found here to be more suitable to ye volume than a greater, & more pleasant to ye Eye. I have sent you like wise ye proof sheet, y^t you may see, what changes of pointing, putting letters Capital, &c I have made, as I hope, much to ye better. . . . Y^e Sections only made wth Def. I. Def.II. which are now made full & in Capitals DEFINITIO. I. &c. Pray look on *Hugenius de Oscillatione*, wch is a book very masterly printed, & you'l discern that is done like this. Compare any period of ye Old & New; & you'l discern in ye latter by ye chang of points and Capitals a clearness and emphasis, y^t the other has not: as all y^t have seen this specimen acknowledg. Our English compositors are ignorant, & print Latin Books as they are used to do English ones; if they are not set right by one used to observe the beauties of ye best printing abroad.[118]

The final stimulus was Bentley's; but the details of seeing the revised text through the press were the responsibility of Roger Cotes, who was engaged in the project by the following spring. Eighteen months after Bentley had arranged for the initial specimen, production was put in hand. Hopes that Livebody, a London compositor and wood engraver, could be employed on the new edition were confounded. His skills in setting text to block were marred by other weaknesses:

> I proposed to our Master printer to have Lightbody come down & compose, which at first he agreed to; but the next day he had a character of his being a mere sot, & having plaid such pranks yt no body will take him into any Printhouse in London or Oxford; & so he fears he'll debauch all his Men. So we must let Him alone.[119]

Instead, he was employed in London to provide the cuts. The task of ensuring that compositors and pressmen were regularly supplied with copy and with corrected proof fell to Cotes (figs. 5, 6, 7). Thanks largely, but not exclusively, to Newton, there were pauses in production of several months in winter 1709–10, most of the latter part of 1710, the first half of 1711, the winter of 1711–12, summer 1712, and winter (again) 1712–13. The programme depended not only on Cotes's ability to coax copy from Newton, to revise it as necessary, to secure Newton's agreement to such changes, and to see proof dealt with expeditiously. It also depended on the programme of the press itself, dependent on weather as well as on the ordinary hierarchy of priorities among jobs.

The book (fig. 8) was completed in May 1713, and on 30 June Bentley wrote to Newton explaining that he would soon receive six copies in quires (there being no binder in Cambridge who would 'either work well or quick'). Cotes had received a dozen copies, and presentation copies had gone to Harley, Thomas Trevor (later Attorney-General and Chief Justice of the Common Pleas) and John Moore, Bishop of Ely. He had also already sent two hundred copies to France and the Netherlands, and had fixed the retail price in England at 15s. in quires.[120] Though Bentley had thoughtfully left it to Newton to present a copy to Halley, the failure to send authors' copies out before gifts to influential recipients, and before the first main export shipping, merely emphasises the spirit in which Bentley was now working. He not only commanded the press, dealt with the trade and organised publicity. He also controlled the circulation of

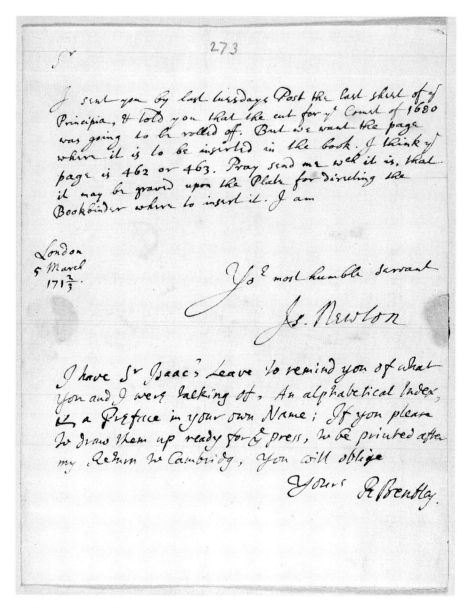

Fig. 5 Letter from Sir Isaac Newton to Roger Cotes, concerning printing the *Principia*, 5 March 1712/13, annotated by Richard Bentley (Trinity College, MS R.16.38b(273)).

copies among a circle of admirers that was defined more by Bentley's friendships and acquainatances than by Newton's. It is almost as if the book itself was Bentley's.

Cotes himself crowned his work with a lengthy preface. His reward from Newton was discouraging, and mean-spirited. If any letter of thanks was sent, none has survived. Instead, through Crownfield, he received a list of errata and addenda composed by Newton. After working through them, pointing out Newton's own errors and

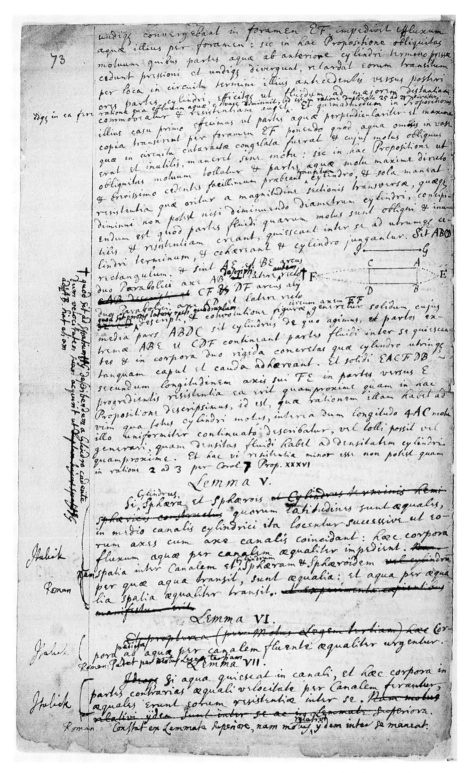

73

...undiq; convergebat in foramen EF impedivit effluxum aquæ illius per foramen: sic in hac Propositione obliquitas motuum quibus partes aquæ ab anteriore cylindri termino pimæ cedunt pressioni et undiq; divergunt, retardat eorum transitum per loca in circuitu termini illius antecedentis versus posteriores partes cylindri...

...Lemma V.

Si Sphæra et Sphærois quorum latitudines sunt æquales, in medio canalis cylindrici ita locentur successive ut eorum axes cum axe canalis coincidant: hæc corpora fluxum aquæ per canalem æqualiter impedient. ...spatia inter Canalem et Sphæram & Sphæroidem per quæ aqua transit, sunt æqualia: et aqua per æqualia spatia æqualiter transit.

Lemma VI.

...corpora ab aqua per canalem fluente æqualiter urgentur.

Lemma VII.

Si aqua quiescat in canali, et hæc corpora in partes contrarias æquali velocitate per Canalem ferantur, æquales erunt eorum resistentiæ inter se. ...Constat ex Lemmate superiore, nam motus idem inter se maneat.

Italick
Roman

Italick
Roman

Italick
Roman

Fig. 6 Part of the printer's copy for Sir Isaac Newton, *Philosophiae naturalis principia mathematica*, second edition (Cambridge, 1713) (Trinity College, MS R.16.38a(73)).

101

314   PHILOSOPHIÆ NATURALIS

De Motu   tium *HG*, defcribendum a Cylindro
Corporum. cadente dum velocitatem fuam ac-
quirit, ut *HG* ad ½*AB*. Sint etiam
CF & *DF* arcus alii duo Para-
bolici, axe *CD* & latere recto
quod fit prioris lateris recti qua-
druplum defcripti; & convolutione figuræ circum axem *EF* ge-
neretur folidum cujus media pars *ABDC* fit Cylindrus de quo
agimus, & partes extremæ *ABE* & *CDF* contineant partes fluidi
inter fe quiefcentes & in corpora duo rigida concretas, quæ Cylindro utrinque tanquam caput & cauda adhæreant. Et folidi
EACFDB, fecundum longitudinem axis fui *FE* in partes ver-
fus *E* progredientis, refiftentia ea erit quamproxime quam in hac
Propofitione defcripfimus, id eft, quæ rationem illam habet ad
vim qua totus Cylindri motus, interea dum longitudo 4*AC* motu
illo uniformiter continuato defcribatur, vel tolli poffit vel generari,
quam denfitas Fluidi habet ad denfitatem Cylindri quamproxime.
Et hac vi Refiftentia minor effe non poteft quam in ratione 2 ad 3,
per Corol. 7. Prop. xxxvi.

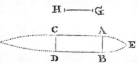

LEMMA V.

Si Cylindrus, Sphæra & Sphærois, quorum latitudines funt æqua-
les, in medio canalis Cylindrici ita locentur fucceffive ut eo-
rum axes cum axe canalis coincidant : hæc corpora fluxum
aquæ per canalem æqualiter impedient.

Nam fpatia inter Canalem & Cylindrum, Sphæram, & Sphæroidem per quæ aqua tranfit, funt æqualia : & aqua per æqualia fpatia æqualiter tranfit.

LEMMA VI.

Iifdem pofitis, corpora prædicta æqualiter urgentur ab aqua per
canalem fluente.

Patet per Lemma v & Motus Legem tertiam.   Aqua utique &
corpora in fe mutuo æqualiter agunt.

LEMMA

Fig. 7 The equivalent page, in its published form, Cambridge, 1713.

suggesting improvements, he allowed his irritation to spill into a final paragraph accus-
ing Newton of failing to spot further errata, and claiming to have made 'some hundreds' of corrections in the course of printing, which he had never thought it necessary
to communicate to Newton.[121]

Differences over 'trifles' had clouded the correspondence between the two men as

PHILOSOPHIÆ
NATURALIS *Ri: Bentley.*
PRINCIPIA
MATHEMATICA.

AUCTORE
ISAACO NEWTONO,
EQUITE AURATO.

EDITIO SECUNDA AUCTIOR ET EMENDATIOR.

CANTABRIGIÆ, MDCCXIII.

Fig. 8 Newton, *Principia mathematica*, second edition (Cambridge, 1713), Richard Bentley's copy.

the text had been edged through the press, revised and subject always to Cotes's punctilious eye. The disputes were now brought into the arena of the reader: 'Such Errata the Reader expects to meet with, & they cannot well be avoided.' The view that the reader should not only expect a list of errata, but that such a list would not include the more trivial examples that could be easily identified, was deeply rooted in assumptions about the nature of printing in the seventeenth century. The *Principia* has an established position, at the threshold of modern scientific thought. But Cotes and Newton, in their different ways and in their dispute, were also signalling an end to a world of textual approximation, where texts (other than classical and biblical) were assumed to exist in an incompletely defined state, fluid in the sense that readers were required and expected to interpret the minor variations of the mediating printed word.

Bentley's surviving accounts with Crownfield provide so unusual an opportunity to observe the initial circulation of a major scientific work at the beginning of the eighteenth century that they are worth printing at length.[122] This portion of the accounts bears a receipt dated 25 November 1715, a few days after the last charge by Crownfield to Bentley for the purchase of a book. It may be assumed, therefore, that the following represents the position by the autumn of 1715, that is, nearly two and a half years after the book had come from the press in May 1713.

Sir Isaac Newton's Principia sold, to ye following
Persons, (viz)

26	To Mr Laughton of Clare hall, and were paid to Dr Bentley
12	To Mr Cotes, for himself, and not paid for
6	To Sir Isaac Newton, and not paid for
2	sent to be bound by Mrs Steele for Dr Bentley –
2	sent to Dr Hare, for him and Bishop of Ely

Sept:29

  1714 –

| 4 | sent to Sir Isaac Newton |
| 13 | To Mr Needham of S:^t John's and paid by him to Dr Bentley |

65

Books deliver'd out by Corn: Crownfield and were
paid to him, or to be paid.

50	To M^r Wm Innys Bookseller in Paul's Churchyard, at 13s: a piece	32	10
50	To Mr Christopher Bateman	32	10
50	To Mr James Knapton	32	10
50	To Mr John Churchill	32	10
25	To Mr Daniel Midwinter	16	5
25	To Mr Paul Vaillant	16	5
25	To Mr William Taylor	16	5
13	To Mr Professor Saunderson, at 9^{l.} pound for 13	9	
13	To Mr Warren of Jesus, at 9^l: for 13	9	
13	To Mr Newcome of S:^t John's, at 9^{l.}: for 13	9	
13	To Mr Allen of Sidney, at 9^{l.}: for 13:	9	
12	To Mr Henry Mortlock	7	16
12	To Mr Benjamin Tooke	7	16
12	To Messieurs Moetjens & Le Cene in ye Strand	7	16

12	To Mr Jonah Bowyer	7 16
375		205 19
65		
200	Sold to Corn^s: Crownfield, at 11s: per Book	110
640	sum Total	315 19
71	Remains unsold	
Total 711		

The retail price of copies, 15s. in quires, left Crownfield with a somewhat larger profit on each copy than the London booksellers, who may perhaps have charged a higher price as a consequence. Bentley made himself responsible, at least initially, for relations with the booksellers, corresponding with them and arranging advertisements in the *London Gazette*, the *Post-Boy*, the *Daily Courant* and the *Evening Post*: the bills for these advertisements amounted to £1.12s.6d. He, too, paid the few shillings for packing materials, and allowed Crownfield a shilling a copy for factorage, or commission. No separate charge appears for carriage of those books that had to be sent to London, and so this must have been absorbed by Crownfield.[123]

Of the booksellers featuring in Crownfield's invoice, Paul Vaillant of the Strand had substantial interests in overseas trade. He took twenty-five copies – hardly enough for adequate distribution abroad of an author with a European reputation. Jacob Moetjens and his partner Michel Charles Le Cène, too, were well known as booksellers with a good foreign stock at their shop – likewise in the Strand.[124] But it was David Mortier, also in the Strand, who was named as supplier in the long review in Le Clerc's new journal, the *Bibliothèque Ancienne et Moderne*, published in The Hague in 1714.[125]

Meanwhile those who had received copies as gifts began to acknowledge them. Among the first to write was Charles Morgan, Fellow of Clare College and one of the circle closest to Bentley. Writing to Cotes from Ely House in Holborn, home of John Moore as Bishop of Ely, he spoke for several at once:

> I rec^d this day the five copys of Sr Isaac's Principles directed to me & return you my hearty thanks for the kind Present of one them [*sic*] which you are pleased to favour me with. I shall esteem it the more, not only on account of ye great improvements which the book that was so much & justly admired before must have received from y^r care in this edition of it, but as it is a mark of y^r friendship for me in which I always did & shall think my self extremely happy.
>
> My Lord presents his service & thanks to Dr Bentley for the Present to him. Mr Whiston does the same to you. Dr Hare & Dr Clarke are both out of town, but I have writ this post to Dr Hare to acquaint him that his book is in my hands, & Dr Clarke is expected in town this week. The mistake in y^r orders may easily be set right; but I suppose it will be time enough to do that when we come into ye country, which I hope will be soon, that I may have an opportunity of thanking you in person for a favour in which you have drawn y^r self into a snare that perhaps you was not aware of. for you have thereby laid an obligation upon me to endeavour to become Master of the book, which will prove an occasion of my putting many such impertinent questions to you as I have been used to trouble you with.[126]

The letter emphasises how far Bentley was determined to reward his own friends and supporters. Of all men, Moore was of immediate and critical importance to him. The two had long respected each other. Moore had been among those who had recommended Bentley to the Mastership of Trinity, while Bentley turned repeatedly to his library for early manuscripts and printed books. With Bentley now at odds with the fellowship at Trinity, this old friendship had assumed even greater moment. Since the Bishop of Ely was required to sit in judgement on the Master of Trinity, and there were several people ready to pass judgement prematurely, Moore and Bentley had to behave punctiliously towards each other; but there was never any suggestion that Moore's legal position in this respect ever compromised his generosity in allowing Bentley and his associates, such as John Davies, to work in his library.

Among the recipients, Francis Hare, royal chaplain, Fellow of Eton and prebend of St Paul's, was among Bentley's particular friends, and had been instrumental in the publication of his work on Menander. In 1713, the year of publication of the Cambridge edition of the *Principia*, Bentley addressed to him his anonymous attack on Anthony Collins's subversive *Discourse on free-thinking*. William Whiston, though expelled from the University in 1710 for his Arian beliefs,[127] had retained Bentley's respect: Bentley had taken no part in his prosecution, and made unsuccessful attempts to dissuade him from certain ruin by persisting in his determination to publish his beliefs. Though no friend of the established church, Whiston, like Bentley, joined in the attack on Collins in 1713. Finally, Samuel Clarke, long a member of the Moore circle and friend of Bentley, had paid Bentley more than a compliment when, in acknowledging those who had helped with his monumental edition of Caesar published by Tonson in 1712, he had drawn especial attention to Bentley's generosity and learning as Keeper of the Royal Library: many of Clarke's readers will have noted the contrast with the allegations of discourtesy made during the Phalaris controversy almost twenty years previously. Now, once again, Bentley was at the centre of controversy, as his disputes with the fellows of Trinity moved into the Court of Queen's Bench. The publication of the edition of the *Principia* financed by himself was an opportunity to remind friends and enemies alike of his achievements rather than his quarrels. In its way, it was another part of his determination to defend himself by actions that would set him in the best possible light. In this it was akin to his arranging in the previous year for the University to present a loyal address to the Queen, congratulating her on her efforts to win peace in Europe: the sentiments could hardly be denied, but the timing and its phrasing made clear that this was a document designed to support the government.[128] So, as the case against him in Trinity gathered strength, the work of Newton himself, the most celebrated of all members of the College, was manoeuvred so as to form silent encouragement for the defence.

The total of ten copies sent to Newton fell far short of the list of possible recipients across Europe that he had had in mind.[129]

William Jones acknowledged his gift, from Newton himself, on 11 July, expressing the hope that it would prove possible to publish the new preface in 'some of the foreign journals'.[130] The allusion to overseas interest in Newton was well made. Bentley had provided for the Cambridge Newtonians; but he had taken no account of their foreign equivalents. Newton's own list of proposed recipients of the second edition makes it clear that he had overseas readers especially in mind. It contains about seventy names, beginning with six copies to be sent to Russia and eight to France. Copies were also to go to Tuscany, Venice, the Duke of Savoy, the Kings of Denmark and Prussia, the Elector of Hanover, the universities of Leiden, Utrecht, Franeker, Groningen, Paris, Toulouse, Bordeaux, Poitiers, Orleans, Montpellier, Rheims, Douai, Avignon, Lyon, Aix and Uppsala; to the libraries at Vienna, Liège, Leipzig, Prague, Mainz, Cologne, Trier, Zurich, Berne, Basle and Milan, as well as to individuals including Leibniz, Bernoulli and Count Herberstein in Prague.[131] Yet Bentley had in effect seized control of distribution, allowing his author too few copies to distribute so many gifts. So, in a less ambitious way, Newton took such steps as he could to ensure that the book became known in circles that he valued. In 1713, Jean Anisson, former Director of the Imprimerie Royale, visited England, and took back copies to Paris in order to explore the possibility of another edition to be published by the Académie Royale des Sciences. Among those who received copies as a consequence, the Abbé Bignon and Pierre Varignon, Professor of Mathematics at the Collège Mazarin, acknowledged these gifts in November.[132] In January, Bernard le Bovier de Fontenelle wrote as Secretary of the Académie Royale des Sciences to thank Newton for the Académie's copy, and took the opportunity to hint that whatever Leibniz's claims and quarrels with Newton, France at least recognised proper achievement. 'Il y a déja plusieurs années que cet excellent ouvrage est admiré dans toute Europe savante, et principalement en France, où l'on sait bien connoistre le mérite étranger.'[133] Others were les fortunate. Johann Bernoulli, in Basle, whose comments on the first edition of the *Principia* had been published in the Leipzig *Acta Eruditorum* in February–March 1713 – just before the publication of the second edition – was still impatiently awaiting a long-promised copy from Abraham de Moivre in the following spring.[134] After repeated pleas, William Burnet finally sent him a copy that arrived, somewhat battered in transport, in May.[135] The delay, and his disagreements with Newton, left him aggrieved.

Meanwhile, the Company of Booksellers in Amsterdam made any thoughts of further publication by the Académie Royale des Sciences unnecessary.[136] Notwithstanding the absence of foreign addressees in Crownfield's list of members of the trade to whom the new edition had been distributed, the Cambridge edition of the *Principia* quickly attracted notice overseas. In March 1714 it was reviewed in the Leipzig *Acta Eruditorum*, probably as a result of action by Newton rather than Bentley.[137] But the intentions of the Amsterdam booksellers to prepare their own edition had been announced as early as the summer of 1713. 'Deux presses roulent continuellement pour avancer cet Ouvrage', remarked the notice of this project in the *Journal Litéraire*.[138] So far as is at present known, it appears that no authority for this was granted by either Newton or Bentley. The new edition, a page for page resetting on paper inferior to that from Cambridge, and with a new set of woodcut figures, appeared in Amsterdam in 1714. Thus the ordinary book trade took up what Bentley had kept to himself in Cambridge, and the Académie Royale des Sciences had considered as another form of private publication in Paris. The need for such an edition (a further one appeared in 1723, also from the Amsterdam booksellers) is itself evidence of the interest that Newton's work commanded, even if most of his serious readers on the Continent supported Leibniz's part in his argument with Newton. But in the late summer of 1713 the Cambridge edition was still far from exhausted. And even in the autumn of 1715, as Crownfield's account to Bentley shows, there still remained more than seventy copies lying unsold at Cambridge. The Amsterdam edition was not prompted by an absolute shortage, but by difficulties in obtaining copies even in the principal commercial centre of Europe's most important bookselling nation. It was also prompted by price.

English-printed books were expensive. In 1710, Uffenbach remarked the difference between Dutch and English prices as he browsed among new books in the London bookshops, and he summed up the position:

> Latin books may be bought far cheaper in Holland than here; english books however must be bought here, as they do not go out of the country; when I began to study english at Frankfort, I could meet with nothing but a bible. Widow Swaart, behind the exchange at Amsterdam, is the only dealer in english books there, and she has nothing but sermons and the like.[139]

In Oxford, he returned to the theme. 'Latin books it would be folly to buy, for they can be bought in Holland for a third of the price which must be paid here.'[140] Import duties on paper and books, and export charges on books, combined to make both imports and books printed in England expensive. Uffenbach was searching out English-language books, and therefore thought also of the limited stocks held by the widow Swart who, notwithstanding interests in Bible printing and in the work of William Sewel the lexicographer, was catering primarily to a well-defined and small readership in the Low Countries[141]; but his remarks on price were equally applicable to books in Latin. Other foreigners, too, noticed the high price of books.[142]

The reasons lay very largely in the cost of paper. English mills, whose paper was subject to excise duty, did not produce enough white paper at the end of the seventeenth century or in the early eighteenth century for the needs of the domestic trade; and it was often inferior in quality to that from France or Italy. Though the number of paper-mills grew not only in response to demand, but also, and crucially, with the aid of the skills and investments of Huguenots displaced by the revocation of the Edict of Nantes, most paper used in England had still to be imported from abroad.[143] At the same time, English governments pursued a broadly, if sometimes muddled, protectionist policy.[144] Most imported paper (especially in time of war with France) came through Holland. In the late seventeenth century French paper, of high quality, could be cheaply obtained there; but when it was imported to England it was subject to greater import duty, while its price was also to some extent controlled by Dutch merchants – who also controlled the price of Dutch paper. The French paper industry declined after 1685 on a scale that alarmed the government;[145] and Holland and

England benefited in particular. The difficulties in England of domestic manufacturers of white paper,[146] the varying tariffs imposed at several times between 1690 (when import duty was doubled) and 1712 (when new import and excise rates were set, to be increased again by 50 per cent two years later), and the attempts to meet government demands for revenue (especially in war-time), led to confusion for importers and printers alike; but the resulting high price of paper was clear enough.[147]

Since paper accounted for about half of of the production costs in printing books, wholesale and retail costs for books alike soared, making it difficult in turn to sell books from England in Holland. 'Pour un livre qu'on imprime ici pour 2½ sols, personne ne payera sept sols . . . les hauts prix sont pour la plupart, les Causes qu'on peut a peine debiter les Livres imprimes en Angleterre.'[148] In this way, with the support of successive British governments who imposed excise duties on home manufacture and duties on imported paper, and quite apart from its geographical position on the threshold of Europe, the Dutch book trade was often able to determine the English export trade of just those books that might have a European interest.

Amidst all their various difficulties in reaching readers overseas, those responsible in Cambridge for the several books discussed in the last pages were more fortunate than others who tried without success to sell their work abroad. In Oxford, Benjamin Marshall arranged for copies of his chronological tables (1712) to be printed both in English and Latin versions, the latter for the foreign market. But by 1725, 'for want of Correspondence abroad, and the Charge of Exportation not answering', he still had not sold 1,000 copies of the 1,500 he had paid to have printed of the Latin version.[149]

Both in England and on the Continent, prices of books tended to vary, according not only to distance (and hence cost of carriage), but also according to the policies of individual booksellers and according to local scarcity. Undercutting was commonplace, and not only when booksellers banded together to spoil sales by subscription. But so too was setting a premium. As the Amsterdam bookseller Jean Louis de Lorme explained in 1708 to Mme Boudot, bookseller in Paris, as he sought for her a copy of the Cambridge *Suidas*,

> Je vois bien madame, que vous ne connoisé pas encore la politique de certains libraires de chez vous, qui donnent les livres, que les autres ont, a un prix modique et ceux, qu'il savent estre les seuls qui les ont, ils savent y mettre un bon prix. Vous jugez bien madame qu'il est cette politique. Je l'ay eprouvé moi-meme, estant a Paris et surtout en Suidas etc.[150]

De Lorme was Leers's principal rival in the supply of books from Holland to France, so it was not only the Parisian booksellers who were a source of worry. Only a few months earlier, he had complained of a shortage of copies of the *Suidas* in Amsterdam, as he sought to obtain a copy to send to France for the orientalist Michel Pinart: 'Je n'ay pu trouver Suidas ici', he wrote to Toussaint Rémond de Saint-Mard – a mere sixteen months after the Curators of the press at Cambridge had agreed to supply no less than a hundred copies to the Amsterdam bookseller Rudolph Wetstein.[151] It seems improbable that Wetstein can have sold so many copies already; and it is far more probable that the Cambridge press was falling victim to deliberate attempts in the Amsterdam trade to keep up the price of an expensive book. In the case of the two other books that caused most interest in the continental market, Bentley's Horace (1711) and Newton's *Principia* (1713), different tactics were adopted, and each was printed in a new edition in Amsterdam, by Wetstein and the Company of Booksellers respectively. But for each of these books the investment was much less, and the customers could be expected to be more numerous. In the case of Bentley's work, Wetstein was even able to obtain (it can only have been from Bentley himself) the same copper-engraved title that had graced the Cambridge edition. Meanwhile, for the Curators in Cambridge the effect was very similar: that while some books might be expected to command attention overseas, there was little chance of obtaining very great export sales. De Lorme might be expected to supply a copy of Davies's edition of Caesar (1706) to Copenhagen; Claude Jourdan, another Amsterdam bookseller, might advertise Pearce's edition of Cicero, *De oratore* (1716) in the Amsterdam *Gazette*, next to Montfaucon on Greek palaeography; and Waesbergh might advertise the same book in the *Journal des Sçavans*.[152] But there was no large-scale trade; and even in the cases of most of the books that were treated in the several overseas reviewing journals, sales were probably modest indeed.

The foundation of the Press coincided with a new national confidence. In government, the accession of William and Mary not only brought a glorious revolution. It also brought England closer intellectually, socially, economically and politically to the cities that controlled much of the northern European economy. The subsequent accession of the Hanoverians brought northern Germany closer. Political isolation was impossible, and the spectacularly successful campaigns of the Duke of Marlborough during the War of the Spanish Succession further emphasised not only the place of Britain in Europe: they also bred pride in achievement. In letters and in the sciences, there were ample examples of names that won European reputations. Dryden and Pope were both reviewed in the Leipzig *Acta Eruditorum*, as well as Newton, Locke, Cowper, Tyson, Lister, Boyle, Whiston and many others. Scarcely a month passed without there appearing in the *Acta Eruditorum* a review of one or more books published in England. In November 1698, as work got under way on the first major project of the new Cambridge press (Talbot's quarto edition of Horace), the *Acta Eruditorum* included reviews of no less than five books published and printed in London, including Stillingfleet on the Trinity and four recent works on medicine. In addition, space at the end was used to notice William Cowper's large folio *Atlas of humane bodies* and the latest part of William Cave's *Scriptorum ecclesiasticorum historia literaria*. No doubt the presence of Mencke's son in London at this time was a help; certainly this month was exceptional. But the tendency was clear. Whether in Latin or in English, the works of the London, Oxford, and now Cambridge presses were regularly being brought to the attention of the European scholarly world through this and other journals, as well as in correspondence. Within a few years, the position semed still stronger, at least in the eyes of the editor of *The Present State of the Republick of Letters*. Ignoring a widespread convention that the republic of letters existed independently of national boundaries, he puffed this new journal launched by the booksellers William and John Innys with encomia that made plain the disadvantages under which some foreign countries laboured:

No country in the world furnishes greater plenty of good materials for such a work [as *The Present State* . . .] than England, as there is none where arts and sciences are cultivated with greater encouragement, or better success. Here the greatest men in the State, are often also the brightest ornaments of the Republic of Letters, and promote learning as much by their example, as by their protection. Where do we meet with such noble foundations as in our Universities? or where can a man study with so great advantages in every respect? And where can merit hope to be rewarded with better preferments, either in Church or State? Nor can we, like other nations, complain of the want of liberty, which is the nursing-mother of knowledge, and absolutely necessary both to the discovery and progress of truth . . . Every man may think as he pleases, and publish his speculative opinions whatever they be, without the difficulty of obtaining a License from a partial or superstitious Censor, or standing in fear of an Inquisition and an *Auto da Fé*. So mild is our Government, both in Church and State; as being fully convinced of this maxim, That truth needs neither force nor artifice to support it.

'Tis to this happy liberty, both of conscience and the press, so much envied by our neighbours, that we owe those many excellent books which are daily printed in England. This has enabled us to make those discoveries and improvements in almost every part of knowledge, which have gained so great a reputation to the English writers abroad, that our language is now studied by foreigners as a learned one. No Englishman can wish this liberty abridged, but he who envies the glory of his country, and the advancement of learning and of truth.

To this liberty we are also indebted for the free importation and use of foreign books, by means of which we reap the benefit of all the improvements made by the learned in every part of Europe . . .[153]

Newton had died the previous year; Voltaire had chosen exile in England; Defoe's manifestly partisan *Tour thro' the whole Island of Great Britain* had been published in 1724, written partly to gainsay hostile or ignorant foreign accounts. But Swift's *Modest proposal* was to be published in 1729. The Innys' new reviewing journal caught a national mood, even if the details of political, ecclesiastical and everyday life would not always bear examination. *The Present State of the Republick of Letters*, ever alert for support in its commitment, quoted a correspondent from Hamburg at length a few months later:

No Country in the world abounds more with great originals than England. In Poetry they have a Milton, as yet outdone by no body: even the great Homer, and Virgil his noble Imitator, team not with so many real beauties and soaring thoughts, as are to be found in the inimitable English Epick. In Philosophy and Mathematicks, who among the Antients and Moderns can vye with their immortal Sir Isaac Newton, Dr. Cudworth, &c.? In Philology, Natural Philosophy, &c. Spelman, Selden, Lock, Sir Hans Sloane (whose cabinet of Curiosities is not to be parallel'd in Europe) &c. have hardly their equals.[154]

The increasing presence of the English language, both in continental Europe and across the world, was a clear reflection not only of political and military success. It was also acknowledgement of the declining importance of Latin; and it represented an increasingly powerful challenge to French. Close business connections had meant that in commerce there had been for generations a working understanding of English in trading circles.[155] But beyond the immediate contacts between importers and exporters, between captains of ships and those with whom they had to deal in the ports, the dominant international language of the book trade was French. The dispersal of Huguenot refugees hastened the process. 'All the world grows so very much French here', wrote Roger Gale from Amsterdam in 1699, 'that you shall meet with nothing else almost in any bookseller's. In this city, where there are two hundred of that trade, there are but two that have almost anything to do with the learned languages; the rest shall tell you they are French booksellers.'[156] Gale's impression was correct. As already noted, the Dutch book trade witnessed a long series of special journals, most of them in French, designed to direct attention to recent publications.[157] In Paris the *Journal des Savants* was edited for several years after 1701 by one of the most energetic of all Bibliothécaires du Roi, the Abbé Bignon: the royal library profited as never before.[158] But among readers and customers, and not only in Holland, there was a growing demand for books in English.

❦ 5 ❧

Crownfield's later years

Crownfield remained in office until he retired in 1740. By the 1730s, however, his interests had long since become more those of a bookseller than a printer; and in this the University could have no formal interest. Instead, the last years of his office as Printer (he died in 1743[1]) were dominated by the University's anxiety at a Press that stood once again in need of reform.

Long before even 1720, the University faced once again questions that had dogged its printing ever since Thomas Thomas had established his press and other equipment in a converted set of rooms near Great St Mary's in 1583. Now, the refounded University Press had enjoyed specially built premises since early in the eighteenth century, premises that were widely admired and that formed a part of visitors' tours round Cambridge: a place to print keepsakes, but also a place of work excellently suited to efficient production. John Hudson, Bodley's Librarian, who took an informed interest in such matters as one who was exceptionally active in the affairs of the press at Oxford, had described it in 1708 as 'a pretty, large & lightsome room: wth another over it, very convenient for drying ye sheets'.[2] At the time, Hudson found Crownfield and his staff at work on three books: Barnes's Homer, and editions of Hierocles (by Peter Needham, Fellow of St John's College) and Cicero's *Tusculanae disputationes* (by John Davies, Fellow of Queens' College). Though Hudson did not mention them, the Press was also at work at that time on an edition of Sallust by Joseph Wasse, a further edition of Le Clerc's *Physica* and *A brief history of the joint use of set forms of prayer* by the prolific Rector of St James's, Colchester and former curator of the Press, Thomas Bennet. The second edition of Newton's *Principia* had been started a few months earlier, though work on Bentley's Horace had been temporarily suspended.

Ten years later he would have found much less activity. The year ending November 1708, in which Hudson's visit took place, was by no means the busiest in the first years of the eighteenth century. Expenditure of £179 on workmen's wages was, apart from the previous year, the lowest since 1699 – the first year of the Press's operation, and therefore not a full year. In 1709 it was to be £252. The value of work done in the years ending November 1708 and 1709 respectively was £269 and £378. But a decade later, in the year ending November 1718, the Press accounts recorded wages of only £99, for work valued at £148. The annual wages bill rose above £200 in only one year during the 1720s, in that ending November 1726; and for eleven years from 1728 it remained well below a hundred pounds, dropping to a low of £30 in 1735. In Crownfield's time, it recovered to over £100 only in 1739 and 1740 – that is, after the University had set in motion an enquiry into the Press's affairs.[3]

Since Crownfield and his workmen had little control over the speed at which authors were willing to release their texts, the annual wages bill is a more reliable way of measuring overall activity than examining the numbers of titles published. Nonetheless, the latter emphasised in a much more public way how little was being produced at the Press. Sermons accounted for too high a proportion of the output; but they had the advantage of requiring little of their authors, when compared with the prolonged investment of time in (for example) editing major classical texts; and they required little investment on the part of the book trade. From about 1711–13 (the years that saw the publication of Barnes's Homer, Bentley's Horace, and Newton's *Principia*), the Cambridge press was under-funded, under-exploited by the University, and under-used by authors and booksellers alike.

The reasons for this decline in output are complicated only in some respects. It was not a regular decline. Some projects foundered even before they had been launched, such as the proposal in March 1712/13 that Crownfield should print a new edition of Stephanus' Latin thesaurus, edited by Kuster.[4] Scarcely anything was published in 1717 apart from sermons by Richard Laughton of Clare College and Daniel Waterland of Magdalene; but the following year saw editions of Cicero, Lactantius and Clemens Romanus.

In themselves, the details of publication dates are often misleading, since, as we have seen with Bentley's Horace, some books were in the press for several years before they were published. As we have seen, there was intense interest in Moore's manuscript of Bede as early as 1702.[5] Three hundred pounds of Saxon type were authorised for purchase in 1713/14.[6] The death of the editor supervened, leading to further delay, and the book did not appear for another seven years. Subscriptions seem to have been fewer than anticipated, for as late as October 1721 – that is, with printing well advanced – advertisements offered copies on large paper at 50s., or on ordinary at 30s.[7] Subscriptions were to be taken in either by William Bowyer in London or by Crownfield in Cambridge. The book was published in the winter of 1721–2.[8] Thus a book published in 1722 had taken up part of the Press's energies, money and time for at least eight or nine years, and its interests for twenty. Moreover, in 1722 it was followed by another substantial work, a folio edition of John Covel's *Some account of the present Greek church*, as well as Cotes's *Harmonia mensurarum* and half a dozen other books. The year 1722 was an active one for publications; but these represented the consummation of work over long periods. By itself, the measure of new publications in any given year was not a true representation of the Press's work.

Many of the University's affairs seemed to be in a state of crisis. The effects of the departure of Newton from Cambridge to London in 1696 had been postponed by the efforts of Bentley to promote his college as a centre of mathematical and natural sciences. With the help of Roger Cotes, the first to hold the new Plumian chair of astronomy and experimental philosophy (founded in 1707), he had seen through the Press a revised and corrected version of the *Principia* for a new generation, and for a much wider audience. But Cotes died in 1716, provoking Newton's much-quoted reaction, 'Had Cotes lived, we might have known something.'[9] The observatory above Trinity's Great Gate, whose construction Cotes had overseen, was to be little used for its original purpose after his death. Another of Bentley's protégés, J. F. Vigani, died in 1713, leaving the teaching of chemistry in the hands of John Waller, Fellow of Corpus Christi College, who has left no trace of any enthusiasm for the subject. Ludolph Kuster, whom Bentley had attracted over from the Low Countries, had returned to the Continent once his edition of *Suidas* was completed: he died in 1716. William Whiston of Clare College, Newton's successor as Lucasian Professor of Mathematics and one of his most enthusiastic exponents and popularisers, was ejected from the University as an Arian heretic in 1710. Henry Sike, from Bremen and a gifted linguist, committed suicide in his rooms in Trinity in 1712, and was succeeded as Regius Professor of Hebrew by a man who was later to be dismissed by the gossipy William Cole as 'an old miserly refugee, who died rich in College'[10]: certainly Philip Bouquett left little mark on his subject in the University. Events at Trinity College inevitably had a disproportionate effect on the University as a whole. But above all, the unresolved disputes between Bentley and the Fellows of the College, as well as between Bentley and the University, drained energies and distracted attention away from what otherwise might have been pursued. Even so valuable a windfall as the gift of Moore's library, widely believed to be the finest private collection in the country, threw the University Library into a state of crisis prolonged until the 1730s, where proposals by the *protobibliothecarius* Conyers Middleton, printed at the Press in 1723, had much good sense, but little hope of effecting immediate remedy. Meanwhile, the neglect shown to the books was at once a source of scandal and an opportunity for theft.[11]

In all this, the decision to found a regius chair in modern history at both universities in 1724 initially offered little help.[12] Yet as the first new chair for seventeen years after Cambridge itself had established a professorship of Anatomy in 1707 (the post was held by a notorious absentee, George Rolfe), the new Regius Professorship offered a sign of life. Indeed, three new posts followed rapidly thereafter: in Arabic and in botany (both in 1724) and in geology (by the bequest of John Woodward, in 1728).[13] But the professorship of modern history was designed with more complex ends in sight. In an initiative inspired as much by nationalist sentiment as by educational needs, Professors of Modern History were to be appointed with responsibility not only for teaching this subject, but also for ensuring that England would not remain destitute of competent linguists. In the royal view, one of the University's duties was perceived as sending forth 'constant Supplys of learned and able Men to serve the Publick both in Church and State', a task that was prejudiced by the habit of employing foreigners for tuition, either in England or, still more unsatisfactorily, during overseas travels. Thus the Universities lost pupils, and the Crown lacked the requisite numbers of those possessing modern languages. In order to remedy this, each University was to have someone 'skilled in Modern History and in the knowledge of Modern Languages'; and under this person there were also to be two further language teachers. As a result, it was anticipated that there would be a supply of suitably qualified entrants to the diplomatic and civil services.[14]

The first to hold the new chair at Cambridge was Samuel Harris, of Peterhouse. His publications proved to be on the Old Testament, not on modern history. In itself, Harris's appointment made little difference to a university that was showing itself in much more general need of reform. For the University Press, there was little perceptible difference as a result of this royal intervention apart from an Italian edition of Bentivoglio printed in 1727, fruit of the regius chair's obligation to provide for modern languages. This small book was an early venture for William Thurlbourn and through its London booksellers Groenwegen and Prévost was clearly intended for an international clientèle. One of the first students to benefit from the new royal arrangements was Samuel Edwards, of Trinity College, the title-page of whose poem *The Copernican system* (1728) drew attention to his status as 'one of His Majesty's Scholars on his Royal Foundation of Modern History and Languages'. But the poem was occasioned more by the recent death of Newton than by historical animus. The only book of a historical nature printed at Cambridge in the following few years was Samuel Knight's life of Erasmus – the work not of a Regius Professor but of a prebendary of Ely, 'an Englishman, a Protestant, and an Antiquary'.[15]

The appointment of a distinguished scholar, David Wilkins, or Wilke, to the new chair of Arabic suggested more seriousness of purpose, especially perhaps in that a royal charter for it had existed since 1714 but had never been acted on.[16] Wilkins's appointment was but one example of increasing interest during the 1720s in oriental studies, from various quarters. Apart from purchases of Hebrew from Athias in Amsterdam and from Elizabeth Grover in London, Crownfield had bought no oriental type. The little Arabic needed for University verses and for the work of Simon Ockley derived from Hayes; and when in 1714 a poem in Ethiopic was submitted for the verses on the death of Queen Anne, it was printed in Hebrew characters.[17] The Syndics, seeing no pressing need, did not seek to add to their store, and build up a range of exotics such as that assembled at Oxford. For the University as a whole, the gift to the University Library by George Lewis, formerly of Queens' College, and for many years chaplain at Fort St George, of a cabinet of manuscripts and various curiosities gathered from India and the Far East, provided both novelty and encouragement to further work. The University Librarian, for one, saw the connection between the Chair and the cabinet.[18] Meanwhile in London, the SPCK faced a request from Salomon Negri for editions of the Psalter and New Testament in Arabic. For help in printing them, the Secretary, Henry Newman, turned to Crownfield amongst others. Crownfield was obliged to decline since he had too little type of the right size. One consequence of this was that the Society asked the young William Caslon to cut a new fount of a suitable size, and the work was instead printed in London by Samuel Palmer. In recognition of the University's supportive interest in the SPCK, the Society subsequently presented a fount of Arabic to the Press.[19] However, its generosity was not to be properly justified, since the type was scarcely used save by Leonard Chappelow, Sir Thomas Adams's Professor of Arabic since

1720, and that simply for contributions to the University's books of verses on public occasions.

Thus, attempts to breathe fresh vigour into the University by these several different means all proved of distinctly limited effect. Wilkins was an absentee, and ceased to hold the chair after five years; the Press scarcely used the type; and though a catalogue of Lewis's manuscripts was printed in 1727, the cabinet seems to have been most successful as a tourist attraction.[20] When in 1729 Wilkins vacated the Lord Almoner's professorship, his place was taken by Chappelow, who henceforth held the two chairs in Arabic simultaneously, as did his successor from 1768, Samuel Hallifax. Though some of the fundamental means to serious attention to the subject were available, there was no will to put them to use.

In the 1690s, the revival of the Press had depended very largely on Bentley, who engaged the energies of a group of scholars able to provide books of a kind proper to a learned press. But with Bentley's energies dissipated by argument, and the University riven by dispute, any policy that had been apparent in the first years of reform was now allowed to wither away. In some respects, naturally, Bentley's influence lived on. John Davies repeatedly acknowledged his help as he advanced with successive editions of works by Cicero, a course that had been begun in 1709 with the appearance of the *Tusculanae disputationes* [21]: this reached a third edition in 1730, in the same year as there appeared a second edition of *De divinatione et de fato*, while his *De natura deorum* reached a third edition in 1733. Zachary Pearce's edition of *De oratore*, first published in 1716, was republished in 1732. Davies himself was also responsible for editions of Minucius Felix in 1707 and 1712, and of Lactantius in 1718. Much more important, Bentley's own edition of Terence was published in 1726, handled in London by Knapton, Knaplock and Vaillant: an Amsterdam edition quickly followed. The Press's ability to print Greek was an advantage that London booksellers were as willing to exploit as were local editors and authors. Plato's *Republic*, edited by a young graduate of Trinity College, Edmund Massey (1714), Clement I's *Epistolae ad Corinthos*, edited by Henry Wotton, Fellow of St John's in 1708–17 (1718), three plays by Euripides, edited by John King of King's College (1726), Aristotle's *De rhetorica* (1728) and Demosthenes, edited for beginners by Richard Mounteney, also of King's (1731),[22] were all printed by Crownfield not only for Cambridge, but also for booksellers in London. So too, at last, was a second edition of Barnes's Anacreon, which had been first published in Cambridge by Edmund Jeffery in 1705. Nine years after his death, in 1721, his work was issued by a London bookseller, James Knapton.

Printing for schools had been among the most lucrative of all of the University Printers' activities in the seventeenth century. Following the death of Hayes, in 1706, the University had forsworn the most popular (and therefore profitable) parts of this market, leaving them to the Stationers' Company.[23] Although there was thus no benefit to be found here, there remained opportunities for more personal enterprise. In his last years, Hayes had benefited from printing some of the various schoolbooks compiled by Edward Leedes, of the grammar school in Bury St Edmunds; and in 1706 Crownfield printed an index by Leedes to Ovid's *Metamorphoses*, presumably to accompany

Leedes's own edition of the *Metamorphoses* printed by Hayes two years previously. From Newcastle, Thomas Rudd required a thousand copies of a Latin *Syntaxis* in 1700, and a further thousand in 1707. From Canterbury, in 1715 there came a call for a selection from Herodotus. And in 1723 Arthur Kynnesman was supplied with copies of a short Latin grammar for Bury St Edmunds.[24] At undergraduate rather than schoolboy level, in 1703 the first edition appeared of Whiston's successful edition of Tacquet's Euclid: another appeared in 1710, the local booksellers Richard Thurlbourn and William Dickinson joining Crownfield as its promoters, and yet another in 1722. But the English version, which only appeared in 1714, was printed and published in London.

Such local demands from schoolmasters, using their Cambridge connections to meet their printing needs, had long been familiar. In a similar way, the Press was also the most convenient vehicle for printed sermons delivered by fellows of colleges, either in Cambridge itself or in churches many miles away. The separately printed sermon remained a familiar feature of the printing house for most of its history until the late nineteenth century, though from the later part of the eighteenth there was a choice of local printers. Sermon printing was usually straightforward, and sales were predictable. In many respects other than the fact that sermons were by acknowledged authors, they had much in common with jobbing printing. Thus they remained a mainstay of the Press, even when most people's attentions were focused on a more diverse range of books and subjects. To authors, those who were most immediately affected, it therefore seemed all the more offensive on the rare occasions that a sermon preached in the University Church was refused by the University Press. This was the lot of the prickly John Edwards, of St John's, who preached the 5 November sermon in 1709. As he explained subsequently,

> I flatter'd myself that it would easily find Admittance to the University-Press. But this common Favour, yea, this Right which is generally claim'd by those who think fit to let their Friends have a sight of those Discourses which were Acceptable to them in the Delivery of them, was denied me.[25]

Whatever the custom (Crownfield had printed Edwards's own commencement sermon in 1699), there was no question of any right. Edwards's Gunpowder Plot sermon was forthright in extolling the benefits of the reign of Queen Anne, and acclamatory on the blessings of England, whose climate and soil, as well as scholarship, were unparalleled. His attacks on Louis XIV ('the Great Goliah of these Philistines'), on Jesuits, ('those Frogs of the Mystical Aegypt') and on Papists in general, not least those who had clancularly plotted against King James I, were quite as spirited as the occasion required. But Edwards wanted a sense of proportion and judgement. His enthusiasm for England could be comical, as in his praise of its climate: 'By reason of our happy Situation, we are neither scorch'd with excessive Heat, nor pinch'd with extreme Cold; we stand in need neither of Grotto's nor Stoves.' More seriously, he had not hesitated to remind his congregation of the difficulties experienced by William III, 'being unkindly treated by some, and treacherously by others, and denied those Aids and Assistances which were necessary for completing that Work which he had undertaken'[26]. News that the sermon was not to be printed at Cambridge spread quickly, and reached the ears of the first-year undergraduate John Byrom by mid-December.[27] Edwards vented his feelings in his dedication to his fellow-Johnian, the Earl of Orford, First Lord of the Admiralty and High Steward of the University: 'In my own Vindication, I am necessarily obliged to fly to Your Lordship's Patronage, and to present this Sermon to Yours and the Publick View, from another Press, lest the refusal of allowing it that of the University, should encline any persons to imagine that there was some Good Reason for that refusal.' Was this, he asked, a fit time to 'stifle and suppress the Publication of it (tho'-modestly requested) when there are so many Prints flying abroad every day of a quite contrary kind, libelling the Publick Administrations, and vilifying the Church, and religion itself'.[28]

Not to be printed by the University Press, on request, was thus to arouse suspicion, and potential damage to reputation. Few in Cambridge might have cared to insist on their case with the same gusto for publicity that so frequently characterised Edwards's stormy relations with the book trade; but by casting the argument in terms of religious and political orthodoxy, he raised questions of concern to all in the University. By implication, personal or merely political attachments, quite apart from academical, scholarly or commercial considerations, were to be subsumed by these greater arguments. It was a course of reasoning that could do the Press no good.

Edwards seems to be have been an exception; certainly he was a noisy one. More straightforwardly, a collection of Daniel Waterland's sermons preached at St Paul's Cathedral was printed in 1720 for the London booksellers William and John Innys. The principle that many Cambridge authors found it more convenient to have their work printed, if not published, in Cambridge rather than London, remained a powerful asset for the Press's well-being. So in 1724 Crownfield printed Waterland's *Critical history of the Athanasian Creed* for a consortium of London booksellers:[29] it required a second edition, again printed in Cambridge, four years later. In 1728 he printed, for the London booksellers William and John Innys, Susannah Newcome's *An enquiry into the evidence of the Christian religion*. The work of the wife of John Newcome, later Master of St John's College, it was published anonymously – though its authorship seems to have been an open secret.[30] It appears to have been the earliest work emanating from the Cambridge University Press to be written by a contemporary female author. Those who were prepared to be impressed noted her theological abilities, and her 'sound sense and masculine judgement', while one admirer confessed that she put him constantly in mind of Madame de Maintenon in more humble style. In the eyes of many, her literary judgement seemed superior to that of her husband.[31]

The Press was a convenience, nearer and more accessible than those in London. Barnes had realised this and had exploited it, with both Hayes and Crownfield. The scholarly pursuits of the University, encouraged by Bentley and the others who had established Crownfield as University Printer, were echoed in the more mundane institutional and personal needs of the University and its members. In the year 1713–14, which seems to have been quite typical, Crownfield's bill to the University included printing combination papers for both Masters of Arts (in January) and Bachelors (in

April and May), an order to barbers not to trim hair on Sundays, 100 notices about undergraduate behaviour, 400 copies of tripos verses (twice over), commencement verses for three members of the University on their taking advanced degrees, several separate notices about assizes of bread in December, April, May, July and September, and an order to return books to the University Library. The last was unusual; but the order concerning barbers was a regular feature of Crownfield's jobbing work, which in many respects traced the course of the academic calendar. While the University and colleges employed the Press for notices, tripos poems, collections of poems on national occasions, and the papers increasingly found to be necessary in local administration, private individuals also found Crownfield to be of help. In 1724, Beaupré Bell, who though not a fellow of his college spent much of his time in Cambridge, had a few copies printed for his friends of his poem *The osiers*, based on the work of Jacopo Sannazaro.[32] This and such vanity printing as Samuel Edwards's poem *The Copernican system* never produced much work for the printing house; but it was not a long step from this to many a sermon.

In some of the sciences there were various evidences of activity. On the one hand, little is known of George Rolfe's contribution as the first Professor of Anatomy beyond a syllabus of his lectures that he had printed in 1724,[33] and nothing is recorded of Charles Mason's teaching as Woodwardian Professor of Geology from 1734 beyond his inaugural lecture. Yet in mathematics and astronomy the situation looked very different, as Crownfield responded to the University's needs. The continuing traditions of Newton and Cotes produced a series of books at several levels, from undergraduate instruction to more advanced work.

In these areas in particular, and thanks not least to Robert Smith, successor to Cotes as Plumian Professor and to Bentley as Master of Trinity, the Cambridge press attracted much of the local contribution, work that was often directly inspired by Newton. In 1707, Cotes and Whiston began their joint course of lectures and experiments in hydrostatics and pneumatics.[34] Until his dismissal from the University prevented his books from being published in Cambridge (and even in 1708 the Vice-Chancellor, Edward Lany, refused to allow his *Essay upon the Apostolical constitution*[35]), William Whiston saw that his own lectures were printed at Cambridge – for publication in London by Benjamin Tooke. Those on astronomy appeared in 1707, and those on physics and mathematics in 1710. The revised English version of the latter was printed and published in London in 1716, by which time Whiston had become firmly established in a new career unembarrassed by the obligations of Cambridge theology.[36]

In London, and in other centres, the sciences became topics for lectures well attended by polite society.[37] Meanwhile, partly under the enthusiastic guidance of Roger Long, Fellow of Pembroke College from 1703, Master from 1733, and from 1750 the first Lowndean Professor of Astronomy and Geometry, astronomy in the University flourished as never before, even if the observatory built above the great gate at Trinity under Cotes's guidance was not much used. In 1730, Long issued proposals for a *System of astronomy*, intended to offer a more readily intelligible series of figures and instructions than those currently available.[38] Instead of the Trinity observatory,

Long relied on, and gave most of his attention to, apparatus designed by himself. The largest was a sphere about 20 feet in diameter that he had constructed in the grounds of his college, and in which he could present lectures demonstrating the movements of the heavenly bodies to about twenty people at a time. As his prospectus also explained, he had besides this various orreries, glass spheres and 'other machines, of an invention entirely new'. His book would include illustrations of this equipment, as well as the customary astronomical diagrams. Richard Dunthorne, a member of the college staff at Pembroke, was retained as his assistant; and in 1739 he in turn had printed in Cambridge *The practical astronomy of the moon: or, new tables of the moon's motion* – the results of his study of Newton's theories. The book was very properly dedicated to his employer. As for Long's own book, which he planned apparently from the first to publish himself but for which subscriptions had been collected by Innys in London, nothing appeared until twelve years after the proposals had been issued; and then only a first volume appeared. His faithful readers had to wait a further twenty-two years for part of the second volume, and that incomplete. He died with the project still unfinished, with copies distributed to his readers in haphazard states.

Even to generations used to delays and alterations between the issuing of proposals and final publication, Long was eccentric. He was wealthy enough to ignore both the ordinary conventions of the book trade, and the costs that impelled most people towards publication. For other authors it was usually very different, for reasons that related partly to local politics, partly to individuals' ambitions for their books, and partly to the abilities and inabilities of printers and booksellers. With improved financial, as well as geographical, communications, the book trade tended to distribute risk as well as profits. In London, the most obvious manifestations of increasingly distributed publication arrangements were to be seen in the emergence of booksellers' congers, whereby a system of half, quarter, eighth and smaller shares meant that costs and profits could be shared systematically, and shares could themselves be bought and sold.[39] For the Cambridge booksellers, most of them with little capital to invest heavily in publication, arrangements with London publishers became ever more regularised. Robert Green's *Principles of natural philosophy* (1712) was printed at the Press for the local bookseller Edmund Jeffery; but like many other of the books whose title-pages bore Jeffery's name it was also available in London from James Knapton in St Paul's Churchyard and from Benjamin Tooke in Fleet Street. Green was a Fellow of Clare College. Fifteen years later, his most ambitious and most eccentric work, *Principles of the philosophy of the expansive and contractive forces*, a folio of almost a thousand pages proposing a philosophy which was 'truly English, a Cantabrigian, and a Clarensian one', was likewise printed by Crownfield; it was sold also in Cambridge by both Jeffery and Thurlbourn, as well as in London by Knapton, Knaplock, the Innys brothers and Benjamin Tooke.[40] These particular London stationers were repeatedly associated with Cambridge booksellers and with Crownfield's work: they formed, in various permutations, a group who found convenience in familiarity and also, no doubt, in credit arrangements.

As mathematics for Cambridge undergraduates concentrated increasingly on a few topics, so there was a call for convenient aids. Some were speculative on the part of the booksellers; others were published initially by subscription. Both in his own work and in handling that of others, Robert Smith seems to have preferred the latter. His own books, the *Compleat system of opticks* and (in very different vein, reflecting his interest in music) his *Harmonics, or the philosophy of musical sounds*, appeared from the Cambridge press in 1738 and 1749 respectively.[41] Luke Trevigar's work on conic sections, published in 1731, was less ambitious, and was perhaps addressed primarily to his own and his colleagues' pupils in Clare College and elsewhere in Cambridge: 'the demonstrations will be clear and easy, and the foundations so order'd, as to be obvious to almost every capacity'.[42] His *Sectionum conicarum elementa . . . in usum juventutis academicae* was available in London from Prévost and Vandenhoeck, as well as from Cornelius Crownfield's son John Crownfield. But it had been first published by subscription, and the list of subscribers in Cambridge is remarkable for the numbers of those who took multiple copies, as if to pass some on to their pupils: William Greaves, Fellow of Trevigar's college, took no less than twenty copies, and John Colleton, also of Clare, took six.

While Trevigar's book never reached a second edition, two other publications of the early 1730s were both widely taken up. *Quaestiones philosophicae in usum juventutis academicae collectae & digestae*, by Thomas Johnson, Fellow of Magdalene, enjoyed a decade of success both at Cambridge and Oxford. It was first published by William Thurlbourn in 1732 as a shilling pamphlet. Three years later, when a second edition was called for, it had reached over two hundred pages; and it had grown still further by the third edition of 1741 – price now 3s.6d. Though the title-page did not say so, arrangements were made from the first to sell it in Oxford; and Fletcher and Clements's name appeared on later title-pages. The other book of this kind also came from Magdalene. In 1734 Crownfield printed the first edition of the first part of John Rowning's *Compendious system of natural philosophy*, the work of a Fellow of Magdalene whose subsequent career as a lecturer in London and as Headmaster of the grammar school at Spalding in Lincolnshire (where he was prominent in the Gentlemen's Society) was to help popularise his book. The fact that it was in English rather than Latin was no doubt a help in its continuing popularity. Its complicated bibliographical history (it eventually ran to four parts) took it to at least an eighth edition by 1779. But the Oxford and Cambridge booksellers did not figure on the title-pages after 1735 despite Rowning's explanation in his preface that the book was drawn up from papers he had prepared for his own pupils at Cambridge.

Not all such work was printed initially in Cambridge. Although in 1722 Smith arranged to have printed there his edition of Cotes's *Harmonia mensurarum*, in 1738 he went to London to have William Bowyer print (again at Smith's own expense) his edition of Cotes's *Hydrostatical and pneumatical lectures* delivered in Cambridge in about 1706.[43] Like Smith's own *Compleat system of opticks*, printed partly in Cambridge in 1738,[44] copies of Cotes's work were to be sold in London by Stephen Austen, in St Paul's Churchyard. Austen's list at this time also included Barrow's Cambridge lectures on mathematics and geometry, as well as the recent volumes of the abridged

Philosophical Transactions, Newton's *Method of fluxions* and Voltaire's *Elements of Sir Isaac Newton's philosophy explained*.[45] Copies of Cotes's lectures were also available from 'the Booksellers at Cambridge'. The book proved a success. Like much other mathematical and scientific work from the University at this time, it was designed as much for an audience outside Cambridge as within. Smith described himself on the title-page of the *Hydrostatical and pneumatical lectures* not as a Fellow of Trinity College, but as 'Master of Mechanicks to His Majesty' – a title that both laid claim to royal interest, and also avoided the suggestion that the contents of the book were of interest only to those who sat in the same Cambridge rooms where Cotes had once lectured. As one of the London reviews explained,

> As to the lectures themselves, the Editor tells us, they are compiled with great Freedom and Diffusiveness of Thought and Expression; the Writer condescending to clear up every Appearance of Difficulty, as designing the Instruction either of Beginners, or People of common Understanding; and he has render'd them more entertaining and useful than ordinary, by enlivening the Science with a mixture of Literature, and the History of the Inventions he treats of . . .[46]

The book was translated into French in 1742, and a second edition in English was printed at Cambridge in 1747. But, like Bentley, Smith was able to ignore the ordinary routes of the trade if he so wished. His edition of Cotes's letures was first published at his own expense, and the copper engraved plates used for that passed in turn to the University Printer Joseph Bentham when the second, Cambridge, edition was called for, and then back to London again for the third edition in 1775 – seven years after Smith's death. His own lectures appeared in similarly independent fashion.

Others besides Whiston (who had been excluded from the University) found it necessary, or more comfortable, or more profitable, to have their books published in London rather than Cambridge. Conyers Middleton, one of Bentley's leading adversaries, saw his pamphlet of 1723, advocating improvements in the University Library, printed by Crownfield. But his other work, including his much reprinted *Letter from Rome* on popery and paganism, his celebrated life of Cicero (published by subscription, 1741[47]), his opinions on miracles in the early church (1747) and his *Treatise on the Roman senate* (1747), quite apart from his *Miscellaneous works* in 1752, was virtually all printed and published in London. Bentley, whose Terence appeared in Cambridge in 1726, saw his old Boyle lectures issue from Crownfield's press only in 1724, and then, in its sixth edition, from that of Mary Fenner in Cambridge in 1735.[48] The fault was the bookseller's, not Bentley's. In practice, authors were not necessarily able to influence the place of printing. In 1732, Bentley's version of *Paradise lost* was published by Jacob Tonson and a group of other London booksellers, and was printed in London. To have published Milton in Cambridge, even in a misguided attempt to restore a 'genuine Milton',[49] would have been a radical departure for the University Press; and Tonson, who controlled the copyright in Milton, had no need to face the inconvenience of printing in Cambridge a book that would have its principal sales in the metropolis.

It will be seen from the last paragraphs that there was no regular arrangement between Crownfield and any London publisher in particular. In the late seventeenth century, Hayes had been employed by the Stationers' Company, the largest publisher in London. Earlier in the seventeenth century there had been occasional arrangements, whose details have now been lost. In 1698, Tonson had reached a limited agreement with the new press, which was not extended. But though some London booksellers' names subsequently turned up regularly in imprints, there seems to have been no further regular arrangement, formal in the sense that it was sanctioned by the Curators. In this, the University Press was like any other printer. James Knapton, and Robert Knaplock, two of the most frequent to collaborate with Crownfield, had both been well established since the previous century. William, and later his brother John, Innys were of a younger generation, and by the late 1720s were among the largest booksellers in London, with a commensurate demand on printers. By means of their reviewing journals, the *Memoirs of Literature*, the *New Memoirs of Literature* (1725–7) and the *Present State of the Republick of Letters* (1728–36), which paid attention not only to new publications in London, but also to reports in foreign equivalents from Germany, the Netherlands, France, Italy and Switzerland, they established themselves on a scale hitherto unfamiliar in London publishing. Their catalogue dated 1726[50] listed about 400 works, and revealed a firm interested principally in theology, natural philosophy and medicine. As Printers to the Royal Society, their list was in some measure predictable. Newton, Flamsteed and Ray were each strong presences, Flamsteed's *Historia coelestis Britannica* having been published only the previous year, and his *Atlas coelestis* being announced as in the press. But other parts of the list included Dryden, Dugdale, a valuable cache of educational books for schools and a smattering of architecture including Palladio and Pozzo. Among the books of particular interest to Cambridge were Cotes's *Harmonia mensurarum* (completed by Crownfield in 1722), various works by Daniel Waterland and Davies's edition of Caesar, of which a new edition was published in 1727. William Stanley's anonymous catalogue of the manuscripts in Corpus Christi College (1722) had been printed and published in London, rather than Cambridge.[51] The list included many of which the Innys brothers had bought stock subsequent to publication, as well as the books, such as Newton's *Opticks* (second edition 1718) or the third edition of the *Principia*, in whose publication they had invested initially. Thus Crownfield's books were absorbed into the London trade, not as part of a strategy such as had been envisaged in the mid-1690s, but in the piecemeal manner that characterised the book trade in general. The distinctive nature of the University Press had been eroded.

Of all the London printers, William Bowyer was at an immediate advantage. His connections with Cambridge were strong. Though it was unusual for the sons of printers to be sent to university, his son William was educated partly at St John's College, which he entered in 1716, and where he seems to have spent as much as five or six years. In 1712/13, when Bowyer's printing house had suffered a disastrous fire, the University contributed £40 towards his relief.[52]

Among the works by resident members of the University that passed through the elder Bowyer's hands at about the time his son was at Cambridge were works by Robert Jenkin, Master of St John's; by John Newcome, Samuel Drake and Paulet St John, Fellows or former Fellows of the college; by Conyers Middleton of Trinity (critical of Richard Bentley); by Richard Crossinge, of Pembroke; by Daniel Waterland, of Magdalene; and by William Willymott, of King's. The advertisements for the 1722 edition of Bede by a yet further member of the younger Bowyer's college, John Smith, likewise bore the elder Bowyer's name, as agent. Other books followed in the next few years, notably William Stanley's catalogue of the manuscripts in Corpus Christi College in 1722, and an edition of Matthew Parker's *De antiquitate Britannicae ecclesiae et privilegiis* by Samuel Drake of St John's in 1730, published by subscription and many years in the press.[53]

Not surprisingly, the younger Bowyer considered himself to have a particular call on Cambridge authors. His education had given him both acquaintances among the University, and an understanding of its preoccupations. Many of those whose books he printed were from his own college. In 1730 he went so far as to phrase the title-page of John Taylor's *Music speech at the publick commencement* 'Printed by William Bowyer, jun., sometime student of the same college' – a statement akin in its claim to institutional association to Crownfield's habitual 'Impensis Cornelii Crownfield, celeberrimae Academiae Typographi'. Bowyer's mingling of piety with business also gave rise to occasional jealousy, in which he was not above reminding his correspondents of their mutual background. 'I understand I am not to have the favour of printing your Sermon', he wrote once to Samuel Squire, fellow Johnian and now Dean of Bristol, 'which gives me reason to fear that I have behaved in such a manner as to forfeit a friendship which was founded on a natural, I may say, a *trading* principle, considering I was a pupil of Dr. Newcome.'[54] Bowyer's remarks on the extent to which an author could specify a printer are not disinterested; but they do illustrate that such questions could be posed, given appropriate circumstances. In another heated exchange, on this occasion with Thomas Stackhouse, he opined, 'It is a mere joke for you to say you have not interest to recommend a Printer of your own work. You should have made it, as I told you in your other work, a previous condition of the contract. You might have urged, that, for a solitary guinea, you had unhappily sold to me all your future productions; and that, though it was reward not adequate to them, yet the least you could do was to insist on my printing them.' Stackhouse's rejoinder was courteous:

> I sometimes meet with returns from you that I neither deserve, nor expect. When an author prints for himself, doubtless he can choose what printer he pleases; when he sells the copy, the printer is at the option of the bookseller; and here he can do no more than *recommend his friend*; which is as much as you, or any other reasonable man can desire.[55]

The Bowyers became major competitors, while Crownfield's work declined as he lost interest and those who had promoted him were distracted by other matters, or died. At first, much of this decline in the Press's activities was obscured. Established books and authors or editors such as Bentley and Davies were printed in new editions; and there were sufficient major new projects, such as William Reading's three-volume folio edition of Eusebius and other historians of the early church (1720), Smith's Bede (1722) and Leonard Chappelow's new edition of Spencer's *De legibus Hebraeorum* (1727).[56] Both the Bede, based on Moore's manuscript, and Chappelow's new edition of Spencer, based on Spencer's own notes recently bequeathed to the University by Thomas Tenison, Archbishop of Canterbury, drew directly and fundamentally on materials in the University Library. Thus one aspect of the University fed another, in the way that Bentley, and others before him such as Laud or Fell at Oxford, had originally envisaged for a university press.[57] Bentley's own eagerly awaited edition of Terence was published in 1726 (fig. 9), and copies were handled in London by Paul Vaillant, one of the principal foreign booksellers.[58] The Press continued to receive extended notices, and often plaudits, for these and other books in the foreign reviews.[59] Had proposals in 1734 by the Norfolk antiquary Beaupré Bell to print a survey of Roman coins, based largely on his own collection, come to anything, the Press would have become involved in a distinguished project in a fashionable field, likewise of more than only British interest. But Bell, who had in him not a little of the dilettante, died prematurely, in 1741, and the project was abandoned.[60]

Various indicators of commercial and practical well-being could obscure the true dangers. Most obviously, Crownfield had to keep himself constantly supplied with equipment wherewith to print to an acceptable standard; and this required repeated investment in freshly cast type to replace what had been worn out. By the winter of 1713–14, he needed new type not only for the planned edition of Bede, but also 500 lb of English and brevier, Roman and italic, and 300lb of Greek. At least some of his needs were supplied by the Voskens typefoundry in Amsterdam.[61] For so long as he wished to avoid the expense of wholesale reinvestment in new designs, Crownfield was obliged to return to the same firms or their successors to replace his worn-out metal. In 1703 and again in 1709–10 he obtained further supplies of ordinary text sizes from the Schipper typefoundry in Amsterdam, which after the death of the Widow Schippers in November 1699 was largely run by the foreman, Jan Bus.[62] In 1723, 1,223 (Amsterdam) *ponden* of pica Roman and italic were forwarded from London to Crownfield by Gijbert Dommer, grandson of the Widow Schippers.[63] Two years later, Crownfield was again in touch with the Schipper establishment, seeking over 1,300 *ponden* of Roman and italic in English and great primer.[64] More, this time mainly of long primer, followed in 1726.[65] Thus, in four years, Crownfield had taken steps to replace much of the type most used for ordinary text setting.

But there were also less welcome signs. In 1725 the Curators reviewed stocks of books whose sales had either almost or completely ceased. Davies's edition of Caesar, published in 1706, was one; and the remaining 66 copies on large paper and 394 on ordinary paper were sold to Davies for £100.[66] As copies had been offered originally at 18s.6d. and 12s. respectively,[67] it was as disappointing a price as it was a disappointing sales history. Wasse's Sallust, published in 1710, had performed similarly weakly, there remaining 10 on large paper (out of 150) and no less than 444 on ordinary paper (out of 1,000). Crownfield himself agreed to buy this stock, for £115, presumably in the expectation that a low remainder price would rejuvenate sales.[68] The *Suidas* was a

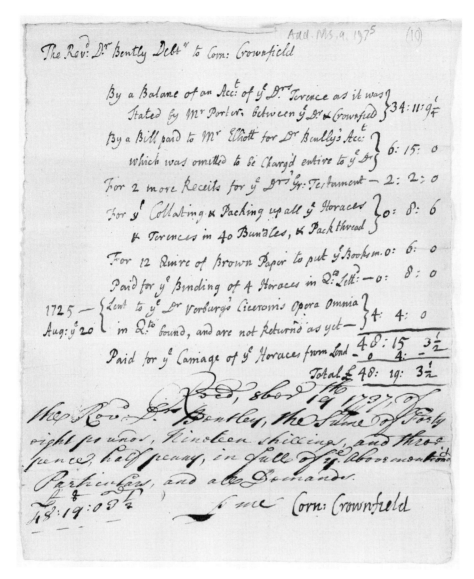

Fig. 9 Bill by Cornelius Crownfield to Richard Bentley, paid in 1737, including money outstanding on
Bentley's Terence (1726) and for handling copies of his Horace (1711)
(Trinity College, MS Add. a.197(5)).

larger, and less tractable, problem. Sir Theodore Janssen, whose timely help had saved
the project when John Owen had failed the University, had himself been financially
ruined, as a Director of the South Seas Company.[69] Janssen's stock of unsold copies of
the edition that he had in effect financed now lay in the warehouse of the Company in
London. The Vice-Chancellor was empowered to purchase this dead stock.[70] The
embarrassment remained, for when Crownfield's affairs as University Printer came
under scrutiny in 1737, there still remained 425 copies unsold.[71]

By this time, the Press was manifestly not meeting the needs of the University. Robert Smith, Plumian Professor of Astronomy, and one of those in Cambridge most alert to the University's (scarcely less than his College's) well-being, expressed his disquiet by example when he wished to find a printer for two of his major projects. First, in spring 1738 he turned not to Crownfield, but to William Bowyer, in London, to print an edition of the *Hydrostatical and pneumatical lectures* by Roger Cotes, his predecessor in the Plumian chair. In the same year, Smith's own *Compleat system of opticks*, published by subscription, was being printed by the University Press. But Crownfield did not complete the task; instead it was handed over to Bowyer, who printed the last several sheets in the late summer that year.[72]

The University Press, in the hands of a man who had served the University well, had degenerated as a result only partly of Crownfield's declining energies. Without the support of the University more generally, and with the orphans of a programme that had taken too little notice of the practicalities of publication or distribution, he was set an impossible task.

On 23 November 1737, a Syndicate was appointed with the task of enquiring into the losses incurred over the past forty years. It found a Press whose business had decreased and whose losses had increased, equipped with type and presses in urgent need of replacement.[73] Perhaps to spare a long-serving official of the University from criticism, the Syndicate offered no explicit opinion as to where responsibility lay for such circumstances; but the fault lay as much with the way in which the Press had been organised, and its activities deliberately curtailed, as with the execution of its business by any particular person. The report came, moreover, shortly after the University had faced a difficult series of legal squabbles following the death of William Fenner, who had been licensed in 1731 to print Bibles and Prayer Books.[74] The report dwelt on the aftermath of this affair also, and to this work we shall return. But the critical problem was the running of the Press itself.

The results of ignoring the Press were plain to see, as even the most senior members of the University took their work elsewhere. There were few more prominent than John Taylor, Fellow of St John's, University Librarian from 1732–4 and Registrary of the University since 1734.[75] He had entered St John's in 1721, and graduated in 1724, his time as an undergraduate thus overlapping that of Bowyer. The first of his work to pass through Bowyer's hands was his much admired speech delivered at the public commencement in July 1730, followed a few days later by his speech delivered earlier in the year commemorating the execution of King Charles I.[76] William Thurlbourn, the Cambridge bookseller, figured on the title-pages, and in 1732 he was named as one of those to whom those wishing to subscribe to Taylor's projected edition of Lysias should address themselves. Both the proposals and the edition (which did not appear until 1739) were printed by Bowyer.[77] By this time the two men had more than printing in common, for Bowyer also acted as Taylor's agent in other matters.[78] But thereafter, for so long as he was in Cambridge (he resigned as Registrary on taking up a new career as clergyman outside the University in 1751) he turned to the University Press, beginning with proposals for an edition of

Demosthenes in 1739 and a further edition of Lysias 'in usum studiosae juventutis' in 1740.[79] Taylor's transition from an old college loyalty to support for the University Press in which he, as University Registrary, had some interest, offers a more than usually dramatic example of the manner whereby the changes introduced in and about 1740, including the retirement of Crownfield and the re-equipping of the Press, prompted a re-examination of printing arrangements by authors and booksellers in Cambridge alike.

⚛ 6 ⚛

The mid-eighteenth-century printing house

The crisis in the 1720s and 1730s that faced those in the University who cared about the Press had its roots in the 1690s and in the early eighteenth century. The faults lay not with any individual; and they lay only partly with the failure, analysed in the preceding chapters, of Bentley and his contemporaries seriously to consider how the books were to be paid for, and published, rather than simply the needs for proper academic supervision and for the mechanics of printing.

In 1696, the University had affirmed its wish only to print 'some Classick Authors, and such Books of learning as they [i.e. the University] shall find to be wanted'.[1] This remained the Press's firm policy. Though many of the classical authors included in the Stationers' Company's publishing interests were printed in substantial fresh editions at Cambridge, the Press never sought to trespass into the general market for elementary editions of the classics, or of grammars or other schoolbooks. As if to remind the University of the Company's interests, as well as what it had to offer, and even of the advantages of selling books through its agency, an advertisement at the back of an edition of Ovid printed by Hayes in 1703 listed not only classical texts published by the Stationers, but also a number of books printed by the Oxford University Press and offered for sale through the Company in a scheme that was in fact already proving an abject failure.[2]

Much of the history of the Cambridge press from 1583 onwards had depended on accommodation or collaboration with the interests of the English Stock, to the point, in Hayes's hands, where the Company owned the press, employed the University Printer and provided much of his order book. It was not a situation that some in Cambridge relished; and it was one of the principal considerations behind the new foundation in 1698. Though the new Cambridge press was intended to break with past inadequacies, it continued to respect the interests of the Company's English Stock. Until his death in November 1705, Hayes continued to print almanacs, as an employee of the Company. But after his death (those for 1706 also bear his name, but were printed as usual in the early autumn of the previous year), no more were printed by the University Press for the present. Instead, in 1706 the University secured a covenant of forbearance whereby Cambridge was to receive £200 per annum in lieu of exercising its right to print what had by the beginning of the eighteenth century become a very substantial list.[3]

The agreement was an ungenerous one, and it was criticised from the first. It also ignored the real needs of Cambridge. In the early eighteenth century, the Stationers' Company sought to retain its long-standing control of some of the most popular and widely selling books in the English-speaking market. Almanacs, schoolbooks, elementary editions of classical texts and the Psalms in metre, all featured in its claims to a monopoly. The schedule attached to the covenant when the agreement of 1706 was repeated in 1726 included New Testaments, psalms in metre, 'all Psalters', all primers, the ABC, horn-book prints, Lilly's grammar, almanacs and prognostications, all conceivable Latin authors that would be suitable for study at school, Aesop in Latin, Homer, Hesiod, Demosthenes, Isocrates and Hippocrates in Greek, Erasmus, Lipsius, manuals of Latin composition, and an assortment of works including Foxe's *Book of martyrs* and Thomas à Kempis (in both Latin and English), as well as others that had by this time fallen out of general fashion.[4] At various periods in the seventeenth century, University Printers at Cambridge had either challenged or contrived to accommodate some of these claims. In the eighteenth century, the battle was fought on different fronts, as the Stationers' books gradually either fell into disuse, or were replaced by quite different editions, or (as in the case of the extremely profitable business in almanacs) were declared as a genre to be a common-law right.[5] Their position became untenable, not simply as a result of the increasing reluctance on the part of the universities to refrain from venturing more independently, but as a result of a looser publishing structure throughout Great Britain. At the beginning of the century, Cambridge first took advantage of the situation by agreeing to receive money in return for compromising where a battle would have been a distraction from learned publishing; and then, in 1781, the University accepted an annual payment from the government in compensation for the loss of a privilege to print almanacs.

On the one hand the Cambridge policy was astute; on another, and particularly with respect to the successive covenants of forbearance in 1706 and 1726, it failed to acknowledge an essential truth: that without a regular supply of cheap work, with an assured market (such as schoolbooks, for example), a learned press would usually run at a loss. Such agreements, while they secured peace with the Stationers' Company, prevented the University from using its Press to the best advantage. Instead, Crownfield was restricted to work that was rarely likely to achieve steady and substantial sales over a long period and to a wide audience, and prevented from that which would secure a regular, assured and speedy return on expenditure such as could be used to subsidise the production and sale of slower-selling scholarly books.

Edward Bentham, of Christ Church, Oxford, and brother of the then University Printer at Cambridge, explained the matter at Oxford in 1756:

> Tis to be observed that the chief gains of a master printer arises from the quantity of work & not from the goodness. And the U[ty] by not admitting low & trivial things of quick sale to be printed at its press, thereby precludes itself from a great & perhaps the most profitable branch of printing.[6]

By the 1720s, and still more by the 1730s, Crownfield's early successes had receded into the memories of a dwindling number of members of the University. As his business diminished, so his later career was much criticised, particularly among the younger members of the University. It hardly mattered that some of the reasons for its diminishing lay with the University itself. In 1732, Bentley reached the age of seventy (he died in 1742). Crownfield seems to have been almost of an age with him.[7] Those who now dominated the University were no longer of the generation that had seen Crownfield established, and the newly founded Press enjoy its first years of glory.

The lead for reform came not from among those long resident in Cambridge, but from one who had until recently been an outsider. In 1736, William Richardson, a former scholar of Emmanuel College, was elected its Master, an event remarkable enough in itself since he had never been a Fellow.[8] He had spent most of his short career away from Cambridge, in Lincoln (where he was a prebendary in the Cathedral) and in London, where his work on editing his uncle's papers had brought him contact with the printer William Bowyer.[9] But he was familiar with Cambridge in other ways, since he had recently returned to live there for the sake of the libraries, in order to pursue his work on a revised edition of Francis Godwin's account of the English and Welsh bishops. He was born in 1698, the year that the Press was established, and he was thus still aged less than forty when, unexpectedly, he was elected Master of his college. Thanks to the customs of the University in ordering the colleges from whom the Vice-Chancellor was chosen, he became Vice-Chancellor almost immediately, in 1737. In this capacity he took the opportunity to investigate Crownfield's business, though his interest was to last long after his year of office. As Master of Emmanuel, he was ambitious for improvements, whether in the size of the Master's Lodge (a proposal that the Fellows' combination room should be given up to the Lodge was abandoned) or in the restoration and rebuilding of decayed parts of the College more generally. He brought the same firm practical approach to the needs of the Press and the University as he did to those of his college.[10] To a new generation, it was natural to speak of Crownfield's increasing age, as well as infirmity, in seeking to arrange a pension and thus clear the way for a younger man.[11] For the University in general, it was difficult to ignore allegations that the Press had been mismanaged for forty years; and in November 1737 a syndicate was appointed to investigate its affairs.[12]

The moment was opportune, as the University turned its attention for the second time in a generation to improving the space between the University Church and the Schools. The Senate House, built between 1722 and 1730, faced a motley array of old buildings, on which the University had cast its eye. In the early 1720s, James Burrough of Gonville and Caius College and the architect James Gibbs had put forward proposals for a court bounded by senate house, schools and (on the south) a building that was to contain the University's court and offices on the ground floor, and the Press above.[13] This scheme remained live in the public mind, illustrations of the proposals being displayed, for example, on the title-page of Bentley's Boyle lectures (printed by Mary Fenner) and of Conyers Middleton's *Dissertation concerning the origin of printing in England*, both published by Thurlbourn in 1735. A slightly revised version of the scheme was brought forward again in 1738, in Richardson's year of office as Vice-

Chancellor. With the needs of the Press now critical, the Grace appointing a syndicate to buy up the properties to the south of the Senate House placed especial emphasis on its particular claims. A new building such as this, belonging to the University, would mean that rent would no longer need to be paid to Queens' College.[14] But though some properties were acquired soon afterwards, this scheme petered out; the new east front of the schools (including the east room of the University Library) was completed to designs by Stephen Wright in 1754–8, but the south building was never built.[15]

The Syndics appointed in 1737 to investigate the Press thus worked in a university that was prepared to countenance change, but was cautious and divided about implementing it. Their report of 1741, its signatories headed by Roger Long, did not mince matters. They wrote of having discovered 'great disorder and confusion', worn-out type, increasing losses and decreasing business. On inspecting the accounts from 1698 to 1738, they alleged that printing house expenses had exceeded income by over £3,000. But they also wrote of the urgent steps recently taken to remedy matters. Old type had been sold off, and new type bought (fig. 10); two old presses had been replaced; and whereas when the Syndics had been appointed they had found only three men employed, 'not half supplied with work', they could now report that there were seven or eight men constantly employed. In the Syndics' opinion, printing was now so much improved that authors would think it in their interest to have their work printed at Cambridge.[16]

The new University Printer, Joseph Bentham, was of a clerical family from the Isle of Ely, son of the registrar of Ely Cathedral and one of ten children. He was a younger brother of James, minor canon of Ely from 1737, who was to devote much of his life to improving the roads across the fens and to compiling an original and pioneering history of the cathedral. Their brother Edward, educated at Oxford and later Regius Professor of Divinity, was a Fellow of Oriel College at the time of Joseph's election as University Printer at Cambridge. They were a tight-knit family, and well known. Local gossip supplemented the remark that God made men and women and the Herveys ('a species between man and woman') with the further observation that he made the Benthams as well – 'as' (in the words of William Cole) 'they are as unlike in all their actions to the rest of mankind as it is possible to conceive, though without guile, and quite inoffensive'.[17] Joseph Bentham had been apprenticed to the London printer Edward Say in 1726;[18] he was well placed as a candidate for the post of University Printer, having both the skills and the necessary local and academic connections. In due course he was to serve also as alderman and mayor in Cambridge, and he was frequently referred to as Alderman Bentham. The *Cambridge Journal and Weekly Flying-Post* greeted his election to the common council with satisfaction: 'If a true Attachment to the present happy Establishment, a benevolent Temper, a correct Judgement, and a humane Disposition can recommend a man to the Public, the Corporation on this Occasion have certainly fulfilled the Desires of every Individual.'[19] In his private life, he married late (there were no children),[20] while George Dyer remarked both his sense of humour and his taste for gardening.

A SPECIMEN of the Letters belonging to the University of CAMBRIDGE.

ABCD

ABCDE

ABCDEF

ABCDEF

Two Lines English.

Quousque tandem a-
butere, Catilina, pati-
O dii immortales! ubi

Double Pica.

Atque super vitâ plaudere,
morte queri.   mmoda vixit
Tros Tyriusque   Britannis

Paragon.

Death only now appears to
ease their Grief, Death, the
Jove's Osiers Woods, Floods. Powers

Best Great Primmer.

Manner of Yard-Wide Stuffs whatsoever all Black Durants, and Rashes
Features of Him here, tho' true, but

Old Great Primmer.

is now compelled by his great Losses,
to implore the Relief of Charitable
Anno Dom. 1730. *December, Novem-*

Oldest Great Primmer very much used.

mention'd in a Statute made in the first
Year of the Reign of our most gracious
Prince of Wales, *and his Open and Se-*

Best English.

valetudinum. Democritus, luminibus am
istis, eraa scilicet discernere olbvbona, mala; *
If thou doest well shalt thou not be accept-

Old English N. 1. much used

vine Perfections of our Lord, and the all-
2. *That Part of it which is Duty, is not a*

Old English N. 2. much used

ens aut infelix ego sum, ut, cum nullâ spem
qui hoc fece- optimam sententiam amplecti, de

Old English N. 3. very much used.

ACCA AUREUS videbir sic tamenduas
Baccalaureus in actum per se vel quàm ju

Best Pica much used.

956 Cicero de Divinatione a Davisio   *Cant.* 1721
91 *Lucien de la Traduction de N. P. Sieur D'Ablan-*

Old Pica very much used.

Homas Edwards Arm. Ballivus Libertat' Epis' Ee
de ssign. ad om' pred' tenend. Om' *G* ad respontn

Best Long Primmer.

nus; quare legit, *ille in insinita*-II. pag. 17. Sane, quod mo
nuit *tem omnem peregrinabatur.* Viro*Vellcius Paterculus* lib. I

Old Long Primmer N. 1. much used

valente *dialectico* magna lustatio est. In coelo autem crasso &
Et valentes] Robusti, fortes. Infra: *In qua tibi cum*

Old Long Primmer N. 2. very much used.

Ex his intelligi potest Arist. sub Propositione arrnationem
tanquam Probationi subjectam. Hec enim est qua constituit,

New Brevier.

Dru, inaugura illa vetus Zenonis Ipsum enim Agedum, inquit, sermo
CAPUT I.   RINCIPIO creavit a Quum autem esset

Old Brevier.

nPsurma. roo&nquusiulijsand   ia, ecasuiv Airuoest iriiuvigh uucxrle-tino
umi urpeisim, sou nloomadsu rroepniat, decronnuslnrceulsome &dr,sevs jm

Minion.

V. 1. Act. 1, 15. Psal. 1lege.35. 6. 8E11. | V. 2. Hebr. 21. 3. | V. 6 sul. 11. 1
5, 10, 12. Psal. 148, 5. | 1. Psal. 32, 6. Job. 38, 11, & 30, 7.   V. 3 1714. Psal. 35 1

Paragon Greek.

῍Οκκα κεν ἀγ῾σελίας καῖζακεσεις τᾶς ἀλ
εγεινᾶς·   Κᾶτθανεν ἁ ΚΑΡΟΛΙΝΑ·

English Geeek much used.

γὰρ ἀπη῾γειλέ μοι, ἐν σὺ τῷ δεραπίῳ διελάσας
ματαξὺ δακτύλα ἐφόνευσας, ὅτι μὶ πω῾ς τᾶς

Long Primmer Greek much used.

τόφον αὐτὸν ὑπηλάρσον καὶ ὑπ' ἄρα ᾗ ἄπερ ρὸς ΟΥΑΠΟ μὶ ᾔ
εἴσσει, παδαλλῶ· ὑφερφορέοντες, αὐτὸν η ψυψυβφλεσιαν. ὑπὶς τοῦ,

Brevier Greek.

Περδικος δ ουθέν ἐν τῆ συψλέφαμμεν τῷ περὶ τῆ Ηραηλίεος ὑπερ ᾗ ᾔ
πλειίσυς υπαδάνευτα ὅτας περ τῆς ἀρ῾τὶς ἀνοριλιτου ἀρε και λ

Long Primmer Hebrew.

אָנֹשׁ תְּבֻשָׁנָה תַּגְשֻׁנָה תַּגְשֻׁנָה תַּגְשֻׁנָה
תְּנֻשִׁי יֻנְשׁוּ נֻשַׁי נֻשׁ

English Arabick.

نسل مهلك يابسي لازم
يعول اثرعا كل ملائها

English Saxon.

ða he ða mið ᵹnimmum ꝺ cint peᵹum
þæcco þær ꝺ he ealſe þa þitu ðe him

Pica Saxon.

Dı he ða mıð ᵹnimmum ꝺ cint peᵹum þreeð
þær ꝺ he ealſe þı þitu ðe hım man ðybe ᵹe

Fig. 10 *A specimen of the letters belonging to the University of Cambridge* (*c.* 1740). Reduced. (Cambridge University Library).

Not surprisingly, the terms of the University's agreement with Joseph Bentham were partly the result of observing past mistakes. His appointment was agreed by the Syndics on 28 March 1740, and passed by Grace on 31 December.[21] Among the provisions for his work were that he was to be allowed 2s. a ream for overheads such as fire, candles, balls, ink, parchment, paste, lye, lye brushes etc.; that he should be paid 4 guineas a year for 'papering up Letter, and keeping it in order'; that he should be allowed sixpence a ream for outside quires, to be used for proofing paper, and a shilling a parcel for packing parcels (defined as consisting of between four and six reams); that he was to have sole profit on anything taking up under three sheets; the University was also to allow him one chaldron of coals a year; and, most importantly, that if profits in any year did not amount to £60, the University was to make good the deficiency.[22]

He was much liked, if the gossipy William Cole (who claimed to have been responsible for finding him a wife) is a reliable authority. Horace Walpole stayed with him, and found it agreeable.[23] It was no doubt a help that, though not a notable collector himself, he was prepared to take an interest in the antiquarian interests of others,[24] while Cole records a number of carved or glazed coats of arms that had survived in the house of the University Printer opposite the entrance to Queens' College.[25] Cole's own experience of the printing trade was limited; and he therefore had few people with whom to compare Bentham once he reflected on his printing. But his observation that Bentham was noticeable for the care with which he completed his books is a reminder of the assumptions in the printing trade that were by no means confined to printing in Cambridge.

> For Mr. Joseph Bentham, a conscientious good man, and extremely punctilious in his business, was never satisfied with his printing, always cancelling sheets and reprinting them, which consumed much time and paper, and in other respects made not those advantages that others would have done in his profession; for which he suffered in his pocket, which I know was not well filled at his marriage.[26]

Bentham was a more acute businessman than Crownfield had been in his latter years; he had the advantage of being a member of a local family with many connections both in the county and the University; and he was of an obviously amiable disposition. All these circumstances contributed towards the well-being of the University Press in the decades of his office as University Printer, from 1740 until his retirement in 1766.[27]

During the period that Bentham was University Printer, the Press did not always prosper as some would have liked. Its printing of Bibles and prayer books brought both profit and embarrassment. Further aspects of this are described below, in a separate chapter. Its printing for authors remained a service, an essential part of a press in an academic community, rather than a very lucrative part of the business. There was little money to be made from printing books for private customers who were then permitted long periods before their bills were called in. But more importantly, the Cambridge press once again became a notable presence in the book trade at large, with established London connections to some of the most powerful booksellers in the country, and with a significant proportion of the trade in privileged books. Under Bentham's eye, the foundations were laid for some of the principal features of the Press during the coming century and more. Above all, the quantity of work passing through the Printer's hands increased vastly.

This may be measured most readily in the quantities of paper that had to be moved between Cambridge and London for the University and for privileged work. For the whole of Bentham's career, the Press used a single carrier, Edward Gillam, or (later) his son. Gillam's waggons set out for London three days a week, and returned from the so-called Cambridge warehouse in Bishopsgate Street on four days a week, while once a week he also employed a horse-carrier for smaller messages and packages.[28] In 1740–1, Gillam's bill for the entire year's carriage was £5.8s.8d., including 16s.1½d. for a hamper containing a new printing press, weighing just over 8 cwt. The only charge for carriage of paper supplied to Cambridge was of £1.18s., for 15 cwt. in September 1741. In 1755–6, the total bill was £54.15s.9d., most of it for carrying paper; and in 1765–6 it reached £117.3s.1d. Most of this was for the privileged books, and most of the London deliveries that year were to the Press's recently appointed agents: Beecroft, Rivington, Waugh, Dilly and White, while virtually all the 'up' trade (that is, from London) consisted of white paper. Scarcely a week passed without a transaction, and in some weeks Gillam's waggons were kept very busy. In November 1765, a total of over 4 tons of books in sheets were delivered from Cambridge to various London booksellers, and in December about 2 tons. Even in January, when the roads were not at their best, a further 2 tons and more were shipped to the capital. Most of these shipments were fairly modest: it was rare for a bookseller to be sent more than ½ a ton of printed sheets in a single consignment, though White in January and Rivington and Beecroft in October 1766 each received over a ton. For the 'up' journey, on the other hand, there were different reasons for parcels to be quite modest. Because of the cost of paper, the Press preferred to order what was required immediately; and inevitably the suppliers could not always provide everything in a single batch from the mill. Nevertheless, in November and December 1765 there were shipments of well over 1 ton on two occasions; in May 1766 a single shipment of paper weighed 2¼ tons; and two in July weighed over 1 ton each.[29]

Like most printers, the Press preferred to keep little white paper in stock, and instead ordered it for each task, thus avoiding the danger of having unnecessary capital tied up in the warehouse. All paper supplies (Dutch or English) came from agents in London: the Press did not customarily buy direct from the mills. When Bentham took over, the usual supplier was John Rowe; but as demand was increased, so others were applied to. In 1755–6, these included the firms of Johnson and Unwin, Rowe & Webber, Grosvenor & Webber, Baker, and Herbert & Durnford. By the mid 1760s, the names of the stationers and paper-makers included Vowell, Bayles, Bowles, Unwin, Field, Tassell, and Fairchild, of whom the last two (William Tassell and William Fairchild) were paper-makers at the mills at Sawston, near Cambridge.[30] In 1757–8, apparently for the first time, Tassell supplied about 10 per cent of the paper charged to the University. In the following year his bills accounted for about 40 per cent, and in the next about 45 per cent, as his business increased rapidly. Deliveries cannot always be correlated with individual editions, but a few were recorded more particularly. John Rowe supplied Dutch demy and crown paper for the Bible in 1740.[31] English demy was ordered in 1743 for a prayer book.[32] In 1744 paper was ordered from Theodore Janssen.[33] Responsibility for the choice of paper and supplier was usually the responsibility of Bentham and Bathurst, as printer and agent, and the Vice-Chancellor was expected to pay the bill. Bathurst was as alert as Bentham to the quality. 'I can furnish you with 30 Rh more for 12° C Prayer', he wrote to Bentham in 1747. 'I could wish it a little thicker; but must take up the best can be had.'[34] The Syndics do not seem to have taken a very close interest in paper quality, until in 1765 the appointment of a number of new agents made them perhaps more alert. For the first large order of Bibles and prayer books to be placed subsequently, the Syndics asked that samples be obtained from a number of sources: orders were placed with three: Bowles, Field and Tassell.[35] But inevitably, given the large impressions that were going through the Press, there were overruns, and there had to be reconciliations. Bathurst himself made up stock in 1748,[36] and in 1751 paper that had been ordered for an octavo Bible was ordered to be cut down so as to be used for a small duodecimo prayer book and psalms.[37] Since the repetitious nature of the successive editions of the smaller formats in particular of the Bible and prayer book brought with it identically organised formes and sheets, it was an easy matter to carry over unused sheets from one edition to the next. This procedure was agreed formally by the Syndics on occasion,[38] but in practice it was quite frequent, and copies varied slightly accordingly.

Changes to staff had begun well before Bentham took office. In 1737, the Syndics appointed to investigate Crownfield's affairs found 'only three Men employed in the House, and they not half supplied with Work'. Soon after Bentham's arrival, in 1741 they spoke of 'seven or eight men constantly employed'.[39] Thus, for the first time for a generation, the size of the workforce was comparable with that in the first decade of the century, when there had regularly been half a dozen compositors. In the 1730s there were still only two presses. They were under-used, and the men were under-employed. Though books did not by any means take up all the energies of the printing house, in 1729–30 it appears that the equivalent of less than a hundred days' work was put through the two presses, the six books concerned including a catalogue printed in a short run of four hundred copies for Crownfield himself.[40] That year, six men were employed. Of the three compositors, John Thorn, Thomas Kippey and Adrian Crownfield, Kippey had been with Crownfield since 1708, and Crownfield's son Adrian since 1717. Of the two pressmen, Richard Gathurn and John Rumball, Gathurn had been with Crownfield ever since he had been apprenticed at the beginning of the century. These five were helped by a further long-serving workman, Robert Nicholson, who ran errands. By 1733–4, the number had been reduced to three, consisting of Thorn, Gathurn and Nicholson: that is, including just one compositor and one pressman; and Gathurn appears to have been employed for only half the year.[41] The bill for their labour at composition, correction and presswork amounted that year to just over £33, while Crownfield continued to draw his salary of £26 per annum as University Printer. Nicholson was soon succeeded by a younger man, Robert Hibble; but it was this situation, in which but three men were inadequately employed, that faced the Syndics when they examined the Press in 1737.

For the first time for many years, in 1737–8 Crownfield himself took on an apprentice, Frederick Bingey, though it is not clear how many years he had to serve. In August 1738 a new compositor and a new pressman were recruited, Bircket Wheaton and Matthew Whalley. Their arrival signalled the beginning of improvements in staff numbers, new investment in equipment, and a greatly increased output.[42] In autumn 1740 nine people were eligible for wages for long or short periods. Thorn and Bingey were joined by a further compositor, Orian Adams. Of the pressmen, Whalley had by then gone, but Gathurn and Wheaton remained. Two boys were recruited, namely Gathurn's son (also called Richard) and Moore Aungier, son of a local carpenter: both worked in the printing house for a while before being formally apprenticed to Bentham in November 1743. A third apprentice, Robert Moore, from the nearby village of Linton, followed in September 1744.[43]

For generations, journeymen had moved among London printing houses; and as the number of presses outside London increased, so they moved round the countryside also. While Crownfield had been able to recruit and keep some of his men for many years, the increasing numbers of men employed in the printing trade who had worked in several houses gradually undermined ingrained habits.[44] Fresh expectations, fresh standards and different practices all made their mark in Bentham's printing house. Many were no doubt Bentham's own, and some he shared. William Godbed, who joined the press in August 1740, came from a very similar background to Bentham's own: both were sons of clergymen from Ely, and both had served their apprenticeships, at almost exactly the same time, in the printing house of Edward Say in London.[45]

In the following year, Bentham recruited two further pressmen, Henry Doyle and J. Gawthorpe, and in 1742 yet another, George Pinches. At the end of the year, a further pressman named Crage was recruited in London.[46] Most, like Crage, came from London, those that did so being paid a standard fifteen shillings for removal expenses. Brooker, Whalley and perhaps Doyle had worked for William Bowyer,[47] while Bentham turned to his old master Edward Say for Godbed. Pinches may be identified with the person of that name who had been apprenticed to John Baskett in 1724.[48] Some were temporary. Benjamin Lyons worked for eight weeks in 1740–1 as a compositor with knowledge of Hebrew and Greek.[49] And as usual, not all the new staff stayed. Adams disappeared after being advanced some cash because of the severe winter of 1740–1, when it was too cold to work. John Brooker, an Irishman who appeared briefly in 1740–1, likewise went off without notice.

By November 1741, the University Press possessed four presses, though not all were used all the time. For some of the time at least, particular journeymen appear to have been regularly charged with particular presses.[50] In autumn 1742, Bentham had seven journeymen on his staff, besides various assistants. During the year, he had lost two men, Gawthorpe (in January) and Godbed (in March), while Pinches had arrived as

Gawthorpe's replacement. Of these men's assistants rather less is known. Moore Aungier, 'the person who hangs up, gathers &c. the Books in the warehouse, goes of Errands &c. &c.' was paid just five shillings a week for his work – and not surprisingly, for a while required the help in the warehouse of the more experienced Gathurn. But these men between them were not sufficient to run at full stretch a printing house containing four presses, setting and distributing type, and printing off editions. In the absence in the accounts of further charges for labour, here, in other words, is confirmation that the printing house was not working to capacity. The new presses, costing about £14 each, were made by Thomas Smith, blacksmith, and Richard Purcer, joiner, in London.[51] Both Say and Purcer were regular suppliers of other printing materials, including composing sticks and milled lead for spacing.

The supply of work in the printing house was irregular, and its execution depended on the weather. Bentham on occasion found himself with men only recently recruited yet who could not be kept fully employed. In 1741 Henry Doyle received the equivalent of about three weeks' pay for 'deficiency of work' after he arrived from London. In the same year, a total of £31.10s.9½d. was lent to the journeymen 'chiefly in the time of the Frost last winter, and when work was deficient, which Sum they promise to pay at small weekly payments'. In February 1741/2, and again in the summer, when times were again lean, Henry Doyle and George Pinches shared £6.15s.3d. between them: about half that sum was also, again, lent out among the journeymen. Bentham introduced new methods of management, in a systematic attempt to keep men once they had been recruited. Copy-money, that originated as money paid in lieu of books to compositors and pressmen for copies of books on which they had worked, and which since the mid-seventeenth century had been treated as a regular wage,[52] was halved under Bentham to 2d. per week. Separate charges were now made systematically for such essential operations as cleaning out old letter, keeping type cases in order, and the somewhat nebulous 'taking care' of particular presses – nebulous because payments were irregular and not all presses seem to have required such attention. Benjamin Lyons, whose most valuable skill was his ability to set Hebrew type, was paid specifically for setting a specimen of it: for men who were not such birds of passage, no such payments were recorded in the accounts.

It is almost certainly due to the influx of new journeymen from elsewhere, and especially from London, that from 1743 onwards some books printed at Cambridge bear press figures, numbers set at the feet of pages (normally versos) whose purpose was to record details of printing, and which were not, like signatures, catchwords or pagination, for the use of binders or readers.[53] The annual accounts, recording such matters as the provision of new friskets, working presses down, and caring for them generally, indicate that at least in the early 1740s Bentham's presses were each numbered.[54] It seems reasonable to suppose that in this period the press figures refer to these presses, not the men. These numbers were not applied systematically, though they seem to have been used more in Bibles and prayer books than in other work. Their use also appears to have been a matter of personal preference on the part of the pressmen concerned. Certainly the practice was never enforced at Cambridge. The early and repeated use of the figure 2 seems also to suggest that one particular pressman was attached to this press. Thus we may perceive how in printing a single book the various sheets and formes were not printed consistently at a single press, or even a pair, but at several, with the work shared out.

For reasons no longer entirely clear, these numbers were employed only intermittently even within particular books. The figure 2 appears sparsely, and with no others, in Cicero, *De natura deorum*, the first volume of Butler's *Hudibras*, Rutherforth's *Essay on the nature and obligations of virtue* (all 1744) and William Smith's *Natural history of Nevis* (1745). In 1745, numbers 1, 2 and 3 were used in the small prayer book, yet in Edmund Law's *Considerations on the state of the world* only 3 appears, and that again very rarely. By 1746, figures 1 to 4 were all used for the Welsh Bible and prayer book; but even in 1747 their use in the duodecimo English Bible was intermittent. By 1758, the prayer book included figures 1 to 5, and by 1764 the octavo prayer book of that year included figures 1 to 7.

In some of this at least, the evidence of what was not printed may be as significant as what was. Perhaps most of the formes without numbers were machined by pressmen who had been longest at Cambridge, while increasing frequency indicates recent arrivals. Though we can only speculate on the reasons for these irregular appearances, the figures do permit other observations on the organisation of the printing house. The various issues of the Bible and prayer book on different sizes and qualities of paper, and the practice of printing a few copies of some other books on large paper, meant adjustment at press with change in paper size, or in extreme cases even a return to the imposing stone. Some books were straightforward. Zachary Brooke's *Two sermons preached before the University of Cambridge* (1763), a quarto, was altered at press for the large paper copies, the change involving little more than changing the arrangement of the furniture on the bed of the press, and replacing the frisket: the press figures are the same in both the large and the ordinary paper issues. The two issues of the octavo prayer book, 1751, published on two qualities of paper, were likewise printed consecutively at the same presses. But the two issues of the duodecimo Bible of 1747, one price 2s. unbound and the other half a crown, though in fundamentally the same setting of type, have differently organised press figures: the implication is that the two differently priced issues were worked off independent one of the other, probably because of the long press-runs involved.

In one crucial respect, however, the University Press seems to have been at a disadvantage. There is no firm evidence that there had ever been a rolling-press at the University Press for more than a very brief period.[55] Encouraged not by the need for books, but for separate engravings and etchings, Sarah James, owner of the *Cambridge Journal and Weekly Flying-Post*, and others in Cambridge, offered the means to print from copper-plates, on a rolling-press. Despite the existence of such facilities so near to Bentham's own premises, nothing has been discovered to suggest that Bentham ever used them. Perhaps it was to Sarah James, too, that amateur artists among undergraduates and recent graduates from the late 1740s onwards turned for pulls of their imitations after Rembrandt, portraits of Cambridge figures, and local landscapes. The books published at Cambridge in these years seem to have been little affected; but by February 1757 William Davenport, journeyman to Thomas James, had established a rolling-press at the Green Dragon in Walls Lane (modern King Street), where he offered 'all manner of Copper Plate printing, as neat and cheap as in London'.[56]

The trade in engravings, so closely allied to that in books in some respects, was quite separate in others, and the printing of engravings required quite different skills: journeymen were said to be able to earn 30s. a week, or even (if they were exceptional) half a guinea a day, compared with a compositor or pressman who might earn 1 guinea a week.[57] Instead, any engraved illustrations had to be printed in London, usually after the text had beeen printed in Cambridge if the page to be printed was part of a sheet also bearing text. Engraved frontispieces, printed on separate leaves, such as Grignion's engraving after Francis Hayman at the front of the 1762 quarto Bible, or the two maps inserted into copies of the Welsh Bible published in 1746, were thus more economical to print, since the weight of paper to be transported was so much less. But for engraved ornaments on title-pages, or engraved headpieces, there was no alternative to moving printed sheets from and to Cambridge. The volumes of university verses prepared for the marriage of the King in 1761, the birth of the Prince of Wales in 1762, and the peace in 1763 were all decorated with the same engraved plates: a vignette on the title-page by P. S. Lamborn depicting King's College chapel and the University buildings, and a plate of the royal arms at the head of the dedication. These were printed in London by one of the members of the Ryland family, who was presumably also responsible for printing other engravings for the Cambridge press. After 600 copies of the 1761 verses had been printed, Lamborn and another man named Stevens were paid to touch up these plates in 1762, when 500 more pulls were taken; by 1763 the plates were looking distinctly worn when they were used in what proved to be the last volume of its kind.[58]

By 1757, insurance on the Press's property (including goods stored in the warehouse over the printing office and in a second warehouse opposite) had to be raised from £2,000 to £2,500.[59] Three years later, it was thought desirable to increase the insurance further still, the equipment of the printing house now being valued for the purpose at £700, other goods (presumably principally paper) at £1,500, and goods in warehouses, including one in Black Lion Yard, at £800.[60] A yet further revaluation eighteen months later caused the Syndics to order that the 'utensils' in the printing house should be insured for £700, the 'goods' in the printing house and in the warehouse above it for £1,500, the further 'goods' in the warehouse opposite for £400, and that a second policy should be taken out for the 'utensils in the new Printing house in Silver Street, late the White Lyon', valued at £100, together with goods there valued at £600.[61]

The move across to the south side of Silver Street, first (by June 1760) to a warehouse in Black Lion Yard opposite the end of Queens' Lane, and then, by November 1761, to a branch of the printing house itself, established in the former White Lion, did not in itself mark a sudden expansion of the Press's business. As we have seen, there had been thought of moving the Press to a building opposite the Senate House since the early 1720s, and the need for better accommodation had been publicly acknowledged in 1738.[62] But the completion of the new east front of the University Library, and the decision *ex silentio* not to proceed with the southern building that would have housed the Press, were instrumental in the University's taking steps, by now long overdue, to find other space for printing and kindred activities.[63] The management of the Press had for too long been overshadowed not by the requirements of a business, but by the University's architectural ambitions, and its final abandoning of a project after almost forty years. The Press's acquisition of property on the south side of Silver Street marked the beginning of a sequence of expansion and relocation that was eventually to lead to the relinquishing of the site on the corner of Queens' Lane and Silver Street, and the establishment of the printing house on the site that it occupied until 1963. The White Lion was bought for £170 in 1762, and alterations were put in hand to convert it into a second printing house.[64] It was a poor substitute for the sentiment and topographical prominence once hoped for: a printing house in the same group of buildings as the University Library, offices, church and Senate House, one whose central importance to the University's activities and perception of its interests would have thereby been unmistakably emphasised. But converted inn buildings, instead of new ones by Gibbs or Wright, could be made to serve their everyday purpose.

The local architect and contractor James Essex undertook most of the work, charging *inter alia* for putting up drying poles as early as November 1761, which suggests that the new premises were already in use as a warehouse by that time. By May 1762 he was 'fixing' a press (that is, anchoring it by stanchions to the floor and ceiling, so that it would remain stable and take the strain of impressions). A frame for compositors was charged for in the same month. A new press was installed in June, when it was also discovered that the floor had to be strengthened; and yet another press was moved from across the road at the end of the month. Further items in his account in August referred to the new press, and to alterations to another; it seems that by the late summer there were three presses in working order.[65]

All this activity was not only to meet the need for Bibles and prayer books. There is some evidence to suggest that from the first it was intended that the new premises should be used for printing the law books that Bathurst and the Press so ardently desired to develop.[66] In 1742 Bathurst had issued an edition, printed by Bentham, of the excise laws on beer and other liquors. Printer and publisher were met by an injunction brought against them by the King's Printers, who considered their privilege to have been infringed. The ensuing legal wranglings were not resolved until 1758, when the Court of King's Bench found that the University possessed a concurrent authority with the King's Printers, a decision based on the same letters patent of Henry VIII that had proved the University's bulwark in the past.[67] But once resolved, the University and Bathurst were at liberty to proceed with plans to print not just a selection, but a complete new edition of the Statutes, to be edited by Danby Pickering, a London barrister known for his editorial skills.[68] Proposals were issued in 1761, and the first volumes appeared in 1763, in an edition of 1,250 copies.[69] It was an ambitious undertaking, for which the new premises were essential, and for a few years the buildings on the south side of Silver Street, 'small, but handy' in the words of one visitor from London accustomed to more spacious premises, became known as the law printing house.[70]

However, while the University had won its point, the projected edition was not the success that Bathurst and his allies in Cambridge had hoped. Like Baskerville, Bathurst had to pay the University for the privilege to publish the Statutes, the fee being 3s.9d. per sheet, additional to printing charges of £1.19s.6d. per sheet,[71] plus the cost of paper and, as usual, the cost of transport from and to London. When he had embarked on the project in March 1741/2, the edition of the excise laws had been but one part of the larger scheme for Bathurst to act as the Press's London agent, for which it had been agreed that he should be allowed 14 per cent profit.[72] But while the lawsuit had dragged on, circumstances had changed; Bathurst parted company with the University as its agent; and by 1763 he had little more claim on the University for special treatment than had Baskerville. The project was in effect brought to an end in May 1766, as the Syndics reviewed the Press in the light of Bentham's illness. At the same meeting that ordered that the executors of John Taylor should be charged for warehousing unsold stock of his books, the Syndics showed themselves in similarly determined mood in ordering that no further volumes of the statutes should be printed without further instructions.[73]

When Bentham was appointed in 1740, he inherited reforms that had already been put partly in place. New equipment had been purchased, and major new projects begun. Most of them were the suggestions of just those same energetic Syndics who had been charged with investigating the Press's affairs: part of their remedy was actually to provide new work. John Taylor, who had continued to catalogue John Moore's vast collection of books in the University Library after he had been appointed University Registrary in 1734, was instructed in May 1738 'to finish it with all possible expedition' and there was even talk of publishing a catalogue.[74] So large a project would have brought welcome work to the Press. Taylor's own quarto edition of Lysias, for which he had issued proposals in 1732, was printed not by the Cambridge press but by William Bowyer, in London: 'I am glad Mr. Taylor is got into your press: it will make his Lysias more correct', wrote one of Bowyer's correspondents.[75] But Taylor's subsequent work came to Cambridge, beginning with an octavo Lysias approved by the Syndics of the Press (including Taylor himself) in December 1739 and published in 1740.[76] In 1739 he also issued proposals for his more ambitious project, an edition of Demosthenes to be published in three volumes, in quarto. For this, the paragon Greek obtained in 1699 still served for the main text, to magnificent effect; but it was accompanied by Caslon's noticeably less heavily ligatured long primer and English, ordered by the Syndics in 1738–9.[77] Other substantial books approved during these months as the future of the Press was under review included Nicholas Saunderson's quarto *Elements of algebra*, published also in 1740,[78] and Richardson's own folio edition, much expanded, of Francis Godwin *De praesulibus Angliae*, published in 1743.[79]

For a London bookseller, to print in Cambridge was potentially more expensive than to print in London, especially if most copies were to be sold in the capital, or via the London trade. The cost of transporting paper, already referred to,[80] was a major factor;

but there were other inconveniences and charges as well, such as the need to print engravings in London, or the need for travel back and forth for consultation: those responsible for the SPCK were not alone in their anxiety to keep in touch with their printer.[81] Though the Oxford press was not strictly comparable in the mid-eighteenth century, being differently equipped and enjoying established and straightforward connections with London for heavy traffic by the River Thames, the differences between Oxford and London occupied William Blackstone as they occupied the Cambridge authorities when they found themselves in competition with others. Blackstone considered Oxford prices 'a Matter of Complaint'. 'For Instance we pay 17^s 6^d per Sheet for Printing an 8vo. in English-siz'd Letter, No. 500, usually done in London at 15^s per Sheet, without Notes.'[82] At that rate, Cambridge was at first glance slightly cheaper than Oxford, though it must be stressed that such elementary comparisons may be seriously misleading. In practice, Bentham seems to have made little or no allowance in attempting to entice London booksellers to his door. His prices for printing were comparable, and often identical, with those charged in the major London houses. But although there is some evidence to suggest that his prices rose, like the cost of paper, in the middle years of the century, there is none to suggest that he was seriously affected by the labour unrest among compositors in 1748 that obliged some London printers to dismiss their staff.[83] Most of the work for which charges are recorded was for Thurlbourn, the local bookseller, who frequently acted in concord with London stationers. However, since nothing is known of the financial details of Thurlbourn's business, it may be that differences in cost between London and the country were hidden in his own shares, profits and losses.

When the Syndics accepted a book to be printed by Bentham, they also agreed the price of the work. For a period in 1741–2, the customer (Thurlbourn) signified his agreement by signing the figures with the Syndics, though this rapidly went out of practice. Not all books printed by Bentham in the 1740s and 1750s were included in the Syndics' record, but the costs noted at this time offer the essentials of his cost structure. It was divided between composition, correction, presswork and a profit or overheads cost intended for the University. Since paper was the customer's responsibility, little evidence remains of this save when the University itself was customer in, for example, books of congratulatory or mourning verses.

Composition charges were fundamental. They related not to the format, but to the size, or sizes, of type (fig. 11) in relation to the format: to the amount of setting per sheet. Thus a lay-out with ample interlinear spacing, or short lines, could appear to be cheap in the accounts. Conversely, a lay-out with longer than average lines, and more lines on the page than average, would cost more, a feature that Oxford compositors seem to have claimed in their favour.[84] Correction charges were set according to the formula usually employed in London, at one-sixth the charge of composition.[85] The charges for presswork varied with each job, in ways that are not always easy to follow, but again these charges were close to those customary in London. The supposed University profit was regularly calculated at 50 per cent of the charges thus accumulated, again according to a formula familiar in London.[86]

Though much of this was formulaic, in practice there was considerable room for manoeuvre, both in charges for composition and in charges for presswork. Each book had to be taken on its own terms. As Samuel Richardson remarked when asked as a London printer to comment on a series of complicated calculations by Blackstone respecting the charges that should be properly applied at the Oxford press, he had 'generally fixed . . . Prices by Practice, by Example, by Custom, and by Inspection'.[87] In this way, and perhaps fearing some difficulty from one of their number, John Taylor, the Cambridge Syndics (still, at this time, called curators) agreed on Christmas Eve 1741 'that for extraordinary alterations in Composition, the Author &c be charged, for ye Use of ye University, one fourth of what is p^d the Compositor for such alterations'.[88] Taylor's specimen of his edition of Demosthenes was published within a few weeks of this meeting, and its address to the reader was warning enough to the printer. Quite apart from editorial improvements, Taylor remarked, 'To this let me subioyn the Typographical Correctness of what is here offered, the Beauty of the Character, and the Uniformity of the Pages. Great care has been taken to maintain a consonance of Printing and Pointing (as far as the Nature of the two Languages would admit of it) in Text and Translation.'[89] In 1748, he was rewarded when the first volume to appear of his (now) projected five reached the hands of a reviewer.

> A tant d'avantages qui distinguent cette Edition des précédentes, il faut joindre la beauté du papier & du caractère & surtout l'exactitude de l'impression.[90]

The records of costs in the University Press reveal an overall evenness within a context of many slight variations.[91] Composition charges per sheet depended on the number of ens to be set, and thus to a great extent on type size and on whether or not there were notes. These distinctions were clearly laid out in the costs established in 1741 for the printing of Taylor's quarto Demosthenes, of which a substantial specimen was printed in that year. The main Greek text, in paragon (fig. 25a, p. 290), was to be charged at 10s. a sheet; the notes, in small pica, at 18s.; and the scholia (not included in the specimen of 1741), at £1. Once the costs of correcting, printing and the University's share had been taken into account, the respective costs per sheet were £1.2s.7d., £1.15s.3d. and £1.18s.5d.[92] Quarto or octavo books set in English (the type size most used for bookwork at the Press at this time) tended to cost about 6s. a sheet in the 1740s, or 10s. or 10s.6d. with notes in a smaller size such as long primer.[93] There were many exceptions. The setting of Zachary Brooke's *Defensio miraculorum*, a quarto published in 1748, with footnotes, was charged at 9s. a sheet, while some books were charged in half sheets, such as two octavos both published in 1750: John Michell's *Treatise of artificial magnets*, in English, at 3s.6d., and Zachary Grey's anonymous *Chronological and historical account of . . . earthquakes*, in English and long primer, at 4s., were at the same rate as Rutherforth's *Defence of the Lord Bishop of London's Discourses*, an octavo set in English and published the same year. William Barford's *In Pindari Primum Pythium dissertatio*, a quarto printed in half-sheets (1751), was in the same size type as a visitation sermon by Rutherforth, also in quarto, and published in the same year; but it was charged at 4s.6d., the equivalent of 9s. a sheet, compared with 5s.6d. for the

DOUBLE PICA ROMAN.

Quoufque tandem abutere, Catilina, patientia noſtra? quamdiu nos etiam furor iſte tuus eludet? quem ad finem ſeſe effrenata jac-

ABCDEFGHJIKLMNOP

GREAT PRIMER ROMAN.

Quoufque tandem abutêre, Catilina, patientia noſtra? quamdiu nos etiam furor iſte tuus eludet? quem ad finem ſeſe effrenata jactabit audacia? nihilne te nocturnum præſidium palatii, nihil urbis vigiliæ, nihil timor populi, nihil con-

ABCDEFGHIJKLMNOPQRS

ENGLISH ROMAN.

Quoufque tandem abutêre, Catilina, patientia noſtra? quamdiu nos etiam furor iſte tuus eludet? quem ad finem ſeſe effrenata jactabit audacia? nihilne te nocturnum præſidium palatii, nihil urbis vigiliæ, nihil timor populi, nihil conſenſus bonorum omnium, nihil hic munitiſſimus

ABCDEFGHIJKLMNOPQRSTVUW

PICA ROMAN.

Melium, novis rebus ſtudentem, manu ſua occidit. Fuit, fuit iſta quondam in hac repub. virtus, ut viri fortes acrioribus ſuppliciis civem perniciofum, quam acerbiſſimum hoſtem coërcerent. Habemus enim ſenatuſconfultum in te, Catilina, vehemens, & grave: non deeſt reip. confilium, neque autoritas hujus ordinis: nos, nos, dico aperte, confules defumus. De-

ABCDEFGHIJKLMNOPQRSTVUWX

Fig. 11 Specimens of type, shown approximately actual size, cast by William Caslon in the mid-eighteenth century. These were the most common sizes used in books.

SMALL PICA ROMAN. No 1.

At nos vigeſimum jam diem patimur hebeſcere aciem horum autoritatis. habemus enim hujuſmodi ſenatuſconſultum, verumtamen incluſum in tabulis, tanquam gladium in vagina reconditum: quo ex ſenatuſconſulto confeſtim interfectum te eſſe, Catilina, convenit. Vivis: & vivis non ad deponendam, ſed ad confirmandam audaciam. Cupio, P. C., me eſſe clementem: cupio in tantis reipub. periculis non diſ-
ABCDEFGHIJKLMNOPQRSTVUWXYZ

LONG PRIMER ROMAN No 1.

Verum ego hoc, quod jampridem factum eſſe oportuit, certa de cauſſa nondum adducor ut faciam. tum denique interficiam te, cum jam nemo tam improbus, tam perditus, tam tui ſimilis inveniri poterit, qui id non jure factum eſſe fateatur. Quamdiu quiſquam erit qui te defendere audeat, vives: & vives, ita ut nunc vivis, multis meis & firmis præſidiis obſeſſus, ne commovere te contra rempub. poſſis. multorum te etiam oculi & aures non ſentientem, ſicut adhuc fecerunt, ſpeculabuntur, atque cuſtodient. Etenim quid eſt, Cati-
ABCDEFGHIJKLMNOPQRSTUVWXYZÆ

BREVIER ROMAN.

Novemb. C. Manlium audaciæ ſatellitem atque adminiſtrum tuæ? num me fefellit, Catilina, non modo res tanta, tam atrox, tam incredibilis, verum, id quod multo magis eſt admirandum, dies? Dixi ego idem in ſenatu, cædem te optimatum contuliſſe in ante diem v Kalend. Novemb. tum cum multi principes civitatis Rom. non tam ſui conſervandi, quam tuorum conſiliorum reprimendorum cauſſa profugerunt. num inficiari potes, te illo ipſo die meis præſidiis, mea diligentia circumcluſum, commovere te contra rempub. nôn potuiſſe; cum tu diſceſſu ceterorum, noſtra tamen, qui remanſiſſemus, cæde contentum te eſſe dicebas? Quid? cum te
ABCDEFGHIJKLMNOPQRSTVUWXYZÆ

Nonpareil Roman.

O dii immortales! ubi-nam gentium ſumus? quam rempub. habemus? in qua urbe vivimus? hic, hic ſunt in noſtro numero, P. C., in hoc orbis terræ ſanctiſſimo graviſſimoque conſilio, qui de meo, noſtrumque omnium interitu, qui de hujus urbis, atque adeo orbis terrarum exitio cogitent. hoſce ego video conſul, & de republica ſententiam rogo: & quos ferro trucidari oportebat, eos nondum voce vulnero. Fuiſti igitur apud Leccam ea nocte, Catilina: diſtribuiſti partes Italiæ: ſtatuiſti quo quemque proficiſci placeret: delegiſti quos Romæ relinqueres, quos tecum educeres: deſcripſiſti urbis partes ad incendia: confirmaſti, te ipſum jam eſſe exiturum: dixiſti paululum tibi eſſe etiam tum moræ, quod ego viverem. Reperti ſunt duo equites Romani, qui te iſta cura liberarent, & ſeſe illa ipſa nocte paulo ante lucem me in meo, lectulo interfecturos pollicerentur. Hæc ego omnia, vix dum etiam cœtu veſtro dimiſſo, comperi: domum meam
ABCDEFGHIKLMNOPQRSTVUWXYZÆ

Pearl Roman.

O dii immortales! ubi-nam gentium ſumus? quam rempub. habemus? in qua urbe vivimus? hic, hic ſunt in noſtro numero, P. C., in hoc orbis terræ ſanctiſſimo graviſſimoque conſilio, qui de meo, noſtrumque omnium interitu, qui de hujus urbis, atque adeo orbis terrarum exitio cogitent. hoſce ego video conſul, & de republica ſententiam rogo: & quos ferro trucidari oportebat, eos nondum voce vulnero. Fu-

Pearl Italick.

O dii Immortales! ubi-nam gentium ſumus? quam rempub. habemus? in qua urbe vivimus? hic, hic ſunt in noſtro numero, P. C., in hoc orbis terræ ſanctiſſima graviſſimoque conſilio, qui de meo, noſtrumque omnium interitu, qui de hujus urbis, atque adeo orbis terrarum exitio cogitent. hoſce ego video conſul, & de republica ſententiam rogo: & quos ferro trucidari oportebat, eos nondum voce vulnero. Fuiſt

sermon: the setting of extended quotations in Greek must be presumed to have added to the costs on this occasion. In general, smaller type cost more, and larger less. Well spaced pages, involving less type-setting, similarly cost less, and the extra complication of setting William Green's translation of the song of Deborah (1753), with the original Hebrew and a commentary, was thus offset by generous white space, resulting in a charge of 8s. a sheet.

Thus the cost of poetry could be noticeably lower. The first volume of Grey's

Hudibras, at 10s.6d. a sheet, was comparable with other ordinary books in prose, since although the text was in English, there were many footnotes: it was 6d. a sheet dearer than another octavo of the same time, the fourth edition of Davies's edition of Cicero, *De natura deorum*, set solid in English and with double-column footnotes in long primer. But the quarto edition, 1746, of Smart's Latin translation of Pope's 'Ode on St Cecilia's Day',[94] published with his own ode for the same festival, set in double pica with interlinear spacing, cost 5s. a sheet, the same as Joseph Beaumont's *Original poems* (1749), equally generously spaced, set in great primer and with a long introduction in a larger size.

The printing of Christopher Smart's successive exercises in 1750–55 that repeatedly won him the Seatonian prize, first awarded in 1750, was charged, as in other years and by the terms of Seaton's will, to the University.[95] Editions were of 500 copies, including 50 or 75 on large paper. The poems were set according to a style that remained very little changed: quarto, in double pica. This standard work reveals a gradual increase in price from year to year, between 12s.3d. in 1750, 1751 and 1752; 12s.6d. in 1754; and 14s. in 1756.[96] In some years there were extra charges for correction, suggesting last-minute thoughts on Smart's part.[97]

The University verses were set in great primer, a smaller size of type than the Seatonian poems; but they were printed in folio, as they had been since 1697. Between 1748 and 1763 (the date of what was to prove to be the last of this series with a pedigree stretching back to the sixteenth century) the basic cost of printing rose from 10s.6d. per sheet to over 13s. Both in 1762 and 1763 (the dates of the bills were only five months apart) the cost was 11s.7½d. a sheet, and in 1761 it reached 13s.1½d. – curiously precise figures, unparalleled in the charges levelled for ordinary books. Here, the extra costs of correction, inseparable from the need to compose these books of topical moment, remained endemic, and the bills to the University repeatedly included special charges. In 1755, the cost of 'extraordinary work' on the verses and the Orator's speech to mark the opening of the new buildings for the University Library added approximately 15 per cent to the cost of composition and printing. Reprinted sheets and cancelled leaves added to the complications of printing, while the bill for the volume of 1755 includes money paid 'for Meat & Drink for men Working in the Night'.

In both the bills for the Seatonian poems and in those for the University verses, further elements in the price structure may be perceived. First and largest was the cost of paper. The edition sizes of these volumes were not large (500 in the case of Smart), but paper costs still exceeded the cost of printing by 25 per cent and more. The same was true to an even larger extent of the University verses, printed in editions varying from 250 (for the University Library verses addressed to the Chancellor, the Duke of Newcastle, in 1755) to 600. The price of 12s.6d. a ream for ordinary crown in 1748 was never again so low, and by the early 1760s the University was paying £1.15s. a ream for good quality fine writing demy, ordinary copies being printed on second quality writing demy, at 18s. As a result, paper costs were as much as double the basic cost of printing.

Smaller sums had to be found for printing off title-pages as advertisements, and sticking them up or otherwise distributing them. In the case of the University verses, engraved ornaments had to be prepared and printed. Gribelin's device, employed on the title-page of the 1748 verses, was printed by Edward Ryland, in London; and Ryland also printed Lamborn's new engraving of the Schools, Senate House and King's College Chapel, as well as the royal arms at the head of the dedications, for the 1761 volume marking the marriage of George III, that of 1762 marking the birth of the Prince of Wales and that of 1763 celebrating peace. The cost of the engravings was not separately recorded, but as printing and carriage for the two plates cost well under one pound for slightly smaller editions in 1762 and 1763, it seems that the materials, design and engraving cost about £8 apiece.[98] Once bought, the plates could be used again for other jobs, but only if they were touched up from time to time. The plates of 1761 had to be touched up by Lamborn and another local engraver, William Stevens,[99] in order for them to be used the following year – not surprisingly after 600 impressions. Binders' bills were separate; and while the bindings on the Seatonian poems were generally minimal, many copies of the University verses, intended for presentation to the royal family or to political or ecclesiastical dignitaries, required more lavish expenditure. The University employed the aged Henry Crow, one of the less accomplished local binders, for the Seatonian poems, and most were issued simply stitched up or in marbled paper wrappers.[100] But the University verses, issued in a variety of bindings including some of velvet, commanded work of a much superior quality, especially those of goatskin finished by Edwin Moor.[101]

Presswork was usually charged, as in London,[102] at 2s.4d. for 500 sheets, regardless of format (most work was in octavo, quarto or folio). But, again, there were exceptions, and it is sometimes difficult to know whether these were the result of error or policy. An edition of an account by Richard Allyn, of Corpus Christi College, Oxford, of his naval experiences, *A narrative of the victory obtained by the English and Dutch fleet, over that of France, near La-Hogue, in the year 1692*, printed for a London bookseller in 1744 and with no acknowledgement on it of Bentham as printer, was charged at only 1s.4d.[103] Parts of tokens (a token being 250 sheets) were usually charged as a whole, so that 350 or 400 were charged as 500. For printing, as for composition, Bentham exercised a measure of discretion, and (with the agreement of the Syndics, who constitutionally controlled the prices) applied varying charges within a context of a normal regularity. There is no evidence that he applied a fixed scale of rates, such as that established at Oxford in 1758,[104] or that he varied much from ordinary trade practice. But by the end of the 1740s there is some evidence to suggest that prices were beginning to increase, and that the rate of 2s.4d. was no longer being applied so regularly. John Ross's octavo edition of Cicero's *Epistolae ad familiares* (1749), of which 500 copies were printed on demy paper and 50 on royal, was charged at 4s.6d. for the 550. Masters's history of Corpus Christi College (4°, 1753) was charged at 3s.4d. for 450 copies on demy and 50 on royal, and by the mid-1750s a charge of 2s.6d. for 500 had become normal. In other words, costs of materials and charges for labour both increased in the mid-century; and though the University had little control over the cost of paper, it reaped a modest reward in that the profit charged to each job was calculated wholly as a proportion of the price of labour.

The last pages have been concerned with the equipment, premises and men with whom Bentham worked. They have concentrated on some of the ways in which reform was approached, and achieved. It remains in the next chapters to examine the place of authors, and to show how the greatest change of all was achieved: the printing of Bibles and prayer books on an immense scale. It also remains to determine the extent of the Press's success with these books.

☙ 7 ☙

Booksellers and authors

To most of its authors, the University Press was more important as a printer than as a publisher. Hence the question of payment by, rather than to, the Press did not arise. Traditionally, the reward for the kind of books with which University Printers were most concerned was composed partly of a number of authors' copies, for presentation or for further sale, but more importantly of an increased reputation. Authors publishing their own work, or at least paying for all or some of the printing costs, could not in any event expect a reward as authors either from the Press or from the booksellers. In the eighteenth century, as payments to authors by booksellers became more common, the question could not escape Cambridge; but it could be, and was, ignored. Rewards for writing remained elusive, and the debate was not finally brought into open discussion until long into the nineteenth century.[1] The following chapter is concerned with the position of authors in Cambridge as they saw a world of bookselling and publication defined ever more by monetary values.

In the mid-eighteenth century, Cambridge was dominated by two booksellers. Since 1729, the shop at 1 Trinity Street had been occupied by William Thurlbourn, in succession to Edmund Jeffery. In the early 1730s, Thurlbourn steadily expanded his business, engaging both Crownfield and William Fenner as printers until in 1735 his name appeared on the title-pages of both Bentley's Boyle lectures and his adversary Middleton on the history of printing in England, as well as works by Thomas Johnson, Fellow of Magdalene, who had been with him since 1732 and was one of the editors of Stephanus' Latin *Thesaurus*. From 1741, Thurlbourn also began to issue catalogues of auction sales. In autumn 1756 he entered into partnership with John Woodyer. With Woodyer's brother William they extended the premises, taking in 2 Trinity Street in 1757. The Woodyer and Thurlbourn partnership remained until Thurlbourn's death in 1768.[2] Thomas Merrill, later joined by John Merrill, was to be found in Regent Walk, until their shop was demolished in 1769 to make way for the new Senate House. They too were thus at the very centre of the University. The Merrills subsequently took number 3 Trinity Street. Thomas died in 1781,[3] and the firm was then run by John and Joseph Merrill. Further south, on the west side of Trumpington Street (now King's Parade), and beside the old Provost's lodgings of King's, Robert Watts had opened the first circulating library in Cambridge in the mid-1740s. Following his death in February 1751/2, his daughter married John Nicholson, from Leicestershire, the most familiar of all Cambridge booksellers.[4] Of the other firms in the mid-eighteenth century, and apart from bookbinders such as Francis Hopkins who also dabbled in bookselling, Richard Matthews was established by the end of the 1750s. On his retirement in 1778 he was to be succeeded by John Deighton, who then for the present retained his premises in Great St Mary's Lane.[5]

Although Thurlbourn commissioned some books from the University Press in the expectation that he would sell most of the copies by retail, like other booksellers he expected to pass on stock, as a means of credit. In return he was able to gain wares from London. A catalogue of 1735 listed many books of which he had simply acquired stock – not only recent works such as Theobald's edition of Shakespeare (1733), but also older works such as the works of Joseph Bingham (1726) and of Richard Crossinge of Pembroke College on the duty of charity (1722), apart from Amsterdam editions of Cicero and Horace and either a Leipzig or Amsterdam edition of Faber's Latin Thesaurus.[6] Another catalogue, of 1741, listed twenty-nine books 'printed for' Thurlbourn in Cambridge, and John Beecroft in London: apart from books that bore their imprints, the list also contained several that had been published by others, and of which one or other man had acquired stock.[7]

The eighteenth-century imprint is frequently an imperfect guide to how a book was financed or distributed, as credit was exchanged and parcelled out in a web of inter-dependent booksellers. In 1745 yet another catalogue advertised books 'printed for J. and P. Knapton' in London, and Thurlbourn in Cambridge; but if the imprints of the books listed are evidence, the two firms had not collaborated in the publication of all the works mentioned.[8] This was not peculiar to Thurlbourn, or to country bookselling. It was the very foundation of the trade in books. According to one estimate, booksellers expected actually to sell only a minority of copies of an edition they had commissioned: 'and that two Thirds, if not three Fourths of those you [i.e. booksellers] put off are exchanged among yourselves for others, which would have no Sale at all, were they not thus push'd and dispersed abroad by the Members of your Society, whose particular interest it is so to render Copies that lie in Obscurity more universal'.[9] In Cambridge, the Merrills sometimes signified their interest in the informal way of adding a manuscript inscription to the foot of the title-page. 'Sold by T. (or T. and J.) Merrill' may thus be met with on copies of which the printed imprint made otherwise no mention of the firm.[10]

In Cambridge as elsewhere, the press depended on the goodwill of authors. Whether in London or in smaller centres, the fragile relationship between the two parties, mediated by the booksellers or publishers, assumed a willingness on the part of authors either to write, or, having written, to revise, make fair copies and finally submit their work to be printed. In many respects those who wrote in Cambridge were unusual. Few of them wrote (at least obviously) at the behest of political party; few of them could expect financial reward from their booksellers, whether as hired hacks or as established literary figures; as clergy, many of them saw their sermons into print almost as a matter of duty. Most importantly, they had independent means of support.

The Fellow of a college, supported by his stipend and maintained (whether frugally or comfortably) by his foundation, who addressed himself to some question, or pursued his researches in the library, in antiquities, or in the natural world, was subsidised in ways that the increasing numbers of professional authors, especially in London, were not. As a result, many of the arguments about authorship and its rewards in the eighteenth century provoked very little interest in Cambridge. Some members of the University, and in particular Edmund Law,[11] studied the question of copyright closely. But though for many authors and booksellers alike this was the dominant issue in the book trade for almost three-quarters of a century, most authors – whether in Cambridge or not – were more immediately concerned with the conduct of the booksellers into whose hands they delivered up their manuscripts. Booksellers were to be viewed with anxiety, and often with jealousy at their seeming or real meanness. In this at least, there was common ground between authors in the university, and authors elsewhere. 'In much wisdom is much grief: and he that increaseth knowledge increaseth sorrow.' The relevance of Ecclesiastes was not lost on authors in eighteenth-century Cambridge, though few pursued the text with such jaundiced persistence as John Edwards, Fellow of St John's College, who at his death in 1716 left much of his life's work unpublished.[12]

'No man but a blockhead ever wrote, except for money.'[13] Samuel Johnson's opinion, delivered in 1776, was that of one who well knew the London book trade: it is not clear whether at this point he thought also of his acquaintances in Cambridge or Oxford. For authors in the universities there was usually little choice. Authors in eighteenth-century Cambridge could not ordinarily expect great financial rewards. The Copyright Act of 1710 had emphasised the interests of authors, establishing a term to copyrights and, to some degree, also identifying an author's writing as a property. However, most of the books written in Cambridge during the next half century could command little interest for the sake of their copyrights. Bentley, exceptional as so often, received 100 guineas for his revisions to Milton; but that was from Tonson, in London.[14] One of the few to receive a fee from the University Press in Cambridge was Ludolph Kuster, who was paid £200 for his work on the *Suidas,* and allowed eight copies on ordinary paper and four on large.[15] Forty or so years later, F. S. Parris was paid a fee of £40 for his work on the text of the Bible. Both were editing tasks, and both were for books in which the Press had an interest as publisher. But in the main the Press existed to print, not to publish, and so it could have no interest in the rewards of authorship – either financial or in critical or social renown.

With the means to hand to print in Cambridge, and with a local bookselling trade that was increasingly willing to invest in the cost of publication, authors in Cambridge had by the middle of the eighteenth century a context in which choice was possible: between publication in Cambridge or London, printing either in Cambridge or London, or some other form of publication such as subscription. Until this time, and thanks principally to the less capacious nature of the University's press, as well as to the lack of capital among local booksellers and to their weak links with their London equivalents, this choice was not so obvious. Conyers Middleton, Fellow of Trinity

College and as an author versed both in the London trade and in the University Press, phrased his quandary explicitly when in 1738 he was pondering how his forthcoming life of Cicero should be brought to birth. By this stage (the work was not to be published until 1741) he had determined on publishing by subscription.

> I begin to think of printing at this Place [Cambridge], where it will be most convenient to me, and where we have a Syndicate on Foot to regulate the Press, and bring it again into Credit and Order; and my neighbour *Thurlborn*, whom I am dispos'd also to oblige, has been making Proposals to me. But I shall not think of taking any Resolution, till I can compute the Size and Charge of printing my Work, and see a little forward into the List of Subscribers; as far as I can guess at present, it will make a large Volume in 4to, which being handsomely printed may demand a Guinea for the Subscription Price.[16]

The reform of the University Press under Richardson may have offered a strong inducement; but in the end Middleton turned to the London printer James Bettenham. His decision to publish by subscription was to be expected, and it was a course commonly followed in Cambridge at a time when it had found widespread national popularity.[17] For some books, such as Masters's history of Corpus Christi College (1753), for which proposals were issued in January 1749/50,[18] or, in different vein, a monograph on *The scripture-doctrine of the existence and attributes of God* (1750) by Thomas Knowles, Fellow of Pembroke College and rector of Ickworth in Suffolk, there was an obvious and easily identifiable audience. Knowles was also chaplain to Lady Hervey, and her support is to be seen plainly in the social backgrounds of the subscribers who mingled with the local clergy and gentry in a gathering that had unusually few names of individuals or libraries from Cambridge itself. Overall, the small, tight-knit educated population in and around Cambridge, or linked by a national network of family and informal connections across the country, was ideal for subscription publication. When in 1747 Thomas Rutherforth prepared to publish his lectures given in St John's College as *A system of natural philosophy*, he found bodies of subscribers in Cambridge, Oxford, south-east England (especially Kent), Wales and the north of England, as well as in Holland. Of the 1,250 copies printed,[19] only about 100 were left for sale, once subscribers had been supplied and Rutherforth had his own copies to give away. The imprint, 'for W. Thurlbourn . . . Cambridge . . . and sold by J. Beecroft . . . London' suggests a larger involvement in the book's financing than can have been the case.

Publication by subscription could be beset by difficulties.[20] By no means everyone necessarily wished to be included in a printed list,[21] yet success depended on a network of friends willing to promote the project and to gather subscriptions. For Middleton and Knowles, the connections with the Herveys were essential. Subscriptions for Zachary Grey's annotated edition of *Hudibras*, of which Bentham printed the first volume in 1744, were promoted by, among others, Edmund Law (then Archdeacon of Carlisle) in Carlisle and Conyers Middleton in London.[22] Copies of the prospectus, when they arrived in New England, were thought to be too late to be of effect, but Timothy Cutler, rector of Christ Church, Boston, promised to encourage interest as much as he could.[23] For books of a predetermined length, it was a comparatively easy matter to establish the manufacturing cost, and therefore the price to be asked of sub-scribers. But some kinds of books were less straightforward. In 1732, John Taylor's proposals for his editon of Lysias, to be printed by Bowyer, announced that it would 'by moderate computation, contain above 70 sheets': the price was to be 12s., or 18s. for copies on large paper.[24] In the end it contained 105¾ sheets (charged as 107), and Taylor was responsible for meeting the difference in cost. By the time the book came to press, it had also been decided to print copies on not two, but three sizes of paper, including 25 on writing royal.[25] Disappointments always lurked in wait. Even by publishing by subscription, in such a way as to suggest that the author would have control over the book's appearance, Taylor found himself dissatisfied at the unequal disposition of his notes across the openings.[26] Typographically, his unfinished edition of Demosthenes, printed by Bentham at Cambridge, brought him more satisfaction.

James Bentham's *History and antiquities of the conventual and cathedral church of Ely* was published only in 1771, after his brother's retirement. It was one of the last books on which Joseph Bentham had worked. Preparations for it had begun in the early 1750s. In September 1756 James Bentham had issued a *Catalogue of the principal members* of the cathedral clergy. Like a similar document prepared by Robert Masters for Corpus Christi College a few years earlier, the pamphlet was part information, part an appeal for help in historical enquiry, and part a preliminary appeal for subscriptions. In par-ticular, Bentham's plans for a heavily illustrated book required 'publick-spirited Lovers of Antiquity' who would be prepared to meet the cost of preparing and printing the various plates, in return for the addition of their names beneath the pictures. He expected about forty plates in all. It was a straightforward scheme, and having issued his pamphlet Bentham began to write to possible contributors – some, such as William Stukeley, more for the sake of obtaining or checking information, others, such as members of the families whose ancestors' monuments were to figure, sometimes wholly unknown. Old, half-forgotten acquaintances were approached, and packets of the pamphlet were sent to Oxford, London and elsewhere to be distributed to best advantage.[27]

The challenges were both financial and practical. Bentham spoke with feeling of the difference between arranging a series of illustrations in London, where there were suit-able artists in plenty, and doing the same in Cambridgeshire, where the only available person – and he not always – was a portrait painter, Heins.[28] Since most custom, and most work, was in London, there were few trained engravers or woodblock cutters in the country.[29] For an engraver, he turned to Peter Spendelowe Lamborn, a native of Cambridge and trained in London under Isaac Basire before he had returned to Cambridge by the winter of 1756–7 and began work on the first of Bentham's plates.[30] These limitations inevitably delayed publication of a book that depended on the accu-racy of its illustrations, quite apart from the need to raise money to meet production costs. But the speed was set more by the author than by Lamborn. Bentham worked deliberately and slowly, sharing his antiquarian enthusiasms in Cambridge with William Cole and with Thomas Gray.[31] 'He is one of the slowest of mortals', Cole later commented to Horace Walpole.[32] Though Bentham told expectant booksellers that he hoped to see the beginning of printing the book in January 1763, very little had been achieved two years later.[33] 'Are we never to have the history of that cathedral?', Walpole asked William Cole in 1769.[34] Its eventual appearance in June 1771, delayed even at the last minute only partly by the death of the Bishop,[35] fully vindicated Bentham's care. At £1.11s.6d. for a large quarto volume containing forty-eight plates, many of them folding out, it was remarkably cheap. As for the content, it was immediately realised that Bentham had achieved his ambition: to write not simply about the history of the cathedral and those who had served it, but also to make an original contribution to the hitherto neglected history of gothic architecture in England.[36]

The cost of the illustrations had preoccupied Bentham in the early stages. By the time he could begin printing, he was able to expect widespread support. Robert Dodsley, Charles Bathurst, William Sandby and Benjamin Dod in London, William Chace in Norwich and Wilson in York all had to be kept abreast of developments.[37] But the engraved plates were paid for by individual patrons. The opening headpiece, of Augustine's reception in England, was the same plate as had been used in Richardson's edition of Godwin in 1743. Others cost more. Initially, the standard charge for the simple plates of monuments was 4½ guineas, including drawing, engraving and printing. This was later raised to 5 guineas.[38] But the so-called 'capital' plates, that is the folding illustrations principally of the architecture, cost 18 guineas.[39]

Bentham, Bowyer, Thurlbourn and the London booksellers involved in the Cambridge trade all depended on a network that was established on a social footing before it became an economic one. College loyalties or enmities, political party that had so firm a grip on patronage and on appointments to professorships, and the less formal links of friendship now recoverable principally through surviving correspondence, defined the manners whereby books were printed and published in Cambridge or for Cambridge authors. Manuscripts unsolicited in the sense that they came without introduction were few; and encouragement to undertake or complete work already begun came not from the Press – either Bentham alone or the Syndics as a body – but from individual application and patronage of sundry kinds.

Dedicatory epistles required of the author and dedicatee alike a mutual understanding of rhetorical procedure, in which personal relationships and public positions were linked in varying degrees. Richard Bentley's nephew Thomas dedicated his edition of Horace, printed by Crownfield in 1713, to Lord Harley, and resorted to language so inflated that it earned him a place in the *Dunciad*:

> Bentley his mouth with classic flatt'ry opes.[40]

Middleton's dedication of his life of Cicero to Lord Hervey became celebrated. But his comparisons with Scipio and Lelius, Polybius and Terence, were well understood – overseas as well as in Britain:

> Telle fut la manière dont ces illustres *Romains* furent mettre à profit des momens de loisir, qui sont aujourd'hui si fort à charge à presque toute la Noblesse. Ils se livroient au commerce savant des plus Beaux-Esprits, & des meilleurs Ecrivains de leur Siècle, & se perfectionnoient eux-mêmes dans l'étude, & dans le gout de Belles-Lettres, en dirigeant la

plume des autres. Qu'ils ont laissé peu d'imitateurs, & qu'il y a des Pais où les *Harvey* sont rares![41]

There was an increasing disparity between practices in Cambridge and those in some parts of the London trade, where authorship became more and more firmly established as a paid profession, whether in Grub Street, in political propaganda, or in literature more generally. So, too, in Cambridge the process of judging a book in manuscript was different, in that formal evaluations were made not by the publisher (be it the Syndics or even Thurlbourn or one of the other Cambridge booksellers) but by the author's acquaintance, those he consulted, or those whose intellectual, social or financial patronage he sought out. Much of this academic scholarly world remained a self-governing one, existing side by side with, though dependent on, the book trade. In some respects, it was akin to the great expansion in London of literature for the professions. But to generations that witnessed the increasing power of what would now be called the publisher's reader, this distinction between two different literary worlds was a defining one. In 1738 the practices in this respect of the London trade caused comment: 'of leaving an Author's Manuscript in the hands of a Bookseller, in order to be examin'd by a Person in whom he greatly confides':

> 'Tis true, Gentlemen, that it is your common *Plea*, that you are not sufficient Judges yourselves of the generality of Subjects, and therefore must consequently refer it to some proper Judges, on whose Opinion you can safely rely: But do you know, Gentlemen, that *it is even as difficult a thing to know Men, or their Knowledge, that is, to know a proper Judge, as it is to know Books*. And therefore it may probably prove as difficult a Task for you to find out a proper, knowing, and unbiass'd Person, carefully to examine and judge of such a Work, as it is for yourselves to form a Judgement; and oftentimes much more difficult, since a Person must be knowing to know a good Judge, and not depend on common Vogue, or Fame, a common Lyar.[42]

Whim, chance, envy or ignorance were but some of the dangers to which such a proceeding exposed manuscripts; and there was always a risk of intellectual theft by the referee. But much of the danger could be avoided, in this polemicist's view, by frankness and openness:

> I must own I have ever thought, that the plain and open Method is the fairest and best, and I should always most readily choose it myself, and recommend it to others. The bringing the Author and Examiner, Face to Face, I have known more than once to be attended with a good Effect; and I particularly remember, that a Copy of my own, in my younger Days, was referred to Mr. *Prior*, a Gentleman with whom I had never spoken before; who, having received me at his House, in the most obliging and polite Manner, over a Dish of Tea, pointed out to me some Faults, but with the utmost Candour; and tho' I doubt not he could have made many other Remarks, which he probably omitted, on Account of my being a Youth and an absolute Stranger; had he been never so frank and open, I could not have taken it amiss, being fully convinced of his Judgement as well as Integrity.[43]

Of those in Cambridge whose work was regularly published in London, Thomas Gray was one of the few to find a place as an author of general appeal. But the 40 guineas he received from Dodsley in return for the copyright of two odes in 1757 was an exception, and he was more often criticised by his friend William Mason for failing to insist on proper financial reward.[44] William Whitehead, fellow of Clare College, and later Colley Cibber's successor as poet laureate, left Cambridge soon after Dodsley published his *On the danger of writing in verse* in 1741 – for which Dodsley paid him 10 guineas, the same as Johnson received for *London* (1738).[45] The same fee was paid by Dodsley to Whitehead for his *Essay on ridicule* (1743). But in 1743 Dodsley also agreed to pay Edward Young 160 guineas for the copyright for the first five books of *Night thoughts*. In 1769, Whitehead was to receive 100 guineas from James Dodsley for his highly successful play *The school for lovers*.[46] Authors who remained in Cambridge never commanded such figures; indeed, the kinds of less popular literature on which they tended to concentrate could not warrant them. Richard Hurd anticipated a fee for his translation of Horace, though his comments to William Bowyer suggest that he did not appreciate, or perhaps wished not to seem to appreciate, that this included both his translation and his copyright:

> You say, if you purchased the edition, you should expect to have *the right of the copy absolute*. I suppose you only mean the right of 750; that is, of this edition. Pray let me have your final answer as soon as possible. What I propose is to have the new edition printed off directly, so as to be finished at the farthest this summer . . . And I am sensible, as you say, of the difference betwixt a piece of dry criticism and a novel. I should not insist on the payment of the 40*l.* till a year after the time of publication, if that would make any difference.[47]

Even when Hurd was being courted by Bowyer, he still threatened to sell it to a local Cambridge bookseller, Thurlbourn, for less than he would to London. A few years later he wrote, tongue in cheek, of how having written his *Moral and political dialogues*, he 'sent them to a bookseller of good credit', requesting 'but a moderate share of the profits', but a 'pretty large impression'. The bookseller, in this prefatory dialogue, thought 250 copies preferable to 2,000. The dialogues were published by Millar in London, and by Thurlbourn and Woodyer in Cambridge, without comment.[48]

Zachary Grey, of Trinity Hall, though never a Fellow of his college, involved himself closely in Cambridge life, as incumbent of the adjoining parishes of St Peter's and St Giles's, to which he devoted the winters, and passed the rest of the year as rector of the St John's College living of Houghton Conquest in Bedfordshire, which he served from the neighbouring and better appointed town of Ampthill.[49] By the time he saw into the world the book for which he is principally remembered, an annotated edition of *Hudibras* with illustrations after Hogarth, he had been responsible for about two dozen publications. The book could expect widespread sale, and Grey was eager that his work on this most popular of poems should be properly acknowledged by the booksellers. His emissary to them was James Tunstall, Fellow of St John's and University Orator, whose mild character made him perhaps singularly suitable for such a purpose. Grey's proposals to Bathurst, one of those who eventually shared in its publication, met with a cool response, as Tunstall reported:

He peremptorily rejected your proposals in every form. Your first proposal insists on 600 copies certain, and half the number of copies subscribed for that exceed 1000, with the 'General Historical Dictionary,' neatly bound, gilt and lettered; and 13 copies in large paper, bound in red morocco leather, gilt and lettered; and 12 copies in calf-skin, gilt and lettered. You had said, that Mr. Bathurst offered you 600 copies, provided there were 1000 subscriptions. You do not express in the said proposal whether you intend absolutely to part with the property of the Notes; but I must acquaint you that Mr. Bathurst is utterly against any agreement whereby you shall retain any property in any future impression, either of the notes separately, or together with the text of Hudibras. Understanding then that you intended to part with the notes absolutely, and thinking that your subscription might amount to 1500, I put this supposition – that you would ensure to the Proprietors 650 subscriptions, and asked whether they would allow you 850 copies, free of all charge, out of an impression of 2000, which were all to be sold off before any new impression was made; and allow you farther the 25 copies, and the 'General Historical Dictionary,' bound as aforesaid. I did not pretend to make this proposal, because you had given me no commission for it; but said I would communicate their answer upon this head to you. Mr. Bathurst excepted against giving in the 'Historical Dictionary;' and said, that, if you would ensure him 650 subscriptions, he would give his consent, and endeavour to prevail upon the rest to do the same – that you should have the 850 copies and the 25 copies bound, &c. as above, free of all charge, out of the impression of 2000, under the circumstances mentioned: but, as he obliges himself to have no second impression till the first is sold off, so he would have you obliged to sell none of your 850 copies under the market price, if any should chance to continue in your hands by your not having the complete number of 1500 subscribers, or by their not paying in their second payments . . . One proposal I mentioned more, that they should print the text in conjunction with your notes, and divide both the expence of the impression and the number of copies between you, each party retaining your respective properties in the text and notes in future impressions; but this, though apparently very fair, Mr. Bathurst would not hear of. In short, I believe your number of subscriptions may make your bargain worse with Booksellers, if after all you think it expedient to make any bargain.[50]

Grey's *Hudibras* (1744), quite unlike any other book printed by Bentham both in its appearance and in its nature, was an exception. Indeed, the second volume was not printed by Bentham at all, but in London, perhaps in order to meet the need for simultaneous publication of the two volumes in a minimum of time.[51] But like others who published their books by subscription, a measure of independence was possible in the specifications for the design of the work – not only, in this instance, Hogarth's illustrations, but also the quality of the paper to be used: Grey seems to have rejected several examples before he was satisfied.[52] His negotiations with a bookseller, even as he saw to the work's publication by subscription, offer a glimpse of the tensions between the interests of authors and booksellers, the reluctance of large booksellers to encourage publication of potentially popular books in a way that would undermine their position, and the determination that a text (in this case Grey's extensive notes, that formed much of the reason for the edition in the first place) once parted with, an author could not expect to receive further reward other than literary fame. Nor was payment necessarily wholly in money. It was still the case, as it had been for generations,[53] that to an author who was otherwise adequately supported, books could prove a powerful incentive, whether to be kept (as, surely, in the case of Bayle's dictionary, suggested here) or to be given away or sold. Presentation copies, on large paper, suitably bound and decorated, could provide both reminders and acknowledgements, whether to patrons or to friends.

For many an author, booksellers were to be treated with caution and even suspicion. Samuel Johnson, like many another, altered his opinion in the light of experience, writing of their 'avarice' in 1744 and some years later remarking, 'The booksellers are generous liberal-minded men.'[54] For the poets associated with mid-eighteenth-century Cambridge, none among the London booksellers enjoyed such status as the Dodsleys, publishers of Thomas Gray, William Mason, William Whitehead, Christopher Smart and Christopher Anstey. Yet Robert Dodsley himself was cautious. Despite his long-standing position as Baskerville's London agent in the 1750s, when the quarto Virgil was published in 1757 Dodsley preferred to subscribe for twenty copies, rather than become more closely involved in the risks of publication. In Cambridge, Smart published for himself the first edition of his translation of Pope's 'Ode for St. Cecilia's Day' in 1743; and when in 1746 he wished to issue a further edition, linked to his own ode for the occasion, he persuaded Dodsley to share in the venture. But, for all the detail of his instructions to London, the critical part of the agreement was on Dodsley's terms:

> I sent you this morning, by the coach, an hundred copies of my affair, which, I suppose, will be as many as you will be able to dispose of. I wou'd have it advertised but for three days, & only in one paper each day. The price of 'em is two shillings a piece . . . If you find they go off tolerably let me know.[55]

Perhaps Dodsley eventually took further copies; but he was clearly not committed to them. Moreover, as the edition consisted of 1,000 copies it is evident wherein Smart's tone of command lay: it was more than that of the author, anxious as he was that his book should be properly presented to the world.

> Deign on the passing world to turn thine eyes,
> And pause awhile from letters, to be wise;
> There mark what ills the scholar's life assail,
> Toil, envy, want, the patron, and the jail.[56]

The difficulty for authors, whether at Cambridge or elsewhere, lay in discovering the requisite capital, resources or attention to publish their work. To emphasise once again: publishing was under-capitalised; paper was expensive and had usually to be paid for long before costs could be recovered; and the successful sale and distribution of books depended always on a mixture of commercial and private connections, fed by interest or enthusiasm. For all these reasons, subscription publication (which made it possible for authors to recover the cost of paper early in the proceedings) offered an attractive means.

Other experiments were tested outside the ordinary book trade, most obviously in the work of the major publishing societies such as the SPCK. In 1735 a group of professional and literary men, scientists and scholars joined with a group of noblemen to found the Society for the Encouragement of Learning, to print books at the expense of, or subsidised by the Society in return for the author's interest in his work. Selection was to be in the hands of a committee; and no member of the society was to receive any private profit or advantage. The project had much in common with the non-priv- ileged work of the University Press. Richard Bentley not only refused to be associated with it (there were hopes of his still unpublished Manilius) but was also adamantly opposed to it.[57] Its books, mostly printed by Bowyer, were the epitome of a learned press: editions of Maximus Tyrius and of Aelian's *De natura animalium*, Thomas Carte's *Collection of original letters . . . 1641 to 1660*, Alexander Stuart on muscular motion, a translation of Newton on the quadrature of curves, and both Tanner's *Notitia monastica* and his *Bibliotheca Britannico-Hibernica*. But the Society suffered the same failings as Cambridge University Press in the first half of the eighteenth century. While a few of its books, such as Stuart on the muscles, sold out, others did not. Booksellers, receiving discounts that had to be divided between several agents, were given little incentive. In 1746, when the Society was facing bankruptcy, a large stock was sold off at low prices. Many of these books had never promised rapid returns, and remaindering was merely an encouragement to booksellers to wait their chance. The Society was wound up in 1749, and Bowyer had to be paid off for printing Tanner's *Bibliotheca* partly with unsold copies of his own work. Though the reasons for the Society's collapse were several, including a falling-off of interest among the members on whose subscriptions it depended, a principal difficulty was the bookseller, able to determine the success or failure of a book – 'by strongly recommending it to his Customers, but also taking the most prudent Steps in exchanging it with his Brethren', in the words of a pamphlet itself inspired by the Society.

> That many Copies are damned by Enmity, or lost for want of proper Support, is not to be doubted; whilst others, vastly inferior, succeed by the Power of Friends . . .
> A Bookseller of Capacity, Integrity, and Diligence, especially if he have a brisk Trade, may push off a small Impression of almost any Thing tolerable, whilst the very same Performance would intirely miscarry in the Hands of another, who is ignorant, slothful, and of little Credit and Business.[58]

In University circles, as in metropolitan ones, publication was a means not only to literary (or theological or other) fame, but also to possible patronage and even inde- pendence. In 1768, Christopher Anstey celebrated the author's mixture of emotions and aspirations in the appendix to his poem *The patriot*, printed by Fletcher and Hodson and sold by four London booksellers. His fictional author, discovering his bookseller's lack of interest (copies of his poem lay still in a bundle in the corner of the shop) and the mockery of those for whom he had thought to write, reflected not just on being laughed at 'by Women, and vile Poetasters' but also on his undone hopes:

All chance of the Toadland Preferment is gone![59]

Patronage remained, as it had been for generations, of vital importance. For long after its form had changed in literary circles, it survived in the penumbra of the universities and in some of the professions at which their members aimed, especially in the church and in politics. The colleges themselves were sometimes major patrons in their own right. In the mid-eighteenth century, Trinity had the presentation of over sixty livings, and St John's of three dozen. King's had two dozen. As usual, there was a noticeable discrepancy between the largest and many of the other colleges: Jesus had a dozen, Pembroke, Corpus and Clare eight each, Trinity Hall five, Peterhouse four and Queens' three.[60]

Of many examples of authors in search of patronage who figure in Nichols's *Literary anecdotes*, that of Zachary Pearce is one of the more notable. After graduating from Trinity in 1713–14, in 1716 he published an edition of Cicero *De oratore*, part of the programme of editions of Cicero printed by the University Press in which John Davies was the leading figure, encouraged by Bentley. He dedicated his work to Lord Parker, though at the time the two men were, according to Nichols, strangers to each other. Parker not only gave Pearce 50 guineas, but also persuaded Bentley to arrange for him to be elected a fellow of Trinity. When Parker became Lord Chancellor in 1718, he took Pearce into his household as his chaplain, and between 1719 and 1724 Pearce was presented to a series of livings, first in the Essex countryside and then in London, culminating with St Martin in the Fields. Pearce responded by dedicating to his patron (now Earl of Macclesfield) an edition of Longinus (1724). At Macclesfield's house a meeting with the Duke of Newcastle, with whom he had been at Westminster school, led to an appointment as royal chaplain. Marriage to the daughter of a London distiller brought wealth. But now, following the disgrace of Macclesfield, a further avenue appeared, as Pearce attracted the interest at court of Lady Sundon, one of his parishioners, and through her was brought to the notice of Queen Caroline. The deanery of Winchester came in 1739, the see of Bangor in 1748, and then in 1756 the see of Rochester and the deanery of Westminster. By now in advanced age, he declined to allow his name to be put forward for the diocese of London, and instead sought to resign from his positions, apparently in order to pursue his studies. He died in 1774, and is commemorated by a monument in Westminster Abbey. He had proved himself an able scholar, and much of his literary energy was taken up in religious controversy. After early support (albeit perhaps reluctant) of Bentley, he became his antagonist. But in his public career he had been more fortunate than many, particularly in his choice of his first patron; his series of promotions offered an example to those still left to hope in Cambridge.[61]

The interplay of social expectations and obligations could complicate relationships. In 1751 Francis Coventry, author of *The history of Pompey the Little* and who had recently graduated from Magdalene College, cast an eye at the Cambridge practice of admitting Fellow-Commoners, many of them from the families of the nobility and gentry, who paid to enjoy the privilege of dining at high table in their colleges. There was more than a modicum of truth in his scandalised remarks:

> For as Tutors and Governors of Colleges have usually pretty sagacious Noses after Preferment, they think it impolite to cross the Inclinations of young Gentlemen, who are Heirs to great Estates, and from whom they expect Benefices and Dignities hereafter, as Rewards for *their Want of Care of them*, while they were under their Protection. From

hence it comes to pass, that Pupils of this Rank are excused from all public Exercises, and allowed to absent themselves at Pleasure from the private Lectures in their Tutor's Rooms, as often as they have made a Party for Hunting, or an Engagement at the Tennis-court, or are not well recovered from their Evening's Debauch.[62]

Many of the fellows of Cambridge colleges in the eighteenth century looked either east to the Herveys of Ickworth, near Bury St Edmunds, or west to the Harleys and, after the house was bought by Lord Hardwicke in 1740, the Yorkes at Wimpole.[63] Four of Hardwicke's sons, including his heir Philip Yorke and Philip's younger brother Charles, later Lord Chancellor like his father before him, attended Corpus Christi College as Fellow-Commoners. Philip Yorke, in particular, evinced interests in literature, modern history and classical scholarship.[64] From 1749 to 1790, and from 1806 to 1834, the office of High Steward of the University was held by successive Earls of Hardwicke.[65] For all the vicissitudes of their libraries since, the books by Cambridge authors still on the shelves in these two great houses (the present house at Ickworth was built later, in 1795 to c. 1830), often on large paper and handsomely bound by Cambridge bookbinders, are reminders of the importance attached to dedication and presentation copies. John Taylor, University Librarian, Registrary, and Fellow of St John's College, dedicated his edition of two orations by Demosthenes and Lycurgus (Cambridge, 1743) to Charles Yorke, but he also made a practice of presenting his other books to Wimpole as well. Other authors included Richard Bentley, whose presentation copy of his Terence (Cambridge, 1726) to Philip Yorke is still in the house, as is the presentation copy of the *Dissertation on the Book of Job* (London, 1749) by John Garnett, Fellow of Sidney Sussex. Not all who gave such books sought presentation to benefices or cathedral canonries; but they did clearly anticipate some more or less tangible social advantage.

More prominent in many people's minds than either the Herveys (who did not invariably control great wealth or patronage[66]) or the Yorkes were the successive Chancellors of the University. Between 1689 and 1811 this office was held by only three men: the Duke of Somerset until 1748, the Duke of Newcastle until 1768, and the Duke of Grafton until 1811. Though the Duke of Somerset was instrumental in refounding the Press, he later withdrew himself from much of Cambridge and public life. His successors were quite different. They both relished careers in politics, where they each wielded immense influence and achieved high office; and they were both perceived from the first as possible patrons, especially but by no means exclusively in the Church.[67] For many, the Duke of Newcastle, who in addition to his political position also had the gift of no less than twenty-seven livings,[68] dominated the University from the time of his election as its High Steward in 1737.[69]

As a consequence, books became vehicles for appeals for patronage and escape from the trammels and travails of college fellowships. Patronage could also bring other, less direct rewards than, for example, lucrative appointments to prebendal stalls. Conyers Middleton was commented on as one who, despite his assiduous attendance on successive patrons, yet failed for many years to acquire a living.[70] But as he frankly remarked in dedicating his life of Cicero to Lord Hervey in 1741, the interest of a prominent patron could also generate subscriptions:

> The chief Design of my Epistle is, to give this public testimony of my thanks for the signal marks of friendship, with which Your Lordship has long honoured me . . . and what many will think the most substantial benefit, it's large subscription to Your authority. For though, in this way of publishing it, I have had the pleasure to find myself supported by a noble list of generous friends, who, without being sollicited, or even asked by me, have promoted my subscription with uncommon zeal, yet Your Lordship has distinguished Yourself the most eminently of them . . .[71]

It was Hervey who had encouraged Middleton to think of publishing by subscription; it was Hervey who had suggested improvements to the prospectus; and it was Hervey who had assiduously sought out subscriptions among people whose interest Middleton could not otherwise have engaged.[72] He was not the only prominent figure to have helped. In 1739 Middleton had written to Warburton,

> I am oblig'd to you for my Rt. Revd. Subscriber, and the more so, for the Pains that it cost you to draw him in. Episcopal Gold, like that from the Royal Hand, may help to cure the Evil, with which I am said to be infected.[73]

By the time he published his life of Cicero, Middleton was a nationally celebrated figure. His part in the disputes with Bentley had taken him to the brink of disaster in the London law courts, while his combination of classical researches and unconventional religious opinions had brought him fame and notoriety of a different kind. It is therefore not surprising that the list of subscribers to his latest work, on which he was known to have been long engaged, should have been unusually extensive, and socially remarkable, for an academic book: Lord Hervey certainly helped, but Middleton's own reputation was no mean recommendation. Well over a thousand, more than half the total, of the subscribers opted for copies on large paper. Dedicatees were expected to take more copies than were necessary for their own shelves; and when a few years later, in 1750, Thomas Knowles dedicated his book to his employer and patron Lady Hervey, she took forty. For Middleton's work, Hervey, as dedicatee, took twenty-five; Henry Bromley, the Lord Lieutenant of Cambridgeshire, took twenty; and both the Duke of Newcastle and Arthur Onslow, Speaker of the House of Commons, took five each. The list was headed by seven members of the royal family, each of whom subscribed for a copy on large paper. Apart from the nobility and the loyalty or interest of colleagues in Cambridge, Middleton also found a following among the Inns of Court. Booksellers in Salisbury and York, as well as in Oxford and London, likewise showed an interest.

Middleton's life of Cicero, which proved highly profitable, was printed not in Cambridge but in London. The principle was the same as it had been developed in the late seventeenth century: that it was possible for an individual to publish his own book, and it was possible thereby to reap a profit.[74] Subscription publishing reduced the element of risk; but though it allowed the possibility of abandoning a project, and returning monies received, if sufficient interest was not forthcoming, it could never eliminate risk altogether. It would, moreover, always be a tempting alternative to negotiations with booksellers, so long as booksellers seemed mean in their fees or remained so poorly capitalised that they could not afford to take even a subsidised chance. Middleton's Cicero was immediately taken up by the booksellers in London and Dublin, and it had reached a sixth enlarged edition by 1757. For any Cambridge author, Middleton's work was a poignant reminder of how successful an academic writer could become. Most were perforce obliged to remain content with lesser prizes, in a university world where books did not normally generate riches. Moreover, there seems to be substance in the frequently heard complaint that, by refusing to promote sales, or even boycotting books altogether, booksellers actively discouraged authors either from retaining their copyright, or from publishing their own works by subscription. Barnes had encountered just such difficulties at the beginning of the century; and as a correspondent remarked to Zachary Grey in 1747, 'You know the booksellers will not promote anything that is not their own.'[75]

For any author seeking to publish his work by subscription, the labour of assembling customers' promises was considerable. In 1733, Francis Blomefield, isolated in Norfolk and preparing to print as well as publish his history of the county, summarised to Thurlbourn what he had so far accomplished in Cambridge. Prudently, he had waited until October, when senior members of the University would have returned from their summer absence, and suitable undergraduates might be approached as well.

> I have taken care by my own acquaintance and my friends to gett a subscription paper into every college among the fellows. I should take it as the greatest of favours if you would lay me out one into every college among the undergraduates. I am sensible you know some one in every college, and the little time I have left the town I know none.[76]

Two copies of the proposals were to be kept in Thurlbourn's own shop, where customers might put down their names; two were to be pasted up in public places (Blomefield suggested the 'School doors'); half a dozen were to be disposed among colleges where Blomefield considered his links to be weak; and sixteen were to be disposed as Thurlbourn thought fit. By this stage, Blomefield had already written to some of those most likely to be interested, including Thomas Baker at St John's and James Burrough at Caius.

Eccentric, learned and isolated, Blomefield had more in common with his acquaintance among fellows of the colleges than shared antiquarianism. As for all authors who sought subscriptions, every possible contact was a potential supporter and means to further support. To publish by subscription meant certain independence; but it also emphasised the ambiguous relationship between author and printer: of trust and mistrust, of different viewpoints in evaluating fairness, sincerity or meanness, of each party challenging the other.

William Richardson's folio edition of the account of the English and Welsh episcopate, De praesulibus Angliae commentarius by Francis Godwin, the seventeenth-century Bishop of Hereford, was published at the end of 1742, but with a title-page dated 1743.[77] It was one of the most ambitious of all the books that appeared from the Cambridge press in the mid-eighteenth century, and it was one of the most handsome. As some others contrived in publishing by subscription, Richardson was able to exercise his own judgement for the type, paper and design for his book, with the added advantage of his position as Syndic. The new type from Caslon was brought into use, and in its ornamental use of Caslon's flowers the book's typography had an air of modernity.[78] The project was intended as a measure of the claims of the Press as a learned publisher. Richardson, whose interest in the forms and means of publishing was by no means limited to Cambridge,[79] was one of the most active advocates of the post-Crownfield reforms, and this was his *magnum opus*. At the request of Edmund Gibson, Bishop of London, and John Potter, Archbishop of Canterbury, he had revised and extended Godwin's work down to the present; and he now proposed a book on a grand scale, amply laid out and ornamented with engravings. The result was to be impressive.

Intimately acquainted with the Press and its workings, Richardson was unusually well placed as an author. But in all fundamental respects he was treated exactly as other authors who sought out the Press to print their work. The Syndics agreed to print the book on 11 February 1739/40.[80] The details of the agreement were much as usual. Composition, mostly in great primer and long primer, was charged at a basic 6s. a sheet, with a further shilling for corrections. Presswork was to cost 3s.6d. a sheet, and since some of the 750 copies were to be on large paper there was to be a charge of 1s. for altering the margins: this last charge was high, or even excessive, for a simple and speedy adjustment, compared with the rest of the cost. Out of these charges, a total of 11s.6d. per sheet, Bentham had to pay his workmen and find his profit. On top of this, the University levied its normal bill for overheads, expressed in the accounts as the use of its types, amounting to half as much again per sheet. Thus Richardson had to find a total of 17s.3d. per sheet for his work to be printed, plus the cost of paper and its transport. But Bentham was unable to print the proposed engravings, comprising a frontispiece portrait of Godwin by Vertue, and about sixty headpieces and tailpieces by Hubert Gravelot and François Vivares.[81] So Richardson had also to meet the cost of commissioning and printing these, and of yet more transport from and to Cambridge, where (except for the frontispiece, which was on a single leaf) the letterpress was printed before the sheets were sent to London for the engravings to be printed on a rolling-press.

In the absence of a bookseller to provide capital, for a folio that was to run to over eight hundred pages, in two volumes, the only practicable way for Richardson to publish the book was by subscription. By the time the book was nearing completion, he had gathered in almost 280 orders, including 40 for large paper copies. He had the names of most of the colleges at Cambridge and Oxford, and of the bishops; the Bishop of Norwich took 2 copies on large paper, and the Earl of Gainsborough, to whom Richardson was chaplain, no less than 6. In Cambridge itself, Conyers Middleton, who likewise employed Gravelot for the decorations to his *Life* of Cicero, printed in London at about the same time, also took a copy on large paper. By Richardson's own statement, the 40 subscriptions for large paper copies represented all that were to be printed in that manner: there may have been a few more in practice. But although by the time he had seen the last proofs through the press he probably had sufficient money to meet the printing bills, it is noticeable that the list of subscribers includes hardly any copies for booksellers. This was an expensive book, one that could expect a specialist market, and the booksellers had no reason to encourage a project that came into the world by a means they disliked. The residue of the edition not taken up by subscribers was advertised as a new publication in the *Gentleman's Magazine* in November 1742, price two guineas in sheets. Copies were available in London from J. and P. Knapton and from Charles Bathurst; in Oxford from James Fletcher; and in Cambridge from William Thurlbourn.

Authors could thus look for rewards quite other than simple sums of money, paid out by booksellers who bought their copies. Grey hoped to add an expensive *desideratum* to his own shelves, the ten folio volumes of Bayle's *Dictionary*; and he hoped, too, for specially bound copies that he could either give away (so engendering new possibilities of patronage) or sell. Others, such as Pearce, looked for patronage – in the form of money but also, and no less eagerly, in the offer of ecclesiastical preferment. Yet others, like Middleton, resorted to publishing their own work by subscription in hope not only of selling enough to recover costs, but also to make some money. The risks involved in such proceedings were many, as Joshua Barnes had discovered to his and his widow's loss earlier in the century.[82] But for most authors in Cambridge, the continuing and direct support of a college fellowship was itself a form of patronage. The colleges, and the university, existed in order to teach and to educate; but they also existed for the support of learning – of letters, of theology, of mathematics, of the sciences. In themselves, the emoluments of college fellowships were usually modest enough. To escape to a living might mean both more money and an end to enforced bachelordom. The attractions of a fellowship often palled; but such an existence provided sustenance and respectabilty for authorship in a manner wholly unknown to most authors in the country.

The continuing lack of capital in the book trade, partially met in London by booksellers who organised themselves into groups for particular projects, and so parcelled out the risks and the possible profits, meant that some of mid-eighteenth-century Cambridge's most considerable scholarly achievements could never be serious propositions as local publications or (thanks, as always, to the weight of paper that was involved) as products of the local printers. The new edition of Stephanus' Latin dictionary, the first major revision since the sixteenth century, and much augmented, was the work of a group of Cambridge classicists: Edmund Law of Peterhouse, John Taylor of St John's, Thomas Johnson of Magdalene, and Sandys Hutchinson of Trinity. Proposals were issued in London in 1732, and the whole was published in four volumes in 1734–5 by Samuel Harding.[83]

There were many lesser examples, some printed in London out of convenience, some from eccentricity, and some for the sake of the probable market. In 1724, with the help of Bentley, Richard Bradley was appointed the University's first Professor of Botany. But the University's hopes both of lectures by an acknowledged authority and of a benefactor who would provide a botanic garden were disappointed, and Bradley remained an absentee in London.[84] Opinion was scandalised. It can hardly have been surprised when in 1730 his notes of *A course of lectures upon the materia medica*, read at Cambridge and founded on the collections assembled by Vigani in Queens' College and John Addenbrooke in St Catharine's, were printed and published in London.[85] Successive sermons preached in the University Church during the 1720s and 1730s by Robert Leeke, Fellow of St John's College, were printed in London. So, too, were sermons preached in the church by Samuel Drake (1719) and John Mainwaring (1765), both also fellows of the college. The practice of turning to London printers was not limited to periods when the Cambridge press was at its weakest, and not all of these are examples of Bowyer's maintaining connections with his old college. For the Cambridge booksellers, the choices were very similar. Thurlbourn became a regular and heavy customer with Bentham, arranging for books to be printed a few minutes' walk away from his shop at 1 Trinity Street, opposite Great St Mary's church. But a few books for which he was primarily responsible, such as Conyers Middleton's lecture on John Woodward's bequest of his geological collections to the University, with provision also for a professorship (1732); or the 1751 and 1753 editions of Richard Hurd's translations of Horace;[86] or the *Imitations of Horace* by a shy and retiring Fellow of Jesus College, Thomas Nevile (1758),[87] were printed by Bowyer. Nevile's translation of Virgil's *Georgics* (1767) was printed by the University Printer, for Thurlbourn and Woodyer; but it was Bowyer, again, who printed Nevile's subsequent imitations of Juvenal and Persius in 1769 for Thurlbourn's successor John Woodyer.[88]

Much of this had to do with the convenience of authors. But Hurd, Fellow of Emmanuel College, turned to Bowyer as a possible publisher as well as printer when he found Thurlbourn unsatisfactory: 'As he grows old he grows lazy', he commented to Bowyer as he sought to find excuses for poor sales of his book after nine months. 'One reason at least for the Epistle to Augustus not going off was, I think, Thurlbourn's neglect to advertise it properly when it was published . . . I have lately met with some of my own friends who never observed it in the papers till the other day, when it was advertised more carefully.' Hurd's hopes that Bowyer would publish an edition proved fruitless, and worse. In the end, the first volume was printed in London, by Bowyer, and Thurlbourn had the second printed at Cambridge. It is not clear whether this was because Bowyer took offence, or Thurlbourn preferred Bentham, or extra speed was thought necessary. But to Hurd, at least, and for whom perversely Bentham was the more convenient printer, the experience was disagreeable.

Most saw the choice of printer as lying between Cambridge and London. Few took the further course. In the mid-eighteenth century the private press re-emerged as a means to publication, brought into use as it had never previously been in England, though it had figured prominently in the introduction of printing to many small towns of fifteenth-century Italy: in both periods, the concept proved attractive both to those wishing to promote scholarly writing and those who sought lighter diversion. In England, Francis Blomefield in Norfolk, Charles Viner in Aldershot, and, most celebrated, Horace Walpole at Strawberry Hill, all chose to establish their own presses on a smaller or larger scale, principally as a means of printing their own work.[89] In Cambridge, Roger Long, Master of Pembroke College, attempted the same, and obtained type with which the sheets for his *Astronomy* could be set and proofed in his Master's lodge, before the type was carried the few yards down the road to be printed off by Bentham. It was a characteristic arrangement, for Long was fascinated by mechanical contrivances, whether musical instruments or, more spectacularly, a water velocipede in the Master's garden and, most celebrated of all, a very large hollow sphere in which the viewer, once inside, could observe the relationships of the heavenly bodies.[90] The first volume of Long's *Astronomy* was dated 1742. Long died without seeing his work completed, and it was left to John Archdeacon, Bentham's successor, and the bookseller John Deighton, to see the second volume to publication, printed by the University Press and issued in 1785.[91]

Others were less ambitious, but they often encountered difficulties in the face of a book trade reluctant to admit the financial interest of authors, and that found much academic publishing unattractive. It was partly a matter of capital. It was also a matter of willingness. The London booksellers, who still controlled most of the British book trade, resented the privileged position in which the learned presses had been placed, which gave them some of the most lucrative books. By agreement and licensing, the highly profitable trade in almanacs remained in the control of a cartel. For more ordinary books, there was little incentive to encourage the presses at Cambridge and Oxford by promoting the books printed there either by subscription or as their own publications. The only practical means of overcoming this prejudice was by offering higher profits, which was not always possible. In 1776 Samuel Johnson reflected on the question as it affected the Oxford press; but his remarks were also apposite for Cambridge:

> The Booksellers who like all other men have strong prejudices in their own favour are enough inclined to think the practice of printing and selling books by any but themselves an encroachment on the rights of their fraternity and have need of stronger inducements to circulate academical publications than those of one another; for of that mutual cooperation by which the general trade is carried on, the University can bear no part. Of those whom he neither loves nor fears and from whom he expects no reciprocation of good offices, why should any man promote the interest but for profit. I suppose with all our scholastick ignorance of mankind we are still too knowing to expect that the Booksellers will erect themnselves into Patrons and buy and sell under the influence of a disinterested zeal for the promotion of Learning.
>
> To the Booksellers if we look for either honour or profit from our press, not only their common profit but something more must be allowed . . .[92]

For so long as this was the case at the university presses (and the position at Cambridge was substantially the same in this respect), there was little point in Cambridge University Press's publishing books that could expect scant interest from the London booksellers. Thus authors were left to seek out their own means of publication, and the Press gave no lead. The reasons given, perfectly truthfully, were related to shortage of capital; but the book trade itself was inimical to the Press's publishing on its own account. As a consequence the Cambridge press remained primarily a printing concern, not a publishing one.

In this way, too, it remained as it had been in the sixteenth and seventeenth centuries, essentially in competition with the London printers. For a century and a half after Thomas Thomas's appointment in 1583, there were no printers in Cambridge other than those sanctioned by the University. Robert Walker and Thomas James, from London, established the *Cambridge Journal and Weekly Flying-Post* in 1744.[93] Their printing house, 'next to the Theatre Coffee House', was on the west side of Trinity Street, between the top of Trinity Lane and Senate House Hill – that is, within a stone's throw of the principal local booksellers. Though Thomas James himself did not die until 1758, his name was soon replaced by that of Sarah James, who advertised both letterpress and a rolling-press for copper-plates.[94] Among the books to appear from the premises were two intended to promote sales of the newspaper, a history of the civil war by Jacob Hooper, and a *History of the life of Queen Anne*, by Conyers Harrison. Otherwise, there was little printing that could in any way challenge the position of Bentham as a printer of books and pamphlets. An octavo *Letter to his subscribers to the plan and elevation of an intended addition to Corpus Christi College*, printed in 1749, was a rare sortie for Walker and James into this field: the pamphlet, a frank attack by James Essex on the amateurish attempts at architecture by Robert Masters, was hardly to be printed at the press of which Masters, as head of a college, was a syndic.

In 1762, a rival newspaper, the *Cambridge Chronicle*, was founded by Thomas Fletcher and Francis Hodson at the New Printing Office, Market Hill. In 1767, it was amalgamated with the older *Cambridge Journal*. Fletcher and Hodson became much more important than Walker and James as book printers, and established themselves as another resort for authors unwilling or unable to use the University Press or to go to London. Like their rivals, they too offered the services of a rolling-press; but their prime business was as newspaper and general printers. Apart from works by Christopher Anstey (author of *The new Bath guide*, of which they printed editions in 1766 and 1768), their work included Agostino Isola's *Italian dialogues* (1774) and Rowland Rugeley's translations from La Fontaine and others (1763). They became the first real alternative printers in Cambridge.

Thus, by the later years of Bentham's term of office, printing in Cambridge had changed fundamentally. The University Press, reinvigorated, had grown considerably, and was at work on two sites. Nearer to the centre of the town, small printing houses had been established, equipped with the minimum necessary for particular projects, whether newspaper or jobbing work, modest book printing, or printing copper-plates. These smaller presses did not all survive for long. Depending partly on their owners' health or ambitions, unprotected by any institutional assumptions, and prey to bankruptcy, they existed in the shadow of the University. Most of their work came from members of colleges, or was sold to them. Though there were occasional exceptions (*The new Bath guide*, printed by Fletcher and Hodson, bore the imprint of Dodsley), in the mid-eighteenth century these were publications principally for local distribution. But in offering, however modestly at first, an alternative local printer to Bentham and then to his successor John Archdeacon, smaller printers such as these, like some of the local booksellers who were increasingly well capitalised or otherwise financed, began to establish a pattern of publishing that was to dominate the Cambridge book trade for a century.

The local printers never posed a major challenge either to the University Press itself or to printers in London. Their use remained casual, to substitute in an emergency or for cheapness' sake, or to provide when the University Printer might not be expected to act, as with Essex's pamphlet against Masters. Members of the University and residents of the town alike employed them, and much of the ephemeral printing of advertisements, forms, letterheads and notices emanated from their presses. But for the mass of book-printing the principal alternative to the University Printer remained London.

Books remained in print for many years, despite the efforts of booksellers and their fears of piracy. The Cambridge *Suidas*, which proved almost immovable for a generation, has become the most celebrated,[95] but other smaller works remained available for sometimes surprisingly long periods. Stock of Bentley's Horace (1711) was still being advertised by Thurlbourn in 1735, together with the Amsterdam edition of 1713.[96] The difficulty for Cambridge University Press was that there was no mechanism for agreeing to destroy or reduce unsold stock. It took a longer view of its publications than those booksellers in London who, to some observers, seemed to lose interest after as little as six months, and expected authors to take up any remaining copies. As, again, it was remarked of London booksellers:

> I know not whether, as a Sort of Punishment on yourselves for the Error of printing too great a Number, you ought not, as the *Dutch* are reported to do with their Spices, destroy some, in order to give an additional Value to the rest.[97]

In this view, it was the author rather than the publisher who suffered, who sustained damage when his works were 'prostituted' as the booksellers sold them off at less than anticipated. The author retained an intellectual and moral interest in his property even after he had sold or otherwise made over his work to the bookseller. 'For the sake of your private Interest, you too frequently print more Copies than you ought, without duly considering the Author, or his Subject, or what Demand there may be for so great a Number. The Want of this Precaution often occasions the whole Impression to be damned or lost; especially when, as is the usual Practice in such Cases, the Bookseller, having sold a Part, and the rest not having the Run he expected, sells them all at any Rate to the first Purchaser, excepting a few which he reserves, in case they should ever become scarce or saleable Books.'[98] To an author contemplating such a member of the London book trade, the Syndics of Cambridge University Press could offer little financial gain, but they could offer convenience and prosaic safety. By convention, members of the University whose books were printed at the University Press were not charged for warehousing during their lifetimes. The less tangible advantage, of being published under the auspices of the University, does not appear to have been an issue for the greater part of the eighteenth century.

Robert Smith, Bentley's successor as Master of Trinity College since 1742, died in 1768. His term of office thus coincided closely with that of Bentham. His *Compleat system of opticks* had been printed for him in 1738, when Crownfield was still University Printer. But Bentham had printed the first edition of his *Harmonics, or the philosophy of musical sounds* in 1749, as well as a second of his edition of Cotes's lectures in 1747. These books were published in English, but they gained a European reputation. As modern languages gradually replaced Latin as the international means of communication, so the need for translations grew, and demand for language skills increased. Notwithstanding the occupation of the throne by the Hanoverians, longstanding interests and traditions died hard. German did not become a fashionable language in Britain. Instead, the stimulus of travel to France and Italy in particular continued to encourage study of these languages especially. Winckelmann's *Geschichte der Kunst des Alterthums*, published at Dresden in 1764, was known to most people through several editions in French or Italian translation.

Among works from the Cambridge press, Smith's *Opticks* (1738) was published in Dutch at Amsterdam in 1753 and at The Hague in 1764; in German at Altenburg in 1755; and in French at Avignon and at Brest in 1767.[99] Cotes's *Hydrostatical and pneumatical lectures* was published in Dutch at Leiden in 1740 and at Amsterdam in 1752, and in French at Paris in 1742 as *Leçons de physique experimentale*. Nicholas Saunderson's *Elements of algebra*, printed at Cambridge in 1740–1, appeared in French in 1756, published in Amsterdam, Leipzig and Paris. A German edition appeared rather later, at Halle in 1798–1805. Newton's *Principia*, from an earlier generation, remained unavailable in English until 1729, and in French until 1759. By contrast, his *Opticks*, published originally in English in 1704 and in Latin two years later, also appeared during the 1740s in various editions in Latin in Switzerland and Italy, while two French translations were published at Paris in 1720 and 1722. No German editions of either the *Principia* or the *Opticks* appeared until the late nineteenth century.

For German-speaking Europe, the route to English books tended to lie either through Latin or, for increasing numbers both of academic works and of other forms of literature, through French.[100] For much scientific publishing, Latin remained the primary medium in Germany:[101] in Leipzig, the *Acta Eruditorum* and its successor the *Nova Acta Eruditorum* continued unchanged in that respect until the periodical was brought to an end in 1782. The choice of French for the *Nouveaux Mémoires de l'Académie Royale des Sciences* in 1772, published in Berlin, offered eloquent witness to the shift in linguistic priorities and (in the sciences especially) adequacy. Edward Gibbon was characteristic of many: able to write fluently in French, but ignorant of German.

In Cambridge there is only fragmentary evidence of a taste for German before the last years of the century.[102] But there was an increased interest in other languages. The foundation of the Regius chairs in modern history at Oxford and Cambridge in 1724 brought the means and (for a while) the obligation to appoint teachers of modern languages.[103] John Green, Bishop of Lincoln, wrote with some, if perhaps exaggerated, claims to truth when he reflected on how heavy drinking and violent sports had given way to more gentle pursuits. 'A taste for *Musick*, modern *Languages*, and other the polite *Entertainments* of the *Gentleman*, have succeeded to Clubs, and *Bacchanalian*

Routs', he wrote of Cambridge in 1750.[104] By then, teachers of modern languages had become familiar, if intermittent, figures. Girolamo Bartolomeo Piazza and F. Masson were appointed by the first Regius Professor of Modern History; and though Piazza had no immediate successor following his death in 1741, French teaching continued. The most notable exponent was René Labutte (or La Butte), who found his position challenged by a new arrival, James Fauchon, in 1746.[105] The two men soon argued, each claiming the other was incompetent (their pronunciation differed noticeably); and in due course each issued a French grammar. Fauchon's *French tongue made easy to learners*, printed by Bentham, appeared in 1751; and René Labutte, after teaching the language in Cambridge for forty years as well as earning a living partly as a printer,[106] produced his own, printed by Archdeacon in 1784. French became fashionable, though disappointingly little is known of Rowland Rugeley, whose *Miscellaneous poems and translations*, drawn partly from La Fontaine, was printed by Fletcher and Hodson in 1763.[107] Meanwhile Italian gained a new advocate with the arrival in 1764[108] of Agostino Isola, who by the time of his death in 1797 had not only established his family in the university, but had also published a series of books on his own behalf. After a slim collection of *Italian dialogues* intended for beginners and printed by Fletcher and Hodson (1774), he continued with a selection from Italian poets, a translation of Gray's *Elegy* (1782) and editions of Tasso (1786) and Ariosto (1789), all of the latter being printed at the University Press. The local trade left Isola to publish his own works, but his pupils included those who, like William Wordsworth, sought some relief from the ordinary demands of the curriculum.[109]

Though it published a few books, the Press was established in 1698 primarily as a printer. It remained so until the end of the eighteenth century and even beyond. The mishandling and misfortunes of *Suidas* were caution enough against the Syndics' pursuing too adventurous a path in publishing books, rather than simply printing them. At another extreme, in a market where sales could be (and were) assured, they preferred to sell even Bibles and prayer books through an agent. With little capital, the cost of paper alone, amounting to about half the cost of production, was discouragement enough against the Syndics' wishing to publish on their own behalf, and hence be obliged to finance the whole of the cost of an edition before any copies could be sold.

In the mid-eighteenth century, as Richardson's reforms took hold, and Bentham proved to be an accomplished businessman, it increasingly seemed that the Press existed for profit. It was a view that became more widespread as the printing of Bibles and the prayer book not only proved a success, but also in effect – for these books – made the Press a London publisher in all but name. The University was willing to lease out its privileges, whether to Mary Fenner and her partners in the early 1730s, or to Baskerville in the 1760s. It was willing, by a series of agreements linked to annual payments, to refrain from printing almanacs, from which printers in Cambridge had made large profits a hundred years earlier. Those who took advantage of this attitude might complain at the charges or at the University's refusal to give quarter. But the assumption underlying all the various agreements was that these were profitable enterprises.

Bentham left a press that bore little resemblance to that with which he had been charged in 1740. But his reputation had been established long since – not only in the University, in the politics of local government, and in London, but also in the eyes of a shrewd Oxford bookseller. In 1756, as a part of his suggestions as to how the Oxford press should justify its 'great name', Daniel Prince found it pertinent to refer to Cambridge:

> Twelve years ago, at Cambridge, Printing was at the lowest Ebb. They did not farm-out their Patent. All lay motionless; till Mr. Bentham, their present Manager, reviv'd it, and that in so prudent a Way, that he has brought it to an Income of at least £500 per Annum clear to the University, from neat Workmanship. He did not only acquaint the Governors with his Design, but put the Project in Execution by Degrees, so as not to dishearten the Gentlemen by any excessive disbursements . . .[110]

Prince wrote of the privileged books, the Bible and the prayer book, in particular. But his admiration for Bentham, his skill as a printer and his skill both with the Syndics and with his customers, was more generally based. He allowed it to overcome the wariness with which the two universities customarily eyed each other. The extent to which the succeeding generation profited from Bentham's work will be examined below.

❦ 8 ❧

Bentham and Bibles

For much of the first half of the eighteenth century, the trade in Bibles and the prayer book was dominated by John Baskett, supported by continuing imports from the Netherlands. As printer both in London and in Oxford, Baskett was in a commanding position in a trade where accuracy was sought to a degree greater than in almost any other kind of book, and yet where the profits to be obtained from cheap printing were very considerable. Accuracy and profit were often at odds with each other, and critics were always forthcoming. The reasons for the Cambridge Syndics' eventual wish to enter this sector, which had not been a preserve of Cambridge printers since the late seventeenth century, were straightforward: it offered an assured market, structured in a way that other parts of Crownfield's business conspicuously were not. But in order to operate successfully, there had either to be a growth in demand for a book that was already in sufficient supply, or the Cambridge product had to be superior in some way, whether in quality of printing or materials, in keenness of price, or in quality of texts. The timing of Cambridge's entry was in fundamental respects controlled by the degree of interest in those who controlled the press, the Syndics. As we have seen, the extent of the Press's difficulties under Crownfield was not grasped until the late 1730s. The penultimate paragraph of the report on the state of the Press alluded to the recent lease to William Fenner, 'for printing Bibles &c. by Blocks or Types'. As will be seen, it was an experiment that had failed; but it was one that had brought to a head the question of printing the English Bible and the prayer book, privileged books which Bentley and Crownfield alike had ignored. Notwithstanding the past few years, the more general lesson could not escape the Syndics: that there existed a need for Bibles and the prayer book, and that there was a strong case for investment.

In Bentham's hands, the Press once again became a major printer of these books, and came to rely on them for a substantial portion of its activities and income. The printing of Bibles and prayer books became a central focus of policy, and has remained so virtually ever since. But the preliminary skirmishes with their printing, when the University leased out its rights to a group who thought to invest in methods that had proved successful in the Low Countries, were discouraging, and finished in mutual dissatisfaction. Moreover, Bentham's own work has been much obscured by the brilliance of John Baskerville, whose Bible of 1763 is treated in the next chapter.

No Bible was printed at Cambridge between 1683 and 1743. As Henry James, President of Queens' College, realised in 1705, while the Oxford University Press could come to advantageous arrangements with the Stationers' Company, the greater cost of transport between London and Cambridge, by road rather than river, placed Cambridge at a disadvantage. As a result, he saw little hope of a Bible trade for the new University Press. By ending their agreement with Cambridge after Hayes's death, the Stationers had gained freedom: they no longer had to keep a printer supplied with new type; no longer had to pay for the upkeep of a printer's house; and no longer had to meet the salary of a workman; nor did they have to pay for the carriage of paper. In 1692, the Stationers had come to an agreement the results of which were to subsidize learned printing in Oxford with £200 per annum, and to see a series of Bibles printed at Oxford from 1695 onwards.[1] In James's view, it was a better bargain that that struck for Cambridge. Bardsey Fisher (Master of Sidney Sussex College), Richard Bentley, and Charles Ashton (Master of Jesus) had 'soe order'd matters that ye youngest child is never likely to hear of another bible printed at Cambr. and yet Cambr. has heretofore been famous for printing Bibles correctly.'[2] He was unnecessarily pessimistic.

The right to print Bibles in England, held since the sixteenth century by the two universities and by the King's or Queen's Printers, was dominated by the beginning of the eighteenth century by just two interests: the heirs (and their assigns) of Christopher Barker, who had purchased the patent in 1577, and the accommodation of 1692 between the Stationers' Company and the University of Oxford. In 1709, these interests were complicated when John Baskett purchased a share in the reversion of the interests of the Queen's Printer; following further negotiations, in 1712 he was sworn as Queen's Printer, a title that in due course passed to his heirs and then, in 1769, to Charles Strahan.[3] Rather than challenge Baskett (which they could only have done by persuading Cambridge to print on their behalf), the Stationers' Company came to an agreement with him that left the interests of the English Stock intact.[4] Accordingly, for much of the first half of the eighteenth century, Baskett's name appeared on Bibles printed both in London and in Oxford. In 1711 he also obtained a share in Bible printing in Edinburgh. In England, he held all but a monopoly in printing both Bibles and Books of Common Prayer so long as Cambridge refrained from doing so.

The weakness in his position, so far as there was one, lay in the long-established trade in English Bibles emanating from Holland. For generations, the market for the English Bible and prayer book had been supplied, in varying degrees, by printers in the Low Countries, who employed a form of stereotype printing to manufacture tens of thousands of copies for the English-speaking world – in the British Isles and in an increasing colonial market. The Dutch printers had overcome the expense either of keeping standing type from which to make repeated printings, or of the need for resetting, requiring time-consuming and costly proof-reading.[5] The Schipper printing house in Amsterdam, which had been able to print Bibles from cast metal plates since

1673, maintained its interest in both Bibles and Books of Common Prayer even in the mid-eighteenth century.[6] Among the several books printed from plates listed in 1714 in which the Leiden bookseller Samuel Luchtmans had an interest was a folio edition of the English Bible.[7] The true dates of these Dutch-printed Bibles are not clear, since there had long been a tradition amongst Amsterdam printers of leaving in dates older than those of publication; as a consequence, it is not obvious that the quarto editions dated 1730 and printed probably in Amsterdam were indeed the last of their kind to appear, or that copies of the pocket edition dated 1732 were not in fact also printed for some years afterwards. But the decline of English-language Bible and prayer-book printing in the Netherlands both acknowledged the increasing capacity of printers in the British Isles (in Scotland as well as England) and encouraged others to enter an expanding market. In view of the fact that Bibles, and other books, were printed from plates in Holland, it is remarkable that similar techniques do not appear to have been applied in England until the 1730s.

This was the background against which in 1731 the University leased out its right to print Bibles and prayer books, to a consortium who appeared to offer an answer to a difficult problem, and a fresh approach to printing the most reliable of all books.

William Ged, who was the first printer in Great Britain to print from stereotypes, and who has been credited in much of the secondary literature with the invention of the process, was an Edinburgh goldsmith, born in Dunfermline in 1690.[8] His interests seem to have moved to the printing trade in the mid-1720s, and after a brief partnership in Edinburgh formed to develop his scheme for printing from cast metal plates, in 1729 he agreed with a London stationer, William Fenner, to enter into another partnership for twenty-one years. In 1730, these partners brought in first the London typefounder Thomas James and then James's brother John, a successful London architect who had a few years earlier been responsible for alterations in the chapel of Gonville and Caius College.[9] John's connections with Cambridge seem to have been critical in Fenner's obtaining the University's licence. The partnership also seems to have been thus extended to meet the need for money and materials wherewith to develop the invention. Thomas James was to provide type, while John, who subsequently showed himself to be particularly aware of the financial implications, was perhaps the principal investor. By early in 1730 the partnership was strong enough to challenge the London trade. It is not clear why John Baskett did not enter into an agreement with the partners at this stage. As King's Printer he had an obvious interest in a method that would reduce his printing costs for Bibles. Instead, and perhaps in the hope of better profits, Ged, Fenner and their partners negotiated an agreeement with Cambridge, who though it had the right to print Bibles had not exercised it since the previous century.

The approach had been made by April 1730, when Conyers Middleton reported events to Lord Harley:

> There is now a proposal made to ye University of purchasing a lease of us to print Bibles & Common Prayer books from our Press, a power we have reserved out of ye last lease granted to ye Stationer's Company; 'tis made by persons who pretend to be Masters of a new discovery & rare secret in ye Art of Printing by Plates of a hard metal cast for each

Page, wch is contrived cheifly for books of constant & standing sale, & will make ye impressions vastly cheaper than in ye common way, & as they say, more beautifull too, & do not question but y^t when their method is once experienced in their Bibles, it will be made use of in all other great Works: one of ye Proposers is Mr James ye Architect, & most people here seem at present disposed to embrace ye offer.[10]

Middleton, who as the most recent authority on the work of Caxton had an especial interest in printing, spoke with a prescience that would have astonished him, in that within a century the University Press depended on stereotyped Bibles, and various versions of the technique were transforming the printing trade as a whole. But Ged and his partners rapidly found themselves in difficulties. Their agreement with the University excluded Crownfield, the University Printer; and instead, the University was to receive £100 per annum in return for licensing its right to print the Bible and the Book of Common Prayer. The partners found premises in Cambridge, recruited printers from Holland,[11] bought one or more presses and appear to have begun to print two books: a Bible in nonpareil and a Book of Common Prayer. Their optimism was premature. Disputes with the workmen, disagreements between the partners themselves, the inconvenient distance between Cambridge (where a foreman was in charge) and London, the inevitable clash of interests between traditional typefounding and a process that was designed to reduce the need for new type, and the manifestly poor quality of what was printed ('done in so bad a manner, and so far inferior to those sold by the King's Printer'), combined to bring the experiment to a premature end.

In 1733 Ged returned to Edinburgh, where a few years later he was to complete his celebrated Sallust, printed 'non Typis mobilibus, ut vulgo fieri solet, sed Tabellis seu Laminis fusis'. In Cambridge, William Fenner, now established with a printing press, found a living as a printer; and over the following months a handful of books appeared bearing his name, printed either privately for subscribers[12] or for Thurlbourn. He died in the winter of 1733–4, leaving his widow to conduct a vociferous, bitter and unrewarding campaign of her own against both his erstwhile partners and the University. After the partnership had also failed to keep up with the necessary payments the University refused to extend the licence after 1737. Nothing is known to have survived of the Bible; but it appears that a few sheets were salvaged of an octavo Book of Common Prayer, which were made up with sheets printed conventionally and published with a title-page dated 1733.[13]

Half a century later, Edward Rowe Mores recalled being told by a 'straggling workman' who had been employed in Fenner's venture that:

> both bibles and comm.-pr. books had been printed, but that the compositors when they corrected one fault (which was only to be done by perforation) made purposely half a-dozen more, and the press-men when the masters where absent battered the letter in aid of the compositors: in consequence of which base proceedings the books were suppressed by authority and condemned to *et piper & quicquid, &c.*, and that all the chandleries in *Cambr.* were full of *James's* bibles, and that the plates were sent to the King's printing-h. and from thence to *Mr Caslon's* founding-h. to be melted; an inspector standing at the furnace to see the order fully executed.[14]

While clearly not complete, the essentials of this account, noting the printing of part at least of both the Bible and the Book of Common Prayer, are probably correct. But even so, it is not clear why Dutchmen who had been brought over because of their special expertise should set about destroying their work, unless they had been suborned into doing so; and the introduction at the conclusion of the King's Printer (who had no authority whatever in the affair) was entirely unnecessary. The tale had become adapted, no doubt as a result of much retelling among fellow printers, whose own interests had become reflected in the account.

In fact, it seems that not all of the Cambridge stereo plates were indeed melted down. Specimen blocks of both Bible and prayer book appeared in the London sale rooms in 1786;[15] and in 1825 T. C. Hansard was able to include in his *Typographia* pulls from two pages that he claimed to have escaped from 'Caslon's cormorant crucible'.[16] If indeed these pages were, as he claimed, surviving examples from James's experiments at Cambridge, then those experiments may have been more ambitious still: to include not only a Book of Common Prayer and a Bible, but also a duodecimo Book of Common Prayer of which Hansard's pages now afforded the only clear evidence. Moreover, since the pages in question are taken from the order of service instituted by George II to celebrate his accession to the throne on 11 June – that is, one of the very last sections of the prayer book – then they offer the possibility that other, previous parts of this duodecimo prayer book had been plated, and perhaps even printed. In other words, the investment had been triply abortive, in that none of three separate projects had been successfully executed.

Whatever the true extent of the hopes and experiments of Ged, James and Fenner, the unique survival of the opening sheets of a single copy of a prayer book is witness today of the beginning of a process that was eventually to place the University Press on a firm financial footing for the first time in its existence. Technically, the beginning was abortive; and while the work had been licensed by the University, the University Printer had had no part in it; and it had been made on premises apart from his own, with equipment brought specially to Cambridge. But the decision to use this unfamiliar technique to print Bibles and Books of Common Prayer was of fundamental importance.

In a forlorn effort to protect his interests, John Baskett had greeted the project by Fenner, Ged and their associates to print the Bible by joining with the London stationers William Mount, John Coggs and William Davis in an action brought in Chancery. But there could be no doubting the University's legal right to print the privileged books, or even to do so through its nominated agent; and Baskett was quickly seen off.[17] At Oxford, Baskett rented the Bible Press from the University for £200 per annum, though this was paid only irregularly, and his relations with the University were often strained. But in the early 1730s his business (now carried on with two prominent London booksellers, Samuel Ashurst and Robert Gosling) showed signs of improvement; and when a new lease was agreed in 1734 the number of presses to be used by the partnership was increased from four to five.[18] Though little record seems to have survived of the quantities of the privileged books that he printed, he was by 1720 already printing octavo and duodecimo editions of the Bible in 10,000 copies apiece, while a duodecimo New Testament was said to be 'always printing'. The quality of his work in the smaller formats left much room for improvement, the small, poorly printed type rendering them sometimes illegible, while the quality of his texts was cause for scandal.[19] Ged and Fenner sought a share of this market, and their failure suggested a way forward to others at Cambridge. Instead of licensing a further University Printer, or of following the Oxford practice of permitting a separate business for privileged books, the Cambridge authorities chose that the printing of Bibles and the Book of Common Prayer should be a part of the ordinary activities of the University Printing House.

Bentham's appontment as University Printer in 1740 offered a clear statement of intent by the University. As Printer, he was to restore order and vitality to the Press. As a person with established local interests and connections, he was to restore confidence. Such qualities were urgently needed.

The Syndicate established in 1737 to enquire into the University Press included William Richardson, the new Master of Emmanuel, and F. S. Parris, of Sidney Sussex College.[20] In one respect, expectations of them were unequivocal; and less than a year after their appointment a further Grace approved a further Syndicate to direct the printing of Bibles on the expiry of the Fenner lease.[21] Eager to redeem the situation, on 26 October 1738 the Syndics ordered '1000 Weight of Brevier Letter' from William Caslon, 'for printing Bibles & Common Prayer Books in 12°'. A year later the order was countermanded – on the advice of Caslon himself – to the same weight of the smaller nonpareil: that is, the size of type used by John Baskett for printing the duodecimo Bibles with which any new Cambridge Bible would be in competition.[22] It was an odd mistake to have made, and probably reflects the inexperience of the Syndics, who in the circumstances may not necessarily have had Crownfield's whole attention. Joseph Bentham was thus approached not only to succeed the aged Crownfield, but also to bring much-needed experience. His first task was to print the Bible.

By May 1740 (that is, after the decision to appoint Bentham[23]), it had been agreed that the new Cambridge Bible should be printed on two sizes of paper, demy (for the large) and crown (for the ordinary): paper was ordered from John Rowe, in London.[24] On 11 December the price was set at half a crown and 2s. respectively: 1,000 large and 9,000 small were to be printed.[25]

The reasoning behind these decisions, following the Fenner affair, was straightforward, and was presented to the University:

> The Syndics thought it would be adviseable for them to undertake the printing a Bible of such a Size as is of most general Demand, and this they did, 1. in order to serve the Public with a more beautiful and correct Edition than can easily be found. 2. For the Honour of the University, which would be advanced by such a Work being well executed at their Press. 3. That, by their being secure of constant Employment for them, they may be always able to retain a number of good Hands ready for any Work that shall be brought in. 4. Because they believe a considerable Profit may accrue to the University by printing Bibles, though it cannot yet be estimated how great it will be, nor is expected to be equal to that of a private Trader.[26]

Except perhaps for the Book of Common Prayer, the Bible had for generations been available to retail purchasers in a greater choice than any other book – not only of bindings (which were not to be taken generally into publishers' hands until the nineteenth century, and even then often remained in the hands of wholesaling agents), but also of size of type and size and quality of paper. For some editions, there had been a surprising range of choice in the seventeenth century.[27] But what in the seventeenth century seems to have been underplayed was made explicit and emphasised to purchasers in the eighteenth. From 1724, and in order to control unreasonable variation and exploitation by the trade, Bible printers were obliged by law to set the price of each copy on the title-page.[28] At the time, the printing of Bibles in England was in the hands of Baskett, at whom the order was therefore directed. Baskett obeyed the order irregularly from the first, and by the late 1730s usually ignored it. The order had no effect on printers outside England, in Amsterdam, Edinburgh and Dublin, who also supplied the English market; but once the Cambridge press entered this market it had, like London and Oxford, to abide by the rule.

More than any other book, the Bible and the prayer book were thus sold on their visual appearance and their physical characteristics: their typography, their materials and their cost. Like the Bible, the prayer book was also turned into an object in which taste and money were as important in determining choice among an extraordinary variety of finished objects as were religious preferences or anticipated purposes. Conventions and individual taste played complementary roles, in which owners of these books required that they should be immediately identifiable for their religious content, and yet often wished to demonstrate their decorative, religious or financial distinctiveness. As the manufacture of Bibles and prayer books increased, so also many of the traditional freedoms in this respect were gradually abandoned. The great numbers of copies required by charitable societies required cheap, and inevitably uniform, bindings. In 1747, asking for a further consignment of Bibles from the Cambridge press, the London bookseller Charles Bathurst undertook that they would be bound up only in his own house.[29] Demand led to shortages, and hence either to higher prices or to lower standards. In 1760, the Society for Promoting Christian Knowledge agreed that in view of the current expense of leather, its agent should be allowed extra for binding, provided he reduce the price once the cost of leather dropped again.[30] Different degrees of decoration and quality of materials and workmanship in the binding were but the most obvious external attributes of a book, such as the Bible, that possessed significances in its exterior appearance just as much as its internal.

Within the book there were other opportunities for taste, adornment and religious inclination. John Sturt's two series of engravings published originally in the 1720s remained available in debased versions long after his death in 1730. They could be bound into Bibles, or (supplied with a title-page of their own) they could be bought as a separate series.[31] In 1751, when the Bible trade was still dominated by Baskett, an advertisement for Bibles listed quarto copies from Oxford, suitable for families, either in plain calf, or with cuts, with a gilt spine, or with Sturt's engravings and in Turkey leather. Copies were available in a similar range in small quarto as well.[32] As if in confirmation that the customer was no longer entirely free to choose, but was being shaped in his or her choice by suppliers – in this as in other consumer goods – these various guises of the Bible were all offered at fixed advertised prices. For both the Bible and the prayer book, the engraving trade offered more sets of illustrations, to be bound in, organised according to the lectionary or other parts of the contents.[33] Inevitably, the quality and price of these engravings also varied. Since their production was not restricted to the learned presses, and they emanated from the engraving trade rather than that for ordinary books, these series of engravings enjoyed a life cycle quite independent of the dates of publication on title-pages. Surviving copies attest to the fact that suites were bound up frequently an appreciable number of years after their first publication, as booksellers or binders used up their stocks, or engraved plates were reprinted without change of date.

As costs and production standards for some of the most popular formats were driven down, the several publishers discovered that competition could be increased if they each offered a choice among their own wares. In 1736, the SPCK, founded in 1699 and designed partly to promote charity schools and partly to publish works that would encourage piety and Christian behaviour, was also anxious to encourage the study of the Bible among the general population in Britain as well as to promote missionary activity overseas.[34] Accordingly it offered 'for the use of the poor' two editions in duodecimo, one set in minion and one in nonpareil, price 3s. and 2s. respectively. Either could be purchased with the Book of Common Prayer bound up with it for a total of 3s.9d. or 2s.8d. – the same as the price of a grey cloth waistcoat or a pair of breeches for a charity school boy, advertised in the same document.[35]

Moreover, and as the SPCK advertisements made clear, the trade in the Bible and the trade in the Book of Common Prayer were closely linked, by their status as privileged books reserved to the King's Printer and the two university presses, and (for many customers) by their shared place in the worship of the Church of England. Like Bibles, from 1724 prices of prayer books had to be printed on their title-pages. Fenner had wished to print both at Cambridge. They could be marketed together or separately, and customers expected a similar choice of format and appearance. In 1736, the SPCK list offered the prayer book in pica octavo, brevier or minion duodecimo, minion 24°, and nonpareil 24°, at prices between 2s.4d. and 9d.

Rather than follow Oxford, and establish a separate Bible press, the Cambridge authorities envisaged that any printing of privileged books should be within the same printing house. There were good organisational reasons for this, since it would ensure that workmen would be kept fully employed, rather than shifted constantly from job to job. On piece-rates, as the compositors were, lost time was lost income.[36] Quite apart from the interest of the employee, in a generation that was beginning to pay increasing attention to the management of time as a part of industrial production, this was an important consideration. As Bentham's brother Edward, canon of Christ Church, put it when he was asked to comment on proposals for the Oxford press in 1756:

Authors & Editors, tis well known, unexpectedly to ye Printer every now & then give themselves, some hours at least, if not half a day or a whole day's, Holiday.

Some time must be lost to the Compositor in transporting himself to t'other side of the house & settling himself in a new piece of work; by which time perhaps ye Author returns & expects the Compositor should be immediately ready to attend him.

Q. If, instead of sending its Compositors to t'other side of ye House, the University was to reserve to itself the Liberty of printing in its own house any such sort of Bible or Common Prayerbook as the Delegates should think proper, paying themselves & their workmen according to ye rate of ye Tables, & leaving the trouble & profits of sale to Basket. Thus, the University would have always stock-work in hand, & might occasionally throw out Editions of ye Bible & Com. Prayer, wch might do it credit.[37]

It seems probable that the canon of Christ Church consulted with the University Printer on a matter requiring a professional opinion.

The first Bible to be printed at Cambridge under the auspices of the Syndics rather than (like Legate in the 1590s, or Buck and Daniel in the 1620s and 1630s) of a University Printer acting in his own capacity, or at the expense of the Stationers' Company (like Hayes), was published in 1743, in duodecimo. Although it had been agreed in 1740 that the edition was to consist of 10,000 copies, this order was increased to 12,000 in June 1741, sure sign of confidence by its promoters.[38] By then, composition had already been in progress for some months:[39] by November 1741, the first ten sheets had been printed off, matters not helped by a recalcitrant new printing press.[40] The text was checked and proofed by F. S. Parris, who was paid a fee of £40.[41] But though in 1762 it became known that Parris had devoted much labour to ensuring as correct a text as possible for the edition of that year, in which he was further helped by Henry Therond of Trinity College, nothing was said of his work on this earlier edition. In 1743, the more immediate question was one of marketing, and of disposing of an edition larger than of any book ever before published by the University. Much of the edition was sold for distribution in accordance with the terms of the trust of Philip, 4th Baron Wharton,[42] while others were taken by the SPCK, through the London bookseller and agent for the Press, Charles Bathurst.

Like other publishers of the Bible, the Syndics had agreed to print copies of their new edition on both small and large paper. In 1743 the SPCK had extended its range to include a brevier octavo edition of the Bible, at 6s., a price that is impossible to reconcile with an audience solely of the poor. But the appearance of a Cambridge Bible was made the occasion of a wholesale revision of prices downwards. Though the Syndics had set the prices of their duodecimo Bible at half a crown and 2s., the SPCK offered them (likewise unbound) at 2d. less in each case. At the same time the prices of other editions in duodecimo were reduced, from 3s. to 2s.9d. and from 2s. to 1s.8d.[43] Much more important than the fact that Cambridge Bibles were more expensive when compared with others in the list of one of the country's most powerful publishers, was the fact that the SPCK was thus subsidising and undercutting a book of which the University's agent had anticipated sole charge in London.

Although the Bible was chosen first, attempts at stereotyping had also concentrated on the prayer book. In the early eighteenth century, the place of the prayer book in public worship was emphasised with renewed zeal. William Beveridge's *Sermon concerning the excellency and usefulness of the Common Prayer*, originally preached in London in 1681 and first printed the following year, was an immediate success. By 1700 there had been at least seventeen editions, and by 1800 the number had grown to over forty. Copies were printed in different formats and sizes of type so as to reach different audiences, and the SPCK added it to its list of publications, offering copies at 2¼d. each. Like others, Beveridge also emphasised the importance of the Holy Communion, though weekly practice varied in different parts of the country, depending on the availability of clergy and on the customs of individual parishes.[44]

The Cambridge Syndics were entering as assured a market for the prayer book as they had for the Bible. To a great extent the two went together, since so many of those who bought the Bible required a prayer book (and the metrical psalms) to be bound up with it. From the outset, when Caslon was asked to provide a thousand pounds weight of nonpareil type specifically for the Bible and prayer book, it was anticipated that the two would be printed together.[45] So, when on 22 October 1741 the Syndics at last agreed the edition sizes, they agreed not only to print 6,000 copies of the prayer book in nonpareil type, but also 12,000 of the services only, in the same type, to be bound up with Bibles. Less than twelve months later, they agreed to print 2,000 copies each of the prayer book in octavo and in duodecimo, and eleven months later again they agreed to 1,000 copies in folio, on two sizes of paper.[46] These were but preliminary skirmishes. By 1744–5 the Syndics had gained confidence, and were placing orders for far larger editions: of 24,000 copies of a 24° edition in June 1744, of 3,000 of a duodecimo edition in March 1744/5. Within a few years, numbers had risen again. Between May and October 1747, it was agreed to print 4,250 copies in octavo; 10,000 copies in duodecimo, set in minion type in double columns, and 5,000, employing the same type but in single columns; and 4,000 in duodecimo in long primer. In the same months it was further agreed to print 10,000 copies of the metrical psalms to be bound up with the 24° prayer book and 15,000 copies of the psalms in duodecimo.[47] At a single meeting of the Syndics in May 1758, orders were given to print four separate editions of the prayer book: in quarto on two sizes of paper (500 large and 1,500 demy), in octavo (5,000 copies), in duodecimo (10,000 copies in brevier), and in 24° (20,000 copies). A further order for 15,000 copies, small duodecimo, followed in October.[48] By the mid-1760s, orders had increased still further, and editions of 15 or 20,000 of the smaller formats of the Bible and prayer book had become frequent. Prices were driven ever downward, in attempts obtain further markets. In 1743, the price of unbound copies of the smallest format of all, in 24°, was 1s.2d. in sheets; by 1753, copies in the same format were available for sixpence. Duodecimo editions were available in the 1740s and 1750s variously (according to the size of type and quality of the paper) at 9d., 1s., 1s.3d. or 1s.8d.

All this was not accomplished without some difficulties. Although the Syndics and Bentham rapidly achieved an unprecedented importance in the market, and eventually began to realise substantial profits, they did so only after coming to terms with the complications of regulating paper supplies and arriving at agreements over agents and discounts. In order to bring some supervision to matters, in October 1741 the Syndics determined that two of their number should attend the press monthly in rotation, to inspect workmen and the Press's activities generally.[49] Profits depended on tight margins, and on as economical use of paper as possible. There was more profit in large paper copies, and so there was every inducement to encourage customers to expect variety, and to buy more expensively if they could. In March 1745/6, when it was realised that there was a likelihood of a larger demand than had been anticipated for the Bible on demy paper, printed in nonpareil, and that the profit on that was much larger than that to be obtained from printing on the smaller crown paper, the order given the previous autumn for an edition on demy was increased.[50] In June 1751 second thoughts similarly resulted in 1,000 copies on large paper being added to an order to print first 12,000 and then 14,000 on small paper.[51]

Most of all, the Press depended on its London agents. Charles Bathurst, the bookseller with whom the Syndics reached agreement in March 1741/2, was experienced in ways that Bentham and, still more, the Vice-Chancellors of the day, were not. Tensions were inevitable, and particularly so in dealing with a printer who had very little capital on which to draw at any one time. Such difficulties were not unique either to Bathurst or to Bentham; there were plenty of others who faced cognate problems in the book trade, at a time when it was changing fundamentally during the middle years of the eighteenth century, and when fresh contrivances had to be made to create sufficient working capital.[52] Bathurst was not only to maintain a warehouse in London for books (including, but by no means solely, Bibles and prayer books) printed in Cambridge; he was also to indemnify the University against bad debts. In return, the University undertook to pay for (but was not obliged to undertake) initial advertising, would pay the cost of carriage from Cambridge to London, and would allow him 14 per cent.[53]

Most of Bathurst's interests were in Britain; but with the development of British interests worldwide, the market for books was gradually changed. In this, the missionary societies were of fundamental importance – the SPCK in the eighteenth century and the Bible Society in the early nineteenth. Commercial exploitation by booksellers on a scale sufficient to influence the home market tended to develop much later. The SPCK had been founded to pursue its work both at home and in the colonies. It quickly focused its attention on North America and on India, supplying books and encouraging missionary work. In its hands, books printed at Cambridge made their way overseas in increasing numbers. The *Suidas*, no longer in much demand in Europe, was provided for missionaries in India in 1719,[54] among other foundations for a serious library; but most books were cheaper, and intended for more general enlightenment. The Lutheran mission at Tranquebar, and the English mission at Fort St George (Madras) to the north, were both objects of the Society's support: for books, educational and domestic supplies as well as equipment for the printing press established by Bartholomaeus Ziegenbalg and Johann Gründler in 1712.[55] In November 1744, the Society agreed to send out not only printing equipment, but also a dozen Cambridge printed Bibles, bound in parchment, to Madras, and a further dozen duodecimo Cambridge Bibles to Cuddalore, just to the north of Tranquebar.[56] These Bibles seem to have been the first multiple shipment of Cambridge printed books to India. Until 1776, it was illegal to print the Bible and prayer book, both privileged books, in America; and though there may have been a pirated Bible in 1761 the limitation seems to have been generally observed: no New Testament was printed there until 1777.[57]

Accordingly, those who supplied to the Society were contributing substantially to its overseas interests. It was a market that commanded respect, but the Society was commensurately demanding in its needs: not only for cheapness (since the books were to be sold as widely as possible), but also for a reasonable quality. The acceptance by the Society of Cambridge Bibles and prayer books into its catalogues was an event of some importance, that was to have repercussions. But it seems to have happened with such suddenness, and the ensuing events moved with such rapidity, as to make it probable that matters were guided by individual and forceful influence. Any inroads into the Society's interests in these books had to be at the expense of Baskett, just as it had to be in the wider, more general, trade. Although it was agreed by the Society in May 1744 that Cambridge Bibles and prayer books should be included in its catalogues, it was only in October following that formal complaint (by Vincent Perronet, Vicar of Shoreham in Kent and one of the Wesleys' most devoted supporters) was recorded of misprints in several recent editions of Baskett's New Testaments printed at Oxford and London. The matter was referred to the Archbishop of Canterbury, and in December a decision was reached that augured well for Bentham: that none but Cambridge editions be sent in future to members, 'on Account of the many & gross Errors in the Editions publish'd by Mr Basket'. In some of this, the Cambridge press may have had a sympathetic advocate in the person of the powerful treasurer to the SPCK, John Denne, former Fellow of Corpus Christi College. But the storm blew over as quickly as it had arisen, and Baskett was restored to favour the next month.[58]

It was not the last time that Baskett was criticised. Further complaint reached the Society in 1757, respecting an octavo edition of the Bible dated 1751, and in 1758 objections were made both of the quality of his paper and the quality of his printing in a New Testament printed at Oxford in 1757.[59] In 1759 the Society went so far as to insist on inspecting a sample of paper before printing commenced.[60] It is difficult to reconcile such complaints with Scrivener's remark that in the mid-century 'the Bibles of the Basketts . . . earned a fair name both for the beauty of their typography and their comparative freedom from misprints.'[61] Bathurst's printing was poor, and occasionally so poor in the smaller and cheaper formats that it was illegible. But Bentham was not blameless either in this cut-throat business.[62] He was in many ways fortunate that in 1760 the SPCK agreed to place various new editions of the Bible in octavo printed at Cambridge on the list of available publications. The list is a reminder of what, even in one format, was by now being offered to the world. The title-page quoted the price unbound at 4s. or 6s. But the Society offered copies bound: on fine paper, with or without the Apocrypha, at 5s.6d. or 6s.6d., or printed in brevier, on crown (smaller) paper at 3s.8d. or 4s.6d. or on the same paper, including both the Apocrypha and the services and the psalms at 4s.10d.[63]

In challenging Baskett's dominating position, Bentham and the Cambridge authorities had taken on a powerful adversary, and forged for themselves a respected position. The timing of some of the complaints against Baskett was in important respects supremely fortunate. For quite apart from the trade to be obtained in English Bibles, there was also a chance to print the Bible in Welsh. In itself this can have offered little profit, and certain anguish. In 1727 the SPCK had arranged for an octavo Bible in Welsh to be printed by Baskett, and it remained committed to supplying further copies as required. In 1741/2 stock of the 1727 edition ran out,[64] and by the end of the following year a committee had been recommended to oversee a new edition. But in December 1743 the Society discovered that Baskett already intended to print a new Welsh Bible on his own account.[65] It seems that at this stage Baskett preferred to set aside this project for the present; and with remarkable expedition (it was agreed at the same meeting that heard of Baskett's second thoughts) the Society agreed instead to approach William Richardson, at Cambridge.[66] In this way the Society made its first formal contacts with Bible printing at Cambridge, contacts that were to be maintained for generations to come. By the beginning of April following, after a brief skirmish as to the price of printing 15,000 copies in octavo, agreement had been reached and matters had been so far advanced that an advertisement could be placed in the London newspapers.[67] The same year, Cambridge Bibles were added to the Society's lists for the first time, and complaint was made of various of Baskett's Bibles. Thus Bentham could be presented as a responsible alternative to an inaccurate printer; his willingness to co-operate over the Welsh Bible, and Richardson's receptiveness and support as head of a house and a syndic, helped to promote his interests in English Bibles.

After setting out the reasons for printing the Bible in Welsh, and so meeting the needs of 'vast numbers of inhabitants of several parts of Wales', the proposals turned to the edition in question, and to the allied question of the prayer book:

> The Society for Promoting Christian Knowledge being fully persuaded of ye Excellence & Necessity of such a Charity have not only Agreed to recommend & encourage it: but have likewise undertaken ye management of this good work, under the direction of the Right Rev^d. the Bishops, in whose Diocese the Welsh Language is used – and accordingly they have already made a Contract with ye University of Cambridge for an Impression of fifteen thousand Bibles & Common Prayer Books together with ye Psalms in metre on a good Letter and Paper, not doubting but that the same gracious Providence which has prospered all their other Undertakings for the Glory of God, & ye Salvation of Souls, will also raise up Benefactors to enable them to complete this, notwithstanding the Expence of it will amount to a very Large Sum . . .'[68]

Of the need for such books there seemed no doubt, and Isaac Watts asked to reserve 1,000 copies each of the Bible and the prayer book. But as the Bible progressed through the press, its London sponsors repeatedly found themselves critical of their printer. In order to expedite printing, Bentham began at several places simultaneously, and this puzzled the Society. Since it had been decided to use the London edition of 1717 as a model, and Bentham was able to reset the Bible line for line, in fact this presented very little difficulty. More awkwardly, concern was several times expressed over the press-work and the quality of the ink. Even the typography came under criticism, as

Bentham was instructed to set the marginal notes further away from the text so as to produce a less crowded effect. Bentham retaliated by complaining of the quality of the paper. Over it all hung the ordinary seasonal dangers of any printing house at the time, of damp paper becoming mouldy in summer, or freezing and cracking in winter.[69] The printing of the Welsh Bible and prayer book dated 1746 proved to be a prolonged affair. At the last minute, it was decided to include two maps in the Bible, engraved by Nathaniel Hill and the gift of William Jones, FRS. These were printed by the London rolling-press printer Edward Ryland at a rate of 18s. per hundred, excluding the cost of paper. The whole project had proved to be more expensive than had been antici-pated by the time the books were published in June 1748 at prices between 3s.6d. for the Bible (including the Apocrypha), prayer book and psalms bound up together, and 5s. for the same bound into two volumes. But by the end of March 1750 the edition of a little over 15,000 copies had been virtually sold out.[70]

Bentham's triumph was short-lived, for the next octavo edition was commissioned from Baskett, and the SPCK was to provide a fresh fount of type for the purpose from Caslon.[71] Together with the prayer book and metrical psalms, it appeared in London in 1752, following Bentham's example line for line in the prayer book as well. Nevertheless, the 1748 edition had brought assured income. It had allowed men to be retained at the Cambridge press who would otherwise have been laid off. Paper was supplied by the Society, and Bentham printed the edition at a rate of £14.10s. per sheet – slightly more than had been originally hoped by the SPCK. Apart from small dona-tions of 3 or 5 guineas from various colleges, designed to encourage the project, money was paid on account by the Society: £435 in 1745–6, and £584.10s.10d. in 1746–7: the final balance in 1748 brought the printing bill up to £1,160, for a total of eighty sheets.[72]

While it was a great advance on previous arrangements, which had been irregular and intermittent at best, the agreement with Bathurst tied the University's hands more than it wished once it was realised how successful the English Bible and prayer book business could become. With the advent of sales through the SPCK in 1743–4, the University arranged to sell direct to the Society, as well as to Bathurst.[73] But whereas the authorities at Cambridge wished to control their press, Bathurst considered that they had insufficient understanding of the needs of the London (and hence overseas and to a great extent country) trade. It was also in Bathurst's interest to obtain as many books as possible to sell, provided that he had a market: the temptation to force the pace, and to lecture Bentham and others at Cambridge on the management of the book trade, was on occasion overwhelming. In 1747, matters came to a head when Bathurst seems to have mistaken a suggestion for a formal agreement by the Syndics that more paper should be ordered. The first consignment of paper intended (according to Bathurst) for a Bible in minion type was sent to Cambridge,[74] only to be returned by F. S. Parris, now Vice-Chancellor, whose letter of protest to Bathurst reveals much about the fragile existence of the Press during these years when (to judge by the healthy number of its publications) it might appear otherwise to be in a singularly successful period.

We have above £500 worth of paper by us already for several works, most of which particularly near 500 Rh: for the 8ᵛᵒ Bible tho paid for on delivery, can't in all probability be employed this twelvemonth: And our press expence yᵉ last year has quite drained us, having exceeded our receipt I think above £800. Our workmen's wages I find at yᵉ rate of £16 a week; these, tho reduced much, as they must be out of hand, I find no money to answer. The Welsh Bible is paid for within a trifle: works of authors bring in but a trifle; our chief dependance must be on what our books in your hands produce. The last half year you know brought us no money; the next I find will not bring us quite £200; which were little more than enough to answer this paper of your's, & another parcell from Mʳ. Rowe about 3 weeks ago. So yᵗ I am reduced to yᵉ necessity of either returning your paper, or, what is still worse, putting an intire stop to yᵉ press: thô in truth I wish as well to it as any man; & have done as much as most to support it; and am still ready to do so on any practicable footing.[75]

The truth was that receipts from Bathurst were irregular. In 1745–6 the University received £298.2s.9d. for Bibles sold by him up to May: no further money had been received by the time the accounts were made up in November. The following year was better, and showed receipts of £740.1s.6½d. 1747–8 brought a reduction again, to £353.17s.3¼d.[76] Bathurst could do little but accept the Vice-Chancellor's summary. But in doing so he felt bound to point out the true position if examined from the point of view of the possibilities and realities of the market as he saw them:

I did not in the least expect the Case to be as I now find it; because there were (I believe) the Folio, octavo, & twelves Com prayer (now all out of print) in the market at the same time as well as the Bible. These Books having been out of print together with the Bible make my returns much smaller than I wish they were. Sixteen pounds a week is a great Expence; it will maintain about twenty Men upon the common footing, & they should do a good Deal of Business. Mʳ. Bentham writes me, that you think proper to have the Nonpˡ.12° psalms done the next thing, & enquires how many should be printed on Crown paper & how many on Demy. According to my Judgement 6,000 upon Crown paper & 4,000 on Demy: these will take up 80 Rheams of paper in the whole, which according to the common way of working, will be wrought off by two Presses in a fortnight, or by one Press in a month. And I beg Leave to offer it to your Consideration, that of the Folio C Prayer (which was about half printed in May, & the whole paper provided) there may be about 100 Rh. now to work, which is but five weeks Employment for one Press: & but half the time for two – The Common prayer 12°: for which I sent the Demy Paper, will take up 90 Rh. or if this Impression is enlarged, as I think it is, 120 Rh. which is three Weeks works for two Presses, & Six Weeks for one. Which ever of these you choose to do first, if you please to order one to be finished at a time without interruption, something will be coming frequently to Market to bring in the Money again, & a little profit.[77]

There were some straightforward principles here, and some good common sense. Most importantly, if the Cambridge press was to succeed it had to be as well organised as the busy London printing houses, paying its men similar wages and achieving a regular output at press: Bathurst considered that a single press, worked by two men, should produce three reams of sheets printed on both sides per day. The point that once work was begun, it should not be allowed to lie around uncompleted and therefore unsaleable, was an obvious one. So too was the desirability of keeping books in print, and the market therefore constantly, rather than intermittently, aware of Cambridge Bibles and prayer books. But without the right paper little could be achieved, and the Cambridge press was in a cash flow crisis.

Parris's solution was to lay off men, and employ the others either on the independently funded Welsh Bible or on such books of the Press's own as had paper available. Neither he nor Richardson, in whom he usually found an ally in the Press's affairs, found Bathurst's insistence on further investment realistic:

> I might too in my turn, Sir, think it very hard to be thus teized by you against all reason; and might fairly content myself with reminding you of your proper concern, to sell our books during pleasure, & be thankfull for the great advantages you receive at our Expence, without fancying from thence, yᵗ you are to command us or our purse. But I rather chuse to shew you, what you have made me see very fully, & what I hope to satisfie others of, yᵗ we are in no condition to execute these your schemes.
>
> Our utmost receipt from our press this year, thô you make me two payments, as indeed you ought, & I must desire you to do, can't I find be £600. Our expence, on yᵉ present footing of yᵉ press, without any new project, or more paper than is necessary to compleat yᵉ Folio & small twelves com: prayer, can't be less than £850. we have really no money to spare to answer this excess of expence, if indeed it were prudent to lay out all here, & reserve nothing for any extraordinary emergences. What then had been yᵉ case, if we had proceeded in yᵉ way I found the press, paying for paper without end to carry on Bible work without Measure? Our expence (I don't guess, but have computed it carefully) had then exceeded our receipt this year above £2000: or rather, we had by this time wanted money even for our necessary Expences, our press had been shut up, & yᵉ poor Syndics ridiculous. A Printer & a Trader, who knew our small stock & small returns of money, should have been aware of this.[78]

In the end, a compromise was reached, and a few weeks later, in May 1748, the Syndics quietly agreed to order paper from Bathurst sufficient to make up what was already in Cambridge in order to complete the duodecimo prayer book.[79] But the pause in the headlong production of the privileged books had drawn attention to its dangers; when the Syndics resumed production they also ordered Bentham to seek to recover all outstanding debts by authors whose work had been printed at their own expense.

As a bookseller, Bathurst could reasonably complain. The Press had allowed its supplies to fail, in a healthy market. According to him, even the 24° prayer book, one of the most popular lines of all, had by October 1751 been out of print for eighteen months. The duodecimo edition had been out of print for a year; that in octavo for three and a half years, from summer 1747 to Christmas 1750; and that in folio for fifteen months. The Bible had been out of print for fourteen months, and by October 1751 it was out of print again. Instead of being supplied with regular parcels, Bathurst had found himself with a thankless and (in his view) poorly rewarded task that the University could not do without. There was some justification here, and not least in that within the space of about thirteen years the University had seen its assumption disproved: that the power of the King's Printer, and the failure of attempts at Cambridge to print the privileged books under licence, were reasons enough not to encourage the University Printer to embark on such a difficult market. Thanks to Bathurst, an entirely new perspective had been created; but in return he claimed that by the time he had taken into account necessary trips to Holland for paper and to Cambridge for more general questions, he was receiving a smaller annual income from the business even than the wages paid to a journeyman working for his principal rival in this market, the King's Printer.[80]

In all of this, he rightly recognised that the principal difficulty lay in the cost of paper, and the University's inability to invest in sufficient supplies. His solution was straightforward. He would undertake to print up to 1,000 reams of privileged books each year, he supplying the paper and paying the University 50 per cent more than the journeymen's wages for composition, correcting and presswork. In light of the Press's current shortage of suitable type, he would also undertake to buy sufficient for this purpose.[81] He did not welcome the suggestion that a second agent be employed, for he was unconvinced that sales would thereby increase, and he was proud of his own reputation.

Bathurst remained the University's London agent for the Bible and prayer book until 1751. By then, the tensions between the University, who had to invest in paper, and Bentham, who had to make no investment of his own (though he protested that in practice he did) and whose task it was to sell most (but by no means all) of the finished Bibles and prayer books, had become intolerable. The University's decision to impose on Bathurst a reduction in his commission to 10 per cent no doubt forced the issue, but it was one born of practical financial analysis;[82] and in October a new agent was appointed. The new man, Benjamin Dod, had been bookseller to the SPCK since 1744/5,[83] and was therefore well used to much of the Cambridge trade. He was prepared to accept just 7 per cent, exactly half what had been first agreed with Bathurst.[84] It may have seemed harsh, and it was certainly ungenerous when compared with the allowances paid to the warehouse keeper in London for the Oxford press, agreed by the Delegates at Oxford in 1758.[85] But Cambridge was, for the present, in a strong position.

Dod brought fresh ideas, and fresh money. By 1760, the market for Bibles had become saturated with cheap editions, many of them poorly printed, and with texts that had become corrupt. Baskerville's celebrated folio Bible of 1763, discussed more fully in the following chapter, was one attempt to meet a need for a fresh approach – by the University as well as by Baskerville, whose interests have more generally been emphasised by historians. The University itself had already by then instigated a new edition in quarto that was to be textually and decoratively superior to the many that had been printed in the past two decades. On 17 June 1760, the Syndics agreed to share with Dod the costs of printing a quarto Bible, the two parties each to own half of the edition. Subsequently, it was further agreed to provide an engraved frontispiece and title-page for the Bible:[86] the frontispiece was engraved by Charles Grignion, after a design by Francis Hayman. The text seems to have been the responsibility of F. S. Parris, Master of Sidney Sussex College, who had corrected the edition of 1743 and had been much involved in that of 1747 also. His work of 1760–2 on marginal annotations and italicisation lived on in numerous subsequent editions, whether printed in Cambridge, Oxford (where in 1769 Benjamin Blayney took over many of his suggestions) or London.[87] The project, which began with a new quarto edition, was subsequently enlarged so as to include an edition in folio as well, printed from reimposed formes of the same setting of type.[88] Both editions were published in 1762, and thus appeared a few months before Baskerville's folio.

The impression of continuous and increasing activity in the sphere of Bible and prayer book printing has, however, to be countered. The Cambridge press was embroiled in a trade where critics were ever at the ready – and in London especially. 'Truly the jests People make here of the negligence of our Advantage & Honour are very irksome', wrote Bathurst to Bentham in December 1747, commenting on the steps taken in Cambridge to bring to order a confusion in the printing house that seems to have led to nothing being completed for sale.[89] Printing of privileged books had to be fitted in with other work, on the same presses: there was no press specifically for Bible or prayer book printing. Thus, when in 1760 it was decided to print a new quarto Bible (eventually also to be printed in folio, and published in 1762), it was ordered that one press should be devoted to this project, with a second occasionally, so that the edition could be finished eighteen months from the time it was started.[90] The arrangement, designed to produce the Bible with a minimum of delay, was evidently exceptional.

Dod's death in 1765 brought a need for yet further arrangements with London. The year was complicated by Bentham's illness; and the University faced a dilemma once again. By this time, the decision to appoint Dod as London agent, and the terms agreed, had been fully vindicated. Using a system of promissory notes which allowed him to delay payments until the following financial year, the University had watched its income from the printing of Bibles and prayer books rise steadily, quadrupling to £3,000 between 1752–3 and 1763–4.

From the early 1740s, under Bentham's auspices, the Press once again became one of the country's leading suppliers of the Bible and the Book of Common Prayer. Eventually such a policy ensured that the Press would escape financial ruin. The anxiety with which the early years were meanwhile viewed is recorded in a small notebook covering 1740–4, now in the University Archives, in which costs and receipts were set out in minute detail.[91] In reality, it was impossible to unravel the true costs of any of the Press's operations, whether for printing the privileged books, for printing the University's own very occasional publications, or for printing for private customers – that is, booksellers and authors. Bentham, like other University Printers in the eighteenth century, was permitted to work on his own account; but he used the University's premises, the University's type, and the University's presses. Paper and labour were the only elements in a job that could be costed independently, since paper was bought against each job, and composition and presswork could be measured – either by time or, more usually, by the length of setting or by the sheet printed off. Nonetheless, some calculation was necessary; and to one witness at least this suggested that the printing of privileged books could be measured against work for authors and other private work. So it seemed, after due account had been taken for paper, printing charges, packing and carriage, and discounted charges to booksellers, that the duodecimo Bible of 1743, which with the services cost £1,100 to print and send to London, made a clear profit of £195. On a duodecimo prayer book, printed in an edition of 6,000 copies, the profit appeared to be £130. For a folio prayer book, printed on more expensive paper stocks in an edition of 1,000, the profit appeared to be £98. Beside these sums for the privileged books one could set the annual profit accruing to the Press from private work. In 1740–4 this averaged £162 per annum.[92] For a press that had been, and threatened to continue to be, a burden for the University, the conclusion was inevitable: that the printing of the Bible and prayer book must be of primary concern.[93]

Dod's death brought an opportunity for reappraisal. By 1765, Bentham was still only in his mid-fifties; but he was unwell.[94] The experiment with Baskerville was of recent memory. His celebrated folio Bible had been published in 1763, and in 1760–2 he had printed four editions of the prayer book in Cambridge. Idiosyncratic, querulous in some of his dealings with the University, an absentee and, though a University Printer, wholly independent of Bentham's printing house, Baskerville had nevertheless proffered an alternative strategy for the University. His books found many admirers, though they also found detractors. Neither party was eager for a further agreement. But other printers, some jealous of his advantage and others perceiving longer-term benefits, were readily forthcoming.

The suggestion that the University should lease out its privileges to print the Bible and the prayer book met with immediate enthusiasm in the London trade, where it was believed that the annual profits had been £1,300 for the past seven years, and where it was also observed that a further £200 resulted from farming out the almanac privilege. Among those interested, William Strahan and Robert Collins[95] were thought to have bid £800 per annum, an anonymous consortium £900, and another anonymous party £1,000. Thomas Fletcher and Francis Hodson, printers of the *Cambridge Chronicle*, offered £100, as did J. Wilson and Isaac Fell, from London. The London firm of Mount and Page was also interested. In September 1765 John Nichols was sent by Bowyer to present their own joint proposals to the Vice-Chancellor. Notwithstanding the figures, the University was as much interested in a creditable agreement and in reliability as in maximum profit. Bowyer clearly believed himself to be in a privileged position, as a member of St John's, and for these reasons he and Nichols considered that a comparatively modest bid might secure the lease.[96]

Most in the trade saw the need for a joint approach: a printer and a bookseller who would work in partnership. It seemed to Nichols (as no doubt it did to some of the others who bid) that the trade in privileged books could be greatly increased. By extending his business as a bookseller, and for all the inherent dangers in partnerships where accounts might never be properly settled, Bowyer also hoped for 'less trouble than I have now with Authors & Booksellers'.[97] Meanwhile Nichols also noted who might be of advantage to them in Cambridge. René Labutte had moved from London to Cambridge as an assistant to the printer of the *Cambridge Journal* and had established himself as a teacher of French.[98] But above all, it was necessary to secure the co-oper-ation of John Archdeacon, who seems already to have become a central figure in Bentham's printing house. 'Whoever has the Lease, Mr. ArchDeacon MUST be a LEADING person', wrote Nichols to Bowyer on the first afternoon of his visit, before calling on him both on the day following and the next.[99]

Nothing came of the trade's hopes. At the end of October the Press Syndics decided, for the first time, to employ more than a single agent. More importantly in the longer term, and in the aftermath of the half share dealing with Dod, they also deter-mined to proceed henceforth by agency, rather than (as they had in the 1730s and with Baskerville in the 1760s) farm out their rights. In autumn 1765, agreement was reached with no less than five London booksellers: John Rivington, James Waugh, Benjamin White, John Beecroft and Edward Dilly. Thomas and John Merrill, the Cambridge booksellers, were added to the group. The list, involving some of the largest London booksellers, is a measure of how profitable the trade in the Bible and prayer book had now come to seem. By confirming that there should be agents rather than licensees or other partners, the Syndics could expect to benefit from these profits. Archdeacon's position was clarified by his appointment as Bentham's assistant in what became a period of transition.[100] A year later, on 13 December 1766, with these various negotia-tions and suggestions now brought to an end, Bentham resigned his office.[101]

By this date, John Baskerville had left Cambridge, triumphant and yet disappointed. His truncated career as University Printer forms the subject of the following chapter.

Baskerville and Bentham

The last chapter was concerned almost wholly with the reintroduction of Bible and prayer book printing at Cambridge under the guidance of Joseph Bentham. It dealt with the production of books for a part of the book trade that was unusually demanding, and with the right judgement could be unusually profitable. Bentham's task was to make a place for himself in a market that was conservative and established, albeit one that was growing apace thanks to changes in population structures and distribution, and thanks to the withdrawal from the English-speaking market of the Dutch Bible trade. Ever since the eighteenth century, this workaday process has been over-shadowed, the commercial skills of Bentham in conjunction with a handful of senior members of the University (notably Richardson and Parris) outshone by the brilliance of John Baskerville (fig. 12). Yet there was more to the brief period when John Baskerville was University Printer than simply the production of a handful of books that were in almost every way better designed and better printed than those of Bentham.

Baskerville's Bible of 1763 has been justifiably praised ever since its appearance, as one of the finest books ever to have been printed in Britain. As such, it must take pride of place in the history of printing in Cambridge.[1] Baskerville had turned to printing after a successful career in Birmingham first as a writing master and then, probably from the early 1740s, in the japanning trade, meeting a demand for decorative and highly finished household wares. Then, in the early 1750s he turned his attention to printing: to improvements in type design, and improvements in paper, to ways of imparting an evenness on the printed page both in appearance and in impression, of a kind not to be found in the work of his contemporaries. His quest took him not only to improvements in type design (using the skills he had learned as a writing master) and in developing with James Whatman a means of making a smoother paper, made on a new, wove, mould (rather than the usual laid mould), but also to new standards in the construction and use of the printing press, and to improvements in the manufacture of ink.[2] By 1754 he was able to issue a specimen of a projected edition of Virgil; when the edition appeared three years later, type, paper and ink were seen to be combined to demonstrate the revolutionary nature of his achievement, one that has affected many of our expectations respecting the appearance of printing ever since.

Even before he had completed his quarto Virgil in 1757, Baskerville had begun to

Fig. 12 John Baskerville, by James Millar.

think of printing a prayer book, of a size 'calculated for people who begin to want Spectacles but are ashamed to use them at Church'. But in order to do so he had to come to an agreement with those who already enjoyed the sole rights, either Baskett or Cambridge; and the latter's 'patronage', as he phrased it, seemed more probable.

> If I find favor with the University, & they give me a Grant to print an Edition of a prayer book . . . I would as soon as Virgil was finished & a proper place could be found for their Reception, send to Cambridge two presses, Workmen & all other Requisites, but should be glad to take the Chance of the Edition to my Self, & make the University such Considerations as they should think fit to prescribe.[3]

Baskerville was appointed University Printer on 16 December 1758, in order to allow him to complete specific projects: the printing of two octavo prayer books, and a folio Bible.[4] When he was appointed, his other business in hand included an order from the Oxford press for Greek type, which was not delivered until 1761.[5] Both in his eyes and in those of the University, the Cambridge appointment was no more than a form of licence, for which he had to pay. The order of the University's decisions, in which consent was sought first for the terms of his agreement, and only then was he elected 'one of the Stationers & printers of this University' for a term limited to ten years, makes clear the unusual nature of his position.[6] Indeed, he was specifically not to use the University's name in his other work, and could print nothing more at Cambridge without the permission of the Syndics. Apart from the celebrated Bible and (eventually) three editions of the prayer book in octavo and one in duodecimo, he is only known to have printed one further item at Cambridge, a broadside address dated 30 April 1762 to Ferdinand, King of the Two Sicilies, acknowledging various gifts to the University.[7]

The printing house that Baskerville established at Cambridge in the spring of 1759, and where he installed his assistants Thomas Warren and Robert Martin,[8] was quite separate from that of Bentham. He found the arrangement tiresome:

> I then applied to the University of Cambridge (Oxford having farmed their Priviledge to the Patentee) & with difficulty obtained their Licence to print an octavo Edition of a Common Prayer book in two Sizes of Characters, on the hard Condition of paying to the University twenty pound the thousand, & the expensive Inconvenience of setting up a compleat Printing House there; & the double Carriage of Paper to & from Cambridge, & afterwards to London &c.[9]

His intentions to print works distinctive both for their design and for their workmanship had little in common with the more everyday needs of Bentham's press. Nevertheless, he was from the first in competition with Bentham. By agreeing to license him, the University chose to risk its profits for the sake of the fee it exacted from Baskerville. 'It is not my desire to print many books; but those, *books* of *Consequence*, of *intrinsic merit*, or *established Reputation*, such as the public may be pleased to see in an elegant dress, and to purchase at such a price, as will repay the extraordinary care and expence which must necessarily be bestowed upon them.' Here, in his proposals of 1757 for an edition of Milton, he shared his ambitions with the general public, whose approval of the Milton would encourage him further:

> But if this performance shall appear to persons of judgement and penetration, in the *Paper, Letter, Ink* and *Workmanship* to excel; I hope their approbation may contribute to procure for me what would indeed be the extent of my Ambition, a power to print an Octavo *Common-Prayer Book*, and a FOLIO BIBLE.
>
> Should it be my good fortune to meet with this indulgence, I wou'd use my utmost efforts to perfect an Edition of them with the greatest Elegance and Correctness; a work which I hope might do some honor to the English Press, and contribute to improve the pleasure, which men of true taste will always have in the perusal of those *sacred Volumes*.[10]

He brought his own equipment to Cambridge – not only his type, but also, most probably, his printing presses constructed to his own modification.

> 'My Presses &c are exactly on the same Construction of other Peoples. But perhaps more accurate than any ever formed since the Invention of the Art of Printing; to explain myself, I have been able to produce three more perfect Plans than have ever before appeared in a Letter Press, (to wit) the Stone, the Platten, (mine are all of Brass an Inch thick) the two first may be produced by any Man who has some Ingenuity, and much attention; But for the third, all printers must depend on the Letter-founder. All my presses were made at Home under my own Inspection . . .'[11]

Much of the appearance of Baskerville's books was the result of his using a much harder support to the paper as it was printed, packing the tympan with a doubled sheet of 'the finest flannel' rather than the two or three layers of swanskin (that is, a very thick and spongy flannel) used by others.[12]

Unlike the University Press, Baskerville could only proceed in his project by borrowing the necessary capital. Proposals for the Bible were issued in the summer of 1759, though by the time the volume was published he had considerably modified the design (fig. 13).[13] The first octavo prayer book appeared in July of the following year.[14] But while these books (with the subsequent prayer books, published in the autumn of 1760, in February 1762 and (in duodecimo) in April 1762) were sufficiently different from the ordinary Cambridge books to cause notice, the Syndics seem to have been determined that Baskerville should not be left to himself in this market. He had printed 2,000 copies of the first prayer book; and in December 1759 the Syndics agreed to print 8,000 copies of an octavo edition. In November 1761 they agreed to another edition of 5,000, and eleven months after that they agreed to another of the same size.[15] Thus, between December 1759 and October 1762, they had agreed to print 18,000 copies – numbers far in excess of Baskerville's. In July 1761 the University agreed that he should print 4,000 copies of a duodecimo edition (published in April 1762, price 4s.6d. in sheets);[16] and in November the Syndics agreed that they should themselves print an edition of 10,000, set in the same size of type as Baskerville's.[17] Whatever allowances are made for the differences in price (Baskerville's being somewhat more expensive) and in quality, the University was giving Baskerville no quarter even as University Printer.

Similar tactics were adopted for the Bible. As already mentioned, Baskerville was already in touch with Oxford on other matters when he was appointed to Cambridge. It is not impossible that his enquiries there as to the possibility of printing a Bible under the auspices of Oxford (and therefore Bathurst) alerted the Oxford delegates to their own position, and that this, coupled with Baskerville's appointment to Cambridge, led directly to their decision to enquire into Baskett's performance.[18] Certainly the events in Cambridge coincided with a renewed interest in the subject in Oxford, and the decision there in July 1759 to print a new quarto Bible, in English on a pica body (that is, with good interlinear spacing): as those reporting to the Delegates put it, 'We find that all the best sorts of Bibles and Common-Prayer Books are and have been for some years last past printed in London, and none for many years printed at Oxford.'[19] Whether or not this revived pride was coincidence, Baskerville himself had grander ideas in mind. In his first formal approach to Cambridge, in 1757, he had explained his hopes in some detail:

> But my highest Ambition is to print a folio Bible, with the same letter of the inclosed Specimen, which would allow a handsom margin, besides Notes, & which I would decorate with a neat black Ornament, between & round the Colums & marginal Notes, about a quarter as broad as the inclos'd Specimen, which may serve to give a rude or imperfect Idea of what I mean & will appear more agreeable to every Eye than the coarse red lines in the best Editions. The Reason of my mentioning a bible at this time is this; that if it was

PROPOSALS

For *PRINTING* by *SUBSCRIPTION,*

THE HOLY BIBLE.

CONDITIONS.

I.

AS the University of Cambridge has done **Mr. Baskerville** the honour to elect him one of their Printers; this Work will be printed there in one Volume Folio, with the same Paper and Letter as this Specimen.

II.

The Price to Subscribers will be four Guineas in Sheets; one half to be paid at the time of subscribing; and the other at the delivery of a perfect Book.

III.

It will be put to Press with all possible Expedition, and delivered to Subscribers in three Years from the date of these Proposals.

IV.

Some will be printed with an Ornament, like the first Page of this Specimen, and some with plain Lines, like the second; the Subscribers are desired to mention at the time of subscribing which sort they choose.

V.

After the Subscription is closed, the Price will be raised.

VI.

Those who subscribe for Six shall have a Seventh gratis.

To the PUBLICK.

THE great Expence with which this Work will necessarily be attended, renders it not only imprudent, but absolutely impossible for the Editor to venture on it, without the Assistance of a Subscription. And he is encouraged to hope, as he has already received the publick Approbation of his Labours, that they will continue to favour his Ambition, and to enable him to render this one Work as correct, elegant, and perfect as the Importance of it demands. To this End, he is determined to spare no Expence, no Care, nor Attention. He builds his Reputation upon the happy Execution of this Undertaking; and begs it may not be imputed to him as a Boast, that he hopes to give his Country a more correct and beautiful Edition of the *SACRED WRITINGS,* than has hitherto appeared.

ADVERTISEMENT.

TWO Editions of the Book of common Prayer in large Octavo, are preparing at Cambridge, by the said J. BASKERVILLE; the one, printed with long Lines, is now in the Press; the other in Columns, will be put in Hand as soon as the first is finished. He hopes the first will be ready in about four Months, and the other in four Months afterwards.

The new Edition of *Milton's* poetical Works in large Paper will also be ready early this Winter, at the Price of one Guinea in Sheets. Those who have already taken the small, may exchange it if not damaged, on paying the difference.

Many Gentlemen have wished to see a Sett of the Classicks from the *Louvre* Edition in the Manner, Letter and Paper, of the *Virgil* already published; if they could be purchased at a moderate Price: *J. BASKERVILLE*

therefore proposes to print the same, if he finds proper Encouragement; and to proceed with the Poetical Classicks first; and as *Juvenal* and *Persius* in one Volume, is wanting to compleat the Cambridge Sett; he intends publishing that first, at sixteen Shillings in Sheets; one half to be paid at the time of subscribing, the remainder on Delivery of the Volume. Gentlemen inclined to encourage his Undertakings are desired to send early their Names and Places of abode (which will be prefixed to the Work) to the Publisher at his House in *BIRMINGHAM,* and their Favours will be gratefully acknowledged by

Their most obedient

Humble Servant

JOHN BASKERVILLE.

17 Received of Two Pound and two Shillings; being the first Payment for a Bible in one Volume in Folio; which I promise to deliver in Sheets on payment of the like Sum.

Subscriptions are also taken in by *Mr. Tonson* in the Strand: *Mr. Dodsley* in Pall-Mall London; *Messieurs Hamilton* and *Balfour* in Edinburgh: *Mr. Faulkner* in Dublin; and most other Booksellers in Town and Country. MDCCLIX.

Fig. 13 John Baskerville, preliminary proposals for a folio Bible, 1759.

the pleasure of the University to give me a Power to print it, it would be at least twelve months before it could be begun, as it must be printed by Subscription, & about a fourth part of the price advanced as my Capital would not carry it without; the price I imagin would be three and a half Guineas in Sheets, everyone of which I would endeavour to make as perfect as the Specimen; it would be two years in the press . . .[20]

Baskerville hoped for co-operation; and he received it – at a price. By the agreement reached with Cambridge in December 1758, he was required to pay for the privilege to print the prayer book (at a rate of £20 per 1,000 copies), though he paid nothing for the Bible.[21] But he was in a weak position in other ways, and his letter to the Vice-Chancellor meant that the University itself was fully aware of his plans – plans that in the circumstances of ordinary publishing would have been kept secret from competitors as far as possible. The agreement of December 1758 even specified details of the design of his Bible: 'the Margin to be a little enlarged and the Ornaments (if any) to be such as the said Syndicks for the time being shall approve'.

With the specimen page that he issued in 1759 before them, the Syndics agreed on 18 December 1759 to print a new edition of the Bible, including 250 copies as a small folio on superfine crown paper. They were planning to offer customers a book specifically alternative to that produced by the other University Printer.[22] The subsequent agreement with Dod, providing for one press to be continuously employed and a second occasionally, and the Bible to be completed if possible by Christmas 1761, gives a clear indication of the University's and Dod's anxieties.[23] This was to be a race against Baskerville. But though his was the later to appear, Baskerville offered a better design, on a grander size of paper; and it was printed in an edition of only 1,250 copies. The decorative typographical borders shown in the specimen, not having found favour, had been abandoned: what was arguably appropriate for a prayer book was simply a distraction in a folio Bible. The revised proposals issued by Baskerville in August 1761 acknowledged the strength of readers' opinion:

> As many Gentlemen have objected to every Kind of Ornament round the Page, the Work will be printed quite plain, with the marginal Notes all at the bottom.[24]

His great primer type was larger; he dispensed with the central rules that had become so regular a feature of Bible printing; and he set his notes at the foot of the page, leaving only dates in the margins. Bentham, having to print both a quarto and folio from the same setting of type, would have found it inconvenient to treat his notes in this way, since it would have meant some resetting, and he therefore left them in the margins. The Syndics offered a text that had been reviewed by a member of the University, F. S. Parris, and typography that had also been reviewed so as to display the linguistic history of the text more accurately; but there could be no doubting Baskerville's triumph in design. The whole was made for clarity: a book to be read without danger of losing one's way. Parris's edition was published in 1762, and Baskerville's in July of the following year. Thereafter both Bentham and his successor John Archdeacon refrained from printing folio editions of the Bible; and Baskerville found copies of his own expensive edition difficult to sell.

THE

CONTAINING THE

OLD TESTAMENT

AND

THE NEW:

Tranflated out of the

AND

With the former TRANSLATIONS

Diligently Compared and Revifed,

By His MAJESTY's Special Command.

APPOINTED TO BE READ IN CHURCHES.

CAMBRIDGE,

Printed by *JOHN BASKERVILLE,* Printer to the UNIVERSITY.

M DCC LXIII.

CUM PRIVILEGIO.

Fig. 14 The Bible, printed by Baskerville (Cambridge, 1763).

Fletcher and Hodson, printers of the *Cambridge Chronicle*, and who described themselves as Baskerville's publishers in Cambridge, took in subscriptions for the folio Bible.[25] However, the list of subscribers reveals how little support for his greatest project he had found in Cambridge itself, or indeed in Oxford.[26] This was not surprising, for few individual members of colleges can have wanted such a book. More seriously, the universities' connections with the clergy and their patrons in the rest of the country had not been exploited. Baskerville had found a warmer welcome from gentry, professionals and wealthier members of the merchant classes around the country and, noticeably, in Ireland. But his short list of subscribers was no basis for success for a book that would, in any case, not sell fast; and he had few means of supporting a slow seller. Only three years after publication, more than 40 per cent of his edition remaining unsold, he disposed of the stock to a London bookseller who offered it at a reduced price.[27] Baskerville had achieved his ambition; and the University had demonstrated its commitment to printing the Bible as accurately as possible. The price had been high.

For many readers of newspapers in and around Cambridge, Baskerville's name was better known for writing paper ('gilt or plain, equal in fineness to the best abortive vellum') than for printing.[28] The Baskerville episode, when the University once again farmed out its right to print privileged books, does not, strictly speaking, form a part of the history of the University Press. Baskerville became University Printer, but never printed with Bentham; the association of his name and that of Cambridge on the title-pages of the 1763 Bible (fig. 14) and the several octavo editions of the prayer book have over the centuries brought some undeserved lustre to a university press whose first business (at least as regards the printing of these two titles) was profit. Bentham was a competent printer, but neither as keen-eyed nor as ambitious for the appearance of his work as was Baskerville.

An age of ferment

In the early 1770s the British publishing trade was in turmoil. The previous decade had marked the passing of a generation that had shaped and dominated the book trade in the aftermath of the Copyright Act of Queen Anne. It was a generation that had seen authors given new status and (in some cases) new scales of financial reward; the solid establishment of retail trade by printed catalogue; and ever growing importance accorded to magazines in which reviews, extracts and comment shaped taste and success. It was also a world in which a small group of London booksellers still held most of the reins of power and therefore of money. Robert Dodsley died in 1764; Jacob Tonson, Thomas Osborne and John Newbery all died in 1767; Andrew Millar in 1768; and John Knapton in 1770. Bankruptcies; arguments over book pricing; arguments over copyrights; jealousies between long-established parts of the trade and newcomers with fresh and seemingly threatening ambitions; doubts among printers: all these fuelled a period of anxiety in the book trades. 'By the failing of several booksellers, I have met with very great losses, and am at present much distressed for want of cash', wrote the London bookseller Thomas Davies in February 1770, on James Granger's enquiring of him when he might expect to receive £50. Sales of Granger's history of England had been disappointing. 'Many of the booksellers have not sold a single set, particularly Mr. Baker in York-street, and Mr. Newbery, in St. Paul's Church-yard; therefore, we must be very cautious how we talk of another edition, for fear of injuring those subscribers who have many copies remaining.'[1] While we may recognise in this the reluctant tones familiar among publishers even in less stressful times, Davies had reason to be cautious.

The several crises in publishing and bookselling occurred at the same time that increasing demand for printed matter was placing heavier requirements on the printing trade, thereby introducing its own crises and opportunities. A burgeoning newspaper trade, in London and in the country, and a market for weekly and monthly periodicals both for a general readership and for more particular interests or sections of the population, helped to encourage a market for more books.[2] Of what proved to be the longer-lived magazines, the *Monthly Review* was founded in 1749, Smollett's *Critical Review* in 1756, the *Town and Country Magazine* in 1769, and the *Lady's Magazine* in 1770. Many others existed for shorter periods. Circulating libraries and philanthropic societies, organising and orchestrating clamour whether for novels,

Bibles or sermons, contributed further to this expansion by their own particular requirements.[3] Above all there was a demand for cheaper books, especially in the wake of the case of Donaldson versus Becket in 1774. Smaller formats, cheaper paper and cheaper bindings all marked a craving for books of a kind that could be bought privately, at lower cost, by a wider section of the community.

While to a great extent many of these various new expectations could be met, and were encouraged, by the establishment of presses in small towns across the country, where newspapers and local literature could be produced to fuel readerships over sometimes unexpectedly large areas (newspaper printers were especially quick to point out the extent of their circulation[4]), most of the requirements for increased production came from, and were met in, London and its satellites. For the purpose of supplying the Bible and the prayer book, the Cambridge press was a major satellite. Both in the course of events at Cambridge under Archdeacon, in the crucial years covered by his period as University Printer between 1766 and 1793, and in the manner whereby London needs were met, the Cambridge press was in large measure led by events that were outside its control. But the consequences were inescapable. While clamour for the privileged books increased, offering a means for the Syndics to concentrate on a relatively straightforward business, where costs, demand and sales offered a compact and easily understood model, scholarly printing, and especially scholarly publishing, was allowed a comfortable second place. Though the Press expanded its premises (mainly, at first, for the sake of warehousing), there is no record that it invested in any new press between the end of the 1760s and the beginning of the 1790s. The printing of the privileged books was highly competitive, and both in its quality and in its pricing was subject to constant monitoring by the larger customers. It was self-contained, and its risks were measurable. The result was that, in a university where only a minority of dons were energetic in their research and in their teaching, few were prepared to exploit the Press. Changes were in a considerable measure forced on the University by public opinion after Parliament in 1781 voted a grant of £500 per annum as compensation for the loss of a share in the almanac monopoly. For the first time in its history, the University Press came under public scrutiny as the employer of public money.

In other respects too, the fundamental changes in the scale of the country's printing, publishing and bookselling trades in the second half of the eighteenth century brought long-term consequences for Archdeacon and his successors as University Printers. The search for new methods and new materials was persistent. Many experiments proved fruitless, and the printing trade in particular was not changed fundamentally, either in its technology or in the organisation of its labour force, until after Archdeacon's death. The type used for printing, methods of printing, designs and principles of presses, and the quality and sources of paper all came under scrutiny and were subject to change. Individually, fellows in their colleges, and undergraduates in their often casual attitude to their studies, might remain isolated from the rest of the country. The University Press, caught up in national (and eventually international) changes had perforce to respond in a specialist printing business, for Bibles and prayer books, that had its own momentum.

The late eighteenth-century growth in the book trade was driven by questions of price, whether for Bibles and prayer books, for scholarly books, or for more general literature. At one end, fine printing encouraged, and was encouraged by, bibliophile demand for books that were out of the ordinary – on large or fine paper, in new fashions of type (frequently of a large size) and with expensive illustrations – some even printed in colour. At the other, the scramble for markets and for profits forced prices down. Smaller formats and smaller types provided part of the means to do so. The established booksellers also faced an outright attack on their price structures. In the 1760s, the assault on London prices was led by John and Alexander Donaldson, booksellers from Edinburgh who in 1765 opened a shop in the Strand, and campaigned with the help of prominent newspaper advertisements to demonstrate the difference between 'Donaldson prices' and 'London prices'. Their argument was straightforward: that by, in effect, permitting the superior position and capital of London booksellers to establish a perpetual monopoly, bookselling as a whole suffered, and printing tended to become slovenly and inaccurate. Most importantly, the price of books would be driven upwards by such a monopoly,

> the infallible Consequence of which is to retard, and indeed stop altogether the Progress of Learning. This has been complained of as the Consequence of Patents and Privileges, from their first Introduction; and that there is as much Reason, if not more, for exclaiming against that Abuse at present, than formerly, must be felt by every Man, who is desirous of having a tolerable Library of Books, and is not possessed of a most opulent Fortune.[5]

The argument was brought home in Cambridge by means of a newspaper campaign. A notice in the *Cambridge Chronicle and Journal* in 1771 set out the figures, as they offered editions of *Emile* in English for 7s. instead of 12s., of Stackhouse's history of the Bible for 27s. instead of 3 guineas, of Winslow on anatomy for 10s. instead of 15s., and of Marquet's chemistry for 7s.6d. instead of 10s.[6] No doubt the Donaldsons had a university readership in mind in choosing their titles for advertisement in Cambridge. Certainly their policy offended the established London trade, who sought to dislodge Alexander Donaldson by a campaign of vilification. In 1764, William Strahan wrote of his 'pyratical scheme', based on his having 'printed a good Many Books in a cheap Manner, by reducing their Size from 4to to 8vo or from 8vo to 12mo but in general so wickedly incorrect and such indifferent Paper that Gentlemen are much disgusted at them'.[7] Donaldson triumphed. James Rivington was declared bankrupt after an inglorious career in which he failed to gain business by selling cheap.[8] But the mood of many customers was unmistakable, and booksellers and printers alike strove to meet the expectation for reduced prices.

By the 1760s, the University Press had established for itself a place in the national book trade that was based principally on the Bible and the Book of Common Prayer. These are discussed in the following chapter.[9] Although there were always academic and scholarly books among its work to which it could point if necessary as the kind of book expected from a learned press run by a university, the trade in the essential books for the church was of far greater importance. Indeed, as we have seen, while many scholarly books were printed by Bentham and his staff, in practice only a very few were actually published by the Syndics. Authors, or their Cambridge or London booksellers, remained the more usual customers for the printing facilities in Queens' Lane and Silver Street other than those already employed on the privileged books.

Among the Cambridge booksellers, Thurlbourn, most successful and from whom Bentham had received so much of his work, died in 1768. His business was taken over by John Woodyer, his partner for many years. Woodyer was bankrupt in 1779.[10] On 1 January 1780 John Deighton moved into his premises on the corner of Trinity Street and St Mary's Street.[11] In 1785 Deighton moved to London,[12] and meanwhile in turn produced more booksellers, of whom the most prominent in Cambridge (at least for a short while) was his apprentice William Lunn, who soon after marrying a widow from Wisbech opened a shop on Peas Hill in January 1787.[13] By the autumn of the same year Lunn was at a more promising address opposite the Senate House (fig. 15).[14] In 1790, he established his reputation as a bookseller not only on the size and quality of his varied stock, but also on two fundamentals of business practice: to deal only in ready money, and to sell at the lowest terms possible – that is, at less than the normal London rate.[15] Lunn was among the new men, who saw the future in ideas and practices more familiar to the London trade than to country booksellers; eventually he was to move there. But his early Cambridge career belongs only to Archdeacon's last years as University Printer.

Meanwhile, in the older generation, the Merrills continued successfully in business, though when the Regent Walk was demolished in order to make way for the new Senate House at the end of the 1760s, Thomas Merrill, who had been in the Cambridge book trade as binder and bookseller since the 1730s, was obliged to move the few yards to 3 Trinity Street.[16]

For many members of the University the person who came to dominate the local book trade in the seventies and eighties was John Nicholson, who first made his presence known in the 1750s, when he wheeled his books round the colleges for sale.[17] At first he had no connection with the University Press. His first publication, poorly and cheaply printed in London in 1757, seems to have been *The history of Israel Jobson, the wandering Jew . . . translated from the Chinese by M.W.* Little more than a pamphlet, it was designed to cash in on the taste for so-called Chinese tales and on the comet expected in 1758. But, at the end, this wretchedly printed little book included an advertisement that contained the germ from which he was to make his name and his wealth. Nickolson (his name was thus spelled both on the title-page and in the advertisement) offered

> all Sorts of Books in most Languages and faculties, and has great Choice of Second-Hand School-Books; also lets out Books to read by the Year, Month, Week, Day, or Volume. Sells all Sorts of Maps and Prints, with Frames, or without. Where gentlemen &c. may have Books neatly Bound in all Sorts of Binding at the Lowest Prices.[18]

Fig. 15 Shops at the corner of Trinity Street in the 1760s, seen just to the left of the tower of Great St Mary's church. Detail from an engraving by P. S. Lamborn.

As a further sideline to bookselling he also offered 'Pieces of Plaster of Paris'.[19] In due course he opened a bookshop and circulating library[20] on the west side of King's Parade, by the old Provost's lodge of King's College. From there he published a succession of books intended to meet the requirements of undergraduates at a time when there is evidence to suggest that there was actually a shortage of books in some subjects.[21] Not all of his books were of the cheapest, though they were never lavish. Thomas Hutchinson's edition of Xenophon *De Cyri expeditione*, printed at the University Press, was available in three forms: quarto on fine demy or crown paper at 10s.6d. or 8s., or in octavo on fine demy, price 6s.; and the best copies had a coloured map. By the 1780s he was advertising elegant and fashionable bindings, as well as plain ones, and could boast the work of John Bowtell, the most skilled local bookbinder of his generation.[22] Ever alert to possible sales, Nicholson regularly took a booth at Stourbridge Fair.[23] He also continued to hawk his stock in the colleges: apart from new and secondhand books, he was willing to supply exercises and (it was said) even sermons in manuscript for those unable or unwilling to compose them for themselves. The necessary subterfuge in this business is said to have given him his nickname, as he walked round hawking 'Maps!', though he seems to have been so celebrated that it can have fooled no-one.[24] His circulating library was likewise calculated to meet the needs of the University well beyond the ordinary educational ones that might have been anticipated: 'consisting of the most Capital Books in History, Mathematics, Antiquities, Law, Physic, Voyages, Novels, Dictionaries, Grammars, &c. &c. in various Languages'. Catalogues were to be had, price sixpence.[25] Unlike the Merrills and Deighton, Nicholson rarely advertised in the newspapers: his market was well defined, and deliberately local, whereas the other booksellers hoped to draw attention to their books throughout the very considerable part of the country penetrated by the *Cambridge Chronicle* during the last third of the century.

John Woodyer was born in about 1720; John Nicholson in about 1730; John Merrill in about 1731; and Joseph Merrill in about 1735. These men, middle-aged when Archdeacon was appointed University Printer in 1766, dominated the Cambridge book trade. Archdeacon was born in about 1725. The principal local booksellers were his near, if slightly younger, contemporaries. They became his principal and (apart from the University itself) most regular customers, through whom, still by exchange of credit and stock, his work reached the London trade. Few books were commissioned directly by London booksellers, however large a part their orders might represent of a total edition size.

Some of the changes to the appearance and marketing of books have already been discussed. In few ways was the University Press's innate conservatism more noticeable than in its attitude to illustrated books. Though eighteenth-century Cambridge could seem remarkably isolated from the rest of the world, it would have been difficult for many resident members of the University not to be aware of, even if they were not familiar with, the designs by Richard Bentley, son of the late Master of Trinity, for poems by Thomas Gray, then still at Peterhouse, published by Dodsley in 1753. The volume, extravagant by English standards in its design, but bringing to English idioms a welcome Italianate influence, found instant acclaim, and three editions were called for in the year of publication.[26] For Cambridge, the book had some personal curiosity; for the reading public as a whole, as well as for book illustration, it was a publication of key importance, that was to affect taste for generations to come.

Gray could not bear to think of his portrait as a frontispiece to the volume.[27] But he was eager enough as a collector of prints, and in this he was less idiosyncratic. The numbers of rolling-press printers, engravers and print-sellers in Cambridge in the 1750s, 1760s and 1770s suggests that there was a substantial local demand. In 1757–8, William Davenport, first in Walls Lane (modern King Street), then in Bridge Street and then in Petty Cury, offered a service as copper-plate printer 'as neat and cheap as in London'.[28] It is not clear from the wording of his advertisement whether he was still at this time also employed as a journeyman by Thomas James, printer of the *Cambridge Journal*. From the beginning in 1762, Thomas Fletcher and Francis Hodson, printers of the newly founded *Cambridge Chronicle*, advertised that they were able to execute 'all manner of business on the Letter or Rolling-Press, elegantly and expeditiously'.[29] Sarah James, printer of their older rival, the *Cambridge Journal*, offered in 1764 to print 'Copper-plate Coats of Arms, Shop-bills, Bills of Parcells &c. &c, &c. worked at the rolling-press neatly and expeditiously'.[30] The University Press, still relying for its engraved illustrations and decorations on the London trade, remained unable to offer such a service until 1768, when the Syndics agreed to the purchase of a rolling-press, and obtained one from London.[31]

By the time of Bentham's retirement, both the University and other parts of the local population were alert to the attractions of engravings not only as decorations in books, but also as decorations in the home, and as, like books, objects even to collect. The enthusiasm for engravings, fuelled by imports from continental Europe, was nation-wide. For some, including William Cole of King's, George Ashby of St John's, Michael Lort of Trinity, Richard Farmer of Emmanuel, Robert Masters of Corpus, and W. H. Ewin, a local businessman, this took the form of iconomania, concentrating on portraits,[32] while others were more venturesome. To meet the popular demand for information, William Gilpin finally published his *Essay upon prints* in 1768, two years after Archdeacon's appointment.[33] By 1792, a year before Archdeacon was in turn suc-ceeded as University Printer, it had reached a fourth edition. By 1775, the catalogue of the specialist London print dealers Sayer and Bennett ran to 150 pages. In 1763, Horace Walpole drew together George Vertue's notes on the subject for inclusion in his *Anecdotes of painting in England*. Joseph Strutt provided yet further guidance in his *Biographical dictionary of engravers* in 1786. These several works were by no means alone among the manuals and opinions offered to those who sought guidance. In 1772 William Cole thought that the 'rage for head-hunting seems to be cooled in Cambridge',[34] but he was premature. Whether the taste was for etched or mezzotint imitations of Rembrandt, for the large reproductions of paintings published by Boydell, for portraits, for plates of Hogarth's work, or simply for decoration or comic amusement, the print trade transformed the visual education of virtually every kind of society in the mid-eighteenth century. James Granger's *Biographical history of*

England, first published in 1769 and containing particular words of thanks to Cole and others in Cambridge, offered connoisseurs a convenient method of identifying and organising their portraits. It further popularised the study of 'heads' among a clientèle of enthusiasts whose forebears included John Evelyn, Samuel Pepys, the Harleys and James West.[35] Cambridge fell easily into the fashion; the local newspapers were full of advertisements; and some of the more enterprising even tried their amateur hands at making prints, usually etchings, themselves.[36]

Enthusiasms were not limited to iconomania, and taste for prints of virtually all kinds inexorably permeated attitudes to printed books. Collectors were encouraged by the prominence given in local auctions to the prints offered for sale, whether from local private collections or from imported consignments.[37] The presence of sufficient connoisseurs in the university and neighbourhood attracted artists and engravers to Cambridge. Of these the most celebrated was Peter Spendelowe Lamborn, miniature painter, artist and engraver,[38] whose hand, as we have seen, is to be found throughout Bentham's history of Ely cathedral as well as (on a rather smaller scale, and much less ambitiously) the local guidebook *Cantabrigia depicta* (1763 and later editions). But besides his work for books, he also published various separate plates, including in 1762 a series of views of Cambridge and nearby.[39] In 1767–9 he published further views, arranging for subscriptions to be taken not only in Cambridge and Oxford, but also by Boydell in Cheapside, Sayer in Fleet Street, Spilsbury in Covent Garden, and Austin in Bond Street – thus including some of the largest of the London print dealers.[40] Gradually he extended his stock-in-trade, advertising lists of his work in the local newspaper.[41] Lamborn remained active in the town until his death in 1774, longer than some more peripatetic artists, but he was by no means an isolated figure. James Bretherton, drawing master, offered etchings after Dürer, Piazetta and Carlo Maratta, as well as landscapes, from 1768 to 1771, when he left for London.[42] By the end of 1770 he had been joined by his son Charles.[43] In 1770, Alexander Bannerman, who worked for Boydell, was offering an engraving of a fiddler after Ostade, besides scenes from *Macbeth*, the Old Testament and elsewhere.[44] The amateur Christopher Sharpe was offering copies of his work in the same year;[45] and by that autumn Lamborn was advertising a list of his work offered for sale in a print shop opposite the Senate House, the existence of such a specialist shop in itself being a clear sign of local enthusiasm.[46] William Henshaw, son of a Cambridge gunmaker, had embarked on his career by early 1773, when he advertised some of his work and offered to teach either drawing or etching at his father's house in Trumpington Street. He advertised his engraving after a Poussin Holy Family (then in the possession of John Hinchliffe, Bishop of Peterborough) in 1775.[47] Henshaw's career was cut short when he died in London shortly after he had gone there to learn further from Bartolozzi.[48] Other engravers were simply visitors to Cambridge, such as A. Polack, who in 1773 advertised that he could be contacted either through the inn opposite St Catharine's College or through a silversmith in Petty Cury, and that apart from engraving stone or metals he was also prepared to execute bookplates and billheads.[49]

Letterpress printers and rolling-press printers, possessing very different skills and for most of their time pursuing very different markets, formed two usually distinct parts of the printing trade as a whole. The career of Davenport, as he moved his rolling-press between three addresses in Cambridge within two years, is a reminder of a further fundamental difference: he had no type, chases, imposing bench or heavy equipment other than his rolling-press (itself smaller than an ordinary common press) to move with him, and the nature of his work required much less paper. In the early 1790s, A. Macintosh offered his services as rolling-press printer in Green Street, in what must have been quite modest premises.[50] The largest printing houses were able to employ a rolling-press as well as their common presses, and in 1699 it had been expected that this would be the case at the Cambridge University Press. But the tendency was for the two distinct skills to be organised into separate establishments where each could follow its trade according to its particular needs and conventions.

The same was likewise to a great extent true of the retail trade in the metropolis. Though there were specialist print shops in Cambridge, and artists such as Lamborn traded from home as well as from shops, the connection between the book and print trade was in one respect more obvious in Cambridge than it often was in fashionable London. Booksellers outside London were more likely to sell patent medicines than engravings. Nicholson, searching for business, offered maps and prints, framed or unframed, in company with his circulating library and his stock of books for sale. Other Cambridge booksellers similarly sought to supply both markets. Lamborn's and Henshaw's work was to be had from Merrill and Woodyer, and in 1788 Lunn was to take up the residue of Lamborn's stock.[51] Richard Matthews, beside Great St Mary's, was similar in that his stock included both books and prints when it was sold to the newcomer John Deighton in 1778.[52] It was from Deighton's shop that Joshua Baldrey, one of the most celebrated of all the Cambridge engravers, launched his career in 1781 by offering to draw likenesses at 15s. each and to give eight drawing lessons for 1 guinea.[53] By November the following year he, too, was advertising a print shop opposite the Senate House.[54] Lunn's printed catalogues, in which he was prepared to offer even a stuffed squirrel, listed substantial holdings of prints, as well as drawings and on occasion a few paintings.[55]

The Cambridge book trade responded with *A chronological series of engravers from the invention of the art to the beginning of the present century*, written anonymously, published by Woodyer in 1770 and printed by Archdeacon, with three plates of engravers' marks at the end.[56] It took its place next to Gilpin and the other authorities, but like Middleton's account of the origin of printing, published in Cambridge thirty-five years before, it was an isolated if learned contribution.

Together with this taste in furnishings and in collecting, the appearance of books was transformed as readers likewise expected, and were supplied with, engraved illustrations of a quality and in numbers unknown to previous generations. Topography, archaeology and classical antiquity, natural history and travel were some of the subjects in which this was most obviously and most lavishly to be seen – sometimes at an extreme, as the cumbersome series of plates that accompanied the account of Cook's voyages demanded special treatment on library shelves. These were expensive, commensurate with the very considerable cost of engraving.[57] But the large-scale introduction of engravings into even quite small and modestly priced books both created and sustained a taste for more general illustration that persisted to be developed in books and periodicals alike, and also answered the urgent need of the publishing trade. For in part this new attention to illustration, especially in popular books, introduced marks of individuality in publications, and thus a means of protecting copyright.

For his study of Ely cathedral, James Bentham sought out patrons for the individual engravings, and expected contributions of 18 guineas for the folding 'capital plates' such as that showing the south elevation of the cathedral.[58] Many engravers worked both in the book trade and on plates intended simply for decoration or other pictorial record. But costs remained a problem, one that was solved for booksellers by the introduction of smaller formats and the practice of engraving (and then printing) several images on a single plate.[59] Hence the costs of illustrating could be dramatically reduced, to perhaps as little as a penny an image. This was exploited to the full in the 18° editions of established authors, issued by John Bell, Charles Cooke and others in the wake of the Becket versus Donaldson judgement – a judgement that removed perpetual copyright and allowed considerably more competition in the book trade.[60] The reasons for the appearance of these books, thus dressed up with engraved frontispieces, had as much to do with protecting their publishers' interests as encouraging possible customers and readers. For though perpetual copyright in authors had been abolished, the Engraving Copyright Act of 1734/5 (often referred to as Hogarth's Act) offered protection in the illustrations for fourteen years.[61] But whatever the immediate needs of the trade, the ubiquitous presence of these books, printed in large numbers and available either stitched in paper wrappers or in cheap leather bindings more or less ornamented, was a constant reminder of the way the trade led readers to expect illustration – whether to poetry, essays or the novel – where it had not formerly been customary.[62] From the middle of the century, Thomas Boreman's, John Newbery's and others' books for children had made much of their cheap (usually woodcut) but nonetheless attractive illustrations,[63] and the many works of Mrs Trimmer, daughter of the engraver John Joshua Kirby, were to do the same both for children and for those with weak reading skills. The universal expectation was for illustration.

For the University Press, these changes impinged to very varying degrees. Bentham had demonstrated that it could sustain a successful role in the book trade, and prosper commercially. Yet there was an alternative view. The decision by the Court of King's Bench in 1758 in the University's favour, confirming its right to print the Statutes, was not based on commercial considerations, nor solely on precedent (Cowell's *Interpreter*, 1607, being the obvious example[64]). It was founded on Henry VIII's letters patent of 1534 and on the confirmation of the University's position by Charles I in 1627/8 – that is, on the University's privileged responsibility. In the words of the judgement, 'the Chancellor, Masters and Scholars of the University of *Cambridge* are INTRUSTED, *with a concurrent Authority*, to print Acts of Parliament and Abridgments of Acts of

Parliament'.[65] In a letter to Blackstone at Oxford, one of those delivering the judgement, Sir Michael Foster, provided a gloss lest the point be missed:

> The Words underlined were thrown in, by way of an Intimation to the University, that we consider the Powers given by the Letters Patent, as a Trust reposed in that learned Body, for publick Benefit, for the Advancement of Literature, and not to be transferred upon lucrative Views to other Hands. I hope both the Universities will always consider the royal Grants in that Light.[66]

It was a timely reminder, as much an admonition to the two university presses as a declaration of support. In distinguishing the university presses from the ordinary London trade, it was also a reminder that too close an association with such trade might compromise Cambridge's commitment to the objects implied in the charter of 1534. More obviously, the judgement was also one of several measures taken in the second half of the eighteenth century to promote the universities' distinctive responsibilities for the advancement of learning, and to protect their interests by financial means also. In particular, the University Press remained able (like that at Oxford) to claim drawback on tax paid on paper, provided it was for printing books in Greek, Latin, oriental or northern languages. This right was confirmed by the paper duty legislation of 1758–9, 1780–1 and 1787.[67] It was a right to which the University had become accustomed, so much so that the implicit trust, similar to that of which Foster and his colleagues had thought in 1758, was little considered.

But the University's press benefited from national legislation in another way; and when this was changed the University could not avoid taking heed. For many years the University, like Oxford, had come to an accommodation with the Stationers' Company concerning the right to print almanacs. By this means, Cambridge had received an annual income of £250 during Bentham's term of office, raised in 1767 to £500.[68] But in 1775 a judgement in the Court of Common Pleas determined that the right to print almanacs was a common one.[69] The two universities thus had no claim to the payments to which they had likewise become accustomed, and which had formed an appreciable part of their income. The possibility, in cases where the donor wished it, that perpetual copyright might be granted to Cambridge and to the other English and Scottish universities, offered in the same year,[70] was poor compensation – particularly since it was unpredictable. An attempt in 1779, led by Lord North as both First Lord of the Treasury and Chancellor of the University of Oxford, to vest the right to print almanacs solely in the two English universities and in the Stationers' Company, proved to be a misguided failure. As was pointed out in the debates in Parliament, whatever the desirability of promoting the well-being of the universities, it was wholly undesirable to promote a monopoly in doing so.[71] Much noise was made during the debates as to the necessity and faults of existing almanacs; but the matter was succinctly put by Thomas Erskine, speaking on behalf of his client who had brought the original action, Thomas Carnan:

> If the Universities have lost an advantage, enjoyed contrary to law, and at the expence of sound policy and liberty, you will rejoice that the courts below have pronounced that wise

and liberal judgement against them, and will not set the evil example of reversing it here. But you need not therefore forget, that the Universities have lost an advantage, – and if it be a loss that can be felt by bodies so liberally endowed, it may be repaired to them by the bounty of the crown, or by your own. – It were much better that the people of England should pay 10,000*l.* a year to each of them, than suffer them to enjoy one farthing at the expence of the ruin of a free citizen, or the monopoly of a free trade.[72]

By further legislation in 1781 an attempt was made to reconcile these various developments that had left the University exposed. According to George Borlase, Registrary of Cambridge, one result of the cessation of the annual income from the Stationers had been that the Press was no longer able to continue to print learned books, but had had to concentrate on those that would produce a profit. It was a convenient argument, but one that could have been put forward equally well on the basis of many other years' work in the Press's history. Of Oxford, meanwhile, it had been alleged that part of the income had been spent on public feasts.[73] The Lord Chancellor, Lord Thurlow, found ready weapons wherewith to mock the attempt to right a matter – the claim of the universities to a monopoly – that had no basis in law. Nonetheless, the preamble acknowledged that the two universities had been accustomed to receiving at least a thousand pounds a year by farming their privileges to the Stationers' Company, and that this had been spent 'in promoting different branches of literature and science, to the great increase of religion and learning, and the general benefit and advantage of these realms'.[74] Henceforth, Cambridge and Oxford were each to receive £500 per annum from the government, from money collected as duty on almanacs. It was the first time that income from a tax voted by Parliament was used on a regular basis to fund activities of the University; and it was perhaps for this reason, as well as to prevent use of the money in ways contrary to that clearly intended by Parliament, that on 11 June 1782 the University made the arrangement a formal one internally as well, placing the money granted by 'munificentia publica' in the hands of the Syndics of the Press.[75] Whatever past practice, there had been no such explicit commitment previously. Newly reminded of their obligations, and the public trust placed in them, the Press Syndics gradually took fresh interest in what, and how, books were to be both printed and published under their auspices.[76]

John Archdeacon

John Archdeacon, Bentham's successor as University Printer, was reported to be an Irishman, though nothing is known of his career before he arrived in Cambridge shortly before he took over the Press.[1] In 1766 he seems to have been aged just over forty.[2] He was appointed University Printer on 15 December 1766, on the recommendation of the Press syndicate.[3] Cast into an arena where the assumptions and practices of half a century were being questioned or destroyed, his terms of appointment differed from those of Bentham in 1740 in several revealing respects.[4] His salary was to be £100 per annum (or £130 maximum in case of particularly profitable years), compared with Bentham's £60; but as Bentham was still in the Printer's house, Archdeacon had to find his own accommodation. Bentham had been able to supplement his income with the smaller jobs in the printing house, had enjoyed various allowances to be paid for by the University which were of disadvantage to the University in having no limit, and he had been able to charge for some services. For Archdeacon, a further attempt was made to separate salary from expenses.

Although much that he inherited from Bentham could be allowed to continue, both the University and the book trade were to witness profound changes during his term of office, and there were already signs of these.

A university press could ignore most of the changes in illustrated books. Bentham and then Archdeacon issued few books, other than in the sciences and mathematics, in which illustration played an essential part; and few of the Press's books bore even much engraved decoration in the last forty years of the eighteenth century – the very period when other books were changing so dramatically. Apart from the history of Ely Cathedral, published in 1771 but begun while Bentham was still in office, the principal illustrated work other than in mathematics to be issued from Bentham's press in the 1760s was Sandby's editions of Juvenal and Persius, decorated with engravings by Lamborn after published illustrations of classical sculpture.[5] When in 1769 it was agreed to print the prayer book in Welsh, it was at the instance of the London engraver and printseller William Ryland, who published the book in 1770 with series of engravings after Samuel Wale by Ravenet, Grignion and others dating from 1755 and 1765.[6] In other words (and as usual for Bibles and prayer books), the Press was content to watch others ornament its work.

The Press's attitude to illustration and ornament suggests aesthetic caution of a kind that was at odds with its more liberal attitude to type design, for many readers the most obvious visual property of a book after its illustration. More importantly, the increasing emphasis on illustration was but one aspect of a gradual separation in the book trade at large in the appearance of books, linked to longer established identities of authors and their audiences. Illustration, and the kindred importance of the design of a page or of a volume, marked differences not only of taste or of equipment, but of culture. In the second half of the eighteenth century the visual distance grew between the appearance of books of general literature and of those intended for an academic audience. Conventions of page size, of page lay-out and of the use of white space further emphasised this division. The process was not of course even or uniform; but gradually there emerged a distinction of appearance between quite different groups of books. For this reason, at one of the turning points in the history of publishing, it is important to examine also the ways in which choice of type changed during this period.

The purchase by the University Press of Caslon's types in the 1720s and 1730s had, certainly, been made necessary because the older sources of supply, of Dutch designs, were no longer so straightforward; but they had also placed the Press among the foremost of English printers, employing a new and distinctive design. So powerful was the appeal of Caslon's design, after only a very few years, that change was essential if the Press was to retain its customers. Even by 1733, Henry Newman, secretary of the SPCK, was speaking of him as 'the greatest artist in Eng[ld], if not in Europe, since Elzevir, for Letter-Founding, who furnishes all our Presses here, so that the Printers send no more to Holland as they used to do'.[7] Baskerville's appointment in 1758, and with it an inseparable commitment to his new type designs, likewise suggests that the University was not intolerant of change in typographical taste.

Despite some efforts, difficult today to judge how serious, Baskerville appears not to have sold the ordinary sizes of his roman type to other printers. 'I have never sold any Types,' he wrote in 1773, 'nor do I intend to sell any to London Printers, as my Labours have always been treated with more Honour abroad than in my native Country.'[8] This absolute claim was not quite true, for a large size had been used for *Aris's Birmingham Gazette* in 1760–7. But it certainly seems the case that having failed to interest British printers he had already by 1762 – that is, before he had finished his Cambridge Bible – turned to possibilities overseas.[9] He had done more than design type. Both in his development of the use of wove paper and in his work to improve the accuracy of the printing press itself he had cause to hope to be honoured. He complained, too, of the booksellers who had not taken his publications, though their reasons for failing to support him probably resulted more from not wishing to support so individual a publishing enterprise than from an innate dislike of his type-faces or hot-pressed paper.

'Mr Baskerville of Birmingham that enterprizing place, made some attempts at letter-cutting, but desisted and with good reason . . . indeed he can hardly claim a place amongst letter-cutters. his typographical excellence lay more in trim glossy paper to dim the sight.'[10] The opinion was delivered by Edward Rowe Mores, antiquary and eccentric. British printers likewise remained suspicious, and the more familiar type-faces of Caslon stayed a staple part of printers' equipment. In a trade that by the 1770s was no longer dominated by a single typefounder, others imitated the Caslon designs, and in 1785 the Fry foundry was explicit, writing of its

> great Satisfaction to observe that the original Shape of their Roman and Italic Letters continues to meet the Approbation of the Curious, both in and out of the Printing Trade: nevertheless, to remove an Objection which the difference in Shape, from the letters commonly used, raised in some, whereby their Introduction into several Capital offices has been prevented; they have cut entire new sets of Punches, from Gt. Primer to Brevier both Roman and Italic . . . and they flatter themselves they have executed the Founts, as far as they are done, in an elegant and masterly Manner . . . which will mix with, and be totally unknown from, the most approved Founts made by the late ingenious Artist, William Caslon.[11]

It is a mark of the strength of the Caslon foundry that no imitations of its designs dating from the 1720s were cut by rivals until so long afterwards. But it is altogether less clear how this relates to popular taste – so far as popular taste could distinguish the two. Certainly Caslon had familiarity as his ally, and Benjamin Franklin was quick to report ignorant prejudice against Baskerville's designs, when he ensnared a critic into thinking that Baskerville's type was that of Caslon.[12] Nonetheless, though the only books set in Baskerville's types that appeared during his lifetime were those that he printed himself, he set a fashion. In Birmingham, rival printers brought out a cheaper imitation of his folio Bible, issued in parts and in a type-face and lay-out that deliberately aped his own design. It was a compliment that Baskerville saw no need to appreciate; he met it with another Bible of his own and with vitriolic public attacks. The rival Bible was poorly printed, and on inferior paper, but it stood as testimony to the contemporary admiration commanded by Baskerville's own Bible of 1763.[13] Baskerville died in 1775; but by the early 1770s imitations of his designs by other typefounders were already available either from Alexander Wilson in Glasgow or from Isaac Moore in London.[14] Wilson's and Moore's (later the Fry foundry) types belatedly found widespread approval, and further imitations became available from Thomas Cottrell in London and Robert Martin in Birmingham.[15] Baskerville had set a trend, though the prophet was indeed not honoured in his own country, and his punches were sold abroad.

In all this, despite the examples before them of a Bible of generally acknowledged supreme beauty, and several elegant editions of the Book of Common Prayer, the Cambridge press chose to remain staid, and to follow a familiar path rather than risk venturing too quickly into new tastes. Consummately conservative, it also acknowledged the conservatism of its most important market: that for Bibles and prayer books. Yet to do so was to ignore other opinion. The simultaneous existence of two so clearly different designs of type, both popular and both marketed competitively, introduced a situation with which neither printers nor readers were familiar. In time, and like the major typefounders, the larger printers found themselves obliged to offer both, until a true modern face, developed further from Baskerville's pen-inspired designs, eventually dominated the trade. Meanwhile, by responding with noticeable caution to popular expectations for standards in book presentation, the University Press placed itself further in a backwater.

Though the Press did gradually install new type-faces on the model of Baskerville, the contrast with other local printers was marked in both content and appearance. In politics, the University Press was obliged to be conservative: to support the foundations of church and state on which the University itself was established. Accordingly, nonconformist, radical, or even mildly reforming, opinion tended to Fletcher and Hodson, or later to Francis Hodson.[16] But whether nonconformist or not, those who turned to other printers found that their books looked different, in fresh idioms increasingly familiar as the expanding British typefounding trade made its presence seen among printers who might previously have turned to Caslon. In the mid-century, Caslon's influence had been all but universal. From the 1730s to the 1750s, when Chambers's *Cyclopaedia* needed to include type specimens, it was Caslon's work that was laid before the public to be educated in the ways of typography.[17] Changes in typographic taste, the dismissal in 1757 of Joseph Jackson and Thomas Cottrell from Caslon's foundry (both of them were to set up their own businesses, in competition with their former master), and the establishment by Joseph Fry of a type foundry in Bristol in 1764, under the management of Isaac Moore, from Birmingham, were all signs that Caslon's stranglehold was weakening, as the printing industry became more disparate and more demanding.[18] In Cambridge, the departure of Baskerville, and the residual influence of the appearance of his printing among the local printing trade, may have prompted Fletcher and Hodson to install the close imitation of his type cut by Isaac Moore (who had by then moved to London), and to use it, for example, in the edition of Roger Cotes's *De descensu gravium* they printed for Nicholson in 1770.[19]

Newspaper printers, aware of the demands brought by familiarity and by daily close scanning, were likewise alert to changes, and trumpeted improvements or investments accordingly. In July 1763 the *Cambridge Chronicle* announced that it had 'procured an entire new letter, contrived on purpose by Mr. Caslon, by means of which this paper will contain near four hundred lines more than it has hitherto done'.[20] When in January 1792 the *Cambridge Chronicle and Journal* bought new type, readers were informed of the 'new and beautiful letter, cast by Mess. Fry & Co. letter-founders to his Royal Highness the Prince of Wales': a patriotic reference to the Prince of Wales could do no harm.[21] It was by such daily means, as well as by books and pamphlets, that the reading public was educated to believe in change as an improvement. But as the advertisement of 1763 also explained, the real virtue of a change in type could be an increase in the number of words that could be fitted onto a page, and hence (in the case of newspapers) more reportage or (in the case of books) a saving in paper.

For a press whose output consisted overwhelmingly of large editions of two books, the Bible and the prayer book, the savings to be achieved by investment in types of strong construction and of an economical design were of the very greatest potential interest. But there were other considerations as well. Type for these books had to be hard enough to bear repeated use in editions of 10,000 copies. Hence both the quality of the metal and the design of the type were of importance. Type with thin walls would break too easily; and type designs whose smaller sizes contained letters with bowls (such as a, e, g) so small that they would fill with ink during printing were likewise to be avoided. As printers' manuals continually stressed, it was essential that such bowls should not only be of a sufficient dimension on the face of the type; they should also be deep enough.

> Accordingly, the goodness of printing-letter being not confined to true shape alone, consists also in having a *deep* face; which depends, first, upon the Punches being cut to a reasonable depth, and their Hollows deepened in proportion to the width of the respective letters; and secondly, upon the Punches being sunk *deep* into Matrices: for if either of these two requisites is neglected, the Letter, in course, will have a shallow face, and prove unprofitable to the purchaser; as it is in France, where Printers have very great reason to complain of the shallowness of letter cast by their founders.[22]

For decades, the Press had relied exclusively on printing type supplied by Caslon. The Syndics' minutes do not reveal explicitly what caused them to turn in June 1769 to the foundry of Alexander Wilson in Glasgow, and to cancel an order agreed the previous October for Caslon. Apart from a few small parcels (presumably to make up particular letters), the Press had obtained no new brevier type for some years. Since his appointment as Printer in 1766, Archdeacon had bought only modest quantities of any types, apart from a new fount of minion, weighing 816 lb, in February 1769 – for which he had obtained the approval of the Syndics the previous October.[23] But the order to Wilson was both substantial and specific, and suggests a new broom at work. Moreover, Archdeacon was particular, and sought a type from Wilson that would give a large size face, but on a smaller body than usual. Wilson explained:

> We should have sent the inclosed Receip[t] for the Italick sooner, but found it necessary since writing last to make new all the ascending Letters, on purpose that the same might come in upon Y[r] small body; our ordinary Bourgeois being too tall – this has been the reason of the delay – you'l please transmit this to Y[r] Correspondent in London who may receive y[r] box – with them is another assortm[t] of Roman Capital A upon a narrower form than that formerly sent; w[c] will save room in the Line, as so many of the Verses begin w[t] this Letter.
>
> I hope the seven Boxes of Roman have arrived safe. annexed is Y[r] Accompt and you'l please state the Charges w[c] you have disbursed before the boxes were given into the Waggon. After which we shall expect Y[r] orders for drawing for the ballance, when it may happen to suit Y[r] Convenience.[24]

The seven boxes that Wilson mentioned had arrived safely, by sea from Glasgow and by road from London: 982 lb 6 oz of roman bourgeois on a brevier body, to be followed by 84 lb 12 oz of accompanying italic, and a further plentiful supply of the letter A to meet the particular needs of setting the Bible. The reasons for Archdeacon's interest in this new supplier were not only connected with design. Wilson's type was sixpence a pound cheaper than Caslon's (2s., rather than half a crown), and was thought to be of a superior hardness.[25] In summer 1771 the foundry of John Baine, Wilson's former partner but now trading independently in Scotland, supplied a fount of nonpareil, weighing 1148 lb, at 3s.6d. a pound, with 5 per cent discount for prompt payment.[26] Again Scotland was cheaper, at 3s.6d. a pound compared with 5s. in

London.[27] A further fount of nonpareil was bought from Wilson in 1782;[28] and in 1783 the Syndics agreed both another font of nonpareil and a new fount of bourgeois on brevier to replace that bought in 1769.[29] But though the Scottish founders thus supplied a substantial quantity of small type for use in printing pocket editions of the Bible, New Testament and prayer book, they did not displace Caslon as the usual source. Apart from the repeated needs for small parcels of type to replace worn letter, Caslon supplied founts or substantial quantities of pica (478 lb) in 1770; of English (518 lb) in 1771; of nonpareil (500 lb) in 1775; of minion (883 lb) in 1779; of pearl (130 lb) in 1781; of small pica (523 lb) in 1782.[30] The Syndics gave further orders for a 1,000 lb each of minion and nonpareil in May 1787, and the same of brevier a year later.[31] He gave credit for old metal, and on one occasion instructed that a compositor was to receive 3 guineas: no reason for this was recorded.[32]

Much of the demand was for the smaller faces, those least easy to print and yet most needed for the tens of thousands of duodecimo, 24° or small octavo editions of the Bible and prayer book that formed the mainstay of the University Press. In such a business, it was not surprising that there was a constant tension between reasonable clarity and the quality of paper required for an edition. This had been part of the reason for the interest in Wilson in 1769; and the several varieties of casting gradually introduced by the Caslon foundry were watched with attention. But larger text faces were also of interest. Desire for changes in the appearance of the printed page seems to have been driven not only by the need for economy, but also by the typographically fashionable interlinear space. Amidst this mixture of interests, in 1785 Caslon provided large-bodied English, and in 1792 the Press agreed to purchase large new founts of pica and long primer, specifying 1,000 lb each of full-faced long primer and of lean faced pica (the latter intended for an octavo prayer book), as well as 700 lb of common-faced long primer.[33]

Much of the success or otherwise of the smaller types in particular had to do with paper quality, as well as with type design, the casting of type, and the skills of the pressmen. Though the smallest Bibles printed by the University Press in the last third of the eighteenth century were not of as poor a quality as some that had been printed in the 1740s, it remained that damaged type, poor locking up of formes of type and poor make-ready all contributed to inconsistent, if nonetheless generally improved, quality. Other type was necessary as well. The special demands of the Codex Bezae are discussed below.[34] Mathematics was a more everyday problem, and William Ludlam, of St John's, recorded his own suffering at the hands of the press, in self-complacent detail:

> I am sometimes forced to make types, which are commonly brass, of which I here send you a specimen ($\pm a \pm b \pm c$). It is called *plus-minus* $\pm$. I printed my first Tracts at Cambridge, when Archdeacon (not Bentham) was their printer. I was very sick of it; the University meanly provided with mathematical types, insomuch that they used daggers turned sideways for *plus's*. They were sunk into arrant traders, even to printing hand-bills, quack-bills, &c. which they then for the first time permitted for Archdeacon's profit. As to table-work, of which I had a deal, they knew nothing of it; and many a brass rule was

I forced to make myself. Sometimes long ones with notches to appear like short ones set exactly under each other. I complained of this to Mr. Bowyer, and would have had him print my Essay on Halley's Quadrant; but he was too full of more important work. I remember I told him I had marked all Archdeacon's damaged letters; which were not few, especially in the Italic. To which the old Gentleman replied, 'I don't like you the better for that.'[35]

Ludlam's *Astronomical observations*, with extra matter involving the setting of complex mathematics, taxed both the ingenuity and the resources of Archdeacon's men. But though the old competition remained between Bowyer and Archdeacon, it was not to be exploited unjustly.

Until the late 1750s, the Press obtained its paper through London stationers. In the mid-1750s the University was calling on up to five separate suppliers in any one year.[36] But there had been a paper mill at Sawston, about five miles to the south of Cambridge, since the seventeenth century, which by this time was in the hands of a paper-maker named William Tassell.[37] Between 1757–8 and 1785–6 he continued to supply paper, until the mill was taken over by Charles Martindale, who then took up the Press's business. Under Archdeacon's aegis the former London stationers were gradually abandoned in favour of local manufacturers. Apart from the mill at Sawston run by Tassell, there were also two built more recently, with one vat each, a little upstream, in the hands of a local businessman named William Fairchild. From 1777–8 onwards, Fairchild likewise became a regular supplier, and by 1779 there were three: the two Sawston paper-makers and the London stationer John Vowell.[38] Then in the early 1770s Vowell's name disappears, until in 1774–5 he took over from Fairchild who henceforth invoiced no more paper at least for the University's own printing needs. By the late 1770s, Fairchild's business was in distress. In 1778 and again in 1780 his two mills were offered for sale;[39] he was bankrupt in 1779;[40] and by 1785 John Vowell, now installed as paper-maker at Sawston, was also able to move into the Cambridge retail trade and to take over Deighton's shop opposite the Senate House on Deighton's removal to London.[41] Thus, from 1775–6 until Vowell gave up his business to Martindale in 1792 the University Press depended on two suppliers only, both of them local paper-makers, for the printing of its Bibles, prayer books and other books accepted for publication by the Syndics. The only exception was Kipling's edition of the Codex Bezae, published in 1793, for which paper was obtained from the London stationers Wright and Gill.

Baskerville had demonstrated the difference that could be achieved by the appropriate use of paper – but at considerable, and for the purposes of Archdeacon and the Syndics unjustifiable, expense.[42] For the vast majority of the Bibles and prayer books printed at Cambridge, the Syndics were in another kind of market, one for which a low final price was fundamentally important. In 1766 and 1767 the Syndics considered at some length specimens of paper both from London stationers and from the local paper mills. The context of their deliberations in March 1766, a meeting at which it was also decided to proceed with editions of 20,000 copies of the prayer book in 24°, and of 15,000 copies of the Bible in small octavo, suggests the nature of their anxiety.[43] One result was that purchases of paper were spread amongst several suppliers, who had access in their turn to different mills. So a London stationer, Bowles, was to supply it for the 24° prayer book; Field, also of London, for an octavo prayer book; and William Tassell of Sawston for the small octavo minion Bible.

Much of this, again, had to do with costs. Consciously gracious, the Syndics agreed to take 200 reams from Tassell at the old price of 10s., where now they expected to pay 10d. less.[44] Again, interest was not restricted to the smallest formats. When in the following autumn it was agreed to print a fresh edition of the Bible in quarto, including 250 copies on fine royal paper, specimens were likewise called for from several stationers. Not surprisingly, but perhaps not before time, the Syndics also ordered that a paper stock book was to be kept henceforth.[45] Thereafter, with quality subject to constant monitoring, there were fewer causes for complaint, though a plaintive note in the Syndics' minutes in 1777 noting that the next edition of the 24° prayer book should be on better paper than the last suggests that the process was not infallible.[46]

Apart from type and paper, ink was delivered from London, usually in barrels: Archdeacon's men do not seem to have mixed it themselves.[47] It was an expensive item in the accounts: in November 1785 Archdeacon acknowledged payment by the Vice-Chancellor of £100 to meet journeymens' wages, and of £51.5s.6d. to meet a bill for ink.[48] There were other constant demands for building and repairs, for regular needs such as paper for the windows, and an assortment of tasks by carpenters, joiners and blacksmiths, most of whose energies were directed at repeated minor repairs to the presses: there is no evidence in the vouchers for these years that a new press was ever bought. In the detailed accounts submitted year by year by the local smiths, James Fowle and then James Fuller, there emerges a clear portrait of equipment that required frequent attention so as to be kept in working order. Friskets and tympans broke constantly, chases needed either to be mended or altered, points were either worn or broken. From time to time bars of the presses were either lengthened or shortened, perhaps (no reason is recorded) according to the height of the pressmen, and spindles of the presses had to be new pointed. The carpenter had to supply girths, to repair cheeks and to plane platens.

The Bible trade was (and is) uniquely competitive. For a generation and more, the main competitors were members of the Baskett family, and the Oxford press. They were to remain so. But in the mid-century the Bible trade underwent a profound change. While demand for smaller formats increased more or less continually, partly as a result of the activities of missionary societies and other philanthropic bodies, demand for the larger quartos and folios increased as well, but for different reasons. The privileged presses made little attempt at first to exploit what was to prove a resilient and popular market, and one that was to remain so until the early years of the twentieth century. Instead, their position was challenged by innovations designed both to escape the legislation that restricted Bible printing and also to appeal to a middle-income market. Legislation was evaded by offering Bibles attended by commentary, rather than consisting of the text alone. Sales were found by appeals to the aspirations – social, educational, religious, economic and family – of possible buyers. The books were marketed so as to appear reasonably priced; and they proffered a means whereby families (who were regularly featured in the titles of these elaborate editions) might emphasise their corporate identity by recording events such as births or deaths. While Bentham and Baskerville were in competition both with each other and with the Basketts, others offered cheaper Bibles in quarto and folio, making them additionally attractive not only by commentaries of varying authority but also by inserting engravings as a part of the basic price (rather than to be chosen and inserted as extras) and, crucially, by publishing in parts. By part-issue, manufacturing and retail costs could be spread over a period. So, for less money, an apparently superior object could be acquired. These Bibles, sold in parts, were deliberately offered in a way that had by the mid-century become an accustomed method, especially in the more popular market, of buying many of the longer books, a method employed for the sale of an assortment of dictionaries, histories of England and other long works.[49] For those who promoted such Bibles, the market must sometimes have seemed insatiable. In some respects, the inspiration for the many editions of the Bible accompanied by commentaries and illlustrations may be perceived in Philip Doddridge's *Family expositor*, published in six volumes between 1739 and 1756. John Marchant's *New family Bible*, published in the mid-1740s in 140 folio weekly parts at threepence each,[50] was printed by Robert Walker, who for a time had printing offices in both London and in Cambridge, where he printed the *Cambridge Journal*. By the close of the 1750s the market was becoming established, with works such as Samuel Nelson's *Universal Bible, or every family's best treasure* (1758–9) and the several editions issued by Robert Goadby, in Sherborne.[51] In 1764–5, the *Cambridge Chronicle* carried advertisements for four such projects, their timing no doubt partly inspired by the recent appearance of Parris's edition of 1762 and of Baskerville's edition of 1763, both of them more expensive. Bibles in part-issues were kept available: it was assumed that subscribers would join at different times. Francis Fawkes's *Complete family Bible* was first published in sixty weekly parts in 1761–2. When it was relaunched in spring 1764 it was explicitly aimed as a challenge to a more expensive equivalent by William Rider, a master at St Paul's School, marketed as *The Christian's family Bible*.[52] Both cost sixpence per week and both offered copperplate illustrations, but Fawkes's work (in quarto) comprised fewer parts than Rider's (in folio); and Rider found himself obliged to justify his higher cost:

> It was intended to have been comprised in One Hundred Numbers, but the large and elegant Type on which the Text is printed, has extended it more than was imagined. It will, however, be the cheapest Bible with Notes that ever was published, considering the Excellency of the Copper-Plates, the Paper, and the Type, and the Care and Abilities that have been displayed by the Author.

The engraver Grignion had been engaged for the plates, and the revised calculations suggested that the whole would take 120 parts – compared with the 80 advertised for Fawkes.[53] By spring the following year, two further competitors were being advertised. Like Rider, Samuel Rogers, author of *The elegant family Bible*, realised the importance of appealing to quality, as well as to price. His version was planned to contain fifty copper-plates and to be completed in a hundred sixpenny numbers, making up two quarto volumes. But the advertising was explicit in stating wherein the appeal at least partly lay, in linking the project with two of the most fashionable names in contemporary typography. The work would be

> printed in a most elegant Manner, illustrated with a great Variety of Copper-Plates, and every Page ornamented with a Border of Flowers, in the same manner as Mr. Baskerville's elegant Book of Common Prayer, printed at Cambridge . . . The Bible will be ornamented with a Border of Flowers on each Page, most elegantly designed by Caslon.[54]

Thus, by an irony, the idea of a border that Baskerville had shown in his original specimen of his Bible, but had later abandoned, was taken up by a competitor. By this time the market was offered ample choice, but in April advertisements appeared for yet another, this time by the indefatigable William Dodd and emanating from the West End address of Robert Davis, in Piccadilly, rather than Paternoster Row. The commentary was to be drawn from Locke, Daniel Waterland, the Earl of Clarendon and other authorities, but the price of each part was still to be 6d. a week, or 2s. for monthly parts.[55]

Whether or not the optimism of the projectors of these various editions, and of others like them, was justified, the effect on the market for large-format Bibles from the privileged presses was almost inevitable. The Cambridge press withdrew from the market in folio Bibles; Baskerville's, reduced from 4 to 3 guineas in 1767, was being offered at a remainder price of 36s. in London by 1770;[56] and though Oxford retaliated with a revision by Benjamin Blayney (heavily influenced by the work of Parris), printed in folio in 1769, only one further folio Bible (1786) was printed at Oxford after that until 1794.[57]

Type and paper both controlled costs – the latter more than any other element in production. But to sell the Press's publications in a world already so crowded required entry into the less predictable part of the sequence linking word and reader. The Syndicate's decision in 1765 that there should in future be several agents could be no more than an experiment.[58] Relationships with Bathurst and with Dod had been complicated by the University's reluctance to acknowledge the complexity and strategies of the wholesale and retail book trade.[59] But in the late 1760s and 1770s a series of decisions and measures taken by the Syndics attest to a conscientious attempt to come to terms with a competitive market-place, in which old and sometimes informal agreements had too easily led to misunderstanding. In large part this was prompted by Dod's death in 1765 and the winding-up of his estate, in which the University took back into its care the residue of unsold stock, with the exception of the folio Bible of 1762, which was to be divided between the University and Dod's executor.[60] So, in April 1768 the responsibilities of the (now) four London agents and of Merrill were apportioned, each agent to be allowed 10 per cent above a stated minimum. By this arrangement, Rivington and Beecroft were expected to sell £600 worth of books before this discount applied, Dilly £200, and White and Merrill £400.[61] Perhaps not surprisingly, the

Syndics were immediately forced to revoke this discriminatory arrangement, and to settle on an overall 10 per cent.[62] The booksellers had won, and the booksellers remained to instruct the Syndics on the management of the market. In the absence of any relevant experience either among the Syndics or on the part of Archdeacon it could hardly have been otherwise if the Press was to continue as one of the country's, and the empire's, principal suppliers of Bibles. On the recommendation of the London booksellers Rivington and Beecroft, the price of the newly printed large quarto Bible was reduced from 15s. to 14s. In 1776 the Apocrypha printed in 1773 was reduced from 1s. to 10d.[63] Expenditure by the agents on advertisements in the London and country papers was sanctioned in 1771.[64]

The Bible trade, ostensibly controlled by the two university presses and by the King's Printer in an arrangement confirmed in successive legal cases during the eighteenth century,[65] was largely a trade cartel of which the Cambridge press and its agents were only a part. The disputes at Oxford following the expiry of Baskett's lease in 1765, and the eventual appointment of the London paper merchants Wright and Gill as the new lessees, proved to be episodes that led to the ending of the Oxford practice of leasing out the rights to print the Bible and other privileged books. More, apparently, than Cambridge, Wright seems to have found a successful market in the American colonies, that was inevitably affected by the war of independence. This, together with a discouraging outlook in respect of the Stationers' Company and of infringements of the patent on Lily's Latin grammar, led him to withdraw from Oxford.[66] In 1780 his printer and agent in Oxford, William Jackson, became a partner in the Bible Press. So the University took back to itself the business of printing Bibles and prayer books, and thereby transformed its press into one that was to become dominated by these needs.[67] Hence when in 1781 the duty on paper was increased, what formerly had seemed straightforwardly competitive and commercial, seemed now to take on an aura of joint interest. Historically joined with Cambridge in legislation, facing an unfamiliar task in a hostile world, the University of Oxford now sought to combine with her sister university in fixing the prices of Bibles and the other privileged books.[68] Rivington and the King's Printer were soon included in the discussions, but Archdeacon was in a commanding and well established position, and in the end Cambridge offered no more than a compromise, leaving some prices as they were.[69]

Proportionate to the size of the editions, the number of copies still in existence of the smaller formats of the Bible, New Testament and Book of Common Prayer printed by the privileged presses places them among the books that have survived least well. They have, quite simply, been read to pieces. As a result, and in the absence of complete records of production, it is now difficult to recover the overall size of the trade in these books in the 1770s and 1780s, the period when, under Archdeacon, the Cambridge press turned itself into a business whose primary commercial concern was their printing. Nevertheless, much can be determined of the extent, if not the share, of this trade as it was perceived from Cambridge. Not surprisingly, most demand was for pocket editions, in octavo, duodecimo and 24°. The quarto Bible, used so often as a family Bible and hence carefully preserved, was much less in evidence on the presses.

Between Parris's edition of 1762 and the first to bear the name of John Burges alone as University Printer in 1798, the University Press printed editions only in 1768, 1769, 1776, 1789 and 1796.[70] In the same period, Oxford or its licensees printed more than three times as many editions in this format.[71] Instead, Cambridge concentrated on the smaller formats. Between 1766 and 1795, the Syndics gave instructions for the printing of about 460,000 Bibles and over 350,000 copies of the New Testament in octavo or smaller. Orders were given approximately every two years to print editions of 15,000 copies of the Bible in duodecimo, set in nonpareil; and after 1776 similar orders were given for editions in 24°. Editions of the New Testament alone were frequently even as large as 20,000. In the same period, well over half a million copies of the prayer book were printed – most of them, again, in duodecimo or 24°.

It is not straightforward to collate the Syndics' instructions with surviving Bibles, Testaments or prayer books. Some editions did not appear until years after the order had been given, and others were divided like the duodecimo prayer book published in 1771, which appeared in both long primer and bourgeois editions. But the underlying assumptions and ambitions of the Press are clear: that it was answering a demonstrable public need, using its obligations as a privileged printer to supply a market that was much less elusive than that for scholarly publishing.

In such a context, the needs of Cambridge authors were, not surprisingly, at risk. Indeed, they were put in second place, since Bibles and prayer books were of consummate importance. In 1785, Archdeacon was rebuked by the Syndics for printing 'private work', that is pamphlets and books (many of them by resident members of the University) other than those ordered by the Syndics themselves, but from which he was expected to make his living. Apart from works for local authors or for local booksellers, such printed work also included William Ludlam's typographically demanding quarto volume of *Astronomical observations* from the new observatory at St John's College, published in London by Cadell in 1769.[72] For the Syndics, however,

> The Quantity of private work lately done at the University Press has interfered in a very considerable degree with the printing of Bibles & Common Prayer Books; Agreed, that the Printer be ordered for the future not to begin the printing of any private work, exceeding three Sheets, without first satisfying the Syndics, that it will not impede the Public Business of the Press.[73]

The preponderance of books published by third parties (especially local booksellers, either singly or in consortia with members of the Cambridge and London trade) and by authors themselves (frequently by subscription) was a direct result of the lessons learned and remembered from the disaster of the *Suidas* of 1705. But whoever was the financially responsible party, sales had to be engendered. Subscription proposals, newspaper advertisements, listings in magazines (the *Gentleman's Magazine* ran a monthly list of new books from 1731; the *Monthly Magazine* from 1732) and the long-standing practice of pasting up title-pages as advertisements were all familiar to the eighteenth-century reader. Reviews of books from the Cambridge press were not common, but the effect of even a favourable review could not be counted on. Moreover, the Press's books were rarely advertised in the local papers, and for reasons that were straightfor-ward. The London periodicals enjoyed a wider circulation. In this, Cambridge readers were very similarly placed to those at Oxford. 'I cannot think', wrote the London bookseller and publisher Thomas Davies to one of his authors, 'that advertising the Sermon in the Reading and Oxford papers will produce any thing but a further increase of charges. Consider, the London papers reach both those places, and are, I suppose, more read than those of the Country.'[74]

The regular route for goods to and from London was by Gillam's waggon, which set out three times a week and set down goods at the Cambridge warehouse beside St Helen's church in Bishopsgate.[75] From the Bishopsgate warehouse unbound sheets were taken to the London booksellers, agents or wharves as necessary. Every year, Gillam charged the University for carriage during the previous twelve months, and from this it is possible to obtain a clear picture of one part – including financially the most important part – of the Press's operations. Because his bills were to the University, they did not normally include carriage for private work – that is, for private individuals or for booksellers. Hence the invoices are very substantially for carriage of the privileged books. Occasionally there was also type to be charged for – either fresh from the founders or else returned to be melted down for credit. But in the absence of any evidence that the Press sought to recover charges from third parties, it does not seem that Gillam included in his annual invoices (except by very occasional mistake) parts of editions other than those apportioned to the Press itself that had been printed either for their authors or for other booksellers. In this way, Gillam's invoices provide a guide to the quantity of work produced by the Press on its own account. Save in a handful of instances they do not include copies of these books sold to local booksell-ers. In the case of the privileged books this was principally to Merrill, who in 1768 per-suaded the Syndics to increase the edition size of a 24° Bible so that he could take no less than 5,000 copies.[76] The weight mainly of paper carried from Cambridge to London showed an increase of over 50 per cent between the appointment of Archdeacon in 1766 and the appointment of his successor in 1793. In the late 1760s between 17 and 21 tons were carried annually to London at the Press's expense. By the early 1790s this had risen to 29 or 30 tons.

In 1764–5, as in 1763–4, the only bookseller to whom Bentham sent printed paper was Benjamin Dod, the University's agent. Two years later, in 1766–7, the list of addressees on Gillam's invoices was still dominated by his successors as agents. The arrival of Archdeacon coincided with a change of practice that may have been prompted jointly by the new agents and by pressure from Cambridge. In 1767–8 there were fifteen or sixteen booksellers in Gillam's list of addresses, and by 1770–1 the number had risen to about thirty.[77] Furthermore, the list now included destinations for books beyond London. While the vast majority went straight to London booksellers, either for local sale or for onward transmission (in Britain or overseas) by their agency, others avoided the London trade, and were sent to London simply in order to be for-warded by water to other towns in Britain. Both the Merrills and Woodyer were active in this trade; but so, too, was the University Press. In the 1770s and 1780s Gillam's invoices included notes of parcels sent to booksellers in Chester (Broster; Lawton; Poole), Halifax (Binns), Leeds (Binns), Newcastle upon Tyne (Akenhead; Chalmers; Charnley; Slack), Pontefract (Lindsey), Preston (Binns), York (Sotheran; Tesseyman; Todd), Edinburgh (Balfour; Tait), Glasgow (Bryce) and Aberdeen (Angus). The geographical emphasis in these lists on northern England and on Scotland not only reflects the organisation of the British book trade. In particular it expresses the limits of London booksellers' influence as sources of supply. The list of addresses is puzzling in that though carriage was charged to the University, there is no sign that it was repaid unless (and this must be presumed to have been the case) it was included in the annual receipts from the appointed agents. Certainly it was the University's bill, and not that of Archdeacon on his private account or that of the other booksellers for whom he printed. Perhaps most probably, since there would have been no real reason not to send books to London agents rather than their customers, these northern addresses represent part of the business of the Press's Cambridge agents, the Merrills.[78] But the clear implication is that for these northern booksellers named in Gillam's invoices it was both more convenient and also cheaper, at least for carriage, to deal directly with Cambridge than through a London agent.

Work for the University remained in many respects much as it had since the days of Crownfield, save that volumes of verses were no longer printed after 1763. In this jobbing printing, hardly any of which has survived, there are also clear signs of changes in both administration and social organisation, both for the town and for the University. Among Archdeacon's earliest work of this kind, the establishing of the new hospital under the terms of the will of John Addenbrooke brought a flurry of demands for printed matter: 700 copies (some as broadside advertisements, others as handbills) of the rules; printed letters concerning patients; a form of prayer for the hospital; 1,500 tickets, 650 posters (in two sizes), 80 forms of receipt, and 750 copies of the *Te Deum*, all for a concert in June 1766; and then, in September, 1,000 printed letters to admit patients.[79] Religion, medical treatment, fund-raising and musical enjoyment were all dependent on the printing press. In a university of sixteen colleges, and of about 1,400 resident members, it was usually the practice to print one or two hundred copies of public notices, whether to warn against gaming, to announce prizes, or to announce (in January 1773) 'Rules and orders for choice of pupils to attend lectures in modern history'.[80] In the winter of 1785–6, in attempts to regulate the lives of undergraduates, orders were printed forbidding dining in inns or taverns, and then (no doubt as a result) to suppress 'irregularities' in giving dinners in rooms of undergraduates. Further notices followed a few weeks later reminding publicans of the need to have their licences signed. It may be a measure of the growing irritation of the authorities in these months that with each successive notice the number of copies printed was increased.[81] Other notices, such as orders to return books to the University Library, required as many as 500 copies, and were perhaps sent to individuals as well as being posted in public places. For years, the volumes of university verses had been advertised by posting up their title-pages. But it is quite clear that the University as a whole was depending ever more on notice boards as, like the country more widely, it became

assumed that ubiquitous printed notices and advertisements were a part of the everyday environment.

However great an effect such changes may have wrought on everyday surroundings,
they were changes in detail rather than of policy. For generations, the Press had prospered from its right to print almanacs, another form of ephemera. Latterly this had
been an easy form of income, as compensation from the Stationers' Company in return
for desisting from exercising that right. No special account was made of this income,
so the Press neither profited from it nor was encouraged to suggest ways in which it
might be employed. The circumstances of how this moribund income was first taken
away and then rediscovered from the public revenue and used to promote learning have
already been described.[82] The consequences were radical, and basic to the organisation
of the Press as public obligation became linked with opportunists in the university
community to impose their own programme of a kind not seen since the beginning of
the century.

On 8 June 1782, in a departure from usual practice which did not normally require
the printing of such documents, Archdeacon printed a hundred copies of a Grace 'to
impower the Syndics for the Press to dispose of the 500£ pr. an. given by Government,
in the printing of Classics'.[83] The government grant, enabled by the Almanac Duty Act
in 1781, was intended as compensation for loss of the University's longstanding privilege to print almanacs. Though it was awarded by Parliament to Cambridge and
Oxford without prejudice as to how exactly it might be applied, in June 1782
Cambridge decided that its portion should henceforth be spent on printing either new
editions of early writers, or more recent work.[84] By legislation passed just before the
Almanac Duty Act, the two English and the Scottish universities were allowed a drawback on paper: that is, they could recover duties on any that was used for the printing
of 'any Books in the Latin, Greek, oriental or Northern Languages'.[85] Together, these
two decisions in Parliament provided the stimulus as well as the mechanism for the
Press to embark on a programme which, for the first time in many years, had a coher-
ence and clear commitment to the promotion of literature and science and of the
increase of religion and learning. Such was the vocabulary of the preamble to the
Almanac Duty Act, reminder of the standards by which the universities were to be
publicly judged.

In this way, by omitting to allow English as a medium for the subsidised publication
of scientific work, Parliament helped to place part of the University's learning at a disadvantage. As recently as 1770, the *Monthly Review* had welcomed Ludlam's observations based on work at the new St John's College observatory, referring specifically to
the public benefit to be gained from private wealth:

> In the noblest parts of science, natural and moral philosophy, the reputation of the
> present age is little inferiour to that of any which have preceded it; not even in astron-
> omy, where the fame of a Newton may seem to eclipse all other merit; for we still may
> promise ourselves the most important and useful improvements, while, aided by geom-
> etry, we continue to tread in the sure paths of experiment and observation. – This laud-
> able spirit of philosophizing is happily promoted by that assistance which wealth can

bestow, in the erecting observatories, furnishing them with their expensive apparatus, and liberally providing for the maintenance of those who shall be chosen to conduct the observations.[86]

The reviewer, George Walker, a dissenting clergyman, went on to allude to Ludlam's keenness, widespread in contemporary scientific and maritime circles in particular, to discover a method of determining longitude. It was an irony that, either by carelessness or deliberate omission in drafting an Act of Parliament, allowing cheaper paper to the Press, work of such inherent public interest and benefit should be set at a disadvantage compared with literary or philological scholarship.

The new monies from the government grant were not to be used for printing the privileged books. It was a measure of the University's determination that the Syndics were made answerable not only to themselves, but also to the University as a whole: that the Grace promoted to govern the almanac compensation income incorporated a requirement that the Syndics should submit an annual report on the ways they had spent their grant. A year later, they could report the purchase of new Greek type, expenditure of 50 guineas on the latest edition of Edward Waring's *Meditationes algebraicae* (originally printed at Cambridge in 1770), printing in progress of a fresh edition of Aristotle *De poetica*, edited by William Cooke of King's College, and intentions to proceed with editions of Plutarch and Aeschylus.[87] Expenditure amounted to just £137.3s. In the following year the Syndics confused agreement to spend money with actual expenditure. So they agreed on a subsidy of £250 for a new edition of Tanner's *Notitia monastica* and of £50 for George Atwood's *Treatise on the rectilinear motion and relation of bodies*, but returned no account of printing costs for books already agreed. In the third year their report made it clear that they were prepared to interpret their brief generously, in that for just under £300 they had bought heavily and usefully at the sale of the library of Anthony Askew, settling the books in the University Library and so investing in a store from which future editors of classical texts could benefit.[88] It was only in the fourth year, with grants allocated to Richard Relhan's *Flora Cantabrigiensis* (published in 1785, with several supplements from 1786),[89] Agostino Isola's edition of Tasso's *Gerusalemme liberata* (1786), a fresh edition of Waring's *Meditationes analyticae* (1785) and payment of part of the expenditure on Nasmith's edition of Tanner agreed two years previously, that the Syndics began to present the kind of details of actual expenditure that might ordinarily have been expected. But so far their expenditure, however interpreted, showed no danger whatever of approaching the £500 awarded annually to the University by Parliament.

The public eye was drawn to the Cambridge press, but it was drawn to a press that had not had the benefit of Blackstone's thorough-going reform at Oxford. In the eyes of a reviewer of a new edition of Cicero, published by Oxford in ten volumes in 1783, there was a clear hint that Cambridge too ought to follow, and in particular attend to literature. This was, after all, the University that could boast Dryden and Milton, Middleton and Gray, Bentley and Markland, as well as contemporaries such as Richard Farmer, Master of Emmanuel, and William Barford of King's, John Barlow Seale of Christ's and Richard Porson, or Jacob Bryant of King's and Richard Hurd of

Emmanuel.[90] In the sciences, a new Society for the Promotion of Philosophy and General Literature failed to make headway.[91] Its members were drawn from across the academic spectrum, but the only papers ever to be agreed for an intended volume of proceedings were on earth sciences, mathematics, astronomy and an ascent in an air balloon. The papers were agreed in 1785, and some were printed; but the society was dissolved in 1786 and it was over thirty years before the foundation of the Cambridge Philosophical Society.

A new edition of Aeschylus had been among the first projects considered in 1782–3; and though it quickly foundered on disagreements with the young Richard Porson, the scheme was pursued into the choice of purchases at the Askew sale in March 1785.[92] In that sale, most of the purchases were of Greek literature or other related materials. They were orchestrated by Richard Farmer, as University Librarian, and by Michael Lort, formerly Regius Professor of Greek. Their acquisitions for the University Library brought both a wealth of early manuscripts and the notes of John Taylor, former University Librarian and editor of Demosthenes. The purchases drew attention to the University's new mood, and prompted from a correspondent in the *Gentleman's Magazine* an informed and not unsympathetic assessment.

> After having taken measures for putting their press on a respectable footing, they have paid a proper tribute to the memory of their late illustrious member [Taylor], by possessing themselves of all his MS notes; and you may congratulate the public on the approaching prospect of seeing them issue, with due honour, from the University-press, in new and correct editions of Aeschylus, Apollonius Rhodius, Pindar, Juvenal, Terentianus Maurus, and other classic authors. After so long an interval since any thing more than Bibles and Common Prayers have proceeded from that press (for, I believe, Dr. Taylor's own works, printed there, almost half a century ago,were its last classic labours); we may hope the students of this university will give such specimens of their taste for, and proficiency in, the literature of Greece and Rome, as will show them not a whit behind the sons of their sister. Comparisons are invidious . . .[93]

As long ago as autumn 1782 Caslon had supplied a fount of great primer Greek type, the first substantial purchase of its kind for many years. Further purchases of long primer, pica and small pica followed.[94] By no means everything that was planned was completed, or even launched. The special long primer Greek on a small pica body, intended for the notes to Aeschylus, was put to other uses. Thomas Edwards's ambitious edition of Plutarch's *Moralia*, designed on the same lines as the edition of the Lives published in the 1720s by Tonson and edited by Augustine Bryan of Trinity, proved to be a fancy, as in yet another sign of change of pace the Syndics for the first time set a delivery date for his manuscript.[95] Porson's edition of Aeschylus, agreed at the same meeting, was to have been delivered by Christmas 1785, save that the project collapsed in recriminations.[96]

Understandably, authors were ready to acknowledge this new-found generosity. In 1784, Atwood wrote of the 'liberal assistance' (it was £50) he had received towards the expenses of printing his work.[97] In 1789 Gilbert Wakefield dedicated the first part of his *Silva critica* to the Syndics of the Press, and was rewarded with support for the second. William Falconer, a successful doctor in Bath, wrote fulsomely of the kindness of Samuel Parr in recommending to the Syndics his *Miscellaneous tracts and collections relating to natural history*, 'to be printed by their Authority and at their Expence.'[98] Relhan published the first edition of his *Flora* partly by subscription, but in the preface to the second edition (1802) wrote of the Syndics' *benevolentia*. J. D. Carlyle, who in 1795 was appointed Professor of Arabic, wrote of their *liberalitas*, perhaps not unmindful of his particular need for exotic type. In 1787, James Nasmith, noting that he had had the use of William Cole's annotated copy of Tanner's *Notitia monastica* in the University Library, also acknowledged the liberal encouragement of the University at large. These subsidised books were by no means the only books of consequence that passed through Archdeacon's hands in these years; and those that were subsidised may represent conclusions reached only after some difficulty. The output of Bibles and prayer books continued, but among the sermons and notes of courses of lectures other 'private' work also came from Archdeacon's presses. The almanac fund supported Isola's Tasso, but not a selection from the Italian poets printed in 1784, or Ariosto in 1789, or Labutte's French grammar, printed in 1784 and again in 1790.[99] Robert Masters's account of the life and collections of the antiquary Thomas Baker (1784), Richard Watson's six volumes of his *Theological tracts* (1785) and his *Chemical essays* (1786) all had to find their own way in the world.[100] So, almost, did Thomas Parkinson's introductory *System of mechanics and hydrostatics* (1789), of which too few subscriptions had been received to meet the cost of production. For this, the Syndics were persuaded of a last-minute need and so rescued the project with a timely subvention.[101]

Gilbert Wakefield, no impartial observer since he had benefited from the arrangements, nonetheless both summarised the practical means by which the Syndics established that what they approved was reputable, and also recorded his own – if not necessarily others' – experiences once a book was printed.

> The work is proposed to the *syndics*, or *curators* of the *university-press*. One of their body is requested to read the performance, in order to form an estimate of it's merits, and to judge of the expediency of printing it, with respect to the credit, or discredit of the work, to their body and the *university* at large. Upon his approbation the work is consigned to the press; the whole expence is defrayed by the *university*, and the entire copy presented *gratis* to the author. The only interference of the *syndicate* on these occasions is, to fix the price of the volume, which is usually, but not much, below the current rate; that the public, on the one hand, may be accommodated, and no inducement, on the other, holden out to the speculating monopolisers of these articles of trade.[102]

His account made the Syndics sound a charitable body indeed, but also, and no less importantly, one from whom much of the further responsibility of publication, of achieving sales, had been removed. In these circumstances, the established processes of publication by subscription became less essential; and when subscriptions were collected, it was either a simple saving on the account or (as in the case of the *Codex Beʒae*) permitted lavish expenditure. An Act of Parliament had relieved the Syndics of commercial obligation, the rock on which earlier attempts to promote the Press as a publishing body had foundered repeatedly through the eighteenth century. Now, there was a further benefit in that it was by these new publications, quite independent of the continuing business of printing Bibles and prayer books, that the Press's and the Syndics' reputation and achievement were mainly judged.

By 1793, the Syndics had made grants from the almanac compensation fund to over twenty books. They had also begun to bring before the English-speaking public the work of German theologians, through J. D. Michaelis on the New Testament,[103] and had printed Carlyle on Arabic literature.[104] But Edwards's proposed quarto edition of Plutarch had been reduced to an octavo edition of *De educatione puerorum* only (1791),[105] and the list had not been without controversy. Apart from Kipling's work on the *Codex Bezae* (by far the most ambitious project in these years, and to which we will return), Samuel Vince's *Treatise on practical astronomy* enjoyed less than universal enthusiasm amongst those who considered that others beside Vince deserved credit for it.[106] Gilbert Wakefield's edition of the *Georgics* (1788) had been followed by his *Silva critica*, but of this Archdeacon printed only the first three parts before Wakefield, non-conformist in his religion and in his politics, and the University finally parted company: the two concluding parts, issued after Porson, Wakefield's most vehement critic, had become Regius Professor of Greek in 1792, were printed in London.[107] Other hopes, apart from the Aeschylus, had been fruitless. Although the Chancellor, the Duke of Grafton, lent his manuscript of Statius so that an edition could be prepared, none appeared; and though James Tunstal of Christ's was engaged to prepare an edition of Terentianus Maurus, using the materials obtained at the Askew sale, this too proved over-sanguine.[108]

There was in the publication of some of these books more than the pursuit of learning for its own sake. To an extent not perhaps envisaged by Parliament in 1781, the fund was manipulated and directed towards undergraduate desiderata, as well as wider scholarship. Herbert Marsh, the translator of Michaelis, had found himself embarrassed when asked in Germany how the University prepared ordinands, and had been obliged to admit that 'theological learning forms no necessary part of our academical education'.[109] William Ludlam's *Rudiments of mathematics,* which the Syndics had accepted as a textbook suitable for undergraduates in their first year, proved to be the success that had been hoped, and after its initial publication in 1785 remained in use well into the nineteenth century.[110]

Whatever these particular needs and interests, above all, and despite all the criticisms, there was at last a momentum in publishing books where subsidy could encourage, even if it could be no substitute for a coherent publishing strategy for the Press as a whole.

Public money helped. But as so often the sharpest criticism came from the University's own members. In a university that was increasingly self-conscious as demands increased, even from its own members, for reform, and the question of the exclusion of nonconformists moved higher up the agenda, the Syndics were in an exposed position. William Frend, Fellow of Jesus College, expressed his irritation in an anonymous pamphlet printed not, as was common for documents critical of the

University, by Hodson, but in London. His primary target was not the Press in itself, but that part of the University which had become identified as most staunchly and unsympathetically conservative:

> This body has not given in proper accounts of the expenditure of that money [the almanac compensation]; nor has any one useful work been yet produced in consequence of it. Many useful books, and valuable books, are become extremely scarce: of some we have no good editions at any price: they might be printed with some propriety: But how far a *facsimile* of the Beza manuscript, or Italian sonnets, are consistent with the appropriation of the money, any one may judge. The *University* should take care that it be not used to serve private views more than general utility.[111]

It was easy to ridicule by reference to Isola's editions of Italian poetry. But the main fault of the proposed facsimile of the *Codex Beʒae* was that it was to be edited by the conservative and reactionary Thomas Kipling. Frend's remarks were intended *ad personam*. Seen in the light of reports detailing low expenditure even in the context of a grace so loosely worded in 1782 that it permitted the purchase of manuscripts and adversaria for the University Library (the same fund was also to be used to support Robert Holmes's work on collating the text of the Septuagint), the printing and publication of the *Codex Beʒae* is all the more understandable. The University was underspending a public grant, and needed a large and visible project. There is no evidence that expenditure in the first years after 1782 was deliberately held back so as to save money for such a project: there would have been no need or advantage in doing so.

An anonymous pamphlet, published in London in 1792, spoke – not without justification – of the 'indolent uselessness' to which college fellowships were liable, and of the 'corroding rust of inactivity' in resident Fellows. 'A foreigner would scarce believe that fewer works of learning are published from our Universities, than from the same number of men of liberal education anywhere in the kingdom.' Comparisons with Oxford were no encouragement whatever, and in particular the almanac duty fund had produced no perceptible improvement:

> Since the act of Parliament . . . Oxford has produced but very few learned publications from its own body, and Cambridge, I believe, none. This demonstrates, that the freedom from necessary employment, which the founders of the University doubtless thought would be productive of the most beneficial effects to learning, especially when assisted by a constant intercourse with a learned body, and the liberty of admission into an extensive public library, is, in fact, the most stubborn enemy that science has, and is, I am convinced, the sole cause why the resident members of the University are, taken in the mass, slower in their progress to literary eminence, and less often arrive at it, than those whose minds are rendered active by necessary business.[112]

The major project to which the Syndicate turned their attention was a facsimile of the *Codex Beʒae*, the fifth-century manuscript of the Gospels and Acts of the Apostles in Greek and Latin parallel texts, and the University's greatest treasure. As a member of the Press Syndicate, Thomas Kipling had been privy to decisions on the use of the almanac compensation money ever since its beginning. The consistent underspending of the fund was public knowledge. Kipling was in a position to understand the reasons for this, and its implications. In 1779 he had taken the degree of BD, but so far his sole book had been a summary, *The elementary parts of Dr. Smith's compleat system of opticks*, printed by Archdeacon in 1778.[113] In 1782 he had succeeded Richard Farmer as Lady Margaret's Preacher, and he was ambitious for advancement, taking his DD in 1784.[114] In spring 1786 a type facsimile of the *Codex Alexandrinus* appeared from the press of John Nichols in London, so bringing to fruition an idea that had been in circulation since the 1640s.[115] The *Codex Be*ʒ*ae* was an obvious successor, and one that Kipling seized on with energy.

The suggestion that the Press should embark on so major a project was first recorded in the Syndicate minutes in May 1786, when the impetus seems to have been a letter addressed by Kipling to the Vice-Chancellor.[116] A month later it was agreed that the Press should defray all costs of paper and presswork. Though examples of the *Codex Be*ʒ*ae* had been included among the engraved illustrations in Astle's *Origin and progress of writing* in 1784,[117] it was quite another proposition to engrave the whole manuscript. To prepare and then print from engraved plates would entail costs akin to those that had been rejected for the facsimile of Domesday Book in the 1760s: of 4 guineas per plate for tracing and engraving, about £3 for each copper plate, and about £2 per plate for printing: a total of over £9 per plate, with further costs for work in colour on the few pages that required it.[118] From the beginning, an engraved facsimile (such as John Pine had executed of *Magna carta* in 1733) can hardly have been a possibility. The review of the *Codex Alexandrinus* facsimile in the June issue of the *Gentleman's Magazine* alluded to the considerable expense involved in such a means of publication, and commended the effect achieved by the typefounder Joseph Jackson, who had engraved the punches especially for it in imitation of that manuscript.[119] Jackson's success in this, as in his earlier work on the similar facsimile of Domesday Book published in 1783, exposed him to further demands for such projects. He was a well-known figure, of whom anyone interested could read in Nichols's recently published life of William Bowyer — and there was much in this book, concerning so many local authors, to interest a Cambridge audience.[120] Kipling and the Syndics may well have heard of him in this way.

It was a further seven months before the Syndics agreeed to print the *Codex Be*ʒ*ae* in a facsimile type, and gave Kipling authority to negotiate with a suitable typefounder. Again, considerations of cost intervened. In the event, only a few lines from the *Codex Be*ʒ*ae* were published in engraved facsimile, included in the introduction and printed — with an assured attention to detail — in brown rather than black, so as to imitate the manuscript more closely. Everything was left to Kipling, to such an extent that at the same meeting when he was given authority to choose the paper, it was also agreed that the published price should be two guineas.[121] Whether the Syndics were simply confident of their resources (the almanac subsidy was substantially underspent at this time), or merely foolish in giving such a hostage to fortune, it is clear that they were not prepared to take a responsible joint interest in that with which they had been

Fig. 16 Punches, matrices (to the right in each group) and type (at the front) for the facsimile of the *Codex Bezae* (1793).

charged by the University. Instead they left it to one of their number. However, the fixed price enabled Kipling to organise subscriptions. For paper he settled on the finest available: a wove super royal made by Whatman and supplied by Wright, Gill, Son and Dalton, who submitted their bill for 108 reams in July 1787. Of the £405 payable, the University could expect to recover tax of £72 on publication.[122] Vellum for the copy for the royal library was delivered gradually between January 1788 and January 1789 from Street and Starkey, in London. Printing of this copy in itself presented particular problems. Not only did the limited quantity allowed mean that there was little margin for error; but the sheets themselves measured just the size of the finished page. So, instead of printing a folio in the ordinary way, two pages at a time, each page had to be printed from a separate forme. It was a time-consuming and costly undertaking.[123]

For a punchcutter (fig. 16), the letter-forms – Greek and Latin – of the *Codex Bezae*, involving several scribes and annotators of varying accomplishment, presented a more complicated challenge than those of the much more consistently formed hands of the *Codex Alexandrinus*. They were irregular, and were not simply to be copied (figs. 17, 18). Nonetheless, by November 1787 Jackson was able to submit a bill for a substantial delivery of double pica Greek, with smaller quanities of pica and brevier, as well as a bill for cutting ninety-six punches at 5s. apiece.[124] Gradually the rest of the type and the punches were prepared, the constant re-supplying of double pica during 1788–91 suggesting that it proved a difficult face to print without damage.[125]

The evidence of the suppliers suggests that printing of the facsimile part of the project was virtually completed in the later part of the winter of 1788–9; but the whole was not published, in an edition of only 250 copies, until 1793. Most copies were bound up in two volumes, to be properly admired, even (if with some surprise) for the sake of the large type – double pica – used to print the introduction.

By the time the work emerged, the University was distracted by matters having much to do with Kipling and little with New Testament studies. By then, Kipling was the appointed substitute of the Regius Professor of Divinity and former Professor of Chemistry, Richard Watson. For all his attainments, Watson was in the eyes of many unpopular, despised and increasingly discredited. For them, the lead he took in the prosecution of the unitarian and radical William Frend, resulting in Frend's expulsion from the University, only tainted him still further. Kipling's politics obscured his own achievement, and so critics fell with glee on the few mistakes in his transcription, and on his Latin.[126] Presentation copies were dispatched, including (apart from that to the King) one to the Vatican, and copies were bound up specially for the King of Denmark (as benefactor to the University Library)[127] and (at Kipling's own request) for the Duke of Marlborough. Copies were despatched across Europe.[128] The University, and Archdeacon and his men, could take a justifiable pride in their achievement. As for Kipling, those copies of the facsimile not subscribed for were allowed to him to sell at three guineas a copy.[129] Five years later he was rewarded with the deanery of Peterborough, though many preferred to see in his appointment a retreat from Cambridge and from the academic world.

The edition of the *Codex Bezae* was a triumph for all who had been concerned in its manufacture, whether paper-maker, punchcutter, or compositor or printer. From the beginning there had been those who were prepared to carp. Readers of the *Gentleman's Magazine* were reminded that Beza himself had been apprehensive lest its unauthorised readings might do harm.[130] Another correspondent wrote, 'I cannot but think that the university press might be much more laudably employed than in the exhibition of a transcript of this MS.'[131] Though partly in Greek, it had been written in the west, 'by a man more skilled in the art of writing a fair and beautiful character ... than either in the Greek or Latin language'. Blunders and ignorance suggested that Wettstein's opinion of the manuscript was all that was required, save perhaps for a fac-simile copy of a specimen chapter or two to satisfy curiosity. Both the manuscript and Kipling were quickly defended, but in a manner sometimes intended to sting. Porson, in ironic mood, acknowledged a few weeks later that the manuscript was inaccurate; but so were all ancient manuscripts; it was full of interpolations; but these were in themselves of interest, as emanating possibly from apocryphal gospels. In any case, the work was almost half printed (this by October 1788). As for Kipling, he was in Porson's view

> without any question, furnished with every accomplishment necessary to get honour for the University, and money for himself. He has, from his earliest youth, applied himself diligently to all sorts of critical learning, but most diligently to sacred criticism, and, from a long acquaintance with MSS. aided by natural sagacity, is become such an adept at Greek palaeography, as few know, and few would believe.

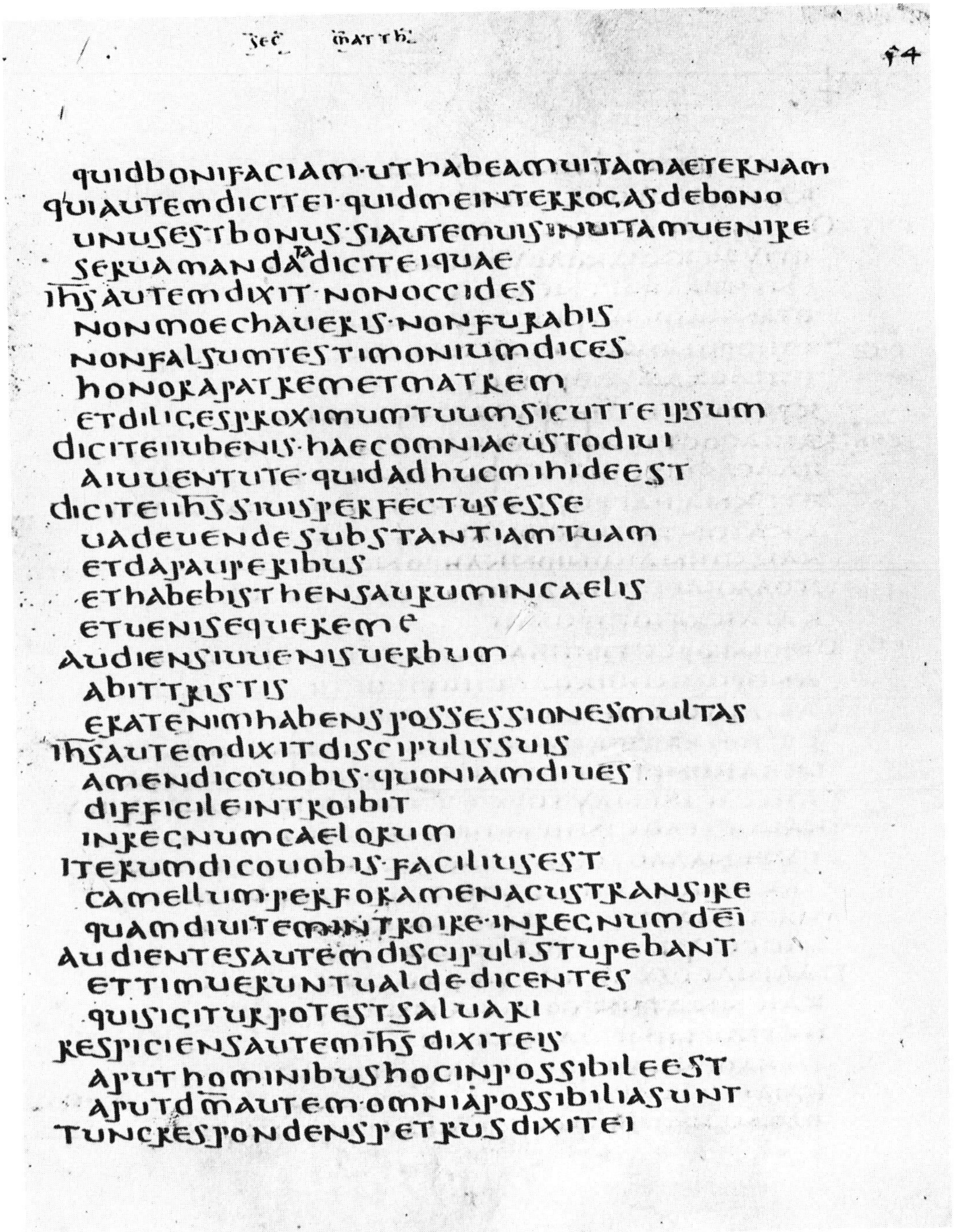

sec̄ Matth̄

54

quidbonifaciam·uthabeamuitamaeternam
quiautemdicitei quidmeinterrogasdebono
unusestbonus siautemuis inuitamuenire
serua manda diciteiquae
ihsautemdixit nonoccides
nonmoechaueris nonfurabis
nonfalsumtestimoniumdices
honorapatremetmatrem
etdiligesproximumtuumsicutteipsum
diciteiiubenis haecomniacustodiui
aiuuentute quidadhucmihideest
diceiihs siuisperfectusesse
uadeuendesubstantiamtuam
etdapaueribus
ethabebisthensaurumincaelis
etuenisequereme
audiensiuuenisuerbum
abittristis
eratenimhabenspossessionesmultas
ihsautemdixitdiscipulissuis
amendicouobis quoniamdiues
difficileintroibit
inregnumcaelorum
iterumdicouobis faciliusest
camellumperforamenacustransire
quamdiuitemintroire inregnumdei
audientesautemdiscipulistupebant
ettimueruntualdedicentes
quisiciturpotestsaluari
respiciensautemihs dixiteis
aputhominibushocinpossibileest
aputdmautemomniapossibiliasunt
tuncrespondenspetrusdixitei

Fig. 17 Matthew xix.16–27, from the *Codex Bezae*, Cambridge University Library, MS Nn.2.41.

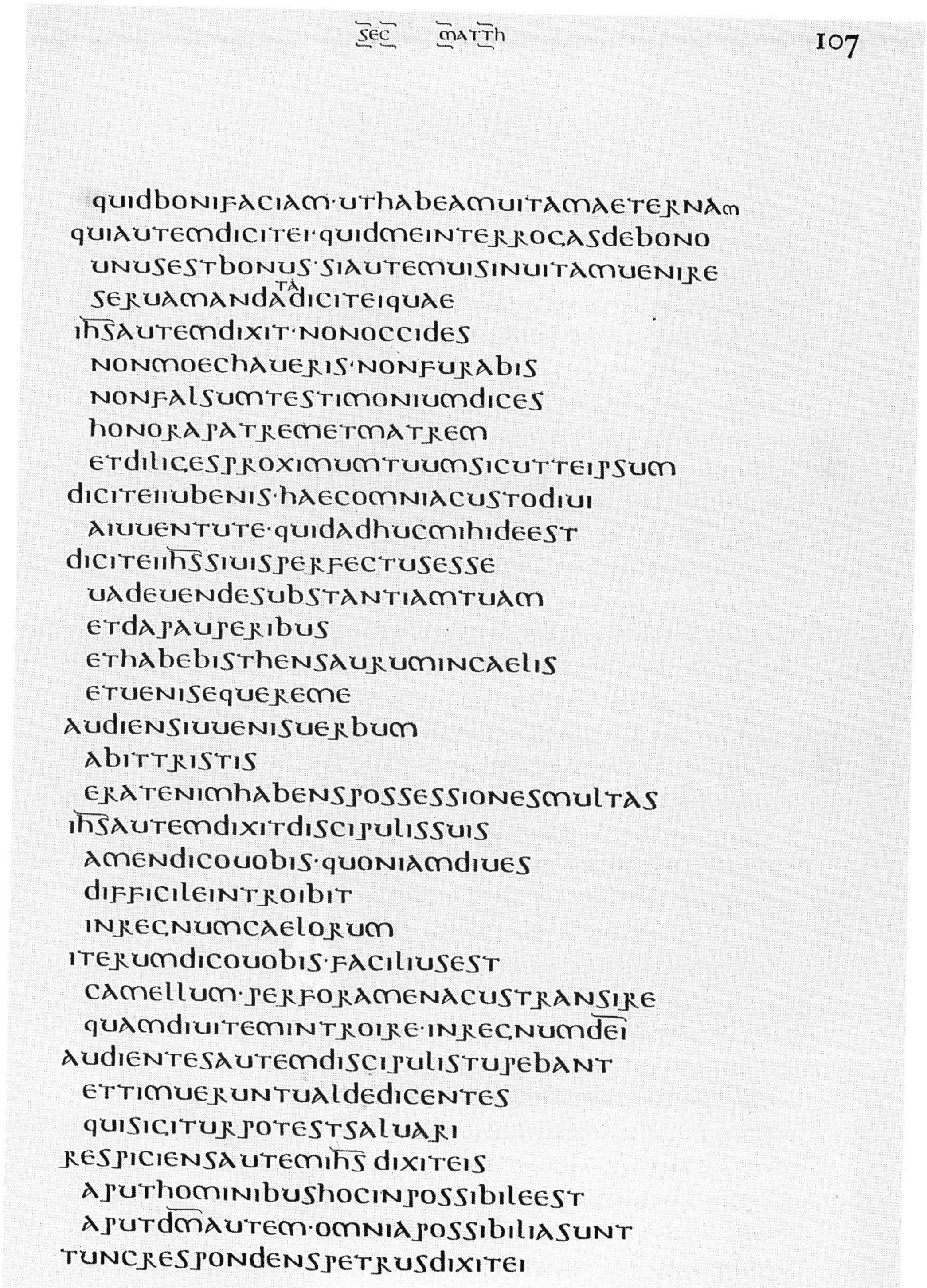

quidbonifaciam·uthabeamuitamaeternam
quiautemdiciter·quidmeinterrocasdebono
unusestbonus·siautemuisinuitamuenire
seruamanda͞ta͞diciteiquae
ih̄sautemdixit·nonoccides
nonmoechaueris·nonfurabis
nonfalsumtestimoniumdices
honorapatremetmatrem
etdiliresproximumtuumsicutteipsum
diciteiiubenis·haecomniacustodiui
aiuuentute·quidadhucmihideest
diciteiih̄s͞siuisperfectusesse
uadeuendesubstantiamtuam
etdapauperibus
ethabebisthensaurumincaelis
etuenisequereme
audiensiuuenisuerbum
abittristis
eratenimhabenspossessionesmultas
ih̄sautemdixitdiscipulissuis
amendicouobis·quoniamdiues
difficileintroibit
inrecnumcaelorum
iterumdicouobis·faciliusest
camellum·perforamenacustransire
quamdiuitemintroire·inrecnumde͞i
audientesautemdiscipulistupebant
ettimueruntualdedicentes
quisiciturpotestsaluari
respiciensautemih̄s dixiteis
aputhominibushocinpossibileest
aputd͞mautem·omniapossibiliasunt
tuncrespondenspetrusdixitei

Fig. 18 The same page in type facsimile, 1793.

Porson went on to comment on the way in which even in speech Kipling reminded him of the man for whom he deputised, Richard Watson.[132]

By a mixture of Kipling's determination and commendable scholarly fortitude that the better course was to share knowledge, and allow others to judge for themselves rather than to suppress it, the manuscript was published. The critic who thought it should be suppressed was easily silenced by quoting from Beza's own carefully phrased and cautious words, and by drawing attention to the fact that it had never been published accurately.[133] Having printed a correspondence on the subject, the *Gentleman's Magazine* contented itself with a noncommital review by Richard Gough, who did little more than quote former scholarship and acknowledge the beauty of its printing.[134] Porson, needing more space than the *Gentleman's Magazine* could offer, returned to the attack in an extended notice in the *British Critic*, and systematically undermined Kipling's work.[135] But even he could not deny the value of the principle on which the whole enterprise had been founded, and on which he realised manuscript studies had to depend.

> The practice of publishing whole MSS. in such a manner that every page, line, word, letter, and point, shall, as far as types can imitate hand-writing, completely answer to the original, is as yet in its infancy, though it has been publicly and strenuously recommended by Michaelis, and other critics. For since all MSS. are liable to accidents from fire, water, different animals and the ravages of war; since, even if they escape these accidents, they must ultimately be destroyed by time, as the colour of the ink gradually fades, and the traces of the letters become less and less visible: it is much to be wished, that persons possessed of sufficient leisure and learning would provide against this evil, by a timely diffusion of copies so accurately taken, as to prevent us from regretting the loss of the original.
>
> If such a scheme had been conceived in the last century, supported by proper encouragement, and executed with due care and fidelity, it is not unreasonable to suppose, that every scholar in his study might, by this time, have had access to many MSS. of the earliest ages, which he is obliged to seek in strange countries with great loss of time and money, perhaps of health, or to collate by the means of a mercenary, negligent or ignorant proxy.
>
> The late Dr. Woide undertook to publish the celebrated Alexandrian MS. upon this plan. He has performed his task with incredible labour, and as we are willing to believe (for we certainly have not taken the trouble of examining) with sufficient accuracy.[136]

By 1793 the use of facsimiles – usually engraved – for the history of manuscript illumination was well established, while Montfaucon and Mabillon had demonstrated their fundamental importance in palaeographical studies a century previously. Maffei, Baring, Tassin and Toustain had all exploited the medium.[137] Such facsimiles were by their nature selective. The creation of facsimiles of entire volumes was a costly affair; but so, too was the textual collation of originals by scholars obliged to attend foreign libraries. The edition of Plutarch planned by Thomas Edwards had been aborted by the failure to see the necessary manuscripts. For generations, even Biblical scholars had relied on collations and notes made by intermediaries of indeterminate skill and aptitude. Gough, writing his review of the *Codex Bezae* a little before Porson, had ventured the hope that Alexandrinus and Beza would be followed by Vaticanus. But the problem was no less central to other literature, and in these words we see also the Porson who was to transcribe the whole of the Trinity College manuscript of Photius twice over.

Meanwhile the bibliophile in Porson, noting that even in the few months since publication the price had risen from 2 guineas (the subscription figure) to 7 or 8 guineas, was unstinting in praise of the work's appearance:

> The university, so far as it depended on that venerable body, has most amply performed its part. The paper is of the finest quality that could be procured. The types represent, with sufficient exactness, the letters of the MS. which of themselves are not inelegant. In short, it is, with respect to outward appearance, one of the finest books that have appeared since the aera of printing, and far exceeds the *fac-simile* of the Alexandrian MS. in splendor. No wonder, therefore, that it should have greatly risen in its price, at a time when the value of books is almost wholly measured by their magnificence and rarity.[138]

Other, apparently more ordinary, books brought their own difficulties and criticisms. The compositors at the University Press were unused to setting complex mathematics, and the results were not always felicitous. It was acknowledged that, however great Edward Waring's reputation was in Europe as well as in Britain, his handwriting was very poor. The Syndics recorded that the 'peculiar nature of the work itself, & the singular advances he has made in that science' were reasons for subsidising his *Meditationes algebraicae*.[139] But they cannot have envisaged just how difficult the compositors would find their task either on this occasion or three years later on his *Meditationes analyticae*. His calculations spread out into the margins and required fold-out leaves. The *Meditationes analyticae*, with afterthoughts printed on a leaf to be inserted, required almost three pages of corrigenda, set in small type on a quarto page. Readers still found further corrections to make for themselves. These books were by no means the only ones to fall into difficulties. Atwood, too, found renown on the Continent and difficulties at home. His *Description* of experiments in natural philosophy, conducted in the course of lectures at Trinity College, was translated into Italian and printed at Pavia in 1781.[140] But in Cambridge, his *Treatise on rectilinear motion* was delayed by 'extraordinary Expences'.[141] Corrections were made at press, and this book too had a lengthy list of corrigenda; yet further amendments were made before copies were issued to the public, corrections being either stamped in with type or entered in manuscript.[142] The reasons for such awkwardnesses no doubt lay partly with the authors, as well as with the compositors, but the incidence of mistakes was certainly a discouragement.

Archdeacon's work was divided between the printing of privileged books, which occupied most of his men's time, and from which assured payments satisfied the needs of the University; the printing of what became known as private work, that is work on behalf of booksellers (in Cambridge and in London, but also, occasionally, elsewhere) or individuals; printing for the University's everyday administrative needs; and printing those few books that the Syndics themselves sanctioned.

In all this there was ample room for disagreement, not only in the time occupied under these various heads at the composing cases and on the presses, but also, and even

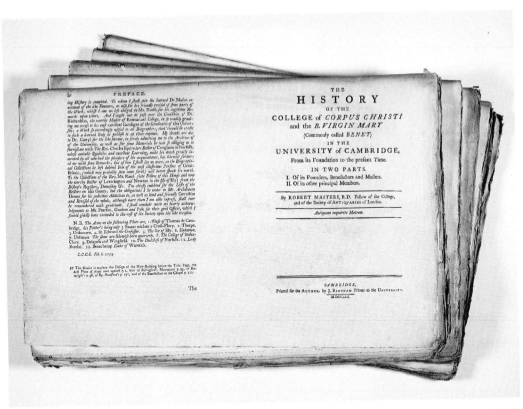

Fig. 19 Sheets of Robert Masters, *The history of the college of Corpus Christi* (Cambridge, 1753), folded for storage. Published copies have an engraving of the seal of Henry, Duke of Lancaster, in the blank space above the imprint.

more particularly, in the warehouse, where it was more difficult to cost different jobs. In the view of at least one member of the University, the University Printer benefited more than the University – so much so that its trade had shrunk to the point which in an ordinary business would have forced its closure.[143] In 1792, in the wake of the London scale of 1785, the Syndics agreed detailed rates for the setting of Bibles.[144] By the early 1760s the warehouse was becoming increasingly decrepit, letting in water which damaged the stock.[145] Here, with space at a premium, work done on private account could pose a direct threat to the needs for storing tens of thousands of copies of prayer books, Bibles, New Testaments and Psalters (fig. 19). Furthermore, since gathering and collating of sheets was the responsibility of the warehouse-keeper, who usually worked on his own, there were also occasional clashes of interest in the apportioning of his time. In 1774 the Syndics dismissed the warehouse-keeper for having failed to keep up with gathering the books as they came in from the printing house, but the task had in truth become more than a single person could manage, and his successor was allowed to engage extra help.[146] Not surprisingly, the Syndics were alert in particular to bulky books, and both Taylor's Demosthenes and Anthony Shepherd's *Tables for correcting the apparent distance of the moon and a star from the effects of refraction*, printed in 1772 (the latter published by order of the Commissioners of Longitude) were subjects for criticism. The stock of the Demosthenes was sold off to the local bookseller John Woodyer, who in 1774 reisssued it with fresh preliminary pages so as to give the impression, to a casual observer at least, who did not bother to glance at the clear references to volumes two and three in the signature lines, that the second and third volumes of the set (all that had been originally published) now constituted an orderly two volume edition.[147] Shepherd's work, on the other hand, was that of a man deeply unpopular in his college for the aggressive tenacity with which he held on to all available preferments, so denying them to others.[148] In 1782, ten years after publication, the sheets of his tables had still not been properly gathered, and it was found necessary to engage a boy specially for that purpose: it was estimated, so large was the work, that the task would take six months. But the decision by the Syndics that Shepherd should also remove the stock from the warehouse so that the University's work could be stored was almost certainly driven both by personal dislike and by need.[149]

Archdeacon's term of office, dominated by the printing of Bibles, New Testaments and prayer books, and in its latter years increasingly affected by the University's rekindled interest in the support of scholarly publishing, had seen practical changes both in the printing house and in its supplies. New typefounders, new suppliers and sources of paper, and even new expectations on the part of its employees, who from the 1780s compared their earnings with national scales, all affected the working of the Press. By summer 1793, there were two printing houses in the town apart from the University Press: of Francis Hodson, printer of the *Cambridge Chronicle and Journal*; and of Benjamin Flower, newly arrived in order to establish a radical newspaper, the *Cambridge Intelligencer*, and who soon turned to book printing as well.[150] In publishing, beside the major local booksellers led by Merrill, the Syndics were at last emerging as an independent force. The stark choice offered to members of the University, to publish for themselves or to persuade a local or London bookseller of the worth of their manuscripts, was no longer so simply put.

The establishment of a new generation of publishers in London offered authors further opportunities.[151] But in printing it remained that the Press was yet to see still greater changes – changes that had their origins, again, in the last thirty years of the eighteenth century. The need to speed production, apply cheaper materials, provide acceptable or even improved quality, and enable the printing industry to meet still further increasing demand, had been perceived for a generation. The practical needs of printers to have a standard measure of type, addressed by Fournier le Jeune in 1737, was answered in France by François-Ambroise Didot in 1775, though in Britain the typefounding trade was to remain unstandardised throughout the nineteenth century. In France and then in England attempts were made in the 1780s to speed composition by the introduction of logotypes – that is, groups of letters cast as single units.[152] In America, France and Scotland, renewed attempts were made to invent a successful means of casting stereotyped printing plates.[153] Proposed improvements to the design of printing presses, practical or otherwise, were a measure of the need of the trade, and in England dated from at least the theoretical work of the typefounders and printers Isaac Moore and William Pine of Bristol, in the early 1770s.[154] In Basle in the 1770s, Wilhelm Haas's iron press contained the germ of ideas that were to be taken up in England at the end of the century. In France, members of the Didot family experimented to develop the wooden press with the aim of printing a full forme at just one pull of the bar, rather than the two that were necessary for the familiar common press; and in 1783 the director of the Imprimerie Royale, Anisson-Duperron, published designs for one that was built and put to work. A further design, introducing a cam mechanism rather than the traditional screw, was published by Philippe-Denis Pierres in 1786.[155] In London, and even more ambitiously, William Nicholson patented methods by which the common press would have been displaced by a cylinder or rotary press.[156] In papermaking, Whatman's experiments in the manufacture of wove paper, and Baskerville's application of it, combining it with hot-pressing so as to provide the smoothest possible surface, had met with very little encouragement among ordinary printers. On the continent, Pierre Didot took a lead in employing *papier vélin* in the 1780s.[157]

Not all of these many experiments proved successful; but they expressed the mood of a generation faced throughout western Europe with fundamentally the same printing needs. With these investigations into the more obvious practical requirements there went parallel changes in tastes for printing types, the two considerations – practical and aesthetic – often marching together, but also tending too often to be separated by commercial needs: 'I have perceived with regret that the Art of Printing has been very much neglected in England', observed the printer, publisher and typefounder John Bell in 1788, introducing his specimen of types 'cut upon new and I flatter myself very improved principles', 'and that it is still in a declining state – expedition being attended to rather than elegance – and temporary gain is preferred to lasting advantage and reputation'.[158] After 1763, Baskerville had turned his back on Cambridge; and following the sale of his punches to Beaumarchais his type-face reappeared in the Kehl edition of Voltaire, printed between 1784 and 1790. Both Fry's and Wilson's imitations of Baskerville's type-faces were conservative in their intent, and neither foundry sought the revolution in design introduced by the brothers Didot in the early 1780s.[159] It was for the London punchcutter Richard Austin, working with the printer John Bell who was acquainted with the Paris trade to introduce similar ideas into Britain.[160] Archdeacon had ventured into modern tastes. As for Greek, the edition of the *Codex Beʒae* had used a type especially commissioned. Soon after his death, the University Press was to see both an entirely new Greek introduced for everyday use and new roman types; and it was to be embroiled in the latest, ultimately successful, attempts to increase production by means of stereotype plates in the world's first successful iron presses.

The ways in which the University Press exploited these new ideas, and laboured to introduce technical innovations, form the substance of the following two chapters.

12

John Burges

The aftermath of the French Revolution, the constitutional experiments that led to the execution of Louis XVI in January 1793, the subsequent declaration of war by France on England, and the ferment of political debate that accompanied all these events, placed old habits in a new light – for university, town, county and country alike. The war was to have a profound effect – socially and financially – on the book trade, as the need for money obliged the government to increase duty on paper, and the debate on the war, revolution, government, taxes and the cost of food demanded a large proportion of the trade's energies, capital, labour and equipment. Overseas trade was disrupted, and the import of raw materials for paper-making was prevented. The Press could not escape national affairs. Winters brought demands for the relief of the poor,[1] the price of food was kept under control sometimes only with difficulty, or even with local subsidy,[2] and the fear – in 1792–3 especially – that Britain would follow the French in its own revolution was not far from many people's minds. Wartime brought demands for money, for equipment and for troops, and by the end of the 1790s the financial crisis faced by the country was having its inevitable effect on the Press.[3] Political agitation, made the more threatening by the success of its principals in harnessing the printing and bookselling trades to its cause, led in turn to increasingly desperate measures and attempts by a frightened government to control the press. By an irony of timing, the retirement and death of Archdeacon, University Printer since 1766, likewise marked the death of an old régime.

When John Burges was appointed University Printer in partnership with Archdeacon on 1 July 1793,[4] the two men had been working together probably for the whole of Burges's career, since he had been apprenticed to Archdeacon in 1763.[5] By 1789, Burges was taking responsibility for what would usually have been done by the University Printer. Gradually Archdeacon withdrew from the Press; and he died after a short illness at the age of seventy on 10 September 1795.[6] He was buried not, like so many other University Printers, in St Botolph's church, but where he had died, at Hemingford Abbots, on the River Ouse, near St Ives.

The emphasis was to be on continuity, not on change; and in principle this proved to be the case. Like others before him in their first few months, Burges oversaw the introduction of new equipment. A new large press was supplied by William Morton, specialist pressmaker of Shoe Lane in London, in summer 1796.[7] This brought the total temporarily to six, though one was soon discarded.[8] But all could not quite continue as it had developed under Archdeacon.

To the changing emphases of the University in its teaching and in its learning were added the requirements of a war that increasingly demanded men and money.[9] The decade after Burges's appointment also witnessed a revolution in paper-making, with the introduction of machine-made paper and its rapid acceptance by much of the printing and publishing trade; the invention of a successful iron press offering precision unobtainable with the old wooden common press; and the development of a method of stereotyping that by reducing the costly requirement to keep quantities of standing type for books that might be reprinted, offered a promise of savings in money.

The Cambridge booksellers in the 1790s were dominated by three businesses: those of the Merrills and of W. H. Lunn, neighbours at the corner by Great St Mary's church, and then that of John Deighton, on the corner of Green Street, further along Trinity Street. Deighton's name had appeared on books printed by Archdeacon as early as 1780, when his shop was opposite the Senate House; but he did not live continuously in Cambridge. At the end of 1785 he left to establish himself in London, where he opened a bookshop in High Holborn, taking over that of William Cater.[10] There he remained until 1794, when he returned to Cambridge.[11] In London, Deighton made the most of his Cambridge connections. His catalogue for 1792 included a group of editions of classical authors from the estate of Henry Homer of Emmanuel College, and another group of publications by Gilbert Wakefield, lately Fellow of Jesus College. Stock from the late Lockyer Davis (d. 1791), whose premises also Deighton took over, was offered at reduced prices; and a glimpse of him outside the bookselling world is afforded by the half-dozen Swedenborgian works offered at the conclusion of the same catalogue.[12] In keeping with his aspirations, the catalogue for 1794 included a smattering of medieval manuscripts, as well as copies of three early Shakespeare quartos at 10s.6d. apiece.[13]

He left in Cambridge what was generally regarded as the most desirable bookselling address. Meanwhile his former assistant, William Lunn, after opening a shop in the less fashionable Peas Hill in 1787, moved after only ten months to his master's old shop. In 1792 Lunn moved again, this time to one 'near the Public [that is, University] Library', recently occupied by a Miss Lord; and then, in 1797 and with a clear eye on the developing fortunes of the capital's west end, he removed to Oxford Street, in London, taking a shop near the fashionable Argyll Street.[14] In his business practices he had much in common with the well-known London bookseller James Lackington, of Finsbury Circus.[15] While in Cambridge, his rule (following Lackington's example) of selling for ready money only, rather than credit, and of issuing substantial annual catalogues, had ensured that he would be a formidable figure, though he took little part in the publishing of new books compared with the sustained policy of his principal local rivals, and neighbours, the Merrills.

Deighton had also continued to maintain some of his old links, partly through advertisements in the local newspaper. When in 1794 the opportunity came to buy the

Merrills' stock, he seized it. In an advertisement in the *Cambridge Chronicle* he explained his new situation:

> J. Deighton respectfully begs leave to inform the Gentlemen of the University, Town, and county of Cambridge, that he has purchased of Messrs. Merrill, booksellers and stationers, their stock in trade . . . The premises of Messrs. Merrill being no longer used as a public shop, J. Deighton has taken the house lately occupied by Mr. Hovell, sadler, Trumpington-Street, the corner of Green-Street, where the above business will in future be carried on.[16]

John Merrill died in 1801, aged seventy; and his brother Joseph died in 1805, wealthy enough to leave over £3,000 to local charities.[17] By the early years of the nineteenth century Deighton was solidly established, a leading supplier of books to the University Library and able to advertise that, thanks to a newly established foreign connection, he was able to obtain foreign books as cheaply as anyone in the kingdom.[18]

Lunn, Deighton's former assistant, retaliated by taking bookselling into the world of furniture, and announcing that he had 'furnished a room in his house, at a very considerable expence, with a large and elegant mahogany library case, in which he has deposited for sale an assemblage of superb and rare books, that will be found on inspection to merit a particular degree of attention'.[19] But Cambridge proved a discouraging place for such a venture, and Lunn never succeeded in obtaining the agency of the University Press.

Besides these large booksellers, in the early years of the nineteenth century there was the business of John Nicholson, to which his son succeeded in 1796.[20] The smaller shops included those of Barrett in All Saints church-yard; of J. Gee, formerly a journeyman to the Merrills, in the market-place;[21] and of Benjamin Flower, who ran a bookshop in conjunction with his printing business in Bridge Street. Nicholson's circulating library was by far the most prominent and most successful; but there was also another, principally of novels, run by William Page, whose family combined bookselling and a circulating library with confectionery and the skills of the pastrycook, in premises divided between Shoemaker Row (modern Market Street) and a shop opened in 1796 opposite Holy Trinity Church, a few yards away.[22] In Trinity Street, John Bowtell had been established opposite the end of Green Street since the early 1790s, in a shop with a binding premises attached, having moved there from the adjoining parish of All Saints. Like his friend Nicholson, Bowtell was also able to supply transcriptions of manuscripts or printed books. But though he was a bookseller, and so became embroiled in the Frend affair, his main business was in bookbinding, and in this he was the leading Cambridge figure of his generation.[23]

The centuries-old isolation of colleges such as Emmanuel, Christ's, Jesus, Peterhouse and Pembroke from the centre of the book trade remained unbroken, as the pull of the two most populous colleges, St John's and Trinity, dominated the topography of the trade. To a great extent this was also true of printers. The University Press itself was isolated from the centre of the book trade in and around Trinity Street, while Hodson was on the corner of Green Street, M. Watson in the Angel Inn yard, on the west side of Trinity Street, and Flower in Bridge Street.

Fig. 20 Richard Corbould Chilton (Sidney Sussex College, B. A. 1785), *Helluones librorum* (Devourers of books). Aquatint by Francis Jukes, engraving by J. K. Baldrey. The works of Newton, Locke and Vince figure prominently in the undergraduate's study.

The lists of books offered by the local booksellers reflected local needs (fig. 20), though these varied greatly in a university where study was not essential. 'It would scarcely be believed how very little knowledge was required for a *mere* degree when I first knew Cambridge', remarked George Pryme, many years later. 'Two books of Euclid's *Geometry*, Simple and Quadratic Equations, and the early parts of Paley's *Moral Philosophy*, were deemed amply sufficient. Yet in the year 1800 three students failed to pass even this test.'[24] Nicholson had made his name by books for undergraduates, and by 1804 his successor, anxious to provide for the more studious, could offer translations of Juvenal and Persius, of Cicero, Xenophon and Aeschylus, as well as elementary works on mathematics, physics and astronomy by James Wood and others, a range of books on kindred subjects by Samuel Vince, helps to French and Hebrew, and cribs for Locke and Paley. Though Deighton's and Nicholson's names frequently appeared together on the same title-page, the two had established very different traditions. As agent for the University Press's Bibles and prayer books, Deighton was in a powerful financial position, which he developed. In 1803 he took over the publication of the *University calendar*. On these connections he built up a list that came to epitomise some of the principal strands in the University's interests. Like many another bookseller, the books he advertised as being 'printed for' him consisted of a mixture of stock bought in, books in which he had a share as publisher, and books he had commissioned outright. The list of over fifty titles at the end of *A description of the University, town, and county of Cambridge* (1796) included Shakespeare in fifteen volumes, a biographical dictionary also in fifteen, Murphy's edition of Samuel Johnson in twelve, and Zouch's edition of Walton's *Lives* (York, 1796), besides Wood, Vince, Ludlam, Paley and other undergraduate needs. Nicholson, too, counted Vince on his list. Gradually Deighton accumulated lists of members of the University, the semi-official account of ceremonies in the Senate House, Relhan on Cambridgeshire flora, a catalogue of the botanic garden by its curator James Donn, the University Librarian (Clarke) on antique sculpture in the Library, Joseph Milner on the history of the Church, Michaelis on the New Testament, and Porson's Euripides, as well as the annual sheet almanac (first published for 1801), a guide to Cambridge, and a manual of university slang. In that his list included Herbert Marsh, Edward Maltby and the more evangelical Charles Simeon and Isaac Milner, he showed no theological favours.[25] Much of Deighton's sober list, and rather less of Nicholson's, was printed at the University Press.

Bookselling and publishing were drawn ever more towards London. The several years' sojourn there of John Deighton was to have a long-term effect on the fortunes of the University Press, as he gradually established himself as the first Cambridge bookseller whose aspirations were as a national publisher.

For the present, the Press was to be concerned with two priorities: the maintenance and exploitation of the Bible and prayer-book privilege, and a restricted choice of books to be printed and published with the aid of the Government Annuity Fund (GAF). These reflected some of the preoccupations of the University itself: its concern with evangelicalism manifest in figures such as not only Milner (who died in 1820) but also including Charles Simeon of King's, and William Otter of Jesus, and in countries overseas in the stimulus afforded by Claudius Buchanan and Henry Martyn. On the other hand, the GAF books reflected the unique status afforded to Greek classical literature and culture in a generation inspired by Porson and, in different vein, Wilkins and Clarke. With the emergence of a new generation of London publishers, the University Press was also drawn closer to the centre of the book trade.

For printing in Cambridge, these changes in direction were most noticeable initially not in the death of an aged University Printer, nor in the election of one of his journeymen as his successor. There had long been two printers established in Cambridge. By 1793 Francis Hodson depended partly on occasional pamphlets or short books, but still mainly on his newspaper, the *Cambridge Chronicle and Journal*. This in turn relied for much of its support on the conservative instincts of the University. There now arrived a third printer, of radical ideas and national interests.

The first number of the *Cambridge Intelligencer* appeared on 20 July 1793.[26] Its printer was Benjamin Flower, a Unitarian who came to Cambridge not only as an experienced printer seeking fresh markets, but also as the author of a substantial book on the French constitution, published in 1792, in which one of his most urgent purposes was to argue for a constitutional reform in church and state in Great Britain. While any new press in Cambridge might pose a commercial challenge – potential or actual – to the University Press itself, a press owned and run by a nonconformist and declared reformer posed a constitutional challenge as well. Flower's book had been reviewed at length in the *Monthly Review* by a Fellow of Peterhouse, Thomas Pearne, also a Unitarian, whose interests as a student of politics were well known.[27] Whether or not Pearne played any part in Flower's decision to come to Cambridge, the establishment of a new and reform-minded press coincided with a summer and autumn in which printers and booksellers across the country were pursued through the courts for printing radical literature, and that of Tom Paine in particular.

In an affair widely followed elsewhere, the same seasons also saw the aftermath of the trial before the University of William Frend, Fellow of Jesus College, who refused to allow his outspoken radicalism to be contained within his college walls.[28] Amidst acrimonious proceedings, Frend was expelled from his college and then, at the end of June, from the University – only a month before the first number of the *Cambridge Intelligencer*. Frend's case divided the University, and provided ample opportunity to goad two of its most senior and (for some) least respected members, Thomas Kipling, editor of the *Codex Bezae*, and the absentee Regius Professor of Divinity for whom he acted, Richard Watson. Flower printed the fullest account of the proceedings against Frend; and while he developed his newspaper into one of the country's most successful and widely read organs of radical opinion, he also established himself as a printer and publisher of books and pamphlets in Cambridge itself. Later, in 1800, he was also briefly to open a bookshop.[29] Coleridge, who came up as an undergraduate to Frend's college in 1791, contributed poems to the *Cambridge Intelligencer*, and in 1794 Flower printed his first separate work (written jointly with Southey), *The fall of Robespierre*. 'I cannot but think my poetry honoured by being permitted to appear' in the *Cambridge Intelligencer*, wrote Coleridge a little later, reflecting on Flower's conduct of his newspaper.[30] Flower found most of his work among dissenters and evangelicals, counting both George Dyer and Mrs Barbauld among his friends. In 1794 he also printed a new edition of Chatterton's Rowley poems; and his name became familiar to many more undergraduates as the printer of analyses of Paley and of Locke.

Apart from the local booksellers, Lunn, the Merrills and Deighton, Flower's connections in the London book trade were principally with G. and J. Robinson, of Paternoster Row, who in August 1793 had been found guilty of selling *The rights of man* to a country customer and who in November that year had been fined by the Court of King's Bench.[31] Chatterton's poems, seeking a genteel market, were sold by Edwards in Pall Mall, while others of Flower's books were handled by Thomas Conder in the City, a member of a well-known nonconformist family. In most respects there was a gulf between Flower's interests in bookselling and his interests as a newspaper proprietor. There is no evidence that he became much involved in the circulation of the undergrowth of the seditious pamphlets and broadsides at which the government took particular alarm; and when he was finally arrested he was accused of libel, not of sedition or treason. The excuse was an attack in the *Cambridge Intelligencer* on Richard

Watson, the 'Right Reverend time server and apostate' whom Pitt had promoted to no higher office than the see of Llandaff. It was in Watson's capacity as Bishop of Llandaff, rather than as absentee professor, that the House of Lords found its excuse in resolving that Flower had committed a 'gross and scandalous libel' on one of its members. Flower's imprisonment in 1799, and his departure from Cambridge to Harlow in 1804, removed from Cambridge not only a radical but also a printer, just before the time when the University Press was to become preoccupied with the introduction of stereotyping and an overwhelming demand for Bibles.[32]

Like other printers in the town, he was always in some measure dependent on the University, and therefore susceptible to its requirements with all the advantages of yet being unofficial. So in 1796 he was instrumental in launching the first issue of the University *Calendar*, printed for the local bookseller W. Page. The book's fortunes followed Flower's own: no edition was published in 1798, and the last to be printed by him appeared in 1799. For the next three years it was printed by Hodson, who gave it a more authoritative appearance by introducing the University Press's 'Hinc lucem' device on the title-page; and then from 1803 it was printed by Watts, at the University Press. Its publication, for many years in the hands of Deighton, was not taken over by the University Press until 1914.

While much of Archdeacon's printing had been workaday, with its emphasis on privileged books in cheap formats, the continuing practice of printing copies on large or fine paper, and the achievement of the *Codex Beʒae* in 1791, were reminders of a bibliophile market as well as one for religious or scholarly necessities in their most basic forms. Occasionally, copies were printed on vellum – of the *Codex Beʒae* for the royal library, and two copies of Porson's *Medea* in 1801. In some at least of the preservation and enlargement of Porson's reputation there was an element of bibliophily, a taste for copies on vellum and large paper that was by no means restricted to antiquarian gentility. In a generation bred on the tastes of Mead, Askew and Pinelli, all of whose library sale catalogues, recording a culture that depended much on appearance, were widely read and referred to, the cult of vellum and large-paper copies was natural. 'There are few who object to the decorating *a good picture* with an *elegant frame*,' wrote the young T. F. Dibdin in 1802, 'and in purchasing a *vellum* or *large paper* copy, we are guilty of no more absurdity than adorning the pencil of a Raphael, or a Teniers, with a frame in proportion to its magnitude and beauty'.[33] Porson had been notoriously slovenly in his clothes; but he was well acquainted with the fashionable London book trade. In this, his taste was furthered by his contemporary and close friend Matthew Raine. Porson gave to Esther Raine, 'puella doctissima et dilectissima', one of the vellum copies of his *Medea*.[34] The folio Glasgow Aeschylus of 1795, anonymously edited but in which Porson's part was never doubted, included eleven copies on large paper.[35] So fashion further required even after his death that his *Adversaria* should be printed on large as well as ordinary paper. In the 1790s, this market assumed greater importance. Among the London printers, William Bulmer's Shakespeare Printing Office, opened in 1791, set standards which few managed to equal but many aspired to.[36] Bulmer was to have a direct influence on the Cambridge press, in that the equipment in which he invested was emulated by first Burges and then Burges's successor, Richard Watts.[37] As Dibdin, arbiter of taste in such matters, was eager to point out, the taste for large-paper copies or for copies on vellum, was not confined to older books – as the extravagant prices realised in 1804 for recent books printed on vellum seemed to prove.[38]

The appearance of the paper used for books, and not just its effect on their legibility, had by the time of Archdeacon's death taken its place firmly on the Press's agenda. Kipling's choice of the finest paper available for the *Codex Bezae* had been little more than the reputation of the manuscript and the University required. But now a wider and more general interest in wove paper, with its smoother surface more sympathetic to smaller or thinner-faced types, was transmuted to instruction for printing. For this, Burges turned to Grosvenor & Chater rather than the local suppliers, paying as much as 33s.6d. a ream for their Extra thick wove post, used to print Carlyle's *Specimens of Arabian poetry* (1796).[39] The qualities offered by wove paper also suggested that Bibles might be printed on it to advantage. Usually, the Press's 24° editions of the Bible and prayer book were printed in nonpareil; but in October 1795 the Syndics agreed to print the Bible in pearl, the smallest size of type practicable, and specified that it should be printed on wove paper.[40] Type for the purpose was supplied by Caslon, and paper ('Extra large extra thin Wove Royal') at 38s.6d. a ream by Grosvenor & Chater.[41] In February 1796 the Syndics agreed the purchase of a hot press, so as to add a sheen to the printed sheets and make binding easier.[42] Richard Farmer, Master of Emmanuel, University Librarian, student of Shakespeare, early English literature and printing, and book collector, was not at this meeting; but the fact that he was given responsibility for procuring this expensive equipment suggests that he was forward in proposing it. It may well be that he, the most cosmopolitan and probably the best informed about modern fine printing, was the prime mover in many of the investments in new equipment and different paper. If so, his death in September 1797 deprived the Press of crucial advice, for Burges by himself was incapable of achieving much further.

It is not clear that the University Press always took the lead in such matters among the printers in Cambridge. In June 1794, the *Cambridge Intelligencer* announced an edition of Chatterton's poetry, to be printed by Benjamin Flower, of which some copies (price 10s. rather than 7s.) were to be printed on 'superfine Royal, and hot-pressed'.[43] In April 1795 – still almost a year before the Syndics agreed to purchase equipment for hot-pressing paper, the *Cambridge Chronicle and Journal* carried an advertisement for a collection of *Academical contributions of original and translated poetry*, printed by Flower and of which 'a few copies are printed on superfine wove royal, and hot pressed.'[44]

Not surprisingly, these extra features, including expensive paper, more difficult presswork and further attention to the printed sheets, resulted in noticeably higher-priced books. The price of Busick Harwood's *System of comparative anatomy and physiology*, to be published by subscription, had to be increased before the first fascicle had appeared, because of the cost of the drawings and engravings, obliging the Syndics to issue a printed statement to that effect. But they made sure to emphasise that it was the author, not the Syndicate, who was obliged to raise the price.[45] Nor could supplies always be relied on. The paper trade was unaccustomed to keeping large quantities unsold for long periods; but rapidly increasing national demand in the publishing industry for wove paper rendered it even more vulnerable to the seasonal difficulties of the weather for which paper-makers usually allowed. Damp or exceptionally cold weather brought difficulties. In January 1797 Grosvenor & Chater explained to Burges that they would complete his order as soon as they could possibly get it finished: 'but the Weather is much against us'.[46] Wove paper was increasingly fashionable, and the better makes of it were both attractive to customers and practical for more ambitious printing. So it was introduced into the wording of advertisements, with other distinct physical attributes including hot-pressed and superfine, as well as less tangible adjectives such as elegant.[47] But demand and supply were not always in pace in this period of change; and more ordinary royal paper was to be had for 16s. to 18s. a ream, rather than twice that and more. Amongst Cambridge-printed books, the price of the duodecimo prayer book set in brevier on bourgeois, on wove paper and hot-pressed, was set at 4s.6d., compared with 1s.2d. for the ordinary duodecimo printed in bourgeois. For the octavo prayer book, in an English-sized face on wove demy, hot-pressed, the cost was 8s., compared with the ordinary octavo editions at 3s.8d. for the larger in great primer, or 2s.2d. for the smaller in pica. Throughout the second half of the century, the Press had laboured to reduce the cost of the privileged books. Not since the prayer books issued by Baskerville in the 1760s had the octavo edition cost so much.[48]

The only reasons for such ventures among the Bibles and prayer books (and even Farmer's influence, by itself, could scarcely have carried the day) can have been those having to do with a constant search for fresh markets. In similar vein, the decision in 1798 to print an octavo Bible, set in English-faced pica, on three varieties of paper, was a response to others: the Press was wary of innovation for its own sake, and so long as its monopoly, shared with Oxford, was not breached, had no need to take a lead. The new Bible was to cost between 16s. and 28s.; but almost immediately this was reduced; and so was the price for the 24° pearl Bible. In fact, none of these speculations with the privileged books sold well. They required extra advertising; by the end of 1800 the octavo Bible had been further reduced, now without the Apocrypha, to between 12s. and 18s., and in 1803 the remaining stock of the octavo Bible was sold off.[49]

These ventures had been driven by two winds. First, the Press had not escaped criticism for the quality of its printing; and second, much more importantly, the monopoly was being challenged more blatantly and on a scale far greater than had been known since the days of wholesale imports from Amsterdam in the late seventeenth century.

Criticism of quality was not new. The SPCK had complained in the middle of the century; and it complained again now, of the 'coarse, bad coloured & very bad paper' used in the 24° prayer book of 1796, set in nonpareil, and in the duodecimo minion prayer book of 1798: the two were among the very cheapest that the Press had to offer. The Syndics' response to such criticism was much as might have been expected. In their opinion, while the paper was certainly browner than that used in the equivalent books from Oxford, the type was arguably superior. But they agreed to change papermaker.[50] Within a few months, paper was also being supplied from Thetford in

Norfolk, though Martindale's position was never under serious threat.[51] As usual, difficulties arose not with the more expensive books, but with the cheapest.

The quantities of these and other books that the Syndics were ordering at this time posed considerable demands for quality control on any paper-maker; and the challenge was the greater in that customers expected even these exceptionally cheap books to be of reasonable appearance. In the 1790s, the Press sold 20,000 copies of the 24° non-pareil prayer book annually. In 1798 the edition size was increased to 40,000, so as to avoid the annual process of printing fresh editions. When in 1800 a further edition was commissioned, the order was for 40,000 copies, with the proviso that the paper should be finer than previously.[52] In the 1760s, editions of half that size for the same book had been large by the standards of the day. All this was accomplished at a time when, thanks to increased excise duty, the cost of paper was rising dramatically. The change in 1794 in the method of calculating duty, by the pound weight rather than by the ream, meant that the onus of tax fell more heavily on printing paper than on writing paper.[53] The University could claim drawback on tax, but it had first to meet the bills submitted by the stationers or paper-makers, and so there was always some burden of tax to be carried. One result, and not only in Cambridge, was to determine still more firmly the distinction between those books that were to be printed in the best possible way – for example, the *Codex Bezae* or Carlyle's Arabic poetry, on Whatman's wove paper – and those for which costs had to be kept down – like most of the privileged books.[54]

A further question, respecting the Oxford and Cambridge monopoly, was more generally serious, not only because it posed a greater threat to the privileged presses, but also because it was so widely rooted in the book trade at large. The privileged position of the two University Presses had been exposed to parliamentary debate in the 1780s, when they had gained compensation for the loss of almanac privileges. Now it was exposed again, as increasing numbers of booksellers and printers challenged the monopoly of the privileged presses to print the Bible and prayer book, and so posed a direct commercial threat to a vital part of their business.

William Jackson, proprietor of the *Oxford Journal* and partner in the Oxford Bible press, died in April 1795, five months before Archdeacon; but the trouble with rival Bible printers had begun before then. Jackson had failed to stop publication of a family Bible printed in Dublin known by his surname.[55] His failure in the Irish courts led others to hope for similar leniency in mainland Britain. In London, Millar Ritchie offered a further threat with his well-printed annotated Bibles, published in 1795–6.[56] It was by no means universally the case that challenges to the monopoly were mounted by printers of the cheapest editions.

To protect their monopoly, it was of importance that the Cambridge and Oxford presses should collaborate, and not least in legal matters. In the face of attack from the book trade, and in the face of increasing wages and of increasing duties on paper, the two universities determined on a joint front to the trade, and agreed on a unified price structure for Bibles and prayer books. For a few years, competition was abandoned. In May 1795, soon after Jackson's death, Joseph Jowett of Trinity Hall and Regius

Professor of Civil Law was instructed to consult with the Oxford delegates.[57] The initial proceedings cannot have been straightforward, but in February 1800 the two presses agreed on prices to be charged on Bibles, New Testaments, Tate's psalms, and the prayer book. Most Cambridge prices were increased, by 3s. (for the medium quarto Bible in pica), by 8d. (2s.4d. to 3s.) for the demy duodecimo Bible in nonpareil, by 4s. (from 17s.) for the medium folio prayer book, by 2d. for the duodecimo prayer book in minion set in columns. Altogether, the prices of some sixty books were tied in this way – virtually the entire range of Bibles, prayer books and associated publications offered by the Cambridge press.[58]

This was only the beginning. By the end of the same year, the two university presses had agreed to co-operate in seeking to prosecute printers offending against their privilege, and to seek injunctions against booksellers who handled such illicitly printed books.[59] Their target by this time was the King's Printers in Scotland, whose duodecimo Bible of 1799, offered for sale in London, posed a direct threat to the English privileges.

The production of Bibles and prayer books was greatly increased at both Oxford and Cambridge during the 1790s and early years of the nineteenth century; but it remained that the supply was unequal to the demand. So, increased output at the two presses was in a very real sense a struggle not only to overcome technical limitations, but also one to maintain a monopoly. The law would support their position, but it could not prevent repeated challenges, some of them ingenious, in a market to whom an ancient monopoly was at best an irritant and more usually an irrelevance. Few of the ruses adopted by rival printers were new. Annotated editions of both the Bible and the prayer book had been common since the 1730s, and in some cases the notes were so placed on the page that they could easily be cut off if so desired.[60] In an attempt to protect their position, the two university presses acted together, in 1802 obtaining injunctions against Charles Corrall, bookseller in Charing Cross in London, and the King's Printers in Edinburgh. But in a market where demand was high, and prices were competitive, the privileged presses found themselves obliged to be both vigilant and willing to spend considerable legal fees in defending their position, as their argument made its way gradually to the House of Lords.[61]

Legal proceedings were expensive, unsatisfactory, and a distraction. In practice, they were frequently inconclusive. But they had one advantage in that the process even of appeals eventually had an end, whereas the problems of ever larger edition sizes, of heavier demand, of difficulties over paper supplies, of wear on type, and of wages in a period of inflation, all remained. At the end of the seventeenth century, strains on the book trade had eventually broken, with the lapsing of the Licensing Acts. Growing demand for print, and official restraint on the number of printers in an artificial environment where the interests of booksellers and government, once in tandem but now at odds, found relief in an industry that at last permitted printers to discover their own markets. From this, coupled with an increase in demand in a century when the population of England increased from about 5 million to about 8.6 million, the printing and bookselling trade prospered. The world-wide settlement and exploitation of colonies, with their own special as well as more general needs for printed matter, in lands where there were as yet next to no presses and none on any great scale, increased demand on domestic production still further. For the first time, Britain came to depend on her own typefounding trade, and very largely on her own paper-makers. By the 1780s, imported type was a rarity, and imports of white paper had slumped.[62]

Prices had to be re-examined; and just as the London printers had combined to nego- tiate a wage scale for compositors, so likewise the two university presses consulted increasingly on matters of common interest. The strong element of competition with Oxford never disappeared, and Isaac Milner, President of Queens' College, felt any disadvantage to Cambridge acutely. But collaboration became preferable to defeat.

By the closing years of the century, the edition sizes of the privileged books were being driven ever upwards. This was partly in response to demand; but it also coincided with changes in the cost of labour. At the end of 1792, the Syndics agreed not only to increase wages for Bibles and prayer book work,[63] but also, for other work, to pay composition rates as agreed by the London master-printers in 1785. The distinction between wages for work on privileged books and other work was drawn clearly in the Syndics' minutes of 26 December:

> Agreed . . . the Workmens Wages in the printing office shall in future be, for Bibles and Prayer Books, according to the underwritten Table; which was made out on the supposi- tion that it would be reasonable to advance the wages in the proportion of eight to nine on an average.
>
> Agreed also, that, in printing what is usually called Authors Work, the price of all such work, when paid for by letters, be the same as was agreed to at a meeting of the Master- printers in London on the 25th of November 1785.

The reasons given – seven years after London – were humane: 'in consideration of the high price of provisions, and of the Increase of Taxes'.[64]

Composition charges were kept down proportionate to edition sizes. Although against this had to be set the possible disadvantage that more had to be invested in paper, and in storage, in practice the books that were immediately affected were all fast sellers, and therefore not likely to be embarrassments. Among the most popular books, the 24° prayer book has already been mentioned. The duodecimo minion prayer book, which sold in many fewer copies, nonetheless was printed in a new edition of 30,000 in 1798 instead of the customary 20,000. The 24° nonpareil Bible, printed in editions of 15,000 every two or three years through the 1790s, was printed in editions of 20,000 in 1800, and of 25,000 in 1801–3.[65]

In this way, only partial protection was offered to journeymen, including any tramp- ing printers travelling the country in search of temporary work. The Cambridge press still had to contrive to live with the expenses of transport. It is difficult to ascertain how much this affected the everyday working of the press in other respects, or its profitability. With the development of easier transport by water by the canal system (a link with London that Cambridge never enjoyed), the disadvantages to country print- ers, or, more often, to printers in towns other than London, were much reduced.

London publishers came to rely on some printers outside the capital, such as Samuel Hamilton at Weybridge in Surrey, and easily accessible by the river Thames, who became well-known for printing books in small formats, but who also printed one of the volumes of Mitford's quarto edition of Thomas Gray published by Mawman in 1816. Mawman's involvement with Cambridge is discussed further below. The decision at Cambridge to increase edition sizes of privileged books, and therefore to print new editions slightly less frequently, was taken in this context, as well as in one of better capitalisation by the Press and its agents alike.

Most of these sales were to Merrill, the local bookseller who in 1801 was succeeded by John Deighton; but after about 1800 the dominant force was the new London agent, Joseph Mawman, who in 1799 succeeded Charles Dilly in this, and in 1801 was to succeed to Dilly's entire business.[66] Over the next few years, Mawman not only established a list in ancient history and literature, led by books printed at the University Press, but also developed his business alongside his Cambridge interests and sometimes built on them: John Eustace's *Classical tour through Italy*, the *Remains* of John Tweddell (former Fellow of Trinity College), Clarke's *Tomb of Alexander* and Edward Chappell's *Narrative of a voyage to Hudson's Bay* were all joined by a common thread linked to the university and to the circle of Clarke in particular.[67]

By far the greater part of the Press's work was in the privileged books, even as the number of books printed on behalf of authors gradually slipped back, and the Syndics themselves, with the help and inducement of the almanac money, took on a more active role as publishers in their own right. So the disparity of edition sizes became ever more noticeable between the more popular formats of the Bible, New Testament and prayer book, and the other books printed at the Press. Successive parts of the Statutes were issued in editions of 1,000; and so, too, were Porson's editions of Euripides in the first years of the nineteenth century. Samuel Butler's quarto edition of Stanley's much heralded Aeschylus finally came out in an edition of only 250 copies, and Catherine Collignon's translation of Ladvocat's *Historical and biographical dictionary* in 750. The quarto edition of Vince's *System of astronomy* consisted of 500 copies only. But generally Vince's several handbooks, all in constant demand in the undergraduate trade, were printed in editions of 1,000. So too was the second edition of James Wood's *Elements of algebra* in 1798: originally published in 1795, and printed under the joint auspices of Archdeacon and Burges, it became a fixture on undergraduate reading lists, and by 1841 was to reach an eleventh edition in a revision by Thomas Lund. The University calendar, founded in 1796 and not printed by the University Press until 1803, appeared in editions of 500. Charles Simeon's *Psalms and hymns* was unusual in that its third edition consisted of 3,000 copies – reminder of the trade in service books of which it was in many ways a part.[68] Simeon apart, these and others printed in editions of similar size were linked to the limitations of the hand press, on which it was difficult to print more than between 1,000 and 1,500 sheets a day – figures that had been acknowledged in labour agreements since the sixteenth century.

Much more remarkable is the fact that, even in a press that was equipped to print larger editions, and in its printing of privileged books was constantly engaged in editions of far greater magnitude, it was still thought adequate to print editions comparable in size with those that had been sufficient for much smaller populations one and two hundred years previously. At the beginning of the century, Crownfield had printed Barnes's *Odyssey* (1711) in an edition of 1500, Bentley's Horace (1711) in one of 1,000 or a little over, and Newton's *Principia* (1713) in one of 700. Le Clerc's *Physica*, used as an undergraduate text but also, like Vince's work at the end of the century, in some demand elsewhere, was printed successively in 1700, 1705 and 1708 in editions of 750, 750 and 1,000 respectively. The population as a whole had increased, but though the size of the University had actually decreased, most copies of many of these books were not sold in Cambridge.

The approximate similarity in edition sizes was not simply a function of what was economically feasible at a hand-press; it also suggests that there was not necessarily a direct correlation between the putative number of readers and the number of copies that they might require. For some books, sales were always assured, even in an environment such as a university where it was accepted that many copies would survive second- or third-hand in circulation among successive owners. So, although the size of the University in the 1790s was only about 75 per cent of what it had been in the early years of the century, when measured by the numbers of matriculands,[69] the edition sizes of Vince were actually greater than those of Le Clerc. But for other books, necessities in some sense to scholars and others outside the confines of Cambridge, it might have been expected that demand (and hence edition sizes) would be larger than was the case. In practice, the situation that faced all publishers was more complicated. Although by the end of the eighteenth century editions tended to be more frequent, there remained much in the economics of printing to encourage caution in the size of print-runs. Porson's edition of *Hecuba*, printed initially in London in 1797, was republished at Cambridge in 1802 in an edition of a thousand,[70] and again in London in 1808 and 1817.

Capital investment in paper remained critical, as employers accommodated themselves to the wage structures agreed among the compositors and master printers. Only in some instances, and not in most academic publishing, were printers and publishers prepared to launch larger editions than those of traditional size – even in an environment where the number of customers was measurably greater. The lengths of time that a publisher was prepared to allow for sales to recoup at least the basic costs, or that he would let a book remain in print, had much to do with the decision to remain ultimately conservative in establishing edition sizes. Unless sales could be unusually large, and very rapid, it was cheaper to reset a new edition than to invest in paper and pay for extra presswork against sales whose slower pace would entail warehousing and interest charges. One way in which this difficulty could be overcome was by partnerships which would share the cost of printing large editions: the bookselling congers of the eighteenth century proved effective in this respect. But Cambridge University Press had no partners. It depended for its excess of income over expenditure on its own efforts alone.

Richard Watts and the beginning of stereotyping

For long periods during the eighteenth century, the Syndics of the University Press took little interest in their reponsibility, or in the University Printer. Meetings were held at irregular intervals, sometimes to approve decisions in arrears, and their minutes tended to be summary in the extreme. While this might be construed as an advantage to their Printers, who were thereby left to pursue their own business untrammelled by serious interference, such intermittent attention led to a strategy that was ragged and full of weaknesses. In many ways it was sufficient for a press that no-one wished to develop. But once, after the early 1780s, public money was to be spent, there had to be some better policy. This emerged not on the basis of any document, but through the energies of a few individuals, members of the Syndicate who made it their business to attend closely and consistently to the affairs of the Press.

By the last years of the century, the Syndicate was dominated by Isaac Milner (fig. 21), President of Queens' College since 1788. Appreciated by his friends for his manner as well as widely respected for his ability, Milner was an autocrat in many of his college's affairs, and firm in his determined evangelicalism.[1] He had been elected the first Jacksonian Professor of Natural Experimental Philosophy in 1783; and after resigning it following his appointment in 1792 as Dean of Carlisle, he succeeded Edward Waring as Lucasian Professor of Mathematics in 1798. He was to hold this chair until his death in 1820. He served as Vice-Chancellor twice, in 1792–3 and 1809–10, but his influence in the University, and not least in the University Press, was sustained. The combination of literary opportunities (he edited his brother's work on the history of the Church, published at York in 1794–1809), of publishing, of the complexities involved in even the most basic question of whether or not the Press was making any profit on a particular book, and – perhaps above all, for a few years – the technological problems to be addressed in establishing the new process of stereotyping on a firm technical and financial footing, all appealed to his interests. In the Press's affairs, he moved apparently easily from the details of preparing stereotype plates to calculations of the cost of printing to correspondence with solicitors and consultations with the book trade.

Burges's death at the age of fifty-four, on 16 April 1802, caught the Syndics unawares.[2] Unlike the handover from Archdeacon less than a decade before, there was no chance to ensure personal continuity. Milner, taking the lead, sensibly sought out

Fig. 21 Isaac Milner, by John Opie. Mezzotint by Facius after the painting in Queens' College.

advice in London and in Oxford. His eye fell on two men. The first to be recommended to him was Richard Watts, agent for Samuel Hamilton, the latest in a dynasty of printers established in Falcon Court, Fleet Street, and who in the following year was to leave London and settle in Weybridge in Surrey.[3] Watts's father was a shopkeeper at Abingdon, near Oxford, and for a year or so in 1795–6 he had conducted a newspaper, the *Oxford Mercury and Midland County Chronicle*, a short-lived venture founded in opposition to the long-established *Jackson's Oxford Journal*. Besides Watts, Milner also thought of a former journeyman named Andrews, aged forty-four, who had worked for three years at Cambridge under Archdeacon and Burges. Burges had encouraged him to leave, and since then he had been employed at the Bible Press in Oxford. There he had given satisfaction, but Milner also noted the words of a referee: 'modest, honest, – sober, – but heavy: plodding'. Watts was a risk; but at least there was no suggestion that he was plodding.

Burges's death came at a deepening crisis in the English book trade. As indicated in the last chapter, rises in wages and in the price of paper, the one to meet the demands of organised labour and the other to meet the cost of war, had had their effect on printing and publishing alike. In giving evidence to a Parliamentary committee of enquiry established in response to a petition from the trade, some of the largest London publishers and booksellers – Thomas Hood, Owen Rees and Robert Evans – all testified that their trade had declined in the past year. Hood claimed to have refused between fifteen and twenty new works that he would otherwise have taken, unable, like other publishers, to risk books that would not sell sufficiently quickly. It was a symptom of the trade's straits that William Cobbett was the lone voice to report increased trade: much of his business was with the United States, and in remainders. From booksellers, paper-makers, stationers and printers the tale was repeated. Eliezer Chater (from whom the Cambridge press bought its wove paper) calculated that the average cost of printing paper rose from 1s.2d. to 1s.5d. per pound between 1799 and April 1801, when new duties were introduced. With a reduction in demand for paper there went a reduction in the number of men in paper-making. Luke Hansard, speaking as a printer, opined that demy printing paper had roughly doubled in cost between 1793 and 1801. Among the printers, William Bulmer claimed that whereas it had cost him 25s. to print an octavo sheet set in pica in 1791, it now cost him 26s.6d. The combined effects on the price of books were calculated more generally by Owen Rees. According to him, Walker's *Geography*, one of the most popular of all school textbooks, increased in cost between 1800 and 1801 by 53 per cent; and in a basket of thirty-eight 'common books, chiefly on Education', the increase overall was 40 per cent. The situation was merely aggravated when one looked overseas: at wages said to be half those in England and yet where printers' profits were 10 per cent more; where ordinary printing paper cost one-third of the price in England; and where printers and publishers were able to reprint English works at low prices with no fear of infringing copyrights.[4] These claims were unsubstantiated, but they could be easily checked. Their message was clear: that the book trade was very seriously embarrassed.

The events following Burges's death suggest that the Syndics were not unaware of the critical importance of finding a person who would be capable of carrying forward changes that were in some respects already in hand. So, for caretaker, they turned to the familiar figure of John Deighton, who was a bookseller (and also agent for the University Press) but no printer. He was elected on 28 April – twelve days after Burges's death. Day-to-day running of the press was placed in the hands of two of the senior journeymen, Thomas Eadson and John Smith. Deighton, no more than a figurehead, resigned on 11 December, having allowed time for a search for a printer. Richard Watts, his successor, was elected on 16 December.[5]

Immediately after Burges's death the Syndics made two decisions that were to have major repercussions on the running of the Press. Firstly, they agreed to ask their agent, Rivington, to recommend a person capable of surveying the stock and goods. Secondly, they agreed to discover more concerning the management of the Oxford press as it was seen from the point of view of one of its London agents, probably William Dawson of Paternoster Row.[6] Milner depended greatly on Dawson's advice, and it was due largely to him that Watts was appointed University Printer at the end of the year. In this way too, Rivington introduced to Cambridge the ambitious and deter-mined figure of Andrew Wilson, whose involvement with Lord Stanhope and the development of stereotyping was soon to dominate the affairs of the University Press.[7]

Wilson's first assignment, before there was any formal talk of a further connection with Cambridge, was to report on the state of the Press in the wake of Burges's death. His discoveries, presented with the same air of proficiency that was to mark his later work, suggested that such a review was overdue, though by no means everything can have been the fault of Burges himself:

> I have inspected the Printing Materials belonging to the University of Cambridge with as much care and attention as the wretched state of the greatest part of those materials, and the shortness of the time occupied in doing so, would permit.
>
> I beg leave to report, that the condition of these materials is such as to fix a charge of most unpardonable neglect somewhere; and that for a series of years. I have, for instance, discovered large quantities of new Types, as if just received from the Founder's, belong-ing to Founts of letter which have already either been melted, or are fit only to be melted, from the circumstance of their being worn out; – and some very good Founts have been completely – spoiled, as well by mixing older and otherwise bad letter along therewith, as by the culpable conduct of the Founder in supplying Imperfections of quite a different face from that of the Founts with which they were intended to be mixed. As a professional man, therefore, I cannot help expressing my indignation that a property which must have been so liberally supported, should have suffered so much by carelessness in the manage-ment as to be rendered comparatively of little value.
>
> I have selected the letter which may be deemed *Good*, and that which is partly *spoiled* and partly *two-thirds worn*, from all the rest, which is certainly of no further use but as *old metal*. Of the former there is about 3000 w^t.; of the second description, about 5000; and of the latter, about 10,000 w^t. – Adopting this principle for the valuation, I think the whole of the materials may be considered as worth Six Hundred and Fifty Pounds . . .
>
> Perhaps I ought to mention, that there is only one good Press in the office; and farther, that in a House in such bad condition as the University Printing Office at present is, the Presses particularly must be much injured by dampness.[8]

The type spoke for itself; and the single press deemed in acceptable condition among the five to which their number had been reduced in the summer of 1798 was presum-ably the one bought from Morton in 1796.[9] As for the premises, the annual accounts rendered by carpenters, plumbers and builders (including major re-tiling work in 1798[10]) were constant reminders that the buildings were old and fragile.

Watts brought the fresh air of an outsider as well as ideas from the London trade. Records were improved so that it was possible to see clearly for each sheet the costs of setting, presswork and correction, as well as their relation to the total expenditure and timetable in the course of printing a book.[11] A new fount of brevier type was bought from the Wilson letter foundry in Glasgow in March 1803, and in June the Press acquired a stove on which to melt type-metal for itself, partly so as to cast leads for interlinear spacing.[12] In the same year it also invested in a new crown press, apparently of a modified design. It was bought from Thomas Aspinshaw, and at a cost of £32 was considerably more expensive than that bought in 1796 for 18 guineas.[13]

The carpenter's bills in this period offer some guidance on the arrangement of the Press. At the end of the century most of its activities remained on the north side of Silver Street, principally in the building erected by John Field in the 1650s.[14] The building in which Crownfield had begun work, to the north of that on Queens' Lane, had been given over to anatomy and chemistry in 1716; but the old printer's house and premises remained on the corner of Queens' Lane and Silver Street, and the Press also fronted Silver Street further up the road, towards St Botolph's church.[15] The extra space acquired on the south side of Silver Street was used mainly for storage, and the new warehouse built in 1786[16] was a lasting reminder of the arguments and accusations that had marked its birth. In the old building, press room and room for compositors were separate. Besides this there was a 'letter house' (presumably for storage of type), an office, a warehouse over it, and various smaller rooms.[17] Thanks to the poor condition of the premises, and the heavy wear to which they were subject, the floors near each of the presses and at compositors' places required annual attention.

In the late 1790s, the bills for repair mention the floor at the presses of Brand, Parks and Pleasance. Besides these men, the names of other pressmen in 1797–9 included Hancock, McGowen, Reeve, Ship and Yaxley. Eadson and Smith, to whom was entrusted the running of the Press after Burges's death, were both compositors, a task generally acknowledged to be superior to that of pressmen. Their immediate colleagues included men named Allen, Bastie, Bowes, Brand, Douglas, Gee, Kettlewell, Mair, Metcalfe, Rowell, Rutherford (or Rutherforth) and Taylor. Most of the Greek setting, now and in the following years, was in the hands of Douglas and Metcalfe. Not all of the compositors (in particular) seem to have stayed at the Press for many years, and it was presumably the custom here as in other printing houses to take on temporary labour when occasion required.[18] Outside these two key activities, there were a warehouse keeper and two warehouse boys, and an errand boy.[19] Overall, this list of employees is incomplete. However, it offers some indication of a business where the speed of printing had not been dramatically increased, yet where the sizes of editions of the most popular of the privileged books were now to be counted by the ten thousand. Both composition and printing were shared out, though for the shorter books in particular the same compositor or pair of compositors would work together for the entire work. At press, teams were responsible for both the inner and the outer formes of a sheet, though there were occasional exceptions, and after the arrival of Watts, Burges's successor, it became the practice to count work by the forme rather than by the sheet for the privileged books. Two men working together at press on one of the larger editions usually managed from 10,000 to 12,000 formes in a week, though more than that was not unknown.[20]

Each man was expected to work at several jobs in the course of a month. But the pace of a book through the Press depended also on authors and on proof-reading. For some authors, there were many corrections to be made, including cancel leaves. The corrigenda pasted onto several slips of paper in the second edition (1800) of Vince's *Principles of fluxions*, and the manuscript corrections in the text, are reminders of the several returns that one author – fortunately he seems to have been unusual – made to his proofs.[21] In normal circumstances, and for ordinary books, there was an interval of between about a week and a month between composition and printing. For Bibles and prayer books, where accuracy was at a premium, six weeks to three months was more typical, and six months or more was not unknown. The edition of 40,000 copies of the 24° nonpareil prayer book begun in the summer of 1797 was not completed until June 1798, having been set mainly by three men and printed by four different pairs of press-men. Composition was paid for by the sheet or by the forme, depending on the size of type and the complexity of the matter; but correction was paid for by the hour – fivepence in 1798, and later raised to sixpence.

Burges and Watts both had charge of the University Press at a time of rising prices and of rising expectations from their journeymen. In 1800 a pair of pressmen working on books other than Bibles and prayer books were generally paid 5s.4d. per thousand perfected sheets of straightforward work. In 1801 it was increased to 6s., and in 1802 to 6s.8d.[22] Compositors' rates, much more complicated in that they depended on the size of type and on the complexity of the matter, rose as well, and in most respects were the industry's benchmark.[23] In London, as we have seen, booksellers and printers combined to protest to Parliament about the increase in excise on printing paper, which in April 1801 was increased to 2½ d. per lb.

Such were the circumstances and the environment in which Watts and Wilson set to introduce their changes. Both men had been trained in London. They not only brought to Cambridge knowledge of some of the discussions already afoot in the capital, but also developed an acute appreciation – if not entire understanding – of the need for change in what had become one of the most important printing houses in the country thanks to its virtually constant output of Bibles and prayer books. Thus far, attempts to make an improved printing press that would be both more durable and allow faster work had met with little success. William Nicholson's patent in 1790 for a printing machine was premature, and was a disappointment even when it was finally developed several years later, while Thomas Prosser's improvements to the ordinary hand press, put forward in 1794, were never widely adopted.[24] In typesetting, the experiments of John Walter with logography, involving composition partly by clusters of letters rather than by individual characters, had proved impractical. In most of these inventions, the emphasis was on the need for speed, and on the need to minimise damage to type during long press-runs.[25] Yet, at a time when improvement seemed to imply progression forward, some of these ideas seemed merely retrograde. 'It is rather painful to see intelligent men take up a subject for improvement under mistaken ideas, and misapply ingenuity, time, and money, by treading backward the road that experience hath passed forward', remarked a reviewer of *An introduction to logography* in 1784.[26]

Recently rekindled interest in another old idea, printing from stereotype plates, promised more practical results. In a generation that had largely forgotten the processes of the Dutch printers who in the late seventeenth and early eighteenth century had produced Bibles and other works in such quantities, much had to be reinvented. Likewise, they had no experience (other than such as could be gained by their eyes) of the work of Ged and his followers in the 1730s. The survival of worn stereotype plates in the hands of the firm of Luchtmans in the Netherlands for several versions of the Bible seemed an anachronism.[27] But even as Edward Rowe Mores wrote in 1778 of James's 'unlucky attachment to a method of printing long since rejected, and at variance with the improvements of latter times',[28] others saw possible advantages. The patents taken out for methods of stereotyping by Andrew Foulis and Alexander Tilloch in 1784[29] mark the interests of a much wider spectrum of the printing trade than just those few members who had the Bible and prayer book monopolies. In France, F. I. J. Hoffmann, from Alsace, resumed the problem in the early 1780s, while the need between 1789 and 1796 for huge numbers of assignats brought about practical application (for a strictly limited purpose) of a process whose principles had been abandoned by most of western Europe during the eighteenth century. The several other experiments in different stereotype processes being carried out during these years in France were detailed by A. G. Camus, Garde des Archives de la République, in 1802.[30] The prospectus issued by Pierre Didot and his associates in year seven of the Republic [1798–9] summarised the advantages to the book trade at large: accuracy, cheaper books, and – since books could be printed off as needed – an end to the need to buy and store large quantities of paper. For some people at least in Cambridge, these were of practical as well as academic interest. Michael Lort, Regius Professor of Greek, who took a leading part in acquiring Askew's Greek manuscripts in order that they should underpin a programme of scholarly publishing at the University Press, attended also to possible improvements in methods of printing, including the experiments of John Walter.[31]

Watts and the Syndics may have dreamed of accuracy and speed; and Milner seems to have known of Didot's work in Paris.[32] For the present, the person who had most to gain was Andrew Wilson. Since 1799, when he had separated from his business partner, a printing ink manufacturer named Joseph Cooper, he had been running his own firm in Wild Court, Lincoln's Inn Fields. In 1802 he had complained to Parliament that whereas at the beginning of 1801 (that is, before the increase in excise charges on paper) he had counted forty-five compositors, pressmen and apprentices in his employ, he was by 1802 reduced to twenty-three, with four presses.[33] At present, it is not known how he was introduced to Lord Stanhope, who had learned of Tilloch and Foulis's work on stereotyping; but the two men were working together by June 1802.[34] For Wilson, the opportunity at a time when business was depressed must have been welcome. By August 1803, with the new process presumably somewhat developed, he was able to address a circular 'to the Authors, Booksellers, Printers, and Schoolmasters throughout Great Britain and Ireland', in which – after rehearsing the names of those who had attempted it without success – he revealed that he had established a Stereotype office in Duke Street, Lincoln's Inn Fields. So he extolled stereotype printing, or 'fixed type printing; because all the letters in one Page form but *one piece*'.

> Accuracy, and the securing publishers against the usual *risk*, and the great advance of capital which would otherwise be necessary, together with the saving of the *interest* and *compound interest* thereon, are amongst the striking advantages of Stereotype Printing. This valuable Art will enable me to afford, at any time or times, an equal Number of copies of any Work which has a very extensive Sale (such, for example, as the Bible, or the Book of Common Prayer,) Twenty-five *per Cent*. cheaper, than I could do if the same Book were to be printed by me in the usual manner; supposing that the work, were to be, in both cases, printed wholly at my own expense and risk. For *School Books* this model of print-ing will be peculiarly excellent. Such books are in general, inaccurate, ill printed, and dear. These objections will be removed, by means of this new invention. I have in contempla-tion to Stereotype several Books for the use of Schools . . .[35]

Wilson presented his work on stereotype in the context of other measures designed to improve the process and quality of printing. By means of 'panatypes', he claimed, engravings could be multiplied a hundred thousand times without deterioration. A new iron printing press, designed on new principles and manufactured by Robert Walker under the direction of Stanhope, was already in use at Bulmer's printing house in St James's.[36] Ink had been made to Stanhope's specification by Mark Graham, of Lincoln's Inn Fields. 'It is pleasing to reflect', enthused Wilson, 'how the abovemen-tioned Inventions, when properly combined, might tend to give new vigour to many important Branches of the Printing Business; and in what manner, they might afford fresh employment to Compositors, Pressmen, Type-Founders, Printing-Press-Makers, and Artists of various descriptions.'

At a time when the trade believed itself to be under threat, with publishers turning away books, the price of paper and labour climbing, and the expectation of foreign printers intruding their editions of English-language authors into the British market, Wilson's words were aptly chosen. But most of all, and as he went on to rehearse at length, the threat lay in the tax on paper, the principal reason for the petition of the London trade to Parliament in 1802. It was a tax on education and a danger to religion 'literally beyond the bounds of calculation'. Wilson spoke not only as a possible bene-factor to printers and publishers, but also as a victim looking for a fresh start. The opportunity to work at Cambridge must have been welcome not simply for the sake of developing new technology.

It is difficult not to believe, on reading this document, that Wilson had less the trade at large in mind, than one particular part, and even one particular printing house. His remarks on the cost of schoolbooks may have been directed to Rees's calculations for the parliamentary committee in 1802;[37] but his emphasis on the Bible and prayer book trade was of potential benefit only to the privileged presses; and he already knew much about the state of that at Cambridge.

The principle of stereotyping was straightforward, and was described by Hansard a few years later:

> The pages must be set up in the usual way with fusil types of the common make, but cast higher shanked, and supplied with spaces, quadrats, &c. of a peculiar height ... The pages are impoosed, one, two, or more together, according to their size, in a small chase. From this forme a mould is taken, *en creux*, in calcined gypsum, or plaster of Paris; and from this mould a cast of metal, having the face of whatsoever types it contains, *in relief*, in one plane surface, forming a plate of metal about a Pica or Small Pica in thickness.[38]

The details were less straightforward, as Hansard proceeded to explain. Irregularities in type, small pieces of rubbish left on the imposing stone, imperfect application of oil to the type in order to prevent adhesion to the plaster of Paris, the importance of even casting of the plates, and the difficulty of handling the plaster casts, the importance of excluding air bubbles in casting both the plaster and the metal stereotype plate (fig. 22): all caused difficulties at the simplest technical levels. It was problems such as these that led to delays and divisions that dogged Wilson and the University over the next many months.

On 6 February 1804, the Syndics agreed to employ Wilson 'to execute a set of Stereotype-plates for a new Edition of the 8vo brevier new Testament'. The decision was apparently the only business of the meeting; and though the Minutes were signed first by Martin Davy, the Vice-Chancellor, the most powerful voice among the half-dozen who attended was that of Isaac Milner, who had chaired the previous several meetings (and was to chair subsequent ones) as Vice-Chancellor's deputy. In April, the Syndics set out their understanding in fuller detail:

> Agreed that Mr Wilson & Mr Watts be appointed Joint Agents for the sale of the present Stock of Bibles & Prayer books at a discount to be regulated by them under the direction of the President of Queens' the Master of Catharine & Mr Creswell.
>
> Agreed that Mr Wilson on condition of putting the University in possession of the Art of Stereotype printing shall receive one third of the annual savings arising from this mode of printing for the term of fourteen years commencing at Lady [Day] last – that the method of estimating the savings shall be determined by two persons to be nominated one by the Syndics the other by Mr Wilson, and that these persons in case of any difference of opinion shall have the power of appointing an Umpire.
>
> Agreed that Mr Wilson engages that if he shall communicate the above Art to the University of Oxford he will not treat with them on the principle of receiving any pro-portion of the savings.
>
> Agreed that Mr Watts is directed to purchase two new Presses of Lord Stanhope's construction and to order new types to be cast and the apparatus for the Stereotype process to be executed.
>
> Agreed also that the President of Queens the Master of Catharine and Mr Creswell are desired to determine the best place for erecting a foundry.
>
> Agreed also that Mr Watts with the assistance of Mr Humphreys shall prepare a plan for altering the Warehouse into a Printing Office.
>
> Agreed that the sum of five hundred pounds shall be advanced to Mr Wilson on account.[39]

No doubt the Syndics hoped that, by recording their decision so fully, they would avoid misunderstanding; and that the decisions of the arbitrators in so experimental a

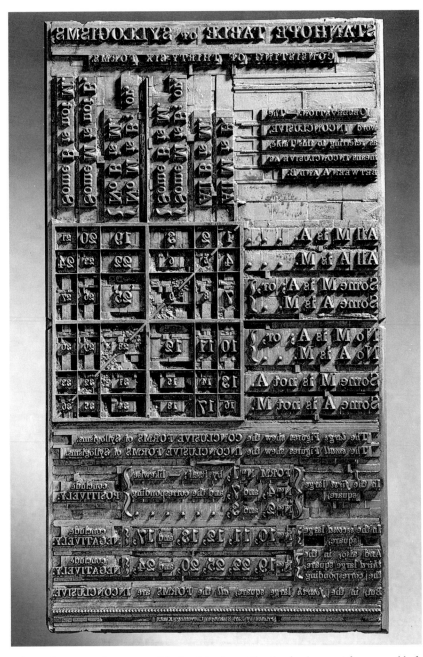

Fig. 22 Stereotype plate, prepared for Lord Stanhope. The plate has been cast from a mould of set type, leaving the individual characters and other pieces of type, as well as the botched spacing in the tabular work, clearly identifiable.

proceeding would safeguard their own, as well as Wilson's, interests. The hand of Milner is clearly visible, guiding the University with respect not only to costs and premises, but also to the competing hopes of Oxford. The stereotype secret was, for the present, to remain a secret between Wilson and Cambridge.

The direction that stereotype printing at Cambridge might have taken had the Press wished simply to continue with its established programme of Bible and prayer-book printing, on a scale similar to that in the 1790s, can only be guessed. There is no suggestion in the surviving records that there was any wish to pursue the other course offered by Wilson, in schoolbooks. Nor did the Syndics record any interest in the possible advantages, notably in improved accuracy, that might be discovered in the printing of mathematics, and of which Firmin Didot had written in 1795:

> J'espère que les amateurs de la Typographie s'appercevront que, pour la première fois, elle aura répandu sur un ouvrage de mathématiques une élégance qui portera avec elle son utilité; et peut-être qu'entraîné par les avantages que mon procédé peut procurer au public, je pourrai, après avoir été utile aux mathématiciens, l'être un jour aux littérateurs, en stéréotypant Virgile, Horace, et les bons auteurs de l'antiquité . . .[40]

Instead, all was changed by the foundation of the British and Foreign Bible Society on 7 March 1804. Though other societies had been founded with the object of distributing the Scriptures on a charitable basis, and for many years in the eighteenth century Cambridge Bibles had been widely dispersed by both the Society for Promoting Christian Knowledge and the Society for the Propagation of the Gospel, the foundation of this new body brought fresh impetus and enthusiasm born of its promoters' determined interdenominationalism. Though initially innocent of many of the details of publishing, the Bible Society committee brought the skills and attitudes of successful businessmen as well as of the churches. The University Press soon found itself dealing with a major publisher whose need for absolute accuracy, clear printing, reasonable paper, promptness and minimum cost forced new attitudes on Cambridge. Henceforth, whereas the Syndics had previously treated with Wilson in the hope of improving their own business, via their normal agents in London and Cambridge, the existence of a customer dedicated to the purchase and dissemination of cheap Bibles on the largest possible scale now introduced an air of urgency. The new mood was none the less keen for involving a society whose even-handed ecumenism appeared to some (most vociferously Herbert Marsh, translator of Michaelis on the New Testament, and from 1807 Lady Margaret's Professor of Divinity) to be at odds with the commitment of the University to upholding the established Church.[41] By May 1804, and with the shriller parts of these arguments still in the future, the Society was already expressing interest to Watts and Wilson in Welsh, English and Gaelic Testaments and Bibles.[42] Its wish for expedition accorded with Wilson's initial enthusiasm, as well as with the somewhat tight timetable the Syndics had set themselves as a consequence of their decision to invest so wholeheartedly in a new and expensive process.

Wilson received his £500 from the University immediately; but the conversion of the warehouse to a printing house took rather longer, and with it new premises to

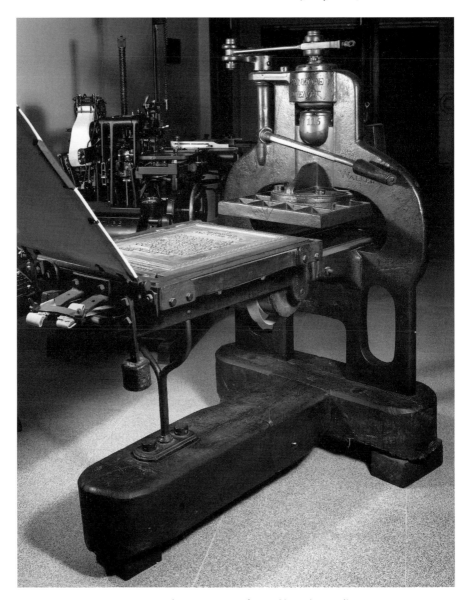

Fig. 23 A Stanhope press, manufactured by Robert Walker.

contain the stereotype foundry. A plan was sent to Stanhope, and by July work had begun on an ambitious stone and brick building. The iron Stanhope presses (fig. 23) weighed much more than the old wooden presses, but the new building also had to withstand heat and fire. All costs of construction were, naturally, met by the University, and by 1806 it was calculated that the new foundry building had cost £1759. To this had to be added not only the £500 advanced to Wilson, but also £450 paid to Watts for 'apparatus' received for the foundry.[43] Inexorably, the costs mounted as the building was brought into use. The foundry required much more coal than the old printing house, and Stanhope's new presses were five times the cost of the old common presses. The first, made by Robert Walker in London, was delivered in the winter of 1804–5. Two large models delivered in 1806 cost £200, and the two further ones of a modified design, delivered in January 1807, £90 each.[44] It is less clear how far Watts was prepared simultaneously to move his existing equipment across the road: the annual carpenter's bill for repairs in 1804–5 includes charges both for the customary repairs to the floor in the old printing house, and also for taking down and repairing the rolling-press, and for treating the proofing press similarly.[45]

Though both Bulmer and Charles Whittingham had installed Stanhope's iron presses in London a little previously, the new presses were to some extent still unproven.[46] But the real difficulties that Watts and Wilson faced lay in typefounding, in metallurgy, and in casting the stereotype plates of which Wilson had promised so much.[47] When questioned about delays or costs, as both mounted up over the next few months, Wilson was always ready with answers, so much so that Milner confided to his notebook his anxiety as to whether he was not 'an advent[r]. – without Judgm[t].' Wilson was never elected a University Printer, and his position as agent placed him in an invidious position which Milner did not shirk from describing as evil. Perhaps it did not help that although the University had entrusted so much to him, Wilson spent relatively little time in Cambridge. Between April 1804 and July 1805, by his own account, he attended the printing house and stereotype foundry at Cambridge on only forty-seven days.[48] But even while keeping the upper hand in the original agreement with Wilson, the University had placed itself in his hands. So long as the stereotype process was not fully understood, it had little option but to co-operate with him. Once the process was proven – technically if not necessarily financially (and there was ample room for debate on the latter), Wilson's co-operation would no longer be necessary.

No book appeared from the new process until the summer of 1805, and the agenda set by the Syndics (advised by Wilson) and the Bible Society alike anticipated an earlier return. In August 1804 the Bible Society wished for an estimate of the cost of printing 10,000 and 20,000 copies of a 24° nonpareil Bible, of 20,000 duodecimo minion New Testaments, and of 10,000 or 20,000 octavo bourgeois Bibles, and when they could be completed. Failing that, could the sale prices of the old stock be further reduced in return for ready money?[49] A month later, it was agreed to seek out somewhat smaller quantities (the largest was for 5,000 duodecimo brevier New Testaments) of the English version; but in acknowledgement of the continuing urgency to meet demand for the Welsh, on which the Society had been largely founded, to order 20,000 duodecimo nonpareil Welsh Bibles.[50]

In the Syndics' agreement lay some of the difficulties of the following months. They agreed to supply to the Society six books in stereotype which would have to be set, corrected with unusual attention, and then printed by a technology that was largely unproven.[51] There was some justice in Wilson's view that matters could be hastened if a corrector was constantly to hand: much of the reason for the length of time it took to print the Bible conventionally lay in the delay between composition and going to press. The Society found it as difficult to accept delay in the stereotype editions as did Milner. By mid-May, Wilson claimed that the brevier New Testament would be ready about a month hence; a long primer New Testament would be ready in about ten days, and that about seventy pages had been finished of the nonpareil Bible and New Testament. Deliberately or not, he promised too much, and none of the books was finished by the end of the following month: the long primer New Testament was not now expected until mid-August.[52]

Eventually the first books were finished. The first to be both stereotyped and printed at Cambridge was a duodecimo minion edition of the prayer book, of which 2,000 copies were set, stereotyped and printed between March and mid-July. In late summer 1805 the Press also issued a first impression, of 1,000 copies, of an octavo bourgeois New Testament, of which the type had been set and the plates made in London. A nonpareil duodecimo New Testament followed in August.[53] In the space of about six weeks, the Press completed and published four separate editions of the New Testament in octavo and duodecimo, set in long primer, bourgeois, nonpareil and brevier. For a new process, it was an ambitious programme of production, that had required relatively little labour at press compared with the task of preparing stereotype plates for three long books.

In the face of criticism at the months of delay from both the Bible Society and informed opinion in Cambridge, it is difficult to understand why so many were carried forward simultaneously. Without the large orders and constant pressure from the Bible Society, Watts, Milner and Wilson might have developed a different pattern of publication. But the Bible Society was clear in its own mind as to the need for dispatch, even to the extent that when in 1806 the Welsh Bible was delayed as a consequence of Wilson, the Society entertained the possibility of reverting to old methods. As John Owen, the Society's secretary, explained to the Vice-Chancellor, stereotype would be acceptable 'provided *expedition* could be obtained by such means'.[54] The same need for speed meant that the sizes of the first impressions were reduced to as little as 1,000 copies, so as to begin to fill orders as quickly as possible.[55] The whole had been achieved at the cost of lost sales, and by making some of the plates in London, and some at Cambridge,[56] while the entire proceedings had become embittered as early hopes were almost inevitably proved too great.

Meanwhile, Wilson also communicated with Oxford, where the Delegates of the Press agreed that in view of Cambridge's now possessing the means of stereotype printing, it was 'not only expedient, but necessary' that Oxford should follow.[57] A hasty series of meetings through the spring and early summer of 1805 led to an agreement with Wilson; but though so much had been discovered by experiment at Cambridge the process proved to be no less recalcitrant at Oxford. As at Cambridge, several books were forwarded simultaneously, but it was only in October 1806 – well over a year after the first stereotype books had come from the Cambridge presses, that a prayer book was eventually completed. As at Cambridge, the promised savings proved elusive, perhaps especially (at least in the case of a long primer New Testament) as a result of the superior quality and size of the necessary paper, 'the quality being nearly the same with that of the books printed in Stereotype by Cambridge, and the very size wch. in paper of the same quality entitling the Paper-maker to an higher price'.[58] The spirit of guarded co-operation that marked the dealings of the two university presses when they were faced with challenges to their monopoly among booksellers, or when establishing the rates of pay for their journeymen, was not to be seen in the outright competition which marked the attitude of Cambridge and Oxford alike in the adoption of new and – possibly – advantageous technology.

Milner noted the events of the autumn of 1805 with some anxiety, as he heard Wilson claim that there would be a profit of £30,000 in eight years (surely, in Milner's eyes, proof of want of judgement), and saw old stocks of the privileged book sold off cheaply in preparation for the promised new work. As Cambridge disposed of its stock, and was thus left unable to fill orders, so Oxford gained. Further hands were drafted into the stereotype foundry – a man and two boys in the summer and autumn of 1805 – to help with the new process. For Milner, a former professor of chemistry, the temptation to experiment was irresistible and only slightly related to any administrative need. His niece later compared his enthusiasm for the process, and his willingness to spend long hours in the foundry, with Peter the Great's attention in the Amsterdam shipyards.[59] Nonetheless, or perhaps as a result, progress seemed discouraging indeed, as Milner noted on 22 November that Watts and his staff had cast twelve plates, five or six of which had failed, while of the ten cast apparently by Milner and his assistant or assistants two moulds had broken, and of the remaining eight only seven were perfect.[60]

The first edition of a Bible to be published by the Bible Society rather than by the Press appeared in 1806: a duodecimo set in nonpareil of which – after many delays and much complaint – the Society received the first 1,000 copies in July.[61] They came almost exactly a year after the New Testament in the same format had been published; and meanwhile the latter, together with the duodecimo in brevier, had been much reprinted.

Impressions of these first books were initially small, at first of 1,000 or 2,000 copies and then increasing from the winter of 1805–6. Of the 3,500 copies of the bourgeois New Testament first published in July 1805 in an impression of 1,000 copies, two further impressions had been completed by November. The Bible Society took 2,000 copies, more than half the copies printed, but giving no hint of what was to come. Sales by spring 1806 of the duodecimo brevier editon were more encouraging, totalling 11,540 out of 12,000 copies printed in four impressions. By then, the advantage of printing shorter runs so as to respond more quickly to immediate demand, and to keep to a minimum unreturned investment in paper, had been amply demonstrated. The Bible Society was an established customer. By June 1809 – that is, in the space of four years – the Press had printed 147,500 copies of the duodecimo brevier Testament alone, and between the summers of 1806 and 1809 it printed 55,000 copies of the duodecimo nonpareil Bible. Most, again, had been taken by the Bible Society, whose demands governed some editions of the Bible and of the New Testament.[62] The Press's agents – Rivington and Mawman in London, and Deighton in Cambridge – continued as before. But other societies needed copies of the scriptures as well, notably the Sunday School Society[63] and the smaller Naval and Military Bible Society. Their needs, heavy enough in comparison with demand in the previous century, never exercised control in the same way.

Yet the Bible Society was also a selective customer, as it sought out the best value for books that were, in many thousands of cases, to be given away. While it bought massively for some editions, for others its demand was smaller, and irregular; others again it ignored altogether. John Owen, the Society's secretary, well realised the need for editions to suit varying demands, and indeed the Society's first orders had demonstrated this. When in Cambridge in July 1806, in pursuit of the elusive Welsh Bible and New Testament, he was shown a specimen of a pica New Testament in English, and he was quick to report:

> I could wish the Com^ee. to pay particular attention to this specimen. It was my intention to have recommended the University to print such a one. It is greatly wanted by the aged, the young, the slow reader and indeed by families in general. 5000 would be soon disposed of, and would be a kindness to the world. If the Com^ee. authorize me, I would avail myself of my situation here, and secure priority in this beautiful book.[64]

Owen's desire to secure priority is a reminder of the commercial context in which the Society was working, perceived by the London agents as a competitor not only in selling books to which they had been accustomed to enjoy a privilege, but also jockeying for a strictly limited amount of space on the presses of the two universities. By 1808 the Society was taking annually over 20,000 copies of the duodecimo brevier New Testament alone, and in the six months between Michaelmas 1809 and Lady Day 1810 it took 25,000 copies. The nonpareil duodecimo edition first issued in July 1806 was its own publication.[65] But though the Society dominated sales of some of the octavo pica editions, it bought less of many others, and of some only intermittently. Owen's aesthetic judgement of the 'beautiful' pica Testament that he was shown in July 1806 could not increase sales. Cost (which usually meant compactness), combined with acceptable quality, remained critical factors, and the Society bought the complete Bible in both the demy octavo brevier and the crown octavo minion editions. It ignored the octavo bourgeois New Testament of July 1805. At the end of 1806 it similarly ignored the rather grander royal octavo pica edition, and in 1809 the somewhat experimental duodecimo nonpareil Bible on fine paper. The rest of the trade was usually able to choose more widely, and so support a diverse range of editions in various formats and type sizes.

Nonetheless there were failures. Of the first New Testament of all, printed in a first impression of 1,000 copies in July 1805, the Bible Society, in urgent need of supplies for which it had waited months, took 2,000 copies of the 3,500 that had been printed by the end of the year; but then stock was allowed to run down, and the book was not reprinted. It had fallen victim to the arguments with Wilson, who had made the plates in London. A duodecimo edition in August was even less successful. Of 1,000 copies printed, 38 had been sold by Michaelmas 1806, all to Deighton. A survey of old stock in 1827 revealed that no more were sold subsequently.[66]

When the Bible Society had first thought of approaching Cambridge, its interest was as much in Welsh as in English. The matter was complicated by arguments over translations, in which the Press could have no opinion other than the fact that the text was still subject to the approval of the Bishops of Hereford and the dioceses in Wales. Matters were further complicated by the fact that the SPCK was already strongly – if clearly inadequately – established in Wales, and had recently printed an edition of the Welsh Bible at Oxford.[67] So the Bible Society's wish in September 1804, to obtain 20,000 copies of a duodecimo Welsh Bible and 5,000 New Testaments,[68] was delayed from the beginning. Then the Society found itself further embroiled in the dispute between the Syndics and Wilson, as Wilson tried to retain the stereotype plates as a bargaining counter. The Society's first edition of the Welsh New Testament, a duodecimo in brevier, was completed in August 1806 and published in September,[69] and the pattern of an initial small printing followed by reprints in small quantities was again partly in response to impatience to see some results rather than wait for a large edition. The first two impressions, in August and September, were each of 2,000 copies, and the three of the following year of 5,000 and 6,000.[70]

It had always been agreed that in case of dispute, Wilson and the Cambridge Syndics should go to arbitration. Wilson was entitled to one-third of any profits, but no agreement could be reached on how great such profits might be. The costs of stereo plates, type-metal and time were straightforward. Less easy to calculate were the savings that arguably accrued from the facts that Cambridge no longer needed so much warehousing (in any case, it had converted some of its warehouse space into a printing house); that paper no longer had to be bought in such bulk, since impressions could be smaller; that insurance was thereby saved; that type did not become worn so quickly; that setting and correction charges were reduced; and that interest costs were reduced.[71] Here there was ample room for dispute. Matters came to a head in spring 1806, and Wilson was loud in his own defence. To him, even the extra cost of the stereotype plates was such an advantage that it could be construed almost a saving:

The Stereotype art will not only effect a considerable reduction in the prices of books; but these books will possess a *uniform beauty*, and a *security against error*, which must stamp every stereotyped work with a superiority in value of no small estimation . . .

What an important security it is, that the inaccuracies of language, the incorrectness of orthography, the blunders in punctuation, and the accidental mistakes that are continually occurring in the printing of works by movable types, and to which every new edition superadds its own particular share of error . . . what a security it is, that, in a work of such importance as the Bible, all these descriptions of error are not only completely cured by the Stereotype invention, but that the certainty of the Stereotype plates remaining correct may be as fully relied on as if the possibility of error did not at all exist!

And when it is said that one third of the savings between the two plans is to be ascertained, it must mean *between works equally well printed*; . . . not between works beautifully printed upon the Stereotype plan, and printed on the old plan with types that are worn! In Stereotype, every page of the most extensive work has a separate plate: all the pages, therefore, from the first to the last, must be equally new and fine. By the old method, when one sheet is worked off, the types are taken down, and the next sheet is composed with the same types that have been used in the preceding sheet; so that although the first sheets of a Bible may happen to be printed from new types, these, it will be allowed, are in a gradual state of wear as the volume proceeds, and the last sheets of the said Bible will appear to be worked from types that are old and worn-out.[72]

Eventually, in August 1807, Wilson agreed to instruct the Press in the details of stereo-typing;[73] and though he was still in touch with the University in 1810,[74] the need for his skill went. In the trade at large, the secret became open knowledge, and the cost of pre-paring stereotypes eventually diminished. Connections seem to have drifted apart rather than terminated formally. Wilson had never given up his own business in London, and with the decline of demand on his time by Cambridge and Oxford he returned to it. Relations with Stanhope soured, as they had with Cambridge, and Wilson turned to developing a publishing trade by which to promote his own stereo-type work.[75]

Wilson himself claimed that in 1802 he had been lured to Cambridge partly by the suggestion that the University Press might print Greek and Latin classics by his method – and that as a result he had been obliged to refuse enquiries for such books from the London stationers.[76] Instead, efforts remained concentrated on the privileged books, in the case of the Bible principally to meet the demands of the Bible Society who also turned to Oxford as a supplier once it too had introduced stereotyping.

Quite apart from the new and unfamiliar technical processes of stereotyping that so intrigued Milner and caused such difficulties for the journeymen as they strove to master a new technology, there were other organisational innovations that came with the Stanhope press and the stereotype plate. In a printing house where large editions (necessary in every other year, for some of the more popular works) had become cus-tomary for Bibles, prayer books and the metrical psalms, stereotyping made it possible to print in smaller impressions, but more frequently. The best-selling duodecimo brevier New Testament was reprinted five times in 1806, in impressions of between 2,500 and 5,000 copies. This, with the reduction in time necessary for proof-reading and correction, made it easier to maintain a varied stock, as well as to respond to demand as it developed. The duodecimo Welsh New Testament, of which 2,000 copies were first printed in August 1806, was reprinted in the same number in September and then, in impressions of 5,000 or 6,000, three times in January to August 1807. But grad-ually, and with demand, the impressions of the more popular editions grew. The same duodecimo English New Testament was reprinted six times in 1807, up to 10,000 copies on each occasion. Under Watts's successor John Smith, impressions of 10,000 for this and the minion prayer book became commonplace; the five impressions in 1809 of the New Testament included two of 15,000 each, in a year that saw 55,000 copies of this book alone come from the Stanhope presses.[77]

Time was also saved in composition, though as critics repeatedly pointed out, initial costs were noticeably higher. With careful handling, stereotype plates could last for many years. For the most popular of all the early stereotyped books, the duodecimo brevier New Testament, no new plates were thought necessary until January 1814. By then, the original set had provided 300,500 copies, in thirty-eight impressions. The costs at press were not noticeably changed, in that each press still required two men to work it efficiently. But here the larger platen area of the Stanhope presses (at which the stereotype editions were usually worked), and the fact that a whole sheet could be printed at a single pull of the bar, both helped. The University Press obtained elephant-size paper from Martindale, and so was able to make more effective use of press time.

There were, however, unexpected consequent awkwardnesses, in that the Bible Society insisted not only on cheap printing, but also on cheap and serviceable binding. It was soon pointed out to the Society by one of its binders, David Nelson, of Kirby Street, near Hatton Garden in London, that by printing thirty-six pages to a sheet (rather than the usual twenty-four) for the duodecimo edition, the Press was making difficulties for the binder. It was agreed that in future type should be imposed so as to provide three half sheets to each gathering, and the binder should receive a halfpenny extra for each copy.[78] In a further decision likewise prompted by the needs of binders and, linked to them, the convenience of readers, Watts was instructed in 1808 to allow a larger inner margin than he had hitherto.[79] So binders' needs, in London, dictated what the Cambridge printer should provide, as the different activities in book manu-facture were drawn closer together and each party found itself obliged to consider the implications of individual changes for related industrial developments. In printing, the general conservatism of most of the process through four and a half centuries meant that such questions – respecting relationships rather than practices discrete to each par-ticular trade – had hardly occurred since the fifteenth century; and even then the transi-tion from manuscript to printed book had incorporated ideas, such as imposition and format, familiar to at least some of those involved in the making of manuscripts.

For the coverings of books, some parts of the eighteenth-century trade had already become accustomed to a degree of uniformity, especially in cheaper books for which printed paper bindings were appropriate, or for schoolbooks and some practical hand-books, for which canvas bindings had been in use since the mid-century. But the Bible Society, anxious for a robust, stylish yet cheap product, and applying the principles of mass-manufacture, established its own house style of cheap leather, and employed several binders on whose work was imposed such a degree of uniformity that it required special marking to identify each firm's output.[80] Not all of its books were bound in the same way; but the sense of conformity as well as the message of author-ity linked to the name of the society was one of the most important innovations for most readers. In this manner, the Bibles issued by the Bible Society, and other books issued by other charitable societies like the SPCK, paved the way for later assumptions attaching styles, patterns and appearances of bindings to particular publishers and their publications. The Bible Society was punctilious about the wording of the title-pages of its own Bibles, lest there be some misunderstanding.[81] It was no less punctilious about the outside of its books, for this reason and for reasons of economy. The indirect encouragement this gave to a leaning towards edition binding, and with it the conse-quences of how books were marketed, recognised on bookstalls and in shops, chosen and then read with expectations already aroused in some degree by outside appearance, proved to be as critical a contribution to publishing and reading as the society's support of the stereotype process itself.

The quality of paper, of which Watts's predecessors had periodically received complaints from the SPCK, had become a yet more serious issue by the end of the eighteenth century as supplies of rag diminished and war with Europe prevented imports on the scale necessary. Efforts to discover alternative materials such as straw or nettles were only partially successful, and advanced little beyond an experimental stage, while efforts to use second-quality rags combined with chlorine bleaching produced paper often distinctly brown in tone, and that foxed easily.[82] Attempts were made to use jute, straw and other materials. Unbleached wood-pulp made perhaps its earliest commercial appearance in an edition of John Wilkins's *Mathematical and philosophical works*, printed by Charles Whittingham in 1802.[83] So far as printers and publishers were concerned, the difficulty lay in the materials, not so much in the method of manufacture. When in December 1807 the Bible Society criticised the quality of a recent shipment of the nonpareil Bible and the long primer New Testament, it focused on both the paper and the presswork:[84] the two, of course, were linked in the very process of printing. Again, the desire for economy competed with that for quality and appearance, while the demands of the binders, expected to work at a rate that left little margin for difficulties, were never far away.[85] Initially, the large sheets required for the books printed on the Stanhope presses cost 40s. per ream, though they later dropped to 36s.[86] Substantial savings in the cost of paper for the duodecimo brevier New Testament were only achieved when, from January 1807 and after seven impressions on elephant paper, the size of sheet was dropped to demy, at 20s. per ream.[87]

Some of the greatest difficulties in quality control stemmed from the fact that the Press had been so much enlarged within a very short time. At the end of 1806, as he strove to meet demand for English and Welsh editions, Watts summed up his position in a letter to Joseph Tarn:

> We have 5 Stanhope presses and 6 Common ones now employed, 3 of these are at present getting forward with 5000 Welsh Testaments and 2 others are engaged in completing your orders for Pica & Long Primer Testaments, 1000 of the Pica Testam[t] is at this time packing for the Society to be forwarded to M[r]. Smith to-morrow morning.
>
> I have been expecting more Stanhope presses from M[r]. Walker agreeably to a strict promise he made in September last – and in consequence of the great demand for our editions I commissioned M[r]. Matthews in Duke street Lincolns Inn fields to send me any second hand common presses he might meet with, he was unsuccessful however & is now about to forward two new Common presses to me – these I expect next week or thereabouts, and if these be not sufficient I will continue to procure others.[88]

A few months later he was no less embarrassed by all that was expected:

> I am in great hopes of material assistance in the warehouse department from M[r]. Gibson. You would pity me, if you witnessed the pressure of business now upon me – I believe near a dozen works besides the Staple Articles of Bibles, &c, in several languages. I have

engaged an excellent classical scholar to assist me in the Reading department as soon as he has taken his degree at Xmas next. I hope to be able to bear up till that time, with continuance of help.[89]

It is not surprising in the circumstances that mistakes were made in the very books that the Bible Society had expected would benefit from the promise of accuracy in a new technology. Human error led to the omission of a chapter from the Book of Judges, the omission of a verse from the Psalms, and the omission of a few words from Jeremiah, all in the Welsh Bible published in 1807.[90]

Though Wilson had from the first associated stereotype printing with the Stanhope press, in practice Watts had discovered that it was possible to work plates (provided the sheet was not too large) on a common press.[91] Extra drying space for printed sheets was constructed in the new foundry building,[92] and new men were taken on; but the Bible Society orders were overwhelming the Press, and were damaging the balance of work that would have to be maintained if the printing of academic work, supported by the Almanac Duty fund, was to be continued, and if the University's senior members were not to be alienated. The advent of the Oxford press as another supplier for the Bible Society must have brought relief, even if pride and rivalry in other matters meant that it could not be widely expressed at Cambridge. As for languages other than English and Welsh, those unaffected by legislation that restricted who might print them, none was printed at Cambridge for the time being. The SPCK retained a strong interest in Scotland, as in Wales, and in 1807 printed an edition of the Old Testament to accompany the New Testament of eleven years previously: both were printed at Edinburgh. The Bible Society had made initial enquiries of Cambridge about Gaelic in 1804, but in the end it turned to Stanhope and Tilling, printers in Chelsea, who completed the Bible for the Society in 1807. And though Wilson became involved in the French scriptures, Watts did not. He was already overburdened.

Who bought or received the hundreds of thousands of copies of the Bible and New Testament printed by Watts? The story of Mary Jones and her Bible in Welsh seems to have been a fiction developed subsequently; and the tale of how the first cart-load of Cambridge-printed New Testaments was received at Bala was not put down until several years later, when memory may have played tricks.[93] But there is no doubting the demand for these books. The Society's anxiety to supply copies as quickly as possible, and the irritation that welled up even in the pages of its annual reports, were matched by the speed with which copies were taken up once they did become available. 'The 500 test: were disposed of immediately. I hope you will be able to send me 500 or 1000 more *very soon*', wrote Thomas Charles to London in October 1806, before going on to request large parcels to be sent to Machynlleth, Llanidloes and other towns in Montgomeryshire, and Barmouth in Merioneth. Those for Bala were to go by the Chester canal, from Paddington, and those for Montgomeryshire and Merioneth by the Shrewsbury waggon. At the beginning of November he was asking for parcels of 500 copies apiece for Caernarfon, Pwllheli, and Llansannan in Denbigh.[94] A year later, when the whole Bible was published, 400 went to Bala, and 100 to Anglesey, but most of the first 2,000-odd went mostly to parts of the country further south:

to Carmarthenshire, Brecon, Aberystwyth, Lampeter and other parts of Cardiganshire.[95]

The stereotyped English Testaments and Bibles bought by the Bible Society were quickly spread across the world. One of the largest early consignments of the New Testament consisted of 1,000 copies sent to Ireland, in December 1805. Within a year, and apart from another 2,000 shipped to Ireland, copies had also been sent to convicts at Woolwich, prisoners in Newgate and soldiers at the Cape of Good Hope. In April 1807, 150 Bibles and New Testaments were sent to Tasmania, and 250 to Nova Scotia.[96] The annual report for 1808 listed copies sent to the English garrison at Gibraltar, to Sierra Leone, to New Brunswick, to Samuel Marsden for New South Wales (500 Bibles and 1,000 Testaments), to convicts sailing for the same place, and to prisoners in Newgate and Chelmsford gaols. The loss on the sale of 20,000 copies of the Welsh Bible at reduced prices amounted to £1,187.

In less than five years, between 1802 and 1806, the University Press had been transformed. It had a new printing house, converted from the principal warehouse; it had a modern factory building where the new industrial process of stereotyping was to be carried out; it had new and larger presses; it had discarded its past, literally, in disposing of an important part of its old stock of books. The staff had been increased, and one former apprentice was recalled from London in 1805, to become first Reader and then Overseer.[97] Among the apprentices taken by Watts during these years was the fourteen-year-old Richard Clay, who had grown up only a few yards from the Press, near St Edward's Church.[98] Each element in this programme of innovation depended on another, and printing from stereotype plates was most satisfactorily executed on Stanhope's iron presses, whereby pressure could be more evenly controlled than hitherto. The future was secured – so far as it could ever be – by the foundation of the Bible Society, and the resulting renewed and heavy demand for the printed Bible. Despite Milner's justifiable anxieties, and at very considerable financial cost, the Press's investment in buildings, equipment and skills marked a revolution that could be turned to profit.

Stereotyping was no panacea. As had been realised almost from the first, it was only really practicable for the most popular of books, for which was anticipated a prolonged and reasonably heavy demand. So, even for the Bibles, New Testaments and prayer books, only the editions in octavo format and smaller were stereotyped. The list of books printed by this method down to 1809 also included the metrical psalms and (thanks to the Bible Society) the Welsh Bible and New Testament, but these were all. Not all the smallest books were at first thought suitable. For years, the Press had repeated editions of a 24° prayer book, and had printed it yet again in 1801, in an edition of 40,000 copies. Watts did not print it in stereotype, but instead employed standing type to print an impression first of 3,500 copies in April–July 1806, followed by three further impressions of 5,000 by the following April, and another of 7,000 in March–April 1807 – a total of a little over 25,000 copies.[99] The smaller types presented considerable difficulties for stereotyping. When it was further reckoned that up to 120,000 copies might be taken from standing type,[100] there was little advantage in printing a book requiring relatively little metal by the expensive new process.

Wilson's own position in the University, and his attachment to the Cambridge press, were precarious. As costs mounted, delays seemed inseparable from stereotyping. Undertakings were not met, so Milner and the Syndics found increasing reason to wish to sever links with him. There is no record of whether or not the Press ever set or prepared for him stereotype plates for Ainsworth's and Johnson's dictionaries, as was provided for in an agreement in March 1807,[101] though plates of both were offered amongst the sale of his stock in London at the auction of 1816.

More generally, and outside Cambridge, some reserved judgement and others were openly critical of Wilson's commitment to a process on which nevertheless he established his renewed business in London. A contributor to the *Monthly Magazine* in 1807 wrote with what was fast becoming received opinion:

> Stereotype printing has not been adopted by the booksellers of London, because it does not appear that more than twenty or thirty works would warrant the expence of being cast in solid pages; consequently the cost of the preliminary arrangements would greatly exceed the advantages to be attained. On a calculation, it has appeared to be less expensive to keep certain works standing in moveable types, in which successive editions can be improved to any degree, than to provide the means for casting the same work in solid pages, which afterwards admits of little or no revision. As the extra expence of stereotyping is equal to the expence of paper for 750 copies, it is obvious that this art is not applicable to new books, the sale of which cannot be ascertained. Although these considerations have induced the publishers of London not to prefer this art in their respective businesses, yet it has been adopted by the Universities of Cambridge and Oxford; and from the former some very beautiful editions of Common Prayer Books have issued to the Public; probably the art of stereotyping applies with greater advantage to staple works of such great and constant sale, as prayer-books and bibles, than to any other.[102]

Wilson issued an immediate rejoinder pointing out the advantages especially in accuracy, and that stereotyping contributed to savings in much more than basic composition. In his view, the process could be applied with advantage to three-quarters of all books printed in England, Scotland and Ireland. Using the occasion to promote his own business, he declared himself ready to co-operate with both printers and booksellers. 'I am fully prepared to enable them to participate in the advantages to be derived from the Stereotype art, in any way that may be most conducive to their particular interests, either collectively or individually.'[103] But his ambition outran the expected demand, and in 1816, having no obvious successor who wished to take on his business, he was obliged to sell at auction his stock of publications, his stereotype plates, other equipment, and premises.[104] Eight years later, in 1824 the London printer John Johnson summarised some of the arguments against stereotyping, with the conservatism born of hindsight:

> The following arguments have been advanced in opposition to the practice of this invention; First, the expense of composition, and the trouble of proving each page separately for several times, is much greater than in the common mode: Secondly, the composition is charged a higher price, and the expense of Stereotyping, together with the weight of metal (which may be taken at about one-fourth that of type) must of necessity make the

first edition come very high: Thirdly, Stereotype plates must always be done at iron presses, on account of the vast power required to bring them off; the price for printing is necessarily higher than that of type: Fourthly, the plates once cast must ever remain so, as no alteration in the size of the page, or cut of the type can ever take place, without incurring all the original expense: Fifthly, Stereotype work is never taken by pressmen from choice, on account of the trouble and additional labour required; also from the great impression necessary, the plates are more liable to injury; when the pressman must stop while they are repaired, and should several others be before him, he must wait his turn which is sometimes a day, or more, before he can go on again; consequently the pressmen never observe a *batter* (unless it be very glaring), because they would be stopped in their progress; hence numerous errors are likely to arise, even by that process which was stated to be perfection itself, and also one of its greatest advantages: Sixthly, the bookseller has, by the old mode the certainty, or nearly so, of detecting, particularly in town, any unjust advantage which might be taken of him, in point of number, by those with whom he entrusts his work: that important security will be wholly done away by plate-printing. He must also be subject to the loss sustained by the damage of the plates, together with fraud by the "*facility with which Stereotype plates are cast from Stereotype plates.*" We conceive this last objection which is so highly important, and which will bear the strictest examination, is in itself quite sufficient to deter all persons from giving it the least countenance or support in any way whatever.[105]

Biased though it was, Johnson's account reflected widespread suspicion among the more ordinary book printers, and the process remained for some years afterwards much less common in Britain than it was in the United States. For British printers and publishers, it was found useful only for books having the largest sales, as Caleb Stower's words in his influential printer's manual of 1808 took root: 'Many insurmountable difficulties, we are persuaded, attend the adoption of this invention, for *every* department of the printing business. It must be confined to books of standard reputation and extensive sale, and to such as cannot be subject to any alterations. The saving of case-work appears to be the principal advantage in stereotyping; the gain, therefore, on works printed with any letter larger than long primer, must be trifling.'[106]

In 1805–6, with Watts preoccupied with questions respecting the introduction of stereotyping and other new equipment, the amount of non-privileged work diminished temporarily. From the first, Stanhope's presses were intended as an integral part of the stereotype agreement with Wilson, and so few other books were printed on them for the present. Charles Grant's *Poem on the restoration of learning in the east* (1805), which obtained one of the prizes offered by Claudius Buchanan, was a rare exception, and seems to have been the first book printed in this way at Cambridge.[107]

Under Watts's care, the affairs of the Press had on the one hand been irreversibly transformed. For the University, the events of his tenure had implications for its own internal running that carried far beyond the confines of Queens' Lane and Silver Street. The repute of the Press was not in doubt; but the manner by which it had been managed was open to fundamental question. By the spring of 1808 the Syndics could no longer dally with the costs incurred, and the repeated broken promises, of the previous few years. Milner was appointed with James Wood, of St John's College, to examine the Press's affairs. They found much confusion, and they found it difficult to discover the true financial position. Watts's resignation in June 1808[108] proved to be only the beginning of a protracted dispute in which he sought to vindicate himself. After much argument, it was established that profits in the years 1802–7 (that is, before as well as during the introduction of stereotyping) had been only about £640 per annum, compared with not less than £1,500 per annum in the previous fifteen or twenty years. Stereotyping was by no means the entire explanation, at a time when extra salaries had cost about £700 per annum, and the extra apprentices taken on had sometimes been paid by time, as if they were journeymen. The difficulty of discovering the true accounting position, not helped by Watts's obstreperous attitude, made it clear that he could not long continue. He resigned finally on 17 June 1809, though it did not take effect until 30 October.[109]

He left Cambridge soon afterwards, and established himself as a printer at Broxbourne in Hertfordshire, where his first work included the successive volumes of Edward Daniel Clarke's *Travels in various countries of Europe and Asia*, published by Cadell and Davies in 1810–23: the Syndics' reaction to his including a statement on the title page of the second edition of the first part, to the effect that it was printed at Cambridge University Press, whereas (as was clear from the statement at the end of the book) it was printed in Broxbourne, is not recorded.[110]

Among all these arguments, and the introduction of new methods and technologies, the Syndics' closing report on Watts's affairs included one remark that gave a rare insight into the way in which the Press was viewed in the University more generally. It was not only a learned press, to be overseen by a body of the University's most senior members. It did not exist solely as a means to publish the University's work; nor even as one of the country's most powerful supporters of the Christian religion (through the Bible) and (through the Book of Common Prayer) the Established church in particular. There was a further aspect:

> The Press has been the great source of income to the University; and it is chiefly by the Press that the University has been enabled to undertake some expensive buildings, and both useful and ornamental alterations.[111]

This would have been hard to sustain. The University's own summary accounts record a period of mounting costs at the Press, and no proportionate increase in income. Between the four accounting years 1800–4 and those of 1807–11, expenditure more than tripled, while income rose only 2.6 times.[112] In 1810–11, Press expenditure (which of course included matters such as paper, an investment on which there would be an almost immediate return) represented 68 per cent of the total by the University as a whole. The University's increasing interest in its press was not just on scholarly grounds. Success or failure was of critical and immediate importance to the University's economic well-being.

Watts's term of office had been dominated by the introduction of new methods, new machinery and new organisation. Though everyone recognised the obvious innovations, few might have guessed the implications of the experiments for which the University was paying in supporting Wilson. Directly or indirectly, the stereotype experiment was closely watched by the printing trade across the country. As we have seen, within a few years views were sharply divided on the merits of the process, and of the principles behind it. The Press's influence was transmitted in more personal ways as well. One of Watts's apprentices, Richard Clay, did not remain in Cambridge, but went to London, where the firm he established in 1817 became one of the largest and best known of all book printers in the country. The knowledge he had gained in the first years of the century was used to serve London publishers; and after his son became University Printer in 1854 he became the adviser in the background, guiding the fortunes of the Press where he had learned his craft. These matters lay in the future. For the present, and more parochially, although it was not widely appreciated, and Watts suffered partly as a result, different accounting demands were inseparable from the technical changes wrought during his years. However, for most people the questions remained straightforward: the relationship of privileged printing to other work, and the overall profit to be expected from the University Printer. It is the more remarkable that during his term of office, beset by Wilson, Milner and the Bible Society, Watts also produced not only the usual sermons and pamphlets such as were expected, but also William Wilkins's *Antiquities of Magna Graecia* (1807), an imperial folio set in great primer in an edition of five hundred copies.[113] Besides this magnificent book, published by Longman, came other books on classical antiquities, including Edward Daniel Clarke's study of *The tomb of Alexander* (for J. Mawman in London, 1805), a study of a sarcophagus in the British Museum, brought from Alexandria. This book will be discussed further in the following chapter, in the context of the new Greek types introduced during Watts's term as Printer.[114]

14

Hellenism and John Smith

As Watts had given the Syndics ample notice of his wish to resign, there was little difficulty in arranging the search for his successor. But whereas for Burges's replacement Milner had made discreet enquiries, there was no such privacy for that of Watts. The extent of the Press's business had become such as to attract serious attention from outside, and there were several candidates. The competition for Watts's place was the clearest possible indication that the University Press was regarded as one of the country's major printers. The evolution from country cousin to membership of the inner circle was complete. Charles Frederick Barker, who declared himself apparently in June 1808, sixteen months before Watts's resignation, claimed more than fourteen years' experience at unspecified businesses in Bury St Edmunds and in London. Henry Bryer was to be taken more seriously, apprenticed in Woodfall's printing office in London and for many years in charge of it until he established his own business in 1806. He shrewdly arranged for a testimonial from Longman & Co., emphasising his ability in printing classical texts. More importantly he also gained the support of some of the leading London publishers and printers besides Longman, including the Rivingtons and Mawman as the University's own agents as well as Nichols, Hansard, Woodfall and Bulmer among the printers, and Cadell & Davies, Butterworth, Baldwin and Robinson among the publishers. It was a formidable body of opinion; but he chose not to recall that in 1811–12 he had been successfully prosecuted by the University for failing to deliver books to the University Library, as required to do so by copyright legislation.[1] Lawrence Thompson, another London printer, was less well known, and came supported by an assortment of London printers and booksellers of the second or third rank, as well as by a bevy of members of the University not all of whom knew him. The one internal candidate seems to have been John Smith, who had the advantage of being known locally. He obtained not only the support of Samuel Vince, Plumian Professor and one of the Press's best-known authors, but also that of Edward Pearson, the most recent Vice-Chancellor; of Herbert Marsh; and of Thomas Kerrich, *Protobibliothecarius*. Watts also re-offered himself.[2]

Again, having endured a difficult period, the Syndics preferred to seek continuity. Smith, who was elected on 11 November 1809, was a native of Cambridge, and was the senior journeyman at the Press.[3] The memory of Watts left a sour taste for the Syndics, and in arranging for Smith's salary and housing to be established by the University they also stipulated that he 'be not allowed any perquisites whatever, that the number of Apprentices be limited according to the discretion of the Vice Chancellor and the Syndics, and that the advantages arising from them be carried to the account of the University'. Any transgression of these rules, or other misconduct, was to render him liable to dismissal: there was no suggestion of any appeal.[4] With the affairs of Wilson still not settled, and legal proceedings threatening, the Syndics were in no mood to take risks.

Yet Smith's appointment ushered in a period not simply of consolidation, but also of further change in which he was not called upon to account for his actions for almost twenty years. In practice, he regained the trust of the University in its press. He later recalled his career:

> I had the honour of being elected Printer at the close of 1809: at that time the number of Presses employed did not exceed eight: the number increased in 1812 & 1813 to thirteen. At this period, and on to 1815 & 17, &c increased & increasing Orders flowed in from the British & Foreign Bible Society, and also (through Mess. Rivingtons) from the Society for Promoting Christian Knowledge. And it may at first sight appear strange that in the course of three years or more from this period the Receipts of the Press after having been so great should have fallen off – But many Gentlemen of the Syndicate have never been apprized of the manner in which the large orders in the former period were executed. The fact is, that from 1813 to 1815 the demand for Bibles &c. was such, that had the same quantity of work to be executed been required to be finished in the manner in which the same books are now printed, they could not possibly have been done with the means the Press then possessed – "Send up the Books in gatherings" (i.e. divisions) was the repeated order of the Bible Society – "and we will spare you the trouble of booking off, &c. &c." Many thousand Copies were thus supplied, which were never properly dried. – But the manner in which the general Orders for editions are now executed, requires a more considerable degree of time & labour; the Books are now invariably pressed in the Warehouse and when sent off, tied & capped in small parcels, and labelled – previously undergoing many inspections to clear out creased or other defective Sheets. – In short, were the Books of the present day to be compared with those of corresponding editions printed in 1811–14 &c they would pass for *fine* work when contrasted against the latter.[5]

Smith was the first to acknowledge that his term as University Printer, from 1809 to 1836, saw changes greater than any hitherto. His predecessors had seen the introduction of new methods, and difficulties over the development of processes and the introduction of new machines that were in fundamental respects experimental even when they were expected to earn rewards. But it was Smith who saw stereotyping established as a normal means of production; who installed a new generation (the last, as it proved) of reliable iron hand-presses; who faced a major crisis in the supply of paper; who with the other privileged presses faced the most serious challenge yet in the trade in Bibles and prayer books; who finally withdrew from the historic site in Queens' Lane and saw the entire Press established in a group of purpose-designed buildings; who in those premises saw the end of the traditional paper windows and their complete replacement by glass; who introduced gas lighting;[6] and who experimented with an early version of a cylinder press but who remained steadfastly opposed to the introduction of machine printing. His career as University Printer spanned several upheavals in the book trade, at the conclusion of the Napoleonic wars, when printers and publishers on the Continent posed all too clear a threat to some of the Press's established market, and in the late 1820s, when the British book trade as a whole suffered a crisis of confidence. His contemporaries could not but acknowledge his skills. They also realised that the limited nature of these skills (he had been trained as a printer, within the protected environment of a privileged press) exposed the University Press to dangers: by neglect of innovation, by competition from rival printers in both London and the country, and by changes in the structures of London publishing. These several innovations, experiments and changes will be studied in the following pages.

Such was the background in the book trade. Though it affected what they read, how they obtained books, and how books were published, for most members of the university it was of little interest. However, the activities of the Press, and the way in which its affairs were managed, were directly influenced by the course of university taste.

In particular, the attention given to the Greek classics was a part of a wider interest in the survival of Greek antiquity: in manuscripts, in architecture, in sculpture and in the other arts.[7] Wilkins's buildings at Downing College, begun in 1807, remain today as the most visible affirmation of a passion for the achievements of the ancient Greeks. Books, memoirs and collections of artefacts remain as others. Among those who were most to the fore in this new generation of Hellenists was J. D. Carlyle (1759–1804), Professor of Arabic from 1795, who was a member of the Elgin expedition of 1799–1803. Edward Daniel Clarke (1769–1822) of Jesus College, was more strictly a Hellenist, fiercely energetic in his travels and in his collecting, and later University Librarian and Professor of Chemistry. Of the same age as Clarke, John Tweddell (1769–99), of Trinity, died in Greece in the same year that Clarke departed for his major tour there, and left collections of papers that became the subject of prolonged and unresolved wrangling. Slightly younger than him there were William Gell (1778–1836) of Jesus, later a fellow of Emmanuel College and author of *The topography of Troy* (1804); Robert Walpole (1781–1856), who after graduating from Trinity in 1803 also departed for Greece; and the Earl of Aberdeen (1784–1860), Byron's 'travell'd thane', who became one of the most influential of all Hellenists. Byron himself entered Trinity in 1805. William Wilkins (1778–1839, and therefore a contemporary of Gell) entered Gonville and Caius College in 1796, and on graduating was awarded a Worts travelling scholarship in 1801 by whose aid he reached southern Italy, Sicily, Greece and Asia Minor. His *Antiquities of Magna Graecia* was printed by Cambridge University Press in 1807; but in general the books on archaeology and classical art of these years were published in London. With the notable exception of Clarke, most of the so-called Cambridge Hellenists had an influence on taste and on public interest (vigorously fuelled by the public row over the Elgin marbles and the British Museum) more than a direct one on the everyday activities of the University Press. But no-one

Fig. 24 Richard Porson, by John Hoppner, 1796. Engraving
by W. Sharp.

could be unaware of their interests and their actions, an undercurrent and even an
encouragement to printing and to investment in Greek printing types.

Smith inherited a legacy of considerable technical achievement. In the provision of
Greek type for the Press, he also inherited one that had been accumulating for a quarter
of a century and more. We will turn first to this.

Ever since the Syndics had been charged with applying the almanac money principally to the ancient authors, they had interpreted their task as applying to Greek in particular. Their first act in 1782 had been to order new type (both Greek and roman) from
Caslon.[8] The Askew sale in 1785, at which they made substantial funds available to the
University Library in order to support editorial projects, demonstrated their commitment at a time when it had so far proved impossible to spend much on printing.

In this, the ambitions and eventually the influence of Porson (fig. 24) were central.
Dismayed in November 1782 at the restrictive conditions laid down by the Syndics of
the Press for his proposal to edit Aeschylus, in 1795 – and by now Regius Professor of
Greek – he returned with a further, and successful, proposal to edit the manuscript of
Photius' *Lexicon* in Trinity College Library.[9] When Porson was granted permission to
procure a new fount of Greek type for this purpose, the Syndics may not have realised
the extent of their rein, or how many years it would be before anything would appear.[10]
The loss of his transcript in a fire at his house in 1797, and his subsequent resolution in
making another, drew the admiration of his contemporaries; and the second transcript

was presumably nearly or completely finished when, seven years later, Watts was give permission to purchase two Greek fonts towards the planned edition.[11] In fact, matters proceeded no further in this for the present. Instead, the first new Greek type to be used at the Press was a specially commissioned inscriptional sans serif face cast probably by Figgins. It first appeared in a few words illustrating Edward Daniel Clarke's privately produced dissertation on *The tomb of Alexander* (1805), a work that might have been little more than a pamphlet but to which Clarke devoted extravagant care and turned into a large, if thin, quarto volume, its engraved illustrations including one with a colour wash. As part of what even his friends considered vanity printing, Clarke may have paid for the Greek inscriptional type himself, since there is no record of any payment by the University Press.[12] The special type-face was from its inception only likely to be of limited use, and was little employed at Cambridge.[13]

Meanwhile Watts, no doubt aware of Porson's interest, seems to have pursued other avenues for an ordinary text face, and in 1807 seems to have obtained a specimen from Figgins. But this proved unacceptable, principally perhaps because of too great a contrast of thick and thin strokes.[14] Instead, the first size of Porson's own Greek type, long delayed in that he had been given leave to pursue his own choice in 1795, was finally cut by Richard Austin as a private commission for the University Press in 1807. It has proved to be the most enduring of all Greek type-faces ever cut. The model was one version of Porson's own meticulously neat and unambiguous Greek handwriting, though Austin's bill for the English, specifically excluding attendance on him and the many alterations that had been necessary, suggests that the process of translation of written letter-forms to equivalents on steel punches was no easier than usual.[15] The type was cast by Caslon and Catherwood, beginning in December 1807. By the time that the founders submitted their bill, Watts was becoming embarrassed by the Press's constant capital expenditure and slow returns. Milner and the Syndics made most play of the cost of stereotyping, and the much more straightforward Greek types had been contracted in principle long before his appointment. Nonetheless, he took the matter up with Austin, who in 1807 had charged twelve shillings each for the punches of the Greek alphabet. Austin was sympathetic:

> With respect to Mess[rs]. C & C[s]. bill, I am not at all surprised at your not Expecting so high a Charge – but I suppose it is from the trouble & alterations M[r]. Caldwell has had with them & the time spent on them – That Mess[rs]. C & C has charged this price – I know the prices are very materially altered from what they used to be – There is no set prices for making matrices. It rests intirely with the person who is to Make them how he Values his time.[16]

Porson's design (fig. 25) was first used, and there only for a few words, in an account by Clarke of the *Greek marbles brought from the shores of the Euxine*, published in 1809.[17] As in 1805, Clarke's work was the means by which a new type-face was introduced, though on this occasion it was in a book whose production was charged to the Government Annuity Fund established following the demise of the almanac privilege in the days of Archdeacon. The first book to be printed in the new types followed a few

ΟΣΗ μὲν, ὦ ἄνδρες Ἀθηναῖοι, σπουδὴ περὶ τουτονὶ τὸν ἀγῶ-
να, καὶ παραγγελία γέγονε, σχεδὸν οἶμαι πάντας ὑμᾶς
ᾐσθῆσθαι, ἑωρακότας ἄρτι τούς, ὅτε ἐκληροῦσθε, ἐνοχλοῦντας καὶ
προσιόντας ὑμῖν· δεήσομαι δὲ πάντων ὑμῶν, ἃ καὶ τοῖς μὴ δεη-
θεῖσι δίκαιόν ἐστιν ὑπάρχειν, μηδεμίαν μήτε χάριν, μήτε ἄνδρα
ποιεῖσθαι περὶ πλείονος, ἢ τὸ δίκαιον, καὶ τὸν ὅρκον, ὃν εἰσελήλυθεν
ἕκαστος ὑμῶν ὀμωμοκὼς, ἐνθυμουμένους, ὅτι ταῦτα μέν ἐστιν ὑπὲρ
ὑμῶν, καὶ ὅλης τῆς πόλεως, αἱ δὲ τῶν παρακλήτων αὗται δεήσεις
καὶ σπουδαὶ, τῶν ἰδίων πλεονεξιῶν ἕνεκα γίγνονται. ἃς ἵνα κωλύηθ'
οἱ νόμοι συνήγαγον ὑμᾶς, οὐχ ἵνα κυρίας τοῖς ἀδικοῦσι ποιῆτε.
Τοὺς μὲν οὖν ἄλλους, ὅσοι πρὸς τὰ κοινὰ δικαίως προσέρχονται,
κἂν δεδωκότες ὦσιν εὐθύνας, τὴν ἀειλογίαν ὁρῶ προτεινομένους·

Fig. 25a Paragon Greek, originally cut by Robert Granjon in 1565; bought from the Voskens foundry in 1699. From Demosthenes, ed. John Taylor (vol. 2, 1757). *Reduced.*

τῆς ὀρθοβούλου Θέμιδος αἰπυμῆτα παῖ,
ἄκοντά σ' ἄκων δυσλύτοις χαλκεύμασι
προσπασσαλεύσω τῷδ' ἀπανθρώπῳ πάγῳ,
ἵν' οὔτε φωνήν, οὔτε του μορφὴν βροτῶν
ὄψει, σταθευτὸς δ' ἡλίου φοίβῃ φλογί,
χροιᾶς ἀμείψεις ἄνθος· ἀσμένῳ δέ σοι
ἡ ποικιλείμων νὺξ ἀποκρύψει φάος·
πάχνην θ' ἑῴαν ἥλιος σκεδᾷ πάλιν·
ἀεὶ δὲ τοῦ παρόντος ἀχθηδὼν κακοῦ
τρύσει σ'· ὁ λωφήσων γὰρ οὐ πέφυκέ πω.

Fig. 25b Porson's Greek type, in English size, cast by Caslon and Catherwood. From Aeschylus, *Prometheus vinctus* (1810).

months later, an edition of the *Prometheus vinctus* by Charles Blomfield, published in 1810.

The type was the culmination of a long period of development. The Press had been in touch with Austin as early as 1805, when Watts was given permission to employ him 'in making punches & matrices for such a fount as Mr Watts shall judge to be most wanted'[18]: whether or not this somewhat anonymous minute refers to a Greek type rather than Roman, at a period when the Syndics were fully occupied with the introduction of stereotyping, is not clear. However, once Porson's design was before the public, its merits were soon recognised. In an amicable review of Blomfield's work in the *Quarterly Review*, J. H. Monk remarked on the 'beautiful Greek types, cast after the patterns given by the late Professor Porson'.[19] 'We cannot sufficiently recommend to all our future editors of the classics to print their productions in an equally beautiful manner', enthused the *Classical Journal*.[20] George Dyer was more analytical of the specific attractions: 'In the rejection of abbreviations, this type exceeds the Aldine, and seems to have been after the taste of Bodoni, the celebrated Greek printer of Parma: it possesses, too, something of Bodoni's copper-plate appearance.' Dyer also approved of the lack of abbreviations, the treatment of diphthongs as single letters, and the room left for choice in the varieties still offered of gamma, theta, pi and tau.[21] Edward Blomfield, Fellow of Emmanuel College and brother of Charles, recorded the general opinion when he contrasted the type of Wolf and Bekker's proposed edition of Plato, to be published in Germany: that it would be 'delightful for those who are enchanted with the spruce flourishes of school-boy Greek; but it has none of the firmness or distinctness of the Porsonian type'.[22] In a private letter, George Huntingford, Warden of Winchester College and Bishop of Gloucester, praised what he called 'Porsonic' type by contrasting it with that used by Goschen in Leipzig for an edition of the New Testament: 'The very first page of it is offensive in the extreme, so sharp is the Type and so deviating from the Usage of long Time, by the Best Editors, are the Forms of Letters: Letters which a Novitiate could not read.'[23] By avoiding the need for ligatured letters, Porson brought to a conclusion a process of simplification that had been in train since the late fifteenth century. In the mid-eighteenth century, the florid Greek used at Cambridge in the editions of Greek orators prepared by John Taylor had been valued partly for its affinity with sixteenth-century Greek letter-forms. Half a century later, Porson wrought a revolution of which he did not live to see the effect. The English and long primer sizes were cut first, and the printing of his *Adversaria* was delayed until a third size, pica, was available.[24] Within about five years of its first appearance, versions of Porson's design had also been introduced by the typefounders Vincent Figgins and Edmund Fry.[25] The case for reform had been accepted within an astonishingly short space of time.

The publication in Cambridge of Porson's editions of the *Medea* in 1801 and *Hecuba* in 1802 formed a prologue to a concerted effort on the part of the Syndics, encouraged by a vociferous section of the University's own educational and scholarly priorities and interests. The edition of Stanley's Aeschylus which Porson had refused was instead placed in the hands of the young Samuel Butler of St John's, and the first part appeared in 1809, dedicated to Lord Spencer: in keeping with the hope of establishing its place in both the bibliophile and the less wealthy parts of the ordinary scholarly market it was issued simultaneously in both quarto and octavo form. The influence of Porson, who died in 1808, was ever-present, and a spur to his self-conscious admirers.[26]

For once, Press and University interests worked together, in a programme made possible by the Government Annuity Fund. By 1810, the first full year of Smith's office, more than three-quarters of the reported expenditure was on two books, Clarke's account of the Greek marbles recently placed in the vestibule of the University Library, and a study of the metrics of Aeschylus, by Charles Burney, while in the press were the *Prometheus Vinctus*, edited by Blomfield, and further parts of Butler's collected Aeschylus. Porson's *Adversaria*, edited by J. H. Monk and C. J. Blomfield, was published at the expense of Trinity College in 1812;[27] and at the back of the volume the London bookseller Joseph Mawman was able to advertise further the work of Monk, Blomfield and Burney on the Greek tragedians, all printed at Cambridge. By 1814, a summary of the Press's activity reported that a new edition of Monk's *Hippolytus* had just been published, and that an edition of the *Alcestis* was planned; the fourth volume of Butler's Aeschylus was in a state of forwardness, with an index planned to follow (it appeared in 1816); Edward Maltby's edition of Morell's *Thesaurus* was in the press (it was published in 1815[28]); a new edition of Richard Dawes's *Miscellanea critica*, edited by Thomas Kidd of Trinity, had been agreed; and an edition of the *Persae*, edited by Blomfield, would soon go to press.[29] Between 1810 and 1819, almost 60 per cent of the Government Annuity Fund was spent on the classics, virtually all of it on Greek authors. So far as local university events could be influenced, it was a period marred for the advocates of this programme almost only by a single, though major, episode: in 1809, Edward Daniel Clarke, the University Librarian, sold his important collection of Greek manuscripts, including a celebrated Plato, to the Bodleian Library, having apparently failed to arouse sufficient interest when he offered them first to Cambridge. When Gaisford's catalogue appeared in 1812, the *Museum Criticum* recorded the event with caustic remarks on Cambridge's 'ill-judged parsimony'.[30]

At the centre of this generally more successful Hellenist policy stood the influence of Trinity College, exemplified not only in the editorial commitment of Monk, Blomfield, Peter Paul Dobree[31] and James Scholefield – three of them being Porson's successors as Regius Professor, and the first three having been elected to fellowships within five years of each other – but also in the revival of interest in Bentley, whose biography Monk was to publish in 1830. But though Trinity's increasingly powerful voice and interests tended to prevail, it was in a context of rivalries that became sometimes shrill rather than constructive. The tone of the college did not escape George Ticknor, when he dined there in 1819 on his way back to America from Göttingen: 'certainly stiff and pedantic, and a good deal of little jealousy was apparent, in the manner in which they spoke of persons with whom they or their college or their university had come into collision'.[32] The declared aim in editing was textual accuracy; but the several editions of some Greek drama, and the long and detailed reviews accorded them both in the specialist journals and in the more general press, seemed sometimes more nearly to be vehicles for scholarly invective and preening.[33] The exercise became formalised as a part of undergraduate education, and in 1816 Thomas Babington Macaulay reported to his father, 'We have also to draw up a Synopsis of the notes of Porson, Professor Monk, and Bloomfield, to Euripides' plays; a very useful exercise, and approximating very nearly to my annual employment of index making.'[34] But it was not an approach that endeared itself to the young Macaulay, who while he admired Scholefield also thought that he had contracted

> too much of the University style of literature. There seems to me to be the same difference between one of the accurate Cantabrigian Scholars who compares readings and collates Editions, and gives to every Greek particle its due honours and its definite significations, and an elegant scholar who tastes the beauties of the classics without condescending to those minutiae, which there is between a mixer of colours and an amateur in painting, between a labourer who mends the roads on Malvern or Richmond Hill, and the tourist who admires the picturesque beauty of the scenery. The business of the one is to facilitate the enjoyment of the other. But to make that the end which ought only to be the means . . . is a truly deplorable perversion of judgement.[35]

Senior members of Trinity College grouped against each other as Porson's work, reputation and memory became disputed territory; rivalries in the book trade reflected scholarly divisions as well as the established Cambridge habit of looking constantly at the presses of Oxford and – increasingly – London; and English classical scholarship was sometimes perceived in nationalist rivalry with German schools. The foundation in England of two journals devoted to classical studies within a few months of each other provided vehicles for some more domestic aspects of this rivalry. The *Classical Journal*, launched in March 1810 by A. J. Valpy the year after he had graduated from Oxford, was intended as a primary means to establish an ambitious programme of publication in which he engaged the interests of E. H. Barker, George Burges, both of Trinity, and George Dyer, of Emmanuel, among others. The *Museum Criticum* launched in June 1813, printed at the University Press and published in London principally by John Murray, was the work of a group led by Blomfield and Monk. Each journal was designed partly to promote the books either of its particular faction or of its printers and publishers. In the very first issue of the *Classical Journal*, Valpy announced plans including editions of Tacitus, the Greek New Testament, and Schleusner's Lexicon of the same. A hostile review in the *Classical Journal* of Butler's strictly circumscribed Cambridge edition of Aeschylus[36] contrasted noticeably with the innocuous notice accorded it in the *Museum Criticum*. The latter journal was soon referring to 'our Press', and Valpy used the pages of the *Classical Journal* to advertise his own publications. There was a strong, if not always complete, correlation between publisher and critical tone.

Publishers of both classical and English literature in Britain looked always over their shoulder at Germany. In London there were specialist publishers such as Richard Taylor, while German-speaking Europe produced far more than Oxford, Cambridge,

Edinburgh, Glasgow and London combined. 'We wish', wrote the author of a survey of current work on Greek and Roman authors in 1810, 'we could give as ample a list of intended publications in this country'.

> We have as many readers of the classics, as many sound critical scholars, as Germany can boast. We greatly excel the Germans in taste; nor are we deficient in industry; but the repeated taxes on paper, and the price of labor, have almost banished us from the trade of the Continent. We are undersold even in our English classics. The late prohibitions of Bonaparte, unaccountable as far as they relate to the export trade from his dominions, have roused a spirit among some of our booksellers and printers, who are projecting classical publications of importance. Were they certain that the return of peace would not overflow the trade with German classics at a lower price, the most beneficial effects of that spirit would soon appear.[37]

Whatever the possible gain for textual scholarship, for a small group of publishers in Britain and Germany the number of editions of the Greek tragedians was in itself a potential difficulty. Porson's *Hecuba*, published by G. and T. Wilkie at London in 1797, was incorporated into Gottfried Hermann's Leipzig edition, published by Feind, as early as 1800. A further edition, with other plays, appeared from Gerhard Fleischer at Leipzig in 1802, partly composed of sheets printed in England. There it stood beside and to be used in Brunck's established edition, which continued to retain its popularity and to be reprinted several times over. With notes and corrections by Schaeffer, Porson's edition of Euripides was republished at Leipzig. Hermann's *Hecuba* appeared at Halle in 1805. Meanwhile Porson's own work was published at Cambridge in 1802. Further editions of it were published in London in 1808 and 1817, and a yet further one by Fleischer at Leipzig in 1824 as a part of a collected Euripides. The specialist classical booksellers G. and W. B. Whittaker published Porson's *Hecuba* in London in 1821, and when in 1824 it was again published in London, it was 'apud exemplar Lipsianum'. Dindorf's influential Teubner edition, incorporating Porson, appeared the following year.

In the case of the *Prometheus vinctus*, it took a little longer for English scholarship to reach Germany, and for the return voyage to be made. Blomfield was no Porson, as German critics were quick to point out.[38] There was a well-established edition, by Christian Gottfried Schütz, published in Halle and Berlin in 1781; and besides this there was a more elementary edition by G. W. Lange, also published at Halle. Blomfield's Cambridge edition of 1810, printed again at Cambridge in 1812 and 1819, was not taken up by a Leipzig publisher until well after the end of the war, in 1822, when Lehnhold issued it to the accompaniment of Peter Elmsley's work, from Oxford. Further Leipzig editions appeared from Teubner (edited by Dindorf) and Vogel (edited by Wellauer) in the following year.

In an increasingly international world of publishing, fruit partly of the possibilities and demands following the end of the Napoleonic wars, the multitude of competing interests was compounded by the reputation of Porson, whose work, so carefully nurtured by an influential group of members of Trinity, was reprinted in the journals and published in Cambridge, London and Leipzig. The Cambridge press published no text of Homer to set beside the several competing interests in Germany,[39] or that of

Grenville and others from Oxford. Aware of the dangers of duplication, in 1814 the Cambridge Syndics (Valpy's intentions having come to nothing) decided against a new edition of Schleusner's lexicon, on hearing that such a project was already in hand in Scotland: it came from the Edinburgh University Press that year, and Deighton appeared on the title-page as the Cambridge agent. The publicity for the edition remarked on the inferior design and the poor quality ('dusky hue') of the German edition, with which it was in competition in the British market.[40] Nor was competition confined to classical studies. Milton's tract *De doctrina Christiana*, published for the first time in 1825 and printed but not published by the Press, was followed by a Braunschweig edition two years later.[41] In such ways, with just two books, the Cambridge booksellers witnessed a commonplace of the trade in modern authors, where publishers were to some extent protected in their home markets. Home and overseas publishers vied with each other on the same ground.

The web of international connections in the book industry responsible for some of the complexities in the publication of classical texts had taken on some of its shape by the first months of the nineteenth century, before the Napoleonic invasions. On the continent, these connections developed further in French-dominated Europe while Britain remained isolated by war. Foreign books were expensive, and difficult to obtain, as the young Charles Babbage discovered when in 1811 he wished to buy a copy of Lacroix on differential and integral calculus.[42] With peace, the price in England of foreign books dropped,[43] and by the mid-1820s Teubner's classical taxts, printed in Leipzig, were also published in London by their agents Black, Young and Young.

To some extent, the book trade on the Continent was able to continue despite the European wars of the 1790s and first years of the nineteenth century. A few publishers contrived to develop their international connections. The booksellers Treuttel and Würtz, in Paris and Strasbourg, laboured to keep their clientèle informed by means of their *Journal Général de la Littérature Etrangère*, founded in 1801. Throughout the Napoleonic wars they advertised an English subscription rate, the journal covering the sciences, arts and dozens of novels among its international array of new titles. Inevitably there were delays between publication and notice, frequently of several years; and in 1815 there was a conscious effort to catch up with British publications, including the classical texts from Cambridge. Even during wartime, J. A. G. Weigel in Leipzig managed to maintain links sufficient to publish jointly with booksellers in London, Leiden, Venice, Rome, Florence, Vienna, Hamburg and Paris.[44]

Following the end of the Napoleonic wars, the Paris booksellers Martin Bossange and Treuttel & Würtz both established branches in London. By the mid-1820s London booksellers specialising in imports further included Dulau, Zotti, Boosey & Sons, John Bohn and J. H. Bohte – the last three handling German books in particular. The scientific and medical firm of Baillière, founded in 1818, opened in London in 1830.[45] Though the expansion of these international firms was restricted until the mid-century by inadequate international banking, and by the costs of communication and transport,[46] they served markets not only among expatriate communities, and casual visitors to their various cities, but also customers who increasingly assumed access to foreign literatures of all kinds. The dominance of French in Enlightenment Europe gave way to more diverse linguistic skills, and the presence of American publishing, through importing agents such as the bookseller John Souter, became increasingly noticeable. In Cambridge, Deighton's advertisements reflected these continental connections.

Apart from the international market in classical texts, most of these developments in the immediate aftermath of the Napoleonic wars had little effect on the everyday affairs of the Cambridge University Press. But they marked the beginnings of the creation of a world which, by the mid-century, was inescapable.

Between 1806, when Napoleon's armies finally overran Germany, and 1814, most German scholars had been cut off from England by the war.[47] By the time that communication could be partially resumed, Christian Gottlob Heyne had died in 1812; Wolf had moved from Halle to the new university at Berlin, where he was reported to have transferred most of his attention from Homer to Plato; J. G. Schneider, author of a standard Greek lexicon, had left Frankfurt for Breslau, and was working on Theophrastus; and Gottfried Hermann and G. H. Schaefer remained for the present confined to Leipzig by the military campaigns.[48] Gradually, as continental Europe was disentangled from war, travel again became possible, and contacts were resumed. The *Göttingische Gelehrte Anzeigen* resumed its regular notices of books from England. In January 1815 the *Jenaische Allgemeine Literatur-Zeitung* included two articles on Oxford and Cambridge, in a series about European universities, and showed especial interest in the recent differences at Cambridge over the British and Foreign Bible Society.[49] From January 1816 the same journal published regular surveys of recent English books. The process was sometimes slow. Herbert Marsh's *Comparative view of the churches of England and Rome*, published by Deighton at Cambridge in 1811, and Walter Whiter's *Etymologicon universale*, published by the University Press in the same year, were reviewed in the *Jenaische Allgemeine Literatur-Zeitung* only in 1817. A book from Oxford University Press published in 1806 was finally noticed in August 1817. In the *Göttingische Gelehrte Anzeigen*, Burges's *Troades* (published by Deighton in 1807) and Clarke's account of the Greek marbles (1809) were reviewed only in 1816–17.[50]

The restoration of ties was welcomed by classical scholars on both sides of the Channel; but it immediately sharpened old rivalries in the book trade. English editions were expensive, and in short supply on the Continent even following 1815. To meet the need for modern literature, firms such as Galignani were already well established in Paris, undercutting English prices and offering books to the tourists who flooded to the city after 1815, as well as engaging in a trade across mainland western Europe.[51] In German-speaking Europe, firms such as Fleischer or Brockhaus in Leipzig, or Steudel in Gotha were also well established, offering cheap editions, often on poor paper, that were inevitably regarded with distaste by the London trade.[52] In classical literature, Weigel of Leipzig was especially active – and successful.

Davies's editions of Cicero, printed and published at Cambridge in the first half of the eighteenth century, were relaunched with supplementary matter at Halle between 1804 and 1820. Porson's much more recent editions of Euripides were republished at

Leipzig. But the unauthorized publication there of his *Adversaria* from the Cambridge edition, in an 'editio nova emendatior et auctior' brought a forthright protest from his Cambridge advocates.

> Of Porson's notes and emendations it contains not an additional word. Whence then does it derive the epithet *auctior*? Why, from an Appendix containing fifty pages of heavy German commentary upon Lucian, Achilles Tatius, Libanius, &c. from the pen of Frederic Jacobs. And this is the new companion to the remains of Porson!!! This is the *improvement* of a book of which the German preface admits, *Tantum liber eximius thesaurum rerum optimarum tenet -*. Never did we know such an instance of the living and the dead bound together, as this volume presents . . .
>
> The republisher of the *Adversaria* is an able and distinguished scholar, whom we blush to see lending himself to such proceedings of *the trade* at Leipsic. He may aspire with justice to praise of a higher description; but for his vaunted superiority as a corrector of the press we see no ground whatever. The German edition of Porson's four plays, and Matthiae's Euripides were printed under his supervision; each of which has a reasonable allowance of typographical faults: and these are much more inconvenient to the purchaser, than in editions where the error of a letter or an accent can be altered with a pen; such is the quality of the Leipsic paper (in which a reputable grocer in this country would hardly chuse to tie up his customers' tea) that a slight touch of the pen produces a blot which obliterates the whole word.[53]

The view from Leipzig was different, for its editor, G. H. Schaefer, 'educated in the German notions of the importance of an exquisite latinity', had had the boldness to correct the Latin of the Cambridge edition. 'It seemed', reported George Ticknor from Leipzig in summarising the affair to a friend, 'incredible to the classical wits at Cambridge, that a book of Porson's, so carefully and so often revised by those into whose hands his papers came, should contain so vulgar a fault as a grammatical error.'[54] But by then the faults of some of the Cambridge epigones had been well aired, and Blomfield's edition of the *Persae*, published by Deighton in 1814, had been subjected to a vicious review in the influential *Jenaische Literatur-Zeitung* only a few weeks previously.[55]

The pace of the revival in Greek studies at the University Press had been heady. Its effects remained obvious for half a century, and in the case of some of the contributions for longer still. But it depended on only a handful of people.

Through the efforts of Monk and his colleagues at Trinity, the Press became largely responsible for issuing what Porson had left unpublished. However, the long-awaited edition of the Cambridge manuscript of Photius, laboured over by Porson and taken up by Dobree, was finally published in 1822 – in London, by Mawman, rather than in Cambridge itself. In the same year, Monk was appointed Dean of Peterborough. In 1824, C. J. Blomfield was appointed Bishop of Chester.[56]

Thanks especially to a group of members of Trinity led by Monk and Christopher Wordsworth, a classical tripos was established in 1824 – but to be sat only after adequate performance in mathematics.[57] It was a strictly limited achievement, and in many ways a form of defence against those who doubted the essential place of classics in the

University. In 1817, Monk made this the crux of his commemoration sermon preached in Trinity College chapel. After the customary and triumphalist *tour d'horizon* of the college's more illustrious members (the published version of the sermon was provided with footnotes, recording further details), he became more sombre:

> In certain publications, we see the utility of Classical Pursuits denied, and the judgement questioned, which devotes so large a share of the season of youth to these favoured studies. That such attacks should be made, cannot surprise any one, who considers the propensity, too often perceived in men, to vilify attainments of which they are themselves destitute, and to decry advantages, which they have not themselves enjoyed. This propensity is not unfrequently found to be connected with an interested wish to elevate some other system, by the depression of that which has undergone the test of experience, or with a perverse desire of gaining applause by paradox.[58]

The departure of Monk and Blomfield, principals in the sustained attention that had been given to Greek editions by the University Press for several years, helped to further an already established shift in interest towards a more distributed use of the Government Annuity Fund. To those of a critical persuasion, it was an ebbing away. One review described Scholefield's collected Aeschylus, printed at Cambridge in 1828, as an edition 'not . . . of much labour or research': the influence of Wellauer's Leipzig edition (1823) was plain to see.[59] The *Quarterly Journal of Education* was less pusillanimous, and Scholefield's work was castigated for being out of date, out of touch with continental scholarship, and suffering from an inbuilt fault characteristic of Cambridge:

> The University of Cambridge seems to be destined for a long time to feel the effects of her refusal to allow Porson to edit Aeschylus in his own way, inasmuch as every attempt made by Cambridge men to correct or explain this poet has been a signal failure. Butler, Blomfield, and Burges, by their mode of editing the whole or part of his plays, have, as far as in them lay, rendered the study of the finest specimen of the Greek drama unprofitable.[60]

Compared with Dindorf's edition, from Oxford, Scholefield's was expensive, more than twice the price; and though Dindorf's editing could also be disputed, he did not suffer from the same faults as the Regius Professor of Greek at Trinity:

> Mr. Scholefield's edition is incomplete as concerns the fragments; bad as concerns the text; deficient in every kind of collateral information; and accompanied with foot-notes, written in very odd Latin, and of which it is not too much to say that nearly all of them are either trivial or incorrect; that they either contain nothing which is not already known to any well-taught schoolboy, or something to which a scholar will decidedly object.

Classical studies, that had for several years dominated the Press's secular printing, inspiring a new type-face that became the most familiar of all to anyone encountering Greek, and commandeering the Government Annuity Fund, thus slipped from its throne, victim not simply of other subjects and other interests, but of a disabling decline in skills.

Even Trinity College did not speak with a single voice; but the difficulties were compounded, in all subjects, by the differences of opinion and practice among the several colleges, with their various methods of examining. Scholefield's scourge recognised this, in both regretting that such a book should have gained, 'as it appears to have, a firm footing in the university of Cambridge'. But in recognising that many would be led astray, he also took comfort from the fact that the 'better class' of tutors would not fail to point out its errors. How far the dispersed and conflicting interests of the colleges provided a force for conservatism that determined a disabling caution in the University's affairs was a problem that exercised many would-be reformers in the nineteenth century. Indirectly, they could not fail to influence the affairs of the Press, where it was easier to avoid battles by not publishing very much as a University, and leaving questions of the relationship between commercial success, scholarly repute and popular reputation to the slightly distanced ground of the lists of the local bookseller-publishers. Deighton and his lesser colleagues prospered; the University Press was set on a course that threatened eventually to lead to oblivion.

15

John Smith

But there was another way. In the foundation of a succession of societies, like-minded interests in Cambridge (with their allies elsewhere) overcame the parochial differences of colleges and of rank; and with the further establishment of periodicals that could be hospitable to a re-ordering and questioning of established values and academic routines, it proved possible to overcome this inbuilt force of conservatism. Both societies and periodicals relied on the press, and the University Press thus became of formative importance in promoting research, alliances and co-operation, in a manner that was, for Cambridge printers, entirely new.

In November 1819 a group including Adam Sedgwick of Trinity, John Stevens Henslow of St John's and the older Edward Daniel Clarke of Jesus agreed to form a new Cambridge Philosophical Society, whose purposes were soon summarised: of 'promoting scientific enquiries and of facilitating the communication of facts connected with the advancement of Philosophy and Natural History'.[1] In December 1820, the Syndics of the Press agreed to defray the cost of printing its proceedings. At their same meeting the Syndics also agreed to treat a catalogue of the University's anatomical museum in similar fashion, and so to share with the world the recently purchased collection of the late Sir Busick Harwood, the first Downing Professor of Medicine.[2] The foundation of the Philosophical Society was but one manifestation of a change in direction. Thought was also being given once again to the reform of examinations, and to the building of a university observatory.[3] Early in 1823 the Syndics agreed to pay for a treatise on dynamics by a young Fellow of Trinity, William Whewell (fig. 26).[4] In a lean year of expenditure from the Government Annuity Fund (GAF), Whewell's book coincided with an analysis of a course of lectures on human anatomy and physiology by the recently elected Professor of Anatomy, and fellow member of Trinity, William Clark.

Whewell's first book, and for many people his most influential, *An elementary treatise on mechanics* (1819), had been printed by Smith for Deighton in Cambridge, and for G. and W. B. Whittaker in London.[5] Four years later, its continuation *A treatise on dynamics. Containing a considerable collection of mechanical problems* was printed at the expense of the Syndics, but sold by the same firms. Whewell found the path of reform a stony one, and his mentor Richard Jones summed it up. Whewell's difficulty was that he had forgotten

Fig. 26 William Whewell, by James Lonsdale, 1825.

the thick darkness by which you are surrounded – 9 tenths of the people old & young at Cambridge I take it know exactly nothing about the question as to constant successions of phenomena efficient course &c. and you have earnt nothing but abuse & curses by paying them the compliment of supposing they did.[6]

Whewell was well aware of the change in direction, and alluded in his work to the unfamiliarity of some of the continental mathematics he was discussing. Richard Jones heard separately that 'the old mathematics have died & faded away with scarcely an audible groan before the high flood of analytic lore'.[7]

Whewell had graduated as second wrangler in 1816, the year in which the Press printed for Deighton and for Law and Whittaker in London an English version of S. F. Lacroix's *Elementary treatise on the differential and integral calculus*. It was the shared work of Charles Babbage, George Peacock and J. F. W. Herschel who, led (according to Babbage's own account) by Babbage thus introduced 'the Principles of pure D-ism in opposition to the Dot-age of the University'. The punning, and rejected, title, which alluded to notation of which no Cambridge mathematician could have been ignorant, was suggested by Babbage, who claimed to have been inspired to suggest what became called the Analytical Society by the fierce agitation in the University between support-ers and opponents of the Bible Society.[8] As an undergraduate, Babbage found Cambridge mathematics profoundly distasteful, and ignorant of foreign work. Soon afterwards,

I became convinced that the notation of fluxions must ultimately prove a strong impediment to the progress of English science. But I knew, also, that it was hopeless for any young and unknown author to attempt to introduce the notation of Leibnitz into an elementary work. This opinion naturally suggested to me the idea of translating the smaller work of Lacroix . . . I had finished a portion of the translation, and laid it aside, when, some years afterwards, Peacock called upon me in Devonshire Street, and stated that both Herschel and himself were convinced that the change from the dots to the d's would not be accomplished until some foreign work of eminence should be translated into English. Peacock then proposed that I should either finish the translation which I had commenced, or that Herschel and himself should complete the remainder of my translation . . . It was determined by lot that we should make a joint translation. Some months after, the translation of the small work of Lacroix was published.[9]

Babbage's autobiographical mood accorded most of the credit to himself; yet in crucial respects he was accurate, and in none more so than his rueful admission that although the tutors of Trinity and St John's adopted the new notation, others did not: some actively opposed it, and the result for some years was confusion. The ensuing collection of *Examples to the differential and integral calculus*, printed at the University Press in 1820, was designed to remedy matters.[10] Even in 1834, a reviewer in the *Quarterly Journal of Education*, published by Charles Knight, used the opportunity offered by a change that year in the notation used in the University's examination papers, and remarked the divergence of practice as it developed further.

To have no community of system – to have the moderators of one college using one, and those of another using another, each forcing his own upon the whole University during his year of office, – to oblige the same student to read books of different notation, because each happens to be the best of its kind – to keep him in suspense as to what notation he will be examined in, till the beginning of his fourth year, when he ought long before that time to be thoroughly well grounded in one or other – will be no advantage to the cause of science in Cambridge.[11]

The translation of Lacroix, published in 1816, fell on rather variable ground. Of the edition of a thousand copies, the first went to Thomas Underwood, bookseller in London. Law and Whittaker took 315 copies in early 1817, soon after publication. Most copies sold rather slowly, in Cambridge itself: two dozen to Nicholson, and then gradually to Deighton, whose prominence on the title-page obscured the fact that their first thirty copies were not charged to them until sixteen months after publication, in 1818. Thereafter, Deighton was the only, and slow, customer, buying no more until fifty were sent in June 1819; ninety-four in 1820, and a final forty in February 1821. At that point, just over four years after publication, the residue of the edition was wasted.[12] This desultory tale may be contrasted with the career of the fifth edition of Vince's *Fluxions*, published in March 1818 and likewise in an edition of 1,000 copies. In twenty months, Mawman in London took 300, Deighton 210 and Nicholson 200.[13]

The change in the University depended on more than Whewell, Herschel, Babbage and Peacock, those most identified with the new 'analytic lore'. As even the books printed at the Press demonstrated, and quite apart from those whose authors preferred

London printers, publishers and booksellers, the study of mathematics in Cambridge was far from uniformly pursued.

The foundation of the Cambridge Philosophical Society focused many of the scientific interests of the University. The first volumes of its *Transactions*, including papers by Charles Babbage, Edward Daniel Clarke, J. S. Henslow, J. F. W.Herschel, Adam Sedgwick and Whewell, were an obvious cause for the Government Annuity Fund. The foundation of the new observatory in 1822–4, and the beginning in 1829 of G. B. Airy's detailed published accounts of observations there, put the Press to a further test.[14] At a more elementary level, Deighton and the Press collaborated to produce new textbooks: Whewell's *Elementary treatise on mechanics*, first published in 1819, had by 1847 reached its seventh edition, and Airy's *Mathematical tracts*, first published in 1826, likewise became standard reading, attaining a fourth edition by 1858, when it was taken over by Macmillan.

Whewell's own increasingly diverse pursuits took him into the study of Gothic architecture (published by Deighton in 1830, and then revised in 1835 and 1842), while in 1828 Julius Hare and Connop Thirlwall saw published their first volume of a translation of Niebuhr's history of Rome: the work was printed by Smith at the University Press, but published in London by John Taylor, 'Bookseller and publisher to the University of London'.[15] H. J. Rose's *Inscriptiones Graecae vetustissimae*, dedicated to Lord Guilford and the most important work on its subject to have appeared for a generation, was printed in Cambridge, with the aid of the GAF; but Rose arranged for it to be published by Murray, also in London.[16]

At least one of the Press's friends attempted to set his own private agenda. In 1809, Claudius Buchanan, who had spent the past several years teaching at the new College of Fort William in Calcutta, included among his gifts to the University Library a twelfth-century Syriac Bible from South India. According to his widely read autobiographical account of *Christian researches in Asia*, he had been unable to buy a Syriac Bible on his return to Britain. So, using the Cambridge manuscript and other sources, he set about preparing an edition that could be put to missionary – and specifically Protestant – use in India.[17] In a climate of evangelical jealousies exacerbated by Buchanan's own difficult personality, his proposal to the University Press was more specific still: 'I wish not to mention the work to the Bible Society, in the first instance; as it is proper, that it should rather proceed from the Church of England & the Soc[y]. for Promoting Xtian Knowledge.' Buchanan's own first private interest was in the new Church Missionary Society. But this apart, there were difficulties, in that the work would require a new type: Buchanan had in mind one modelled after the New Testament printed for Luchtmans and others at Leiden in 1717.[18] Much delayed, nothing appeared of the project until (notwithstanding Buchanan's initial wishes) the British and Foreign Bible Society published the Gospels and Acts in 1815, the year of Buchanan's death. It was printed not at Cambridge, but by Richard Smith at Broxbourne, where the new type cut by Figgins could expect a more fruitful future in a press that specialised in oriental texts.[19] Cambridge's own exports were more mundane, consisting of copies of the Bible or New Testament sent overseas by the Bible Society.

Without question, the largest part of the Press's exports consisted of Bibles (fig. 27). Others tended to be of most importance to educational institutions, and for these the University also began to make a practice of presenting books to colleges and universities in specific spheres of influence. Perhaps recalling Claudius Buchanan's gift of printed books and manuscripts to the University Library a few years earlier, in 1827 the University sent books to Bishop's College in Calcutta.[20] A decade later, gifts of books were sent to the new theological library at Sydney, the University of Athens, Windsor College in Nova Scotia and the episcopal library in Jamaica.[21] In 1833, the Syndics also agreed to send a set of stereotype plates of the nonpareil duodecimo Bible to Upper Canada. The practice of exporting plates to North America was by then well established in the more ordinary parts of the book trade, but this does not seem to have become regular in that for Bibles.[22]

In these several interests of resident members of the University are to be seen the Press's strengths, and its weaknesses. As Smith, the University Printer, realised, the Press was at an advantage when dealing with local authors. But he and the Syndics could have little control over whom those authors chose as their publishers; and therefore they had, in the end, only limited influence in the development of the Press. Hare had been acquainted with Taylor for several years through the *London Magazine*, and had been instrumental in persuading him to publish Landor.[23] The choice of him as publisher of Niebuhr followed, reinforced by the connections of the London trade, though Hare returned to Deighton (with Rivington in London) when in 1831 he launched the *Philological Museum*, a new (and, as it proved, short-lived[24]) periodical designed to fill the place of the defunct *Museum Criticum*.

As authors in their prefaces repeatedly acknowledged, the GAF enabled the Syndics to meet the costs (or a substantial part of the costs) of printing a limited number of deserving books each year. But the same assured income that made this possible was also a snare, in that by providing a subsidy that did not have to be justified as a cost, it also allowed the Syndics to ignore the wider questions of publishing. In particular, there was no need to consider profit or loss in individual books within the context of the Press's overall turnover. The consequence was an assumption that other publishers would take up what the Syndics did not apportion to the GAF. By allowing this to develop, at a time when the publishing trade as a whole was expanding, the Syndics laid the foundations for a Press that, however worthy, was to seem ever less adventurous and less supportive of the principal everyday concerns of the University. Cambridge University Press had placed printing before publishing, ever since the decision to emphasise the printing of Bibles and other privileged books at the expense of other work. In the generation after the end of the Napoleonic wars, as capital was put into new presses and new type amidst a programme of expansion, it was investment in printing, not in publishing.

The Bible and prayer-book privileges remained under attack. This trade, different in many ways from the ordinary book trade, did not depend only on ordinary booksellers – as the pirates well realised. In 1816, a survey revealed 143 booksellers in different

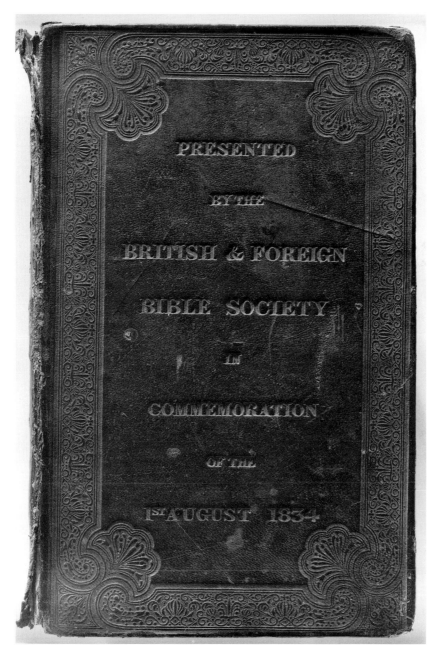

Fig. 27 The New Testament, 1833. A copy of the pica octavo edition printed at Cambridge for the British and Foreign Bible Society. Bound for the Society and stamped on the cover with the date, 1 August 1834, when slavery was abolished throughout the British Empire. This copy was shipped to Antigua, and presented that year by a Wesleyan missionary to a woman who had been baptised into the Moravian church in 1811.

parts of England offering illegal Edinburgh editions.[25] Booksellers were warned off such editions; so the trade moved into the world of pawnbrokers: in 1818 the London bookseller Joseph Mawman, confidant of Oxford and Cambridge alike, had little difficulty in discovering thirty-one such firms so involved. In some instances, false title-pages were printed to suggest that books were printed at Oxford rather than Edinburgh. The core of this illegal activity was among the pawnbrokers of the City of London, but Edinburgh editions were also to be found in bookshops including those of James Bigg in Parliament Street, and of Francis Clark and of Hatchard in Piccadilly. The so-called Parsons' Bristol Bible (named after the proprietor, John Parsons, and printed in Bristol), one of those printed with notes designed to be removed, caused further difficulty and expense, as the booksellers of central London were warned and in nearly all cases pleaded misunderstanding. So, too, the several editions of the Bible and the prayer book associated with the name of William Gurney, either with carefully placed notes[26] or with the normal order of the prayer book slightly changed, were sought out – the more urgently since in Bath one bookseller confessed to having sold a cartload of his cheap prayer books. Other editions of the prayer book, the Bible or the New Testament appeared bearing the names of Tabart (a fashionable bookseller in New Bond Street, who denied any connection), of Thomas Blanshard, and of Richard Edwards, bookseller in Fleet Street.

The stark threat to the privileged presses, represented by a widespread disregard for their position on the part of publishers and booksellers alike, begged more difficult questions: of the ability of these presses to meet demand, and of the wisdom of maintaining a monopoly that that been established in the sixteenth century but for which modern social and industrial conditions were no longer appropriate. Part-publication of the Bible in particular became commonplace. Adam Clarke, author of a widely consulted biblical commentary, reckoned that in less than twenty years at the beginning of the nineteenth century, not less than half a million copies of the Bible in numbers, or parts, had been sold. They were cheap; and because each part was short, it could be read without undue labour. There were advantages to purchasers and evangelists alike.[27] Illustrations became a further weapon against the monopoly. The publication in 1800 of Macklin's monumental illustrated Bible, 'embellished with engravings, from pictures and designs from the most eminent English artists', set a standard which few printers or publishers could hope to afford;[28] but many imitated the principle. For the more ordinary trade, the periodic legal offensives of the privileged presses acting either separately or in concert caused increasing tensions. In January 1819, a gathering of booksellers and others met in protest at the Globe tavern, in Fleet Street. Their number included the radical William Hone, as well as defenders of the *status quo* such as Mawman and Spottiswode. It was pointed out that for selling the Bible, booksellers were being treated more harshly than they had been for selling *The rights of man*. In Hone's view, the universities' privilege actually worked against the sale of Bibles, since the large numbers of editions in parts had increased circulation. In a room said by the *Morning Chronicle* to be 'crowded to excess', the meeting turned into an attack on the universities.[29] Others, some in newspapers and some separately, picked up the attack:

on the accuracy of the available editions, on the editorial principles that were followed, or alleged the superiority of the edition of 1611.[30]

In such circumstances, the edition of a family Bible prepared by George D'Oyly and Richard Mant, for the SPCK, printed at Oxford and issued in 1814–16 in parts, was in some degree a self-defence.[31] It was lavishly prepared, provided with extensive notes, maps and numerous simply engraved copies of paintings. In 1816, a further printing was offered to Cambridge – in the hope that a combination of reduced paper and composition costs would lead to a cheaper product.[32] In the event, the work was delayed; distracted by disputes and prosecutions for illegal editions of the Bible, the Syndics resolved only in May 1819 to print a family Bible for the SPCK. Further delays followed when it was discovered that the original illustrations could not be used by Cambridge, and that fresh ones would be needed.[33] The new Cambridge edition was not completed until late 1823. More than any other book, it involved Smith in the to him unfamiliar London print trade. Copper engraved plates, even quite crude ones, could not provide sufficient impressions of reasonable quality for a work aimed at a large audience, and the illustrations had therefore to be re-engraved.[34] This part of the work was overseen by the SPCK, but the bills came to Smith: from the engravers George Cooke, of Hackney, and Henry Moses, near Wandsworth Road; from the plate printer John Hayward in Tunbridge Street, near King's Cross; for the maps from the engraver Sidney Hall, and from the printers Cox, Barnett, Basire & Barnett. The parts were stitched and pasted into their wrappers by the London firm of John Bird, binder to both the Bible Society and the SPCK and well able to handle almost 50,000 separate parts by 1825.[35] In 1820, it was agreed to print an edition of 10,000, a figure far in excess of the number of illustrations that were actually printed.[36] Compared with the numbers of copies of the Bible that the Press was accustomed to produce for the Bible Society, the edition size of the illustrations was not large: the initial printing was of 2,000 on coloured paper and 500 on white. A thousand further copies were soon called for. But the plates, engraved at an initial cost of 10 guineas apiece, had to be kept in order, and repaired or reworked ready for further printings. It was a field with which Smith was uncomfortable; he found the preparation and printing of the letterpress a distraction from the Press's normal business;[37] and the project seems to have been only a moderate success. A further reprint of the plates for the SPCK was completed in 1829, when binding was placed in the hands of William Wootton, in Cambridge. But in 1836 the remaining stock retained at Cambridge was offered to the SPCK, and no more was heard of the project.[38] The Cambridge press had ventured into a world of part publication, in which other printers had prospered; but the cost had been considerable, and the rewards not worth further pursuit.

For Smith, preoccupied with more ordinary work, and for the Syndics, preoccupied with the threat of Scotch Bibles (a matter on which opinion was divided), the trade looked bleak. Smith's difficulties were compounded by a falling-off of orders from the Bible Society. The country as a whole was much better supplied than it had been ten or fifteen years earlier, but to the Society Cambridge Bibles seemed markedly inferior. Complaint was made of broken letters, inaccurate texts (the minion Bible was said to be 'perhaps the most incorrect Bible in your Stock'), of excessive inking that made reading difficult, of poor editorial design and of poor delivery dates compared with those of competitors.[39] In 1819, the Syndics explored with the Press's neighbours the possibility of acquiring extra property; but they also found it desirable to write formally to the Press's debtors, and in the summer of 1820 to reduce the price of some books.[40]

Affairs between Wilson and the University remained unsettled for several years. By 1812, the list of Bibles and prayer books printed at Cambridge included eight editions or issues of the stereotyped Bible and six of the New Testament alone, besides seven of the prayer book. But there were also ten of the prayer book printed from type, as well as two quarto Bibles and a large octavo Bible.[41] The benefits of stereotyping were difficult to establish, and its cost was difficult to calculate. Then and for years afterwards the book trade argued the case, with charge and counter-charge; but a consensus gradually emerged: that stereo plates could withstand up to 100,000 impressions without serious deterioration, and that while for some much reprinted books there were clear savings, for others, where the cost of paper could be met immediately, there were few. Despite the claims of one of the Press's main Bible competitors, John Childs, printer at Bungay in Suffolk, who alleged that plates could pay for themselves in an edition of as little as 2,000 or 3,000, Smith (like Hansard, with whose opinions he could not fail to be familiar[42]) remained cautious. The costs of the two establishments were scarcely comparable, in that Childs freely admitted that he paid less than London wages: in fact, according to Hansard, his firm made a practice of employing cheap female labour.[43] It was not routine in Cambridge to stereotype editions of the privileged books.

All this depended on raw materials and on the facilities available for their use. Paper costs presented further problems, and opportunities. Childs considered that the price of paper had fallen between 30 and 40 per cent between about 1812 and 1832. By the latter year, John Parker was of the opinion that Cambridge was making books 'much better than formerly, at the same price'.[44] But the process of mechanisation, the changes introduced in the paper trade, the changes forced by the requirements of the various Bible societies, all combined in a context of publishing that had its own agenda of crises and reorganisation. Increasing competition both from the other privileged presses and, more seriously in that no compromise was possible over price, from printers such as Brightly and Childs, further aggravated a period in which reform was hesitant and headlong by turns.

National demand for paper grew at a faster rate than paper-mills were able to meet, while the simultaneous demand for cheaper paper encouraged the use of inferior materials and chemical bleaching methods that resulted in paper of grossly inferior quality. Gypsum was added so as to increase weight, and hence price. In 1823, articles on the subject appeared both in the *Gentleman's Magazine* and in the *Annals of Philosophy*. A copy of the Bible printed for the Bible Society at Oxford as recently as 1816 was found to be already crumbling away.[45] Cambridge University Press's requirements for paper made heavy demands of suppliers, not only on account of the quantity, but also because of quality; the Bible Society in particular was quick to complain, in a market where low prices meant small margins between profit and loss. When Smith took over the Press, paper was bought from three main suppliers: Martindale, Williams & Co. and Jones & Leventhorpe. In this, as in other parts of the Press's business, Smith brought change. In London, Samuel Bagster's successful collaboration with John Dickinson to produce in 1812 a tough, thin and opaque paper for a pocket Bible placed further strains on existing arrangements between the Cambridge press and its customers. During the first five years of Smith's term of office, the paper bill to the Press rose by about 50 per cent, thanks mainly to increased output, and new suppliers were urgently required.[46] With well-equipped premises, and a determined business sense, John Dickinson and his partner George Longman were in a commanding position at their mills for machine-made paper near Rickmansworth, in Hertfordshire.[47] When in 1814 the Syndics decided to end their long association with their supplier Charles Martindale and his predecessors, it was only after prolonged negotiations with Longman and Dickinson: one advantage that the new suppliers could offer lay in their plans to introduce steam drying in the paper-making process, and so overcome the difficulties caused by extremes of weather.[48] In paper-making, as in printing, developments and improvements in machinery marched parallel with efforts to overcome extremes of heat and humidity, and to obtain reliable light. The association with Longman and Dickinson prospered, though at a period when increasing demand throughout the country was being placed on paper manufacturers by the book, newspaper and stationery trades alike, the search for stocks of a satisfactory quality and price remained as a daily feature of running the Press.[49] By the mid-1820s the Press was again placing large orders regularly with another supplier, Towgood's mills at Dartford in Kent.

For years, the Press had depended on paper brought from a distance. As its operations extended, so the number of suppliers of other essentials grew. New iron presses came from Walker and from Clymer in London, as well as the experimental machine by Bacon and Donkin approved by the Syndics in February 1814.[50] Coal for the foundry and for the new steam heating system (agreed in 1832[51]) came via King's Lynn. Type came from Vincent Figgins, from Fry and Steele and from Caslon, all in London, and from Miller in Edinburgh. Other specialist London firms supplied brass rules and leads for composition. Ink came from Blackwell & Colvin, also in London, and later from Grafton, Baker & Biggs.[52] Local Cambridge firms not only continued to keep the premises in good order, and to carry out routine repairs on equipment, but also supplied necessities such as treacle (an ingredient, for a while, in the newly invented composition rollers for printing ink[53]); a range of different fabrics for presses, rollers and paper including flannel, brown holland, kersey and cambrick; pearl ash (potassium carbonate) and turpentine (used for cleaning away ink); and candles, as well as (later) gas for the new lighting.[54]

The premises of the Press, divided by one of the main thoroughfares between the middle of the town and one of its principal wharves, were inefficiently organised, and inadequate for their purpose. This much was clear to the University when in 1821 it was agreed to purchase the old inn known as the Cardinal's Hat, opposite St Botolph's churchyard. The street frontage was not very great; but that gave little impression of the area occupied to the rear by the yard and the associated buildings. The property also adjoined the Press. At the time of the purchase, there was no suggestion of a grand building: merely of practical necessity.

The University's mood was for more general improvements – not just at the Press, where few understood the exact nature of what such a business required. Elsewhere in Cambridge, colleges such as St John's, Trinity and Corpus looked to their own buildings, while the University itself completed the first stage of a new observatory in 1823. In 1824 a syndicate was appointed to examine the needs of the University as a whole. Among its members was William Whewell, whose letter to a fellow member of Trinity summarised some of their discussions as well as more domestic matters, and gave him an opportunity to rehearse a selection of points that he was later to put into print:

> The alterations in progress and in project here are so numerous that I hardly know how to give you an account of them. Our new court goes on prosperously towards its completion. We expect to be able to inhabit three staircases of it in a week or two, and we have had as much difficulty in electing bed-makers as we had in electing the four new Fellows. With the latter election I hope you are satisfied, as, I think, they have taken the four best men. The new buildings at Corpus are going on with equal splendour, and still more at King's. But what is doing bears no proportion to what is hoped to be done, as you probably have heard. The alterations contemplated, of course with various degrees of confidence, extend almost from Peterhouse to St John's. The proposed site of the future "Pitt Press" is the ground opposite St Botolph's Church, where the University have a good deal of land, and where, I learn, as member of a Syndicate for the purpose, we have an opportunity at present of buying more. The houses which narrow the street on each side of Catharine Hall, will, I hope, be removed before we have done, and the opposite side of the street to Rutlidge's corner is to come down in the course of next year. When the old houses at King's are demolished, this will lead us to St Mary's by a fine open street, and then, *en passant*, we will reform the portico and knock off the balls from the steeple. Then we come to the great debateable ground of Caius . . . When people return to the University and meet at Syndicates, we shall see how they have made up their minds upon the subject. There will be great opposition to any plan of raising the requisite sum, and great difficulty in finding an eligible site for the new college, but perhaps both these obstacles may be got over. If it be placed at the end of Trumpington Street, opposite Addenbrooke's (which by the way is also much beautified), it will extend still further our line of improved building. Besides all these plans we have to remove the site of the Botanic Garden; and if, as some propose, we make the present ground into a large square with a good market in the centre, we may turn it to a very profitable speculation, and may perhaps finally convert that part of Cambridge into the commercial and shop-keeping quarter of the town; and by thus diminishing the value of the houses near St Mary's enable ourselves to get some additional openings in the Academical quarter.[55]

As Whewell himself was the first to admit, some of this was visionary. But by no means all of it. In 1828, Whewell himself addressed to members of the Senate a pamphlet summarising the urgent needs for lecture rooms and scientific museums. The colleges and the University combined in the 1820s to redesign and rebuild on an unprecedented scale. They were driven partly by rivalry, and partly by an acute sense of public presence in the townscape; but principally by the needs to replace old buildings that had become decrepit, to offer accommodation for increasing numbers of undergraduates, and to provide working space for the University, be it botanic garden, library, chemistry laboratory or printing press.[56] The decision to abandon the Press's seventeenth-century site completely, and to build anew, was a part of a larger strategy in which architectural considerations and the interests of town planning were at least equally important to those of manufacturing – and, for some people, perhaps more so. The Pitt Press was on a critical site in what some conceived as a wide and magnificent vista that would link Trinity Street at the north with Peterhouse at the south.

To build a printing house in so conspicuous a position was not unprecedented. Indeed, for decades Cambridge itself had thought of placing it even more centrally, as a foil to the Senate House. To build it in a gothic style was in keeping with the same mood that had encouraged Rickman's New Court at St John's, and Wilkins's New Court at Trinity, screen at King's and wholesale reconstruction at Corpus. But the University might also have looked to Oxford, to the plans drawn up in 1825 for a new University Press in Walton Street, much greater in scale than anything envisaged at Cambridge, and as firmly classical in their design as Cambridge was gothic.[57] Plans for the new buildings at both universities were brought forward in the same year.

The proposal that the surplus of the funds for a public statue,[58] gathered by a group of William Pitt's admirers in London, might be used for a new University Press building was made only in May 1824: well after the purchase of the Cardinal's Hat. William Pitt, Member of Parliament for the University as well as Prime Minister, had died in 1806; a statue by Nollekens had been erected in the Senate House in 1812; and a scholarship had been founded in his name in 1813. The suggestion that the residue of the money collected in London should be used for the Press may have been made by J. H. Monk, Regius Professor of Greek until he was appointed Bishop of Gloucester and Bristol in 1830. He, and Lord Camden who was both Chancellor of the University and chairman of the committee to recommend uses for the memorial fund, were well placed to understand the University's needs, and to judge what was practicable. The Press's new land was appropriately close to Pembroke, Pitt's own college.[59]

There could be no doubt of the need. Basing their observations on a well-timed survey commissioned from T. C. Hansard, one of the most respected London printers, the Press Syndics reported to the University that the existing buildings were

> so dilapidated and so inadequate to the effectual conducting of the business, that the University will at no distant period be obliged to incur a very considerable expense in rebuilding the premises situated near Catharine Hall, as well as in making essential alterations in those on the opposite side of Silver Street.[60]

Agreement to spend the Pitt money quickly followed, and in October 1825 plans were exhibited for the new building. The first parts to be completed consisted of the west side of what became a court, with a new house for the University Printer to the south, towards Mill Lane. The old printing house in Silver Street was abandoned soon afterwards.[61] Meanwhile, the extra properties in Trumpington Street, on each side of the Cardinal's Hat, were bought gradually between 1825 and 1830, and Edward Blore was chosen apparently from among seven who were invited to submit designs for the main frontage: the choice of architect was that of the Pitt fund committee, not of the University. Camden sought to be reassuring in stating that his committee was both 'desirous that an handsome Room should be included in the Design, together with a staircase leading to it, but that the Committee would be most desirous any accommodation could be given to the Press in the Building to be erected which did not interfere with those parts which they think should be ornamented'.[62] In other words, there was no question of a grudging compromise between architecture and industry: ornament, Blore's Gothic revival, came first in the minds of the donors. To meet this, a new pressroom and warehouse, separate from the ornamented range, were built to Blore's plainer designs on the north side of the courtyard in 1831–2. On 18 October 1831 the foundation stone was laid for Blore's gothic east side, and it was handed to the University in April 1833.[63] The Pitt Press (fig. 28) immediately featured as one of the sights of Cambridge, depicted on the *University Almanac* for 1834 as well as in a separately published lithograph by F. Mackenzie. Local guidebooks soon included it in their itineraries, undismayed by the fact that much of the Pitt Press was put to uses that had nothing to do with printing or publishing;[64] and the building became familiar the world over when a wood-engraved vignette was brought into use on the title-pages of books printed there.[65]

Internally as well as externally, both the printing house and the Pitt building have been much changed since they were erected. But something of the conception of the new accommodation for presses and compositors survives in Hansard's account of his principles, from which he drew when considering the matter for Cambridge:

> A parallelogram is decidedly the best form for a building for this specific purpose, and a width of twenty-five feet fully sufficient; as more would deprive the centre of the room of the advantage of light from either side. A common press with its bank takes up about eight feet; then say three feet clear passage way; in the centre a range of bulks for wrought-off paper, under which standings and racks for formes, say two feet more. This provides for a range of presses on each side: and in length of room 7 feet 6 inches to 8 feet may be calculated for each press, taking care that the posts or piers between the windows are arranged so that an uninterrupted light is secured to each press. For the composing-rooms the same width will allow a range of frames on each side, a clear passage, and a double row of imposing and correcting stones down the centre. The joists of all the floors should have short bearings, the floor boards to be grooved and tongued, and the ceilings, for many reasons, must be lathe and plaster; any thing more than finishing the walls fair, and lime-washing, is quite unnecessary.[66]

In a further improvement, Hansard insisted on the need to avoid the long-standing practice of hanging damp printed sheets out to dry over the heads of compositors and pressmen:

> First, from a consideration of the health of those employed; secondly, with a view to the danger from the easy communication of fire from their candles, or any other light, to the

Fig. 28 The Pitt Press. Water-colour by George Belton Moore.

sheets on the poles, when, from being dry, and the edges curling, the flames would rapidly spread; thirdly, the dust arising from the various movements about an office; and last, but not least, the safety of the sheets from being either taken off the poles by sudden draughts of air, and becoming soiled in the fall of handling, or for purposes of curiosity or fraud.[67]

The new printing house to the west was of four floors. In the basement were two wetting rooms for paper, and a stereotype and letter store. On the ground floor (fig. 29) were two large press rooms, each capable of receiving eight presses, the ceilings supported by cast-iron pillars and each room lit from both south and north. At the front was the counting house and a large room for reading. At the back of the building were rooms for preparing stereotype plates: a foundry, separate lathe room and a picking room. Upstairs were two more similar press rooms, for a further sixteen presses, and two private rooms for composing and printing confidential work such as examination papers. On the top floor were two large rooms for composition, twenty-seven frames in each, and a series of closets for proof-reading. It will be seen from this that once type was composed it had to be carried down either one or two flights of stairs to the presses or foundry, while all paper for printing, heavy with water, had to be carried up at least one flight of stairs.[68]

By the time that the Pitt Building was finished, the University Press was firmly set on a course that involved little publishing beyond the Bible and the prayer book. It had become a printer whose principal business was in printing the privileged books but who also worked for a small number of publishers of whom the most demanding and regular were the local booksellers J. and J. J. Deighton, and who met a variety of other requirements from the University. Sermons, poems and pamphlets remained the staple fare for resident members of the University; but the amount of jobbing printing for the University and colleges had by 1830 grown dramatically. Examination papers, undergraduate exercises, notices about lectures, and a myriad other requirements took up an increasing number of hours. Where once only a few printed examination papers had been required by colleges (Trinity was celebrated in this respect, employing printed examination papers for scholarships, college examinations and fellowship competitions), by 1830 printed college exercises and examinations of some sort were all but universal.[69] As Smith remarked, 'These papers could only be executed by Workmen competent and accustomed to Mathematical & Greek Composition; and my best mathematical Compositors are those who have been brought up and trained in our own office: London workmen having in several instances left the Office, rather than undertake the Composition of such works.'[70] Their printing placed unfamiliar strains on the Press, entailing all-night working, or even more: 'In one particular instance I did not leave the Office for three days and three nights successively', recalled one employee.[71] In other, more general work, and as a publisher, the GAF enabled the Press to print a small selection of books at little or no expense to itself; but it had no means of advertisement or distribution other than the long-established agency system. The Pitt Press buildings provided a public air of confidence that shielded the reality whose import few in the University were prepared to challenge: that Cambridge University Press was much more important as a printer than as a publisher.

The Press was full to capacity. Over the last decades it had installed new presses, both an improved design of the common press, and a succession of Stanhope's iron presses. Sarah Walker, manufacturer of the Stanhope presses, supplied new ones at a standard charge of £75 or £77 apiece, and submitted heavy bills for the repair of those already in use; but she did not have an absolute monopoly. In 1811 the Press bought from Thomas Smith not only '4 additional Powers for Old Printing presses', at a cost of £29.8s., but also a 'large double Crown one Pull Press with additional Power', price £58 and there-fore substantially cheaper than the Stanhopes. A further similar one was bought for the same price a few months later.[72] By 1813, when a shortage of paper threatened the smooth running of business, Smith was able to write of the danger of there being sixteen or seventeen presses idle.[73] Then yet another Stanhope was bought in 1819. But their continuing maintenance problems, and their high cost, made the Stanhope presses seem less desirable when they were compared with the new lighter design of the Columbian press, developed by George Clymer of Philadelphia and patented in Britain in 1817.[74] With a new building, the University Press was also able to expand; and it bought Columbians. Between August 1828 and September 1832, it installed nine super royal and two double crown Columbian presses, price £65 and £70 apiece with a 5 per cent discount for quantity. Six further presses were bought in 1833–4.[75]

This new investment was a measure of the increase in the business of the Press; but it was also by this date a conservative decision to choose to invest so heavily in machin-ery that, whatever its technical superiority in many respects, remained based on old working practices. The experimental press, with the associated equipment, designed by Richard Bacon and Bryan Donkin to print sheets of paper from four cast formes of type set on a rotating square prism, bought by the University Press in 1814–16, was not a success, and was also perhaps a discouragement to further thought of mechaniza-tion.[76] By 1825 it was merely a curiosity, believed to be the only one of its kind to have survived and 'not being found in any degree useful'.[77] As long ago as 1824, when he had been consulted on the Press's management, T. C. Hansard had confessed that he had, after some uncertainty, installed a 'Printing Engine to work by manual labor only, which appears to be the best was yet put in motion; capable of various degrees of work, from 800 to 1200 perfect sheets per hour.'[78] A little later he warmed to the theme:

> The demand for books and all kinds of printing, is now so increased, that had not machin-ery been brought to aid the trade must have been seriously injured. – There have been no hands unemployed in consequence – and I am perfectly convinced that every printing office of large business, must eventually take that assistance. My work has been increas-ing ever since: and I have for some time been working for another machine, or more Presses – but had I the latter, I could not get hands to work them. – It will be very easy for you to have twenty presses made to add to your establishment, but not quite so easy to get forty pressmen; and one certain effect will follow, you will move under the necessity of submitting to any demands they may be pleased to make, for advance of wages, which will as infallibly cause a less quantity of work to be done . . .[79]

The anxieties and excitements over the opening of the Pitt Press, with its associated buildings behind the Trumpington Street frontage, were in many ways a distraction

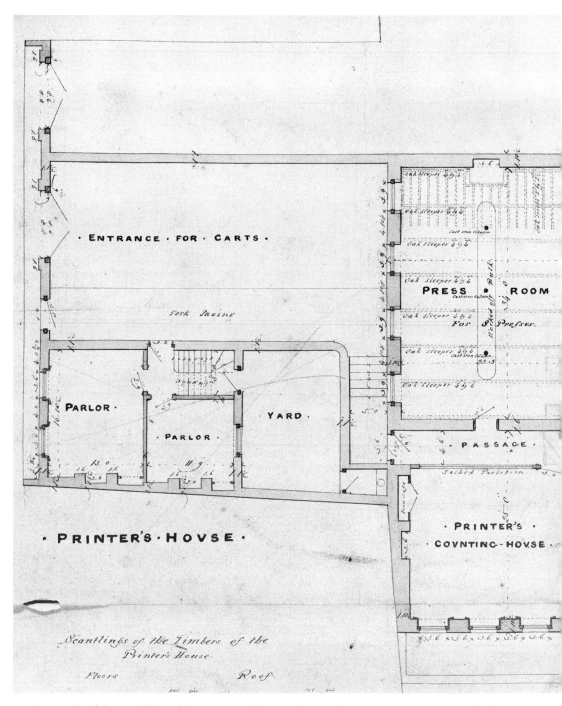

Fig. 29 Plan of the ground floor of the new printing house in the 1820s, looking west. Composition and further presses were accommodated on the upper floors, entailing much carrying up and down stairs of type-metal and of paper. The rooms for preparing stereotypes are in the north-west corner of the building.

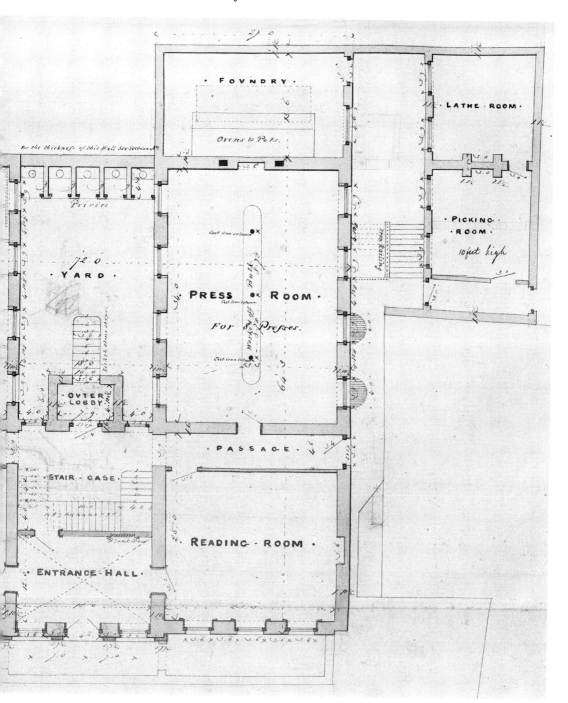

from the questions that Hansard had raised. Much to his dismay and annoyance, and despite his having made clear his own willingness to be employed in the capacity, he was not chosen as manager of the new press in 1829. The rejection was the harder in that the Syndics had employed his skills in fitting up some parts of their new building; but at the age of fifty-three, he may have seemed too old.[80]

As printers, the Press invested in new type, and in new presses; it invested much less in illustration and in the means by which to print it. At a time when the University and town were increasingly supplied with local views, the University Press remained aloof. Richard Harraden's large views published in the 1790s, and his smaller ones published in the early nineteenth century, were succeeded by those of his son and, much more numerously, the engraved work of James and Henry Sargent Storer. By 1830 the directory of local businesses further included the engravers Samuel Coulden and Robert Roe, and three further copper-plate printers, of whom William Metcalfe in Trumpington Street was also able to print lithographs. The Cambridge Philosophical Society's *Transactions* depended on illustration, J. S. Henslow being especially active in this respect. But though the letterpress was printed at the Press, the lithographed illustrations in the first volumes were printed mainly in London – some with spectacular colouring – by Charles Hullmandel and by Rowney and Forster.[81] The engravings, many by J. W. Lowry and E. Tyrrell, were for the most part likewise from London. Roe, the Cambridge engraver, and Metcalfe, the Cambridge printer whose lithographic work appeared in 1835, were the minority. Similarly, the many – and considerably less skilled – illustrations to the Family Bible were printed in London, not in Cambridge. Meanwhile, however, the engraved illustrations to Whewell's work on German churches were printed by the Storers, who became the most successful of the local printers of engravings. The amount of work available through the University Press was strictly limited, and this may have encouraged their active programme in printing local views, whether singly, in portfolios, or as contributions to books. It is not, yet, clear where the many engravings necessary for books on geometry and other mathematical studies were printed, and it may be that the Storers were principally responsible; but it seems unlikely that they were printed at the Press itself. A similarly utilitarian approach was taken by the University Press to wood engravings, for although a vignette of the new Pitt building was introduced to grace some (but not all) title-pages, the bodies of the books printed at this time are noticeably plain. Decorative head- and tailpieces, a feature of many eighteenth-century books, had fallen out of fashion, and Smith was of his time in this: he was not even in the habit of buying cast ornaments from typefounders. The few blocks that were necessary – mainly, again, for mathematics, though a few were cut for Whewell's architectural works – were by D. Dodd, of London.[82]

Though the Press was now even better equipped, there were many anomalies. It remained, as had always been the case, that it could not compete on equal terms for the printing of books that were to be published principally in London. On the other hand, it seemed also to Hansard that there was some prejudice against the University Press among the local booksellers for whom other possible, though less well provided, local printers were John Hall and William Metcalfe, both in Trumpington Street, and James Hodson in Trinity Street, printer of the *Cambridge Chronicle*.

> I have just now began another work for a Bookseller at Cambridge, (on Latin Versification), and saw, at the same time, a Greek work for Cambridge, now doing at Davison's. On expressing my surprize to the Bookseller that works so particularly appropriate to the University Press, should absolutely pass the door, & come to London, just to go back again, I find there is so great a prejudice against the manner in which works are got up through the press there that even this circuitous route is preferred.[83]

Hansard continued to print for the Cambridge booksellers, reporting in 1830 that he was engaged in printing for W. P. Grant[84] and had in hand J. B. Francoeur's *Course of pure mathematics*, translated by Ralph Blakelock of St Catharine's, J. M. F. Wright's *Cambridge tutor*, and the first three sections of Newton's *Principia*, edited by Wright. Grant also used the former University Printer, Richard Watts, and, indeed, seems to have had an aversion to the University Press for the elementary aids in which he specialised.[85] In 1823 he had translations of Tacitus' *Germania* and *Agricola* printed in Bedford, and in 1824 he used J. G. Barnard, in London, for a *Literal translation of the twenty-first book of Livy*. Of the local printers, the most important proved to be Metcalfe, who installed a lithographic press on which the Press called from time to time, and who offered a local alternative for book printing: the edition of Shelley's *Adonais* produced by a group of admirers in 1829, and set from the Pisa edition of 1821, was his most celebrated, but by no means his only, work.

The root of the matter, implied or explicit in these several practices or observations about the Press's printing and selling operations alike, was that Cambridge remained separate from London. The Press was not immune from the difficulties faced by publishers and booksellers in the 1820s, aggravated by the bank crisis of December 1825, that came to all too clear a head in 1826 with the collapse of Archibald Constable in Edinburgh and Hurst and Robinson in London. The trade's confidence in itself was deeply unsettled.[86] It depended on trust, and on credit; and as Charles Knight recorded in his autobiography, these were replaced temporarily by suspicions: by gossip that this or that publisher was about to collapse also.[87] The Cambridge press was little affected directly: the number of new books in which it was involved was small; and the Bible and prayer book trades were sufficiently independent. But the crisis did prompt self-examination, from which emerged a series of changes that lasted for several generations. One result of the lack of adequate communication between the London trade and the Cambridge printers was that by the mid-1820s there were serious overstocks of some editions of the Bible. Those whose advice the Syndics sought were divided as to whether or not Cambridge should employ a special superintendent in London. Rivington, the publisher, and Hansard and Gilbert, both printers, all believed that such a person should reside principally in London, so as to be in constant communication with the established London agents. Others thought he should be in Cambridge. Behind these considerations lay two themes: first, whether or not the University Press should move towards closer involvement in London publishing; and second, a gradual realisation that too much was expected of the University Printer. All the Syndics' advisers were agreed that Smith should be employed exclusively in the printing department.[88] The corollary, that the Press should therefore be divided between its printing activities and its publishing activities, was worked out over the following decade.

With the rapid expansion of the University in the early nineteenth century, changes in the Cambridge mathematical tradition, a generation of classical scholars labouring on editorial projects in the wake of Porson, the establishment of the new classical tripos in 1824, an increase in demand for private coaching, and a recovered seriousness in preparation for ordination to the Anglican priesthood (to which large numbers of undergraduates aspired with more or less enthusiasm), there was a definable and ready market. It was this market that the Deightons addressed: one with strong local connections and interests, but that would also appeal to like-minded readers elsewhere. By the early 1830s, they listed almost 150 works in their catalogue.[89] Editions of the classics included not only the work of Scholefield, Dobree and Kidd, but also that of Gaisford and Thomas Arnold from Oxford. Much, including most of the sermon literature, was locally produced; but multi-volume editions of Immanuel Bekker's Plato (published in London), Kiessling's Theocritus (published jointly with Whittaker, in London), of William Paley, and of Jeremy Taylor (Deightons held only a modest share in this, for which London booksellers dominated) represented projects where they had a smaller interest. Deightons also offered helps to Paley's *Evidences*, to writing Greek verse, to the oriental languages necessary to understanding the Bible, and to studying the Gospels (specifically 'designed for the use of Students at the University, and candidates for Holy Orders'). They were the publisher or part-publisher not only of the most used local guidebook, but also of illustrations of Cambridge, of Dyer's *History* of the University, of the *Transactions* of the Cambridge Philosophical Society, of the University calendar, and of C. H. Hartshorne on the book rarities of the University. In the sciences, they handled Airy's astronomical observations at the new observatory and Whewell's works on mechanics and dynamics, as well as a long list of elementary or intermediate textbooks on mathematics – mostly designed specifically for the mathematical tripos. Whewell's *Architectural notes on German churches, with remarks on the origin of gothic architecture* was uncharacteristic of the Deightons' list in its subject, but his connection with the firm was well established by 1830, the year of its publication.

Though the Deightons published much of this on their own account, or as the major partners, other books in their list depended more on other publishers. The *Encyclopaedia metropolitana*, announced for publication in the early 1830s, and dominated by contributors either from or having close connections with Cambridge, was, as its title suggests, principally a London venture: Deighton had only a part interest. Dyer's history of the University (1814) was published with Longman's and with Sherwood, Neely & Jones, both in London; Hartshorne's *Book rarities* (1829) was published with Longman; Monk's *Life* of Bentley (1830) was published with Rivington; Whewell's works on mechanics and on dynamics were published jointly with Whittaker, and his *Architectural notes on German churches* with Longman. Horne's catalogue of the library of Queens' College (1827) had been printed for the College, and Deighton simply owned some stock. By no means all were printed at the University Press, though in the case of those books by local authors there was a strong practical incentive for this to be so.

Conversely, the Press sometimes printed the work of local authors who were published in London. Cadell and Davies paid for the printing of the first edition of Clarke's *Travels* in 1810; and Blomfield's translation of Matthiae's Greek grammar in 1819 was printed for John Murray, who also took the lead in publishing the *Museum Criticum* and who shared with Mawman Blomfield's *Persae* of 1814. For most books the Press depended directly or indirectly on London booksellers, and on none more than Mawman and Rivington. In the case of Porson's *Adversaria* (1812), Mawman took about 90 per cent of the copies.[90] London publishers were treated quite differently from local Cambridge booksellers. They subscribed for large numbers, in parcels counted in units of not less than fifty. Returns were allowed only if there had been a mistake. As a result, the Press was secure of a return (either as a promissory note not infrequently of as much as ten months or, more rarely, in cash drawn on a bank) immediately after publication. On the other hand, the Cambridge booksellers could both subscribe initially, and buy subsequently in small quantities, as sales demanded, from the Press's remaining stock.

One effect, which exercised the Press continuously, was that it was meeting warehouse costs even for books whose production costs had been met from outside, or that the Syndics had not financed. This was a problem common to other parts of the printing trade. So, too, was the system of credit that allowed long delays in payment for quite large sums. For much of Smith's term of office the annual accounts showed outstanding credit notes of 40 to 50 per cent above the sums actually received in any one year. The largest creditor was Rivington, whose debts totalled 60 or 70 per cent of the total of credit due: Mawman and Baldwin in London, and Deighton in Cambridge, represented much smaller amounts.[91] But the more serious result of all these arrangements, most of them survivals from the eighteenth century, was that the Press remained in isolation. Its preoccupation with privileged printing, with work for Deighton (and, to a much lesser degree, other Cambridge booksellers such as Nicholson or Stevenson), and with printing for the University and colleges, meant that there was little space for other work.

The death in 1827 of Joseph Mawman, who had served the Syndics well as London agent and on whom much of the publishing success of the Greek dramatists had depended, brought matters to a head. Among those who offered themselves was the publisher and bookseller William Pickering, later to be well known for his editions of the classics of English literature.[92] Instead, the Syndics broke with a longstanding tradition, and chose a printer rather than a bookseller. After a period when they had been frequently reminded of their need for Hansard's expertise, it was easily explained. With a new press under construction, and ever expanding demand, they sought refuge with one of the largest London printers of all, William Clowes. Not surprisingly, Clowes himself was unable to undertake the work in person, so instead he appointed his principal assistant, John William Parker, 'an intelligent Man, and an exceedingly good Printer, matured by an experience from his infancy in my office, and having had sole management of the whole of my establishment for the last 15 years'.[93] Parker quickly proved his worth; but the matter had still to be properly worked out. Yet further anxiety came in 1831 over the position of Rivington as the Bible agent, and the threat that the SPCK, to whom the Press had sold Bibles since the mid-eighteenth century, might become a publisher in its own right. The thrust for this proposal had little to do with commerce, and much to do with religion. 'The state of the Christian Knowledge Society . . . is the most miserable of our miseries', wrote J. H. Newman to a correspondent in March 1834.[94] To another, on the following day, he explained: 'As to the Christian Knowledge Society, do you not know the melancholy plight in which it is in? The Evangelicals, taking advantage of the distracted state of the Church, are making a push to get their way in it – and the Bishop of London and Tyler, are temporizing, conceding ½ way, and so making matters clear for their ultimate triumph.'[95] Anxieties over the Rivingtons' cash-flow, on which the Press depended so critically, meant that Cambridge watched the position with attention part ecclesiastical and part commercial. Successive members of the Rivington family had been publishers and booksellers to the SPCK since 1765, when John Rivington had succeeded Benjamin Dod. But the sympathies of the latest generation were with Newman and Oxford, not with evangelicals or those who, as Newman scornfully put it, 'call themselves Churchmen and speak in a sentimental way about the Church yet call any man a papist who begins to act as if he loved it'.[96] The Rivingtons' connection with the Society came to an end in 1835.[97]

But by then Parker had left Clowes, and had in 1832 established his own bookselling and publishing firm in the Strand, retaining at the same time his position at Cambridge. In the same year, he obtained the agreement of Cambridge that he should be a repository for the sale of its Bibles and prayer books; and soon his name was appearing as publisher on other Cambridge books as well.[98] Among the earliest was Adam Sedgwick's *Discourse on the studies of the University*. Henceforth, Cambridge books were to be handled by a London bookseller who, though no less committed to theology, preferred to remain less subject to religious enthusiasm. His list was soon replete with theology, and he was appointed bookseller to the SPCK in place of Rivington, in an arrangement that was incidentally designed to save money;[99] but he had none of Rivington's dedication to an ecclesiastical cause. In large measure, he owed his position, and his success as a London publisher, to the arguments of others; but he also owed them to connections that linked Cambridge to London in social ways as well: to people like William Otter, of Jesus College, biographer of Edward Daniel Clarke, who in 1830 was appointed Principal of King's College, and who was a leading figure in the publishing activities of the SPCK.

Though much of the achievement of Smith, Hansard and Parker at Cambridge was the result of comparisons with London practices, the Press's most obvious competitor – both in a real sense and in the eyes of those for whom the two universities were forever linked – was Oxford. The two presses, more in sympathy with each other than with the King's Printers (though all three were in competition with Samuel Bagster and with Charles Brightly in Suffolk), frequently consulted and collaborated on the prices of the privileged books; and they had a common difficulty in the threat posed to this market by piracies. The more enlightened of the Vice-Chancellors did much to promote such links. Attacks on the accuracy of their texts were met jointly, and particularly successfully, in the face of ill-considered charges in 1832 and more publicly in 1833 by Thomas Curtis, as spokesman for a group of dissenters, that recently printed Bibles were in error because they did not accord exactly with the text of 1611. As was easily pointed out, this text was itself inconsistent.[100] In the contemporary climate of hopes for reform, this particular dispute was, at base, as much about the status of dissenters at Oxford and Cambridge as about the text of the Bible.[101]

None could deny that in the Bible and prayer book market at least the two university presses were in competition. When in 1820 enquiries were made of booksellers in York, Derby and London as to whether they would be interested in becoming agents for Cambridge Bibles, there was much caution. Wilson in York, Mozley in Derby and Whittaker in London all declined, Whittaker explicitly giving as his reason the fact that his firm already acted as Oxford's.[102] At the most simple level, the production figures for Bible printing by Cambridge, Oxford and the King's Printers gave no room for complacency in Trumpington Street. The figures supplied in 1832 by these several printers to the House of Commons Committee appointed to enquire into the King's Printer's patents revealed to the world that during the 1820s Oxford had easily the lion's share of privileged printing, producing three times more than the number of Bibles, New Testaments and prayer books produced at Cambridge: sometimes the discrepancy was even greater. Where Cambridge had once, for a short while, dominated as supplier to the Bible Society, it was now supplying significantly less than the King's Printers.[103]

Smith, defending his position in this and in matters more generally, was able to offer many reasons for this relative decline in importance despite the constant investment in the Press; and much that he remarked was straightforward. But in being called to answer his critics he took the argument into lesser parts of the business, and more secular books:

> In reference to the Compositors department I beg to observe, that many of the works brought to the Press are in the most unprepared state possible: such, I believe, that few Master Printers of the Metropolis would receive. The consequence is, that when proof sheets are sent to the respective Authors, the work is much cut up, & subject to continued over-runnings & Corrections – the Compositors time being in many instances chiefly taken up in effecting repeated Alterations: – so much so, that had the same Volume been printed from Copy duly prepared, the work would have issued from the Press in less than half the time. The practice, I believe, with London Printers is to have the whole of the MS delivered to them at the commencement of the Volume – or at least a considerable portion

of it – & further, an understanding on the part of the Author that when the book is once begun, he will not interrupt its progress. But with the greater part of the works brought to the University Press it is *unavoidably* the reverse. The Authors, for the most part, being Gentlemen of the University, engaged with Pupils during Term-time, furnish their Copy in detail – loosely written – & frequent suspensions of MS., which necessarily occasions great delay and inconvenience. – It is true, that there have been exceptions to this state of MS. supplied to the Printer; and this abundantly proves that the Compositors employed on works of this description can dispatch a Volume with the same expedition as if printed elsewhere. I will cite one or two instances: 1. M^r. Benson's Hulsean Lectures – The Copy of this Volume (1822) was delivered to the Press about the *second week* in *November*, and the work published on the *24th of December* following. – 2. The *Milton MS.* (with all its intricacies) was done at the rate of *five* and sometimes *six* Sheets per week . . . – 3. To this I may add, the work printed last Spring for the Master of Trinity, a closely-printed octavo – in Small Pica & Long Primer, with Minion Notes. The Master's defence of the *Icon Basiliké* passed through the University Press with as much expedition as if it had been printed in Town: D^r. W. attending immediately to his Proof Sheet, & making but few alterations, received, while the work was in progress, 15 new proofs in the course of 14 days.[104]

Smith was too selective to be convincing. Charles Sumner's edition of the newly dis-covered manuscript of Milton's *De doctrina Christiana*, found among the state papers, had been a notable event. Its editor and translator, at least in name, was the King's protégé and librarian; and the King himself selected the University Press. Sumner had been educated at Trinity, and the choice was perhaps at his suggestion. A new large fount of type had been obtained from William Miller in Edinburgh.[105] Rather than trust to a transcript, the manuscript itself had been used as setting copy, protected under glass: the difficulties both in handling this arrangement and in figuring out the text were acknowledged in a premium for composition charges. There were unusually many proofs, but not only because of the difficulty of the copy. Since Sumner was at Windsor, and the University Press could not provide an overseer to check that proof corrections had been made, the publisher of the work, Charles Knight, arranged for the sheets to be seen through the press by W. S. Walker, a young Fellow of Trinity. Walker took upon himself much more than the task of supervision, and revised and improved Sumner's translation.[106] Three copies were printed on vellum.[107] The project had indeed been carried through fast (Knight later recalled that both the Latin and English versions had been completed in a year[108]), but the circumstances were peculiar. As for Wordsworth's rapidly printed pamphlet on the *Eikon Basilike*, the compositors had the advantage of an author no distance from the Press, and one whose forceful and difficult character encouraged speed. The details of such projects, presented in self-defence by Smith, were justifiable in themselves; but they were scarcely typical, and they obscured the main issues: that the Press, like the book trade more generally, was at a turning point; and (ostensibly remarked by Smith only in passing, though it was of central importance) that if it was to succeed it must be in direct competition with London.

By 1832, Smith had been relieved of much of the strategic management of the Press, and it was Parker who faced the House of Commons Committee. On 25 October 1836, four years later, the Syndics accepted Smith's resignation on grounds of ill-health.[109]

How profitable was the Press in Smith's hands? Hansard and Parker constantly compared its working with the printers and booksellers of London. The real interest in Cambridge was somewhat different. This was a part of the University, and its most important source of income: investments yielded little, and legacies were unpredictable. There was no doubt that the amount of Press business, in the sense of administration, increased substantially. In November 1824 the Syndics, who had hitherto met somewhat haphazardly and intermittently, agreed that they would henceforth meet fortnightly during term.[110] According to Smith himself, the nature of the Press's business was also changed. After the lean years of his predecessor, when the introduction of stereotyping brought exceptional costs, the University could in most years look at a surplus of between 10 and 20 per cent, though the audited University accounts ignored much of Smith's daily work. Again according to Smith, writing in 1829, only one year during his term of office showed a deficit, and in most years there was a comfortable surplus – weakened in 1820–2 by the inconvenience (the term was his) of printing the Family Bible. The audited receipts (which included the drawback on paper) told a somewhat less reassuring story. In 1801–3 they were less than £5,000 per annum, a figure that climbed rapidly following the introduction of stereotype printing for the Bible and prayer book, and the receipt of large orders for the Bible Society in the second half of the first decade of the century. By 1810–11 income totalled £14,302; and in the following year, the Press now fully in Smith's hands, it leapt to £23,363. In 1814–15 it peaked at £31,472. This was not to be exceeded until 1833–4 and the last years of Smith's term of office; for many of the intervening years, until the late 1820s, it was only about half this figure.[111] All these figures were obviously subject to the varying costs of raw materials and of labour: paper costs decreased, while rates of pay increased during this period. But the anxieties of the Syndics, and the continuing warnings from Parker especially once he was formally attached to the Press, had some justification. Income rose, and so did the Press's expenditure. Between 1830–1 and 1834–5, the average annual surplus was about £2,520; but in the years each side, 1829–30 and 1835–6 there was a deficit – of nearly £3,000 in the latter year.[112] The question was not simply one concerning the management of the Press. For the University, the income from its operation was of critical importance; and at a time when the rebuilding and extension of the University Library was under discussion, the affairs of the Press came under particular scrutiny. George Peacock, in Trinity, who was deeply involved in Cockerell's ambitious proposals for the new Library, reminded the world in 1830 that the University's disposable capital was no more than £13,000, but that it was anticipated that the annual excess would soon be increased, by the 'increased activities and capabilities of the Public Press, the trading profits of which form the great source of income for the University'.[113] Seen in this light – and there can have been few to whom the care of the University was entrusted who did not see it thus – the affairs of the Press directly affected the well-being of the University as a place of teaching and research, and its ability to develop the lecture-rooms, laboratories, library facilities and museums which became of ever more pressing need. Peacock's hopes of increased Press surpluses proved false. Indeed, the sums provided by the Press, and their inadequacy to meet the construction and investment needs of the University as a whole during the 1830s, serve as a barometer of interest which came to look on the Press less as a means by which to publish work emanating from the University, than as a printing house in which the operative motive was profit. Parker was appointed in 1829 to introduce more efficient working; he was also, both explicitly and by implication, appointed to make money.

Though it was usually able to show a surplus, however modest, for the University, the activities of the Press were in fact limited. The affairs of the first years of the century, when the University had invested heavily in two largely untried innovations, Stanhope's new presses and the modern stereotype process, were warning enough against the kind of speculative investment by which the Press might have prospered. And since money could only be raised either by sales or by internal loans, the Press was in practice prevented from financing large projects, even within the confines of the University's annual budget. It was a commercial publisher, A. J. Valpy, who issued E. H. Barker's new edition of Henri Estienne's *Thesaurus Graecae linguae* in thirteen folio volumes between 1816 and 1828. It was another commercial publisher, Samuel Bagster, who with the help of Samuel Lee, Professor of Arabic and then of Hebrew at Cambridge, issued a succession of large-scale and increasingly ambitious polyglot Bibles from 1822 onwards, and who realised the possibilities of using the same stereotyped settings of different versions and parts of the Bible for several different editions.[114]

Yet a further accusation could also be levelled at the Press: that as a publisher it was not populist enough – not in the sense of appealing to a popular (and therefore extra-university) market, but in that it allowed other publishers to reap easy rewards. As Deighton well realised, but as other local booksellers such as W. P. Grant and T. Stevenson also saw, the market for undergraduate textbooks was well established, and depended on a comparatively restricted list; by the early 1830s it was also helped by the increasing needs of the new University of London, many of whose teaching staff were graduates of Cambridge. With the aid of bookseller-publishers such as the Rivingtons, Whittaker or Simpkin in London, Cambridge-printed textbooks proved to be readily marketable, especially in mathematics. On the other hand, the reasons why the achievements in classical literature were not sustained were more complex. Julius Hare had his own views:

> True, it has much to contend against: the cares and anxieties of political life, – the imperious calls of business, – the pursuit of mammon, from which, when once engaged therein, it is almost impossible to fly, and in which we are borne along every moment more rapidly and more irresistibly, – the ever encroaching intrusions of frivolous society, – the palsying fascination of a frivolous literature, – the vanity that debases us into the slaves of these and so many other tyrants, – all these and a number of other causes are in full action to withdraw us from the calm and quiet groves where we might repose under the shade of antiquity.[115]

Scholarship and mammon might seem incompatible, and education under threat from frivolity. But in a generation that saw the University Press become a major printing house for some of the largest of the London publishers, the vehicle by which an increasing stream of books by Cambridge authors flowed into the national and international book trade, some compromise was necessary. In the end, Smith's defeat was seen as one of finance, and though there were many other difficulties there was much truth in this. Throughout the book trade, and by no means only in Cambridge, under-investment had been endemic for generations. In the first two decades of the nineteenth century the University had invested heavily in equipment, for little financial return, considerable renown, and ultimately at a loss. How far the University, with Smith's successor John Parker, was able to discover a better path, will be discussed in the following chapter.

✎ 16 ✐

John Parker: London publisher and Cambridge printer

By the early 1830s, the book trade had changed in innumerable ways. Smith, who had been with the Press since the beginning of the century, could count as not the least of his achievements that he had seen so much adapted to new needs and opportunities, and perhaps in particular the successful removal to the new premises. But Parker, the younger man, had the energy and the knowledge to carry the process forward, and he gradually superseded Smith. In giving evidence to the enquiry in 1832 into the King's Printer's patents, Parker was clear:

> Now the book trade is undergoing a great revolution at this moment; the publication of the Monthly Libraries, and things of that kind, is destroying the value of the stock books in a great degree.[1]

The connection between a learned press, engaged principally in printing the Bible, the prayer book, classical texts and works of mathematics, and the monthly libraries of general literature issued by London publishers of quite a different hue, might appear to be remote. The immediate context of Parker's remarks was Gibbon's *History of the decline and fall of the Roman empire*, whose copyright had elapsed in 1804 and which had since then been much reprinted.[2] It had been the joint property of William Strahan and Thomas Cadell, who had thereby shared both the risks of printing and the profits of sale. Parker's point was that such 'stock' books, of which the copyright was held by several booksellers and publishers, had value both in themselves and in the sale value that a share might command. The rise not only of the monthly libraries of which he complained, but also, and for the Press more significantly, of publishers such as Murray or Pickering who expected to act on their own,[3] increased the element of risk, but could mean better attention to publicity and sales. As a London bookseller, Parker kicked against the pricks of an old-fashioned system whose complications, set out in confusing detail on title-pages, served to muddle possible customers.[4] In a spirit of independence, in 1834 he offered to purchase, for immediate cash payment, the whole of a forthcoming edition of the Greek New Testament, so as to relieve the Syndics of the task of selling it piecemeal through their usual agents. His letter extolled the advantages to be gained from dealing with a single customer, and

> which necessarily result from the whole impression of a book being in the hands and under the control of an individual, (whose interests are connected with his good management)

as compared with the principle of making the stock equally accessible to various persons, who, from the very nature of such an arrangement, have no direct interest or responsibility, beyond the supply of their own immediate connections. In the one case the book remains comparatively unknown, and inaccessible to a large proportion both of the trade and of the public, while the slower sale and lengthened credit materially diminish the amount of the returns; in the other, there is a motive to make the book well known, and to return the capital invested – the means of so doing depends, of course upon the business power and trade machinery enjoyed by the holder of the stock.[5]

From that, it was a short step to the single commissioning publisher whose kind came to dominate the market for the Press and the rest of the trade alike.

Parker's reforming hand already reached out at the internal organisation of the Press. At his suggestion, the employment in the printing house of children under the age of twelve was ended in 1836.[6] When he looked at the older staff, he found inefficiency, 'a habit of acting as if they considered a situation in the University Press, as one of mere ease and irresponsibility', and that this was especially prevalent among those who had been at the Press longest.[7] However undesirable such an attitude was in itself, the galling effect was to delay work unnecessarily. Unlike anyone so closely concerned with the Press since the seventeenth century, Parker looked on its affairs from the point of view of a London bookseller, not from the point of view of a printer. It was this insight that caused him to make a suggestion that was, in its way, outrageous. Hansard had been disappointed not to be chosen to manage the Press, and he was a printer. Parker, a bookseller but trained as a printer, now put himself forward as University Printer, to replace the aged and infirm Smith. The London connection was of paramount importance, and he submitted the question,

> whether the office of responsible Printer, may not, with advantage, be combined with those duties which are at present entrusted to me – wherein some of the most important interests of the Press are involved – which are as unavoidably transacted in London as the operations of printing are carried on at Cambridge – and upon which the management at Cambridge has so important an influence in producing a profitable result or otherwise? Doubtless such a transaction would impart to the commercial affairs transacted in London, a degree of certainty and of regularity, which would be attended with profitable results, while, at the same time, a more active, efficient, and responsible Establishment than the University has hitherto possessed, would be organized, and kept in a state of activity, to meet its current business.[8]

Parker was elected Printer on 16 November 1836. Within the Press itself, the elderly James Twitchett, overseer since 1807, put his own name forward, and placed on record his long service to the Syndics.[9] But in the final round Parker's opponent was the local printer William Metcalfe. As both men issued handbills appealing for support (Metcalfe's was a lithographed circular), the affair was not just a formality. The choice between a London publisher and a local printer of fifteen years' standing was a distinct one, though experience of the University Press weighed heavily in favour of Parker.[10]

His term of office as University Printer, almost two decades in which the printing and publishing trade expanded throughout the country, was marked by a singular lack of enthusiasm in Cambridge for publishing, and only intermittent enthusiasm for printing. Much of the reason for this lay in the choice of a man in Parker's position: preoccupied with a successful London business, and little interested in promoting or exploiting the University Press. Furthermore, the vacuum remained that had allowed Deighton to flourish as the principal local publisher; it also encouraged outsiders to look to Cambridge, notably the Macmillan brothers and the firm of Rivington. The University as a whole benefited from the interests of these publishers; the University Press became the despair of those who would have preferred to see more investment of time and energy in its well-being.

Parker was right. Without London, the Press could not survive. The University Press had never sought to be the only publisher in Cambridge. The advent towards the end of the eighteenth century of the Government Annuity Fund, and thus of money which could be invested in publishing, had changed the position very substantially, and had been well exploited by several interests for a generation. But in the 1830s there was still no innate expectation that the University Press should also pursue more than a somewhat desultory activity as a publisher in its own right – and that much circum-scribed by the immediate demands of the University itself. In retrospect, the Syndics' failure to build up a more active role might be easily criticised. But at the time there were many reasons against it. Profits, if any, were taken from the Press and put to other University purposes when other University income was small. Capital expenditure on the Press itself was great: on buildings, on presses, on other equipment. The collapse in the early 1840s of demand for Bibles, Testaments and prayer books printed at Cambridge, as the trade passed to Oxford, the Queen's Printers, and, increasingly, to other printers again – in Scotland especially – reduced the Press to a state where there was little to spare and, perhaps in this respect more importantly, little will to muster the requisite energy to take a fresh line.

The arrival of Daniel and Alexander Macmillan(figs 30a and 30b) in Cambridge in 1843 was of vital and lasting importance to the University as a whole. They figure repeatedly in the following pages, as their activities became entwined with those of the University Press. But before them there were others in Cambridge who were prepared to risk capital, and to publish authors who lived only yards from their front doors. J. and J. J. Deighton were the best known, their list of recent books in 1843 including Dobree's *Adversaria*, lectures on modern history by William Smyth, Regius Professor of the subject, Peacock on algebra, works on calculus, and eight books by Whewell including the sixth edition of his *Elementary treatise on mechanics*, the fourth of his *Mechanical Euclid*, and the third of his *Architectural notes on German churches*, as well as a reminder of current ecclesiastical debate in J. M. Neale's novel *Ayton Priory*.[11] The list of W. P. Grant was more restricted, dominated by classical texts, with notes and translations, and other undergraduate aids – to Paley's *Evidences*, to Newton's *Principia*, to Greek metre, to mathematics – but also including a few aimed at the higher forms of schools.[12] That of John Hall, more limited still, likewise offered help to Paley, as well as to Butler's *Analogy of religion*, and specimen answers to Senate House

Fig. 30a Alexander Macmillan. From a
photograph by D. G. Rejlander, taken in
the 1860s.

Fig. 30b Daniel Macmillan. After a
painting by Lowes Dickinson.

examinations in the New Testament and mathematics.[13] Occasionally these smaller booksellers advertised nationally in the specialist press; but their books were unambitious: modestly printed and for a market that was principally a local one – and intentionally so. The Deightons, and later the Macmillans, sought the world beyond Cambridge, and it is with them that comparisons with the University Press were to be made.

More than most of his predecessors, and certainly more than his authors, Parker was a businessman, alert to costs that were sometimes too much ignored. Shortly after he became Vice-Chancellor, William Whewell, so much of whose work had been printed at the Press, and partly published by Parker, received a letter of protest from Parker, who may well have chosen this moment to couch criticisms of an author in a way that, appealing to the well-being of the University, might seem less personally wounding:

> I venture to call your attention to certain customs which prevail in respect to business done at this Press, whereby much loss of the time of persons employed is occasioned, and gentlemen having the business done are frequently put to unnecessary expence.
>
> 1. As to sending for persons, whose time is somewhat costly, to receive directions, though frequently on business of very trifling amount, and requiring such persons to take proofs, when printed. It frequently happens that calls for these purposes are made over & over again before the parties can be met with.
>
> All the real requirements of most cases of this kind, would be fully answered, if a few lines of written directions were enclosed with the MS to be printed, to the Acting Printer, who might be directed to send proofs under cover, and these could be returned for Press, with directions as to the number to be printed, paper, mode of delivery of copies, &c &c. In cases of Examination Papers, or other private matters, all possible secrecy would be ensured by the packets being marked '*Private*'.
>
> 2. As to commencing works which are but in part ready for the press, and feeding the press with copy in small and irregular supplies. Much costly time is wasted, and much valuable material neutralized, by this practice. If gentlemen were charged with all the waste of time & property thus caused they would be greatly surprised at the amount – when it is not charged, a serious loss is inflicted upon the Press. Generally speaking, there is very little practical advantage in beginning to print before a work is sufficiently prepared to keep it going at the rate agreed upon – but when this cannot be done, it is highly desirable for the Press, that the work should be suspended, in order that copy may accumulate, and in the meanwhile both hands and material would be disposeable for other business.
>
> 3. As to the necessity of giving precise directions, in cases of Examination Papers, and other business comprehended under the general term of *job-work*. In want of such directions, it sometimes happens that papers extend to a greater number of pages than have been contemplated by the employer. The expence caused by an error of this kind may be large in proportion to the amount of the job, but it is incurred before the error can be known, and the fair adjustment of it may be difficult. Occasionally, when part of a second page has been occupied, a question has been started as to whether the matter should not have been got into one, or whether the whole, or only the printed portion, of the second page was chargeable. A still greater difficulty has been when exceeding two pages (though making a portion of a third) a job has been charged as *four* pages. Now, by the universal custom of the Printing trade, both man and master are justified in the same charge for a

short page as for a whole one, of the work of which it forms a part, and whenever a job exceeds two pages it is chargeable as four. This custom has all the force of a law in the printing trade, but whenever it is desirable & possible to avoid it by compression of the matter, the printer is always ready to do so, provided he receives previous directions, and a discretion is left him as to making the pages larger.

Trusting you will excuse my troubling you with these technical details . . . [14]

The quirks and demands of authors accustomed to getting their own way in other matters were to be ended. The Press, as printers, was to set the pace, and customary trade practice was to rule. Such an agenda in effect mounted a challenge to Cambridge authors. A new managerial spirit was at large; and in part it was to succeed. The staff of the Press had gradually increased. Parker's deputy in Cambridge for many years, and the person therefore most familiar to local authors, was Thomas Malcom. The composing rooms and press rooms were each in charge of a salaried overseer, each of whom had an assistant. Rather than rely, almost informally, on members of the University, which seems to have been the practice in the eighteenth century, the Press now employed salaried readers, helped by reading boys, to check proofs.[15] The new printing house provided three reading closets, well lit and above the main entrance, as well as another separate room.[16] The numbers of compositors and pressmen varied according to the amount of work in hand, as had always been the case; but in the warehouse the increasing quantities of stock, and the practice of pressing paper, brought an increase in staff there. In the foundry, stereotype plates had to be repaired by skilled hands. Paper had still to be wetted, and in the late 1830s cost 3 guineas a week for the process. The Press's clerk was paid a salary of 3 guineas per week, and had an assistant. In other words, even as the numbers of men directly employed on the central tasks of composition and printing increased, so the numbers of those employed to support them grew likewise.[17]

Most importantly, the introduction of machinery for printing was overdue. According to one of its employees, the Cambridge press was one of the last large printers not to install machine presses.[18] Both Hansard and Parker had long recognised the need, but for different reasons. Hansard, of a slightly earlier generation, believed in them because they offered a chance to be free of the wage demands of pressmen.[19] Parker made a point of keeping himself abreast of developments, and he made clear that as Printer he would introduce machinery.[20] Within a few weeks of his appointment he was asked to obtain estimates for the costs of an engine and four presses, and for the costs of installing them.[21] Some at least were at work by July 1839, in a room equipped specially.[22] At the time, the principal justification for such investment was in the demand for Bibles and prayer books. Eight machines were finally introduced, though not without some changes and difficulty: in 1841, Mr Beales, in a neighbouring property, complained of damage to his premises alleged to have been caused by the rumbling and shaking of the new steam engine that ran the presses and other equipment.[23]

The most popular and reliable machine press available was the Napier double-feeder, which by the time that the Syndics came to consider the matter had been in use in the trade for seven or eight years: a number had been installed at Oxford in about

1837. It was ideally suited to the Press's needs, capable of delivering high quality work from a flat forme of type.[24] But Parker seems, somewhat ambitiously, first to have installed cylinder presses. They had a short life, for in April 1843 he obtained the Syndics' agreement to dispose of one of them, replacing it with two flat-bed presses; then in 1845 the Syndics agreed to sell three further cylinder presses, and to replace them with four flat-beds.[25] Each press required several men and boys to run it: to place paper, to adjust ink, to set pressure, to take off paper, etc. Each was in the charge of an identified individual, though these named men did not remain necessarily with the same machine.[26] The principles of running such equipment had become well established by the end of the 1830s, and were akin to the mixture of adult and boy labour described by Hansard for another of Napier's machines in the mid-1820s.

> Another man of more intelligence acts as foreman, or overlooker, whose business it is to attend generally to the machine and workers, place the paper by tokens on the supplying board, and take away the printed sheets from the other end: a little boy performs the business of the layer-on, but which requires very considerable precision, as the rapidity of the machine will be interrupted if his attention is in the least degree diverted; if any corner should be doubled, or otherwise require particular time for placing, he will be obliged either to throw it to one side, or to cry out "halt," and the machine must stop; it is, therefore, very necessary that the paper should previously have been turned and pressed and laid very even.[27]

Though it was sought to give the impression that the Press was working to the full, and in constant demand, this was in practice unusual; and by the latter years of Parker's term of office it had become rare. By 1840, that is shortly after the installation of a steam engine and printing machinery, the Press had a staff of about 150. At this time there were about thirty Columbian presses.[28] The Syndics' ambitions had, however, outrun the trade. A depression in publishing in 1842 drastically reduced demand on printing houses, and the University Press was left with expensive equipment for which a use had to be found.[29] In 1844, lack of work, and the consequent waste of time and money, became a matter of serious concern to the Syndics, who considered proposals to print editions of historical works so as to occupy men and equipment. The resulting list, though valuable in some respects as a survey of some of the books regarded as more important either to the history of the university or to its study of theology and ecclesiastical history, was disappointing. It included three dozen biographies of figures from Grosseteste to Simon Patrick, authors from the seventeenth century including Pearson, Stillingfleet, Twysden and Willet, and various documentary collections. Deliberately, it was composed wholly of reprints, and this only a few months after the Macmillans had opened their bookshop in Cambridge. Its purpose was primarily to occupy the presses, not to suggest an ambitious programme of publication.[30] Little came of the scheme, and meanwhile business temporarily recovered. When by 1849 the Press's surplus had become seriously depleted it was agreed to reduce wages.[31] The number of the presses in use at any one time, and the amount of work accomplished on each press during a week, both varied. Men and boys were engaged or laid off as necessary, just as the size of the composition department expanded or contracted according to need. The needs were in large measure seasonal, the autumn being more active, and the midsummer months distinctly less so. Work proceeded simultaneously at two or sometimes more presses on the same book (so considerably reducing the number of weeks required for printing), and with all eight machine presses in use it was not unknown in the mid-1840s to achieve a total of 200 perfected reams in a week: the more normal output was between 150 and 200, each press producing the equivalent of up to 25 reams. Individually, press-crews with straightforward jobs, involving little changeover time, could achieve higher figures. In autumn 1846, working on an edition of 10,000 copies of a nonpareil Bible, one crew managed 30 reams in a single week, and others occasionally managed the same for mixed work. In February 1847, a single machine printed 35 reams of a brevier New Testament in a week. But these were maxima, and unusual: so far as it is accurate to use the term in a period of considerable change for the University Press, 20 to 23 reams per week were more usual.[32]

Hansard, whose advice lurked for years behind the running of the printing house, had in 1825 warned of the care with which work had to be managed for machines, so that they were used to best advantage. As in other manufactures, the expense of investment, and the need for returns on it, brought a new emphasis on the value of time. Those who worked the machines were paid piecework;[33] but they served machines whose cost could be measured as a relationship of cash outlay to cash recovery. All the more important, therefore, that work was apportioned between hand-press and machine press in the most economical manner possible, and that sufficient work was found to feed machines' demands.

> After all, in the great variety of forms, and qualities of work passing through any printing-office, recourse must still be had to the aid of good manual presses and experienced pressmen. The serious expense of a printing-machine can only be repaid by executing an extraordinary quantity of work in a much less portion of time than that usually occupied for the same work done by ordinary means. As, therefore, the time consumed in laying-on, or making ready a forme, must be valuable in proportion to the number of sheets which might be struck off in that time; so, frequent repetition of the previous process for short numbers would counterbalance all gains arising from the speed in working. Machine printing will therefore be only applicable to works of extensive scale.[34]

The timing of the introduction of printing machines at Cambridge, though overdue in the eyes of several observers, proved to be unfortunate. It was essential to re-equip the Press, not only with steam presses but also with a cylinder rolling-press to flatten the sheets, replacing (or rather, supplementing) the old standing cold press.[35] Equipment no longer required was sold off. Bacon's experimental press, unused for many years, was finally discarded by the Syndics in 1846 – at the same meeting that agreed the purchase of two new hydraulic presses for paper. Two years later, it was agreed to dispose of up to a dozen under-used Columbian hand-presses.[36]

The new equipment involved major capital expenditure. According to the Syndics' own figures, the number of Bibles printed in 1840 was four times the number printed a decade earlier, and that of New Testaments increased in almost the same proportion. A list of Bibles, prayer books and associated extracts such as Psalters and altar services prepared for the trade in 1839 offered 129 different editions or varieties, in sheets.[37] But in 1839 the Bible trade was thrown into confusion when, after prolonged argument, licences were granted to print the Bible in Scotland.[38] John Childs of Bungay, who had been criticised in 1832 for his remarks to the House of Commons on the cost of Bible printing, claimed that by the end of 1840 the price asked by Scottish printers was 25 per cent less than had been asked by English monopolists. The 'lucrative but precarious' patent[39] even for Spottiswoode, as Queen's Printer, was all the more endangered in the case of Cambridge, as the weakest of the three English patentees. Demand for Cambridge-printed Bibles collapsed, even though the Press responded with a cheap product offered at first one shilling and then tenpence – less than half the previous lowest price. By 1844, with the price of the cheapest Bible at tenpence, only 38,000 Bibles were printed during the year, less than one-fifth the output of the peak year, 1840. By 1850 the figure had fallen lower still, to 31,000. New Testaments, of which it was generally reckoned to sell more, reached 243,000 in 1840; and in 1850 only 35,000 were produced. Production figures for the prayer book slumped by 1849 and 1850 to 1,000 and 3,000 respectively.[40] Though the effects of the loosening of Scottish printing were by no means confined to the northern parts of Britain, the Syndics remarked in particular the effect on sales in the north of England, and on the activities of the various societies.

The initiative for printing the privileged books drifted away, to Oxford, to the Queen's Printers, and to Scottish printers, while a large part of that market was also seized by the firm of Bagster. By the mid-1850s, Bagster's imaginative use of stereotyping, his aggressive marketing skills, and his recognition that by becoming identified as a supplier of Bibles and prayer books he could also gain as publisher of introductions, interpretations, histories and illustrations relating to them, earned for him a place that the ancient privileged presses found impossible to contain. His books were generally considered to be more expensive than those from the privileged printers; but he concentrated on bookshops rather than on distribution through the various societies, and so disproved the opinion of many in the book trade: that demand in bookshops for Bibles was so negligible as to be unprofitable.[41] On their traditional, and legally defined, ground, he challenged the privileged presses directly, with pocket editions of the New Testament, while his diglot editions of the Bible, in English with accompanying German, French, Italian, Spanish or Portuguese, were aimed partly at the cosmopolitan immigrant market.[42] Disinclined to compete, or even to consider it, the Cambridge press not only missed opportunities through lack of imagination, but was also forced into retreat.

Apart from the Bible and prayer book, the Press depended principally on two markets: in mathematics and in theology. The Government Annuity Fund was used towards this end, and regularly in printing the reports of the Cambridge Observatory. The importance attached in the University to the study of mathematics created a demand for textbooks some of which achieved a life of their own independent of Cambridge; but many were directed primarily at the University's own examinations. One of the most industrious contributors was John Hind, of Sidney Sussex College, whose books on arithmetic, arithmetical algebra, trigonometry and differential calculus, all 'designed for the use of students in the University' were handled not only by the several Cambridge booksellers – Deighton, Stevenson, Newby, Hall, Johnson and Hutt – but also by Talboys in Oxford and by Whittaker and by Fellowes in London. Others brought French work to the attention of the University. L. B. Francoeur's *Principles of hydrostatics* was published in Cambridge in 1830, by John Hall, its unfamiliarity leavened by an explanation of the metric system as well as the older *toise*, *pied* and *pouce*. In Gonville and Caius College, Robert Murphy's *Elementary principles of the theories of electricity, heat and molecular actions* (1833), likewise addressed to Cambridge undergraduates, took its cue from Whewell, and built on the work of Poisson, Ampère and Fourier. In Queens', Philip Kelland essayed his own *Theory of heat* (1837) in the light of Ampère and others. In St John's, Charles Whitley translated Poinsot on rotary motion, supplementing his work 'in the hope of rendering this publication useful to Students in the University': as Reader in Natural Philosophy at Durham, as well as Fellow of St John's College, Cambridge, he did not specify his university, but the colophon bore the booksellers' names only of Newby in Cambridge, and Simpkin and Marshall, in London. W. H. Miller, later Professor of Mineralogy, on hydrostatics, 1831, and William N. Griffin (also of St John's) on optics, 1838, both went into second editions within four years, handled jointly by Deighton in Cambridge and by Whittaker or Rivington in London. More ambitiously, the *Cambridge Mathematical Journal*, published from November 1837 by Elijah Johnson and in London by Whittaker (later it was taken over by Macmillan), essayed both to meet local needs for the Senate House examinations and to present new foreign work besides local research.

Not all these books, and others like them, were printed by the University Press. William Metcalfe, at this time in St Mary's Street, became an accomplished book printer, and John Hall, near Pembroke College, though less skilled, was a competitor almost opposite the Pitt Press itself. With a bookshop as well as printing equipment, Hall also developed a list of books intended for undergraduates preparing for the Senate House examinations – classical and early Christian texts, works on the history of the church, and a successful work on arithmetic and algebra by a private crammer, Henry Pix.[43] For so long as Smith, and then Parker, were able to keep the equipment of the University Press fully, or at least adequately, employed, local competition of this kind mattered little: the real competitors were the printers in London, and Deighton could be relied on to continue to provide a succession of publications in Cambridge itself.

London publishers rarely sought to have their work printed in Cambridge. There was no reason why, not linked by the umbilical cord of Deighton, or enticed by the promise of a subvention, or obliged by the personal demands of a Whewell, they should look to Cambridge as a printer in the 1830s any more than they might have done in the eighteenth century. Murray published Christopher Wordsworth's *Athens and Attica*, with illustrations by C. R. Cockerell; but that it was printed by Parker in 1836 was the result of Wordsworth's strong local connections: he was appointed Public Orator that year, and had been a Fellow of Trinity since 1830. In similar fashion, Parker came to be responsible for printing the work of another Fellow of Trinity, Robert Pashley's *Travels in Crete*, published in the same year. One of the most ambitiously illustrated travel books of its generation, it was an unusual commission for the Press. The wood-engravings of the scenery and antiquities, which have captured the eyes of readers ever since, were the work of Samuel Williams, whose fee of £93.10s. was over and above that of the sum of £195 paid to meet the salary and travelling expenses of the artist. The minor engravings, chiefly of the coins, were by Dodd, who was paid £20.5s.6d.[44]

The Press contributed substantially to the cost of printing Pashley's work, so leaving Murray with little more than the tasks of publicity and distribution: because Pashley held much of the stock, it was lost when fire destroyed his rooms in the Temple in 1838.[45] For their printing, the two books had many requirements in common, including Greek inscriptional type and full-page lithographs – prepared in each case by Louis Haghe, partner in the firm of Day and Haghe, successors to Rowney and Forster, in London.[46]

Only one other book to come from the Press in these years was more self-conscious than Pashley's in its decoration and illustration. C. H. Hartshorne's *Salopia antiqua*[47] was the work of an author better remembered in Cambridge for his account of the *Book rarities in the University of Cambridge*, published by Longman in 1829. Once again, Day and Haghe were responsible for lithographs; and the book was given an air of antiquarianism quite unusual in Cambridge printing, by the introduction of black-letter headings, floral ornaments, and woodcuts derived from or suggested by decorative initials in medieval manuscripts. An alphabet of further decorative woodcut initials was used for chapter openings. It lacked the vigour, but the style was closer to that of William Pickering.[48] The book itself was published by Parker, not by the Press.

Though Parker was the Cambridge agent, his list, one of the largest among London publishers, was not by any means confined to Cambridge-printed books. He was, however, at an advantage in that his appointment gave him privileged access to a printing house, thus allowing the possibility of establishing the kind of familiar relationship between publisher and printer to be seen in other parts of the early Victorian book trade, such as between Pickering, Whittingham and the Chiswick Press, or Moxon and Bradbury & Evans.

In the 1840s, with new machines in place and requiring long runs for economical operation, the work presented to the University Press for printing was divided into two: that which could be done on the iron hand-presses, and that which was suitable for the machines. For editions of up to between 1,000 and 2,000 copies, as well as for the multitude of orders for jobbing work and pamphlets, the hand-presses were preferred. Most books were printed in editions of a thousand copies or less, so the hand-presses remained of central importance, worked as an integral part of a business in which machinery became an alternative, not a wholesale displacement of old methods.

The withdrawal of protection against rival Scottish printers of the privileged books coincided, to the Press's relief, with the first months of the contract to print for the newly formed Parker Society, whose first volumes were finished in 1841. As a result, the machines were used mostly for the privileged books, and to meet the requirements of this society.[49] Named after Archbishop Matthew Parker, the Society was founded in

1840 chiefly through the efforts of George Stokes, whose skills and energies as an historical populariser had hitherto found their main outlet in the Religious Tract Society.[50] The Parker Society was a pronouncedly Anglican, and in some respects evangelical, rejoinder to projects such as the Library of the Fathers published by Rivington in London and J. H. Parker in Oxford, and prepared under the auspices of the Tractarians: the first volume, Pusey's edition of Augustine's *Confessions*, had appeared two years previously. In a parallel contribution, the Library of Anglo-Catholic Theology, likewise published by J. H. Parker, issued its first volume in 1841.[51] The urgency with which Pusey and Newman pursued their cause had its effect.

So far as possible, the Cambridge press, like the Oxford press,[52] remained apart from most of these arguments. But as a business it was not immune to the effects of ecclesiastical differences. The contract to print for the Parker Society brought much-needed relief to the University Press, which in 1843 invested in 3,000 lb of small pica type to meet its needs.[53] With a vigorous publication programme designed to bring into print, at a rate of several volumes a year, the principal authors and documents of the English Reformation, the Society quickly attracted 7,000 members, requiring commensurately large editions. The Society's overall printing bill for books in 1844 was £3,996; in 1845, £3,555; in 1846, £3,877.[54] The University Press found its machines ensured of work, and for some years the Parker Society's publications, with the privileged books, dominated the machine room. But from the first the Society had intended that its activities should be wound up once the books it identified had been completed. Although initial plans were modified, the series was concluded, after fifty-five volumes, in 1855, with an expression of satisfaction that returned to its first inspiration: 'It is a curious fact, that the Parker Society publications alarmed the Roman Catholics of this country, and induced them – so it was stated in a prospectus – to establish a counter-society for reprinting the works of Romish writers against whom the reformers had contended. A few volumes were issued; but the plan met with little support, and it is believed was soon given up.' The Parker Society's final report hinted at editorial difficulties, but also alluded to a falling-off in interest:

> If the Society has not accomplished all that it designed, if it has left untouched the works of some valuable authors, if it has in one or two cases been unable to comprehend in its volumes the whole of the writings of divines it undertook to re-print, the Council, though it may feel some regret, cannot express surprise. Such publications could not be of a popular character. Those who were acquainted with the authors of that date knew that their language was frequently uncouth, their learning ponderous and of a scholastic cast, their matter for the most part controversial, and that, in short, they lacked much, from the very fact of their belonging to another age, of that which gives currency to modern literature, even modern theological literature. It was no matter of surprise, therefore, that some of the subscribers expressed a degree of disappointment when the Parker Society volumes began to appear, that men accustomed to the current style of the present day could not bring themselves to grapple with the solid, perhaps heavy, productions of the elder divines. The very cheapness, too, of the Society's publications, multiplying them so rapidly upon subscribers' shelves, was not without its influence.[55]

These avoided the one issue of which no member of the society could have been unaware. Newman's conversion to Rome, and his resigning his fellowship at Oriel College, had brought, in the words of Mark Pattison, a sense throughout the country that the past agitation had been extinguished.[56] It was 'a deliverance from the nightmare which had oppressed Oxford for fifteen years . . . Probably there was no period of our history during which, I do not say science and learning, but the ordinary study of the classics was so profitless or at so low an ebb as during the period of the Tractarian controversy.'[57]

Quite apart from embarrassments over shelf-space, or the theological contrast between sixteenth- and nineteenth-century Anglicanism, or difficulties with sixteenth-century English style, there were lessons for publishing here as well. In important respects, the country as a whole had by the mid-1850s lost its taste for the zeal and fanaticism with which theological argument had been pursued a decade or two previously. In pursuit of its interests, the Parker Society had set a low subscription, but it had flooded the market, and induced a kind of indigestion. Unlike ordinary publishers, who held stock until it was demanded (reprinting as necessary, if feasible), the society had released editions of up to 7,000 copies of books most of which would, even in the most optimistic of ordinary publishing views, have taken several years – or even a generation and more – to sell out. The editions were too large, and the nature of their distribution forced a pace under which the market collapsed once it was no longer enforced by subscription, or supported by the fervour of potential schism.

Apart from the Society, and apart from J. W. Parker, other customers began to figure in the ledgers. Within a short time in the early 1840s, the Press established itself as a printer of examination papers for schools including Sedburgh, Bury St Edmunds, King Edward's Birmingham, the City of London School, Manchester Grammar, and Rochester Proprietary School. Rugby, Eton, Oakham, Uppingham and Blackheath Proprietary School quickly followed. The needs of such schools could be extensive. While Rugby in the summer of 1845 required only eight papers, Leeds Grammar School had 50 copies of papers printed in each of thirty-two separate subjects.[58] The Cambridge Camden Society, taking advantage of the postal system to mount a campaign that depended not only on books, but also on a multitude of brief pamphlets, was one of the Press's most frequent customers during its short life. The Cambridge Antiquarian Society, more local in its interests, provided further work, joining that of the now well established Cambridge Philosophical Society. The edition sizes for most of these books and pamphlets was not great. Even in 1854 the *Transactions* of the Cambridge Philosophical Society was still only printed in an edition of 250 copies; and the annual order for volumes of observations from the University Observatory remained for many years at 211 copies.

When in 1852 the Syndics were called on to answer the investigations of the University Commissioners led by John Graham, Bishop of Chester, they cited the need to protect their interests as ordinary members of the printing and publishing trade as reason to provide only partial details of their affairs.[59] Facts were selected accordingly. There was no difficulty about the equipment owned by the Press. The eight printing machines were said to require about fifty men and boys to manage them; there were hand presses sufficient to employ fifty-six pressmen – presumably twenty-eight in all; and there was space for seventy compositors. Such a staff would have placed the University Press among the very largest in the country.[60] The steam engine, boilers, hot presses and other equipment might occupy just over another hundred men and boys, and ware-housing afforded further employment. The impression that the Syndics wished to give was of a large and busy establishment. But the final sentences of their return to the Commissioners was equivocal:

> The University Press is equal to the execution of a large amount of business; and it need scarcely be added that the annual profits derived from it depend upon the extent to which its capabilities are called into action.[61]

The commissioners, who apart from Graham, former Master of Christ's College, included George Peacock of Trinity, Lowndean Professor of Astronomy and Dean of Ely, Sir John Herschel of St John's and Adam Sedgwick, Vice-Master of Trinity and Professor of Geology, all well informed independently concerning the true position, phrased their report accordingly, warning of the dangers to the Press consequent on the end of the former restriction on Bible printing, and on the 'want of the commer-cial element in the administration of the Press.'[62]

The Press remained acutely under-employed. When the new printing machines had been installed, there had, despite some anxieties, been ample work for them. The Parker Society, together with reduced work on privileged books, continued to ensure that they were fully engaged. By the time the Society published its later volumes, it no longer required editions of 7,500, but of half that figure or less: even the correspon-dence of Matthew Parker himself commanded an edition of no more than 3,750. The large editions for which the machines were best suited had become exceptions, and by the early 1850s it became normal for editions of as small as 1,000 to be placed on the machine presses. Still smaller ones were not unknown, and the new edition of the University statutes, printed by machine in 1852, consisted of only 350 copies. Whereas in the mid-1840s the usual weekly output of the machine presses varied between 150 and 200 reams, the second half of 1853 saw output often less than 50 reams per week, and only three presses at work. In the first half of 1854 it sank to as little as 35 in a week, and only rose above 100 for a few weeks in the summer. Output per machine dropped as well, and by early 1853 it was in some cases as little as 10 or 11 reams per week.[63] Paper size apart, this was less than could be comfortably achieved at a hand-press by two rather than about six employees. Presses lay idle, only three being in use for much of the later part of 1853, and four or five through the summer of 1854.

In 1829, Parker had been expected to introduce a more efficient management, and so to increase the income deriving from the Press to the University. His appointment as University Printer, seven years later, implied similar expectations from the University, when it sorely needed such an increase. In this, Parker's term of office proved a dis-appointment. So far from producing a surplus, the Press showed a loss in 1837–8,

1838–9, 1840–1 and 1848–9.[64] In the context of University finances, this decline was not so much unhelpful, as dangerous. Summarising the overall position in 1841, George Peacock provided a rough estimate: annual income including that from estates at about £1,400, from fees at about £2,000, and from the press ('of very uncertain amount') totalled about £5,500. Given necessary expenditure (not met from other sources) amounting to almost £4,500, the small excess was insufficient to meet public obligations, lawsuits and, most seriously, the urgent need for buildings.

> The necessary consequence of this very inadequate income and great expenditure has been the entire dissipation of the funded property of the university; and during the last year (a precedent full of danger to the highest interests of the university), the appropriation of funds raised for specific purposes (the supply of books to the library), to meet the engagements of the university.[65]

Many sought to explain the reasons for the great difficulties of the University Press. At a period when the printing trade and the publishing trade in the country at large were expanding vigorously, the Press was contracting. In a building specially designated for the Press, some of the best rooms were taken up by bequests of works of art, and by lecture rooms for teaching mineralogy and history.

But it is also necessary to recall Peacock's view of the office of Vice-Chancellor, 'the chief and almost the sole administrative officer of the university, all others being placed under his immediate direction and control'. The University Printer was answerable to him, yet he had no special expertise other than his own experience, and no regular informed advice other than what might be specially sought out from consultants such as Hansard or the London agents. He also chaired the Press Syndicate.

> A necessary consequence of this accumulation of duties upon one person is the neglect or incompetent performance of many of them; for it can rarely happen that this important office can be filled by a person who possesses such an intimate knowledge of the laws and customs of the university, such varied scholarship and learning, such a perfect mastery of the details of business, and such unwearied industry and activity, as to be able to meet the demands which are made upon him by such severe and distracting labours: and we consequently find, when the reins of our academical government are intrusted to hands which are not sufficiently experienced and vigorous to guide them, that the progress of important measures is stopped or retarded, the finances neglected or mismanaged, and the general interests of the university very seriously and permanently injured.[66]

Peacock had no doubt that the Press Syndicate – like other parts of the University – required reform, and pointed out that it consisted (in 1841) of fourteen heads of house, three professors (Divinity, Civil Law and Greek), and the principal Librarian, together with some others 'altogether non-resident': 'It obviously requires to be completely reconstructed.'[67] Inactivity due to old age; want of zeal or aptitude; negligence and indifference; too long exercise of power: these were the terms that came to Peacock's mind as he reflected on a system that embodied a conservatism and lack of skill and imagination of the very worst sort. In the context of a book trade where competition, profit and the exploitation of investments were essential for success, the Press was placed in an impossible difficulty. It was to be some years, and a Royal Commission, before the Press Syndicate was to be reformed, to be replaced with one more flexible and attuned to the business and commerce of printing and of publishing.

Peacock, Fellow of Trinity College, saw the difficulties as an internal university matter. However, the inadequacies of university management were but one part of the difficulty, compounding those over which the University itself had little direct control. When in the late 1830s discussions were afoot to reform the regulations for printing the Bible and other privileged books, they took place in a context that had seen the Scottish Bible trade already restricted. The Bible Society and other societies, anxious to introduce cheap Bibles into Scotland, had been unable to do so because the cheap editions formerly available from Cambridge, Oxford and the Queen's Printers were excluded from a market now the preserve of the Queen's Printers in Scotland – who preserved high prices. Scottish hopes in 1837–8 were for more competition, to drive down prices of what was then privileged printing in Scotland.[68] None of the witnesses called before the committees of enquiry on the subject of Bible printing in Scotland spoke for Cambridge; and what in the eyes of some was to have been an opportunity for competition became a disaster for Cambridge, the worse because its coming seems to have been insufficiently pondered. In 1837, the University Press was more concerned with a specially printed Bible prepared at the wish of the King.[69] The recommendation placed before Parliament, 'that the people of Scotland should have the free introduction of Bibles and Testaments from the presses of the Universities of Oxford and Cambridge, and from Her Majesty's Printers in England and Ireland', so that these books should be more cheaply available, paved the way for cheaper Bibles. But the likely effects on the English privileged presses, once competition was so increased, and which might easily have been deduced from the evidence heard a few months previously, were seriously misjudged. In the summer of 1839, a few months after the publication of the report, the University Press had installed machine presses in an investment whose profits were at first to be short-lived.

In three years during the 1840s the University's cash surplus was below £1,000. In such circumstances there was no question of the Syndics or the University investing further, by borrowing capital. Parker, ever ready to invest in new equipment quite apart from the constant need to replace worn type, reckoned that it would need between £8,000 and £10,000, for new type, for new and larger machines, and for further steam power – all barely more than a decade after the initial investment. Even then, and assuming, very optimistically, that Bible and prayer book business could be won back from Oxford and from the Queen's Printers, the returns would be slow. The stereotype plates used for Cambridge Bibles had become worn, and such Bibles as were now printed were from standing type.[70] The other presses had standing type too, for virtually all editions of the privileged books that were in demand. The investment in type alone was prodigious and, for Cambridge, hardly practical. The alternative was a contracted Press, part of it held in suspension against better times.[71] In May 1849, faced with the insuperable difficulties in the Bible trade, the Syndics decided to put the Press on a reduced footing, and the establishment was reorganised accordingly.[72]

By 1853, in the wake of the Graham Commission, Francis Bashforth, Fellow of St John's, was able to remark that 'the proceeds of the Press now scarcely amount to £900 a year'.[73] There was an obvious comparison with Oxford where, as at least one critic, the ever-alert Robert Potts, was eager to remind his readers, the recent Royal Commission had revealed a University profiting very clearly from the Press's activities. Much of the surplus at Oxford derived from privileged printing,[74] of which it was acknowledged Cambridge had a much smaller share; but much, too, derived from the Press's more general activities. The Oxford press had enjoyed this healthy financial position only for relatively few years: both Oxford and Cambridge had invested in buildings at about the same period.

There were many weaknesses at Cambridge, both in the Syndics, who were inadequately informed and (to many) seemed untroubled by their ignorance, and in the agreement with Parker. Trained as a printer, and appointed University Printer for the sake of these skills, the publishing and bookselling business he established in London seemed at first to offer a further advantage: a route to London booksellers without the complications that previous generations had experienced with London agents. Parker had an interest in selling Cambridge-printed books, as his investments. By 1850, his catalogue contained well over two hundred works printed at Cambridge, from sermons and pamphlets to multiple-volume sets.[75] Yet there were difficulties. From the first, he had shown himself independently minded. So long as this served the interests of the Press, and the Syndics, this was an asset: it was impossible to dispute the justice of his complaints at Whewell and others who treated the Press without consideration of possible wasteful expense. In later years at least, it was his practice to visit Cambridge every alternate week, travelling down on Thursday and returning to London on Saturday:[76] thus he was able to coincide with the meetings of the Syndics. Everyday matters were placed in the hands of trusted deputies – in London as well as in Cambridge.[77] But as his London business thrived, so his interest in Cambridge waned – and waned ever more as he found the Syndics slow to respond to some of the suggestions he put forward for improvements. In 1843 he declined to have anything further to do with Deighton, with whom he had collaborated to publish Whewell, among others: the fact that the two men continued to publish books jointly did not hide the distance between them.[78]

The Graham Commission noticed his detached approach; and the chance to withdraw altogether from Cambridge a few months later seems to have come as a relief.[79] In 1852, Parker was preoccupied with the so-called bookselling question, a complicated series of arguments respecting underselling, discounts and cheap literature. With John Chapman, he took a leading part in promoting underselling, and in May that year published letters from a hundred authors to support this cause (in opposition to most booksellers). In an astutely conducted campaign, those in favour of underselling won the day; and much of this was due to Parker.[80] It is little wonder that the Graham Commissioners that summer found his attention not greatly concentrated on the lesser question of a printing house in Cambridge. It was impossible to be both printer in

Cambridge and bookseller in London, and particularly so when both printing and bookselling required commitment and initiative in a world of free competition. The University Press, cocooned in its eighteenth-century constitution and assumptions, had not yet properly faced a changed world.

Though most members of the University were ignorant of the scale of the Press's difficulties, sufficient was publicly known to cause comment. The Graham Commissioners' recommendation was clear, and the more interesting because, coming from a body of people so many of whom had private local knowledge, it was arrived at not with explicit advice from the book trade but as a result of reflection on local opinion, and local circumstances.

> It is only by associating printers or publishers in some species of copartnership with the University, or by leasing the Press to them, that any considerable return can hereafter be expected from the capital which has been invested in it . . .
> We venture rather to suggest this scheme than recommend it, for we are fully aware of the difficulties which must attend any plan for the satisfactory arrangement of this establishment; but we are satisfied that no Syndicate, however active and well chosen, can replace the intelligent and vigilant superintendence of those whose fortune in life is dependent upon its success; and that in the absence of this essential element of vitality, it will not be long able to maintain its ground against other establishments which possess similar privileges, without labouring under similar defects of administration.[81]

The Syndics' most vociferous critic was Francis Bashforth, of St John's College. He had little direct knowledge, but his response to the Graham Commission's report (printed not at the Press itself but by a jobbing printer, in Market Hill) appealed for a last attempt. The University was faced with a business which, in itself, was difficult to justify. Apart from jobbing printing (examination papers figured regularly in discussions about the Press's future), most printing was for others; and it produced no profit for the University. The investment in plant of the previous thirty years was underemployed, and was under-performing.

The Commissioners' recommendation that the University should enter into some form of co-partnership for the Press was a practical one that the more experienced and thoughtful members both of the University and of the book trade found worth consideration. Bashforth spoiled a useful pamphlet otherwise concerned with the management of the University Library by intemperate and ill-considered remarks about the Press. He laboured with insufficient knowledge: 'the business matters of the Cambridge University Press could scarcely be kept with greater secrecy, if they were the private affairs of the Syndics'.[82] He was also quick to offer opinions, not only on how the true position at Cambridge should be evaluated, but on the future as well:

> As respects the future, it seems to be unadvisable to run the risks of entering into a partnership as has been done at Oxford, and more especially as they are now increasing their interest in the business by purchase. Neither is it desirable to sell or lease the premises, because from the example of Oxford, there is every reason to hope that judicious management is alone required to restore the prosperity of former days. A sufficient motive for

exertion might be expected to be imparted to officers of the Press, who held desirable posts, if it was made known that a thorough casting up of the profit and loss of every year must take place, and that the University would not persist in attempting to carry on the business, unless, on a fair trial, there appeared every probability of a return being received sufficient to yield a moderate profit on the capital invested. If the prosperity became great, there would be every reason for rewarding liberally the officers, whose exertions had been instrumental in bringing about that result.[83]

Yet, following the Graham Commission, and once the principle had been agreed, the Syndics took little time in arranging for a partnership to be established. A committee was appointed to look into the subject in February 1854. The Syndics made their recommendations in May. As they admitted, they had been inspired by an arrangement agreed for the Oxford press the previous year: the partnership documents eventually drawn up for Cambridge made extensive use of the Oxford equivalent. With Parker's advice, and in acknowledging the difficulties inherent in his conflicts of interest, the Syndics recommended a bookseller and a printer. The bookseller was George Seeley, partner in Messrs Seeley of Fleet Street (a firm with whom the Macmillans were well acquainted). The printer, on Seeley's suggestion, was Charles John Clay, who had graduated from Trinity College in 1850 and who was now with his father, Richard Clay, in Bread Street Hill. The University authorised an agreement without delay, and the deeds of partnership were signed on 18 July.[84]

Though the Syndics were clearly determined, and Parker may have been privately relieved, in practice the break was much less rapid, and was to be marked by ill-feeling especially between Parker and the much younger Clay. More importantly in the long term, the attempt to mark a clearer division of the activities of the Press, by establishing two bank accounts – one for the partnership, and one for the Syndics[85] – was a reflection of one of the principal sources of tension that had its origins in the eighteenth century. The Press had always been both printer and publisher, as printer serving several masters yet pretending to serve only one, the University. For Parker's successor, Clay, the clear distinction between his private interests and his duties to the University meant that the Press could become a successful general book printer at a time when its publishing interests sank still further.

In the absence of reliable and consistent figures, it is not straightforward to measure how much the book trade had expanded. By the trade's own count, the number of books, excluding pamphlets, published in 1839–42 was 8,597. A decade later, in 1849–52, the equivalent figure was 13,119. Quite apart from pamphlets, these left out many books from smaller publishers, those not having regular connections with the London trade, and those published outside the ordinary circles of the book trade. They also omitted new editions. But the trend was clear to everyone.[86]

Why then did the Press, with under-used equipment, not find greater favour as a printer for London publishers? One or two books apart, its regular customers for book printing were Parker himself, Deighton, Macmillan, and the Parker Society. By the early 1850s, Bible and prayer-book printing took up relatively little space. With easy access by rail to London, transport no longer presented the challenge that it had in the eighteenth century. London publishers, with growing lists and eager to exploit markets across the world, made unprecedented demands on the printing trade; yet Cambridge had scarcely any part in this. To a very great extent the reasons were personal, and grew from an inward-looking university and its acolytes among the local book trade. Parker was content to fit into such an established view, and for many years he exploited it to his advantage by emphasising his connection and obtaining printing at low rates. There had been other Cambridge agents – and, indeed, there were others among his contemporaries even in London: but none was also University Printer. The Macmillans, with no such institutional attachment though with much closer links spun into a web of friendships and acquaintance both in Cambridge itself and in the wider orbit of its graduates, turned naturally to the local printer, and seem to have obtained favourable rates. With Alexander Macmillan's decision to move to London, taking most of the publishing with him, the connection was to become slightly looser. By then, however, the Press was in the hands of C. J. Clay, and by all estimates in better ones.

It might seem that the question of where to print – in London or Cambridge – was most difficult for Parker, as he built up a list in London far larger than the handful of titles published under the auspices of the Syndics in Cambridge. In fact he used the Cambridge press relatively little, preferring to keep most of his work with London firms. The reasons for this are complicated; but, as for previous generations, they had much to do with the convenience of authors.

It is usually difficult to recover comparative costs among different printers. Though there were agreed trade rates for composition,[87] details of practice varied. Machining costs varied. In face of increasing demands, especially for cheaper makes, the quality of paper varied. As one writer had put it, succinctly, as long ago as 1829, 'Our modern books and manuscripts are in a state of the most rapid decay. The greater part of them will not outlive half a century; many of them not half that period.'[88] The great increase in cheap publications during the 1840s placed still greater strains on machinery and resources. Many of the disputes with the Bible Society were over paper quality. Naturally, some printers were known to be more expensive than others; but much of this was hearsay, or based on experience of which no written record survives. Publishers did not normally bother to keep estimates that were of no importance to the way in which a book was finally manufactured.

In 1854, as the Syndics considered their experience with Parker, and moved towards a partnership agreement, William Whewell raised this question, one of the most fundamental of all. He addressed it to James Cartmell, Master of Christ's College, who though he was not Vice-Chancellor that year was generally – and accurately – considered to be the member of the University most effectively in command of a complex situation. Whewell's *Elements of morality* had been originally published in 1845, and a new edition was called for.

> When I requested Mr Parker to obtain an estimate from a London printer of the expense of printing a new edition of my Morality, I did so, mainly from a wish that the Syndics should have the London price before them. As an author, I have nothing directly to do with the payment of the printer: that falls on the Publisher who undertakes the work. If it

be true that the work of printing can be done cheaper in London, which I understand Mr Parker to assert, I can only insist on the printing being done at Cambridge, by taking upon myself the difference, and making Cambridge printing a condition of the bargain. This in the case of the Morality I am willing to do; but it is not likely that authors in general will do so. Nor would it be proper, I conceive, that the Univ[y] Press should print for me on lower terms than for other persons. What the grounds are of the lower estimate of the London printers, I do not know. Certainly their printing does not appear to be so good as ours. But perhaps some explanation of this may be obtained which may be of use to the Syndics. Mr Parker having superintended the Univ[y] Press, of course has his own view of the ground of the difference. According to my recollection, he has always said that there was such a difference – though I am willing to stipulate with Mr Parker that he should finish this book at the Univ[y] Press, I could not hold out the expectation that I should make the same stipulation in any further publication.[89]

Wage rates among printers in Cambridge were appreciably higher than in any other town except Oxford and some London houses.[90] It was not simply a question of costs in Cambridge relative to those in London. As Clay soon discovered on looking over past records, Macmillan had generally been charged slightly less than Deighton both for printing and for pressing.[91] But Parker's situation was more perplexing, and his attitude to printing costs at the Press naturally changed once he became simply a publisher seeking to have work printed. Whewell's complaint could not be ignored; and in the hands of C. J. Clay, Parker's successor as University Printer, it became a weapon wherewith to confirm his position. The London printer from whom Parker had obtained a quotation significantly cheaper than that from the Pitt Press was Savill and Edwards, of Chandos Street, only a few yards from his premises, who was said to have quoted £2.17s.6d. per sheet against Clay's £3.4s.6d.[92] Having established his own price for Cambridge, Clay now sought out comparative figures from major book printers in London: Clowes, William Rivington, Woodfall and Kinder, Whittingham, Stewart & Murray, and Levey, Robson & Franklyn. Faced with a specimen sheet and asked what a publisher might prudently be charged for setting and printing a thousand copies, all were agreed: that to do so below £3 a sheet would be to court a loss, while the highest estimate was from Levey, Robson & Franklyn, at £3.12s.[93]

As a true means of comparison between different printing houses, such figures were grossly over-simplified. The internal costs of printing a book could by the mid-nineteenth century no longer be calculated under the heads of composition, presswork and paper. An informal note at the back of one of the Press's prizing books (that is, the ledgers in which were recorded the costs of manufacture) set out the various elements to be considered:

> composition; correction; presswork; paper; pressing; binding; extras; posting the title [an accounting charge, normally 5s.6d. per book at this date]; wrappers; postages; woodcuts; electroplates; labels; stereotyping and plates; prospectus.[94]

There were other minor charges as well, since paper had to be damped;[95] and the cost of reading proof is not included here. In 1860, C. J. Clay emphasised the difference between taking a sheet off the end of a machine, folding it and sending it away, as might be done in a cheap house, with simple work, and the way in which the University Press expected to treat work (in this case a Bible, though the practice was the same for other books) once it had been printed:

> this book has to be hung up carefully to dry, and then taken into our warehouse. The sheets are all laid down in succession, and then gathered, and afterwards collated one by one, to see that every sheet is in the book; it is well and thoroughly pressed; and it is then packed in special bales, a certain number in each bale, with printed labels attached before it is ready for delivery. Now all these expenses are very considerable; the expenses of ware-housing bear a very large proportion of our wages paid weekly. The expense of the labour employed in getting up these books after they leave the machine-room is very great.[96]

For estimating purposes, a sum had also to be included for overheads and profit. But though simplified, the figures gathered from the London printers who were asked the cost per sheet of printing Whewell's work established clearly one source of the difficulties that Parker's successor, C. J. Clay, faced when he took over in the summer of 1854.

Disgruntled, Parker accepted the Press's figure for Whewell's book; but the episode brought his connection with Cambridge to an end. He removed all his business from the Press in the late summer of 1854, withdrawing even some work that was only partly completed. By searching back into past charges, Clay and his father, one of the most experienced of all London printers, discovered the nub of the awkwardnesses over charges to Parker for printing, among the several other difficulties facing the Press at this time. Richard Clay explained the position to Cartmell:

> I have no intention to mix myself up with Mr. Parker on the subject of the management of the Pitt Press; but the examination of the foregoing Estimate naturally led me to the consideration of others; and I feel bound to say that I have come to the conclusion, that one of the causes of the unproductiveness of the Pitt Press has been the exceedingly low rate at which Mr Parker's own works have been executed.[97]

His inspection suggested that Parker had paid at rates 10 to 20 per cent, or even more, below those charged for other publications.

Publicly, Parker's reasoning was straightforward; and once he no longer had any responsibility as University Printer, answerable to the Syndics, he finally spoke out. By now he was speaking in self-defence; and he was less than convincing. He also seized on the protection of a man who, being dead, could no longer speak for himself. Deighton's estate when he died in 1854 had revealed the extent to which he had depended on long-term credit,[98] a situation tolerated at Cambridge more than in London and emanating from longstanding custom when dealing with members of the University: the risks had been pointed out specifically by Hare to the Macmillans when they established themselves at Cambridge, and they were assumed to be endemic.[99] Much of Parker's jealousy of Deighton had derived from the fact that whereas, for historical reaons, Deighton had paid the Press by a series of credit notes set at future dates, Parker, the newcomer, claimed always to have paid cash.

> The system has been a beneficial one to the Press, notwithstanding even the present doubt-
> ful state of the late Mr. Deighton's affairs – To myself it has been the reverse of either
> advantageous or convenient – Had the slightest hint of dissatisfaction on the part of the
> Press been given, I should have been but too glad to have availed myself of it, and to
> remove my printing to London, where I could have had it done – as I am now doing – at
> lower rates than I paid the University Press.[100]

It was certainly true that the Press was generous in its allowance of credit: at the end
of 1849, it was discovered that one customer had still not paid for work done in 1831.
Parker had forgotten that the same investigation had found his own debts to the Press
dated in part from two years previously.[101]

The Clays, increasingly irritated by Parker's attitude, and with both a reputation in
London to protect and a position in Cambridge to prove, satisfied themselves that while
printing in London might be available more cheaply, the better book printing houses
quoted figures comparable with those that should be charged at Cambridge. For them,
the question was not what had happened in the past; but how the University Press could
be made profitable in the future.

In the course of the autumn of 1854, suspicions were voiced as to the nature of the
printer from whom Parker had obtained allegedly so low a price. But Savill and
Edwards were straightforward, and Parker used them often. Among their work for him
in the next few months were the 1856 volumes of *Cambridge essays* and *Oxford essays*.
Though he and the Syndics had parted, on far from amicable terms, his list of books as
publisher retained its Cambridge connections. The advertisement sheets in the volume
of *Cambridge essays* for 1856 included notices of a third edition of Whewell's *History
of the inductive sciences*, a second of Robert Willis's *Principles of mechanism* and a cheap
one of E. H. Browne's *Exposition of the thirty-nine articles*. Other titles included
Sedgwick and Frederick McCoy on British palaeozoic rocks, and Trench on the
Gospels, while of the nine contributors to the 1856 volume of *Cambridge essays* six,
including H. J. S. Maine, John Grote and F. J. A. Hort, could be described as fellows
of various colleges. As in Macmillan's list, such books mingled with other subjects,
Parker's ranging from Stirling on Spanish art to Palgrave's and Froude's works on
British history, to works on shipwrecks, as well as C. M. Yonge's *The daisy chain* (published in 1856) and Charles Kingsley's *Hypatia* (1853; cheap edition 1856). While no-
one suggested that novels should be a part of the University Press's list, there was a
discernible pattern in much of this. Like the Macmillans, Parker profited from the
Syndics' difficulties, and he continued to do so after his departure.

As University Printer, Parker had presided over changes in the printing house and
in relations with London publishers. The book trade faced expectations of a scale and
of a nature for which it was obliged to alter many of its established practices, whether
in the specifications of book design and materials or in the management of money or
in distribution. Authors both acquired a new status, and yet saw their position fiercely
disputed. For Cambridge, such changes affected individuals as authors and as readers;
but they also occurred in a context that was summed up by Sir James Stephen, when he
returned to the town in 1849, thirty-eight years after he had graduated, and 'soon ascer-

tained that the revolutionary spirit, which is so active in our courts and parliaments, was not less wakeful in our collegiate halls and cloisters'.[102] It was a long interval between his two visits, and some change was to be expected. But the pace of change, in an environment that in itself seemed so static, took him by surprise:

> All the old text-books in science and in literature had been superseded. All the public examinations had altered their character. Studies unheard of in the first decade of the present century, were either occupying, or contending for a foremost place in our system of instruction. All our academical statutes had undergone, or were undergoing, revision. Reformatory enactments had succeeded each other in such number, and with such rapidity, as to exercise severely the skill of the most practised interpreter of the law. Every principle of education, however well established, and every habit of teaching, however inveterate, had been fearlessly questioned, and not seldom laid aside. And, presiding over all this movement, I found one dominant mind.[103]

The 'dominant mind' was Whewell's. Stephen exaggerated, in dedicating his lectures to him, while the date of his visit, the year after the national and political upheavals of 1848, perhaps made him over-sensitive. Certainly not everyone in the University at this date would have regarded the movement for reform as happening at the same pace as did Stephen. The ways in which the changes of these decades were to be advanced, and incorporated into the publishing activities of the University, remained to be worked out. Before these are examined in the final chapters, the relationship between authors and the new needs of academic publishers in the mid-century remains to be considered.

Enterprise, authors and learning

In the eighteenth century all the evidence suggests that few people in Cambridge expected to receive much income from their writing. Indeed, there are many instances of authors either directly subsidising their work, or taking full responsibility for their publication. Later on, the notes of thanks to the Syndics for agreeing to meet costs, prefixed to so many books especially in the early years of the nineteenth century, were no empty ones.[1] They mark a change in the way that academic books were to be published, as the Press increasingly took over responsibility for the costs of printing and publishing, though in practice these costs continued to be shared among several subscribing bookseller-publishers.

It was a further step for the University actually to pay an academic author for other than (like F. S. Parris in the mid-eighteenth century) correcting the text of the Bible. However, in the second quarter of the nineteenth century there was a gradual change. For authors dealing with Deighton or with Parker, and if any money at all was paid, fees were more usual than royalty agreements. G. B. Airy, who kept careful record of his various earnings as tutor, coach and author (in 1826 he hesitated to apply for the Lucasian Chair in Mathematics, because its stipend was only £99, compared with his current stipend as assistant tutor of £150), noted his receipts as author in spring 1826. Mawman, the London bookseller, paid him £42 for a contribution on trigonometry to the *Encyclopaedia metropolitana*; and Deighton paid him £70 for his *Mathematical tracts*. Airy acknowledged the 'liberal contribution' of the University Press towards the expenses of production of this book; but the hands of Deighton were tied, as usual, in that the Syndics set its price, of 6s.6d.[2] Continuing demand for Airy's work kept it in print, and in 1842 a third edition, of 750 copies, still brought him £50 from Parker, who published it jointly with Deighton.[3] Publication of the second edition of Sedgwick's *Discourse of the studies of the university* was shared between Parker and Deighton, Parker paying Sedgwick £50. By the mid-1830s, Whewell was able to command considerable fees for copyrights in his major books. In 1837 Parker paid him £300 for the first edition of his *History of inductive sciences*; this was followed by £450 for the third edition in 1857. For his *Elements of morality* in 1845, Parker paid him £250, out of a total production cost of £650 for 1,000 copies; further fees were agreed for the following editions in 1848 and 1854, apparently to the point where the £140 paid in 1854 represented almost 40 per cent of the total production cost.

Such figures bore little relation to the earnings possible for works of fiction by successful novelists.[4] None of the authors just mentioned could expect sales on a commensurate scale. Of the mid-nineteenth-century novelists who moved between the academic and the more broadly literary worlds, Charles Kingsley was offered £300 by Macmillan for *Westward ho!*, published in 1855, and a further £250 on reprinting. It was the publishers' first novel, and as a member of the Macmillan circle Kingsley was to be encouraged; yet the sums were tempered by some doubts of his abilities as a popular author. In the end the book proved an unexpected success.[5] In general, publishers' need to avoid high or unnecessary costs encouraged their continuing reluctance to pay authors. Inevitably, this worked to the disadvantage of educational authors, and coloured the attitude taken by publishers of such books. Parker paid Kingsley nothing for *Yeast* in 1851 (it was later taken over by Macmillan, and was much reprinted), and nothing for Holden's edition of Aristophanes in 1848.[6] In 1860, Alexander Macmillan even contemplated that his proposed Cambridge Shakespeare, envisaged in eight volumes, was to be edited without fee: 'The editors do it as a labour of love, and the publisher would only have to risk paper and print.'[7]

For the publishers with which this book is most concerned, much of this had to do with trade rivalry. As publishers found it necessary to search out competent or well-known editors or authors for an intensely competitive educational market, so some inducement became necessary. But the process was a slow one, and was by no means uniform in its application.

Parker's business as a London bookseller was more general than the list of works printed for him at Cambridge might at first suggest. There were similar interests both in Cambridge and at his address in the Strand. Nearby in London, the new King's College, founded in support of the Established Church, offered a ready parallel, and its teaching staff soon appeared on his lists with authors from Cambridge. The junior department, King's College School, provided both everyday custom and, with the Education Committee of the SPCK, an entry into the schools market that was becoming an increasingly important feature of publishing. In this he was in a brisk and highly competitive world, where Valpy in particular was well established (on Valpy's retirement in 1837 the stock was taken over by Longman[8]). There were books of general literature and of popular science. Amongst the works he advertised for the Christmas market in 1837 were many intended for children – illustrated accounts of voyages and of natural history, as well as books with frankly moral titles.[9] In 1847 he acquired *Fraser's Magazine*, founded in 1830 in imitation of *Blackwood's* but recently fallen on difficult times. Over the next few years, contributors to *Fraser's* included F. D. Maurice, G. H. Lewes, Whewell, Charles Kingsley and George Brimley: there was a tone of high moral seriousness.[10] The list of Parker's publications was overwhelmingly directed at the universities and at the Church. In many respects it was plain fare, when compared with that of the publishers of the West End; and in so far as there were comparisons to be made, they were perhaps to be made best with the University Press at Oxford. Possessing a list in which the books from Cambridge both sat comfortably and gained from association, Parker soon became a figure of considerable substance in London publishing. His catalogues were usually divided up amongst several categories for the sake of clarity, but the size of one aspect of his trade may be gathered from the printing orders for the educational catalogue he issued in late autumn 1845. Between November of that year and December of the following, Cambridge printed 32,250 copies.

The advent of Daniel and Alexander Macmillan at Cambridge was initially providential – for the University Press and for local authors. Their work as publishers and with authors is discussed more fully below. Their success in establishing themselves as publishers in both Cambridge and London demonstrated what might be achieved with energy and only a little initial capital: the indirect results of their success in attracting and encouraging local authors are to be seen in the nature of the Cambridge list even to this day. Although Thomas Hughes, as Daniel Macmillan's biographer, said little about the printing of their books, the existence of a local press, known to the very authors whose interest and expertise they courted, provided a convenient route to publication. The beginnings were modest enough. In 1844, F. D. Maurice's edition of Law on the *Fable of the bees* carried on its title-page the imprint of the University Press as printer, and that year the Press also printed for the brothers a half-sheet leaflet on *Questions of conscience suggested by a Catholic to an Anglo-Catholic*: the publishers supplied the paper in each case, and the charges for printing were £20.16s. and 25s. respectively.[11] Other books followed, and by the mid-1850s Macmillan was the most important customer for the printing business other than the Syndics themselves.

In London, and as a publisher, Parker, like Deighton to a lesser extent, relied on the national and increasingly world-wide demand for educational books. The Macmillans realised this from the beginning, and built their list accordingly. In 1849, searching for some means of saving the Press, Parker suggested that it should pursue a series of volumes specially edited and put forth as 'University Editions': the name of the University had a value in itself.[12] Somewhat to the perplexity of educational publishers, the University Press showed itself content to act simply as printer to those from whom it might have learned. Parker's own catalogue exploited the link with the University by emphasising in his announcements books printed at the University Press: and yet the Press had no share in many of them. For some of his list, Parker acted as agent, though the sums he returned each year declined markedly in the 1840s and early 1850s, as did those coming from other agencies. The *cachet* attached to the name of the University became a part of publishers' packaging. For years, Cambridge made no effort to enlist its own members, who were thus enrolled by firms in whose daily success lay part of the explanation for the University Press's decline as publisher.

Much of the trouble lay in an assumption that was shared by Parker and the Syndics alike: 'the special and proper business of the University Press – namely the production of Bibles'.[13] When Parker wrote those words in 1849, the Press had lost most of that business, but the Syndics did not turn to publishing. Questions were put in terms of printing. In 1846, Parker began a series of basic editions of classical texts, printing 1,500 or 2,000 of each title initially, at the University Press. He already had school editions of a few texts, edited by J. R. Major (Headmaster of King's College School in London) and others, but the market was a fluid one, and the choices available to schools were ever greater. In 1846, educational publishers faced a new threat when a reciprocal treaty with Prussia enabled Tauchnitz's and Dindorf's texts to be offered at lower prices than hitherto – in some cases by as much as 50 per cent.[14] By 1854, Parker had published fresh editions of Cicero, Tacitus, Virgil, Ovid, Horace, Aeschylus, Demosthenes and Plautus. But the Syndics had to be convinced:

> I beg you will allow me to say that you would confer a benefit of the highest importance on the Press, and, through it, on the University, were you to undertake the general superintendence of such a series of works.
>
> I have for years foretold that the future existence of the Press will necessarily depend upon the possession of property of this kind – The Syndics are now gradually, but too slowly, acting upon the principle, and a series of classical works, under your auspices, would indeed form an important branch of their operations.
>
> The copyright of such works would necessarily be the property of the Syndics, for the benefit of the University, but there is no reason why they should not [be paid] liberally – handsomely – for writing and Editorship.[15]

It was not only a matter of establishing such a series, or of fitting editors to texts. Like some other parts of the trade, and particularly those that sought large and loyal markets where customers were to be retained, and new customers found, consistency of appearance – format, type and binding – was crucial. This was by no means a new concept in the book trade, though it had been given little attention in recent years by the University Press. Publishers of popular series realised it especially; and so did those of textbooks. Consistency in colour and variety of cloth bindings, and consistency in format and typography, all helped to establish loyalty to particular series. So Parker offered further advice, unwittingly recalling the strength that Porson's Greek type had given to the Press in this respect.

> The decision of the Syndics to purchase new Greek & other types is most cheering, and will, I am sure, improve the prospects & advance the interests of the Press.
>
> In deciding what founts to order, it will, I submit, be well to be guided by the business that may from time to time have to be provided for – Whenever a new book is ready for press, whether one of the Syndics' own, or from a private customer, the style in which it is to be printed being settled, I would select a type most appropriate not merely for that particular book, but for others of the same class, and would furnish the office with a good strong font of the chosen type.
>
> For instance, should a series of Classical works be decided on, a well considered selection of types, for both text & notes, might be made, for the first work, that would secure elegance & uniformity throughout the whole series.[16]

Parker spoke from experience gained in the London publishing trade, and from the knowledge that the results of recent extensions to the plans of Oxford University Press would soon be plain to see. Something of the position was summarised in the opinion offered by *The Publishers' Circular* less than a year later:

The very extensive sale of Tauchnitz's Leipzig editions of the Greek and Latin Classics in England gave rise to the idea, that native enterprise and scholarship might well accomplish for the home market what has been so long done for it by a foreign publisher. The Oxford Series of Classics, now published by Mr. Parker, presenting a correct text, printed on good paper, supplies a rival collection that can hardly fail to beat the Leipzig edition out of the field. In the Oxford edition, a biographical introduction is prefixd to each author, also chronological tables, historical indexes, and brief summaries; these are frequently wanting in the Leipzig editions.[17]

The bogy of Tauchnitz haunted British publishers – in the classics as in contemporary literature.[18] Once again, nationalism was brought to bear on education and learning. William Ewart's foolish exaltation in the House of Commons in 1845 of German universities at the expense of those in Britain was easily answered by Henry Goulburn as Member for the University of Cambridge.[19] Edward Horsman's attack in the Commons, on similar grounds, nine years later was equally misguided. 'All the most approved editions of classic writers which have been produced in modern times are German; all the great commentators are German . . . It is the same with ancient philosophy, and not a little modern . . . We are compelled to follow the Germans as our masters in every branch of philology.'[20] His sweeping claims were countered, this time outside the house, by J. W. Donaldson, former Fellow of Trinity, in his *Classical scholarship and classical learning*, a book mostly concerned with competitive tests and university teaching.[21] Others, more knowledgeable than Horsman, were willing to share his opinion; but the matter was complicated by the political aggrandisement of German-speaking Europe, and the increasing voice of Prussia.

Belatedly, and by the autumn of 1852 with the report of the Graham Commission before them, the Syndics took up the matter. In 1850–1 they had already begun a campaign to build up the Press's list. The printed catalogue of the manuscripts in the University Library was born at this time. It was long overdue, and was to be the first to record in print hundreds of volumes that had been received from the early eighteenth century onwards.[22] In the educational market, there was no reason to seek to rival others directly; but there was equally no reason to ignore a promising market. They sought out editors both for Greek and Latin classics, and for more recent authors; and further well-wishers wrote to offer their services.[23] Whewell, seeing an opportunity, offered an edition of Bishop Sanderson. Editors were sought out not only in Cambridge, but in schools and parsonages as well. The Syndics rose to Parker's challenge, and paid fees for such work. W. G. Humphry, Fellow of Trinity and editor of Theophilus, Bishop of Antioch, was paid £40;[24] and Hubert Holden, now of Cheltenham College, received £50 for his edition of Cicero, *De officiis*, published in 1854.[25] Inevitably, hopes were not always met. Nothing came of a proposed edition of Horace by Benjamin Hall Kennedy, or of an edition of Sophocles by J. W. Donaldson. Of later authors, with some Cambridge connection, Sir Francis Palgrave's proposed collected edition of Newton was over-ambitious, but Alexander Napier's edition of Isaac Barrow was successfully completed, in nine volumes, in 1859.[26]

While Parker remained University Printer, any new arrangements had to be reconciled with his own interests as a London publisher, working in the same field. In any conflict involving the practicalities of publishing, he was in a commanding position, and could in effect control the Syndics. At the last minute, after the price had been fixed, an entire edition of Pearson on the Creed was sold to him at cost price and – on his recommendation – to be retailed at a price 25 per cent below that agreed by the Syndics.[27] But among the books successfully commissioned in these years were some that became stalwarts in the University Press's own list. Cicero, *De officiis*, edited by Holden and first printed in 1854, reached a seventh edition in 1891; and J. S. Purton's edition of *Pro Milone* was among the first titles to be issued in the Pitt Press series in 1875. As always, dates for delivery proved to be flexible. Among editors of books other than those intended primarily for school or university, Henry Griffin Williams, of Emmanuel College, at work on his edition of the mid-seventeenth-century Cambridge theologian John Smith by 1853, delivered his final copy in 1859, yet William Whewell contrived to produce an edition and abridged translation of Grotius, *De jure belli ac pacis* within a few months, having done most of the work for it over little more than a vacation.[28]

Of those who introduced themselves to the Press at this time, none was to have more influence than the 40-year-old headmaster of Falmouth school and incumbent of Penwerris.[29] F. H. A. Scrivener was to become one of the Press's most faithful and productive contributors, an authority on the text of the Bible, editor of the Authorized (King James) Version and a member of the team that prepared the Revised Version. But his first proposal, *A full and exact collation of about twenty Greek manuscripts of the Holy Gospels, (hitherto unexamined)*, though supported by the Syndics, was published by Parker, in 1853. It was one of the last to appear over Parker's name before he and the Syndics went their separate ways.

Bound into the back of Scrivener's book there was a selection from the catalogue of Parker's publications. The titles and the names of the authors were sufficient reminder of the extent to which Cambridge had relied upon him: Sedgwick on the studies of the University; Whewell on the inductive sciences, on the history of moral philosophy, and on other subjects too; Airy's *Mathematical tracts*; Trench's *On the study of words*, *Notes on the parables* and *Notes on the miracles*; Willis's *Principles of mechanism*; Hare's edition of John Sterling; and George Williams's *Holy city*. The list was drawn from Oxford, London and country parishes as well, but Parker's official position at Cambridge gave it a particular resonance. At the end was a column describing just eleven works 'edited for the Syndics of Cambridge University Press', including Napier's edition of Barrow (still very far from complete at this time), Whewell's Grotius and editions of Pearson on the Creed and of the Homilies. There could be no word of the editions of classical authors that Parker was currently arguing for in Cambridge; and meanwhile he was able freely to advertise his own London editions, whether simple texts at 1s. or 2s. each, or the annotated editions aimed at more senior forms and undergraduates.

As both Parker and Deighton demonstrated, the heaviest demand on them was for textbooks, principally in Cambridge but also to a somewhat lesser degree in Oxford, and in the new colleges of the University of London whose early teaching staff was drawn so much from Cambridge.

In Cambridge itself, none was more obviously successful as a compiler of the requisite textbooks than Robert Potts, of Trinity. Potts had graduated as 26th wrangler in 1832, the same year as W. H. Thompson, future Regius Professor of Greek and Master of Trinity, Edmund Lushington, also of Trinity, Professor of Greek from 1838 in the University of Glasgow and brother-in-law of Tennyson, and E. H. Browne, future Norrisian Professor of Divinity and Bishop of Winchester.[30] He remained thereafter in Cambridge, as a private coach, promoting university reform both by correspondence and by printed pamphlets. The most successful of his books, a school edition of Euclid, began in 1845, published by Parker at 10s. and in a version designed for use at university. The smaller school edition, 'designed for the use of the junior classes in public and private schools', first appeared in 1846. Its success was immediate, colossal and international. By 1851, with a second edition, 19,500 copies had been printed, and by 1853 the total stood at over 56,000. Most unusually for such a book, in 1851 the edition was divided between copies on fine and common paper. Potts realised the value of publicity. In 1845 no less than 10,000 advertisements were printed for his Euclid,[31] and in 1850 he emphasised that his book had been taken up by the Royal Military Academy, among others. In Virginia, William and Mary College conferred on him the honorary degree of LLD in recognition of his mathematical works.[32] Though Parker listed it with his other Cambridge books, he did not have control of all copies outside Cambridge. In very large measure, the success of Potts's book was due to its being taken up by various educational interests: in 1850, the edition was provided with variant title-pages, as it was divided between Parker, the National Society, the Council on Education and Ostell & Lepage, booksellers and East India agents in Blackfriars.[33] In the ordinary trade, it was not, at 4s.6d., a particularly cheap book. More curiously, even amidst such achievements, he still felt it necessary to defend the study of mathematics, drawing to his aid Plato, Bacon, Newton, Pemberton, Whewell and John Stuart Mill.

His Euclid began as a Cambridge textbook, and in its shorter form found an international reputation and sale. Apart from America, it was adopted for schools in Bengal in 1853, and translated for German users in 1860.[34] His edition of Paley's *Evidences of Christianity* remained of more local importance, and the sober opening words of his preface were sufficiently parochial:

> By a Grace of the Senate it was decreed on March 23, 1849, that the Holy Scriptures and the Evidences of Christianity should assume a more important place than formerly in the Previous Examination. It is provided by the new regulations, which will take effect in 1851, that the Examination in the Evidences of Christianity shall be extended to three hours, as well as that in Old Testament History; and that the Examination in one of the Gospels, shall be extended at least to two hours.[35]

Potts prepared this book rapidly and under pressure. The end of his preface was dated 20 November 1849: he had taken the opportunity to include further examination regulations agreed at the end of October. The book was published over the name simply of the University Press, and some copies were sold to Longman. The edition, of 6,000 copies, was the equivalent of one copy for every person matriculating in the University for about thirteen years, but Potts also ensured that his book was brought into use by presenting copies to college libraries.

Whatever hopes he had for his handbook, and whatever the success of his school Euclid, for the Press they were fortunately timed. At a period when the printing machines were by no means fully used, and the once large and frequent orders for privileged books had dwindled, the edition sizes of Potts's books were a material, if modest enough, help – comparable only in 1849–50 with an edition of 10,000 copies of a 16° brevier New Testament.[36] They were also a reminder of how much could be achieved if educational publishing were to be developed. But the Press gained relatively little, and lost even the printing of the 'university' edition to Metcalfe. In 1863, on the closing of Parker's firm, the editions of Euclid passed with many of his other titles to Longman, who continued to publish them in various forms, Potts himself meanwhile having been awarded a medal by the jurors of the 1862 international exhibition, 'for the excellence of his works on geometry'. By 1867, the school Euclid had reached 125,000 copies, and the 'university' edition 10,000.[37]

Through his publications, and the way he promoted them, Potts made education a personal crusade. His growing success increased his confidence as he dealt with Parker or with Metcalfe; in the end, his arguments with printers forced him on the attention of the Vice-Chancellor. Parker himself was in an anomalous position, a London bookseller and publisher and (in practice though not by appointment) only part-time printer at Cambridge. The strains between the University Printer and the resident members of the University were usually contained, even in the case of Whewell. Both Potts and Whewell were from Trinity, and it may be that in a letter to Parker, written by a recently graduated member of the college concerning a proposed edition of Aristophanes, there is conveyed something not only of a young man's arrogance, but also of opinions of members of the college more generally. The author, Hubert Holden, had graduated only a year before writing; and in the following year he was to be elected a fellow:

> I was extremely surprised that you did not manage to see me yesterday, the more as my return to Cambridge was hastened by a desire to come to some arrangement with you respecting the publication of my Aristophanes which I concluded from your last letter you were ready to make to-day – If I recollect rightly I expressed to you my opinion that the specimen printed at the Pitt Press would not suit the longer metres.

After expressing to Parker his preferences for format and size of type, Holden returned to his irritation at delay:

> I need not add that this unnecessary delay in the decision of the matter has put me to inconvenience and expense, and will prevent me from bringing out the work at the time proposed: the *early* part of the Long Vacation being the only time which I shall be able to devote to it. I cannot account for it on any other ground than that you are held back by certain misgivings from risking the publication of the book: if so, I shall be ready to engage in printing it at my own expense, & will beg you to be my publisher only – whatever be the result. I trust that I may not be kept any longer in suspense . . .[38]

Holden got his way for the format, a demy octavo; but the type used in his edition (published by Parker and printed at the University Press in 1848) had to remain small.

Not everyone could afford to accept a doctrine that expected work for nothing. In the late 1850s, it was reckoned that a young senior wrangler could earn £100 a year 'with ease' for a few years, by taking in private pupils;[39] such a livelihood, unprotected by colleges, provided few luxuries. Potts relied for his income on private pupils and on his books. For most people in the university who wrote for money either from need or principle, the change came not with books but with the advent of magazines willing to pay fees to authors – not just for fiction, but for essays or other expository prose. In this, the existence of *Fraser's Magazine*, *Macmillan's* and others like them brought a means to an income independent of the writing of books.

The world between the comfort of a college or a living, and the burdens of a life unprotected by such support, was summed up by Stopford Brooke when he viewed the plight of J. R. Green, writing his history of England for Macmillan:

> You see, for absolute want of money, he is forced to give his time, which is wanted for his history, to write petty articles in the *Saturday*. He is without any cure or stipend. And if he had enough to take him abroad and keep him there without his being compelled to produce two articles a week, he could finish his history . . .[40]

Macmillan was persuaded to provide Green with advances before publication. Conversely, the support of a college, or of a university income, in effect meant a subsidy to the publisher, and to his customers.

These changes in attitude and of need were gradually acknowledged by the University Press. The Syndics came to expect to pay editors or authors for work they commissioned. The origins of an organised approach to authors in this respect seem to date from 1852, when they examined practices by other bodies. The Parker Society paid on average £1.11s.6d. a sheet, plus an allowance for transcribing and for a 'literary secretary', perhaps the equivalent of a modern research assistant. Oxford University Press had been paying £100 for editions of other theological texts, or (it was calculated) approximately 50s. per sheet. At this point, the Cambridge press had tended to adopt a more modest scale, though one that was likewise based on a rate per sheet, rather than on any innate comparability in difficulty or complexity. So, Temple Chevallier had received £60 for Pearson on the Creed (approximately 25s. per sheet), and G. E. Corrie had received £75 for the Homilies (or about 35s. per sheet). It was suggested that a more acceptable figure for editing patristic texts might be £4 per sheet.[41] Scrivener was paid £100 in 1871–2 for his work on the paragraph Bible; Walker received £50 for editing Gaius, as did Skeat for editing St Mark's Gospel in Anglo-Saxon: Skeat also received 25 copies.[42] In 1871–2, G. F. Browne was paid £60 annually as editor of the *Cambridge University Reporter*.[43] These scattered examples do not add up to a policy. They do, however, indicate a gradual change in attitude.

In these years, the Press identified – part deliberately and part by accident – three principal areas for development: editions of mainly theological established authors, whether Fathers of the Church or seventeenth-century divines; classical texts; and catalogues of collections in the libraries and museums of the University. The Syndics were cautious, and they preferred editions of established works, rather than monographs. They were inconsistent in their pricing. Of three books published in 1854, Theophylact on Matthew, a volume of Tertullian, and Holden's Cicero, *De officiis*, the first two were similar in that neither could expect a fast sale; yet the manufacturing cost to retail price of one was 3 to 7 and of the other 1 to 2, while for the Cicero it was about 3 to 5. Compared with the ordinary trade, such proportions were narrow.[44] With subsidy from the Syndics, some books were sold too cheaply to support the Press's longer term interests: the first volume of the catalogue of University Library manuscripts was priced at 30s. retail, but the actual cost per copy, including editing, which accounted for well over half the bill, was almost 39s.4d.[45] The Syndics were also variously over-cautious and over-enthusiastic in the numbers they printed. Of the first volume of the new – and long awaited – catalogue of the manuscripts they printed only 250, doubling that number for the second volume after demand had taken them unawares. Only 1,000 copies were printed at first of Holden's *De officiis*. On the other hand, with little regard for the realities of the market, the editions of Barrow and of Irenaeus were set at 1,500 and 1,000 copies respectively, and Barrow was still in print in the 1950s.[46]

Those who felt strongly about the woes of the Press were very ready to air their views publicly. J. E. B. Mayor, later University Librarian for a few stormy years, pressed the case for the history of the University, in which he saw a wealth of literature needing to be republished, or published for the first time. He used the preface to his edition of the autobiography of a seventeenth-century member of St John's College to air his views on the adulteration of food, and on the University Press – his printers:

> The Pitt Press, until very lately, has done scarcely anything for the honour of the sister university [Cambridge]. Let us hope, as loyal sons of Cambridge, that she is awaking to the duty which she owes to the church, whose ministers she is charged to educate; and let us cordially co-operate with our new syndics in their endeavour to efface the reproach under which, as a literary body, we have so long laboured.[47]

Mayor's enthusiasm for his subject was unmatched; his energies in editing were to be proven in such achievements as his massive edition and extension of Thomas Baker's history of St John's College, or his work on Cambridge during the reign of Queen Anne. In quite different fields, he was a notable editor of Juvenal and for the Rolls Series of documents in medieval British history. Like Potts and like Scrivener, he possessed abundant energy, and was irritated by others with less determination or commitment. The reform of the University Press required such qualities from its authors; it also required a re-examination of relationships with members of the University, and with the book trade more generally.

Partnership

As we have seen, the Commissioners in 1852, faced with the collapse of the Press's finances, were unequivocal. 'It is only by associating printers or publishers in some species of copartnership with the University, or by leasing the Press to them, that any considerable return can hereafter be expected from the capital which has been invested in it.'[1] None of the Commissioners had any experience as a publisher or a printer, and they seem to have been unaware that at Oxford, where there had existed such a partnership since the eighteenth century, the system was being seriously questioned.[2] But among those who considered the matter, both in Cambridge and in the book trade, there was overwhelming agreement. If the difficulties of the Press were to be overcome, it would have to be by a partnership between the University and professional skills in printing and bookselling.

Most members of the University found little difficulty in the idea of such a partnership; but some had reservations about its details. Bashforth has already been mentioned. Robert Potts, author of the highly successful school Euclid, doubted whether a partnership would either bring an improvement or was in the best financial interests of the University.[3] The most forward of the critics, Potts was not disinterested, in that rumour suggested to him that his own pocket would be affected.

> When I began printing at the University Press, one of the reasons which induced me to go there, was the great convenience offered of the free use of warehouse room for the books until they were sold off – this I understood was the practice allowed to all Members of the University. It is rumoured that this convenience is not to be allowed when the new Partners come in . . . If such be the intention of the new firm I shall be under the necessity of removing both my stock, my custom and what else I may command, in some other direction.[4]

He set out his case in personal terms. He was also a public figure, who did all that he could to ensure that he had a high public profile. In advertising his books he made full play of reviews and testimonials. It was a position supported, and enhanced, by his appointment as local secretary for the schools examinations instituted by Cambridge in the late 1850s. A little later, full-page advertisements in the educational numbers of *The Bookseller* displayed his name in the size and in the position usually reserved for publishers' own names: in 1860, hinting the way in which Parker's own affairs were moving, the page advertising Potts's various works was shared between Longman and Parker.[5] As for Clay, Potts was as good as his word; when a revised version of his octavo Euclid was called for in 1865, it was stereotyped and printed by Metcalfe, not by the University Press. The longstanding practice of providing free warehousing for books paid for by resident members of the University had been a source of annoyance in the eighteenth century, and was long overdue for reconsideration. Potts lost his battle against change. He also lost the battle over credit. As a necessary preliminary to the partnership agreements, another survey was made of debtors. For years, Potts had exploited the Press in this respect also; and Clay's request to him for payment was met with an intemperate letter, in which Potts expressed himself 'astonished' at being asked to pay his debts. It required several letters from James Cartmell, as chairman of the Press syndicate, pointing out that he had had over two years' credit – much more than normal – before he collapsed.[6] The Syndics concurred with Cartmell, and Potts's departure from the Press's ledgers was a sign of how matters were to be run in future, as Clay looked to orders that would be paid for promptly.

Potts was an irritant, if a potentially embarrassing one. Parker was a much more serious hindrance. His parting with the Press had not been smooth, and he remained an obstacle able to inflict serious harm on its future. In a letter that was lithographed for circulation, Clay set out his complaint in terms that made clear not only that personal relations were strained past endurance, but also that he was well aware of what no reader of Parker's advertisements could have missed. The name of Cambridge, whether in his own title or in his publications, was one to be traded, and Parker worked it hard. But, most importantly to Clay as he sought work for the presses, Parker's orders for printing had all but ended.

> It is with much concern that I have for some time past observed the constant withdrawal of M[r] Parker's business, and his apparent determination to discontinue his connexion with the University Press.
>
> The weight of his influence as a Publisher, which has been mainly established by his former position as "Printer to the University", is thus made to operate most injuriously against the University, by discouraging Authors, even resident here, from employing the Press, who would not only naturally prefer it, but who would also find it most convenient to avail themselves of it – and I cannot conceal from myself that the mere fact of Cambridge men standing aloof as it were from their own Press, must cast a doubt upon the management, and seriously damage the concern . . . I beg respectfully to submit, that if influential members of the University would resolve to support the Press, more would be done towards bringing Mr Parker to pursue a fitter course than by any other means.[7]

Apart from books by Whewell, Parker arranged for few of his later publications to be printed by the Press. In fact, Clay's anxieties at lost business, though real enough, were overtaken by events. On the death of his son, Parker was left in 1861 with William Bourn as his sole remaining partner.[8] The firm was taken over by Longman in 1863. Parker himself died in 1870, and many Cambridge authors had by then long preferred to go to Macmillan instead. The most important independent customers of the Press as a printer were Deighton Bell, and the increasingly successful and imaginative Macmillans.

Clay's background combined practical business with a career at Cambridge that had included a first-class degree in classics, when he was bracketed with his contemporary at Trinity, F. J. A. Hort. He came from a Cambridge family, and his father had served his apprenticeship with Watts at the time when stereotyping was being introduced.[9] Though in 1854 the young Clay was still only in his mid-twenties, he was a person with whom members of the University found it easy to associate. He had all the advantages of his father's accumulated wisdom on which to draw from London. Richard Clay's analysis in the spring of 1854 was straightforward. In his view, the Press suffered notoriously from want of capital, from unsuitable and insufficient plant, and from defective machinery.[10] Under the partnership agreement, the University Press share of £10,000 was represented mostly by the value of the equipment and buildings, while Clay and George Seeley each provided £5,000. Clay was to be the managing partner, and profits were to be apportioned in accordance with the respective investments. At a salary of £400 per annum, he was – as Potts pointed out in his attack – paid almost twice that of the University Librarian. The stipends of virtually all Professors were less, in varying degrees: among the better remunerated were the Regius Professor of Modern History, and the Downing Professor of the Laws of England, at £371.8s. and £200 respectively, while Whewell received about £130 as Professor of Moral Theology, and the ancient Regius chairs were entitled to £40 each.[11] Fellowships, lecture fees and ecclesiastical appointments augmented these stipends, in some cases very substantially indeed; but the fact remained that the University Printer was paid as a businessman, not as a don.

For Clay, the Press provided an increasingly comfortable living. There were complaints at his receiving a salary of £400 per annum; but this was later raised in 1866 to £675.[12] With growing prosperity, he was able to choose his addresses accordingly. Early in the 1870s he moved into a large new house just beyond the Backs, in an area being developed to meet the new needs of academic families.[13] Comparisons may most usefully be made not only with salaries in Cambridge, but also with those for similar positions elsewhere. His father, Richard Clay, died in 1877, a wealthy man. But Clay's equivalent at Oxford, Thomas Combe, partner since 1841, and the largest shareholder in the Oxford press apart from the University itself, appeared even more successful. Bible printing made him rich. He was an early, and notable, patron of the Pre-Raphaelites, and his wife presented Holman Hunt's 'Light of the world' to be placed in Keble College chapel after his death in 1872: most of his collection of Pre-Raphaelite art passed to the Ashmolean Museum on the death of his widow in 1893. A committed high churchman, Combe paid both for a chapel for the Radcliffe Infirmary, and also for the church of St Barnabas ('not a penny was to be thrown away on external appearance and decoration'), nearby the Press: both were designed by the young Arthur Blomfield.[14] Even after these benefactions, at his death in 1872 he still left £80,000.[15] Clay, less flamboyant, was less obviously wealthy; but on matters apart from Combe's ecclesiastical and artistic interests, it was impossible not to compare one man with the other.

Clay adopted the same assumption as his predecessors: that the printing of Bibles and prayer books constituted 'the one great motive for keeping up the Establishment of the Press'. The buildings were, without any doubt, inconvenient, partly because they had been designed before the days of steam presses. But in a business driven by the wish to print Bibles, where profits could, apparently, never be more than very small, and where large quantities were therefore essential, capital expenditure was overdue.[16] There was nothing new in this analysis. The advent of the new partners' capital enabled the Press to reinvest. Five new machine presses – two flat-bed and two cylinder[17] – were bought for £1,500, and new type (Miller & Richard, Stephenson Blake, Caslon and Sinclair had all supplied Clay by 1868) was bought at a cost of almost as much. In 1863, Clay was authorised to replace the engine and boiler.[18] As activity at the Press gathered momentum once more, so paper consumption rose. Before the partnership it had been as little as 74 reams per week. By April 1855 this figure had risen to 135; and by the end of July it was 208. A new programme was introduced for privileged printing. By the end of 1855 this included editions of nonpareil 16° and ruby 32° Bibles (38,000 and 15,000 copies respectively), of a brevier 16° New Testament (60,000 copies), and of a nonpareil 24° prayer book (131,000 copies). Some of these and other editions of these books were electrotyped.[19]

The Bible market, difficult and dominated by the success of Oxford, faced further upheavals when a House of Commons Select Committee was appointed to examine the Queen's Printer's patent soon after Clay had been appointed. Ignorant and prejudiced, Potts did his best to spoil the fragile structure that Clay was rebuilding, and he offered his opinion to the committee:

> Bibles seem to me, so far as regards the men who print them, to be mere matters of manufacture, and come under the same rules as all other manufactures. I think there is no reason that will bear thorough examination for maintaining the patents of privilege for printing Bibles. The tendency of patents and of monopoly appears to me always to have been to produce negligence, inaccuracy, and expensive management: whereas competition, on the other hand, has a tendency to produce energy, economy, vigilance, accuracy, and cheapness.[20]

By ignoring the fact that the cost of Bibles to customers had actually diminished not only because of mechanization in the manufacturing process, but also because of keen competition (often orchestrated by the various publishing and distributing societies) between the privileged presses, Potts attempted to suggest that there was a similarity between outright monopoly and the limited one exercised in nineteenth-century England. 'Under the laws which we are now living, I cannot see the least reason for maintaining the patent; and further, I believe that the interests of the University of Cambridge would not suffer by the privilege being discontinued.'[21] Potts's opinion was misleading, and it was mischievous.

Not all Bibles sold quickly; and for those that did, profit margins were small. James Franklin, of the Bible Society, estimated that the sum allowed for manufacture in a cheap 32° pearl Bible, sold in sheets to the societies at 5½d., was as little as twopence, paper costing at least 3¼d. Even Franklin was perplexed at how it might be done.[22]

The University Press's reputation of having survived, and prospered, on the printing of Bibles and prayer books conceals much, and is misleading for the mid-nineteenth century. It is true that Clay placed this trade at the head of his agenda in the 1850s; but there were special reasons for doing so at that time. Parker's reaction to the new partnership arrangement remained unproven; but it was likely to be unhelpful, even if it was not actively hostile. The success of the Oxford press in printing Bibles and prayer books presented both a challenge and a tempting parallel, though much of what was known in Cambridge of Oxford's affairs seems to have been little more than hearsay. Furthermore, at a period when the ancient monopoly was under attack, the most effective form of defence was to demonstrate a continuing commitment, on a scale and with a seriousness that would ensure a hearing.

In practice, for Clay the printing of the privileged books proved to be of far less everyday financial importance than work for a small group of publishers dominated by Deighton, Bell & Co., Macmillan, and Rivington. In 1854–5, income to the Press from printing the privileged books represented about 40 per cent of that from all book printing; and by the end of the 1860s it had slumped. In 1863–4, the Press received £235 for unwanted stock of printed sheets from various books sold off as waste paper, and only £289 profit from printing the privileged books. In 1871–2, when the list of the Syndics' own books was at its weakest, profits from printing privileged books were still less.[23] But by this date renewed efforts were being made to recover some of the Bible trade. The occasional very large editions – of 30,000 copies of a new nonpareil 32° Bible and of a brevier 32° New Testament, both in 1871[24] – confirmed the traditions of the Press, and by maintaining a presence in the market served as a reminder to other customers of the Press's skills. Among the orders from the Bible Society won by Clay were an edition of 50,000 copies of the New Testament in Malagasy, in 1871, and another of 10,000 French brevier 16° New Testaments in 1872.[25] In the English-speaking market, efforts to sell Cambridge Bibles were desultory compared with the rival Oxford. In New York, Appleton & Co. were unusual in advertising Oxford, London and Cambridge printings seemingly with an even hand, so as to make the most of each other's authority. More usually, Oxford was offered in solitary command.[26] In Cambridge's everyday domestic commercial terms, the contracts to print for the educational market were of far greater consistent importance.

So-called authors' work (including printing for publishers, especially Macmillan, treated in more detail in the following chapter) was greatly increased in Clay's hands, over fifty books figuring under this head in 1854–5. Most were of an educational nature, as Deighton, Bell and Macmillan each pursued their parallel and to a great extent competitive paths. Though most of the edition sizes were not in themselves large – the majority in these first years were between 750 and 1,500 copies, even of schoolbooks – Clay had demonstrated after twelve months that there was work enough.[27]

At the end of the 1860s, though the Pitt Press was by far the largest printer in Cambridge, it was by no means the only one.[28] William Metcalfe, frequently mentioned in previous pages, had premises in both Trinity Street and the adjoining Green Street, where he printed the weekly *Cambridge Express*. Other, general, printers included

Foister and Jagg in Falcon Yard, off Petty Cury; Charles Wharton Naylor, on Market Hill, proprietor of the *Cambridge Chronicle* as well as publisher of the short-lived *Cambridge University Gazette*; J. Palmer in Jesus Lane; Henry Smith in Corn Exchange Street; Frederick Talbot in Sussex Street; John Webb in Butcher Row; Samuel Wheaton in King Street; and Wilson and Son in Jordan's Yard, off Bridge Street. Hatfield and Tofts, proprietors of the *Cambridge Independent Press*, were in Market Hill. Samuel Coulden, copper-plate printer, had premises in Rose Crescent. Apart from Metcalfe's, the size of some of these small businesses, and the restricted space of their premises, few of them in main thoroughfares, are reminders of the kinds of printing on which they relied. In general, they did not have the resources to print large books, though several of them – quite apart from Metcalfe – printed books occasionally. Their principal income was from jobbing printing. Some supplemented their income by printing cheap broadside ballads for sale in the streets: in 1838, Sir Frederic Madden had obtained examples for his private collection from Henry Talbot in Sussex Street, as well as from Sharman in Market Hill and from Samuel Wilson in Bridge Street.[29]

With Alexander Macmillan's decision in 1863 to remove his firm's publishing activities to London, the University Press became, for the first time, the regular and major supplier to a major London publisher – on a scale far greater than in Parker's heyday. There were also other, more occasional, connections with the London trade, with Longman and with Bohn, who published Beriah Botfield's *Prefaces to the first editions of the . . . classics and of the sacred scriptures*, printed at Cambridge in 1861. Clay's father had from 1854 been a friendly adviser in the background; the connection proved to be mutually beneficial, as the Cambridge press came to be relied on as a joint printer – though always a silent one – with Richard Clay and the London firm. Thus, books were set in London, and then printed from plates in Cambridge. In 1861 the University Press became the printer of one of J. G. Wood's popular books on natural history, for Routledge.[30] In some cases the orders for such books were large. In 1865, a new edition of Longfellow by Routledge, set by Clays in London and machined in Cambridge, consisted of 10,000 copies.[31] In 1866, a new *Arabian nights*, for Routledge again, was printed in 10,000 copies.[32] Clay's in London printed regularly for Macmillan, but some of their work was in practice contracted to Cambridge, though there was no statement to this effect in the books themselves. *Tom Brown's schooldays* and Hugh Macmillan's *Bible teachings in nature* were both printed from plates at Cambridge in December 1870, in the same month that Creasy's *Decisive battles of the world* was printed for Bentley.[33] A few months later, again for Macmillan, two volumes were printed for the Golden Treasury series, *Guesses at truth* and Roundell Palmer's *Book of praise*.[34] In November 1871, in time for the Christmas market, Charlotte Mary Yonge's *Chaplet of pearls* appeared for the first time in a one-volume edition, set in London but machined in Cambridge.[35] *Words from the poets*, an anthology 'selected for the use of parochial schools and libraries', was shared between the two printers, father and son, in the same way a month later.[36] The timing of some of this work sent from London suggests the reason for this silent collaboration. It often fell either in November or December, at a time of the year when prompt delivery of finished copies was of critical importance if books were to reach the Christmas trade on which publishers depended increasingly by the mid-century. In other words, the Cambridge press was employed as a supplement when there was too much work in London. Existing or new stereotype or electrotype plates made this relatively straightforward. Though these books were almost all set in London, and machined in Cambridge, in 1872 the tasks were for once reversed: Cambridge was responsible for setting the lengthy notes to a revised and considerably enlarged edition of J. W. Hales's school anthology of *Longer English poems*, also published by Macmillan, the machining of the book being carried out in London.[37]

Working hours were normally from 8 a.m. to 8 p.m. in winter, and an hour earlier in the summer, with Saturday usually a half day. Time was allowed for meals at midday and at tea-time. But as in printing houses elsewhere, these hours were variable according to circumstances. The examination season required later nights of compositors. Machines had sometimes to be run late, though rarely later than 10 p.m. All-night work, common in London (especially towards Christmas) was rare in Cambridge.[38]

The increase in work required more, and more efficient, staff. Clay's London contacts, through his father, were valuable in this respect, and the two men collaborated in arranging for journeymen to move between their two premises. In the Press, conditions of employment gave Clay and the Syndics large powers of discretion. In 1854, the widow of one employee was granted a pension of £25 per annum. Another employee, Israel Harvey, paper-wetter for twenty-eight years, was discharged on account of his lameness. Though he believed that his damp working environment (paper-wetting was done in a cellar at this time) had precipitated the end of his career, the Syndics considered that he had no claim on them for a pension. Another employee was dismissed after being absent without notice one afternoon.[39] As Clay gradually refined the staff, winnowing out those no longer of use, so matters eased, though it was to be ten years before there was a staff sick fund contributed to by the Press itself.[40] Employees could not easily afford to retire, and remained sometimes until within a few days of their death. Baker, the warehouseman, had been with the Press for forty years when he finally retired at the age of seventy, with a specially agreed pension of 10s. a week. Robert Collings, the overseer, was less fortunate, and his pension was paid to his widow.[41]

New people had to be found, both to replace experienced but unsatisfactory men, and to fill new posts. By 1861, printing in Cambridge (not just the University Press) employed 199 people, one a woman and no less than 82 of whom were under the age of twenty.[42] Obviously not all the boys were regularly apprenticed; but in 1867 the proportion of apprentices to journeymen nationally was about 2 to 7¼.[43] The large disparity in these local and national figures suggests that Cambridge was unusual. Boys were required for laying and taking off paper at the machine presses, and for feeding paper to the hydraulic press. Older and stronger ones were put to the iron hand-presses, while the youngest were employed to fold or gather sheets after printing. Others were employed in the counting house, to carry paper, or to run errands. Their weekly wages were from about three shillings, rising to seven or eight shillings by the age of eighteen. Though Clay expressed a preference for employing none under thirteen, in practice many were younger, often sent by their parents at the earliest possible opportunity. As in other industries, the business could not have prospered without such labour, unless there was legislation that would affect its competitors also.[44] So far as possible, Clay employed younger staff, to be trained up, and he was constant in his search for suitable apprentices. He was especially alert to the need to read proofs carefully, and to 'the qualifications of a reader, which are very peculiar'.[45] One of his notebooks contains details of local boys, generally aged eleven or twelve, who might be employed in the reading department.[46]

In 1868 there were four reading closets. Accuracy in the printed text of the Bible was continually enquired into by individual users and by Royal Commissions alike, but other books were also given repeated reading if necessary. The cost of the Globe Shakespeare, printed for Macmillan in 1864, included a charge of £15 for 'extra reading for accuracy'.[47] It was characteristic of Clay's stress on the importance of the best business practice; and it is important in this respect that the suggestion for the Shakespeare came from Cambridge, not from Macmillan, and that Clay's analogy was the text of the Bible.[48]

That in bibliographical terms the practice, when applied to Bible proof-reading, was based on shaky foundations, did not concern Clay – or most of his customers. In 1864, F. H. Scrivener identified the moment when academical interest in the text of the scriptures broke into flower in public consciousness as well. It came with the unexpected announcement by Constantin von Tischendorf of the recovery from St Catharine's monastery on Mount Sinai of the great bulk of what soon became widely known as the Codex Sinaiticus.[49] Tischendorf's announcement was soon enlivened by the counter-announcement by the forger Constantine Simonides that he had written the manuscript himself. Ludicrous as it was, motivated by Simonides' wish to revenge himself on Tischendorf, the claim was conclusively demolished by Henry Bradshaw in *The Guardian* in 1863 after several months in which Simonides had been opposed by Aldis Wright, of Trinity.[50] In itself, the argument was little more than an irritant, for Simonides' claim had been flawed from the beginning. But it gave an airing to textual and palaeographical questions, as they related to the earliest manuscripts of the Bible, among a public more accustomed to accepting textual traditions than to investigating them. It also had an unexpectedly rapid and lasting effect on the English text as well, and led directly to the collaboration of Oxford and Cambridge that was eventually to result in the Revised Version of the Bible.

To an academic audience, Scrivener was for many years an outsider. Though he had graduated from Trinity College in 1835, he had few friends in the University willing to support his cause. The Syndics of the Press were cautious, and Scrivener himself was acutely sensitive to his position. As headmaster of Falmouth school from 1846 to 1856, and rector of St Gerrans from 1862, he relied on others. He wrote of the 'remoteness of West Cornwall from Public Libraries'.[51] Christopher Wordsworth was the more valued by him not only in allowing him advance proofs of his edition of the Greek Testament, but also for years of friendship: the son of the Master, Wordsworth had been a young fellow of Trinity when Scrivener was an undergraduate. Scrivener's methods, and particularly his disagreement on the *textus receptus*, were vulnerable to attack, not least effectively by F. J. A. Hort, in a rivalry that ended only with the death of the two men within a short time of each other in 1891–2.[52] No-one doubted Scrivener's learning, but at least the biographer of Westcott commemorated it as 'slovenly'.[53] Though he continued to revise his work on the early manuscripts of the Bible, for the University Press Scrivener was eventually persuaded to concentrate his energies on the English text rather than the Greek. When in 1876 he accepted the vicarage of Hendon, in Middlesex, a primary attraction was its more convenient proximity to Westminster, and work on the Revised Version.

Scrivener's hopes, tinged with a real personal fondness for the University, were invariably ambitious. In 1853 he had published his collation of Greek manuscripts of the Gospels;[54] but as he explored further he began to concentrate his view on the Codex Augiensis, the ninth- or tenth-century Reichenau manuscript of the Epistles in Greek and Latin in Trinity College library. His programme, entailing detailed examination of early manuscripts, was accomplished thanks to the co-operation of the owners of the most important examples. Distance from Cambridge was little obstruction to his hopes. The local authorities at Leicester had lent him their fifteenth-century manuscript for him to use in Falmouth; and Trinity proved likewise amenable, apparently agreeing even to his arrangement for the manuscript to be transported to and fro by an undergraduate.[55] 'My design', wrote Scrivener

> is to publish, in the least expensive form consistent with accuracy, a transcript of the Codex Augiensis both Greek and Latin, with a full and minute collation of its Greek Text both with our received text and the Codex Boernerianus, and of its Latin version with the Clementine Vulgate.[56]

The whole, including transcript, annotation, introduction and collations with other manuscripts, was to run to almost 700 closely printed pages. This proved too much for the Syndics, who declined the project and gave Scrivener to suppose that it was on grounds of cost.[57] They were helped to their decision by E. H. Browne, the recently appointed Norrisian Professor of Divinity, who had the benefit of knowing Scrivener as a neighbouring clergyman:[58] the difficulty lay not just in cost, but in method. Undeterred, Scrivener thereupon applied to Trinity for a subsidy, estimating production expenses at £200. The College was generous, and offered 50 per cent. But in the discussions between the College, Scrivener, and Browne other questions arose. A transcript such as Scrivener proposed would be complicated (perhaps there was also some anxiety as to its probable accuracy). For the first time in the Press's history, photography was introduced as a possible means of reproduction. Would not a lithographic or a photographic facsimile be more appropriate? A transcript, in Scrivener's eyes, was a necessary second best, not least on grounds of cost.

> The subject of photography I have considered. If any competent number of copies of *the whole MS.* can be made by that means, at a price approaching that of printing, I cannot conceive what advantage my edition (in common Greek type) would have over it: but my

enquiries have led me to believe that such a process on a large scale is too expensive to be thought of, if the book is to appear at a moderate price.[59]

In his view, there was little merit in making only a few photographic copies for the public libraries. Moreover, photography was not in itself a completely satisfactory arrangement. Costs were high: in Cambridge, William Kingsley, Fellow of Sidney Sussex College, not understanding the extent of the manuscript, was at first willing to provide negatives at sixpence apiece, the price of materials.[60] As Scrivener explained, there were also other technical difficulties:

> *Fifty-one* pages of the MS. are thickly overlain with modern scribbling, which a photograph must reproduce: a few pages are so much soiled and worn, that a good photograph will be difficult: but (what is of far more consequence) this copy abounds in alterations, erasures and corrections in every part, by at least three different hands. It is often hard enough to determine the date of these changes with the MS. before one, and with the aid of a glass. No photograph can represent the exact colour of the ink, or the roughness of the vellum. Thus a body of annotations must accompany the photographed no less than the printed volume, or those who use the photograph will often read from the MS. the very text the original scribe did *not* use.[61]

Scrivener's real aim seems to have been a book for the private scholar or student, at fifteen or twenty shillings. Lithography (which at this time would have meant tracing) was a cheaper, but not a better, course. Instead, and with some reluctance on Scrivener's part, the proposed number of photographs was reduced to just a frontispiece (taken by the Revd R. B. Rickards, Scrivener's neighbour at Constantine: 'the reader will find its effect materially improved by the use of a magnifying glass'); three lithographs were provided of the Leicester codex and two other Cambridge manuscripts. Though not published by the University Press, the letterpress was printed by Clay, Scrivener retaining the manuscript in Cornwall for proof correction.[62] The final publication bore Deighton Bell's name on the title-page. By a compromise, it was published by subscription (1 guinea to subscribers, or 26s. thereafter), the list headed by the Royal Library and making a special feature of Trinity's donation. Apart from the 500 subscription copies, Deighton Bell took 500 of the introduction alone, with a new title-page and with the heads altered.[63]

Scrivener meanwhile offered his dedication:

> Whatever be the defects of my Volume, I have striven to be *accurate*; aware that, in these sacred studies, all that is not accurate is much worse than useless.

He found his sternest critic in Hort, whose long notice contributed to the *Journal of Classical and Sacred Philology* acknowledged the scrupulous care with which Scrivener had collated the Trinity and other manuscripts. But in larger arguments Hort found him weaker, as his lack of understanding of the several textual traditions, Greek and Syriac, was exposed. Hort wrote of his 'rashness', the 'random' quality of his judgements, a 'fatal' want of comprehensiveness and his apparent lack of knowledge of some of the most notable scholarship, including that of Lachmann, Tregelles, Tischendorf and Sabatier, on the Fathers.[64]

Scrivener, whose reputation as an authority on the Greek text was therefore some-what equivocal by 1860, offered his own contribution to the debate on the Codex Sinaiticus. The publication of a facsimile of the manuscript in 1862 provided the means for revision of existing editions of the Greek New Testament, and the opportunity for textual re-evaluation. In England, few were more active in promoting such questions, and in 1864 he published a small volume, *A full collation of the Codex Sinaiticus with the received text of the New Testament*. His book, its outside appearance suggesting a clas-sical text rather than biblical criticism, came once again from Deighton Bell, who had published not only his work on the Codex Augiensis but also his Greek New Testament in the series of Cambridge Greek and Latin texts[65] and his *Plain introduction to the crit-icism of the Greek New Testament* (1861). This last book had the misfortune to appear only shortly before Tischendorf's facsimile of the Codex Sinaiticus; but Scrivener was by then already viewed with some suspicion.

Browne had encouraged Scrivener in his work on the Codex Augiensis. Though he recommended his edition of the Codex Bezae to the Syndics of the Press, this too was published by Deighton Bell and printed by Clay.[66] Scrivener was tolerated, and respected for his hard-working diligence, but he was not so much admired as a scholar. In the first sentence of his dedication, he drew attention to the fact that this had been recommended to the Syndics. His acknowledgments were to George Williams of King's and to Henry Bradshaw, besides others in the University Library. Of the pro-fessors of divinity there was not a word. Browne had been appointed to the see of Ely, and Hort was a declared critic of Scrivener's work.

Though his work had so far not found favour for publication (as distinct from print-ing) by the University Press – nor by Macmillan, where Hort's word was also influential – Scrivener was to become one of the University Press's authors most famil-iar to the public. His skills were put to use for the English Bible, and he became the acknowledged expert on the text of the Authorized Version. But his importance was more than this. From the remote west country, newly accessible via Brunel's great bridge at Saltash only from 1859, he had brought to the general public widespread attention to the problems and urgency of textual scholarship of the Bible.

His purpose was simply put:

> an humble yet earnest attempt to revive among the countrymen of Bentley and Mill some interest in a branch of Biblical learning which, for upwards of a century, we have tacitly abandoned to continental scholars. The criticism of the text of Holy Scripture, though confessedly inferior in point of dignity and importance to its right interpretation, yet takes precedence of it in order of time: for how can we consistently proceed to investigate the sense of the Sacred Volume, till we have done our utmost to ascertain its precise words?[67]

Behind these words stood Lachmann and Tischendorf, and their insistence on a return to early manuscripts as a means of recovering texts older still. The coincidence of Scrivener's work on Greek manuscripts in England, the excitement generated by Tischendorf's introduction to the world of the Codex Sinaiticus, and a new generation of textual scholars led by Tregelles, Westcott, Hort and others, brought to public attention what had been long realised by a few: that the received texts of the Bible, and therefore of its English translation, stood in urgent need of reconsideration.

He had also raised the question of facsimiles. The potential applications for photography to the study of manuscripts had been long encouraged,[68] but few had explored them in practice. The appearance of Roger Fenton's photographic facsimile of the Epistles of Clement from the Codex Alexandrinus in 1856 was, claimed Frederic Madden, encouraged by 'the Professors of Divinity and others of the Universities of Oxford and Cambridge'.[69] Scrivener's inclusion in 1859 of a photograph of a manuscript in Trinity College library marked further confidence in the principle, even though it was less than he or some other members of the College might have preferred. The photographic frontispiece of part of one of the Epistles is to be understood in the context of Madden's recent edition of the Clementine epistles; but it was also executed on the eve of Sir Henry James's much-vaunted and highly successful application in England of photography to zincography, a process that dramatically reduced the price on a scale that in 1856 Scrivener had hoped for in vain. The new principles were soon applied to Domesday Book, to early editions of Shakespeare and to facsimiles of 'national' manuscripts. But it was not, for the moment, applied to the Codex Bezae, which in 1864 was published in transcript; the first photographic facsimile appeared only in 1899.

All these considerations came together in renewed and overdue attention to the text of the Authorized Version itself. As Turton, Scrivener and others examined the text of the 1611 edition ever more closely, and considered its inconsistencies of typography as well as its manifest inaccuracies, so it became ever clearer that even the text of the Bible could only be considered static not simply provided it was competently and repeatedly proof-read – or, literally, set in metal plates for stereotyping and electrotyping – but also provided there was agreement on what constituted the textual authority. The Cambridge edition of 1638, and Blayney's printed at Oxford in 1769 were those commonly cited as the most reliable. Scrivener's introduction to the Cambridge paragraph Bible of 1873, and his subsequent revision of this as *The Authorized edition of the English Bible (1611)*, published in 1884, set the arguments of successive Parliamentary committees of enquiry in an appropriate bibliographical context. As Clay explained, the text read by purchasers of modern Bibles was an adaptation – or, in his terms, more 'correct'.

> There is no doubt that the edition of 1611 . . . is very imperfect in those italics. The edition of 1638 was very much corrected in that respect. The intention of the translators was carried out in the 1638 edition, which had been only imperfectly performed in 1611. It appears proved beyond doubt that the edition of 1611 was very carelessly printed, and consequently many words were not printed in italics, which, according to the intention of the translators, ought to have been so printed.[70]

The various witnesses before the House of Commons Committee in 1859–60 found more mistakes to worry over than italics. Dominated by a belief in accuracy as an absolute concept, they never identified properly wherein that accuracy lay. They realised that it informed arrangements for proof-reading; but they made assumptions of a text that had itself been formed and reformed over generations. Multiple proof-reading might remove modern errors, whether in Shakespeare or in the Bible; but it made textual assumptions of the past that the past would not bear.

In practice, the successful prosecution of Bible printing depended on an astute mixture of absolute fidelity to a generally agreed text, some flexibility in its organisation on the page, and, from the 1860s onwards, constant attention to developments in the recovery of the earliest texts. Such matters as chapter summaries not only caused occasional disagreement; their abbreviation or omission also meant that substantial savings in space (and hence paper) could be achieved. The spacial arrangement of the text could also be tinkered with, with relative immunity; and in 1871 Henry Bradshaw, the University Librarian, took a lead in redefining sections of the Bible so as to take account of the divisions in the new lectionary.[71] Such details had important marketing implications. To some extent, the prayer book could be treated in the same manner, and various abridgements or selections were prepared from time to time, whether just of the so-called Service-book or cheaper abridgements that omitted all the offices other than the baptism service.

Clay's position as Printer, increasing the printing work of the Press, was vindicated relatively quickly. That of Seeley, as bookseller and agent, was less comfortable. Quite apart from arguments as to the appropriate level of profit that should be allowed for selling the Syndics' books, it was not appreciated that to sell books takes considerably longer than to print them, and that the bookseller must therefore be at a disadvantage compared with the printer. Moreover, without stock to sell there could be no profit at all. Notwithstanding Clay's efforts, supplies of Bibles and prayer books remained weak in the face of the overwhelming presence of Oxford and the Queen's Printers. Furthermore, as the Syndics quickly discovered when they wished to launch Holden's edition of Cicero *De officiis*, too little thought had been given to Seeley's interests in the Press's publications other than the privileged books.

> If I am to look at it as a matter of business I must say that I could not accept less than 7½ per cent – as we satisfied ourselves long since that 5 p. cent scarcely covers the expences of carrying on business in London in the ordinary course of bookselling. In some few instances in which there was a large amount of ready money – no accounts and no risk of bad debts we have had only 5 p. cent but when credit is given and the ordinary contingencies of travel incurred, it is not sufficient. Mess[rs] Murray & Longman & some other houses charge 10 p.c.[72]

The Cicero, intended as a flagship in a programme of educational publishing, was too important to ignore as an isolated problem. But Seeley found little comfort even in the Bible trade over the coming months, and in 1856 he withdrew from the partnership.[73]

After some debate as to the need for another London partner, Seeley's place was taken by Hamilton, Adams & Co. of Paternoster Row. But this association lasted only a few months. The Bible trade, in which they had hoped to make their principal profits, proved to be more competitive than they had (apparently) anticipated, and required a greater investment than possible returns might justify.[74] They in turn were replaced by George Cox, son of the manager of the SPCK, who proved unsatisfactory and parted in the early summer of 1862.[75] Then the Syndics turned to the larger and much longer established house of John and Francis Hansard Rivington, whose interests in the educational and theological markets offered a more promising relationship. Agreement with the firm was reached in May 1862, and thus an old alliance was revived in a modern form.[76] There the matter rested until 1872, books from the Press being handled through premises at 32 Paternoster Row and in Stationers' Hall Court, while Rivingtons also pursued their retail business at Waterloo Place, in the West End, and increased their activities as publishers. But it proved to be not a situation much relished by the firm. John Rivington retired in 1866. In autumn of 1872 they gave notice, and the link with Cambridge was severed at the end of the year.[77] The difficulties were manifold. For though the London partners were 'sole publishers and agents' of the privileged books, there was little profit in them, and there were few other books actually published by the Press.

Indeed, most profit came not from selling ordinary editions of the Bible, which could be obtained much more cheaply through the various societies, but from the variety with which it could be presented in special bindings (fig. 31). The university presses supplied Bibles in sheets, not bound, so the final appearance of them was at the discretion of agents, wholesalers and retail booksellers. Outlets for these books were not confined to the appointed agents of the privileged presses. The advent of Scottish firms such as Collins and M'Phun, both from Glasgow, in the London market forced prices downwards. In 1858, the wholesalers Barritt & Co. in Fleet Street, who emphasised that their Bibles were printed by Her Majesty's Printers and by the Oxford and Cambridge presses, were offering Bibles 'with clasps, bound in embossed roan, with gilt edges' to sell retail at a shilling. Two years later, noting the general reduction in the prices of Bibles and prayer books, and quietly introducing the cheaper Scottish editions, they reduced many of their own prices to the trade, advertising 'novelties and general binding', and offering styles including 'Morocco antique, velvet, ivory, oak, and tortoiseshell'.[78] Rivingtons, seeking the same market, likewise paid especial attention to presentation, offering bindings in morocco and Russia leathers, in ivory, ebonite, vellum and velvet calf, as well as cheaper styles. They advertised 'Books mounted in gold and silver, jewelled and enamelled mounts, in the best gilt metal work, pierced and engraved from designs made by eminent artists expressly for Messrs. Rivington.' Bibles were also available illustrated with photographs or with steel plates or coloured engravings, at various prices. Members of the trade were invited to view these and other books at the London showroom.[79] Other Bible warehouses offered similarly dressed goods, sometimes illustrated with photographs of old-master paintings, bound up in styles and materials thought suitable for gifts: the Christmas season brought an annual rash of advertising from the many London warehouses and booksellers who by the late 1860s specialised in Bibles and church services, offering them at prices anywhere between a few pence and several guineas. In 1860,

Fig. 31 A Cambridge Bible at the Great Exhibition, 1851. The Bible Society selected for exhibition a copy of the edition printed at the instance of King William IV in 1837, elaborately bound by Hayday in leather and carved and stained yellow deal.

Dean and Son, launching themselves in the Bible trade, offered one in minion 24°, printed at Cambridge and containing twenty-four steel engravings, in a morocco binding with gilt clasps, all for 7s.6d.[80] It was estimated that at this period, in London alone, there were almost five hundred people engaged in binding Bibles and prayer books.[81]

In an age of experiment, and with a list of their own that was largely founded on Oxford theology and on the expanding educational market, the Rivingtons opened branches in Cambridge in 1862 and at Oxford in 1864.[82] In some respects, this was an obvious challenge to Macmillan. As a consequence of Alexander Macmillan's decision to move his firm's publishing to London and separate it from his bookselling in Cambridge, and of his appointment as publisher to Oxford – both events took place in 1863[83] – the two firms were thus each left by the end of 1864 with establishments in all three centres.

The invitation to Macmillan to become London publisher for the Oxford press was an attempt to answer some of the same kinds of difficulties that beset Cambridge. In Oxford, the Bible press was notably successful – and, with at least twenty machines 'constantly employed', according to report,[84] much more considerable than that at Cambridge; but the learned side of the Press was less active:

> The learned side, on the contrary, has been under the management of a board of delegates, gentlemen learned in Greek, Latin, Hebrew, and numerous other creditable studies, but unlearned in the art of making both ends meet; consequently, to use a homely phrase, it has been 'eating its head off'. The managers of the Bible side, although less learned, appear to have been good men of business: they make their own ink, and produce the cheapest Bibles and Prayer-books in the world; and, when the end of their financial year comes round, contrive to show a considerable profit upon their trading. The learned side produces scarcely anything reflecting credit upon the learning of the University, if we except a Greek Lexicon and one or two other books; authors, even those who reside in Oxford, shun the establishment, and prefer to have their books printed in London . . . There is reason to hope that the Oxford imprint will appear a little more frequently than it does at present, and that the creditable character of the work will not be confined to its mere correctness, but that in the quality of the paper used, the taste displayed in the setting-up of the type, and, above all, in the care bestowed upon the presswork, Oxford books may take that place in the estimation of connoisseurs, that they shall feel a pride in pointing to the number of volumes they may possess bearing the much-coveted imprimatur of the University.[85]

The same commentator also remarked on the 'notorious' fact that of late Oxford publications had been selling very slowly. It was a distinctly partial analysis of the situation at Oxford, where Liddell and Scott's Greek lexicon was advertised only a few months later in the context of a list of classical texts (many in Dindorf's editions) that did not deserve such general dismissal.[86] Macmillan's success in Cambridge made him an obvious possible saviour for Oxford, and the improvements at which *The Bookseller* hinted centred on proposals then under consideration. But apart from the fact that the scale of the Oxford press's enterprises was considerably greater (on the learned side as well as in the Bible press) than at Cambridge, the words applied to Oxford might as easily have been applied to Cambridge. The difference was that, for the present, the Cambridge syndics did nothing.

Clay sought competition with Oxford. His concern to revive Cambridge's fortunes in Bible and prayer-book printing amounted to nothing less than a direct challenge.

Inevitably, and relentlessly, comparisons were drawn by critics as well. The results were not always happy, and *The Bookseller* pontificated:

> BADLY-PRINTED BOOKS. – We have at various times drawn attention to well-printed books, but in the interest of both trade and literature we now feel compelled to raise our voice against a most extensive series of badly-printed books issued by three of the most respectable establishments in the kingdom. The books we refer to being the Bibles, Prayer-books, and Church Services issued by her Majesty's printers and by the Universities of Oxford and Cambridge. All the smaller books, with scarcely an exception as regards press work, are but little better than the books issued by the successors of the late Mr. Catnach. We are not speaking without full inquiry, and have now before us three Church Services, one from each establishment. The prices vary from 21s. to 65s., but we find that the price of the sheets of any one is but a few pence, and that it is absolutely impossible at the present time to procure a well-printed book. The reason given is that these books only pay when printed upon the cheap and nasty principle. This must be untrue. There is a demand for cheap books, as cheap as they can be had; but there is also a large demand for the same books in better bindings, and for this purpose it matters very little whether the price be 10d. or 2s. When Mr. Collingwood printed for Oxford, and Mr. J. W. Parker printed for Cambridge, and when the late Mr. Andrew Spottiswoode began to compete with the former, there was a race for quality. Those days are past, but we hope not for ever.[87]

A few months later, the same periodical returned to the subject, remarking some improvement and even suggesting that the pages of a recent Cambridge prayer book reminded it of one of Baskerville's designs.[88]

The same happened for other books where the two presses occupied similar ground. In 1858, concentrating mostly on production values – like most of those who compared the privileged books – a reviewer noted G. E. Corrie's new edition of Wheatley on the *Book of Common Prayer*:

> The Oxford University has long had an edition of this standard work, of which, we believe that we are correct in stating, the only editorial care edition after edition has received has been that bestowed by the printers. The sister university has now entered the field with an edition that is in many respects superior to the Oxford, as may be supposed from the price of one being only 5s., whilst the other is published at 12s.6d. The type is clearer, the paper thicker, the binding better, and altogether the volume is much handsomer. Dr. Corrie, however, appears to have done but little to the book. Some corrections have been made, additional illustrations supplied from notes existing in the handwriting of Dr. Waterland, and from other sources; but the additions are not very numerous . . .[89]

None was more jealous of their differences than the two presses themselves. Through their agents they displayed in advertisements their rival designs of the Bible, the prayer book, and the church services. When in 1875 Henry Frowde, at Oxford, was praised in *The Times* for his initiative in placing the proper psalms for festivals in their appropriate places in the services, Clay immediately pointed out that Cambridge had been doing this for four years – and had advertised the fact at Christmas 1871.[90]

The Press also found new business in printing learned journals. The circulation of the *Proceedings* of the Cambridge Philosophical Society and of the reports of the Observatory had never been great, and in 1854 the print order remained at only just over two hundred for each. The *Journal of Classical and Sacred Philology*, founded in 1854 and published jointly by Macmillan and Deighton, Bell was printed in editions of five hundred. It lasted only until 1860, when there was a gap until it was refounded as the *Journal of Philology* in 1868, under the editorship of W. G. Clark (editor of Shakespeare, and founder of the Clark lectures), J. E. B.Mayor (former University Librarian) and William Aldis Wright (Librarian of Trinity, and editor of Shakespeare). However, these were not published by the Press itself. The names of prominent members of the University graced their covers; but the advertisements which those covers contained stood as a reminder that though the University Press had vastly improved itself as a printer, its policy as a publisher had not kept pace. Long before 1868, Macmillan was dominant, as will be discussed in the next chapter.

Public examinations for schools, organised at Exeter in 1857 and then by the Universities of Oxford, Cambridge and Durham, introduced a new order into so-called 'middle-class education', and had immediate repercussions in the publishing industry. Though the Exeter authorities were careful to emphasise that they were not setting textbooks, they did provide a list of about a hundred recommended books, with a further seventeen for teachers. Parker and Longman were both prominent in this list (there was ample justification in the latter's taking over most of Parker's business a few years later); but there was little from Cambridge publishers: two book by Thring from Macmillan, and two by Pinnock on the Bible from J. Hall and Son. In the list of books for teachers and older students were Procter on the *Book of Common Prayer* (Macmillan) and Harvey Goodwin's *Elementary course of mathematics* (Deighton), the latter intended originally and explicitly for Cambridge undergraduates but now taken up for a further constituency. Both books were printed by the University Press. Procter's work had appeared in an edition of 1,500 copies in 1855, and was stereotyped for a second edition in 1856: by 1869, this edition had been reprinted six times. Goodwin's, first published in 1846, had reached a fourth, and cheaper, edition in 1853; the new edition in 1857 was of 2,500 copies. Thus the University Press gained – as printer, rather than as publisher – indirectly, and increasingly as the new examinations ranged across English and foreign literature, music and the arts, natural science and political economy, history and geography. Set texts (though not, at first, set editions) established an agenda for schoolchildren and for publishers alike.[91] The Cambridge *Regulations for local examinations* in 1864 named almost twenty texts that were to be studied.[92] However, it was to be some years before the Syndics of the University Press established, by a concerted publishing effort, any consistent connection between such lists of books named as set texts, or suggested for background reading, and the possible gain to be found in an educational list.

The advent of Rivingtons in Cambridge and Oxford yet further confirmed the two university towns as centres of educational publishing, on a quite new scale. London educational publishers, needing contacts and also the less easily measurable value of being seen at the right address, required every possible advantage. The title-page of

R. C. Jebb's edition of the *Electra* (Rivingtons, 1867) emphasised many of these points typographically – not only in providing Jebb's degree and position (he was then Fellow and assistant tutor at Trinity), but also in the air of official authority claimed in the black-letter type chosen to record the places of publication in the imprint: London, Oxford and Cambridge. The edition, one of a new series edited by Arthur Holmes (Fellow of Clare College) and Charles Bigg (Senior Student of Christ Church) was intended, like its peers, for undergraduates and for the upper forms of public schools. By 1870, Rivingtons could quote at length from enthusiastic reviewers of Jebb's work in the *Spectator, Guardian, Contemporary Review* and *Athenaeum*. By then, too, Rivington's educational list, dependent for many years on the editorial energies of T. K. Arnold, former Fellow of Trinity, included Christopher Wordsworth's annotated edition of the Bible, and a school edition of Isocrates by J. E. Sandys, and was dominated by Cambridge figures.[93] It was also prescient. Jebb had been a Fellow of Trinity for only four years when his *Electra* was published, and Sandys had graduated only a year before his Isocrates appeared. In engaging young men of such calibre, Rivington showed every sign of looking to develop connections with the University still further. As the publishers of the University's local examination papers and of the *University Reporter*, the firm had within a few years become quasi-official publishers to the University, challenging Deighton, Bell.

Meanwhile, at Oxford the Clarendon Press advertised its school and college books, as well as a growing academic list. In 1869, the new series of educational books included Spenser's *Faerie queene*, a selection from the *Canterbury tales* edited by Richard Morris as well as his *Specimens of early English*, selections from Shakespeare edited by Clark and Wright (the Macmillan connection with Oxford was a direct help in this), a handful of French texts, manuals of book-keeping and political economy, a work on physical education, and basic texts on chemistry, astronomy, heat and logic, besides the traditional Greek and Latin texts.[94] Much of this had been inspired by the needs of the new examinations; and the intentions of the series were more than short-term. Though a few seeds had been sown at Cambridge, no attempt had been made to cultivate these fresh markets. As yet, there was nothing comparable in scale, range, investment or imagination from the Pitt Building. Instead, the pages of advertisements for educational books in the periodical press linked Cambridge with Deighton, Bell ('Cambridge Greek and Latin texts', 'Cambridge school and college text books'), with Macmillan ('Cambridge school class books') and with J. Hall and Son. It is difficult not to suspect that there was an influential body of opinion wedded to the belief that it was not the University Press's business to publish books pertaining to the school examination papers which figured, for example, at the head of the Press's own advertisement in the educational number of *The Bookseller* in January 1860.[95]

The arguments were not straightforward. The old universities' success in establishing public examinations for schools certainly offered opportunities for publishing, where sales could to some extent be predicted. The combination of textbooks written by members of the universities, and printed or published by the university presses, with curricula (or at least an agenda) established and examined by those same bodies, was a powerful incentive to monopoly. But there was a body of opinion to whom this was a route full of dangers – not so much commercial, as educational.

> Education, in fact, in England is what the Universities choose to make it. This seems to me too great a power to be possessed by two corporations, however venerable and illustrious, especially since we know them to have grown up under very peculiar circumstances, and to be fortified by endowments against all modern influences, good or bad. I wish we had several more Universities; I mean teaching as well as examining Universities. I hope that the scheme which was announced some time ago, of creating a University for Manchester, will not be allowed to sleep. I should like to see similar schemes started in three or four more centres of population and industry.[96]

John Seeley – still at that stage Professor of Latin at University College London[97] – wrote this in 1867, in a volume of essays all but one of whose authors had some connection with Cambridge. His target was the division between learning and teaching, exemplified in the system of private tuition; and he was deeply suspicious of examinations whose justification was competition, rather than learning. 'I would deliver education from its dependence, and, without renouncing the undeniable advantages of strict and well-conducted examinations, I would use them as little as possible for the motive or incentive to study.'

Notwithstanding such weaknesses, and in the absence of a better system, the two ancient universities had a duty to lead, their faults becoming the faults of the educational system as a whole:

> Since Education in England is, in the main, what Oxford and Cambridge make it, how important is it that Oxford and Cambridge should disseminate just and profound views on education! There is no greater or deeper subject: there is no subject which demands more comprehensive knowledge or fresh observation . . . Oxford and Cambridge legislate for us, and we may be sure that if those universities labour at present under any serious defect of system, the whole education of the country will suffer for it: our schoolmasters will want just views of their duty, and they will also be fettered in the performance of it.[98]

By his own admission, Seeley's opinions gave offence.[99] But this unease at Cambridge itself engendered a lack of confidence in its notional role, not only as educational leader, but also as publisher. His remarks were delivered in the year that the Taunton Commission published its report, and he was in many respects at odds with the commissioners.[100] However, in his distrust of overly narrow curricula (exemplified, in current practice, in classical education) he was at one with Henry Sidgwick.

The crisis that overtook Cambridge in the 1860s was one of education, and of social and theological awareness. Sidgwick wrote of himself when he reflected on 'bearing the burden of humanity in the lap of luxury'.[101] College reform; tripos reform; statute reform; the education of women; the education of the working classes: all were causes for re-examination. In a commercial sense, the University Press was immune from such movements; but University-wide uncertainty was characterised in the Press's affairs by a lack of direction and of investment. The fault did not lie with Clay, whose energies as a printer were never called in question, and who used a vacuum in the

Syndics' affairs to promote his own interests as a printer to the book trade at large – including the competitors of the Press's publishing interests. Thanks to his energies, men and machines were kept employed that would otherwise have been laid off or left to fall into disuse. In this lay one of the core differences between the mid-eighteenth century and the mid-nineteenth. In the 1730s, the fact that presses stood idle and men were unoccupied became a scandal only after the University recognised it. In the 1860s, Clay, successor to Crownfield as University Printer, discovered how similar uninterest by the University might be turned to advantage, when to do otherwise would be to waste skilled labour and waste the cost of equipment.

In 1866, Clay estimated that the printing business had increased by four or five times its level when he had taken over. It was showing a comfortable profit; part of this was being reinvested; and the University's investment in the partnership could be estimated as being worth more than two and a half times what it had been in 1854.[102] As a printing business, this was highly satisfactory. The publishing side was another matter. Although there were arrangements in place to sell the Press's publications, they were unequal to the task, and editions were in any case too large. In 1863, it was agreed to auction off overstock, some of it printed only very recently: the list included up to 400 sets of Barrow's works (completed in 1859), up to 700 of Wheatley on the prayer book (1858), 300 of Smith's *Select discourses* (1859), 300 of Kemble's edition of St Matthew's Gospel in Anglo-Saxon (1858), and 300 of Whewell's Grotius (1854).[103]

The editions had been put to press in a period of over-confidence, and the Cambridge press was by no means the only publisher to find itself in difficulties. In 1858, the prices of over sixty publications of the Oxford University Press had been reduced, in some cases by 75 per cent and more: the list included not only works dating from the eighteenth century (Wilkins's Coptic New Testament, 1716, was reduced by almost half), but even quite recent books published only in the previous ten years.[104] For all the trade, whether in printing, publishing or bookselling, it was a period of confusion, as a small, well-established group of booksellers complained against the widespread practice of underselling – given legitimacy by Lord Campbell's ruling in 1852[105] – and publishers and printers alike campaigned for the abolition of paper duties, a campaign finally successful in 1861. 'I venture to say', Gladstone protested to the House of Commons in 1852, 'that the whole system of the bookselling trade in this country – except so far as it is partially mitigated by what are called cheap publications – is a disgrace to our present state of civilisation.'[106] Efforts to provide cheap books were not new, and were usually dated by contemporary commentators from the general introduction of machine-made paper, machine printing, paper bindings (characteristically on yellowbacks) and the influence of the railways. By the early 1860s some old-established publishers were also beginning to turn to their back-lists for cheap editions, while striving to maintain their better books. Booksellers, no longer required to maintain prices, had quickly adopted the habit of selling some books at little above cost price; and at least one publisher considered that the effect was to provide a return to publishers of little more than half the nominal selling price. In a turbulent period, the same commentator wondered whether publishers would in time 'fall on the expedient of lowering nominal selling prices, at the same time lessening allowances', or whether they would 'altogether drop the marking of prices'.[107] In the general market, sales for some books were vast, some periodicals achieved sales of over 250,000, and yellowback novels transformed the world of the reading public from the mid-1850s. The university presses enjoyed none of these successes, and faced the difficulties of changing retail prices and changing prices of materials with (in the case of Cambridge) perilously slim reserves.

The Syndics at Cambridge showed no sign of understanding their market, and when they discovered that sales of most of their investments were disastrously low, they preferred to withdraw from publishing almost altogether. In 1871, the only work of any consequence to bear their authority was Skeat's edition of the Gospel of St Mark in Anglo-Saxon and Northumbrian versions, a volume designed to be set beside the earlier work of Kemble and of Charles Hardwick, who had been entrusted with finishing St Matthew following Kemble's death in 1857. Even the new official organ of the University, the *Cambridge University Reporter*, was at first published by Rivington, as part of the ordinary publishing arrangement for London.[108] In a series of short-term agreements to allow it life for a year at a time, the venture was handled with more hesitation than by commercial firms who launched periodicals many times its bulk and circulation. At a time when even quite small decisions had to be presented for the University's approval if they entailed some continuing commitment – whether small building works or the establishment of a journal that did little more than bring within two covers, at regular intervals, what had been an assortment of official notices – the Syndics showed not only an impressive (and frequently puzzling) lack of self-confidence, but also little sign that they wished for enlightenment as publishers.

Printing was more straightforward, and was the Press's main business. Its management required no opinion from the Syndics, provided that the equipment was sufficient and there were no losses accounted to the University. Clay was left to pursue his own interests, and to obtain (apparently with little difficulty) the means to do so. Proposals for an extension to the machine room in 1862 were developed first into a more ambitious scheme, and then yet further land was bought in 1872.[109] The Syndics had invested heavily in machinery on and in the immediate aftermath of Clay's appointment, and they continued to do so. In 1862–4 they authorised the purchase of six machine presses. A further double cylinder press was authorised, for £750, in 1872.[110] Most of these machines were not needed for the publications of the Press, or even for printing the privileged books (though in 1863 the Syndics agreed to an edition of the Welsh New Testament in 50,000 copies[111]), but mainly to print the books ordered by Macmillan.

Among the miscellaneous evidence received by the Graham Commission was a memorandum on various aspects of the management of the University, by Charles C. Babington of St John's, whose principal scholarly interest was in field botany, and who in 1861 succeeded Henslow as Professor of Botany. Among his several suggestions were not only that the University should appoint a 'University Bursar' (no such person was appointed until 1926), but also that the Press Syndicate should become a more flexible body, regularly pruned of those who had served longest.[112] Such a reform was long overdue. With no means of introducing fresh blood other than by death or departure from Cambridge, and depending heavily on heads of houses, the Syndicate had repeatedly proved its weaknesses when faced with challenges from either the book trade at large or from the smaller world of resident members of the University. In 1855 the size of the Syndicate was reduced, and a new system was instigated whereby one-third of the members retired each year, in a three-year cycle. It was effective – even overly so, in that it dispensed too readily with wise heads who might have benefited the Press; and it eliminated useless wood. Yet to introduce fresh heads was one thing. To ensure that they agreed an agenda suitable for a major printing and publishing house was quite another, and here reform was less successful. The Syndics met to consider the formalities of successive publishing agreements and partnership arrangements, as Hamilton, Adams took over from Seeley, and in turn gave place to Cox, until Cox himself was quickly succeeded by Rivington: the rapid turnover is itself some indication of the London trade's view of the management of the Cambridge press. Otherwise, the Syndics' main duties remained to reach occasional decisions on the printing and pricing of editions of the Bible and prayer book, and to oversee the buildings and equipment. In attempts to move stock, prices of several editions of the Bible and prayer book were reduced in the 1850s. A few other books were authorised; but the minutes of the meetings record no discussion of any policy for publishing more generally. Meetings were often poorly attended. In 1852, the Graham Commission had noted that of the eighteen members of the Syndicate, only about half regularly came.[113] In a sequence of four meetings arranged over six months in 1860, one was attended by the Vice-Chancellor and four others, the next by the Vice-Chancellor and three others, the next by nobody at all, and the fourth by just one.[114]

Other reforms, less complicated to achieve and all but revolutionary nonetheless, were directed at the advertisement and sale of the Press's books. In an account of University printing at Cambridge from the earliest times, *The Bookseller* remarked in 1860 on the 'suicidal regulation' that prevented review copies from being sent out, remarking tartly that 'the university, it would seem, is too dignified to recognize the existence of newspapers and magazines'.[115] The criticism was out of date, but not by many months. Indeed, the principle of sending out specimen copies seems to have been established before agreement was reached on review copies. In November 1854, copies of Holden's *De officiis* were sent out to the headmasters of the leading public schools. Only in November 1858 did the Syndics agree, rather cautiously, to send out review copies 'occasionally', 'if thought advisable'.[116] The initial list of putative recipients consisted of the *Guardian*, the *Saturday Review*, the *Athenaeum*, the *Literary Gazette*, the *Christian Remembrancer*, the *Literary Churchman* and the *Bookseller*.[117] It could hardly have been more cautious.

Some of the changes that affected the University Press were introduced by Clay, and others by Cartmell. But some of the most important came with the book trade, and were of quite independent origin. The monthly requirements of Macmillans and of

Deighton, Bell for book printing had a much greater effect on the Press than the deliberations of the Syndics. The demands for examination papers – from the University, from colleges, from schools and from the examining board – were not driven by any decision of the Press Syndicate. In the 1850s and 1860s some of the parts of the book trade closest to the University Press's own interests were transformed by the demand for schoolbooks on subjects well beyond the traditional confines of mathematics and classical texts; yet here, where a decision would have been valuable, the Syndicate was noticeably silent.

✎ 19 ✎

Macmillan

When Daniel Macmillan, aged not quite twenty, left his native Arran and, like many Scots before him, headed southwards, his goal was London, not Cambridge.[1] But after a discouraging search for employment among London publishing houses, he was introduced at Longman's to the bookseller Elijah Johnson, of Trinity Street, Cambridge, who offered him a place at £30 a year, plus board. At the beginning of October 1833 Macmillan joined Johnson, as shopman; he remained with him until October 1836. Compared with the potential and excitement of the London trade, of which the younger man had some inkling thanks to his apprenticeship to a bookseller and bookbinder in Irvine, and (more particularly) his subsequent employment as a bookseller in Glasgow, as well as from his friend James MacLehose in London, Johnson's shop seems to have been something of a disappointment.

However, it had the advantage that Macmillan found leisure there to become well read; and he gained knowledge of the University, as well as the respect of some of its members. These were to stand him in good stead in later years. During his time with Johnson, old-fashioned and limited in his view of the world, Macmillan unwittingly laid the foundations for a business that even by the time of his early death in 1857 was more influential than that of any bookseller in Cambridge before him, and on which the University Press in large measure depended. But in 1837, after a short visit to Scotland, he took a post with Messrs Seeley in Fleet Street, building on the Scottish connection established there by MacLehose, who returned to Glasgow. Macmillan remained with the Seeleys until 1843. His younger brother, Alexander, gave up a modest living as a schoolmaster near Paisley, and joined him there in 1839. In 1843, the two brothers decided to establish their own business; but their choice of premises in Aldersgate Street, near Smithfield in London, all too soon proved unfruitful. Daniel Macmillan, who had first become acquainted with Julius Charles Hare as the joint author of *Guesses at truth*,[2] responded to Hare's remark that they were poorly located with the best defence he could muster:

> We are content to make the best of Aldersgate Street for the present, hoping to move west by and by. We have a very neat shop for a very small rent. It is within five minutes walk of the post office, and Paternoster Row. Nowadays, with penny posts, and Parcels Delivery Companies, it is an easy matter to attend to orders from any part of town or country.[3]

When the opportunity offered to purchase the business of Richard Newby, bookseller in Trinity Street in Cambridge, the brothers consulted with Hare, among others, and took it

> (1) because there is no bookseller in Cambridge, since Thorpe left it, except Stevenson, who knows anything of books. (2) Because the situation is so good, being so near to Trinity and St. John's Colleges. (3) Because I should give careful and constant attention to business. And (4) because in Cambridge one could get sooner known than in London.[4]

The penny post and much improved systems for parcel deliveries transformed the book trade, not just in the new ease with which customers could be accommodated, but also in the relationships between publishers, wholesalers and booksellers. The postal system brought greater opportunities for the use of printed advertisements, prospectuses and catalogues, all of them supporting the established means of sharing information concerning new books in the pages of specialist or more general periodicals. Although special rates for books were not introduced until 1855, practices had changed long before. A few weeks after the introduction of the penny post in January 1840, a London educational bookseller, George Bell, announced that he had opened a depot in London for books published at Oxford and Cambridge designed to avoid 'the delay and disappointment so frequently expererienced by parties requiring these books . . . as a frequent communication will be kept up with the two universities'. It was not entirely fortuitous that his advertisement appeared next to one for a manufacturer of Post Office letter balances.[5] The Macmillans combined their serious-minded approach to literature with these and other developments, working at first within a circle defined by the University and its interests, though encompassing a much wider geographical area. Encouraged by Hare (who advanced them £500) and by F. D. Maurice, and with a loan from W. Burnside, from London, they bought Newby's business and opened their shop at 17 Trinity Street in October 1843.[6] Their first Cambridge catalogue was sent out with the *British Magazine* the following March.

Having made the move, the brothers were even more determined; and when the opportunity came in the autumn of 1845 to purchase Thomas Stevenson's shop, with its stock, at 1 Trinity Street they seized it, raising the money to do so by taking in a partner who otherwise had no interest in the book trade.[7] The shop, neutral in that introductions could easily be made, and yet informed (and frequently entertaining) ground, became one of the most important social centres of Cambridge. It also encouraged the brothers (and Daniel in particular) to develop the publishing side of their business, thereby continuing – though in greatly increased and diversified form – the longstanding tradition among Cambridge booksellers of carrying on a publishing business alongside the sale of new and second-hand books. The Macmillans built on a tradition, and transformed it. 'Here', in the words of Thomas Hughes, drawing on remembered conversations, 'was a mine, hitherto almost unworked, of the best book-producing power of the nation, especially for educational works. There was a great want of these, and in every generation of undergraduates were men specially fitted for writing or editing them.'[8]

In 1843 they had published one book in Aldersgate Street, and one at 17 Trinity Street. Two publications appeared in 1844; seven in 1845; and fourteen, as well as the relaunched *Cambridge Mathematical Journal*, now the *Cambridge and Dublin Mathematical Journal*, in 1846.[9]

Hare did what he could to develop their interests, arranging for them to share one of his books with Parker, and offering advice on whether to accept an offer by the London bookseller and Tractarian sympathiser Edward Lumley, to add their name to the title-page of a new edition of Kenelm Henry Digby's *Broad stone of honour*: the brothers, more at home with evangelical forms of Christianity, did not take up this improbable suggestion.[10] He also wrote to introduce Daniel to Whewell:

> He is a man for whom I have the highest esteem and regards, both morally and intellect-ually . . . he has a high moral purpose, to which he desires to devote his life. Maurice, to whom I introduced him, values him no less than I do; and I really hope it will be a good thing for Cambridge to have so intelligent a bookseller. At present his capital is very small, the result of savings out of a clerk's salary, drained by the necessity of assisting his rela-tions: hence he will not be able to muster a large stock of books: but I hope, and can hardly doubt, that in this respect he will improve. In all others, I believe, he will be incomparably superior to any person of his class in Cambridge.[11]

Whatever the hopes of those who sought the moral high ground, to Daniel Macmillan Cambridge was a puzzle. Local booksellers and the University alike appeared not to realise the potential for a more vigorous attitude to publishing, let alone a proper policy. Deighton was the most active locally, but had little fresh spirit; and while Parker, in London, carried many Cambridge men in his lists, his preoccupations as a major London publisher meant that he could not give his attention wholeheartedly to the university to which he was Printer.

> I wonder that Cambridge University never sends out good editions of English theo-logians, while Oxford sends out so many, and such handsome books, and so many of them by Cambridge men. If Cambridge were to republish the writings of the best of her sons what a noble array of books we should have. It would be an easy matter to do it. The thing might be managed as the Parker Society's books are. With a subscription of £2.2s. a year it would be easy to get nearly all the professional men in England and Scotland who had ever been Cambridge men. Jeremy Taylor, or Fuller, or Barrow, would be good books to begin with, as they are popular writers, better known than many others . . . Donne, Henry More, John Smith, Cudworth, and others might follow. I don't know whether Milton and Howe would have any chance, but a good edition of Milton's complete works is wanted, and it might be so edited as to be for the good of the Church. I should like very much to see Cambridge undertake such a work, and employ the most thoughtful of her sons as editors. There is no need to have commercial men working in it for the purpose of money-making. It were better if the University undertook it for its own honour, and for the advancement of sound learning.[12]

Though Macmillan offered himself to take on the management of such a course, many aspects of it were matters for the University, not necessarily a bookseller with authors and editors – 'commercial men working . . . for the purpose of money-making.' In any case, to believe that so many members of the University would subscribe to such a list, in the way that the clergy and interested laity were moved by religious ideals, conviction or interests to subscribe to the Parker Society, was unrealistic. But once again, the comparisons were with Oxford. The current Oxford edition of Barrow might be 'not very handsome and .. very expensive', but it remained that Cambridge men were not being published where one might expect to look first.

Others in Cambridge were to warm to this theme; but it took some years to take root, and when it did so it developed along some of the lines suggested here by Macmillan. Meanwhile he had other concerns as well, of a more pressing nature. 'I should like very much to see some good Cambridge tracts started. The incendiarism in our neighbourhood, and the discontent of the poor everywhere, call loudly for some mode of lessening the misunderstanding between rich and poor.'[13] Nothing came of such a series of tracts, and as the brothers built up their list two main strands of interest emerged during their first years: in theology and in education – the two subjects in which Deighton had best succeeded, and found the easiest support in the University.

As its critics frequently remarked, the University had allowed itself to fall too much into the grind of examinations. The dearth of leadership was painfully apparent. Cambridge had no Newman or Pusey; more seriously, there seemed no prospect of one. 'Your present divinity professors are not men to stir the minds of the university', wrote Hare to Whewell in 1841, referring also to the 'never-ending still-beginning examinations'.[14] As booksellers, the Macmillan brothers could only provide succour to other interests once they had built up a capital by means of those already established; and so, whatever the moral curiosities of Daniel, and the support given by Hare, the basis of their list depended at first very largely on books previously published, and on kindred new works. Other authors and titles had to be introduced gradually. So, apart from F. D. Maurice, at this time still chaplain of Guy's Hospital and Professor of English Literature at King's College, London, their authors soon included new editions of established works such as the textbooks in mechanics and natural philosophy, by J. C. Snowball, Fellow of St John's. Other textbooks they shared with Deighton; and they also shared with Deighton the pioneering catalogue of the medieval manuscripts in Gonville and Caius College, by J. J. Smith (1849).

The brothers' list was built up by newcomers to publishing; but its foundations were firmly in the past. Kingsley had been first published by Parker, and a substantial group of his books was only taken over in 1863.[15] F. D. Maurice, Hare and Trench had likewise been published by Parker. The need for textbooks in subjects other than the classics and mathematics had long been clear. When F. D. Maurice determined to lecture on the Prologue to the Canterbury Tales at King's College, London, he had been unable to find a suitable text at an affordable price: 'I have Tyrwhitt for my own use, but I doubted whether there was an edition sufficiently cheap to be in the hands of every person in the class. I find there is one – merely of the "Canterbury Tales" – printed at Liverpool, costing about seven shillings.'[16] Daniel and Alexander Macmillan did not publish the kind of edition that Maurice sought (Richard Morris's appeared, in the Clarendon Press series, in 1867). In continuing the assured markets in mathematics, the classics and divinity, they were conservative; but they established a group of schoolmaster-authors who themselves became associated with the firm of Macmillan in particular: Edward Thring of Uppingham, G. F. Maclear of King's College School and Josiah Wright of Sutton Coldfield, as well as Todhunter and Barnard Smith of Cambridge.

The usual printer for the Macmillans became Richard Clay. But many of their books were printed by Clay's son, at the University Press, in an arrangement convenient alike to a publisher only a little along the street, and to authors who lived in similar proximity. Occasionally, Palmer and Metcalfe were also employed, likewise as local Cambridge printers. By the early 1860s, Metcalfe had become an important printer to the firm, with a contract to print the *Oxford, Cambridge and Dublin Messenger of Mathematics*, which made its début in 1861. His situation (by this time he had moved to Green Street; he was later to move again, to Trinity Street) gave him a topographical advantage, close to authors in Trinity, St John's and Caius. Apart from pamphlets, the first book that the University Press printed for the Macmillans was an edition by F. D. Maurice of William Law's *Remarks on the fable of the bees* (1844), in an edition of 500 copies. It was a modest beginning, for within a decade the Press had built up with the firm a relationship on which each depended. The educational list was especially critical at first, and remained so even after the Macmillan list was gradually diversified so as to include literature. Among the regular orders were repeated reprintings, of several thousand each time, of Barnard Smith's *Arithmetic for schools* (first published in 1854): in 1862 alone, 20,000 copies were called for. Isaac Todhunter, Fellow of St John's, became of even greater consequence, both to Macmillan and also to the University Press. His output was prolific, and it was systematic. His *Treatise on the differential calculus*, his *Algebra for the use of colleges and schools* (1858) and his *Elements of Euclid* (1862) became staples for the Cambridge press. The *Algebra*, first published in 3,000 copies, and notwithstanding a well-justified protest that he had relied too closely on the long-established textbook on the same topic by James Wood,[17] by 1862 required a third edition of 10,000, and by 1870 a fifth edition of 10,000; his *Algebra for beginners* was printed 20,000 copies at a time by the early 1870s; the 1871 impression of Euclid was of 20,000. Francis Procter's *History of the Book of Common Prayer*, published in 1855 in an edition of 1,500 copies, and already mentioned, was revised for a second edition the following year, and was repeatedly reprinted with revisions for many years subsequently.[18]

Much of this was the result of successful forays into the expanding educational market. By 1859 the Macmillan catalogue included over fifty titles described as 'class books for colleges and schools'.[19] The Macmillan list, strong in theology and mathematics, was very largely built on authors having some connection with Cambridge; and it was distinctive. In the context of the book trade as a whole, Charles Morgan captured some of its tone in writing of 'the less dazzling but solider truth'.[20] In Daniel's hands in particular there was an air of seriousness about the subjects of the books published. This was also the firm that, venturing into novels, in spring 1855 published Charles Kingsley's *Westward Ho!*; in 1856, *The heroes*; in 1857, Thomas Hughes's *Tom Brown's schooldays*; in 1859, Henry Kingsley's *Geoffry Hamlyn*; and in November 1859 launched a new shilling monthly, *Macmillan's Magazine*, whose pages during the first years serialised *Tom Brown at Oxford*, Henry Kingsley's *Ravenshoe*, and *The water-babies*. It was a determined commitment to contemporary imaginative literature; but such books were also used to consolidate Macmillan's hold on the educational market. Along with Thring's sermons, David Masson's essays, and Westcott on the New Testament, the novels of Charles Kingsley and *Tom Brown's schooldays* were offered as books suitable for college or school prizes, bound either in calf, extra gilt with marbled leaves, or, for a few shillings more, bound in morocco with gilt leaves.[21] The creation of the *Golden treasury series*, in the wake of Palgrave's anthology first published in 1861, led to further commitments in literature. The first to appear after the *Golden treasury* itself were *The pilgrim's progress*, and William Aldis Wright's edition of Bacon's essays. Both were printed by the University Press, and their design was a matter of some concern. The toned paper and the details of the typography selected for the Bunyan reflected a desire to impart an antiquarian flavour, which persisted in the Bacon. The bindings were designed with the same purpose, though Alexander Macmillan, as usual, left most of the detail for this part to James Burn, the binder whom he normally employed. The fine line engravings that feature on the title-pages of the series were, however, not printed by the Press but by the specialist plate printers McQueen, of Tottenham Court Road, to whom sheets of the ordinary copies were sent once the letterpress was completed:[22] the University Press was not equipped for such work.

The books for which Macmillan's became most generally celebrated were not on the whole printed by the University Press. In the early 1860s, Daniel Wilson's *Prehistoric man* (1862) was printed by Constable in Edinburgh; Gilchrist's biography of William Blake and Kingsley's *The water-babies* (both 1863) were printed by Clay in London; and Fawcett's *Manual of political economy* (also 1863) was printed by Spottiswoode. With Alexander Macmillan's removal to London in 1863, the Pitt Building might have seemed, in effect, to have been placed at a disadvantage, though the firm continued to use the University Press, employing it especially for the work of Cambridge authors and editors. In October, the appointment of Macmillan as publisher to the University of Oxford brought the Oxford press within everyday consideration, though in 1865 its printing of the first edition of *Alice in Wonderland* proved a grievous disappointment, made good only when Richard Clay took over.

In practice, the Cambridge press prospered at Macmillan's hands. Reprints from electros of educational books were straightforward. But none of Macmillan's publications made greater demands of the University Press than their collected editions of Shakespeare: first a major new edition in nine volumes, and then the unprecedented success of the popular one-volume Globe edition. In 1852, John Payne Collier's announcement of his discovery of a Second Folio covered in contemporary textual changes created an excitement that reached far beyond the ordinary circles of scholarship and bibliophily.[23] Any doubts over the volume's authenticity only intensified public thirst – whether for new authoritative editions or for more popular and cheaper collections.

In 1864, the firm of Routledge alone advertised six different editions, at prices between six shillings and four guineas.[24] The tercentenary of Shakespeare's birth fell in 1864, and the book trade exploited the occasion. New settings of established editions vied with each other, and new ones were commissioned, of which the most important by far were those of Alexander Dyce and of a team from Cambridge: W. G. Clark, William Aldis Wright and John Glover. There were new monographs and reworked old ones; photographs and engravings of places associated with Shakespeare and volumes of illustrations of his plays. The excitement spilled into other areas of marketing, from playing cards to commemorative china. In Stratford-upon-Avon, recently made accessible by train, the year was marked with a major festival that established a tourist industry on a new scale. Periodicals published special issues to mark the anniversary. A type-facsimile of the First Folio was issued by Booth and a photo-lithographic one by Day & Son. The labours of Collier, suspect and often fraudulent though they were, of Halliwell and of Dyce; the activities of the Shakespeare Society, founded by Halliwell, Charles Knight and Dyce in 1840; and the nascent appeal of Stratford-upon-Avon: all helped to generate a mood of excitement bordering sometimes on mania, from which grew the Cambridge Shakespeare itself.

For most people, the impetus was Shakespeare's. But in 1853, and writing of the text of the Bible, Scrivener had set religious and national interests beside each other. His systematic insistence on reconsideration of Biblical manuscripts, and especially in a context of nationalism ('the countrymen of Bentley and Mill'[25]), coincided with the revived interest in the text of Shakespeare. Textual scholarship was to be on a national agenda. The resulting energy brought new editions of the Bible, both in Greek and in English, and of Shakespeare, that were to stand for generations. The university presses were instrumental in both.

In Cambridge, the seed for a new edition of Shakespeare seems to have been sown in 1860, when at the instigation of W. G. Clark, of Trinity College, Macmillan had a specimen of part of *Richard II* set up at the University Press. At this stage, the editors were to be Clark and another Fellow of Trinity, H. R. Luard, whose interest in textual matters had been aroused by a youthful passion for the work of Porson.[26] For reassurance and advice, Alexander Macmillan turned to his most trusted friend in the trade, James MacLehose:

> I want you to be so kind as to tell me what you think of the chances for an edition of *Shakespeare*, edited like a critical edition of a classical author, with merely the text and such various readings as seemed to have value either from their appearance in early editions or from their intrinsic worth . . . The claims would be that anyone possessing it would have (1) a beautiful book in point of typography, (2) as pure and genuine a text, free from all taints of Collierism and other similar isms as can be obtained from careful scholarship and sound sense, (3) a complete list of all readings both from early editions and skilful suggestion as had any worth.[27]

At 4 guineas a set, and with no fees to the editors who would work 'as a labour of love', Macmillan estimated that he could gain a 'decent profit' with 750 copies. The only risk to him was in paper and print.

Eventually the print order was doubled, to 1,500 copies.[28] It was decided not to stereotype the edition, on grounds of cost: as the charge for stereotyping would be about three-quarters as much as composition itself, and as the University Press charged more for printing from stereotypes, any savings would be insignificant. It was better to risk a larger first impression.[29] At the end of 1862, Macmillan's revealed their hand to the general public, in announcing the first volume of a new edition to be edited by W. G. Clark and John Glover,[30] both of Trinity. The project required careful publicity, not only to excite sales but also to ensure that customers would remain to complete their sets: from the beginning, Alexander Macmillan had been anxious at publishing the volumes at intervals, rather than as a complete group. In mid-November they wrote of their plans to George Robertson, the leading bookseller in Melbourne, promising a supply of circulars by the next mail.[31] There were 24,000 prospectuses printed by the University Press[32] and 100 were printed specially for Calcutta.[33] In Edinburgh, MacLehose received 500 overprinted with his name, as well as 300 circulars and 4 cards on which to gather orders – a favour to an old and loyal friend, in that other Edinburgh booksellers were not to be treated in this way.[34] Bills were inserted in magazines; and the London bookseller Bernard Quaritch was chastised for suggesting that the edition was to be in a smaller format than the demy octavo that was planned. Advertisements explained that the text would be based on 'thorough collation of the four Folios, and of all the Quarto editions of the separate Plays, and of subsequent editions and commentaries'.[35] In March 1863, with publication of the first volume imminent, fourteen travellers' samples were obtained from Burn, the binder.[36]

It was a bold undertaking for the publishers, the more so in that it was planned at the same time that Roundell Palmer's *Book of praise*, Wright's Bacon, and Gilchrist's biography of Blake were all passing through Macmillan's hands.[37] But it was made immeasurably more feasible for the editors by the existence of Edward Capell's collection of the plays, with associated Shakespearean literature, in their own college library.[38] Glover retired from the project soon after it was launched, on leaving Cambridge, and his place was taken by his successor as Librarian, William Aldis Wright – on whom fell most of the subsequent editorial burden, one that continued to occupy him almost to the end of his life in 1914. The first volume appeared in spring 1863, and the ninth and last in September 1866. Even though critics immediately made themselves known ('wretched in the extreme', wrote Dyce: 'a *mumpsimus* edition with hieroglyphical notes'[39]) it was an astonishing editorial feat, and one that laid many of the foundations of work subsequently. The whole was printed at the University Press.

The first volumes of this new and amply annotated edition were followed almost immediately by the single-volume Globe edition, from the same editors: 'the best text in elegant and readable type, very portable in size, strong and handsome in binding, and at a price that will place it within the reach of everybody'.[40] It, too, was printed by the Unversity Press, and it was designed from the first for the Christmas market in 1864. The nine-volume edition was for the library; the Globe edition was for convenience and for economy. 'My eyes being good as ever, I take the Globe volume, which

I bought in days when such a purchase was more than an extravagance', recalled George Gissing.[41]

Even more than the Cambridge Shakespeare, the volume was produced at extraordinary speed. As an edition, the Globe version had a long life.[42] But it was conceived on the sudden; and from among the conflicting demands of Clay as printer, Macmillan as publisher, and William Aldis Wright as principal editor there emerge some of the practicalities of the making of books. In order to get so much type set, proofed and printed in six months, Clay took on extra staff. Having been taken on, these men had to be kept occupied.

Macmillan sent a specimen page to James MacLehose on 24 May, and he was willing to be ingenious. When the Globe edition was proposed, Wright and Clark were immersed in volume four of their Cambridge Shakespeare – and thus had a prepared text of less than half of Shakespeare's works. The ninth and final volume was not to be published until 1866. So there was no authoritative text to which Clay could automatically turn. The help of the two editors was therefore crucial. In order to get round the absence of appropriately authoritative copy-text, Macmillan and Clay hit on the suggestion that proofs should be set up from Knight's Stratford edition, which Clark and Wright could 'tear about for the text'.[43] It was a suggestion that in its acceptance of potentially heavy correction came easily from a publisher who was well accustomed to the expenses and necessities of alterations (not simply corrections) in authors' proofs and revises, to be received with the same generous allowance that characterised so much ordinary setting and proof-correction in the mid-nineteenth-century trade. From London, Macmillan was determined to set the pace early. By late June he was asking whether Clay had copy, and when proofs might be expected.[44] The difficulties were not only editorial, and sprang directly from the printing house, which thus dictated proceedings to publisher and editors alike, as Macmillan explained to Wright.

> The difficulty with regard to the small Shakespeare is this. Clay could not have got so much type set up in the time without employing an extra number of compositors specially for the work. They must *keep the men going somehow* till the end of the book. Clay's plan was to *set up* the work from some ordinary Shakespeare and then *read it before sending you proofs* from your revised copy. If the latter were done properly of course it concerns me that *you* are sure what he does with regard to the first. Indeed he might justly grumble if we demand the book at a specific time & interfere with his private business arrangements for carrying it out.[45]

Not surprisingly, by September, one of the very few letters that survive to Clay from the editors reveals Wright sitting in a slow train crossing Suffolk, and reading proofs: the feat with the small nonpareil types in such circumstances is not to be underestimated.

Notwithstanding Clay's difficulties and demands, and as with the original edition from which it was derived, Macmillan saw the Globe Shakespeare as a book of little risk. 'You see it would be immeasurably the cheapest, most beautiful, and handy book that has appeared of *any kind*, except the Bible.'[46] 'We have little doubt', remarked *The*

Bookseller in September, 'that large numbers of buyers will be found, who will purchase their six or eight copies for the purpose of placing one in every room in their house.' This was never likely; but the volume's success made greater demands on the University Press than any other book to that date. The design of the volume was a typographical *tour de force*. Like other contemporary one-volume editions, it followed the early folio editions in being set in two columns, within rules. At 3s.6d. – later reduced to half a crown – it was not only cheaper than other octavo versions costing twelve or fifteen shillings: it was also within reach of the market for copies costing only two shillings.[47] But unlike its main competitors, the one-volume editions of Payne Collier (Whittaker & Co., 1853), Thomas Campbell (Routledge, 1859), the Memorial edition (Simpkin, 1864) and the Cowden Clarkes (Bickers & Son, 1864), all of which were imperial octavos, the Globe edition was a royal foolscap octavo, less than half the size, while the 1079 pages were made up into a book less than one and a half inches thick. The technical challenges to the Press of thin paper (made by Dickinson: it has generally worn well, though with some browning) and the nonpareil type in which the text was set, were met by compositors and pressmen who were well used to printing long runs of Bibles and prayer books.

It is unfortunate that, so far, little is known of who was responsible for adapting the page design, reducing many of the conventions of the First Folio to a format that would fit into a generous-sized pocket. Macmillan's remarks in his letters to Clay on the subject are concerned principally with the design of the title-page. 'I have forgotten day by day to tell you that I don't much like the two ornaments which you put above and below your own imprint on the back of the Globe Shakespeare. I think I must tell you to take them away as they somewhat mar the title.'[48] The woodcut globe was a late addition, and it was only after several attempts that Clay's men managed to design a title-page that left Macmillan content. As a publisher, Macmillan recognised the importance of initial impressions, and so set great value by the title-page. But the most difficult part, and the most remarkable, was the typography of the text-pages, which required decisions line by line as to how best to fit the text into the restrictions of the margins, while showing line numbers as well.

Marketing for the book was even more demanding, and was based on no less than 225,000 copies of an eight-page prospectus printed at the University Press. Early copies, bound as the completed work but with only the first pages printed and the rest bulked out with blank paper, were prepared in October: among the recipients were Hay & Co. in Calcutta, George Robertson in Melbourne, William Maddock in Sydney, Walsh & Co. in Hobart Town and Rigby in Adelaide.[49] Prospectuses were sent to other firms for insertion in their publications; 45,000 to Smith, Elder (publisher of the *Cornhill Magazine*) and 115,000 to Strahan & Co.[50] The first impression of the Globe Shakespeare was of 20,000 copies. It was printed under some seasonal pressure, because of the impending Christmas market, and it entailed not only extra reading for accuracy (the Press charged £15 for this), but also work through the night – a practice familiar enough for examination papers, but unusual at Cambridge for a book.[51] By the beginning of December, Burn was binding 1,000 copies a day in readiness for publication.[52] The type-setting was electrotyped from the first, but though he hoped to sell 50,000 copies in three years, even Alexander Macmillan cannot have expected the book's runaway success. A further 20,000 copies were printed in February 1865, and the same again in October the same year, June 1866 and February 1867.[53] It began life as a best-seller, and it remained in heavy demand. It was not the year's top seller: in 1864, the first part of *Our mutual friend* sold 30,000 in three days, and *Enoch Arden*, in a first edition of 60,000, sold two-thirds of this in a few weeks. Even for Macmillan, the sale of textbooks was comparable. By the same letter to Clay that he set the print-run for the Globe Shakespeare at 20,000 copies, he ordered a reprint of the same number of Todhunter's small algebra.[54] In the context of the trade at large, the pace of the Shakespeare's sales was comparable with the 60,000 copies of the bound edition of Mrs Beeton's *Book of household management* sold in the first year of publication three years previously.[55] But Shakespeare was not a new work, and in a market where there was plenty of competition the success of the Globe edition was easily as notable.

It is probable that all this, achieved within a timetable that depended on a minimum of delay in the editorial and production process, could not have been achieved but for Macmillan's long-proven and cordial relations with Clay. He relied on Clay not only as printer, but also as one of the few who could hope to make Cambridge authors understand the importance of time, and the damage caused by delay. Wright was straightforward; others, such as J. E. B. Mayor, endlessly fertile with ideas but (as his long-delayed Juvenal proved) no respecter of publishing needs, were not. As printers, the University Press gained a reliable income from Macmillan. The charge for printing the first impression of the Globe Shakespeare was £1,077.10s.6d., which was paid promptly, in cash.[56] For subsequent ones, requiring some correction but no major resetting and no platemaking, it was a little under £520 on each occasion. No other book cost so much. A reprint of Todhunter's *Plane trigonometry*, printed in an impression of 10,000 copies at the same time as the first impression of the Globe Shakespeare, cost £96.0s.6d. At the end of 1865 the Macmillan account stood at over £6,000: the figure was inflated partly by the Globe Shakespeare, but in more normal years it was rarely below £3,000 from 1863 onwards – the year that the firm's publishing was removed to London – and from 1870 it was above £4,000.[57] These figures for printing need also to be seen in the light of others at the Press. The Syndics' receipts from the Bible and prayer book in 1863–4 amounted to a modest £288.15s.8d., the lowest for many years and far short of the registered income of £1,467.16s.11d. from this source in 1855–6.[58]

Daniel and Alexander Macmillan's recognition of the importance of the new postal service informed their later practices. Like London booksellers, they regularly issued catalogues of their stock: in 1865, 18,000 copies were printed of their catalogue of books suitable for Christmas presents.[59] In publishing new books they also made full use of advertisements and of prospectuses, quite apart from insertions in periodicals. Placards were prepared for W. H. Smith's bookstalls; and the University Press was repeatedly called on to produce handbills to advertise new books. Three thousand prospectuses were printed for Smith's *Exercises in arithmetic* (1860).[60] In the autumn of

1861, when a new book by Todhunter on the theory of equations was to be published, 14,000 prospectuses were prepared.[61] The *Golden Treasury series* was launched with the help of 10,000 prospectuses printed in June 1862, and a further 13,500 had been printed within five months.[62] Ten years later, Barnard Smith's works were still being advertised in this way. In October 1871 the University Press printed for Macmillan's 20,000 copies of a leaflet describing his books; and in January following the publishers took 10,000 more detailed leaflets on the same subject – in the same month as the University Press printed a further 10,000 copies of his threepenny *Metric system of arithmetic*.[63]

The departure of Macmillan's publishing activities to London in 1863 did not by any means entail the end of the firm's interest for Cambridge authors. Quite apart from Aldis Wright's continuing commitment, in 1866 Macmillan published a new edition of Airy's *Popular astronomy* and a portion of his long-established *Mathematical tracts*; a summary of the lectures of Henry Bond, Regius Professor of Physic, appeared in the same year. By 1872 the firm could also count among its recent authors the Hulsean Professor of Divinity (Lightfoot), the Knightbridge Professor of Moral Philosophy (Maurice), two Regius Professors of Modern History (Charles Kingsley and his successor J. R. Seeley), the Regius Professor of Divinity (Westcott), the Professor of Anatomy (Humphry), the Professor of Zoology and Comparative Anatomy (Newton), the University Librarian (Henry Bradshaw), the Professor of Political Economy (Henry Fawcett), the Public Orator (W. G. Clark) and the University Registrary (H. R. Luard). John Venn's *Logic of chance* appeared in 1866. J. E. B. Mayor's work on seventeenth-century Cambridge came out with the imprint of Macmillan, like his edition of Juvenal. Seeley's inaugural lecture on *The teaching of politics*, in which he rejoiced at the loosening of the 'artificial values' attached to classics and mathematics,[64] was published in *Macmillan's Magazine* in 1870.[65] The firm had by 1872 also published the inaugural lecture of E. B. Cowell, the University's first Professor of Sanskrit (1867), the *Introductory lecture on experimental physics* by the new Cavendish Professor of that subject, James Clerk Maxwell (1871), and the inaugural lecture by Maurice's successor in the Knightbridge chair, T. R. Birks (1872). Such a summary might be extended further among the resident members of the University; but the Macmillan list was remarkable also for authors from Oxford and London, from Manchester and from the public schools. The decision to establish the publishing side in London brought authors from new places, while also maintaining the powerful Cambridge centre. The firm's future was established during these years as what would now be called an academic publisher, a university press in all but name and organisation.

Overseas sales, and authors, were of increasing importance. The front wrapper of *Macmillan's Magazine* gave the names of agents not only in Glasgow and Dublin, but also in Leipzig, New York, Melbourne, Sydney, Adelaide and Hobart. In North America, Macmillan's initial focus was on bookstores in Philadelphia and New York. The Globe Shakespeare was published by Roberts Brothers, in Boston and comparatively new to publishing; a few months later, copies were shipped from England to Lippincott, in Philadelphia.[66] To the north, Daniel Wilson's *Prehistoric man* (1862;

second edition 1865), written when the author was on the staff of University College, Toronto, was followed in 1863 by a new edition of the same author's *Prehistoric annals of Scotland*. In 1868 the firm published a new edition of *Acadian geology*, by J. W. Dawson, Principal of McGill College and University, in Montreal. Alexander Macmillan's visit to North America in 1867 was coloured by the lack of any copyright agreement between Britain and the United States; but his primary purpose was to extend interest in his firm. 'I hardly anticipate doing much actual business, but only to gain a more accurate idea of what can be done in the future. It will be much to get the good-will of gentlemen engaged in educational work and to let them know what books we already have published, and also what we propose publishing in the future.'[67] In fact he managed to negotiate terms for some books, and he returned with a long list of new acquaintances on whom he could call for advice, for contributions to *Macmillan's Magazine*, and for books.[68] In 1870, J. R. Lowell's collection of essays *Among my books* was followed by a textbook over five hundred pages long, the *First principles of chemical philosophy*, by J. P. Cooke, of Harvard. James McCosh's *Laws of discursive thought*, from Princeton, appeared in the same year. The Scottish connections were strong, and valuable. McCosh had been born in Ayrshire in 1811, and had been first published by Macmillan in 1861, when he was still at Queen's University, Belfast. Daniel Wilson, from Edinburgh, and a friend since the 1830s, had been part of Macmillan's inner circle before he left for Toronto in 1853. Other connections were maintained likewise. Goldwin Smith, who in 1866 resigned the Regius chair of modern history at Oxford for family reasons, and in 1868 was persuaded to join the new Cornell University, was by then already one of Macmillan's authors. In Ithaca, Alexander Macmillan pursued him for a proposed book to be published jointly with Ticknor and Fields, and retained his interest as, restlessly, he moved on to public life in Toronto.[69]

By a web of friendships and introductions, Macmillan built up a North American presence. In 1869, following Cassell,[70] Routledge, Alexander Strahan, Thomas Nelson and Eyre & Spottiswoode, he opened a branch in New York under the management of George E. Brett, who had gained most of his experience with Simpkin, Marshall, in London.[71] It was a sign of the importance attached both to his authors and to a market. The colonies, left to find their books where they would, were turning to the lower prices for copyright British authors available from the United States; and it was estimated that the scale of American reprinting of British copyright works had led to a decline in the purchasing of British books in North America from 70 per cent of entire consumption in 1820 to 20 per cent in 1856.[72] Macmillan had a position to protect, as well as a market to develop.

Other parts of the world were also nurtured. By 1860 Macmillan was in touch with J. C. Juta, who had established his bookselling and publishing business in Cape Town in 1853: Juta went on to become for a while the principal importer of books from Britain.[73] Personal connections were especially important. 'It is refreshing to see some sign of one's oldest friends of any particularly interesting phase of one's life', wrote Alexander Macmillan to W. P. Wilson in Melbourne in 1867. 'Our first going to Cambridge was surely such a phase, and how closely marked your presence in our memory is with it.'[74] The existence of *Macmillan's Magazine* was invaluable. In Melbourne, the principal outlet was the shop of George Robertson, which in 1859–60 took 500 copies of the first two numbers of the journal;[75] Macmillan was careful to inform Robertson as early as possible of his plans for the new Shakespeare. By 1862, Macmillan was also supplying direct to the University of Sydney, as well as to Frederick McCoy, formerly assistant to Sedgwick in Cambridge and now Director of the national museum in Melbourne.[76] In India, quite apart from private customers, the public library at Lucknow was supplied not only with Macmillan's own publications, but also with those of others: again, an old connection helped, in that Macmillan's correspondent Charles Elliott had been at Trinity College in the mid-1850s.[77] Book clubs, popular in India, offered another focus. But the most important part of the trade in India was in educational books, for which much of the market was controlled by committees whose imprimatur was essential. Again, Macmillan used his correspondents, many of whom he had first come to know as undergraduates at Cambridge, to seek out further marketing information, and to elicit manuscripts both for books and for the magazine. 'The information you . . . gave me was very valuable, and continues so,' he wrote to C. B. Clarke, Inspector of Schools in Eastern Bengal, in 1869, 'though one would be glad if there were some Educational register to be got for all the Indian provinces, stating clearly what each man taught.'[78]

Subject-matter was equally important in promoting his international interests. In 1864, there were books and pamphlets on the Australian church, the New Zealand rebellion, and the American civil war, as well as G. O. Trevelyan's Indian essays, *The competition wallah*, originally published in *Macmillan's Magazine*. The following year saw the first appearance of W. G. Palgrave's highly successful *Narrative of a year's journey through central and eastern Arabia*, as well as Lady Duff Gordon's *Letters from Egypt* (the latter an unexpected, and more temporary, success) and Henry Kingsley's novel of Australian colonial society, *The Hillyars and the Burtons*. Mingled with these, with the theology, the schoolbooks and textbooks that formed the spine of the company, were not only the other novels of the Kingsleys and of Charlotte Mary Yonge and the poems of Matthew Arnold, of William Barnes, of Arthur Hugh Clough, but also the beginnings of other interests, in medicine, women's education and the fine arts.

In 1868, the year after his visit to North America, Macmillan published Charles Wentworth Dilke's *Greater Britain; a record of travel in English-speaking countries*. 'I followed England round the world', wrote Dilke. 'Everywhere I was in English-speaking, or in English-governed lands.' He extolled the 'grandeur of our race, already girdling the earth, which it is destined, perhaps, eventually to overspread'. The process, slow and faulty in many places, was plain to see, and in America in particular:

> In America, the peoples of the world are being fused together, but they run into an English mould: Alfred's laws and Chaucer's tongue are theirs whether they would or no. There are men who say that Britain in her age will claim the glory of having planted greater English across the seas. They fail to perceive that she has done more than found plantations of her

own – that she has imposed her institutions upon the offshoots of Germany, of Ireland, of Scandinavia, and of Spain. Through America, England is speaking to the world.[79]

Macmillan's aspirations spanned the English-speaking world, as a general publisher, as an educational publisher, and as a periodical publisher. Month by month, *Macmillan's Magazine* featured in W. J. Linton's decorative border the heads of Alfred, Chaucer, Shakespeare and Milton, the heroes of English culture.[80] Constantly innovative, he launched *Macmillan's* only a few weeks before the rival *Cornhill Magazine* appeared from the house of Smith, Elder. The *Journal of Anatomy and Physiology* made its appearance in November 1866, printed by Clay and under the auspices of a group including three from Cambridge: G. M. Humphry (recently appointed Professor of Anatomy), Alfred Newton (equally recently appointed, as the first Professor of Zoology and Comparative Anatomy) and J. W. Clark (the new superintendent of the Zoological Museum).[81] In 1868 Macmillan launched *The Practitioner*, and in 1869 *Nature*. In 1864 he launched *The Statesman's Year Book*. In June 1868 the first issue of the *Journal of Philology* appeared, edited, again, from Cambridge. Such periodicals promoted and – in their contributors and readers alike – supported his interests as a book publisher.

Inevitably, among the successes Macmillan also counted the difficulties. Contributors to the *Journal of Classical and Sacred Philology* were not paid, but the 500 copies of each issue hardly met its expenses, and it had to be closed. 'Higher learning has few supporters in England', he complained ruefully to one correspondent in 1860.[82] Despite his international success he did not achieve all that he had once hoped. Fresh from his American visit in 1867, and as he contemplated a branch for New York which would overcome pricing and copyright difficulties, he reflected: 'The true idea would be to have a printing office either of one's own or connected with one you could depend on, so as to be prepared to publish there and here at the same time. A great international publishing house is possible, and would be a grand idea to be realized.'[83] For the present, that particular goal eluded him.

His appointment as publisher to Oxford in 1863, the same year as he moved his publishing business to London from Cambridge, gave him a unique position, marked in his tone when he was asked for advice on schoolbooks by Bartholomew Price, Secretary to the Delegates of the Clarendon Press:

> I think the books ought all to be done on a uniform plan, and in each subject the books ought to have a coherent unity. I incline to think that if you had one or two courses of books so constructed they would soon justify their own existence, and need not interfere with existing schoolbooks more than would be quite legitimate. I confess it seems to me we will hardly produce anything worthy of the Universities or equal to the occasion, unless some such coherent plan is followed.[84]

It was the voice not of a single university, but of both Oxford and Cambridge, informed by twenty years' experience as a publisher. At Oxford, a series of schoolbooks was launched several years before there was an equivalent at Cambridge, and some Cambridge authors such as Aldis Wright found themselves published by the other university.[85] They made the journey in the hands of the Macmillan brothers, who almost from their first arrival together in Cambridge demonstrated what an academic publisher might do. Their success, while the Syndics of Cambridge University Press slept, had repercussions for a century.

Gradually, the University Press was to respond to these several wider briefs in publishing, the book trade and subject-matter alike.

❦ 20 ❧

Opening in London

In the Christmas number of *The Bookseller*, 1872, opposite a full-page advertisement by William Collins for variously bound Bibles, prayer books and church services, there appeared an equally large notice by the University Press headed 'Cambridge Bible Warehouse' and stating that

> The University Press of Cambridge will, on the first of January, 1873, open a London depot at 17, Paternoster Row, under the management of Mr. R. C. Lewis, for the sale of Cambridge Editions of Bibles, Books of Common Prayer, Church Services, &c., in sheets, and in every variety of plain and ornamental binding; also for the sale of the other publications of the Cambridge University Press, including local examination papers, reports and class-lists.

Other than a general allusion, there was no mention of the books that had been drawn together and published with considerable effort in the 1850s and early 1860s, of the editions of theologians or of the Press's nascent interests in historical and educational publishing. So far as the publishing side was concerned, the most important features were in the privileged books, and in examinations. It is true that, in a Christmas issue of the leading organ of the book trade, a list – however short – of the Press's other achievements would have made strange reading. The nature of the advertisement was to a great extent dictated by that of those on nearby pages – from Oxford University Press's Bible Warehouse at 7 Paternoster Row, from Henry Frowde's London Bible Warehouse at number 53, and from Courtier & Son's Wholesale Bible Warehouse at number eleven. But in its own way the advertisement was also confirmation of the fact that in the last few years the Press's publishing activities had slowed. Despite earlier and sporadic attempts, there was no concerted effort at publishing the kinds of textbooks from which other firms were greatly profiting; there were few authors coming forward from among the resident members of the University; and there was no sign of the new interests of the University in the now well-established triposes in moral and natural sciences. The Press ventured to London when its publishing was at an ebb. It was obliged to do so after arrangements with London firms, and most recently Rivington's, had failed. These were poor reasons, and discouraging circumstances.[1]

In one very real sense the venture was essential. Rivalry with Oxford had intensified since Clay took office as University Printer, and re-embarked on a programme of Bible and prayer book printing which was closely watched by the trade. The joint body charged with the revision of the Authorized Version of the Bible, already active in its task, was not to complete its work until the Revised Version was published in 1881–5, and the progress towards publication was to be punctuated by inter-university squabbles.[2] The Bible and prayer book trade alone seemed to justify an office in London.

Once again, the move for change was part commercial; and it was part academical. It came as a result of pressures both internal and external to the University, and the Syndics had to meet both. The reformed University administration depended centrally on the replacement of the ancient caput in 1856 by a council of the senate – and with it the demise of the conservatism enshrined in the powers of the heads of colleges. University lecturers, or 'public lecturers', were talked of in the 1850s,[3] though the first were not formally appointed until the 1880s. Curriculum reform, though delayed and often blocked by the voices of traditionalism, arrived earlier, and had more obvious implications for the course to be considered for the University Press. In 1860, the Moral Sciences Tripos (examined by the professors of moral philosophy, civil law, political economy, the laws of England, and English history) became no longer the preserve of those who had already been successfully examined for their degree. The same was true of the Natural Sciences Tripos, from the same year.[4] In 1866–7, the University founded new chairs in zoology and comparative anatomy, and in Sanskrit,[5] and in 1867–71 private endowments enabled chairs to be established in international law, in Latin, in fine art and in experimental physics.[6] In Trinity, Coutts Trotter was appointed lecturer in physical sciences in 1869, and Michael Foster was appointed to a praelectorship in 1870, in order to teach physiology.[7] These various appointments could not fully reflect the multitude of proposals in circulation, designed to encourage subjects, to support individuals, or both. In the 1840s and again in the 1850s, prompted by railway mania, a school of civil engineering had been discussed; now the issue was again raised, by Henry Latham, of Trinity Hall. In 1863–4, the study of fine art was put forward as a branch of academic study. In 1864, Henry Yates Thompson, a wealthy member of Trinity, proposed a lectureship in American history. In 1866, H. R. Luard, University Registrary, circulated a suggestion that there should be a separate historical tripos.[8] None of these came immediately to pass (the Slade professorship, founded by the will of Felix Slade in 1869, was not a full-time appointment[9]); but they were evidence enough of widespread eagerness to diversify the University's studies, and hence responsibilities.

In 1866, Sidgwick wrote, perceptively, of 'new school' professors – those who regarded themselves as being 'as much bound to teach and to write as any other salaried functionary is bound to discharge the duties for which he is paid'.[10] Whewell's death in 1866 eased the way for reform, and not only in Trinity.[11] But the innovations and proposals of the 1860s were given effect properly only in the following decade, whether in tripos reform, changes in college teaching or changes in university administration. The gradual abolition of ordination as a widespread condition for holding a fellowship[12] was of critical importance to individual consciences; but this also implied, even more importantly, that fellowships were no longer to be regarded as staging posts to benefices and marriage. Obviously not everyone wished to model themselves in this new way; but for those who wished, or so aspired, teaching, research and writing became long-term prospects, careers in themselves.[13] In 1854, Clay had been appointed as a businessman and was paid accordingly, though he was careful to retain his identification with his college. By the early 1870s, the same assumptions about the relationship between salary and function, summarised by Sidgwick in a private letter, had gained an unshakeable foothold. From such assumptions and expectations, it was but a step to applying them to running the University Press as an integral part of this process.

It is far from clear how many people in the last months of 1872 understood or anticipated the effect on publishing of recent events in Cambridge itself, and particularly the series of new chairs and other positions that had been created. By their work, and by the ways in which they sought to have it published, the holders of these and yet other posts in the next thirty years greatly determined the strengths and weaknesses of the Press, that remained to identify it for more than half of the twentieth century. The following volume will explore how these and other questions developed, and how the Press strove to become a London publisher controlled from Cambridge.

APPENDIX

Composition and presswork costs for Bibles, 1792

The following composition and printing rates are set out in the Syndics' Minutes (UA Pr.v.2), to accompany the minutes for 26 December 1792. See also p. 256 above.

	Price per sheet at case			price per 1,000 at Press	
	£	s	d	s	d
Bibles folio made up from 4to.		2		3	
Bibles large 4to.		19		3	2
Services Do.	1			3	2
Psalms Do.	1	2	8	3	2
Bibles small 4to.	1	4		3	
Services Do.	1	7		3	
Psalms Do.	1	11	8	3	
Bibles 8vo. with Notes	1	14		3	
Bibles 8vo. Brevier	1	5		2	10
Apoc. Do.	1	5		2	10
Services Do.	1	18		2	10
Psalms Do.	1	12		2	10
Bibles 8vo Minion	1	7		2	8
Apoc. Do.	1	7		2	8
Services Do.	2	2		2	8
Psalms Do.	1	13	4	2	8
Bibles 12°. Nonpareil	2	12		2	10
Services Do.	2	12		2	10
Bibles 24°. Nonpareil	1	15		1	15
Testaments 8vo. Pica		12		2	8
Testaments 8vo. long Primer		18		2	8
Testaments 12°. Brevier	1	4		2	8
Testaments 24°. Nonpareil	1	15		3	8
Prayers folio		5		2	6
Preface to Do.		10		2	6
Canons & Constitutions Do.		12		2	6

	£	s	d	s	d
Psalms to D°.		10		2	6
Prayers 4to.		8		2	8
Act of Uniformity D°.		12	6	2	8
Articles of Religion D°		9		2	8
Psalms D°.		17		2	8
Prayers 8vo. G^{t}. Primer long lines		6	8	2	8
Prayers 8vo. Pica		12		2	8
Forms of Prayer, &c		15		2	8
Psalms D°.		16		2	8
Prayers 12° long Primer		18		2	8
Psalms D°.	1	16		2	8
Prayers 12°. Brevier	1	4		2	8
Psalms D°.	1	16		2	8
Prayers 12°. Minion Cols	1	6		2	8
Psalms D°.	1	16		2	8
Prayers 12°. Minion long lines (overrun^{g})		13		2	8
Prayers 24°. Nonpareil Cols	1	14		3	8
Psalms D°.	2	4		3	8
Prayers 24°. Nonpareil long lines	1	6		3	4
Psalms D°.	1	18		3	4
Tate's Psalms large 12°. to long Prim Pray^{r}	1	4		2	8
Tate's Psalms to 24°. Prayer		17		2	8
The Offices of the Church		6		2	8

[This is followed by a copy of the conclusions of the meeting of the London Master Printers, held at the Globe Tavern, Fleet Street, on 25 November 1785, to consider the propositions of the Compositors: the same conclusions are printed in Ellic Howe and Harold E. Waite, *The London Society of Compositors . . .; a centenary history* (1948), pp. 44–5.]

NOTES

1 A world for books

1 Raymond Astbury, 'The renewal of the Licensing Act in 1693 and its lapse in 1695', *The Library*, 5th ser. 33 (1978), pp. 296–322.

2 Michael Treadwell, 'The English book trade' in Robert P. McCubbin and Martha Hamilton-Phillips (eds.), *The age of William III and Mary II; power, politics and patronage, 1688–1702* (Williamsburg, 1989), pp. 358–65.

3 There is some doubt as to whether Randle Holme's *Academy of armory* (Chester, printed for the Author, 1688) was in fact printed at Chester, rather than London. See the introduction by D. Nuttall and M. R. Perkin to the reprint of part of Book III ('Art of printing and typefounding') issued to the Printing Historical Society, 1972, and D. Nuttall, *A history of printing in Chester from 1688 to 1965* (Chester, 1969), pp. 5–13.

4 David Stoker, 'The establishment of printing in Norwich: causes and effects, 1660–1760', *TCBS*, 7 (1977), pp. 94–111. For newspapers published outside London, cf. Carolyn Nelson and Matthew Seccombe, *British newspapers and periodicals, 1641–1700* (New York, 1987), p. 695.

5 E. A. Wrigley and R. S. Schofield, *The population history of England, 1541–1871; a reconstruction* (Cambridge, 1989), table 7.8, pp. 208–9. For the back projection methods on which many of their figures are based, see *ibid.*, ch. 2 and appendixes 2–3.

6 John T. Evans, *Seventeenth-century Norwich; politics, religion and government, 1620–1690* (Oxford, 1979), pp. 4–5; Wrigley and Schofield, *Population history of England*, p. 571. For smaller communities, see for example Peter Clark, Kathy Gaskin and Adrian Wilson, *Population estimates of English small towns, 1550–1851* (Centre for Urban History, University of Leicester, Working Paper, 3 (1989)).

7 *VCH Cambs*, 3, pp. 97–8.

8 *VCH Cambs*, 2, pp. 138–9. Since the census days fell variously in and out of term, the totals given for the University in the nineteenth century are of limited comparative help.

9 Cf. Peter Isaac, 'William Davison of Alnwick and provincial publishing of his time', *Publishing History*, 40 (1996), pp. 5–32, discussing the output of presses in Alnwick, Berwick and other border towns, Bolton, Chepstow and Newark, and the place in them of cheap editions of classic works. The peculiar status of a thriving printing trade in late eighteenth-century Berwick, in a national context of copyright disputes, became an embarrassment to publishing booksellers in London in particular.

10 *The Athenaeum*, 17 September 1853, reporting the Statistics section of the British Association.

11 David Stoker, 'The *Eighteenth-century short title catalogue* and provincial imprints', *JPHS*, 24 (1995), pp. 9–35.

12 For the scope of the *ESTC*, see R. C. Alston and M. J. Jannetta, *Bibliography, machine readable cataloguing and the ESTC* (1978), pp. 16–17. For the *Nineteenth century short title catalogue*, see the introduction to the *Nineteenth century short title catalogue*, ser. II, phase I (1986): the libraries in the British Isles whose holdings contribute to the *NSTC* are the British Library, the Bodleian, Cambridge University Library, the National Library of Scotland, Trinity College Dublin and Newcastle

University Library. Parts of the Library of Congress and Harvard holdings have also been added from the United States.

13 Simon Eliot, *Some patterns and trends of British publishing, 1800–1919* (Bibliographical Soc., 1994), pp. 24–5.

14 Some of these complexities are addressed in a seventeenth-century context by D. F. McKenzie, 'The London book trade in 1668', *Words; Wai-te-ata Studies in Literature*, 4 (1974), pp. 75–92, which assumes (p. 79) editions of 1,000 copies for each item.

15 These are summarised, with other figures, in Maxted, *London book trades*, p. xxx. Negus's list is in Howe, *London compositor*, pp. 35–9.

16 W. B. Todd, *A directory of printers and others in allied trades, London and vicinity, 1800–1840* (Printing Historical Soc., 1972).

17 The history of credit in the book trade deserves further study. Meanwhile cf. the brief remarks in Bert van Selm, 'Johannes van Ravesteyn, "libraire européen" or local trader', in C. Berkvens-Stevelinck, H. Bots, P. G. Hoftijzer and O. S. Lankhorst (eds.), *Le magasin de l'univers; the Dutch Republic as the centre of the European book trade* (Leiden, 1992), pp. 251–63, at pp. 257–9, with further references.

18 G. A. Cranfield, *A hand-list of English provincial newspapers and periodicals, 1700–1760*, repr. with supplements by G. A. C. and R. M. Wiles (Cambridge Bibliographical Soc., 1961); G. A. Cranfield, *The development of the provincial newspaper, 1700–1760* (Oxford, 1962), ch. 8.

19 Cranfield, *Handlist*, pp. 4, 15, 21, 22.

20 Stoker, 'The establishment of printing in Norwich'.

21 The printers of these local newspapers, and Benjamin Flower, printer of the *Cambridge Intelligencer* (1793–), all printed books as well: see further below, pp. 170, 250. For circulation figures of Cambridge newspapers, 1764–1850, see Michael J. Murphy, *Cambridge newspapers and opinion, 1780–1850* (Cambridge, 1977), pp. 120–1.

22 C. Y. Ferdinand, 'Local distribution networks in 18th-century England', in R. Myers and M. Harris (eds.), *Spreading the word; distribution networks of print, 1550–1850* (Winchester, 1990), pp. 131–49.

23 Tony Copsey and Henry Hallam, *Book distribution and printing in Suffolk, 1534–1850* (Ipswich, 1994), pp. 50, 53.

24 Charles Mitchell, *The newspaper press directory* (1846); Cooper, *Annals*, 4, pp. 523, 619.

25 *Ely diocesan calendar*, 1872, p. 204.

26 For example, *Cambridge Chronicle*, 10 December 1763.

27 *Cambridge Chronicle*, 19 May 1764.

28 *Cambridge Chronicle*, 31 August 1765: the Cawthorne sisters were daughters of the late Mary Cawthorne.

29 *Cambridge Chronicle and Journal*, 5 March 1768.

30 *Cambridge Journal and Weekly Flying-Post*, 27 January 1750, 3 February 1750.

31 A copy of this broadside advertisement was offered in Grant and Shaw's catalogue 32 (1996), item 17, illustrated.

32 Hoh-Cheung and Lorna H. Mui, *Shops and shopkeeping in eighteenth-century England* (Kingston, Ont., 1989), pp. 46–9 etc.

33 Engraved advertisement for Bettison's business, early nineteenth century.

34 *An historical account of Sturbridge, Bury, and the most famous fairs in Europe and America* (Cambridge, c. 1767), pp. 38–9.

35 James Lackington, *Memoirs of the forty-five first years of the life of James Lackington*, 7th edn (1794), letter xl.

36 Few towns could, like Cambridge, retain very many independent print-sellers. *Hodson's booksellers, publishers and stationers' directory* (1855) recorded, exceptionally, no less than seven specialist print dealers in the town. See below, p. 211.

37 Daniel Defoe, *A tour through the whole island of Great Britain*, intro. G. D. H. Cole and D. C. Browning, 2 vols. (1962), 1, pp. 78, 80.

38 Defoe, *Tour*, p. 61.

39 Cambridge University Library, MS Add. 2960, fo. 25r.

40 Cooper, *Annals*, 4, p. 324, with further references.

41 *Ibid.*, p. 86.

42 *Ibid.*, 4, pp. 249–50.

43 *Ibid.*, 4, pp. 355, 365–6.

44 A list of the turnpike bills that were defeated in Parliament between 1696 and 1714 is given in William Albert, *The turnpike road system in England, 1663–1840* (Cambridge, 1972), p. 21n. For the final years of the turnpikes, see David H. Kennett, 'Coaching roads of the Cambridge region, 1820–1850', *Proc. Cambridge Antiquarian Soc.*, 68 (1978), pp. 89–104. The importance to the book trade of national communications more generally is stressed in Nicolas Barker, 'The rise of the provincial book trade in England and the growth of a national transport system' in F. Barbier, S. Juratic and D. Varry (eds.), *L'Europe et le livre; réseaux et pratiques du négoce de librairie, XVIe–XIXe siècles* (Paris, 1996), pp. 137–55.

45 Cooper, *Annals*, 4, pp. 206–8.

46 *Ibid.*, p. 677; 5, p. 69.

47 William Stukeley, reflecting on the ancient Roman practice of setting up monuments beside roads, remarked, 'I have often wonder'd that the cheap and easy method of setting up posts with directions at every cross road is so little practis'd, which methinks deserves to be enforc'd by a law. It would teach the carpenters that make them, and the country people to read, with much more emolument to the publick, than some other methods now in vogue.' William Stukeley, *Itinerarium curiosum* (1724), pp. 77–8.

48 *Cambridge Journal and Weekly Flying-Post*, 16 March 1745.

49 Cooper, *Annals*, gives details of the Acts of Parliament establishing turnpike trusts near Cambridge; but see also *VCH Cambs*, 2, pp. 85–6.

50 *Cantabrigia depicta. A concise and accurate description of the University and town of Cambridge* (Cambridge [1763]), pp. 116, 117.

51 *Cantabrigia depicta*, pp. 111–17.

52 *The new Cambridge guide*, 2nd edn (Cambridge, 1812), pp. 135–6.

53 *The Cambridge guide* (Cambridge [1830]), p. 308.

54 *Letters from Cambridge* (1828), p. 2.

55 Queens' College Archives, Book 80, 2nd pagination, p. 4.

56 See below, p. 221.

57 *The farmers and traders apprehensions of a rise upon carriage* (1752), p. 5, quoted in Albert, *Turnpike road system*, p. 180n.

58 Albert, *Turnpike road system*, pp. 180–7. Transport costs are also discussed by William T. Jackman, *The development of transportation in modern England*, 3rd edn (1966), pp. 348–9; contemporary quoted costs for carriage by land, 1750–1830, are gathered in his appendix 7.

59 Cooper, *Annals*, 4, pp. 44, 48, 53, 172, 250, 385.

60 *Ibid.*, pp. 403, 432, 437, 495, 502.

61 Reginald B. Fellows, 'Railways to Cambridge, actual and proposed: a centenary review', *Proc. Cambridge Antiquarian Soc.*, 42 (1949), pp. 1–7, at p. 1; for proposals in 1825 for a line to Manchester via the Lea Valley and Cambridgeshire, see also Cooper, *Annals*, 4, p. 587n.

62 Reginald B. Fellows, *London to Cambridge by train, 1845–1938* (Cambridge, 1939; repr. Cambridge, 1976). Joseph Romilly, *Romilly's Cambridge diary, 1842–1847*, ed. M. E. Bury and J. D. Pickles (Cambridgeshire Records Soc., 1994), p. 164.

63 Quoted in Arthur Gray and Frederick Brittain, *A history of Jesus College, Cambridge* (1979), p. 165. The previous part of his letter to the Directors of the Eastern Counties Railway reads, 'I am sorry to find that the Directors of the Eastern Counties Railway have made arrangements for conveying foreigners and others to Cambridge on *Sundays* at such fares as may be likely to tempt persons who, having no regard for Sunday themselves, would inflict their presence on this University on that day of rest . . .'

64 *Romilly's Cambridge diary, 1842–1847*, p. 164.

65 Cooper, *Annals*, 4, pp. 586–7; W. T. Jackman, *The development of transportation in modern England*, 3rd edn (1966), p. 568.

66 See the references in Jackman, *Development*, pp. 568–9. Subsequent and further unsatisfactory aspects of the management of the Eastern Counties Railway are summarised in Cooper, *Annals*, 5, pp. 203–4.

67 *VCH Cambs*, 2, pp. 132–3; Fellows, 'Railways to Cambridge, actual and proposed'.

68 The standard histories are D. A. Winstanley's quartet on the eighteenth century, unreformed Cambridge, and early and late Victorian Cambridge. See also the older work by Christopher Wordsworth, *Social life in the English universities in the eighteenth century* (Cambridge, 1874) and *Scholae academicae; some account of the studies at the English universities in the eighteenth century* (Cambridge, 1877). More recently, see especially John Gascoigne, *Cambridge in the age of the enlightenment; science, religion and politics from the Restoration to the French Revolution* (Cambridge, 1989), M. M. Garland, *Cambridge before Darwin; the ideal of a liberal education, 1800–1860* (Cambridge, 1980) and (especially for undergraduates) Sheldon Rothblatt, *The modern university and its discontents; the fate of Newman's legacies in Britain and America* (Cambridge, 1997). But see now Peter Searby, *A history of the University of Cambridge. 3. 1750–1870* (Cambridge, 1997).

69 Willis and Clark, 3, pp. 158–65, followed by a full account of the subsequent delays and difficulties in developing the Museums Site.

70 Membership of the Caput, as its name suggests, depended on the choice of heads of houses, and most university policies were determined by it until the Council of the Senate was established under the statutes of 1856. As a result, heads of houses were able to preserve old practices long after they had been found wanting by those bent on reform. For this and other terms, see F. H. Stubbings, *Bedders, bulldogs and bedells; a Cambridge glossary*, revised edn (Cambridge, 1995). See also Winstanley, *Unreformed Cambridge*, pp. 24–7.

71 Gray to Horace Walpole, 31 October 1734, Thomas Gray, *Correspondence*, ed. Paget Toynbee, Leonard Whibley and H. W. Starr, 3 vols. (Oxford, 1971), 1, p. 3. Gray was mistaken in attempting to distinguish between colleges and halls: in the eighteenth century all were full colleges, whatever (such as Trinity Hall, Clare Hall or Pembroke Hall) their title – common or formal.

72 Lawrence Stone, 'The size and composition of the Oxford student body, 1580–1910', in L. Stone (ed.), *The university in society*, 2 vols. (Oxford, 1975), 1, pp. 3–110, at p. 93.

73 For a summary of the comparative populations of the colleges (including fellows and students) in 1727, see Cooper, *Annals*, 5, p. 504. Statistical information may be most conveniently studied in two summaries by J. A. Venn, *A statistical chart to illustrate the entries at the various colleges in the University of Cambridge, 1544–1907* (Cambridge, 1908), and *Oxford and Cambridge matriculations, 1544–1906* (Cambridge, 1908). Further figures have been drawn from editions of the University *Calendar* and from J. R. Seeley (ed.), *The student's guide to the University of Cambridge* (1862). See also Wordsworth, *Social life*, pp. 639–43.

74 Lodging house papers in the University Archives: CUR 124 (Registry file), T.v.1–3 (registers of licences), etc. The relationship in St John's College between new building work and the size of the undergraduate body is usefully set out in Alec C. Crook, *From the foundation to Gilbert Scott; a history of the buildings of St John's College, Cambridge, 1511 to 1885* (Cambridge, 1980), p. 145.

75 Details taken from Willis and Clark. On Wilkins, see R. W. Liscombe, *William Wilkins, 1778–1839* (Cambridge, 1980). For the Pitt Press building, see below, pp. 311–12.

76 Various college laboratories are discussed most recently in A. L. Greer, 'The Sidney College laboratory', in D. E. D. Beales and H. B. Nisbet (eds.), *Sidney Sussex College, Cambridge; historical essays in commemoration of the quincentenary* (Woodbridge, 1996), pp. 195–221. Apart from the special arrangements made for Vigani at Trinity at the beginning of the eighteenth century, and for Milner at Queens' at the end of the century, the first college laboratory to be established was at St John's College, in the 1850s.

77 Charles Babbage, *Passages from the life of a philosopher* (1864), p. 28.

78 Gray to Horace Walpole, 20 March 1737/8: Gray, *Correspondence*, 1, p. 82.

79 *The new Cambridge guide* (Cambridge, 1804), p. 92.

80 Alan H. Nelson, *Early Cambridge theatres: college, university and town stages, 1464–1720* (Cambridge, 1994).

81 Wordsworth, *Social life*, pp. 192–6. A collection of handbills advertising productions at the Stirbitch Theatre between 1786 and 1803 is in the University Library, Cam.c.211.32.1; cf. Bowes, *Catalogue*, no. 717.

82 RCHM *Cambridge*, p. 369.

83 *The new Cambridge guide*, p. 93. A brief account of concerts is given in Frida Knight, *Cambridge music* (Cambridge, 1980); the pages of the local newspapers provide a more detailed picture. See also Wordsworth, *Social life*, pp. 199–203.

84 *The new Cambridge guide*, p. 94.

85 See below, pp. 210, 245.

86 *A guide through the University of Cambridge*, new edn (Cambridge, n.d.), p. 142. In 1804, the annual subscription to Nicholson's circulating library was 7s.6d. a quarter, which permitted a member to borrow up to fifteen books: *The new Cambridge guide* (1804), p. 97.

87 George Pryme, *Autobiographic recollections* (Cambridge, 1870), p. 156.

88 Clark, *Endowments*, p. 92; *Historical register*, p. 262. For a recent discussion of the 'awkward interval'. see Rothblatt, *The modern university and its discontents*, ch. 6.

2 Changes to books and the book trade

1 See below, pp. 141–2, 311–12.

2 The basic differences between hand-made paper and machine-made paper, and between laid and wove paper, are set out in Dard Hunter, *Paper-making; the history and technique of an ancient craft*, 2nd edn (New York, 1947), especially pp. 114–36, and in Gaskell, *New introduction*, pp. 57–66, 214–28.

3 Hot-pressing was introduced to the British Isles from the continent. Cf. the advertisement by John Chambers in the *Dublin Evening Post*, 22 March 1796, and M. Pollard, *Dublin's trade in books, 1550–1800* (Oxford, 1989), pp. 203–9.

4 Moxon, *Mechanick exercises*, pp. 22–4, 372.

5 E. Chambers, *Cyclopaedia*, 2nd edn (1738), art. 'Letter'. James Mosley, 'The early career of William Caslon', *JPHS*, 3 (1967), pp. 66–81; James Mosley, 'A specimen of printing types by William Caslon, London 1766; a facsimile with introduction and notes', *JPHS*, 16 (1981/2), pp. 1–113.

6 D. B. Updike, *Printing types*, 2 vols., 2nd edn (Oxford, 1937), pp. 116–24.

7 A. F. Johnson, *Type designs, their history and development*, 2nd edn (1959), pp. 85–7. For the old-style revival, see also Janet Ing Freeman, 'Founders' type and private founts at the Chiswick Press in the 1850s', *JPHS*, 19/20 (1985–7), pp. 62–102; D. McKitterick, 'Old faces and new acquaintances; typography and the association of ideas', *PBSA*, 87 (1993), pp. 163–86.

8 See below, p. 197.

9 See below, chapter 13.

10 For the increase in the local print trade, see below, pp. 209–12. The early rolling-press is described in Anthony Dyson, 'The rolling-press; some aspects of its development from the seventeenth century to the nineteenth century', *JPHS*, 17 (1982/3), pp. 1–30.

11 Newton, *Correspondence*, 5, pp. 354, 384, 386, 400.

12 The original copper plates survive in Trinity College.

13 For photography costs and a proposal to publish a facsimile of a manuscript in Trinity College in the 1850s, see below, pp. 370–1.

14 R. Wetstein to Bentley, 23 November 1706: Trinity College, MS R.17.31, no. 27; Bentley, *Correspondence*, 1, pp. 247–8. Wetstein estimated an engraved title-page at 7 or 8 guineas, and a portrait head at 17 or 18.

15 See below, p. 141.

16 [Robert Dossie], *The handmaid to the arts*, 2 vols. (1758), 2, pp. 216–7.

17 King's College, MS Lib.12, page 75 (printed circular).

18 See below, p. 318.

19 Printing houses offering both letterpress printing and lithography appear twice, under each head, in the *Post Office directory of stationers, printers, booksellers, publishers, and paper makers of England, Scotland, Wales, and the principal towns of Ireland* (1872).

20 Gaskell, *New introduction*, pp. 271–2; David Woodward, 'The decline of commercial wood-engraving in nineteenth-century America', *JPHS*, 10 (1974/5), pp. 57–83.

21 Harold White, 'A note on W. H. Fox Talbot and photo-engraving', *JPHS*, 13 (1978/9), pp. 64–5; H. Gernsheim, *Incunabula of British photographic literature* (1984); Henry James, *Photo-zincography* (Southampton, 1860); Brian Coe and Mark Haworth-Booth, *A guide to early photographic processes* (1983).

22 Elizabeth Harris, 'Experimental graphic processes in England, 1800–1859', *JPHS*, 4 (1968), pp. 33–86, 5 (1969), pp. 41–80, 6 (1970), pp. 53–89.

23 See below, pp. 34, 247.

24 Advertisement to John Locke, *The conduct of the understanding* (Cambridge, 1781), at end.

25 C. H. Timperley, *Encyclopaedia of literary and typographical anecdote* (1842), p. 799, remarking that the fashionable London booksellers Thomas Payne and Son were the first in London to display new books in this way.

26 W. H. Lunn, *Catalogue of a select and valuable collection of books* (May, 1788).

27 *Cambridge Chronicle*, 2 June 1798, quoted in A. B. Gray, 'A biography of John Bowtell (1753–1813); and of John Bowtell his nephew (1777–1855)', *Cambridge Antiquarian Soc. Communications*, 11 (1907), pp. 346–84, at p. 360.

28 See below, pp. 355, 391.

29 Some of the more remarkable of these may be inspected in two surveys by Ruari McLean, *Victorian publishers' book-bindings in cloth and leather* (1974) and *Victorian publishers' book-bindings in paper* (1983). See also Douglas Ball, *Victorian publishers' bindings* (1985).

30 Michael Sadleir, *The evolution of publishers' binding styles, 1770–1900* (1930); Esther Potter, 'The London bookbinding trade: from craft to industry', *The Library*, 6th ser. 15 (1993), pp. 259–80, with further references.

31 Graham Pollard and Albert Ehrman, *The distribution of books by catalogue from the invention of printing to A.D.1800* (Roxburghe Club, 1965), especially chapters 4–5. In a large literature since 1965, see for the Netherlands especially the essays collected in C. Berkvens-Stevelinck et al. (eds.) *Le magasin de l'univers; the Dutch Republic as the centre of the European book trade* (Leiden, 1992) and the annotated guidance offered in O. S. Lankhorst and P. G. Hoftijzer, *Drukkers, boekverkopers en lezers in Nederland tijdens de Republiek* (The Hague, 1995), especially pp. 56–60 (catalogues and prospectuses) and 78–86 (international trade; bookselling).

32 Stanley Morison and Harry Carter, *John Fell, the University Press and the 'Fell' type* (Oxford, 1967), pp. 59–69; Moxon, *Mechanick exercises*, pp. 45, 82.

33 *Cambridge under Queen Anne*, p. 350. See also below, pp. 48, 108. For some remarks on the difficulties experienced by Samuel Smith in selling English-language books overseas, see P. G. Hoftijzer, 'The Leiden bookseller Pieter van der Aa (1659–1733) and the international book trade', in *Le magasin de l'univers*, pp. 169–84, especially pp. 176–7; see also below, p. 82.

34 S. Roscoe, *John Newbery and his successors, 1740–1814* (Wormley, 1973).

35 The standard study of the eighteenth-century curriculum remains that by Christopher Wordsworth, *Scholae academicae; some account of the studies at the English universities in the eighteenth century* (Cambridge, 1877); see also John Gascoigne, *Cambridge in the age of the enlightenment; science, religion and politics from the Restoration to the French Revolution* (Cambridge, 1989).

36 See below, pp. 379, 380–1.

37 See below, pp. 213–14.

38 John Edwards, *Some discoveries of the uncertainty, deficiency, and corruptions of human knowledge and learning* (1714), pp. 168–9. For the fashion of turning books round so that their spines faced outwards

on the shelves, see McKitterick, *Cambridge University Press*, 1, pp. 7, 396, and Oates, *Cambridge University Library*, p. 479. The books were turned round in the University Library in 1706.

39 *The first three sections of Newton's Principia* (Cambridge, printed at the Pitt Press for T. Stevenson, and Rivington and Longman in London, 1834).

40 Sir James Stephen, *Lectures on the history of France*, 2 vols. (1852), 1, p. xii. His remarks were addressed to William Whewell, as dedicatee.

41 Oates, *Cambridge University Library*, pp. 443–7, with further references; Isaac Newton, *Optical papers*. 1. *The optical lectures, 1670–1672*, ed. Alan E. Shapiro (Cambridge, 1984), including (pp. 21–2) a list of early manuscript copies and derivations.

42 MS Dd.2.55(2), printed as an appendix to his *Praelectiones physico-mathematicae*, 2nd edn (1726). The manuscript shows signs of having been used as printer's copy.

43 Preface to Roger Cotes, *Hydrostatical and pneumatical lectures* (1738), A3r. Manuscript copies of these lectures have appeared at Sotheby's, 6 June 1966, lot 2184 (sold to Dawson), and at Christie's, 15 March 1995, lot 334 (from the Bute library).

44 See also below, p. 206.

45 Gunning, *Reminiscences*, 1, pp. 199–200.

46 *Cambridge Chronicle*, 6 December 1766.

47 *Cambridge Chronicle and Journal*, 21 March 1789, quoted in Gray, 'John Bowtell', p. 358.

48 *Cambridge Chronicle and Journal*, 23 February 1771. Trusler's *Address* was printed in two forms, one on a single sheet ready for posting.

49 Stanley Morison, 'The Trusler script types', *The Fleuron*, 7 (1930), pp. 157–66. Morison was hesitant to believe that Trusler began his scheme as early as 1771, but the evidence of advertising seems clear enough. I have not sought out other, and perhaps earlier, advertisements in London.

50 *Cambridge Chronicle and Journal*, 23 July 1785.

51 *Cambridge Chronicle and Journal*, 5 March 1796. Cf. Daniel Pape, *Manuscript sermons on several subjects* ([Newcastle upon Tyne], 1787).

52 *Cambridge Chronicle and Journal*, 9 May etc. 1807 (Latin), 27 June etc. (English).

53 Michael Twyman, *Early lithographed books; a study of the design and production of improper books in the age of the hand press* (1990).

54 Cf., for example, the discussion of the relationship between manuscript and printed letter forms in Nicolas Barker, *Aldus Manutius and the development of Greek script and type in the fifteenth century*, 2nd edn (New York, 1992), especially ch. 4, and G. Mardersteig, 'Aldo Manuzio e i caratteri di Francesco Griffo da Bologna', in his *Scritti sulla storia dei caratteri e della tipografia* (Milano, 1988), pp. 107–59.

55 There is a copy in the Rothschild collection, Trinity College, Rothschild 1810.

56 Advertisement by Hollingworth, *Cambridge Journal and Weekly Flying-Post*, 27 January and 3 February 1750.

57 'It was some time in the year 1780 when I resolved from that period to give no person whatever any credit . . . The losses sustained by the interest of money in long credit, and by those bills that were not paid at all; the inconveniences attending not having the ready-money to lay out in trade to the best advantage, together with the great loss of time in keeping accounts, and collecting debts, convinced me, that if I could but establish a ready-money business *without any exceptions*, I should be enabled to sell every article very cheap.' James Lackington, *Memoirs of the forty-five first years of the life of James Lackington*, 9th edn (1794), letter xxxiii.

58 H.-C.Mui and L. H. Mui, *Shops and shopkeeping in eighteenth-century England* (Kingston, Ont., 1989), p. 231.

59 This copy is now in Cambridge University Library, Munby c.375.

60 Matthew Robinson, *Autobiography*, ed. J. E. B. Mayor (Cambridge, 1856), p. xxix.

61 Graham Pollard and Albert Ehrman, *The distribution of books by catalogue from the invention of printing to A. D.1800* (Roxburghe Club, 1965), pp. 175–8.

62 This caused some irritation in the trade.

63 *A reference catalogue of current literature* (1877), advertisement. These bound collections gradually

increased as publishers joined in the scheme, and indeed seem to have induced some publishers to set out their stocks in an ordered fashion for the first time. See also A. Growoll and Wilberforce Eames, *Three centuries of English booktrade bibliography* (1903), pp. 97–9, 156.

64 The increasingly local and individual nature of craft control in the eighteenth century is studied more generally in J. R. Kellett, 'The breakdown of gild and corporation control over the handicraft and retail trade in London', *Economic History Review*, 2nd ser. 10 (1957–8), pp. 381–94.

65 John Edwards, *A brief vindication of the fundamental articles of the Christian faith* (1697), 'The author to the bookseller'.

66 John Locke to John Covel, 29 June 1697: Locke, *Correspondence*, 6, p. 210. The copy in Trinity College has a residue of paste across the page, remaining from when the overlay was removed. That in Emmanuel College has the pasted-on sheet still in place.

67 Covel to Locke, 4 October 1697: Locke, *Correspondence*, 6, p. 217.

68 Tenison to Locke, 21 December 1697, Locke, *Correspondence*, 6, p. 275.

69 Locke to Tenison, 15 January 1697/8, Locke, *Correspondence*, 6, pp. 300–1.

70 See, recently, John Feather, *Publishing, piracy and politics; an historical study of copyright in Britain* (1994), and the review by Hugh Amory, *Times Literary Supplement*, 30 June 1995. For more emphasis on the position of authors, cf. David Saunders, *Authorship and copyright* (1992) and Mark Rose, *Authors and owners; the invention of copyright* (Cambridge, Mass., 1993).

71 Shadwell, *Enactments in Parliament*. The earlier collection, John Griffiths (ed.), *Enactments in Parliament specially concerning the Universities of Oxford and Cambridge* (Oxford, 1869) was restricted to legislation currently in force.

72 *An act for granting to His Majesty an additional duty upon almanacks*, 21 Geo. III c.56 (1781): Clark, *Endowments*, pp. 47–8; Shadwell, *Enactments in Parliament*, 2, pp. 47–9.

73 House of Commons, 6 April 1781; *Parliamentary history of England*, 22, cols. 103–4. See also below, pp. 229–30.

74 House of Commons, 26 April 1781; *Parliamentary history of England*, 22, cols. 105–6.

75 But cf. the remarks by Daniel Prince concerning the Oxford press, 1756: Philip, *Blackstone*, pp. 20–1.

76 Stanley Morison, 'The learned press as an institution', in his *Selected essays*, ed. D. McKitterick, 2 vols. (Cambridge, 1981), 2, pp. 361–82, at p. 381.

77 Cf. Leibniz to Otto Mencke, 14 September 1681, on being asked about the relative appropriateness of German and Latin:

> Wie ich dann auch nicht zweifle, man werde sich einer solchen schreibart, deren eigentliche reinigkeit, den zarthen ohren der frembden mehr als von Teutschen insgemein beschieht, eine gnüge thun könne, befleissigen . . . (Quoted in Hub. Laeven, *The 'Acta Eruditorum' under the editorship of Otto Mencke (1644–1707)* (Amsterdam, 1990), p. 51.)

78 Cf. Anne Goldgar, *Impolite learning; conduct and community in the republic of letters, 1680–1750* (New Haven, 1995).

79 Charles Villers, 'Some account of the researches of the German literati on the subject of ancient literature and history', *Classical Journal*, 3 (1811), p. 349. The remarks were originally published in French.

80 George Ticknor to Elisha Ticknor, Göttingen, 20 June 1816: *Life, letters, and journals of George Ticknor*, 2nd edn 2 vols. (1876), 1, p. 84.

81 These occasions are mostly recorded in successive Graces; but see also the correspondence in Pr.B.4.III.1–12. For gifts from England to Chicago Public Library in 1871, see Gwladys Spencer, *The Chicago Public Library; origins and backgrounds* (Chicago, 1943), pp. 407–10.

3 Founding a new press

1 Carter, *Oxford University Press*, pp. 61–4.

2 McKitterick, *Cambridge University Press*, 1, p. 329.

3 Roger North, *The lives of the Norths*, ed. A. Jessopp, 3 vols. (1890), 2, p. 326; David McKitterick (ed.), *The making of the Wren Library* (Cambridge, 1995), pp. 5–6, 29–30.

4 Celia Fiennes, *Journeys*, ed. Christopher Morris (1949), p. 65.

5 Carter, *Oxford University Press*, pp. 101–2, 133, 140, 147. University of Oxford, *Report of the Committee on the University Press*, under the chairmanship of Sir Humphrey Waldock (*Oxford University Gazette*, supplement, 7, May 1970), p. 19.

6 McKitterick, *Wren Library*, p. 23.

7 *Historical Register*, p. 174.

8 Service for the Commemoration of Benefactors, *Historical register*, p. 174.

9 Monk, *Life of Bentley*, 1, pp. 18–19; Carter, *Oxford University Press*, pp. 140, 147, 222–3.

10 14 Charles II c.33; F. S. Siebert, *Freedom of the press in England, 1476–1776* (Urbana, 1952), pp. 237–63; R. Astbury, 'The renewal of the Licensing Act in 1693 and its lapse in 1695', *The Library*, 5th ser. 33 (1978), pp. 296–322.

11 Locke, *Correspondence*, 5, appendix, p. 789.

12 Locke, *Correspondence*, 5, appendix, pp. 786–7. Smith, a bookseller in St Paul's Churchyard, was a leading importer of books: see Norma Hodgson and Cyprian Blagden, *The notebook of Thomas Bennet and Henry Clements (1686–1719)* (Oxford Bibliographical Soc., 1956).

13 Locke, *Correspondence*, 5, appendix, p. 788.

14 Richard Bentley, *A dissertation upon the Epistles of Phalaris* (1699), pp. lxii–lxiii.

15 Monk, *Bentley*, 1, pp. 57–8; Bentley to Graevius, 15 April 1694: 'Philostrati specimen, quod a Lipsiensibus nuper accepi, non placet: repudio omne edendi consilium, nisi typis elegantiores paraverint'. (Bentley, *Correspondence*, 1, p. 87).

16 UA Pr.v.1(1*); D. F. McKenzie, 'Richard Bentley's Design for the Cambridge University Press *c.* 1696', *TCBS*, 6 (1976), pp. 322–7. The proposals were formerly bound into a volume of miscellane‑ ous papers also including printer's copy for Spelman's *Concilia*, other notes by Spelman, and a series of papers relating to Cambridge including 'Mr Baron's designe for our Physick Garden', poems on William Whitaker, printed notices 1705–17, papers on university discipline after 1660, a synopsis of Hare's collection on the history of the University, a survey of the King's Ditch by Edward Pond, etc. The volume was apparently asssembled by Cox Macro (d. 1767), who also owned other Spelman papers. It then passed to John Patterson of Norwich, and in 1820 was sold to Hudson Gurney of Keswick Hall, Norfolk: for the fullest description see Historical MSS Commn, 12th report, part IX, pp. 137–41. At the Gurney sale (Sotheby's 30–1 March 1936) it was bought (lot 197) by Halliday of Leicester. Between then and *c.* 1969 the proposals were removed from the volume.

17 Leiden, Universiteitsbibliotheek, MS Burm Cod. Fol. no. 11, ii, fo.62, quoted, in translation by Carter, *Oxford University Press*, p. 61.

18 Carter, *Oxford University Press*, p. 161, quoting Pepys, George Hickes, Edmund Gibson and Thomas Hearne. The dislike was shared on the Continent as well: cf. Anne Goldgar, *Impolite Learning; conduct and community in the republic of letters, 1680–1750* (New Haven, 1995), pp. 49–50.

19 Carter, *Oxford University Press*, pp. 150–1.

20 Robert L. Haig, 'New light on the King's Printing Office, 1680–1730', *Studies in Bibliography*, 8 (1956), pp. 157–67.

21 Carter, *Oxford University Press*, pp. 166–8, 235–6.

22 Bentley to John Evelyn, 12 January 1696/7: Bentley, *Correspondence*, 1, p. 133; *The Carl H. Pforzheimer Library; English literature 1475–1700*, 3 vols. (New York, 1940), 3, p. 1152.

23 *Letters of eminent men addressed to Ralph Thoresby*, 2 vols. (1832), 1, p. 268.

24 McKitterick, *Cambridge University Press*, 1, pp. 344–5; Stationers' Company Court Book F, 11 April 1690, 5 May 1690; 4 December 1690, 7 September 1691.

25 McKenzie, *Cambridge University Press*, 1, p. 12.

26 Stationers' Company Court Book F, 7 September 1696.

27 See, for example, among many references to the question, Stationers' Company Court Book F, fo. 263r (decision to prosecute printer in Chester, 22 June 1697), Court Book G, fos. 16v, 59v (John

Bradford to be prosecuted, 5 December 1698, 5 May 1701), fo. 114v (Henry Eyres to be prosecuted, 5 February 1704).

28 Stationers' Company, Journal book for money disbursed, 1656–98; Warden's accounts 1696–7.

29 Carter, *Oxford University Press*, pp. 161–2.

30 The following is based on the much fuller account in McKenzie, *Cambridge University Press*, 1, pp. 28–9.

31 McKenzie, *Cambridge University Press*, 1, pp. 16–34. A few months after Queens' College regained the site, it sold it to St Catharine's College. (McKenzie, *Cambridge University Press*, 1, pp. 34–5; Willis and Clark, 2, p. 85.)

32 McKenzie, *Cambridge University Press*, 1, p. 34. See also below, pp. 311–14.

33 Thomas Smith to Arthur Charlett, 5 September 1695, Bodleian Library, MS Ballard 16, fos. 11–12v: see D. F. McKenzie, 'The genesis of the Cambridge University Press, 1695–6', *TCBS*, 5 (1969), p. 79.

34 John Evelyn to John Place (bookseller), 17 August 1696; John Evelyn, *Diary and correspondence*, ed. William Bray and Henry B. Wheatley, 4 vols. (1906), 4, p. 11.

35 Evelyn to Bentley, 20 January 1696/7; *Diary and correspondence*, 4, p. 14.

36 John Evelyn, *Diary*, ed. E. S. de Beer, 6 vols. (Oxford, 1955), 2, p. 104.

37 Bentley to J. G. Graevius, iii kal. dec. 1695: Bentley, *Correspondence*, 1, pp. 102–3; see also 1, p. 119.

38 Augustin Charles d'Aviler's *Cours d'architecture*, 2 vols., 4° (Paris: N. Langlois, 1691).

39 Bentley to Evelyn, 17 October 1696: Bentley, *Correspondence*, 1, p. 126.

40 See Eileen Harris and Nicholas Savage, *British architectural books and writers, 1556–1786* (Cambridge, 1990), pp. 114–15.

41 Thomas Smith to Arthur Charlett, 5 September 1695; Hugh Todd to the same, 2 June 1696; both printed in McKenzie, 'The genesis of the Cambridge University Press, 1695–6'.

42 Bentley to Graevius, 26 March 1697: Bentley, *Correspondence*, 1, p. 143; see also 1, p. 145. The notes of Thomas Gale (1635?–1702, formerly Regius Professor of Greek at Cambridge), with a further sheet of emendations by Bentley, are now Trinity College, MS O.10.15. A copy of the Aldine edition (Venice, 1514), much annotated by Heinsius and by Gale is now Trinity College, N.4.49. For Bentley, Kuster and Hesychius, see Monk, *Bentley*, 1, pp. 402–5 and J. E. Sandys, *A history of classical scholarship*, 2 (Cambridge, 1908), p. 446.

43 Graevius to Bentley, 9 October 1699: Bentley, *Correspondence*, 1, p. 184. See below, pp. 71–2.

44 R. C. Jebb, *Bentley* (1882), p. 36.

45 Monk, *Bentley*, 1, p. 86. For Bentley and Barnes's edition of Euripides, see *ibid.*, pp. 52–4.

46 Bentley to Thomas Bateman, 25 December 1712: Bentley, *Correspondence*, 2, pp. 448–53.

47 McKenzie, *Cambridge University Press*, 1, pp. 12–13.

48 Euripides, *Tragoediae Medea et Phoenissae*, ed. William Piers (Cambridge, 1703), 'Praeloquium ad lectorem', fo. a3r.

49 Robert Unwin, *Patronage and preferment; a study of James Talbot, Cambridge Fellow and Rector of Spofforth, 1664–1708* (Proc. Leeds Philosophical and Literary Soc., 19 (1982)).

50 Dryden's contract with Tonson, and some related documents, are printed in his *Works*, 6. *The works of Virgil in English* (Berkeley, 1987), pp. 1179–87. See also John Barnard, 'Dryden, Tonson and subscriptions for the 1697 Virgil', *PBSA*, 57 (1963), pp. 129–51.

51 Kathleen M. Lynch, *Jacob Tonson, Kit-Cat publisher* (Knoxville, 1971), p. 42; David Piper, *Catalogue of seventeenth-century portraits in the National Portrait Gallery, 1625–1714* (Cambridge, 1963), pp. 398–403; National Portrait Gallery, *The Kit-Cat Club portraits* (1971).

52 Dickinson left plate valued at £24 and books valued at about £480, in an estate valued in all at £2243.19s.4d. (CUR 21/83; PRO Prob. 4/405). William Graves left an inventory valued at £647.10s.10d. (George J. Gray and W. M. Palmer, *Abstracts of the wills and testamentary documents of printers, binders, and stationers of Cambridge from 1504 to 1699* (Bibliographical Soc., 1915), pp. 128–32.)

53 Carter, *Oxford University Press*, pp. 161–4.

54 The first page of the proposals for the series is reproduced in McKitterick, *Four hundred years*, p. 69. The only known copy is in Cambridge University Library, Cam.b.698.1.

55 Details of the production of these and other books mentioned in the following pages are taken from McKenzie, *Cambridge University Press*.

56 'Jacob Tonson is printing at Cambridg Horace Virgil Terence Catullus Tibullus and Propertius. He proposes as I hear Subscriptions i e one Guinea to be paid in Hand and an other at the delivery of the books I desire you to subscribe for one set of them for me unlesse you hear any thing to discourage it.' (Locke to Peter King, 24 April 1699: Locke, *Correspondence*, 6, p. 606).

57 UA Grace Book Θ, p. 428.

58 UA Pr.v.1, p. 6; McKenzie, *Cambridge University Press*, 2, pp. 1–2.

59 Corporation of London Records Office, assessment for St Anne, Blackfriars, p. 106. He does not appear in the same household (of one William Wragg, or Ragg, victualler) in the assessment of 1692.

60 Note by Beaupré Bell on his copy of *The case of the learned represented* (1724), bought from Crownfield for 6s., unbound, in 1724 (Trinity College T.9.52).

61 British Library, MS Add. 5866, fo.249r.

62 McKenzie, *Cambridge University Press*, 1, pp. 54–5.

63 Enschedé, *Typefoundries in the Netherlands*, pp. 77–80; John Dreyfus (ed.), *Type specimen facsimiles*, 1 (1963), no. 12.

64 Joseph Moxon, *Regulae trium ordinum litterarum typographicarum* (1676), p. 2, quoted in Moxon, *Mechanick exercises on the whole art of printing*, ed. Herbert Davis and Harry Carter, 2nd edn (Oxford, 1962), p. 372.

65 Moxon, *Mechanick exercises*, pp. 22–3.

66 McKenzie, *Cambridge University Press*, 1, pp. 43–4.

67 *Ibid.*, 1, p. 80.

68 R. Campbell, *The London tradesman* (1747), p. 124; McKenzie, *Cambridge University Press*, 1, pp. 89–90.

69 Campbell, *The London tradesman*, p. 123.

70 Moxon, *Mechanick exercises*, p. 76. See also below, p. 64.

71 (James Watson) *The history of the art of printing* (Edinburgh, 1713), Preface, pp. 21–2. For Watson, see D. Wyn Evans, 'James Watson of Edinburgh: a bibliography of works from his press 1695–1722, with an account of his life and career', *Edinburgh Bibliographical Society Transactions*, 5.2 (1982), pp. 1–158.

72 The possible exception was Albert Coldenhoff, who may have been German: see McKenzie, *Cambridge University Press*, 1, pp. 61, 62.

73 McKenzie, *Cambridge University Press*, 1, p. 13. The whole of Somerset's loan had been paid back before the end of December 1697, that is, before any book was printed (*ibid.*, 2, pp. 78–82).

74 An untrimmed copy, in rough boards, is now in Peterborough Cathedral Library (on deposit in Cambridge University Library), Pet. Q.1.1.

75 For Gribelin's work at the Press until 1712, see McKenzie, *Cambridge University Press*, 1, pp. 358–65; for some of his other work, see Sheila O'Connell, 'Simon Gribelin (1661–1733)', *Print Quarterly*, 2 (1985), pp. 27–38.

76 McKenzie, *Stationers' Company apprentices 1641–1700*, no. 473. For the turbulent relationship between Nathaniel Ponder and Braddyll, see Plomer, *Dictionary 1668–1725*, art. 'Braddyll'.

77 McKenzie, *Stationers' Company apprentices 1641–1700*, no. 3748. Details of the staff of the press, and of their work, are in McKenzie, *Cambridge University Press*.

78 McKenzie, *Cambridge University Press*, 1. ch. 4, 'Servants of the Press', provides much fuller details than those selected here.

79 UA Pr.v.1 p. 9; McKenzie, *Cambridge University Press*, 1, pp. 180–1.

80 UA Pr. vouchers, 1699.144; McKenzie, *Cambridge University Press*, 2, p. 110.

81 McKenzie, *Cambridge University Press*, 1, p. 181: even the first engraving, on A1r, was not charged for.

82 UA Pr. vouchers, 1700.23.

83 UA Pr. vouchers, 1705.18.

84 McKenzie, *Cambridge University Press*, 1, pp. 388–9, 2, pp. 119–20. For the Voskens foundry, see

Enschedé, *Typefoundries in the Netherlands*, pp. 108–11, 115–26, and John Dreyfus (ed.), *Type specimen facsimiles*, 1 (1963), nos. 8–9, reproducing specimens of *c*. 1695.

85 Hist. MSS Commn, Longleat, 3, pp. 342–3.

86 Hist. MSS Commn, Longleat, 3, p. 409.

87 Hist. MSS Commn, Longleat, 3, p. 409.

88 See pp. 71–4.

89 McKenzie, *Cambridge University Press*, 1, pp. 398–400.

90 Leonard Forster, 'Henry Sike of Bremen (1669–1712), Regius Professor of Hebrew and fellow of Trinity', *TCBS*, 10 (1993), pp. 249–77. It was Crownfield who discovered Sike's body on 20 May 1712, following his suicide in his college rooms.

91 Sotheby's 17 December 1981, lot 161. For Marsh's library, see Muriel McCarthy, *All graduates and gentlemen; Marsh's Library* (Dublin, 1980).

92 I. Bernard Cohen, *Introduction to Newton's 'Principia'* (Cambridge, 1978), pp. 216–23, and below, pp. 98–108.

93 Bentley's copy of the edition of 1699, with his annotations, is in the British Library (C.20.c.23). A page is reproduced in Robert Unwin, *Patronage and preferment; a study of James Talbot* (Leeds, 1982), p. 15. The volume was once interleaved with copious further manuscript notes, now only visible as stains in reverse on the printed pages. Bentley's copy of his own edition of 1711, with his notes of readings of the Vossius manuscript (Leiden, Universiteitsbibliotheek, Voss. Lat.Q.21) is in the British Library, 679.f.7. See also D. Shackleton Bailey, 'Bentley and Horace', *Proc. Leeds Philosophical Soc.*, 10.3 (1963), pp. 105–15.

94 Bentley to Thomas Bateman, 25 December 1712: Bentley, *Correspondence*, 2, pp. 448–53.

95 Prior to Talbot, 4 October 1700, Hist. MSS Commn, Longleat, 3, p. 423.

96 Term Catalogues 3, 220 (November 1700); McKenzie, *Cambridge University Press*, 1, p. 197.

97 Talbot to Prior, 26 October 1700, Hist. MSS Commn, Longleat, 3, p. 429.

98 Tonson's note to Lucretius, 1712.

99 McKenzie, *Cambridge University Press*, 1, p. 179. A copy of the proposals (UA Pr.B.2(5)) is reproduced in McKitterick, *Four hundred years*, p. 75.

100 Figures from McKenzie, *Cambridge University Press*, 1, p. 163.

101 McKitterick, *Cambridge University Library*, pp. 78–9; John Gascoigne, *Cambridge in the Age of the Enlightenment* (Cambridge, 1989), pp. 155–9.

102 McKitterick, *Cambridge University Library*, pp. 135–7; Terence Towers, 'Smith and Son, editors of Bede', in G. Bonner (ed.), *Famulus Christi* (1976), pp. 357–65.

103 Edward Thwaites to Wanley, 3 July 1702, British Library, MS Harley 3781, fo.212r; Richard L. Harris (ed.), *A chorus of grammars; the correspondence of George Hickes and his collaborators on the 'Thesaurus linguarum septentrionalium'* (Toronto, 1992), p. 372. For de Walpergen's special Saxon small pica sorts cut at Oxford, see Stanley Morison and Harry Carter, *John Fell* (Oxford, 1967), pp. 232, 250.

104 UA Pr.v.1: Minutes of Curators, 27 January 1713/14. See also below, pp. 114, 126.

105 'Owens mentioned in the inclosed is a Dutchman, who trades with Theater-bookes to Holland': George Hickes to Robert Harley, 11 September 1701, British Library, MS Add. 70241; Richard L. Harris (ed.), *A chorus of grammars; the correspondence of George Hickes and his collaborators on the Thesaurus linguarum septentrionalium* (Toronto, 1992), p. 353. The 'theater' refers to the Sheldonian Theatre in Oxford, home of the Oxford University Press; the 'inclosed' has not been identified.

106 Johnson and Gibson, *Print and privilege*, pp. 157–9; Carter, *Oxford University Press*, pp. 182–3. Cf. the remarks by the London bookseller Thomas Bennet: 'Mr Owens sale by Auction at Oxon has done the Latt and Greek Bookes an Injury for they sold most of them much under the Prizes I pay for them in Holland Ready Money though the Charges of selling them cost above 50 pounds Sterling besides the Expenses of bringing them over.' (Bennet and Clements, *Notebook*, p. 58.)

107 British Library, MS Harley 5932(132); Carter, *Oxford University Press*, pp. 183, 254, 437.

108 *Orbis eruditi literatura a charactere Samaritico deducta*. Copy in Cambridge University Library, Hhh.357².

109 UA CUR 33.6(32).

110 *London Gazette*, 3748 (9–13 October 1701). For this and many other details of the progress of the project, see McKenzie, *Cambridge University Press*, 1, pp. 224–33.

111 A copy of the prospectus, 1 April 1701 (not recorded by McKenzie) is in the Bagford collection in the British Library, Harley 5946(131), together with a draft in manuscript.

112 McKenzie, *Cambridge University Press*, 1, pp. 234–5.

113 Queens' College Archives, Book 80, 2nd pagination p. 2. For John Baskett's early career as paper-merchant, see Carter, *Oxford University Press*, pp. 166–7.

114 UA Pr. vouchers 1703, no. 81.

115 UA CUR 33.6(34); UA Pr vouchers 1703, no. 87; McKenzie, *Cambridge University Press*, 2, p. 238.

116 Worth was appointed chaplain to the Bishop of Worcester in 1705, the position that Bentley had once held under Stillingfleet.

117 In 1705, Bennet passed on some to Pieter van der Aa of Leiden: Bennet and Clements, *Notebook*, pp. 64–5. For further remarks on exports, see below, pp. 80–2.

118 The list of subscribers at October 1703 is printed in McKenzie, *Cambridge University Press*, 2, pp. 239–41. Owen's claim to have obtained slightly more subscription money than Crownfield appears to be incorrect.

119 Van Eeghen, *De Amsterdamse boekhandel*, 4, pp. 231–2.

120 Minutes of Curators, 22 September 1704; McKenzie, *Cambridge University Press*, 2, p. 13. Unfortunately, no minutes survive of the meeting on 11 October 1703, when Owen's handling of the *Suidas* was presumably discussed; but see the notes dated 12 October in UA Pr. vouchers, 1703, no. 87.

121 McKenzie, *Cambridge University Press*, 1, pp. 270–1.

122 *Bibliothèque Choisie*, 10 (1706), pp. 297–305, at p. 298.

123 Minutes of Curators, 18 December 1706; UA Pr. vouchers, 1706–7 (schedules of debts); McKenzie, *Cambridge University Press*, 2, pp. 19, 290.

124 *Acta Eruditorum*, January 1706, pp. 1–5; *Journal des Sçavans*, 38 (1707), pp. 70–8; *Bibliothèque Choisie*, 9 (1706), pp. 172–204, at p. 187.

125 Dedication to Léon Modena, *The history of the present Jews*, trans. Simon Ockley (1707), quoted in McKenzie, *Cambridge University Press*, 1, p. 66.

126 Sir Theodore Janssen to Crownfield, 19 October 1704: UA CUR 33.6(35); McKenzie, *Cambridge University Press*, 2, p. 261. It seems unlikely that this letter refers to Bentley's edition of Horace: it was written only a few days after the Curators had agreed terms, on 22 September, for the Caesar (*ibid.*, p. 13).

127 McKenzie, *Cambridge University Press*, 1, p. 56.

128 UA Grace Book Θ, p. 528.

4 Crownfield, authors and the book trade

1 The failure to provide for the costs of publishing is discussed by McKenzie, *Cambridge University Press*, 1, pp. 156–8.

2 McKenzie, *Cambridge University Press*, 1, p. 179.

3 McKitterick, *Cambridge University Press*, 1, p. 358.

4 Francis Hutchinson, *A sermon preached at the Public Commencement* (Cambridge, 1698). Jefferies included a list of some of the books in whose publication he had been involved in Robert Marsden, *Concio ad clerum... Oct.9°. A°. 1700* (Cambridge, 1701).

5 Peter Nourse, *A sermon preached at the publick commencement at Cambridge* (1698): McKenzie, *Cambridge University Press*, 1, p. 177; Karl Tilman Winkler, *Handwerk und Markt; Druckerhandwerk, Vertriebswesen und Tagesschrifttum in London, 1695–1750* (Stuttgart, 1993), pp. 549–50.

6 An elder Richard Thurlbourn died in 1706, aged seventy-three. For details of his wife and children, drawn from the monument in St Edward's church, see Francis Blomefield, *Collectanea Cantabrigiensia* (Norwich, 1750), p. 83.

7 John Dunton, *Life and errors*, 2 vols. (1818), 1, p. 210.

8 John P. Chalmers, 'An addendum to *The Cambridge University Press, 1696–1712*', *TCBS*, 6 (1976), p. 349.

9 William Stukeley, *Family memoirs* (Surtees Soc., 1882), p. 21.

10 Talbot to Matthew Prior, 6 November 1700. Historical MSS Commn, *Bath*, 3, pp. 428–9.

11 *Term catalogues* 3, p. 220.

12 *London Gazette*, 13 November 1707. McKenzie, *Cambridge University Press*, 2, p. 296.

13 *Term catalogues* 3, p. 505 (May 1706).

14 Although, according to their title-pages, there were supposedly four editions in 1713–14, in fact the second and third are substantially from the same type-setting. Part 2 (printed for John Morphew and E. Curl in 1713) includes a catalogue of Crownfield's books; the fourth edition of the *Remarks* was printed for Morphew and Crownfield, 1714.

15 See below, p. 90.

16 Daniel Waterland, *An answer to Dr Whitby's reply* (Cambridge, 1720), 'Books printed for, and sold sold by Corn. Crownfield'.

17 Cicero, *De divinatione et de fato* (Cambridge, 1730), advertisement.

18 William Whiston, *Memoirs*, 2nd edn, 2 vols. (1753), 1, pp. 114–15.

19 *Acta Eruditorum*, October 1706, pp. 457–62.

20 Queens' College Archives, Book 80, 2nd pagination, p. 2.

21 See above, p. 73.

22 Janssen to Crownfield, 17 April 1705; UA CUR 33.6(36); McKenzie, *Cambridge University Press*, 2, p. 275.

23 Janssen to Crownfield, 26 April 1705; UA CUR 33.6(37); McKenzie, *Cambridge University Press*, 2, p. 276.

24 Adalbert J. Brauer, 'Professor Johann Burchard Mencke, F. R. S. (1674–1732)', *Notes and Records of the Royal Society of London*, 17 (1962), pp. 192–7; Hub. Laeven, *The <<Acta Eruditorum>> under the editorship of Otto Mencke (1644–1707); the history of an international learned journal between 1682 and 1707* (Amsterdam, 1990), pp. 155,159.

25 *The History of the Works of the Learned*, 1 (January 1699), preface.

26 Laeven, *The <<Acta Eruditorum>>*, pp. 147–94.

27 *Bibliothèque Choisie*, 3 (1704), pp. 250–1. Le Clerc's later disputes with Bentley, beginning in 1709, are discussed from different standpoints in Monk, *Bentley* pp. 266–80 and Annie Barnes, *Jean Le Clerc (1657–1736) et la république des lettres* (Paris, 1938), pp. 214–24.

28 For more general remarks on the Netherlands' dominant position in Europe, see G. C. Gibbs, 'The role of the Dutch Republic as the intellectual entrepôt of Europe in the seventeenth and eighteenth centuries', *Bijdragen en Mededelingen Betreffende de Geschiedenis der Nederlanden*, 86 (1971), pp. 323–49. For some aspects of the British trade, see Katherine Swift, 'Dutch penetration of the London market for books, *c.* 1690–1730', in C. Berkvens-Stevelinck etc. (ed.), *Le magasin de l'univers; the Dutch republic as the centre of the European book trade* (Leiden, 1992), pp. 265–79.

29 Customs accounts are summarised in Norma Hodgson and Cyprian Blagden, *The notebook of Thomas Bennet and Henry Clements (1686–1719), with some aspects of book trade practice* (Oxford Bibliographical Soc., 1956), pp. 116–18. See also, more fully, Giles Barber, 'Books for the old world and for the new: the British international trade in books in the eighteenth century', *Studies on Voltaire and the Eighteenth Century*, 151 (1976), pp. 185–224, 'Aspects of the booktrade between England and the Low Countries in the eighteenth century', Werkgroep 18e Eeuw, *Documentieblad*, 34–5 (1977), pp. 47–63, and 'Book imports and exports in the eighteenth century' in R. Myers and M. Harris (ed.), *Sale and distribution of books from 1700* (Oxford, 1982), pp. 77–105.

30 Kathleen M. Lynch, *Jacob Tonson, Kit-Cat publisher* (Knoxville, 1971), pp. 108, 109, 110.

31 Bennet to van der Aa, 7 August 1705; *Notebook of Thomas Bennet and Henry Clements*, pp. 64–5. Bennet died soon afterwards, aged forty-one, on 26 August 1706. For van der Aa, see P. G. Hoftijzer, 'The Leiden bookseller Pieter van der Aa (1659–1733) and the international book trade', *Le magasin de l'univers*, pp. 169–84.

32 *Eleven catalogues by Reinier Leers (1692–1709); a reproduction*, ed. H. H. M. van Lieshout and O. S. Lankhorst (Utrecht, 1992). For Leers more generally, see Otto S. Lankhorst, *Reinier Leers (1654–1714), uitgever & boekverkoper te Rotterdam* (Amsterdam, 1983).

33 Talbot to Prior, between 26 October–6 November 1700. Hist. MSS Commn, *Bath* 3, p. 429.

34 *Acta Eruditorum*, July 1701, p. 336.

35 Joseph Guibert, *Le Cabinet des Estampes de la Bibliothèque Nationale* (Paris, 1926), p. 32; Lankhorst, *Reinier Leers*, pp. 93–121; Simone Balayé, *La Bibliothèque Nationale des origines à 1800* (Genève, 1988), pp. 115, 119, 126–7.

36 French purchases, recorded in Bibliothèque Nationale, Archives du Département des Manuscrits, Ancien Régime, 21, are indexed in *Eleven catalogues by Reinier Leers*. For further comment on the Franco-Dutch trade, cf. Françoise Bléchet, 'Quelques acquisitions hollandaises de la Bibliothèque du Roi (1668–1735)', *Le magasin de l'univers*, pp. 33–47.

37 For details, see Jean Sgard, *Dictionnaire des journalistes (1600–1789)* (Grenoble, 1976) and *Dictionnaire des journaux*, 2 vols. (Paris and Oxford, 1991). Though the editors and correspondents of the many journals counted themselves as parts of a 'republic of letters', they depended on their several publishers and hence to a geat extent on the economic forces of the book trade. See Otto S. Lankhorst, 'Le rôle des libraire-imprimeurs néerlandais dans l'édition des journaux littéraires de langue française (1684–1750)', in Hans Bots (ed.), *La diffusion et la lecture des journaux de langue française sous l'ancien régime* (Amsterdam, 1988), pp. 1–9, and H. Bots, 'Le rôle des périodiques néerlandais pour la diffusion du livre (1684–1747)', *Le magasin de l'univers*, pp. 49–70. See also, more generally, Anne Goldgar, *Impolite learning; conduct and community in the republic of letters, 1680–1750* (New Haven, 1995).

38 Apart from the references provided in Sgard, *Dictionnaire*, see Hubert Bost, *Un <<intellectuel>> avant la lettre: le journaliste Pierre Bayle (1647–1706)* (Amsterdam, 1994).

39 Lankhorst, *Reinier Leers*; Hans Bots, *Henri Basnage de Beauval en de Histoire des Ouvrages des Savans, 1687–1709*, 2 vols. (Amsterdam, 1976); Hans Bots and Lenie van Lieshout, *Contribution à la connaissance des réseaux d'information au début du XVIIIe siècle* (Amsterdam, 1984).

40 For Johnson, see also B. J. McMullin, 'T. Johnson, bookseller in The Hague', in R. Harvey, W. Kirsop and B. J. McMullin (ed.), *An index of civilisation; studies of printing and publishing history in honour of Keith Maslen* (Melbourne, 1993), pp. 99–112.

41 Guus N. M. Wijngaards, *De 'Bibliothèque Choisie' van Jean Le Clerc (1657–1736); een Amsterdams geleerdentijdschrift uit de jaren 1703 tot 1713* (Amsterdam, 1986).

42 'Cette langue ne m'est pas assez familière pour oser traduire certains titres difficiles & dont je ne puis pas m'assurer du sens.' (Bernard to Pierre des Maizeaux, May 1700, quoted in Joseph Almagor, *Pierre des Maizeaux (1673–1745), journalist and English correspondent for Franco-Dutch periodicals, 1700–1720* (Amsterdam, 1989), p. 46).

43 *Bibliothèque Choisie*. Tables (Amsterdam, 1718), *4r.

44 *Bibliothèque Choisie*, 11 (1707), pp. 164–5.

45 UA Pr.v.1, Curators' minutes, 7 February 1699/1700.

46 Review of Maximus Tyrius, *Bibliothèque Choisie*, 11 (1707), pp. 287–329.

47 Review of Euripides, *Bibliothèque Choisie*, 11 (1707), pp. 276–87, at pp. 277–8.

48 Joseph Moxon, *Mechanick exercises*, p. 23. See also above, p. 62.

49 Stanley Morison, 'Leipzig as a centre of type-founding', in his *Selected essays on the history of letterforms in manuscript and print*, ed. D. McKitterick (Cambridge, 1981), 1, pp. 132–41; A. F. Johnson, 'The "goût hollandois"', in his *Selected essays on books and printing*, ed. Percy H. Muir (Amsterdam, 1970), pp. 365–77.

50 Review of Horace and Terence, *Bibliothèque Choisie*, 3 (1704), pp. 250–62.

51 Review of Minucius Felix, *Bibliothèque Choisie*, 24 (1712), pp. 120–45, at p. 122.

52 Advertised in the *Amsterdamsche Courant*, 12 October 1713.

53 Bentley to T. Hemsterhuis, 22 February 1712/13: *Some letters of Richard Bentley published from the University Library, Leyden*, ed. Elfriede Hulshoff Pol (Leiden, 1959), p. 34.

54 Review of Horace, ed. Bentley (Amsterdam, 1713), *Bibliothèque Choisie*, 26 (1713), pp. 260–73: see

also Jean Le Clerc, *Mr. Le Clerc's judgment and censure of Dr. Bentley's Horace, and of the Amsterdam edition, compar'd with that of Cambridge* (1738). Le Clerc's correspondents played to his dislike of Bentley's work: see Jean Le Clerc, *Epistolario* 3, *1706–1718*, ed. M. Grazia and M. Sina (Florence, 1994). For comparable remarks concerning the placing of the footnotes in the Amsterdam edition, cf. the *Journal des Sçavans*, March 1713.

55 Review of Caesar, ed. Clarke, *Bibliothèque Choisie*, 1713, pp. 112–49.

56 Bentley to Tiberius Hemsterhuis, 22 February 1712/13: *Some letters of Richard Bentley*, pp. 35–6.

57 Le Clerc to Shaftesbury, Amsterdam, 17 September 1705, and Le Clerc to Gisbert Cuper, 1 November 1705; Jean Le Clerc, *Epistolario*, ed. M. Sina and M. Grazia (Firenze, 1987–), 2, pp. 587–90.

58 *The History of the Works of the Learned*, 1 (January 1699), p. 59.

59 For one example, cf. Joseph Almagor, *Pierre des Maizeaux (1673–1745), journalist and English correspondent for Franco-Dutch periodicals, 1700–1720* (Amsterdam, 1989), pp. 46–7.

60 UA Pr.v.1, Curators' minutes, 14 October 1701 (Kuster), 9 September 1703 (Bentley).

61 A summary is in McKenzie, *Cambridge University Press*, 1, pp. 224–33. See also above, pp. 71–4.

62 *Diatriba de Suida* (1701).

63 *Nouvelles de la République des Lettres*, October 1701, pp. 465–7, April 1703, p. 466. For one London correspondent with journals published in the Netherlands and in France, cf. J. H. Broome, 'Pierre Desmaizeaux, journaliste; les nouvelles littéraires de Londres entre 1700 et 1740', *Revue de Littérature Comparée*, 29 (1955), pp. 184–204.

64 *Bibliothèque Choisie*, 9 (1706), pp. 172–86. Writing from Utrecht, Kuster reported to Bentley on 8 June that the review had appeared: Trinity College, MS R.17.31, no. 23; Bentley, *Correspondence*, 1, p. 239.

65 Two manuscript subscription lists dating from 1701, and clearly far short of the final total, are preserved amongst the Press vouchers: see McKenzie, *Cambridge University Press*, 2, p. 239.

66 UA Pr.v.1, Curators' minutes, 11 May 1705.

67 McKenzie, *Cambridge University Press*, 2, pp. 18 (Wetstein), 29 (Fritsch).

68 UA Pr. vouchers, 1703.87. (McKenzie, *Cambridge University Press*, 2, pp. 239–40.)

69 Queens' College Archives, 'Library account and inventory of furniture', p. 202; Curators' minutes, p. 31; McKenzie, *Cambridge University Press*, 2, p. 18. For a glimpse of Queens' College library at this time, see David Pearson, 'A Cambridge binding of 1700', *The Book Collector* 42 (1993), pp. 553–5.

70 UA Pr. vouchers, 1707.4; McKenzie, *Cambridge University Press*, 2, p. 289; Oates, *Cambridge University Library*, pp. 469–70.

71 Trinity College, Junior Bursar's accounts; David McKitterick (ed.), *The making of the Wren Library* (Cambridge, 1996), pp. 53, 54.

72 Trinity College, MS Add. a.197(4), statement to Bentley, August 1714–November 1715.

73 Kuster to Bentley, 7 January 1707, Trinity College, MS R.17.31, no. 28; Bentley, *Correspondence*, 1, pp. 252–3. For Kuster's career, see J. C. Zeltner, *C. D. correctorum in typographis eruditorum centuria* (Nuremberg, 1716), pp. 307–16.

74 UA Pr.v.1, Curators' minutes, 3 March 1708/9: McKenzie, *Cambridge University Press*, 2, pp. 23–4, 289; Queens' College Archives, 'Library account and inventory of furniture', p. 203. For Crownfield and the University Library, see Oates, *Cambridge University Library*, pp. 469–70.

75 Roberts, *Evolution*, p. 14.

76 Cf. Keith Maslen, 'Printing for the author: from the Bowyer printing ledgers, 1710–1755', *The Library*, 5th ser. 27 (1972), pp. 302–9, repr. in his *An early printing house at work: studies in the Bowyer ledgers* (New York, 1993), pp. 97–104.

77 Barnes to Hearne, 12 January 1707/8: Bodleian Library, MS Rawlinson lett. 24(9).

78 Note of letter by Barnes, 11 June 1707: Emmanuel College, MS James 174.

79 Barnes to Hearne, 12 January 1707/8: Bodleian Library, MS Rawlinson lett. 24(9).

80 Barnes to Hearne, 25 October 1707: Bodleian Library, MS Rawlinson lett. 24(4). The type is shown and discussed in McKenzie, *Cambridge University Press*, 1, pp. 398–400.

81 UA Pr.v.1, Curators' minutes, 17 November 1707. Rudd was the brother of Edward Rudd, Fellow of Trinity College and corrector at the University Press. For Vigani, see L. J. M. Coleby, 'John Francis

Vigani, first professor of chemistry in the University of Cambridge', *Annals of Science*, 8 (1952), pp. 46–60.

82 UA Pr.v.1, Curators' minutes, 15 June 1708.

83 'The Great Frost retarded ye work much': Barnes to Hearne, 8 February 1708/9; Hearne, *Remarks and collections*, 2, p. 167.

84 Summary in McKenzie, *Cambridge University Press*, 1, pp. 306–8.

85 McKenzie, *Cambridge University Press*, 1, pp. 318–19.

86 Barnes to Hearne, 27 January 1707/8: Bodleian Library, MS Rawlinson lett. 24(12); Hearne, *Remarks and collections*, 2, p. 91.

87 Hearne, *Remarks and collections*, 2, p. 91. Cf. the remarks by Edward Lhwyd in 1703:

> English booksellers have a method of setting persons in the coffee houses to decry any book that an author prints at his own charges, so that all may fall to their own hands for little or no consideration. This they call damming a book; and 'tis so common that very few ever escape it. (Lhwyd to Robert Wodrow, 22 December 1703, quoted in *Early letters of Robert Wodrow*, ed. L. W. Sharp (Edinburgh, 1937), p. 263.)

88 Barnes to Hearne, 12 June 1708: Bodleian Library, MS Rawlinson lett. 24(14); Hearne, *Remarks and collections*, 2, p. 113.

89 Barnes to Hearne, 15 May 1709: Bodleian Library, MS Rawlinson lett. 24(19); Hearne, *Remarks and collections*, 2, p. 198.

90 Details of Barnes and the Press are in McKenzie, *Cambridge University Press*, 1, pp. 306–13. The copies of Homer with Barnes's notes and annotated by Roderick are in Emmanuel College, MSS James 145, 146.

91 Barnes to Hearne, 17 December 1710: Bodleian Library, MS Rawlinson lett. 24(24); Hearne, *Remarks and collections*, 3, p. 91.

92 Barnes to Hearne, 15 July 1711: Bodleian Library, MS Rawlinson lett. 24(27); Hearne, *Remarks and collections*, 3, p. 194.

93 Bodleian Library, MS Rawlinson lett. 24(27); Hearne, *Remarks and collections*, 3, p. 202.

94 Barnes to Hearne, *c.* 24 September 1708: Bodleian Library, MS Rawlinson lett. 24 (31); Hearne, *Remarks and collections*, 2, p. 135; *London Gazette*, 21–3 February 1709/10.

95 *London Gazette*, 21–3 and 23–5 February: 10s. was to be paid down, and the remainder on publication.

96 Barnes to Hearne, 15 July 1711: Bodleian Library, MS Rawlinson lett. 24(27); Hearne, *Remarks and collections*, 3, pp. 194, 202.

97 *Bibliothèque Choisie*, 22 (1711), pp. 241–77.

98 For Schelte, see van Eeghen, *De Amsterdamse boekhandel*, 4, pp. 93–5.

99 *Journal des Sçavans*, June 1712.

100 Hearne, *Remarks and collections*, 3, p. 329.

101 *Ibid.*, pp. 429–31.

102 Hearne to Mrs Barnes, 31 August 1712; Hearne, *Remarks and collections*, 3, p. 440.

103 Mrs Barnes to Hearne, 7 February 1712/13; Hearne, *Remarks and collections*, 4, p. 72.

104 Mrs Barnes to Hearne, 9 October 1712; Hearne, *Remarks and collections*, 3, p. 468.

105 Trinity College, MS Add. a.197(2). This and the details of distribution are not printed in McKenzie, *Cambridge University Press*, falling outside the archive of the Press itself.

106 The retail price of his edition, one pound in quires, may have been substantially more than that charged for Talbot's. McKenzie, *Cambridge University Press*, 1, p. 181, quotes the price noted by Edward Rudd, eleven shillings (Trinity College, MS B.7.61). But Rudd did not necessarily buy his copy new, or on publication.

107 *Nouvelles de la République des Lettres*, April 1703, pp. 466–7, March 1705, p. 355.

108 Hearne, *Remarks and collections*, 1, p. 117. See also pp. 58–60.

109 Hearne, *Remarks and collections*, 2, p. 179; see also ibid., p. 103.

110 Details are from Trinity College, MS Add. a.197(1). McKenzie (*Cambridge University Press*, 1, p. 251) assumes that Bentley undertook correction himself. For Hoppe, see *ibid.* 1, pp. 68, 69, 84, 85.

111 Hearne to Roger Gale, 8 October 1711; Hearne *Remarks and collections*, 3, p. 241. For more recent estimates, cf. D. R. Shackleton Bailey, 'Bentley and Horace', in his *Profile of Horace* (1982), E. J. Kenney, *The classical text* (Berkeley, 1974), pp. 71–4, and C. O. Brink, *English classical scholarship* (Cambridge, 1985), ch. 4.

112 Gale to Hearne, 21 October 1711; Hearne, *Remarks and collections*, 3, pp. 247–8.

113 Now Cambridge University Library, Rel.b.71.1; see H. M. Nixon, *Restoration bookbindings; Samuel Mearne and his contemporaries* (British Library, 1974), p. 42.

114 Now Trinity College, NQ.8.3 and Z.2.39.

115 *Memoirs of Literature*, 2nd edn, 5 (1722), pp. 298–313.

116 The timetable of printing is summarised in McKenzie, *Cambridge University Press*, 1, pp. 330–6. See also the detailed study by I. Bernard Cohen, *Introduction to Newton's 'Principia'* (Cambridge, 1971). For Cotes, see Ronald Gowing, *Roger Cotes – natural philosopher* (Cambridge, 1983), and A. Rupert Hall, 'Newton and his editors', *Notes and Records of the Royal Society*, 29 (1974), pp. 29–52.

117 McKenzie, *Cambridge University Press*, 2, p. 291.

118 Bentley to Newton, 10 June 1708, Trinity College, MS R.4.47, fo. 19: Newton, *Correspondence*, 4, pp. 518–19.

119 Bentley to Newton, 20 October 1709, Trinity College, MS R.4.47, fo. 20: Newton, *Correspondence*, 5, p. 7.

120 Bentley to Newton, [30 June 1713], Trinity College, MS R.4.47, fo. 24: Newton, *Correspondence*, 5, pp. 414–15.

121 Cotes to Newton, 22 December 1713: Newton, *Correspondence*, 6, p. 49.

122 Trinity College, MS Add. a.197(4).

123 Trinity College, Ms Add. a.197(4), printed in part in Newton, *Correspondence*, 5, p. 417.

124 For Jacob, or James, Moetjens (d. 1721) and Le Cène, see Katherine Swift, 'Dutch penetration of the London market for books, *c.* 1690–1730', in *Le magasin de l'univers*, pp. 265–79; for his relations with the Harleian Library, see *The diary of Humfrey Wanley, 1715–1726*, ed. C. E. Wright and Ruth C. Wright, 2 vols. (Bibliographical Soc., 1966), pp. 16, 18, 34, 39, 67. Both these authorities are concerned more with the partners' imports than with their exports.

125 *Bibliothèque Ancienne et Moderne*, 1 (1714), pp. 69–96.

126 Charles Morgan to Cotes, 2 July 1713; Trinity College, MS R.4.42(5).

127 For Whiston's subsequent career in London, see Larry Stewart, *The rise of public science; rhetoric, technology, and natural philosophy in Newtonian Britain, 1660–1750* (Cambridge, 1992), pp. 91–7.

128 Bentley's political and legal involvements at this time are described in Monk, *Bentley*, 1, pp. 325–59.

129 Newton retained at least two annotated working copies. One, interleaved, is now Cambridge University Library, Adv.b.39.2; the other (not interleaved) is Trinity College, NQ.16.196. See J. R. Harrison, *The library of Isaac Newton* (Cambridge, 1978), p. 202. Bentley's own copy is in Trinity College, Adv.b.2.3, and Moore's (bound in red turkey leather, gilt, and certainly a gift) is in the University Library, Syn.4.71.2.

130 Trinity College, MS R.16.38(318); Newton, *Correspondence*, 6, p. 11.

131 Cambridge University Library, MS Add. 3965, fo. 358; printed in Cohen, *Introduction to Newton's 'Principia'*, p. 247.

132 (Bignon) original untraced; (Varignon) King's College, MS Keynes 142(A); Newton, *Correspondence*, 6, pp. 40, 41–3.

133 Fontenelle to Newton, 24 January 1714; Newton, *Correspondence*, 6, pp. 59–60.

134 Bernoulli to De Moivre, 9 March 1714/15; Newton, *Correspondence*, 6, p. 73. See also Burnet to Bernoulli, 8 April 1714, *Correspondence*, p. 96.

135 Bernoulli to Burnet, 4 [15] May 1714; Newton, *Correspondence*, 6, pp. 123–5.

136 For the Company of Booksellers in Amsterdam, see van Eeghen, *De Amsterdamse boekhandel*, 5.1, pp. 326–7.

137 *Acta Eruditorum*, March 1714, pp. 131–42; see Cohen, *Introduction to Newton's 'Principia'*, pp. 254–6.

138 *Journal Littéraire*, July–August 1713, p. 476.

139 *Cambridge under Queen Anne*, p. 350.

140 *Ibid.*, p. 383.

141 On Swaart, or Swart, see Paul Hoftijzer, *Engelse boekverkopers bij de beurs; de geschiedenis van de Amsterdamse boekhandels Bruyning en Swart, 1637–1724* (Amsterdam, 1987).

142 See, for example, general remarks on the subject in the review of Davies's edition of Julius Caesar (Cambridge, 1706) in the *Acta Eruditorum* Supplementum IV, sect. VII (1711), p. 297.

143 Coleman, *British paper industry*; A. H. Shorter, *Paper making in the British Isles; an historical and geographical study* (Newton Abbot, 1971).

144 Cf. the remarks by Sir Theodore Janssen in 1713: 'Since the high Duties laid on foreign Paper, and that none hath been imported from France, where 'tis cheapest, the making of it is increased to such a Degree in England, that we import none of the lower Sorts from abroad, and make them all our selves: But if the French Duties be taken off, undoubtedly most of the Mills which are imployed in the making of white Paper, must leave off their Work, and 30 to 40000*l.* a Year be remitted over to France for that Commodity.' (*General maxims in trade, particularly applied to the commerce between Great Britain and France* (1713), p. 17.)

145 Warren C. Scoville, *The persecution of Huguenots and French economic development, 1680–1720* (Berkeley, 1960), pp. 230–7. But as Scovile points out, government interference in the French paper industry from the 1650s onwards coincided with a decline that had already begun before the revocation of the Edict of Nantes hastened the process.

146 For the Company of White Paper Makers, see W. R. Scott, *The constitution and finance of English, Scottish and Irish joint-stock companies to 1720*, 3 vols. (Cambridge, 1910–12), 3, pp. 63–70.

147 Coleman, *British paper industry*, especially pp. 66–70, 124–6. The Paper Duty Act of 1712 provided for the university presses at Cambridge and Oxford to claim drawbacks on tax for paper used to print books in Latin, Greek, oriental and northern languages (such as Anglo-Saxon), but this provision seems to have been little exploited by the Cambridge press in the first years of the Act's operation: see McKenzie, *Cambridge University Press*, 1, pp. 161–2, and also below, p. 213. The cost of paper to the British newspaper trade a little later in the century is discussed in Karl Tilman Winkler, *Handwerk und Markt; Druckerhandwerk, Vertriebswesen und Tagesschrifttum in London, 1695–1750* (Stuttgart, 1993), pp. 297–307.

148 Waesberghe to Samuel Smith, 5 January 1685/6; *Notebook of Thomas Bennet and Henry Clements*, p. 14. Some of the details of paper duties are summarised on pp. 51–2.

149 Benjamin Marshall, *A chronological treatise upon the seventy weeks of Daniel* (1725), 'Advertisement' at end.

150 De Lorme to Mme Boudot, 7 May 1708; van Eeghen, *De Amsterdamse boekhandel*, 1, p. 72.

151 De Lorme to Rémond de Saint Mard, 12 December 1707 (van Eeghen, *De Amsterdamse boekhandel*, 1, pp. 173–4); UA Pr.v.1, Curators' minutes, 30 August 1706.

152 De Lorme to Niels Foss, 20 August 1707: van Eeghen, *De Amsterdamse boekhandel*, 1, p. 87 (Caesar); *Gazette* 16 October 1716: van Eeghen, *De Amsterdamse boekhandel*, 2, p. 264 (Cicero); *Journal des Sçavans*, 61 (1717), opposite p. 483.

153 *The Present State of the Republick of Letters*, 1 (1728), preface, pp. i–ii. In a very large literature, for aspects of the republic of letters, or *respublica litterarum*, see for example Martin Ultee, 'The republic of letters: learned correspondence, 1680–1720', *The Seventeenth Century*, 2 (1987), pp. 95–112, Françoise Waquet, 'Qu'est-ce que la République des Lettres? Essai de sémantique historique', *Bibliothèque de l'Ecole des Chartes* 147 (1989), pp. 473–502; Goldgar, *Impolite learning*, with further references.

154 *The Present State of the Republick of Letters*, 3 (February 1729), p. 151.

155 Some aspects of the early history of English as an international language are studied in P. M. L. Loonen, *For to learne to buye and sell; learning English in the Low Dutch area between 1500 and 1800* (Amsterdam, 1991).

156 Roger Gale to Samuel Pepys, 22 September/2 October 1699; Samuel Pepys, *Private correspondence and miscellaneous papers*, ed. J. R. Tanner, 2 vols. (1926), 1, p. 180.

157 See above, p. 83, and Goldgar, *Impolite learning*, particularly ch. 2, 'Writing to the papers'. As Goldgar emphasises (pp. 66–7), the purpose of many of these journals was not so much to sell books, as to summarise for the benefit of those who would not read an entire work.

158 Françoise Bléchet, 'L'Abbé Bignon, Bibliothécaire du Roy, et les milieux savants en France au début du XVIIIe siècle', in *Buch und Sammler; private und öffentliche Bibliotheken im 18. Jahrhundert* (Heidelberg, 1979), pp. 53–66, with further references.

5 Crownfield's later years

1 He was buried on 4 November 1743: St Botolph's Church registers.

2 Hudson to Hearne, 3 August 1708, Hearne, *Remarks and collections*, 2, p. 123. For Hudson and the Oxford press, see Carter, *Oxford University Press*, pp. 151–2.

3 A summary of annual press accounts, 1696–1740, is conveniently set out in McKenzie, *Cambridge University Press*, 1, pp. 172–3. I have rounded figures to the nearest pound.

4 UA Pr.v.1, Curators' minutes, 2 March 1712/13. Kuster had engaged himself to produce a new Latin dictionary, but then found it impossible to finish the work in time. For Le Clerc's attempt to provoke interest in England to support him, see his letter to an unnamed correspondent (addressed as My Lord), 28 December 1711: Jean Le Clerc, *Epistolario*, 3, *1706–1718*, ed. Maria Grazia and Mario Sina (Florence, 1994), pp. 382–4. For an extended account of the proposed revision of Stephanus, which would have paid particular attention to Bentley's work, see *Memoirs of Literature*, 2nd edn, 5 (1722), pp. 298–313.

5 See above, p. 71. Nichols, *Literary anecdotes*, 1, pp. 233–5; McKitterick, *Cambridge University Library*, pp. 135–7; David C. Douglas, *English scholars* (1943), pp. 73–6.

6 UA Pr.v.1, Curators' minutes, 27 January 1713/14.

7 *The Postboy*, 19 October 1721, 'soon to be published'.

8 Nichols, *Literary anecdotes*, 1, pp. 212–3. A further advertisement appeared in *The Daily Courant*, 3 January 1721/2, and the book was published by 11 January 1722, when Bowyer charged the Revd John Lister for a copy: *Bowyer ledgers*, p. 414.

9 Ronald Gowing, *Roger Cotes – natural philosopher* (Cambridge, 1983). Newton's remark is recorded in Robert Smith's annotated copy of Cotes, *Harmonia mensurarum* (Cambridge, 1722), Trinity College, Adv.b.1.15.

10 *Historical register*, p. 77.

11 McKitterick, *Cambridge Univesrity Library*, pp. 195–200.

12 For Oxford, cf. L. S. Sutherland, 'The curriculum', in L. S. Sutherland and L. G. Mitchell (eds.), *The history of the University of Oxford. 5. The eighteenth century* (Oxford, 1986), pp. 469–91, at p. 474.

13 *Historical register*, pp. 88–91; Clark, *Endowments*, pp. 182–202. Clark summarises the unclear early history of the Lord Almoner's professorship, or readership, of Arabic.

14 Townshend's letter to the University, setting out these hopes, is printed in Clark, *Endowments*, pp. 185–6.

15 Samuel Knight, *The life of Erasmus* (Cambridge [1726]), p. xxx.

16 For Wilkins, see *DNB*. For the Lord Almoner's professorship see Clark, *Endowments*, pp. 193–4.

17 McKenzie, *Cambridge University Press*, 1, p. 37; Edward Ullendorff, 'Two Ethiopic dirges on the death of Queen Anne (1714) and Queen Mary (1694)', *Journal of the Royal Asiatic Soc.* ser. 3, 6 (1996), pp. 1–6. For the Oxford orientals see Stanley Morison and Harry Carter, *John Fell* (Oxford, 1967), pp. 157–65 and appendix iv.

18 See his contribution to *Academiae Cantabrigiensis luctus in obitum serenissimi Georgii I* (Cambridge, 1727), G1r–v, quoted in McKitterick, *Cambridge University Library*, p. 239.

19 James Mosley, 'The early career of William Caslon', *JPHS*, 3 (1967), pp. 66–81; D. F. McKenzie and J. C. Ross (eds.), *A ledger of Charles Ackers, printer of the London Magazine* (Oxford Bibliographical Soc., 1968), pp. 2,11.

20 McKitterick, *Cambridge University Library*, pp. 240–1.

21 Bentley's annotated copies of Davies's work are in Cambridge University Library, Adv.c.52.4, and British Library, 679.d.3–5.

22 The review in *The Present State of the Republick of Letters* 8 (September 1731), pp. 192–8, commented on the 'pretty large character' of the type, the good quality of the paper, and the map, described as 'not bad'.

23 McKenzie, *Cambridge University Press*, 1, p. 27; CUR 33.6(39).

24 UA Pr. vouchers, 1723/21.

25 John Edwards, *Great things done by God for our ancestors, and us of this island*. A sermon preach'd before the University of Cambridge, at St. Mary's, November 5, 1709 (Printed by J. H. for Jonathan Robinson, John Lawrence, and John Wyat, 1710), p. iv.

26 *Ibid.*, pp. 25, 17.

27 'We had a sermon preached at our St. Mary's on the 5th November by Mr. Edwards of St. John's, which was refused to be licensed, but printed by him at London for one of your booksellers (Baker) and one of ours. I never heard of it before I saw the advertisement last night, but will buy it to see why our University refused to license it.' (Byrom to John Stansfield, 17 December 1709: John Byrom, *Private journal and literary remains*, ed. Richard Parkinson, 2 vols. (Chetham Soc., 1854–7), i, i, p. 10.)

28 Edwards, *Great things*, pp. iv, v.

29 James Knapton, Robert Knaplock, William and John Innys.

30 'We have a book lately published from our Press wth ye title of an Enquiry into ye Evidence of ye Christian Religion, wch is said to be written by Dr Newcome's wife & is, I hear, owned by her, being much commended by some, who have read it, wch I have not had leisure for as yet.' Conyers Middleton to Lord Harley, 18 February 1727/8: British Library, MS Loan 29/167.

31 Baker-Mayor, 2, pp. 1026–8. Her book was reissued in 1729 with a fresh title-page and reset preface. But for some people, her reputation seems to have been settled more by curiosity than by perceived achievement. 'In an age when female authors were not so frequent as at present, [her work] conferred on her a greater share of literary reputation than many of her contemporaries were willing to allow.' (Nichols, *Literary anecdotes*, 1, p. 186.)

32 Bell gave a fair copy of the manuscript (rather than the printed edition) to his college: Trinity College, MS R.3.27. Foxon B173 records only one copy, given by Bell to the Bodleian Library.

33 *Syllabus sive Index omnium humani corporis partium* (Cambridge: Thurlbourn, 1724).

34 *Memoirs of the life and writings of Mr. William Whiston, written by himself* (1749), pp. 135–6.

35 *Memoirs of . . . Mr. William Whiston*, p. 139.

36 James E. Force, *William Whiston, honest Newtonian* (Cambridge, 1985), pp. 19–21. For Whiston's own account of his publications, see his *Memoirs*; a more concise 'complete chronological catalogue of Mr. Whiston's writings' is appended to his *Supplement to the literal accomplishment of Scripture prophecies* (1725).

37 Alan Q. Morton and Jame A. Wess, *Public & private science; the King George III collection* (Oxford, 1993), pp. 39–65, with further references.

38 *The Present State of the Republick of Letters*, 5 (1730), pp. 314–5.

39 Norma Hodgson and Cyprian Blagden, *The notebook of Bennet and Clements*; Terry Belanger, *Booksellers' sales of copyright; aspects of the London book trade, 1718–1768* (PhD, Columbia, 1970); Terry Belanger, 'Booksellers' trade sales, 1718–1768', *The Library*, 5th ser. 30 (1975), pp. 281–302; Terry Belanger, 'Publishers and writers in eighteenth-century England', in Isabel Rivers (ed.), *Books and their readers in eighteenth-century England* (Leicester, 1982), pp. 5–25.

40 Green's last work, written on a scale that demanded attention, was reviewed in the *Acta Eruditorum*, June 1729, pp. 241–55. He further emphasised his college connections by dedicating it to another member of the College, the Duke of Newcastle.

41 The copper-plates for these are in Trinity College library.

42 Proposals, printed in *The Present State of the Republick of Letters*, 4 (October, 1729), p. 316.

43 *Bowyer ledgers*, no. 2549.

44 See below, p. 128.

45 Advertisement at the back of Roger Cotes, *Hydrostatical and pneumatical lectures*, 1738.

46 *The History of the Works of the Learned*, May 1738, pp. 348–53, at p. 348.

47 Proposals were printed in *The History of the Works of the Learned*, September, 1739, pp. 232–4. See further below, p. 164.

48 Earlier editions both of the individual sermons and of the collected edition had been published by Henry Mortlock, in London: see A. T. Bartholomew, *Richard Bentley, D. D.; a bibliography* (Cambridge, 1908), pp. 1–7.

49 Cf., for example, the review in *The Present State of the Republick of Letters*, February, 1732, pp. 106–27. For the elder Tonson's reaction to the 'vulture' Bentley, see Kathleen M. Lynch, *Jacob Tonson, Kit-Cat publisher* (Knoxville, Tenn., 1971), pp. 143–4.

50 A copy is in Cambridge University Library, bound up in Cam.d.716.16.

51 *Bowyer ledgers*, no. 827.

52 R. F. Scott (ed.), *Admissions to the College of St John the Evangelist*, 3, pp. 5, 302–4; Nichols, *Literary anecdotes*, 1, pp. 59–63; UA U.Ac.2.(2), p. 406 (1712–13).

53 Nichols, *Literary anecdotes*, 1, pp. 420–1.

54 *Ibid.*, 2, pp. 351–2, italics as in original. Nichols remarks (p. 352) that this was not the only occasion when Bowyer imagined that he had 'a natural claim to favour'.

55 Nichols, *Literary anecdotes*, 2, pp. 399–400.

56 Proposals for Spencer were published in the *New Memoirs of Literature*, 1 (January 1725), pp. 75–6.

57 For Spencer, see McKitterick, *Cambridge University Library*, p. 245.

58 Bentley himself seems to have paid for part of the edition: see Trinity College, MS Add. a.197(5).

59 For example, the reviews of Reading's Eusebius etc. (*Acta Eruditorum*, 1724, pp. 97–9); of Bentley's Terence (*Acta Eruditorum*, January 1727, pp. 18–22 (reviewed just after Francis Hare's edition, London (Tonson), 1725)); of Spencer (*Acta Eruditorum*, May 1728, pp. 204–10); of Davies's several editions of Cicero (*Acta Eruditorum*, May 1727, pp. 216–18, August 1728, pp. 345–7, May 1730, pp. 228–33).

60 A copy of the *Proposals for printing by subscription Tabulae Augustae. Sive Romanorum, Augustarum, Caesarum, Tyrannorum, & illustrium virorum a Cn. Pompeio Magno, ad Heraclium Aug.* survives among Bell's papers, Trinity College, MS R.10.10. Bell's collection of coins, bequeathed to Trinity College, is now deposited in the Fitzwilliam Museum.

61 UA Pr.v.1, Curators' minutes, 27 January 1713/14 (see above, p. 66); Voskens' account, dated 3 November 1714 (UA Pr. vouchers, 1714/30); Crownfield received £100 from the Vice-Chancellor for new types from Holland on 1 November 1714, English style (UA Pr. vouchers, 1714/22).

62 McKenzie, *Cambridge University Press*, 2, pp. 59, 237, 314, 402, 406. For the Schipper foundry at this time, see Enschedé, *Typefoundries*, pp. 86–7.

63 The correspondence concerning half of this order is in Pr. vouchers, 1723/26. Dommer's letter to Crownfield of 21 April 1723 refers to a 'previous bill' of £22; since half of the order for 1,223 lb of type cost £38.11s.4d., this may also have been quite substantial in weight. The Amsterdam pond weighed 492.168 grams (note by Netty Hoeflake, UA Pr. vouchers, 1723/27*). For Dommer (who died in London on 4 October 1725), see I. H. van Eeghen, *De Amsterdamse boekhandel*, 4, pp. 108–10, etc. For remarks on the comparative prices of English and the more expensive Dutch types, see McKenzie, *Cambridge University Press*, 1, pp. 38–9.

64 UA Pr. vouchers, 1725/16. The correspondence from Amsterdam in 1725 and 1726 was signed by Pieter Ouleander, on whom see van Eeghen, *De Amsterdamse boekhandel*, 4, pp. 109–11, 114–16 etc. The Schipper typefoundry was also in touch with John Baskett, King's Printer in London, and with Robert Freebairn, former King's Printer in Scotland, at this time: see Enschedé, *Typefoundries*, p. 86 n.2.

65 UA Pr. vouchers, 1726/11.

66 UA Pr.v.1, Curators' minutes, 31 March 1725. Davies was still a Curator at this time, and was present at this meeting.

67 *Term catalogues* 3, 505 (May 1706).

68 UA Pr.v.1, Curators' minutes, 31 March 1725. The original price had been 14s. and 9s. for large and small paper.

69 W. R. Scott, *The constitution and finance of English, Scottish and Irish joint-stock companies to 1720*, 3 vols. (Cambridge, 1910–12), 3 pp. 344–5.

70 UA Pr.v.1, Curators' minutes, 24 April 1725.

71 UA Min.vi.1, Curators' minutes, 16 November 1737. The stock was to be offered to Wetstein and Smith in Amsterdam.

72 *Bowyer ledgers*, nos. 2549, 2593.

73 UA Grace book I, p. 439. See further below, p. 133.

74 29 October 1730: UA CUR 33.6(45); Grace book I, p. 294; see also below, pp. 177–80.

75 For Taylor, see in particular Nichols, *Literary anecdotes*, 4, pp. 490–535, and McKitterick, *Cambridge University Library*, pp. 186–91.

76 *Bowyer ledgers*, nos 1572, 1577.

77 *Ibid.*, no. 2693.

78 *Ibid.*, microfiches B374, 376 (account for Lysias, payment of stamp duty, supply of books).

79 The proposals for Lysias and Demosthenes are printed in Roger Long and John Taylor, *Two music speeches at Cambridge* (1819), pp. 55–8.

6 The mid-eighteenth-century printing house

1 Stationers' Company Court Book F, 7 September 1696; McKitterick, *Cambridge University Press*, 1, p. 359.

2 Ovid, *De tristibus* (Cambridge: Hayes, 1703), advertisement at end for 'Books Printed for, and Sold by the Company of Stationers'; Carter, *Oxford University Press*, pp. 161–4.

3 UA CUR 33.6(39): the agreement ran for twenty-one years from Christmas 1705. For a list of books published by the Stationers' Company, *c.* 1695, see C. Blagden, *The Stationers' Company; a history, 1403–1959* (1960), p. 187.

4 UA D. I.2, pp. 14–16.

5 Roberts, *Cambridge University Press*, p. 115. The Almanac Duty Act of 1781 granted £500 each to Cambridge and Oxford as compensation for their having lost their payments from the Stationers' Company. See below, pp. 229–30. These payments to Cambridge lasted until 1981, when they were terminated by amicable agreement: Black, *Cambridge University Press*, p. 118.

6 'Remarks by Dr. Bentham, 1756', in Philip, *William Blackstone*, p. 43.

7 McKenzie, *Cambridge University Press*, 1, p. 60.

8 For Richardson, see Nichols, *Literary anecdotes*, 5, pp. 157–9, from which much of the *DNB* notice is drawn.

9 John Richardson, *Praelectiones ecclesiasticae triginta novem*, 2 vols. (1726).

10 E. S. Shuckburgh, *Emmanuel College* (1904), p. 135. Willis and Clark, 2, p. 714.

11 UA Min.vi.1, Curators' minutes, 25 February 1739/40. A glimpse of Crownfield in his old age is afforded by John Byrom, who visited him in 1735:

> There I saw him, seventy-five, and so hearty; he said he went to bed about ten and would sit up for no man's pleasure, and he rose about five and took a walk into the fields, and then a dish of chocolate, and an hour or two after that some tea, and a hearty dinner and no supper, and a glass of wine moderately; that eating an apple-pie once of unripe fruit, he had like to have died but for Dr. Ashurst; that the north-easterly winds were bad for him. (John Byrom, *Private journal and literary remains*, ed. Richard Parkinson, 3 vols. (Chetham Soc., 1854–7), 1, ii, pp. 629–30.)

12 UA Grace Book I, p. 439.

13 Willis and Clark, 3, pp. 44–6; Edmund Carter, *The history of the University of Cambridge* (1753), p. 10.

14 Willis and Clark, 3, pp. 44–7, 54, 61. UA Grace Book I, p. 445 (3 May 1738).

15 McKitterick, *Cambridge University Library*, pp. 256–65.

16 UA Pr.B.2.6. Though dated 1738 in manuscript, the report in facts dates from early 1741. For remarks on the accumulated deficit, see McKenzie, *Cambridge University Press*, I, pp. 147–50, 171–3. McKenzie calculates that the accumulated deficit was £1814.18s.11½d., rather than 'above 3000*l*.'

17 William Davis, *The Olio* (1814), p. 126. A family tree is printed in James Bentham, *The history and antiquities of the conventual & cathedral church of Ely*, 2nd edn (Norwich, 1812).

18 McKenzie, *Apprentices, 1701–1800*, no. 7199.

19 *Cambridge Journal and Weekly Flying-Post*, 30 August 1755.

20 In July 1749 he married Anne Riste, of Sackville Street, London, 'a Lady of great merit and a handsome Fortune' (*Cambridge Journal and Weekly Flying-Post*, 22 July 1749). Her brother George Riste (d. 1761, aged 66) was commemorated by them in a monument in Trumpington church (*Cambridge Chronicle*, 8 June 1765).

21 UA Grace Book I, p. 510.

22 UA Pr.v.1, order book, 28 March 1740; McKenzie, *Cambridge University Press*, I, p. 154 n.4.

23 William Davis, *The Olio*, pp. 118–19; Horace Walpole, *Correspondence with the Rev. William Cole*, ed. W. S. Lewis, 2 vols. (New Haven, 1937), I pp. 178, 185; 2, p. 90.

24 Apart from various allusions in the correspondence between Walpole and Cole, see John Layer and William Cole, *Monumental inscriptions and coats of arms from Cambridgeshire* (Cambridge, 1932), pp. 274, 277.

25 H. P. Stokes, *The Esquire Bedells of the University of Cambridge* (Cambridge Antiquarian Soc., 1911), p. 88; W. M. Palmer, *William Cole of Milton* (Cambridge, 1935), p. 130.

26 Davis, *The Olio*, p. 119.

27 Bentham died in 1778. 'Poor Mr Bentham dined here this day sennight and was well as usual, but died next day of an apoplexy.' William Cole to Horace Walpole, 7 June 1778: Walpole, *Correspondence with Cole*, 2, p. 88.

28 *Cantabrigia depicta* (Cambridge, 1763), p. 113.

29 UA Pr. vouchers, 1740–1, 1755–6, 1765–6. Only the last in this sampling indicates specifically those for whom the parcels were destined.

30 UA U. Ac.2(3), 1754–5–6–7; A. H. Shorter, *Paper mills and paper makers in England, 1495–1800* (Hilversum, 1957), pp. 147–8. Dernford Mill was in the hands of Tassell (or Tassel), and the two Borough mills (later Towgood's) were in those of Fairchild and Joseph Kier.

31 UA Min.vi.1, Syndicate minutes, 21 May 1740; UA Pr. vouchers, 1739–40.

32 UA Min.vi.1, Syndicate minutes, 3 August 1743.

33 UA Min.vi.1, Syndicate minutes, 20 June 1744.

34 Charles Bathurst to Bentham, 4 December 1747: UA CUR 33.7(3).

35 UA Min.vi.1, Syndicate minutes, 14 March 1766, 12 May 1766.

36 UA Min.vi.1, Syndicate minutes, 2 May 1748.

37 UA Min.vi.1, Syndicate minutes, 30 October 1751.

38 UA Min.vi.1, Syndicate minutes, 25 May 1753, 8 October 1754.

39 UA Pr.B.2.6.

40 UA Pr.P.3(22).

41 UA Pr.P.3(26).

42 Details of staff are taken from UA Pr.P.3 and the Vouchers for the appropriate years.

43 McKenzie, *Apprentices 1701–1800*, p. 32. Bentham took on further apprentices in 1751 (Francis Aungier and John Poole: Richard Gathurn and Moore Aungier having served their time) and 1762 (Jonathan Sharp). All three were from Cambridge.

44 Cf. K. I. D. Maslen, 'Masters and men', *The Library*, 5th ser. 30 (1975), pp. 81–94, repr. in his *An early London printing house at work: studies in the Bowyer ledgers* (New York, 1993), pp. 105–22.

45 McKenzie, *Apprentices 1701–1800*, p. 308.

46 UA Pr. vouchers xxvi, 1744–5.

47 Maslen and Lancaster, *Bowyer ledgers*, pp. 484, 507, 595.

48 McKenzie, *Apprentices 1701–1800*, no. 526.

49 A Benjamin Lyon was apprenticed to the London printer Freeman Collins in 1706 (McKenzie, *Apprentices*, no. 1914). I have not been able to establish conclusively whether he was related to Israel Lyons, who made a living as teacher of Hebrew in the University, and whose *Scholar's instructor*, a Hebrew grammar, was printed by Crownfield in 1735. Israel Lyons's son, of the same name, was author of a *Treatise of fluxions* (1758) and of *Fasciculus plantarum* (Cambridge, 1763). See G. G. Gorham, *Memoirs of John Martyn, F. R. S., and of Thomas Martyn, B. D., F. R. S., F. L. S.* (1830), p. 122, and Bowes no. 1232. For notes by Israel Lyons addressed to William Bowyer for an apparently abortive Hebrew almanac for the year 5526 (1766), see Trinity College I.1.58(2a).

50 UA Pr.P.3, Bentham's annual accounts, 1740–2. See also McKenzie, *Cambridge University Press*, 1, p. 131n.

51 'A New Press in Exchange as *per* agreement', £8.8s.od. (UA Pr. vouchers xxvi, 1740–1); Pr.P.3(34). New presses were billed at £14 on 8 August 1740 and £14.15s.od. on 1 January 1741/2 (UA Pr. vouchers xxvi, 1739–40, 1741–2). Purcer (or Purser) appears fleetingly in the Bowyer accounts: see ledger C, fo.1v (C1404 on the microfiche edition by Maslen and Lancaster). New Purbeck stones were bought for the beds of three presses in May 1741 from William Pitch.

52 McKitterick, *Cambridge University Press*, 1, pp. 277–8.

53 K. Povey, 'A century of press-figures', *The Library*, 5th ser. 14 (1959), pp. 251–73; Gaskell, *New introduction*, pp. 133–4. The earliest use of these figures under Bentham's aegis that I have noted are in the Cambridge duodecimo Bible and prayer book, 1743, employing 2 and 4. See also B. McMullin, 'The lingering death of the press figure', in R. C. Alston (ed.), *Order and connexion; studies in bibliography and book history* (Cambridge, 1997), pp. 39–47.

54 McKenzie, *Cambridge University Press*, 1, p. 131. For links elsewhere between presses (rather than pressmen) and these numbers, see D. F. McKenzie, 'Printers of the mind; some notes on bibliographical theories and printing house practices', *SB*, 22 (1969), pp. 1–75, at p. 52.

55 McKenzie, *Cambridge University Press*, 1, pp. 50, 51, 93. Rolling-presses are more easily moved than common presses. See above, p. 65.

56 *Cambridge Journal*, 19 February 1757. In the 1750s and 1760s, etching and drypoint engraving became popular among local amateurs including John Holand (Peterhouse), Edward Haistwell (Corpus), Abraham Hume (Trinity), J. J. Proby (Trinity), John Grove Spurgeon (Pembroke), Charles Tyrell (Emmanuel), and Charlton Wollaston (St John's). See, for example, Christopher White, David Alexander, Ellen D'Oench, *Rembrandt in eighteenth century England* (New Haven, 1983).

57 R. Campbell, *The London tradesman* (1747), pp. 114, 124.

58 UA Pr. vouchers, 1761–2, 1762–3, 1763–4. Harold Forster, 'The rise and fall of the Cambridge muses', *TCBS*, 8 (1982), pp. 141–72. Forster suggests that the increasing prominence of verse in English, rather than Latin, may have been the principal cause for the demise of this tradition that stretched back to the sixteenth century; but it seems more probable that increasing costs were more to blame. The bills for printing the four volumes issued in 1760–3 amounted to between £54 and £66, excluding the very substantial costs of variously ornate bindings and the cost of attending in London to present them. Although some copies were sold, the most expensive ones were given away. In 1763 Bentham recorded having sold copies (presumably unbound) to the value of £28.11s., almost exactly half what it had cost the University to print the edition (UA UAc. 2(3), 1762–3; UA Pr. vouchers, 1763–4).

59 UA Min.vi.1, Syndicate minutes, 23 June 1757. The Press was insured with the Royal Exchange Assurance.

60 UA Min.vi.1, Syndicate minutes, 17 June 1760; a note dated 11 November states that this policy was never taken out.

61 UA Min.vi.1, Syndicate minutes, 11 November 1761.

62 See above, pp. 132–3.

63 Over the next few years, the old buildings south of Regent Walk were gradually removed; the old shops abutting the west end of Great St Mary's, that had once been a centre of the local book trade but were now described as hovels, were pulled down in 1767–8 (Willis and Clark, 3, p. 71).

64 UA Min.vi.1, Syndicate minutes 17 June 1762; Grace Book K, p. 373 (21 October 1762); Willis and Clark, 3, p. 134.

65 UA Pr. vouchers, invoice for 1761–2, paid 24 February 1763.

66 UA Pr. vouchers, invoice for 1763–4.

67 Most of the relevant papers are gathered in UA CUR 33.3; Richard Burn, *Ecclesiastical law*, 2 vols. (1763), 1, pp. 347–74.

68 *DNB*, art. 'Pickering'.

69 UA Min.vi.1, Syndicate minutes, 29 April 1763.

70 John Nichols referred to them thus, evidently picking up local terminology, in 1765: see R. Rabicoff and D. McKitterick, 'John Nichols, William Bowyer, and Cambridge University Press in 1765', *TCBS*, 6 (1976), pp. 328–38, at p. 333.

71 UA Min.vi.1, Syndicate minutes, 29 April 1763.

72 UA Min.vi.1, Syndicate minutes, 11 March 1741/2.

73 UA Min.vi.1, Syndicate minutes, 12 May 1766.

74 UA Min.vi.1, Library Syndicate, 26 May 1738; McKitterick, *Cambridge University Library*, pp. 190–3.

75 Roger Long and John Taylor, *Two music speeches at Cambridge* (1819), p. x.

76 UA Pr.v.1, order book, 7 December 1739. Estimates were based on 500 copies.

77 UA Min.vi.1, Syndicate minutes, 17 August 1738, 2 March 1738/9.

78 UA Pr.v.1, order book, 15 January 1738/9. Estimates were based on 1,500 small and 100 large paper copies.

79 UA Pr.v.1, order book, 11 February 1739/40. Estimates were based on 750 large and small paper copies.

80 See above, pp. 11, 136–7.

81 See above, p. 141.

82 Daniel Prince, 'Some account of the University Printing-House' (1756): Philip, *Blackstone*, p. 19. Blackstone made a more detailed comparison between Oxford and London prices in a letter to the Vice-Chancellor, 21 May 1757: Philip, *Blackstone*, p. 54.

83 'At present we are but settling into a Calm with our Compositors, who have wanted to raise their prices, and combined for that purpose, with as little Reason as Provocation – so that I, as well as others, have been forced to part with some of my Hands, and have not yet got them replaced to my Wish, and go but lamely on, with my Common Business.' (Letter from Samuel Richardson, 7 November 1748, quoted in William M. Sale, jr, *Samuel Richardson: master printer* (Ithaca, 1950), p. 27.)

84 'A third Reason given by the Workmen (i.e. the Compositors) has been, that their Page is *larger* than the London Pages; consequently contains more Work; and, if it has more Work, requires a better Price. But this is a mere Fallacy. In London, and all other Places . . . the Price is not settled according to the nominal Size of the Page, as, so much for a Quarto, so much for an Octavo, &c. which would indeed be most uncertain; nor yet at so much per Sheet, be the Sheet either large or small, which would be liable to the same objections; but the Price of a Sheet and consequently of a Page, is settled according to the Work, (i.e. the Number of Letters) contained in it.' (Blackstone, 1756: Philip, *Blackstone*, p. 24)

85 'The price of the Corrector is governed by that of the Compositor: for, as his Trouble is proportioned to that of the other, so also is his Pay: being allowed a Sum equal to $\frac{1}{6}$ of what is allowed the Compositor: Where the Compositor has 5^s, he has 10^d.' (Blackstone, 'Some thoughts on the Oxford press, 1756', in Philip, *Blackstone*, p. 29.)

86 For the 'rule of thirds', and for other London costing practices at this time, see Keith Maslen, 'Printing charges: inference and evidence', *SB*, 24 (1971), pp. 91–8, repr. in his *An early London printing house at work: studies in the Bowyer ledgers* (New York, 1993), pp. 91–6; see also Samuel Richardson to Alexander Gordon, 9 November 1738, summarising the cost of a book set in pica, repr. in Philip, *Blackstone*, pp. 129–30, and Sale, *Samuel Richardson*, p. 24. Maslen's article is in part a corrective to Patricia Hernlund, 'William Strahan's ledgers: standard charges for printing, 1738–1785', *SB*, 20 (1967), pp. 89–111.

87 Richardson to Blackstone, 10 February 1756, in Philip, *Blackstone*, p. 41.

88 UA Pr.v.1, order book, 24 December 1741.

89 *Demosthenes . . . Graece et Latine*, ed. John Taylor, tomus tertius [specimen] (Cambridge, 1741), p. ii.

90 *Bibliothèque Raisonnée des Ouvrages des Savans de l'Europe*, 40 (1748), p. 469. In fact only volumes 2–3 were ever published.

91 The so-called order book, UA Pr.v.1, from which these details of costs are taken, was in fact used retrospectively: for example, several of the books noted at the meeting on 4 April 1744 had been published the previous year.

92 UA Pr.v.1, order book, 24 December 1741: presumably the charges were recorded retrospectively, since Taylor's address to the reader is dated 25 April 1741. On this occasion it was agreed to deduct the normal one-sixth charge for corrections, since these would be charged separately. Taylor intended ('To the reader', p. iv) that there should be four volumes of text, with notes, and that a fifth volume should contain extra apparatus, including the scholia mentioned in the Press's costing, a thesaurus and an extensive list of variant readings; but only the second and third volumes were ever published.

93 In 1738, Samuel Richardson suggested that his normal charge for setting in pica was 8s. a sheet, or 10s. if there were notes: Philip, *Blackstone*, pp. 129–30.

94 Foxon S491, recording two issues, though the Press's order book (3 December 1746) does not mention this. The edition consisted of 1,000 copies. The first edition of the translation from Pope, in folio, had been printed by Bentham for Smart in 1743.

95 For the foundation, see Clark, *Endowments*, p. 369; for list of early prizemen, see *Historical register*, pp. 289–90. Smart won the prize five times between 1750 and 1755.

96 Vouchers for these several years are preserved in UA Pr. vouchers xxix–xxxi.

97 Bentham charged 1s.3d. extra in 1750 (*On the eternity of the Supreme Being*) and 2s.6d. extra (added to a composition and printing bill for £1.8s.) for alterations in 1756 (*On the goodness of the Supreme Being*). For Smart's practices of revision, and his anxiety at correctness, see Robert H. Mahony, 'Revision and correction in the poems of Christopher Smart', *PBSA*, 77 (1983), pp. 196–206; for further, more general comment, see Arthur Sherbo, *Christopher Smart, scholar of the university* (East Lansing, Mich., 1967), especially pp. 91–3.

98 UA Pr. vouchers, 1762/14. For some examples of the cost of plates, engraving and printing in the mid-eighteenth-century print trade, cf. Louise Lippincott, *Selling art in Georgian London; the rise of Arthur Pond* (New Haven, 1983), pp. 129, 143, 155.

99 UA Pr. vouchers, 1763/30i. Stevens (or Stephens) subscribed to Rutherforth's *System of natural philosophy* in 1748. See also Cole, *Correspondence*, 1, pp. 294, 296.

100 Crow stitched 450 copies for 6s.9d. in 1750 and in 1752, and stitched 51 copies into marble wrappers for 8s.6d. in 1752.

101 For Edwin Moor (or Moore), see especially M. M. Foot, *The Henry Davis gift; a collection of bookbindings*, 2 vols. (1978–83), 1, pp. 80–3.

102 Maslen, 'Printing charges', p. 92.

103 The order book records that 500 copies were printed. For the copy given by Bentham, bound up with some of his other work, to Ely Cathedral in 1778, see Cambridge University Library, Ely.d.449.

104 Philip, *Blackstone*, pp. 84–89.

7 Booksellers and authors

1 See below, pp. 352–3, 356–7.

2 *Cambridge Journal*, 2 October 1756 (partnership); *Cambridge Chronicle and Journal*, 18 July 1767 (death of Thurlbourn on 14 July). See also, with some errors, Henry R. Plomer, *A dictionary of the printers and booksellers who were at work in England, Scotland and Ireland from 1668 to 1725* (Bibliographical Soc., 1922), p. 289; H. R. Plomer et al., *A dictionary of the printers and booksellers who were at work in England, Scotland and Ireland from 1726 to 1775* (Bibliographical Soc., 1932), p. 271.

3 *Cambridge Chronicle and Journal*, 2 June 1781. John Merrill died aged seventy in 1801: *ibid.*, 24 October 1801.

4 Plomer, *Dictionary 1726–1775*; for Nicholson, see above, p. 19 and below, pp. 208 etc.

5 Plomer, *Dictionary 1726–1775* is, again, erratic. For Matthews's retirement and handover to Deighton, see *Cambridge Chronicle and Journal*, 11 April 1778. For Deighton, see further below, p. 000. Matthews seems to have been renowned by some mainly on account of his new young wife: 'where the beauteous Wife's bright visage gives Beauty to Books, and Lustre to their Backs' ([William Dodd], *A day in vacation at college. A burlesque poem* (1751), lines 150–1). He died in December 1783 (*Cambridge Chronicle and Journal*, 20 December 1783).

6 Advertisement in S. Puffendorf, *De officio hominis & vivis juxta legem naturalem* (Cambridge, 1735).

7 Advertisement in James Tunstall, *Epistola ad virum eruditum Conyers Middleton* (Cambridge, 1741).

8 Advertisement in Cicero, *De legibus*, ed. Davies, 2nd edn (Cambridge, 1745). For the need to exercise caution in interpreting early eighteenth-century imprints, and to be alert to anonymity, see D. F. Foxon, rev. J. McLaverty, *Pope and the early eighteenth-century book trade* (Oxford, 1991), ch. 1. For books sold by a mixture of subscription and retail, see Keith Maslen, 'Printing for the author: from the Bowyer ledgers, 1710–1775', *The Library*, 5th ser. 27 (1972), pp. 302–9, repr. in his *An early London printing house at work: studies in the Bowyer ledgers* (New York, 1993), pp. 97–104.

9 *A letter to the society of booksellers* (1738), pp. 43–4.

10 For example, copies in Trinity College library of J. R. d'Arnay, *The private life of the Romans* (Edinburgh, 1761: classmark K.10.47(1)), William Mason, *Elegies* (1763, with a printed imprint that includes the names of Merrill's rival booksellers, Thurlbourn and Woodyer: classmark H.10.144(11)), and *Madge's addresses to Christopher Twist-wit, Esquire* [i.e. Christopher Anstey], *Bath-lauriat, and Plumian Professor* (1777: classmark I.10.95(14)). For further examples, elsewhere, of manuscript alterations to imprints, cf. Foxon D34, H218, L223, V110.

11 Edmund Law, *Observations occasioned by the contest about literary property* (1770). By this date Law was Master of Peterhouse, Knightbridge Professor of Moral Philosophy, University Librarian and Bishop of Carlisle.

12 John Edwards, *Some discoveries of the uncertainty, deficiency and corruptions of human knowledge and learning* (1714), pp. 162–3. For Edwards's strictures on the University, see Henry Bradshaw, 'A view of the state of the University in Queen Anne's reign', in his *Collected papers* (Cambridge, 1889), pp. 69–83.

13 James Boswell, *Life of Johnson*, ed. G. B. Hill, rev. L. F. Powell, 6 vols. (Oxford, 1934), 3, p. 19; A. S. Collins, *Authorship in the days of Johnson* (1927) reviews some of the topics discussed below. But see also, more recently, Mark Rose, *Authors and owners; the invention of copyright* (Cambridge, Mass., 1993), with further references.

14 *An account of the expence of correcting and improving sundry books* [177–], p. 2.

15 Dr James's book, Queens' College Archives, Book 80, last sequence of pagination, p. 2.

16 Middleton to Warburton, 18 November 1738, Middleton's italics; Middleton, *Miscellaneous works*, 4 vols. (1752), 2, pp. 477–8.

17 P. J. Wallis, 'Book subscription lists', *The Library*, 5th ser. 29 (1974), pp. 255–86; W. A. Speck, 'Politicians, peers and publication by subscription, 1700–50' in Isabel Rivers (ed.) *Books and their readers in eighteenth-century England* (Leicester, 1982), pp. 47–68; Larry Stewart, *The rise of public science; rhetoric, technology, and natural philosophy in Newtonian Britain, 1660–1750* (Cambridge, 1992), pp. 151–60.

18 Copies of the prospectus survive in Cambridge University Library, Cam.b.500.11 and Adv.b.54.2.

19 UA Pr.v.1, Syndics' order book, 2 December 1747; the title-page is dated 1748.

20 For one heartfelt and prolonged complaint about the process in a later generation, see Thomas Malton, *An essay concerning the publication of works, on science and literature, by subscription . . . To which is added a true case, between that author, his printer, and paper-merchant* ('1877'[1777]).

21 'I find the printing their names very much Disapproved by some, by others utterly Forbid; and others are so indifferent about it as to leave it entirely to my own Inclination and Conveniency.' Christopher Packe, *Convallium descriptio* (Canterbury, 1743), p. 109.

22 Nichols, *Literary anecdotes*, 2, pp. 535, 537.

23 Cutler to Grey, 24 September 1743: Nichols, *Literary anecdotes*, 4, p. 302. For Cutler, formerly rector of Yale College, who was ordained by the Bishop of Norwich in 1723 and held the degree of DD from Cambridge, see *DNB*.

24 Nichols, *Literary anecdotes*, 2, p. 24.

25 *Bowyer ledgers*, no. 2693.

26 Nichols, *Literary anecdotes*, 2, p. 133.

27 Cambridge University Library, MS Add. 2960.

28 Cambridge University Library, MS Add. 2960, fo. 47*r. For the elder Heins, who worked in Norwich, see Andrew Moore and Charlotte Crawley, *Family and friends; a regional survey of British portraiture* (1992; published in connection with an exhibition at Norwich), especially p. 116.

29 For Francis Blomefield's difficulties in this respect during the 1730s, as he sought to assemble blocks and engravings for his history of Norfolk, see D. A. Stoker (ed.), *The correspondence of the Reverend Francis Blomefield (1705–52)* (Norfolk Record Soc. and Bibliographical Soc., 1992), especially pp. 134–44.

30 John Morris, 'A check-list of prints made at Cambridge by Peter Spendelowe Lamborn (1722–1774)', *TCBS*, 3 (1962), pp. 295–312. Heins and Lamborn also collaborated in the illustrations to *Cantabrigia depicta. A concise and accurate description of the University and town of Cambridge* (Cambridge [1763]).

31 Cole spoke of his 'natural slowness' (Cole to Walpole, 6 June 1769; *Horace Walpole's correspondence with the Rev. William Cole*, ed. W. S. Lewis, 2 vols. (New Haven, 1937), 1, p.160).

32 Cole to Walpole, 3 January 1771; *Correspondence*, 1, p. 210.

33 Cambridge University Library, MS Add. 2960, fo. 68v.

34 Horace Walpole to William Cole, 27 May 1769; *Correspondence*, 1, p.157.

35 Cole to Walpole, 28 November 1770; *Correspondence*, 1, pp. 202–3, with notes.

36 Bentham's own copy, with further notes, is in the Fitzwilliam Museum.

37 Cambridge University Library, MS Add. 2960, fo. 63v.

38 For the Fleetwood monuments, Bentham asked 4½ guineas apiece (Cambridge University Library, MS Add. 2960, fos. 31r, 33r); for the Steward and Moore monuments he asked five (*ibid.*, fos. 34r, 56v).

39 Cambridge University Library, MS Add. 2960, fo. 39r.

40 Pope, *Dunciad* ii. 205.

41 *Bibliothèque Raisonnée des Ouvrages des Savans de l'Europe*, 28 (1742), pp. 147–8. Middleton's relationship with his patron was noticed later in a review of Colley Cibber, *The character and conduct of Cicero considered* (1747): *ibid.*, 38 (1747), pp. 228–30.

42 *A letter to the society of booksellers on the method of forming a true judgement of the manuscripts of authors* (1738), p. 9.

43 *Ibid.*, p. 38.

44 Ralph Straus, *Robert Dodsley* (1910), p. 164; Philip Gaskell, *The first editions of William Mason* (Cambridge Bibliographical Soc., 1951), p. 17.

45 Robert Dodsley, *Correspondence, 1733–1764*, ed. James Tierney (Cambridge, 1988), p. 527.

46 *Ibid.*, pp. 529, 560.

47 Hurd to Bowyer, 14 February 1752; Nichols, *Literary anecdotes*, 2, p. 231.

48 [Richard Hurd], *Moral and political dialogues* (1759), preface, pp. i–ii. Cf. Betty Rizzo, 'The English author-bookseller dialogue', *The age of Johnson*, 2 (1989), pp. 353–74.

49 Nichols, *Literary anecdotes*, 2, p. 533.

50 Tunstall to Grey, 22 February 1742/3. Nichols, *Illustrations*, 4, pp. 372–3. For Tunstall, see Nichols, *Literary anecdotes*, 2, pp. 166–70.

51 The title-page of volume 2 states that it was printed by Bettenham; but part of it may have been printed by Bowyer: see *Bowyer ledgers*, no. 3308. Yet the Bowyer ledgers record only 525 copies as having been printed – not enough even for the very large list of subscribers for over 1,600 copies, let alone the figures spoken of by Tunstall in reporting his conversations with Bathurst. The Cambridge Syndics agreed on 2,000 copies (UA Pr.v.1, Minutes of Press Syndicate, 8 April 1745).

52 Tunstall to Grey, 29 August 1743. Nichols, *Illustrations*, p. 373.

53 McKitterick, *Cambridge University Press*, 1, pp. 250–2.

54 Boswell, *Life*, 1, pp. 304–5.

55 Smart to Dodsley, 6 August 1746; Robert Dodsley, *Correspondence*, pp. 100–1. For an early version of the translation from Pope, see Alexander Lindsay, 'Christopher Smart as reviser; pre-publication texts of two early poems', *The Library*, 6th ser. 17 (1995), pp. 349–54.

56 Samuel Johnson, *The vanity of human wishes*, lines 157–60. The first edition (1749) has 'garret' instead of 'patron'.

57 *Gentleman's Magazine*, 6 (1736), p. 353; Clayton Atto, 'The Society for the Encouragement of Learning', *The Library*, 4th ser. 19 (1938), pp. 263–88. The Society's papers are in the British Library, MSS Add. 6184–92: for further details, cf. *Bowyer ledgers*.

58 *A letter to the Society of Booksellers* (1738), p. 31.

59 [Christopher Anstey], *The patriot; a Pindaric address to Lord Buckhorse*, 2nd edn (1768), p. 63.

60 *The clergyman's intelligencer; or, a compleat alphabetical list of all the patrons in England and Wales* (1745). For the background to some of the following, see Richard Middleton, 'The Duke of Newcastle and the conduct of patronage during the Seven Years' War, 1757–1762', *British Journal of Eighteenth-Century Studies*, 12 (1989), pp. 175–86; Pat Rogers, 'Book dedications in Britain, 1710–1799: a preliminary survey', *British Journal of Eighteenth-Century Studies*, 16 (1993), pp. 213–33; and Dustin Griffin, *Literary patronage in England, 1650–1800* (Cambridge, 1996). Griffin demonstrates the more general abiding importance of patronage after 1755.

61 Nichols, *Literary anecdotes*, 3, pp. 107–11. Pearce's biography is well summarised by Leslie Stephen in the *DNB*.

62 [Francis Coventry], *The history of Pompey the Little* (1751), ch. xii, 'Our hero goes to the University of Cambridge', pp. 232–3; the italics are in the original.

63 Conyers Middleton's letters to Lord Hervey are in Bury St Edmunds Record Office; see McKitterick, *Cambridge University Library*, pp. 182–3 and, more generally, Robert Halsband, *Lord Hervey, eighteenth-century courtier* (Oxford, 1973) and the Earl of Ilchester (ed.), *Lord Hervey and his friends, 1726–38* (1950).

64 Robert Masters, *The history of the College of Corpus Christi* (Cambridge, 1753), pp. 424–6. For Philip Yorke and literature, see Griffin, *Literary patronage in England*, pp. 58–60.

65 Philip Yorke, Baron Hardwicke, was created Earl of Hardwicke in 1754. The office of High Steward, originally a legal one, had become of less practical importance by the late eighteenth century, though the holder continued to wield very considerable influence in the University: see *Historical register*, pp. 64–6.

66 William S. Childe-Pemberton, *The Earl Bishop; the life of Frederick Hervey, Bishop of Derry, Earl of Bristol*, 2 vols. [1925]; Robert Halsband, *Lord Hervey; eighteenth-century courtier* (Oxford, 1973).

67 The Duke of Newcastle served as First Lord of the Treasury from 1754 to 1756 and from 1757 to 1762; the Duke of Grafton served as Prime Minister from 1768 to 1770.

68 *The clergyman's intelligencer* (1745), p. 151.

69 Winstanley, *Eighteenth century*.

70 [James Ralph], *The case of authors by profession or trade stated* (1758), p. 39. For remarks on his failure to be appointed to a bishopric, see Nichols, *Literary anecdotes*, 5, pp. 421–2.

71 Conyers Middleton, *The history of the life of Marcus Tullius Cicero*, 2 vols. (1741), p. xii. Cf. Samuel Johnson's remark on Edward Lye in 1765, 'I think you may be encouraged by the liberality of the Archbishop to hope for more Patrons of your undertaking, and therefore advise you to open your Subscription.' Johnson, *Letters*, 1, p. 250.

72 Halsband, *Lord Hervey*, pp. 242–4.

73 Middleton to Warburton, 4 September 1739. In November the previous year he had reported to Warburton that he had added further to his financial responsibilities by taking his two nieces into his care following the death of their father. Conyers Middleton, *Miscellaneous works*, 4 vols. (1752), 2, pp. 477–8.

74 For subscription publishing in the eighteenth century, cf. Keith Maslen, 'Printing for the author: from the Bowyer printing ledgers, 1710–1775', *The Library*, 5th ser. 27 (1972), pp. 302–9, repr. in his *An early London printing house at work* (Bibliographical Soc. of America, 1993), pp. 97–104; F. J. G. Robinson and P. J. Wallis, *Book subscription lists: a revised guide* (Newcastle upon Tyne, 1975); P. J. Wallis, *Book subscription lists: extended supplement to the revised guide* (Newcastle upon Tyne, 1996).

75 A. S. Collins, *Authorship in the days of Johnson* (1927), pp. 42–5. For Barnes's experiences, see above, pp. 90, 93–5. For Grey, see Nichols, *Literary anecdotes*, 1, pp. 373–4, quoted in Maslen, 'Printing for the author'.

76 Francis Blomefield, *The correspondence of the Reverend Francis Blomefield (1705–52)*, ed. David A. Stoker (Norfolk Record Soc. and Bibliographical Soc., 1992), pp. 70–1.

77 'When a book is not finished till about the middle of November, it is usual to prefix the date of the following year.' Nichols, *Literary anecdotes*, 1, p. 414n.

78 Cf. James Mosley (ed.), *A specimen of printing types by William Caslon, London 1766* (Printing Historical Society, 1983), p. 75.

79 He was one of the early members of the Society for the Encouragement of Learning: see Atto, 'The Society for the Encouragement of Learning', p. 266.

80 Minutes of the Syndics of the Press, 11 February 1739/40: UA Pr.v.1.

81 For Gravelot, see H. Hammelmann and T. S. R. Boase, *Book illustrators in eighteenth-century England* (New Haven, 1975), pp. 39–46. Some of Gravelot's drawings are in the Ashmolean Museum: see David Blayney Brown, *Ashmolean Museum, Oxford; catalogue of the collection of drawings*, 4 (Oxford, 1982), nos. 765, 766, 767.

82 See above, p. 95.

83 For some details, see Nichols, *Literary anecdotes*, 2, pp. 65–74.

84 Nichols, *Literary anecdotes*, 1, p. 709; Winstanley, *Unreformed Cambridge*, p. 162; Blanche Henrey, *British botanical literature before 1800*, 3 vols. (Oxford, 1975), 2, p. 448–9.

85 Printed for Charles Davis by Bowyer: see Keith Maslen and John Lancaster (eds.), *The Bowyer ledgers* (1991), no. 1510. For Vigani see above, pp. 92, 115; for Addenbrooke's chest, see the references in E. E. Rich (ed.), *St Catharine's College, Cambridge, 1473–1973; a volume of essays to commemorate the quincentenary of the foundation of the College* (Cambridge [1973]), pp. 135, 274.

86 D. D. Eddy, 'Richard Hurd's editions of Horace and the Bowyer ledgers', *SB*, 48 (1995), pp. 148–69.

87 Nichols, *Literary anecdotes*, 2, pp. 306–7.

88 *Bowyer ledgers*, nos. 1834 (Middleton), 3684, 3800 (Hurd), 4157 (Nevile, Horace), 4794 (Nevile, Juvenal).

89 Roderick Cave, *The private press*, 2nd edn (1983). Many practical details concerning the establishment of a private press are documented in Blomefield's *Correspondence*, ed. Stoker.

90 Roger Long and John Taylor, *Two music speeches at Cambridge* (1819), pp. liv–lviii. The sphere, now destroyed, is illustrated in Aubrey Attwater, *Pembroke College, Cambridge; a short history*, ed. S. C. Roberts (Cambridge, 1936), opposite p. 93, from a photograph taken in 1871; see also Willis and Clark, 1, pp. 149–50. Long's arrangements for a printer were described briefly by John Nichols in 1765: see R. Rabicoff and D. McKitterick, 'John Nichols, William Bowyer, and Cambridge University Press in 1765', *TCBS*, 6 (1976), pp. 328–38, at p. 333.

91 *Cambridge Chronicle and Journal*, 28 May 1785; cf. the review by William Wales, mathematics master at Christ's Hospital, in the *Monthly Review*, 75 (1786), pp. 273–4.

92 Samuel Johnson to Nathan Wetherell, 12 March 1776, printed in Johnson, *Letters*, 2, pp. 305–6; see also Boswell, *Life of Johnson*, 2, p. 425.

93 For the early history of Cambridge newspapers, see R. Bowes, 'On the first and other early Cambridge newspapers', *Proc. Cambridge Antiquarian Soc.*, n.s.2 (1891–4), pp. 347–58; G. A. Cranfield, *A hand-list of English provincial newspapers and periodicals, 1700–1750* (Cambridge Bibliographical Soc., 1952), p. 4. No copies survive of the earliest numbers of the *Cambridge Journal and Weekly Flying-Post*.

94 See below, p. 209.

95 See above, p. 90. S. C. Roberts, *The evolution of Cambridge publishing* (Cambridge, 1956), pp. 10–14.

96 Advertisement in S. Puffendorf, *De officio hominis & vivis juxta legem naturalem* (Cambridge, 1735).

97 *A letter to the society of booksellers* (1738), p. 51.

98 Ibid., pp. 49–50.

99 For a review in Venice, cf. the *Novelle della Repubblica Letteraria*, 1743, p. 63.

100 Bernhard Fabian, *The English book in eighteenth-century Germany* (1992), pp. 42–5. For the establishment of German, see for example Eric A. Blackall, *The emergence of German as a literary language, 1700–1775* (Cambridge, 1959). A new attitude is evident in Michael Denis, *Einleitung in die Bücherkunde* (Vienna, 1777–8) and in [Leonhard Meister], *Beyträge zur Geschichte der teutschen Sprache und National-litteratur*, 2 vols. (London, 1777).

101 *Ibid.*, pp. 49–52.

102 But, right at the end of the century, cf. the *Concise practical grammar of the German language* (1799), by W. Render, teacher of German in the University, and the (short-lived) successful proposal in 1796 that Trinity College Library should subscribe to the *Allgemeine Literatur-Zeitung*.

103 *Historical register*, p. 88; see above, pp. 115–16.

104 [John Green], *The academic: or a disputation on the state of the University of Cambridge* (1750), p. 22.

105 René Labutte, *A letter to Mr. Fauchon* [Cambridge, 1749]; James Fauchon, *A publick lecture to the clamorous master, La Butte, master of (a) French language . . .* (Cambridge, 1749).

106 See below, pp. 193–4.

107 Rugeley later emigrated to South Carolina: see the account by Christopher Gould and James A. Levernier in James A. Levernier and Douglas R. Wilmes (eds.), *American writers before 1800*, 3 vols. (Westport, Conn., 1986), 3, pp. 1250–2.

108 *Cambridge Chronicle*, 3 March 1764. Isola was appointed to teach Italian and Spanish.

109 Bruce Dickins, 'The teaching of Italian in Cambridge (1724–1962)', in C. P. Brand, K. Foster, U. Limentani (eds.), *Italian studies presented to E. R. Vincent* (Cambridge, 1962), pp. 15–26; June Sturrock, 'Wordsworth's Italian teacher', *Bulletin of the John Rylands Library*, 67 (1985), pp. 787–812; Duncan Wu, *Wordsworth's reading, 1770–1799* (Cambridge, 1993), p. 77.

110 Daniel Prince, 'Some account of the University Printing-House', Philip, *Blackstone*, p. 21.

8 Bentham and Bibles

1 Carter, *Oxford University Press*, pp. 105–8, 159–60.

2 Queens' College Archives, Book 80, 2nd pagination pp. 3–4. He was reflecting on a meeting called by the Vice-Chancellor on 7 December, attended by the three he named: a Grace was passed four days later naming a slightly different group to negotiate details with the Stationers' Company (UA Grace Book Θ, p. 528).

3 Herbert, *Historical catalogue*, pp. 239, 287.

4 Carter, *Oxford University Press*, pp. 168–9.

5 McKenzie and Ross (*Ledger of Charles Ackers*) calculated that a single issue of the *London Magazine* in the 1730s, containing seven half-sheets, 'contained, at 1 lb. per four square inches, 392 lb of type, representing a capital value of perhaps £50' (p.13).

6 Van Eeghen, *De Amsterdamse boekhandel*, 4, pp. 110–11; B. J. McMullin, 'Joseph Athias and the early history of stereotyping', *Quaerendo*, 23 (1993), pp. 184–207, concentrates on the earlier history.

7 Van Eeghen, *De Amsterdamse boekhandel*, 5, p. 134.

8 John Carter, 'William Ged and the invention of stereotype' *The Library*, 5th ser. 15 (1960), pp. 161–92. Carter prints in an appendix the long summary of events in UA CUR 33.6(67).

9 Historical Monuments Commission, *Cambridge* p. 74. James's work in London includes St George's Hanover Square (1721–5), repairs and heightening the tower of St Margaret's Westminster (1735–7), and the completion of the west towers of Westminster Abbey to Hawksmoor's designs (1736–45). See Sir Howard Colvin, *A biographical dictionary of British architects, 1600–1840*, 3rd edn (New Haven, 1995), pp. 536–40.

10 Middleton to Lord Harley, 2 April 1730; British Library, MS Loan 29/167 (not known to Carter).

11 Most of the papers relating to Fenner at Cambridge are gathered in UA CUR 33.6(47–71). Carter ('William Ged', p. 170) suggests that the reason for employing Dutch printers was linked to the strong English trade of the Dutch typefounders; but it may be that those appointed had some more particular knowledge of printing from plates in Amsterdam or Leiden.

12 *A collection of poems. By the author of a poem on the Cambridge ladies*, 8°, 1733.

13 A unique copy is recorded, Cambridge University Library, 7100.d.792.

14 Edward Rowe Mores, *A dissertation upon English typographical founders and founderies*, ed. H. Carter and C. Ricks (Oxford Bibliographical Soc., 1961), pp. 56–7. (1781 edn), p. 35.

15 Among the books of John Henderson, the actor. See John Morris, 'A note on the first stereotyping in England', *JPHS*, 1 (1965), pp. 97–8.

16 Hansard, *Typographia*, pp. 822–3.

17 The various papers relating to this case from the University's point of view are preserved in UA CUR 33.2(114–120) and D. I.24(42–50).

18 Carter, *Oxford University Press*, pp. 173–6.

19 The celebrated remark about 'a Baskett-full of errors' was applied to his folio Bible of 1717. In 1724 George I issued 'Directions to Printers of Bibles and Prayer-books for remedying faulty printing and regulating the prices'. See Carter, *Oxford University Press*, p. 173.

20 UA Grace book I, p. 439.

21 UA Grace Book I, p. 451.

22 UA Pr.v.1, 26 October 1738, 16 October 1739.

23 See above, p. 135.

24 UA Min.vi.1, Syndicate minutes, 21 May 1740.

25 UA Pr.v.1, order book, 11 December 1740.

26 Report by Roger Long et al.: UA Pr.B.2.6.

27 B. J. McMullin, 'The 1629 Cambridge Bible', *TCBS*, 8 (1984), pp. 381–97; B. J. McMullin, 'Paper-quality marks and the Oxford Bible press, 1682–1717', *The Library*, 6th ser. 6 (1984), pp. 39–49; B. J. McMullin, 'Towards a bibliography of the Oxford and Cambridge University Bible presses in the seventeenth and eighteenth centuries', *Bibliographical Soc. of Australia and New Zealand Bulletin*, 14 (1990), pp. 51–73. Choice was not limited to format, type size and paper quality. For an account of the offence caused by the introduction of engravings, see George Henderson, 'Bible illustration in the age of Laud', *TCBS*, 8 (1982), pp. 173–216; for Ogilby and the trade in inserted illustrations in Field's Bibles, see McKitterick, *Cambridge University Press*, 1, pp. 327–8.

28 Herbert, *Historical catalogue*, p. 249; Carter, *Oxford University Press*, p. 173. It was of course an easy matter to paste a slip of paper over the price before a volume was offered for sale, and this was frequently done.

29 Bathurst to Bentham, 4 December 1747, UA CUR 33.7(3).

30 SPCK minutes, 4 November 1760.

31 H. Hammelmann and T. S. R. Boase, *Book illustrators in eighteenth-century England* (New Haven, 1975), pp. 72–3.

32 'Catalogue of Bibles and Common-Prayers', at end of *A catalogue of the most esteemed modern books* (1751).

33 Cf. for example, *The liturgy of the Church of England adorn'd with fifty five new historical cuts*, published by John Sturt and J. Nutt; *The liturgy of the Church of England; illustrated with fifty-five historical and explanatory sculptures engrav'd by Mess. Ravenett, Grignion, Scotin, Canott, Walker and W. Ryland*, published by Edward Ryland, 1755; *The liturgy of the Church of England*, published by Samuel Birt. A set of engravings with captions in Welsh, *Gwasanaeth cyhoedd eglwys loegr*, was published in London in 1755.

34 W. K. Lowther Clarke, *A history of the S.P.C.K.* (1959).

35 *An account of the origin and designs of the Society for Promoting Christian Knowledge*, appended to John Denne, *A sermon preached at St. Sepulchre's Church, May 6, 1736* (1736), p. 29.

36 Cf. the remarks recorded at the SPCK, 1726, concerning Charles Ackers's work on an Arabic New Testament: 'Mr Acres the Arabick Composer had attended about Twenty Times since he was out of Mr Palmer's Service and that such Attendance was always to his Prejudice, as it hindered his dayly Work'. As a contribution towards his inconvenience and loss, it was agreed to give him two guineas. D. F. McKenzie and J. C. Ross (ed.), *A ledger of Charles Ackers, printer of the London Magazine* (Oxford Bibliographical Soc., 1968), p. 2.

37 'Remarks by Dr. Bentham, 1756', Philip, *Blackstone*, pp. 43–4.

38 UA Pr.v.1, order book, 23 June 1741.

39 'Composed in the Nonpareil 12° Bible 2 sh^{ts} A B at 2^s.6^d £4.12.-' Press accounts 28 March 1740–November following: UA Pr.P.3(33).

40 UA Pr.P.3(34).

41 UA Min.vi.1, Syndicate minutes, 3 August 1743; University accounts (UA U. Ac.2(3)), 1742–3. Parris became Master of Sidney Sussex in 1746, and in 1750 was elected *Protobibliothecarius* in succession to Conyers Middleton: McKitterick, *Cambridge University Library*, p. 253. For his part in editing the Bible of 1762, see below, pp. 191–2.

42 The agent was Mr Bangham. In 1662, Wharton (1613–96) settled land in Yorkshire upon trustees to enable the free distribution of Bibles and catechisms in Buckinghamshire, Yorkshire, Westmorland and Cumberland – counties in which he owned land. By 1712 these interests had been extended to other regions, including Wales: see *DNB*, art. 'Wharton', and Mary Clement, *Correspondence and minutes of the S.P.C.K. relating to Wales, 1699–1740* (Cardiff, 1952), pp. 50, 66. For the Welsh Bible, see below, pp. 187–8.

43 *Account . . . of the Society for Promoting Christian Knowledge*, annexed to [Joseph Butler] *A sermon . . . 9 May 1745* (1745).

44 Some aspects of this question are explored in W. K. Lowther Clarke, *Eighteenth century piety* (1944).

45 UA Min.vi.1, Syndicate minutes, 16 October 1739.

46 UA Min.vi.1, Syndicate minutes, 27 September 1742, 3 August 1743.

47 UA Min.vi.1, Syndicate minutes, 27 May, 3 June, 5 August, 7 October 1747. Until the mid 1740s, the Press had been able to print only the Bible and the prayer book in large numbers. The metrical psalms belonged to the Stationers' Company. But when in 1746 occasion came to renew the agreement with the Company, advantage was taken to allow the University henceforth to print numbers of the metrical psalms commensurate with the numbers of Bibles and prayer books printed by the University itself. (Syndicate minutes, 16 October 1746.)

48 UA Min.vi.1, Syndicate minutes, 19 May and 28 October 1758.

49 UA Min.vi.1, Syndicate minutes, 22 October 1741.

50 UA Min.vi.1, Syndicate minutes, 2 October 1745, 12 March 1745/6.

51 UA Min.vi.1, Syndicate minutes, 1 June and 27 June 1751.

52 See, for example, Patricia Hernlund, 'Three bankruptcies in the London book trade, 1746–61: Rivington, Knapton and Osborn', in O. M. Brack (ed.), *Writers, books and trade; an eighteenth-century English miscellany for William B. Todd* (New York, 1994), pp. 77–122.

53 UA Min.vi.1, Syndicate minutes, 11 March 1741/2.

54 Lowther Clarke, *A history of the S.P.C.K.*, p. 66.

55 A. K. Priolkar, *The printing press in India; its beginnings and early development* (Bombay, 1958), pp. 42–3; D. E. Rhodes, *The spread of printing; India, Pakistan, Ceylon, Burma and Thailand* (Amsterdam, 1969), pp. 17–18.

56 SPCK minutes, 20 November 1744.

57 Herbert, *Historical catalogue*, pp. 272–3, 293. See also below, p. 225.

58 SPCK minutes, 5 May, 4 December 1744; 8 and 15 January, 5 February 1744/5. For Denne, see also Robert Masters, *The history of the College of Corpus Christi* (Cambridge, 1753), pp. 277–8.

59 SPCK minutes, 19 April 1757, 19 December 1758.

60 SPCK minutes, 6 February, 6 March 1759.

61 Scrivener, *Authorized edition*, p. 28.

62 See, for example, his edition of the Book of Common Prayer, price sixpence, 1745.

63 SPCK minutes, 4 November 1760.

64 The final copies were given to Mr Jones of Llanddowror (near Carmarthen), for him to dispose of as he saw fit: SPCK minutes, 3 March 1741/2.

65 SPCK minutes, 15 November, 6 December 1743; Welsh Bible minutes, 6 December 1743. A Welsh New Testament had been printed meanwhile at Shrewsbury in 1741.

66 SPCK Welsh Bible minutes, 20 December 1743.

67 SPCK Welsh Bible minutes, 13 February, 6 March 1743/4.

68 SPCK Welsh Bible minutes, 3 April 1744. It was agreed to insert these proposals in the *London Evening Post* and the *Daily Advertiser*.

69 SPCK Welsh Bible minutes, 1744–5, *passim*.

70 SPCK Welsh Bible minutes, 14 June, 12 July 1748, 27 March 1750.

71 SPCK Welsh Bible minutes, 10 April 1750. No Bible in Welsh was printed again at Cambridge until 1806: see below, pp. 271–5.

72 University accounts, 1745–6, 1746–7, 1747–8: UA U. Ac.2(3). SPCK Welsh Bible minutes, 26 April 1748.

73 UA Min.vi.1, Syndicate minutes, 17 March 1743/4.

74 Bathurst to Parris, 4 December 1747: UA CUR 33.7(3).

75 Parris to Bathurst, 8 December 1747: UA CUR 33.7(4).

76 University accounts, 1745–6, 1746–7, 1747–8: UA U. Ac.2(3).

77 Bathurst to Parris, 14 December 1747: UA CUR 33.7(5).

78 Parris to Bathurst, 24 March 1747/8: UA CUR 33.3(51).

79 UA Min.vi.1, Syndicate minutes, 2 May 1748.

80 UA CUR 33.7(7,8) (memoirs addressed to the University by Bathurst).

81 UA CUR 33.7(9).

82 UA Min.vi.1, Syndicate minutes, 27 June 1751.

83 SPCK minutes, 19 March 1744/5.

84 UA Min.vi.1, Syndicate minutes, 30 October 1751.

85 The Oxford figures were on a sliding scale up to books costing 19s.6d.; for those of £1 and upwards the rate was 10 per cent. Ordinary booksellers were allowed half these rates. (Delegates' minutes, 5 July 1758; Philip, *Blackstone*, p. 99.) Less than a year later, the Delegates were obliged to raise the rates allowed to ordinary booksellers (*ibid.*, p. 107).

86 UA Min.vi.1, Syndicate minutes, 17 June 1760, 1 July 1761.

87 Scrivener, *Authorized edition*, pp. 28–35, 238–9. As usual for the Bible, there was also a press corrector, who on this occasion was Henry Therond, Fellow of Trinity College and headmaster of Hull grammar school. Scrivener is mistaken in claiming Parris as Thomas Paris of Trinity College; and he is mistaken in repeating the canard that the folio edition of 1762 is extremely rare. I am particularly grateful to Ronald Mansbridge for his amicable and diligent research into surviving copies of the 1762 folio. For further comment, see B. J. McMullin, 'The 1762 Bentham folio Cambridge Bible and the survival of eighteenth-century publications', *Factotum*, 37 (1993), pp. 5–10, Ronald Mansbridge, 'The Bentham folio Bible', *Book Collector*, 45 (1996), pp. 24–8, and B. J. McMullin, 'Extinguishing the fire at Dod's warehouse in 1762', *ibid.*, pp. 476–84.

88 Articles of agreement between Dod and the Syndics, 28 February 1760/1, UA CUR 33.7(18).

89 UA CUR 33.7(3).

90 UA Min.vi.1, Syndicate minutes, 17 June 1760.

91 UA Pr.P.4(9).

92 UA Pr.P.4(9).

93 Although no proper audit, which would have distinguished capital investment and expenditure more precisely, was ever carried out, the accumulated loss by 1740 has been estimated at £2,419 (McKenzie, *Cambridge University Press*, 1, pp. 172–3). In the eighteenth century, the Press did not calculate depreciation, and it ignored the cost of lost investment opportunities, or of lengthy credit arrangements.

That some of its suppliers in the second half of the century, such as typefounders, were aware of the cost of long-term credit is clear from the discounts offered for prompt payment.

94 Press Syndicate minutes, 7 November 1765.

95 Or, perhaps, Benjamin Collins of Salisbury: Nichols (see below) was not explicit.

96 R. Rabicoff and D. McKitterick, 'John Nichols, William Bowyer, and Cambridge University Press in 1765', *Trans Cambridge Bibliographical Soc.*, 6 (1976), pp. 328–38; Albert H. Smith, 'John Nichols, printer and publisher', *The Library*, 5th ser. 18 (1963), pp. 169–90.

97 Bowyer to Nichols, 15 September 1765. Bodleian Library, MS Gough Camb.70, fos. 23–7; Nichols, *Literary anecdotes*, 2, p. 460. Bowyer was cautious at a partnership, since he recalled Nutt and Gosling, whose affairs had finally to go to arbitration.

98 See above, p. 173.

99 Nichols to Bowyer, 15 September 1765. Bodleian Library, MS Gough Camb. 70, fos. 23–7; Nichols, *Literary anecdotes*, 2, p. 459.

100 UA Min.VI.1, Syndicate minutes, 28 October and 7 November 1765.

101 UA CUR 33.1(41).

9 Baskerville and Bentham

1 'It is one of the great Bibles of all time . . . Since Baskerville, only the Bruce Rogers Bible printed at Oxford in 1935 comes anywhere near him in authority and grandeur.' (Black, *Cambridge University Press*, p. 114.) The Bible and prayer books printed at Cambridge were not, as has sometimes been stated, on Whatman's new wove paper. All of Baskerville's Cambridge books were on laid paper, albeit of a generally high quality.

2 F. E. Pardoe, *John Baskerville of Birmingham, letter-founder and printer* (1975), pp. 26–30. For Baskerville, see in particular also Ralph Straus and Robert K. Dent, *John Baskerville; a memoir* (Cambridge, 1907); Philip Gaskell, *John Baskerville; a bibliography*, repr. with additions and corrections (Chicheley, 1973); J. G. Dreyfus, 'Baskerville's methods of printing', *Signature*, n.s.12 (1951), pp. 44–51; J. N. Balston, *The elder James Whatman, England's greatest paper maker (1702–1759)*, 2 vols. (West Farleigh, 1992), 1, pp. 254–5 etc.

3 Baskerville to an unnamed correspondent, 4 January 1757, Birmingham Public Library: Pardoe, *John Baskerville of Birmingham*, pp. 43–4.

4 UA Grace Book **K**, p. 308.

5 After considering, on 6 June 1758, a proposal from Baskerville to cast new Greek types, the Oxford Delegates agreed on 5 July to order punches, matrices and moulds, and to cast a quantity of type. (Philip, *Blackstone*, pp. 98, 100.)

6 The relevant documents are printed in Straus and Dent, *John Baskerville*, p. 111.

7 Gaskell, *John Baskerville*, no. xii and plate viii.

8 John Baskerville to the Vice-Chancellor, 31 May 1759: Pardoe, *John Baskerville*, p. 64. In 1757 he had announced his intention of sending two presses to Cambridge (Pardoe, p. 43). For Martin, see especially Straus and Dent, *John Baskerville*, pp. 53–9. He died in 1796: 'Wednesday sennight died Robert Martin . . . formerly an assistant in the Printing Office of Mr. Baskerville in this University' (*Cambridge Chronicle and Journal*, 16 April 1796). According to Roberts, *Cambridge University Press*, p. 111, Baskerville's premises were in the old Radegund manor house, Jesus Lane; but no trace of such a tenancy can be found in the Jesus College archives. I am most grateful to Mr E. F. Mills, former Estates Bursar of Jesus College, for searching the college records, albeit in vain.

9 John Baskerville to the Earl of Bute, June 1762; James L. McKelvey, 'John Baskerville's appeal to Lord Bute', *TCBS*, 5 (1970), pp. 138–41.

10 *Proposals for printing by subscription the poetical works of John Milton* (Birmingham, 1757), Rothschild copy, Trinity College.

11 Baskerville to Pierres, 2 December 1773: Straus and Dent, *John Baskerville*, p. 104.

12 *Ibid.*

13 Gaskell, *John Baskerville*, pp. 8–9 and plates vi–vii.

14 *Ibid., pp.* 31–2.

15 UA Min.vi.1, Syndicate minutes, 18 December 1759, 11 November 1761, 27 October 1762.

16 Gaskell, *John Baskerville*, p. 39; UA CUR 33.1(40c).

17 UA Min.vi.1, Syndicate minutes, 11 November 1761.

18 Minutes of Oxford Delegates, 9 May 1759: Philip, *Blackstone*, p. 106.

19 Minutes of Oxford Delegates, 28 July 1759: Philip, *Blackstone*, p. 108.

20 Baskerville to an unidentified correspondent, 4 January 1757, Birmingham Public Library: Pardoe, *Baskerville*, p. 44.

21 Straus and Dent, pp. 110–11.

22 UA Min.vi.1, Syndicate minutes, 18 December 1759. The edition was to consist of 4,000 copies: 3,500 demy and 250 royal in quarto, and 250 superfine crown in folio.

23 Agreement with Dod, 28 February 1761: UA CUR 33.7(18), repr. in Ronald Mansbridge, 'The Bentham folio Bible', *Book Collector*, 45 (1996), pp. 24–8, at p. 24.

24 'As to Mr. Baskerville's *Bible*, he will easily be dissuaded from the marginal ornaments.' Robert Dodsley to William Shenstone, between 18 February and 21 April 1760: Robert Dodsley, *Correspondence, 1733–1764*, ed. James E. Tierney (Cambridge, 1988), p. 438. Part of the proposals of 1 August 1761 is reproduced in William P. Barlow, Jr., 'A Baskerville collection (Contemporary collectors liii)', *The Book Collector*, 38 (1989), pp. 171–91, at p. 179.

25 *Cambridge Chronicle*, 26 March 1763: 'Mr. Baskerville's elegant folio Bible, which will be ready to deliver to the subscribers in a few months, price four guineas in sheets. Those who subscribe for six, have a seventh gratis.'

26 Gaskell (*John Baskerville*, p. 44) has identified three states of the list of subscribers.

27 Gaskell, *John Baskerville*, p. 45. But for further, and apparently conflicting, details regarding the sale of unsold stock, see the review by L. W. Hanson, *The Library*, 5th ser. 15 (1960), pp. 139–40.

28 See, for example, the notice (frequently repeated) by Fletcher and Hodson in the *Cambridge Chronicle*, 15 January 1763. A 'fresh quantity' was advertised by the same in the *Cambridge Chronicle and Journal*, 3 January 1767.

10 An age of ferment

1 Thomas Davies to Granger, 14 February 1770: *Letters between the Rev. James Granger . . . and . . . literary men of his time* (1805), p. 31. In 1772 there were ten bankruptcies in the London book trade alone. The high figures in the second part of the decade (sixteen in 1776; ten in 1777; sixteen in 1778) were not matched again until the 1790s: Maxted, *London book trades*, p. xxxiii. See also William Bailey, *Bailey's list of bankrupts, dividends and certificates from the year 1772 to 1793* (1794), and the (usually monthly) reports in the *Gentleman's Magazine*. Bankruptcies generally soared between 1771 and 1773: see T. S. Ashton, *Economic fluctuations in England, 1700–1800* (Oxford, 1959), p. 129.

2 See, for example, J. R. Raven, *Judging new wealth; popular publishing and responses to commerce in England, 1750–1800* (Oxford, 1992), especially pp. 42–52. Magazines and other miscellaneous journals are conveniently summarised, in chronological order of foundation, in *NCBEL*, 2, cols. 1291–1312, London newspapers cols. 1313–40, English county newspapers cols. 1353–70, Scottish magazines and newspapers cols 1371–78. The growth in the number of periodicals is tabulated in Maxted, *London book trades*, p. xxix.

3 Paul Kaufman, *Libraries and their users; collected papers in library history* (1969); Paul Kaufman, *The community library; a chapter in English social history* (Trans American Philosophical Soc., n.s. 57, pt 7 (1957)); D. P. Varma, *The evergreen tree of diabolical knowledge* (Washington, D.C., 1972).

4 In 1762, the newly established *Cambridge Chronicle* had agents in towns as far afield as Stamford, Newark, Leicester, Boston and Bedford, as well as the newspaper printer Charles Say in Cornhill, London. Within a few weeks, copies were being regularly despatched to York, Newcastle, Carlisle, Bedfordshire, Huntingdonshire, Essex, Suffolk, Norfolk and Rutland (*Cambridge Chronicle*, 30

October 1762, 27 November 1762). The radical newspaper *The Cambridge Intelligencer* (see below, pp. 249–50) circulated widely in the north of England. Cf. G. A. Cranfield, *The development of the provincial newspaper, 1700–1760* (Oxford, 1962), pp. 168–206, and C. Y. Ferdinand, 'Local distribution networks in 18th-century England' in R. Myers and M. Harris (eds.), *Spreading the word; the distribution networks of print, 1550–1850* (Winchester, 1990), pp. 131–49.

5 *Considerations on the nature and origin of literary property* (Edinburgh, 1767), p. 34.

6 *Cambridge Chronicle and Journal*, 30 November 1771. Donaldson's advertisements appeared in this newspaper from 1767.

7 William Strahan to David Hall, 30 November 1764: American Philosophical Soc., David Hall collection, quoted in Robert D. Harlan, 'William Strahan's American book trade, 1744–76', *Library Quarterly*, 31 (1961), pp. 235–44.

8 Rivington's personal life was complicated by gambling. He subsequently established himself as a bookseller in New York and in Philadelphia. See also Edwin Wolf II, *The book culture of a colonial American city; Philadelphia books, bookmen, and booksellers* (Oxford, 1988).

9 See below, pp. 222–6.

10 *Cambridge Chronicle and Journal*, 9 October 1779, 6 January 1781. A dividend was announced, 14 May 1785.

11 *Gentleman's Magazine*, 49 (1779), p. 520; *Cambridge Chronicle and Journal*, 4 December 1779.

12 See below, p. 246.

13 *Cambridge Chronicle and Journal*, 6 January 1787. He had married Mrs Booth of Wisbech the previous October (*ibid.*, 7 October 1786).

14 *Cambridge Chronicle and Journal*, 13 October 1787.

15 W. H. Lunn, *First part of a catalogue of books* (Cambridge, 1790), preliminary notice. Lunn's boasting of the physical qualities of his books drew at least one satirist: see *The sizar* (Cambridge, 1799), pp. 74–6.

16 Plomer, *Dictionary*, art. 'Merrill (Thomas)'. At least in 1761, Thomas Merrill was in touch with Alexander Donaldson, who in that year published, with the translator, *The private life of the Romans*, translated from the French of d'Arnay: a copy with Merrill's name added to the imprint in manuscript is in Trinity College, K.10.47(1).

17 Gunning, *Reminiscences*, 1, pp. 198–200; Christopher Wordsworth, *Social life at the English universities in the eighteenth century* (Cambridge, 1874), pp. 378–85. For his portrait, commissioned by Richard Farmer and hung in the University Library, see McKitterick, *Cambridge University Library*, p. 291 and fig. 12; J. W. Goodison, *Catalogue of Cambridge portraits*. 1. The University collection (Cambridge, 1955) 50.

18 Copy in Cambridge University Library, 7720.d.16^1.

19 *Cambridge Journal*, 18 March 1758.

20 For one example from his circulating library, cf. Cambridge University Library, Cam.d.785.1.

21 Cf. the preliminary remarks to [Thomas Kipling], *The elementary parts of Dr. Smith's Compleat system of opticks, selected and arranged for the use of students at the universities* (Cambridge, 1778). The full edition of Smith's work had become scarce, but (presumably on grounds of cost) no-one wished to republish it. In 1787, it was claimed more generally that many useful books in the classics had become scarce ([William Frend], *Considerations on the oaths required by the University of Cambridge* (1787), p. 39).

22 Advertisement in Cambridge University Library, Cam.d.785.1. For Bowtell, see A. B. Gray, *John Bowtell: bookbinder of Cambridge (1753–1813); biographical notes with a further notice of his nephew John Bowtell the younger (1777–1855)* (Cambridge, 1907) and McKitterick, *Cambridge University Library*, pp. 310, 312–14.

23 Advertisement in the *Cambridge Chronicle*, 14 September 1765; 'at the Upper End of Garlick-Row, the second Booth on the Right Hand'. Similar advertisements appeared in other years.

24 A copy in Trinity College library of Roger Cotes, *De descensu gravium* (printed by Fletcher and Hodson, 'impensis J. Nicholson, Cantab. veneunt apud J. Rivington, Lond.', 1770, has 'Maps' scrawled across the head of the title-page, presumably alluding to Nicholson.

25 Advertisement in Cicero, *De officiis* (Cambridge: Archdeacon, impensis J. Nicholson, 1777).

26 Rothschild, nos. 1061–5.

27 Gray expressed his anguish in a letter to Horace Walpole, 13 February 1753 (i.e. shortly before publication): 'Sure You are not out of your Wits! this I know, if you suffer my Head to be printed, you infallibly will put me out of mine. I conjure you immediately to put a stop to any such design. who is at the Expence of engraving it, I know not; but if it be Dodsley, I will make up the Loss to him. the thing, as it was, I know will make me ridiculous enough; but to appear in proper Person at the head of my works, consisting of half a dozen Ballads in 30 Pages, would be worse than the Pillory. I do assure you, if I had received such a Book with such a frontispiece without any warning, I believe, it would have given me a Palsy.' (Thomas Gray, *Correspondence*, ed. Paget Toynbee, Leonard Whibley and H. W. Starr, 3 vols. (Oxford, 1971), no. 173.)

28 *Cambridge Journal*, 19 February 1757, 11 March 1758. A William Davenport had been apprenticed to John Hughes in London, in 1745: see McKenzie, *Apprentices 1701–1800*, no. 4232.

29 *Cambridge Chronicle*, 30 October 1762.

30 *Cambridge Journal*, 15 December 1764.

31 UA Min.VI.1, Syndicate minutes, 2 April 1768. No invoice for the press seems to have survived; but the Press was charged for carriage of a press from London to Cambridge on 9 May. It may be presumed that it could not be put properly to work until a small grate had been provided (on 19 July) over which to warm the copper-plates for printing. UA Pr. vouchers, 1768/25i and 17689/28ii.

32 G. R. Owst, 'Iconomania in eighteenth-century Cambridge', *Proc. Cambridge Antiquarian Soc.*, 42 (1948), pp. 67–91; Arlene Meyer, 'Sir William Musgrave's "lists" of portraits; with an account of head-hunting in the eighteenth century', *Walpole Society*, 54 (1988 [1991]), pp. 454–502. For Ewin, antiquary, acquaintance of Cole, and usurer, see Horace Walpole, *Correspondence with the Rev. William Cole*, ed. W. S. Lewis and A. Dayle Wallace *(Yale edition of the correspondence of Horace Walpole)*, 2 vols. (New Haven, 1937), 1, pp. 158 etc. and *Letters between the Rev. James Granger . . . and . . . literary men of his time*, pp. 327–8.

33 C. P. Barbier, *William Gilpin; his drawings, teaching and theory of the picturesque* (Oxford, 1963).

34 William Cole to James Granger, 10 July 1772, *Letters between the Rev. James Granger . . . and . . . literary men of his time*, p. 364.

35 For Pepys, see Eric Chamberlain, *Catalogue of the Pepys library at Magdalene College, Cambridge*. III. *Prints and drawings*. ii. *Portraits* (Cambridge, 1994); for details of the Harleian collection of engravings, see Thomas Osborne, *Catalogus bibliothecae Harleianae*, 5 vols. (1743–5) 2, following p. 1034 and 5, at the beginning.

36 The best-known example is the frontispiece portrait by Thomas Orde, an undergraduate, to Henry Malden, *An account of King's College Chapel* (Cambridge: Fletcher and Hodson, 1769): Orde made several etchings of local characters. Michael Tyson of Corpus and William Mason were among others who prepared plates of their own. See also *Letters between the Rev. James Granger . . . and . . . literary men*, pp. 87–8, 152–5, and (for several other Cambridge amateurs) Christopher White, David Alexander and Ellen D'Oench, *Rembrandt in eighteenth century England* (New Haven, 1983).

37 For example 'a fine collection of virtuoso prints' offered from the collection of Thomas Lippyeatt (*Cambridge Journal*, 24 June 1758, sale in Cambridge 26 June: a copy of the auction catalogue (including a notable collection of early printed books) is in the British Library); 'Fine prints, purchased by William Austin . . . consigned to him from abroad by the executors of . . . Sig. Geminiani and Mynheer Van Abell' to be auctioned in Petty Cury (*Cambridge Chronicle*, 13 November 1762).

38 J. M. Morris, 'A check-list of prints made at Cambridge by Peter Spendelowe Lamborn (1722–1774)', *TCBS* 3(1962), pp. 295–312.

39 Advertised in the *Cambridge Chronicle*, 13 November 1762 as 'just published'.

40 *Cambridge Chronicle and Journal*, 9 May and 13 June 1767; *ibid.*, 1 June, 11 November 1769.

41 For example, *Cambridge Chronicle and Journal*, 16 May and 14 November 1772, 20 November 1773.

42 *Cambridge Chronicle and Journal*, 25 June 1768; *ibid.*, 3 June 1769; *ibid.*, 1 December 1770 (also mentioning an etching by his son, C. Bretherton); *ibid.*, 13 April 1771 (announcing departure to Bond Street).

43 *Cambridge Chronicle and Journal*, 1 December 1770, 26 January 1771.

44 *Cambridge Chronicle and Journal*, 4 August and 18 August 1770.

45 *Letters between the Rev. James Granger . . . and . . . literary men*, pp. 307–11. Sharpe also executed an etching of Thomas Gray.

46 *Cambridge Chronicle and Journal*, 3 November 1770.

47 *Cambridge Chronicle and Journal*, 20 May 1775. The engraving was completed by Bartolozzi's pupil, John Sherwin (*ibid.*, 10 November 1781).

48 *Cambridge Chronicle and Journal*, 26 August 1775.

49 *Cambridge Chronicle and Journal*, 23 October 1773.

50 *Cambridge Chronicle and Journal*, 4 June 1791.

51 *Cambridge Chronicle and Journal*, 6 February 1773, 17 December 1774, 28 June 1788; W. H. Lunn, *Catalogue of a select and valuable collection of books* (May, 1788).

52 *Cambridge Chronicle and Journal*, 11 April, 1778.

53 *Cambridge Chronicle and Journal*, 12 May 1781.

54 *Cambridge Chronicle and Journal*, 1 November 1782.

55 W. H. Lunn, *Catalogue* (May, 1788); *First part of a catalogue* (1790).

56 Most authorities attribute this book to Thomas Martyn.

57 Rüdiger Joppien, 'John Webber's South Sea drawings for the Admiralty; a newly discovered catalogue among the papers of Sir Joseph Banks', *British Library Journal*, 4 (1978), pp. 49–77: apart from a payment to Woollett of 150 guineas, the engraving of most plates cost between 30 and 90 guineas.

58 Cambridge University Library, MS Add. 2960, fo. 39r. See above, pp. 155–6.

59 For one survival of 'imposed' engravings, see Iain Bain, *Albert Schloss's Bijou Almanacs, 1839–1843* (1969).

60 Hugh Amory, '"Proprietary illustration": the case of Cooke's *Tom Jones*', in R. Harvey, W. Kirsop and B. J. McMullin (ed.), *An index of civilisation; studies of printing and publishing history in honour of Keith Maslen* (Melbourne, 1993), pp. 137–47.

61 David Hunter, 'Copyright protection for engravings and maps in eighteenth-century Britain', *The Library*, 6th ser. 9 (1987), pp. 128–47; Amory, '"Proprietary illustration"'.

62 For Bell, see Stanley Morison, *John Bell, 1745–1831* (Cambridge, 1930). A selection of his bindings is reproduced in Morison, opposite p. 115; the *Morning Post*, 10 January 1786, offered complete sets of Bell's *Poets of Great Britain* in various bindings, priced between 8 guineas and £33.

63 S. Roscoe, *John Newbery and his successors, 1740–1814* (Wormley, 1973).

64 McKitterick, *Cambridge University Press*, 1, pp. 131–2.

65 Sir William Blackstone, *Reports of cases determined in the several courts of Westminster-Hall, 1746–1779*, 2 vols. (1781), 1, pp. 105–22.

66 Sir Michael Foster to Blackstone, 11 December 1758; Blackstone, *Reports*, 1, p. 122. See also Cooper, *Annals*, 4, pp. 300–1, and C. H. S. Fifoot, *Lord Mansfield* (Oxford, 1936), pp. 222–3.

67 32 Geo. II c. 10; 21 Geo. III c. 24; 27 Geo. III c. 13; Shadwell, *Enactments in Parliament*, 2, pp. 60, 167, 188; Cooper, *Annals*, 4, pp. 301, 402.

68 UA D.1.2(129–32); CUR 33.7; Cyprian Blagden, *The Stationers' Company; a history, 1403–1959* (1960), pp. 203–4.

69 Stationers' Company versus Carnan; Cooper, *Annals*, 4, p. 374 and (for Carnan's inclinations to litigiousness) pp. 390–1.

70 15 Geo. III c. 53. See Cooper, *Annals*, 4, pp. 374–7; Clark, *Endowments*, pp. 46–7; Shadwell, *Enactments in Parliament*, 2, pp. 140–6; Blagden, *Stationers' Company*, pp. 239–41.

71 Cooper, *Annals*, 4, pp. 390–1. House of Commons, 16 April 1779; *Parliamentary history of England . . . to the year 1803*, 20, cols. 602–5. Carnan's petition is printed *ibid.*, cols. 605–8.

72 House of Commons, 10 May 1779; *Parliamentary history of England . . . to the year 1803*, 20, col. 621. For a viewpoint from the Stationers' Company, see Cyprian Blagden, 'Thomas Carnan and the almanack monopoly', *SB*, 14 (1961), pp. 23–43.

73 House of Lords, 20 June 1781; *Parliamentary history of England . . . to the year 1803*, 22, cols. 540, 542.

74 21 Geo. III c. 56. See Clark, *Endowments*, pp. 47–8 and Shadwell, *Enactments in Parliament*, 2, pp. 183–5.

75 UA Grace Book Λ, p. 121 (11 June 1782).

76 Though stamp duty on almanacs was abolished in 1834, the Press continued to receive £500 per annum from the State until it was discontinued by mutual consent (albeit with some regret at the historical break in Cambridge) in 1985: Black, *Cambridge University Press*, p. 118, was correct in 1984 in stating 1981, but the question was finally settled only in 1985.

11 John Archdeacon

1 I am grateful to Mary Pollard for sharing with me – albeit to no avail – her unrivalled knowledge of the eighteenth-century Irish printing trade. The Archdeacons are especially associated with Kilkenny.

2 On his death in 1795, the *Cambridge Chronicle* recorded his age as seventy.

3 UA Grace Book **K**, p. 441. Press Syndicate minutes, 29 October 1766.

4 Bentham's terms of appointment are in the Press Syndicate minutes, 28 March 1740; those of Archdeacon are in the minutes for 29 October 1766. Cf. the remark by Bentham's brother Edward, made in 1756, concerning the salary for an overseer of the Oxford press: 'Supposing the Overseer to be allow'd £80 per Annum (& an able skilful faithful one can scarce be had for less) & computing his clear profits out of the 2s allow'd for each sheet, there must be 1200 sheets annually printed, in order to clear this single article of expence; & whatever deficiency there is, must be made good from the University.' ('Remarks by Dr. Bentham', Philip, *William Blackstone*, p. 43.) Samuel Richardson, too, considered it more appropriate for Oxford to engage a full-time overseer, at a salary, rather than allow someone to be employed at so much a sheet (Richardson to Blackstone, 10 February 1756, *ibid.*, p. 38).

5 There were two editions, one set in pica and the other in great primer. The smaller cost 8s. unbound (Cambridge University Library, Marshall d.5).

6 H. Hammelmann and T. S. R. Boase, *Book illustration in eighteenth-century England* (New Haven, 1975), p. 91; Syndicate minutes, 17 June 1769. See also p. 223.

7 Henry Newman to Benjamin Wadsworth (President of Harvard), 19 October 1733: W. O. B. Allen and Edmund McClure, *Two hundred years; the history of the Society for Promoting Christian Knowledge, 1698–1898* (1898), p. 249.

8 Baskerville to the Académie Royale des Sciences, December 1773: Straus and Dent, *John Baskerville*, p. 105; original reproduced in Maggs catalogue, March 1914. See also Pardoe, *John Baskerville*, pp. 70–1. Baskerville may have been thinking of the remarks by P. S. Fournier in his *Manuel typographique*, 2 vols. (Paris, 1764–6), 2, p. xxxix. See also John Dreyfus, 'The Baskerville punches, 1750–1950', *The Library*, 3rd ser. 5 (1951), pp. 26–48, who remarks (p. 29) on 'the number of Baskerville editions found in continental bindings'.

9 'I have sent a few [type] Specimens . . . to the Courts of Russia and Denmark, and shall endeavour to do the same to most of the Courts in Europe; in hopes of finding in some of them a purchaser of the whole scheme, on the Condition of never attempting another Type.' (Baskerville to Horace Walpole, 2 November 1762: Reed, *Old English letter foundries*, p. 278.) In 1773 he wrote also of having unsuccessfully approached the court of France (Straus and Dent, *John Baskerville*, p. 105).

10 Edward Rowe Mores, *A dissertation upon English typographical founders and founderies (1778)*, ed. Harry Carter and Christopher Ricks (Oxford Bibliographical Soc., 1961), p. 81.

11 Joseph Fry and Sons, *A specimen of printing types* (1785), preface; W. Turner Berry and A. F. Johnson, *Catalogue of specimens of printing types* (Oxford, 1935), p. 41; Reed, *Old English letter foundries*, p. 302. Useful enlargements of Fry's and Caslon's type-faces are given in Philip Gaskell, 'Photographic enlargements of type forms', *Journal of the Printing Historical Soc.*, 7 (1971), pp. 51–3.

12 Benjamin Franklin to Baskerville [1760?]: Straus and Dent, *John Baskerville*, p. 19; Benjamin Franklin, *Papers*, ed. Leonard W. Labaree et al. (New Haven, 1959–), 9, pp. 259–60.

13 The rival Bible (Herbert, *Historical catalogue*, no. 1204) was printed by Nicholas Boden and Orion

Adams, and issued in parts between 1768 and 1770. Cf. Straus and Dent, *John Baskerville*, pp. 58–9, 120–7, and Gaskell, *Baskerville*, pp. 51–2.

14 Alexander Wilson and Sons, *A specimen of some of the printing types* (Glasgow, 1772); Isaac Moore and Co., *A specimen of printing-types* (1768).

15 For Cottrell's type specimens, see James Mosley, *British type specimens before 1831; a hand-list* (Oxford Bibliographical Soc., 1984); for Martin, see *ibid.*, p. 39.

16 Some of the typographical changes in the hands of Hodson may be examined in the long run of programmes for the Black Bear Music Club, 1789–1807, now Cambridge University Library Cam.a.789.1.

17 E. Chambers, *Cyclopaedia*, 2nd edn (1730), art. 'Letter'.

18 T. B. Reed, *A history of the old English letter foundries*, rev. A. F. Johnson (1952).

19 For Moore, see Reed, *Old English letter foundries*, pp. 299–301. The unique copy of his type specimen of 1768 is reproduced in *Biblis* (1958). The reduced reproduction of the 1766 specimen in D. B. Updike, *Printing types* (Cambridge, Mass., 1922), following p. 118, gives an inferior impression of his work.

20 *Cambridge Chronicle*, 9 July 1763.

21 *Cambridge Chronicle and Journal*, 14 January 1792.

22 John Smith, *The printer's grammar* (1755), pp. 7–8. The remark about French founders is based on M. D. Fertel, *La science pratique de l'imprimerie* (Saint Omer, 1723):

> 'Au sujet du peu de *Relief* de l'œil des Caracteres, nous ne sommes pas surpris si les impressions sont si peu nettes; car pour peu qu'un papier trompe la main de celui qui le trempe, ou soit sujet à s'effleurer; pour tant soit peu qu'un noir soit graveleux & pesant, il n'est pas difficile de conçevoir que l'œil s'emplit, & que l'impression ne peut être nette; l'Imprimeur devient un nouveau Graveur, mais avec une main si peu seure & avec si peu de précaution, qu'il interesse très-souvent le trait ou l'œil de la lettre, plûtôt que d'attaquer avec sa pointe l'amas qui s'est formé dans le creux ou à la circonference. S'il y avoit de la profondeur, comme dans les Caracteres étrangers, les impressions de France seroient certainement plus d'honneur. Nous avons vû des Fontes neuves, dont certaines sortes, considerées du centre de la lettre, n'avoient pas de *Relief* l'épaisseur d'un fort papier ce qui est déplorable.' (pp. 3–4.)

For further quotation from Fertel see also P. Luckombe, *The history and art of printing* (1771), pp. 231–2, and *The printer's grammar* (1787), pp. 15–16.

23 UA Pr. vouchers, 1769/15; Min.VI.1, Syndicate minutes, 29 October 1768.

24 Alexander Wilson to Archdeacon, 1 February 1770; UA Pr. vouchers, 1770/3i.

25 UA Pr. vouchers, 1770/2–3, 10.

26 UA Min.VI.1, Syndicate minutes, 29 April 1771; UA Pr. vouchers, 1771/4: the University paid the bill to John Baine & Son the day after the date of the invoice. For Baine, see Reed, *Old English letter foundries*, pp. 260, 340–1.

27 Caslon's price for nonpareil is noted in UA Pr. vouchers, 1772/2i.

28 Syndicate minutes, 30 October 1781; UA Pr. vouchers, 1782/7i.

29 UA Pr.v.2, Syndicate minutes, 29 April 1783; UA Pr. vouchers, 1783/28i. Wilson allowed fourpence per pound for the old metal.

30 UA Pr. vouchers, 1771/7i; 1772/2i; 1777/8i (and Pr.v.2, Syndicate minutes, 15 June 1776: a retrospective decision); 1780/9i (and Syndicate minutes, 28 October 1779); 1781/19i (and Syndicate minutes, 19 May 1781); 1782/15i. For the totals and proportions of various characters in a pica fount weighing 500 lb, see Smith, *Printer's grammar*, pp. 41–6.

31 UA Pr.v.2, Syndicate minutes, 3 May 1787, 1 May 1788.

32 UA Pr. vouchers, 1771/7i.

33 UA Pr. vouchers, 1785/7i; Pr.v.2, Syndicate minutes, 23 April 1792.

34 See p. 236.

35 Nichols, *Literary anecdotes*, 8, p. 414.

36 In 1755–6 these were Johnson and Unwin, Rowe & Webber, Grosvenor & Webber, Johnson & Unwin, Baker, and Herbert & Durnford. (University Accounts, 1755–6.)

37 For the Sawston mills, see Shorter, *Paper mills*, pp. 147–8, partly following T. F. Teversham, *A history of the village of Sawston* 2 vols. (Sawston, 1942–7) and so misnaming John Vowell as Joseph. The Dernford mill (run by Tassell) was closed by the end of the eighteenth century, and now survives in the name of farm buildings. The Borough mills (run by Fairchild and his successors, and still working in the 1970s) are now an envelope factory.

38 By this date, John Vowell the younger had taken over from his father: see Maxted *London Book Trades*, p. 234. For some of the Vowells's other activities as stationers, see Maslen and Lancaster, *The Bowyer ledgers*.

39 *Cambridge Chronicle and Journal*, 12 September 1778: 'To be sold, an exceeding good freehold paper-mill, adapted to make fine paper, situate at Sarston near Cambridge; the erections are commodious, and in excellent condition, there are two vatts, two engines work'd by seperate water-wheels, and supplied by a plentiful spring of the finest water, the presses are iron and of the best make, the drying lofts are spacious, the vatts, engines and chests lined with lead and in fine order. . .'; *London Evening Post*, May 1780, quoted by Teversham, *Sawston*, 2, p. 145.

40 *Gentleman's Magazine*, 49 (1779), p. 328.

41 *Cambridge Chronicle and Journal*, 17 December 1785.

42 Comparisons were not confined to Cambridge. For a complaint by the Delegates at the paper used in Blayney's edition of the Bible printed at Oxford in 1769, see Carter, *Oxford University Press*, p. 361.

43 UA Min.VI.1, Syndicate minutes, 14 March 1766.

44 UA Min.VI.1, Syndicate minutes, 12 May 1766.

45 UA Min.VI.1, Syndicate minutes, 31 October 1766. On 8 December the Syndics agreed that Bowles should supply the paper for 4,000 copies on ordinary paper, at 15s. a ream, and Tassell that for the 250 copies on large paper, at 39s. a ream. The paper stock book has not survived.

46 UA Pr.V.2, Syndicate minutes, 30 October 1777.

47 The *Cambridge Chronicle and Journal*, 10 January 1767, carried an advertisement for Sarah Baylis, printing ink manufacturer, the Golden Ball, Allen Street, Clerkenwell.

48 UA Pr. vouchers, 1785/24i.

49 R. M. Wiles, *Serial publication in England before 1750* (Cambridge, 1957).

50 Advertised, for example, in the *Cambridge Journal*, 16 March 1745. Walker had obtained a royal licence for this work. For a partial statistical analysis of the increasing numbers of such 'non-standard' Bibles, see Jim Mitchell, 'Bible publishing in eighteenth-century Britain', *Factotum*, 20 (1985), pp. 11–19.

51 Herbert, *Historical catalogue*, 1125 and 1126.

52 *Cambridge Chronicle*, 24 March 1764; publication of this version was to commence on 31 March.

53 *Cambridge Chronicle*, 18 August 1764.

54 *Cambridge Chronicle*, 2 March 1765. Publication was advertised to begin on 23 February, the first number costing threeepence rather than sixpence.

55 *Cambridge Chronicle*, 13 April 1765.

56 Gaskell, *John Baskerville*, p. 45; L. W. Hanson, review of this book in *The Library*, 5th ser. 15 (1960), pp. 139–40.

57 Details taken from Herbert, *Historical catalogue*, who lists only a selection of the many 'family' and other annotated Bibles printed during these years.

58 See above, p. 194; UA Min.VI.1, Syndicate minutes, 28 October and 7 November 1765. A single year of accounts for the agents individually survives for 1766–7: UA Pr.P.2. A page of those relating to Rivington is reproduced in Roberts, *History*, p. 114.

59 Cf. Samuel Johnson's summary in 1776 of the press at Oxford and its relationship to its London agent Thomas Cadell and to the retail trade:

> It is perhaps not considered through how many hands a Book often passes, before it comes into those of the reader, or what part of the profit each hand must retain as a motive for transmitting it to the next.
>
> We will call our primary Agent in London Mr. Cadel who receives our books from us, gives them room in his warehouse and issues them on demand. By him they are sold to Mr. Dilly a wholesale Bookseller who sends them into the Country, and the last seller is the Country Bookseller. Here are three profits to be paid

between the Printer and the Reader, or in the stile of commerce between the Manufacturer and the Consumer; and if any of these profits is too penuriously distributed the process of commerce is intercepted.

Johnson considered that the press should allow 30 to 35 per cent profit; that is, a book priced at one pound should be sold to Cadell at about 14s. The distribution would then fall as follows:

> Mr. Cadel who runs no hazard and gives no credit will be paid for warehouse room and attendance by a shilling profit on each Book, and his chance of the quarterly Book [i.e. 104 delivered for each hundred].
>
> Mr. Dilly who buys the Book for fifteen shillings and who will expect the quarterly book if he takes five and twenty will sell it to his country customer at sixteen and sixpence by which at the hazard of loss and the certainty of long credit, he gains the regular profit of ten per cent which is expected in the wholesale trade.
>
> The Country Bookseller buying at Sixteen and Sixpence and commonly trusting a considerable time gains but three and sixpence, and if he trusts a year, not much more than two and sixpence, otherwise than as he may perhaps take as long credit as he gives. (Samuel Johnson to Nathan Wetherell, 12 March 1776: Johnson, *Letters*, 2, pp. 306–8.)

For further comment, see John Feather, *The provincial book trade in eighteenth-century England* (Cambridge, 1985), pp. 56–7. Johnson's account is very much simplified so as to describe the process clearly. In practice many variations were familiar.

60 UA Min.VI.1, Syndicate minutes, 22 October 1767. This clear record, that copies (by implication a substantial number, since it would not have been worth specifying an agreement for only a handful) remained of the 1762 Bible in 1767, makes the celebrated note concerning the rarity of this Bible as a consequence of a fire in Dod's warehouse (see Scrivener, *The Authorized edition of the English Bible* (Cambridge, 1884), p. 29) seem all the more the product of misinformation or imagination. See above, p. 192 and note.

61 UA Min.VI.1, Syndicate minutes, 2 April 1768.

62 UA Min.VI.1, Syndicate minutes, 26 May 1768.

63 UA Pr.v.2, Syndicate minutes, 2 November 1776.

64 UA Min.VI.1, Syndicate minutes, 28 October 1771; Pr.v.2, 26 October 1773. Charles Dilly succeeded Edward Dilly as agent in 1779 and John Fielding succeeded Beecroft in 1781 (Syndicate minutes, 28 October 1779, 19 May 1781). Fielding was bankrupt in 1783.

65 Carter, *Oxford University Press*, pp. 344–52.

66 *Ibid.*, pp. 352–5. The first English New Testament to be printed in America was probably printed by Aitken at Philadelphia in 1777; further editions followed from Aitken's press in 1778, 1779 and 1781, and in 1781–2 he printed his first Bible. But see also Herbert, *Historical catalogue*, pp. 272–3.

67 Carter, *Oxford University Press*, p. viii.

68 UA Pr.v.2, Syndicate minutes, 20 November 1782. For the reform of duties on paper (21 Geo. III c.24), see Coleman, *British paper industry*, p. 133.

69 UA Pr.v.2, Syndicate minutes, 27 January 1783.

70 These dates are taken from Herbert, *Historical catalogue*. While Herbert is in many respects invaluable, his work should be used with caution. In particular (to concentrate on this occasion on but two points) there are inevitable omissions, and some of the formats given as duodecimo should be described as 24°. See also B. J. McMullin, 'Towards a bibliography of the Oxford and Cambridge University Bible presses in the seventeenth and eighteenth centuries', *Bibliographical Society of Australia and New Zealand Bulletin*, 14 (1990 [1991]), pp. 51–73.

71 'Edition' could of course encompass a wide divergence in quantities. At this time, editions of the Cambridge quarto Bible consisted of 4,000 to 5,000 copies.

72 Reviewed by George Walker (see *DNB*) in the *Monthly Review*, 42 (1770), pp. 391–4: see also below, p. 229.

73 UA Pr.v.2, Syndicate minutes, 13 April 1785. No such limitation had been stipulated when he was appointed in 1766: Min.VI.1, Syndicate minutes, 29 October 1766.

74 Thomas Davies to James Granger, 5 January 1753, *Letters between the Rev. James Granger . . . and . . . literary men*, p. 55. On reviews, Davies commented in the same letter, 'We have sold, I believe, no more

than about 100 [of a sermon by Granger] at most, though the Monthly and Critical Reviews have done themselves honour, in bestowing very ample praise upon the "Apology for the Brute Creation".'

75 *Cantabrigia depicta* (Cambridge [1763]), p. 113 and *Cantabrigia depicta*, new edn (1781), p. 113. Gillam's invoices are among the annual series of Vouchers.

76 UA Min.VI.1, Syndicate minutes, 2 April 1768.

77 The largest consignments were sent to Rivington and to Beecroft. It cannot be established from these lists whether any or part of the consignments sent to Dilly were destined for the American colonies, with which the firm had close contacts: cf. L. H. Butterfield, 'The American interests of the firm of E. and C. Dilly, with their letters to Benjamin Rush, 1770–1795', *PBSA*, 45 (1951), pp. 283–332.

78 For one aspect of the Merrills' association with the Scottish booksellers, see *Petitions and papers relating to the bill of the booksellers, now before the House of Commons* (1774).

79 UA Pr. vouchers, 1767/40. For early fund-raising, and legislation for the charity, see Cooper, *Annals*, pp. 342, 344–50.

80 UA Pr. vouchers, 1773/13i. The Regius Professor of Modern History at this time was the recently admitted successor to Thomas Gray, John Symonds.

81 UA Pr. vouchers, 1786/18i.

82 See above, pp. 213–14.

83 UA Pr. vouchers, 1782/201.

84 21 Geo. III c.56; Cooper, *Annals*, 4, p. 401; Clark, *Endowments*, pp. 47–8; *Enactments in Parliament*, 2, pp. 183–5. Grace Book Λ, p. 121.

85 21 Geo. III c.24; *Enactments in Parliament*, 2, pp. 166–8.

86 *Monthly Review*, 42 (1770), pp. 391–4, at p. 391. Cf. B. C. Nangle, *The Monthly Review; first series, 1749–1789; indexes of contributors and articles* (Oxford, 1934), p. 45.

87 UA Pr.v.2 ('Orders for the Press'), Pr.v.3 (accounts).

88 McKitterick, *Cambridge University Library*, pp. 326–34. The Syndics had been prepared to spend £500 at the Askew sale, the whole of their annual allocation.

89 Relhan's *Flora* was republished in 1802, and again in 1820. The illustrations were by James Bolton of Halifax (d. 1799), whose original drawings are in King's College library. Cf. G. C. Gorham, *Memoirs of John Martyn, F. R. S., and of Thomas Martyn, B. D., F. R. S., F. L. S.* (1830), pp. 124–7; B. Henrey, *British botanical and horticultural history before 1800*, 3 vols. (Oxford, 1975), pp. 138–40 and Roy Watling and Mark R. D. Seaward, 'James Bolton: mycological pioneer', *Archives of Natural History*, 10 (1981), pp. 89–110.

90 *Monthly Review*, 72 (1785), pp. 56–63. Porson's name was spelled Pawson.

91 G. C. Gorham, *Memoirs of John Martyn and of Thomas Martyn* (1830), pp. 165–8. The members included J. D. Carlyle, Busick Harwood, Thomas Martyn, Milner, Porson, Relhan and Vince. Printed papers by Vince and Martyn are in Queens' College Library, Gg.1.42.

92 UA Pr.v.2, Orders for the Press, 2 November 1782; J. S. Watson, *The life of Richard Porson, M. A.* (1861), pp. 38–40, quoting Porson's quip about one of the syndics: 'I have heard of a learned Doctor in our University who confounded the *collection* with the *collation* of manuscripts.' Stanley's notes, on which the Syndics required that the new edition would be founded, had been in the University Library since 1715: McKitterick, *Cambridge University Library*, p. 129.

93 *Gentleman's Magazine*, 55 (April 1785), p. 284.

94 UA Pr. vouchers, 1782/15i, 1784/3i,1785/1,11.

95 UA Pr.v.2, Orders for the Press, 2 November 1782. Edwards was to deliver copy for the first volume by Christmas 1784.

96 See below, pp. 291–2.

97 G. Atwood, *A treatise on the rectilinear motion* (Cambridge, 1784), p. xv; summary of almanac duty expenditure, 23 June 1784. The comments in the following sentences are drawn from the respective prefaces.

98 William Falconer, *Miscellaneous tracts and collections relating to natural history, selected from the principal writers of antiquity on that subject* (Cambridge, 1793), advertisement.

99 For Isola, who taught Italian at Cambridge from 1764, cf. June Sturrock, 'Wordsworth's Italian teacher', *Bulletin of the John Rylands Library*, 67 (1985), pp. 787–812.

100 Watson's career as a chemist is described in L. J. M. Coleby, 'Richard Watson, Professor of Chemistry in the University of Cambridge, 1764–71', *Annals of Science* 9 (1953), pp. 101–23.

101 UA Pr.v.2, Orders for the Press, 24 January 1789.

102 Gilbert Wakefield, *Memoirs of the life of Gilbert Wakefield* (1792), pp. 286–7. The Press's reader of the third part of his *Silva critica* was James Fawcett of St John's (Syndicate minutes, 21 October 1791).

103 *Introduction to the New Testament . . .* trans. from the fourth edition of the German and considerably augmented with notes . . . by Herbert Marsh (1793–1801). The reviewer in the *British Critic*, while acknowledging how little England knew of German theology, and therefore praising the significance of Marsh's work, nonetheless found opportunity to criticise him as well as offer encouragement (*British Critic*, 3 (1794), pp. 601–8, 4 (1794), pp. 46–54, 170–6).

104 J. D. Carlyle, *Maured Allatafet Jemaleddini filii Togri-Bardii, seu rerum Aegyptiacarum annales* (1792).

105 A part of the difficulty lay in the fact that the project entailed collating manuscripts in Venice (Orders for the Press, 29 June 1787). The *Moralia* were published in quarto, in eight volumes, by the Oxford press in 1795–1830.

106 Thomas Simpson Evans (1777–1818), who worked at the Greenwich Royal Observatory with Nevil Maskelyne, annotated his copy, sometimes unfavourably, and changed the title-page so as to read 'By the planet Dr. Maskelyne & his satellite Rev. S. Vince.' (Copy offered by the bookseller James Burmester, catalogue 30 (1995), item 217).

107 Wakefield prefaced the fourth part of *Silva critica* with a long valediction.

108 UA Pr.v.2, Orders for the Press, 25 February 1786, 4 July 1785. Gunning gives an unflattering picture of Tunstall, 'the idlest of the idle': Gunning, *Reminiscences*, 1, pp. 33–8.

109 Herbert Marsh, *An essay on the usefulness and necessity of theological learning, to those who are designed for holy orders* (Cambridge, 1792), verso of title-page. Gilbert Wakefield likewise complained of the poor preparation offered for the ministry (*Memoirs of the life of Gilbert Wakefield* (1792), pp. 349–54).

110 UA Pr.v.2, Orders for the Press, 30 November 1784, agreeing to meet the whole expense of paper and presswork; *Alma mater; or, seven years at the University of Cambridge*, 2 vols. (1827), 1, p. 163.

111 [William Frend], *Considerations on the oaths required by the University of Cambridge* (1787), p. 39.

112 [William Heberden], *Strictures upon the discipline of the University of Cambridge* (1792), pp. 47–8. The attribution to one of the Heberdens, of St John's, is on Francis Wrangham's copy of this pamphlet. William Heberden, the physician (1710–1801) as well as three of his sons, Thomas, William and Charles, were all members of the college.

113 This was published anonymously.

114 But he failed in 1788 to be elected to the Lady Margaret Professorship. The fullest account of his career is in Scott, *Admissions to the College of St John the Evangelist*, 3 (Cambridge, 1903), pp. 698–700.

115 Reed, *Old English letter foundries*, pp. 192–5, 315, 316.

116 UA Pr.v.2, Orders for the Press, 24 May 1786.

117 Thomas Astle, *The origin and progress of writing* (1784), tab. V.

118 These figures, quoted by Bayly to the Society of Antiquaries when they were considering the matter in 1767–8, are printed in Sir Henry Ellis's introduction to Domesday Book, 4 (1816), p. cvi.

119 *Gentleman's Magazine*, 56 (1786), pp. 497–8.

120 John Nichols, *Biographical and literary anecdotes of William Bowyer* (1782), pp. 318–19.

121 UA Pr.v.2, Orders for the Press, 24 May, 27 June 1786, 1 February, 30 March 1787.

122 UA Pr. vouchers, 1787/22ai; Almanac fund expenditure accounts, 25 June 1788. The size of the order in proportion to business between Whatman and Gill may be judged partly by the fact that in 1787 Whatman's sales to Gill amounted in all to £4,789 (Thomas Balston, *James Whatman, father & son* (1957), p. 52). The two super royal moulds made for Whatman in July 1786 (*ibid.*, p. 60) were perhaps to meet Kipling's order.

123 UA Pr. vouchers, 1789/3. The invoice quotes the size of the vellum sheets as 19¼ x 13¼ inches: they

were trimmed slightly in binding. George III's copy on vellum is now in the British Library, C.11.e.7–8.

124 Incomplete sets of the punches for the English sizes of Greek and Latin, with some type in English, double pica (small face) and brevier, are now in the University Library.

125 UA Pr. vouchers, 1788/4, 5, 1791/15i.

126 For Watson, see Winstanley, *Unreformed Cambridge*; for Frend, see *An account of the proceedings in the University of Cambridge against William Frend* (Cambridge, 1793), Frida Knight, *University rebel; the life of William Frend (1757–1841)* (1971) and Cooper, *Annals*, 4, pp. 447–50; for the editing and reception of the *Codex Bezae*, see McKitterick, *Cambridge University Library*, pp. 339–42.

127 The binding of the Copenhagen copy is illustrated in A. B. Gray, *John Bowtell, bookbinder of Cambridge* (Cambridge Antiquarian Soc., 11 (1907), pp. 346–84, pl. 25).

128 For one review, see the (Pisa) *Giornale de'Letterati*, 95 (1794), pp. 128–38; the *Codex Alexandrinus* had been reviewed in the same volume, pp. 107–27.

129 UA Pr.v.2, Orders for the Press, 21 June 1793.

130 *Gentleman's Magazine*, 57 (1787), p. 572,

131 *Gentleman's Magazine*, 58 (1788), p. 682.

132 'Cantabrigiensis' in *Gentleman's Magazine*, 58 (1788), pp. 875–7. Porson's 'quiet vein of irony' is discussed appreciatively in H. R. Luard, 'Porson', *Cambridge essays* (1857), pp. 125–71.

133 *Gentleman's Magazine*, 57 (1787), pp. 87–8.

134 *Gentleman's Magazine*, 63 (1793), pp. 732–3.

135 *British Critic*, 3 (1794), pp. 139–47, 361–73.

136 *Ibid.*, p. 139.

137 Cf. also the more recent work of Joseph Strutt: see A. N. L. Munby, *Connoisseurs and medieval miniatures, 1750–1850* (Oxford, 1972), pp. 28–30.

138 *British Critic*, 3 (1794), p. 140.

139 UA Pr.v.2, Orders for the Press, 10 January 1783.

140 George Atwood, *Compendio d'un corso di lezioni di fisica sperimentale ad uso del Collegio della Trinità, e dell' Università di Cambridge*, trans. Gregorio Fontana (Pavia, 1781).

141 UA Pr.v.2, Orders for the Press, 23 February 1784.

142 The copy in Trinity College is a presentation copy; that in the University Library is on large paper. As usual, sheets for the large paper copies appear to have been printed after the ordinary ones.

143 Notes by R. Plumptre, February 1785: Bodleian Library, MS Gough Camb.70, f.14.

144 Details are set out in the appendix.

145 UA UP.2(17), untitled leaflet by R. Plumptre, 1785.

146 UA Pr.v.2, Syndicate minutes, 26 October 1773, 21 October 1774, 29 October 1774 (dismissal of Baily; appointment of Joseph Gee), 2 November 1776, 27 June 1783. Gee was dismissed in 1785, and was succeeded by Robert Rankin (Syndicate minutes, 17 January 1785); on Rankin's resignation in 1792 the Syndics appointed Robert Collings. Until then the warehouse keeper had been allowed perquisites and wages of 12s.6d. per week; in 1792 perquisites were abolished, and wages were increased to fifteen shillings (Syndicate minutes 27 April 1792). The duties of warehouse keeper are described in P. Luckombe, *The history and art of printing* (1771), pp. 487–94.

147 Cf. Charles Johnstone, *Chrysal, or the adventures of a guinea* (first published in 1760), ch. xx.

> 'Now you speak of titles, I want half a dozen directly, this very day, if possible!'
> 'It is rather too late now, but where are the books?'
> 'In the lumber garret, where they have lain this seven years.'
> 'That's well; they are forgot by this.'
> 'Forgot! Why, they were never known! The author was a man of fortune, who printed them at his own expense, but I prevented the sale, and so had them for the publishing, ha! ha! ha! besides a good consideration for buying up at a double price what I had *not* sold of them; so that it was not a bad job, and now he is dead they may safely come out under new titles.'

148 John Peile, *Biographical register of Christ's College*, 2 vols. (Cambridge, 1910–13), 2, p. 241.

149 UA Pr.v.2, Syndicate minutes, 20 October 1782. As Plumian Professor, Shepherd was formally a Syndic of the Press, but he did not usually attend meetings.

150 Michael J. Murphy, *Cambridge newspapers and opinion, 1780–1850* (Cambridge, 1978), pp. 24–30.

151 William Zachs, '"An illiterate fellow of a bookseller": John Murray and his authors, 1768–1793', in R. Myers and M. Harris (ed.), *A genius for letters; booksellers and bookselling from the 16th to the 20th century* (Winchester, 1995), pp. 123–43.

152 François Barletti de Saint-Paul, *Nouveau système typographique* (Paris, 1776); Henry Johnson, *An introduction to logography* (1783); John Feather, 'John Walter and the Logographic Press', *Publishing History*, 1 (1977), pp. 92–134.

153 *Biographical memoirs of William Ged*, ed. John Nichols (1781); *Patents for inventions; abridgements of the specifications relating to printing* (1859), pp. 93–5; George A. Kubler, *A new history of stereotyping* (New York, 1941).

154 *Patents for inventions*, p. 88 (1771).

155 Etienne Alexandre Jacques Anisson-Duperron, *Description d'une nouvelle presse* (Paris, 1783); David Chambers, 'An improved printing press by Philippe-Denis Pierres', *JPHS*, 3 (1967), pp. 82–92; James Moran, *Printing presses* (1973), pp. 41–2; James Mosley, 'The Stanhope Press', in Horace Hart, *Charles Earl Stanhope and the Oxford University Press*, ed. J. Mosley (1966), pp. xx–xxi.

156 *Patents for inventions*, pp. 97–100 (1790); *Repertory of Arts and Manufactures*, 5 (1796), pp. 145–70; Moran, *Printing presses*, pp. 101–4; see also below, p. 264.

157 M. Audin, 'De l'origine du papier vélin', *Gutenberg Jahrbuch*, 1928, pp. 69–86.

158 Stanley Morison, *John Bell, 1745–1831* (Cambridge, 1930), 'Address to the world', following p. 16.

159 A. F. Johnson, *Type designs* (1959), pp. 62–8; J. Veyrin-Forrer, 'Les premiers caractères de François-Ambroise Didot (1781–1785)', *Mélanges d'histoire du livre et des bibliothèques offerts à Monsieur Franz Calot* (Paris, 1960), pp. 67–82, repr. in her *La lettre et le texte* (Paris, 1987), pp. 121–38, and J. Veyrin-Forrer, 'Les caractères de Pierre-François Didot (1783–1790)', *Gutenberg Jahrbuch*, 1962, pp. 57–67, repr. in *La lettre et le texte*, pp. 139–57.

160 Morison, *John Bell*, p. 23, and [Morison], *Richard Austin* (Cambridge, 1937).

12 John Burges

1 Cooper, *Annals*, 4, pp. 433 (1789), 442 (1791), 453 (1795), 464, 469(1800).

2 *Ibid.*, p. 443 (1792), 454–5 (1795), 466–7, 469 (1800).

3 *Ibid.*, pp. 450–1, 453, 458–61.

4 1 July 1793: UA Grace Book Λ, p. 290. On 21 May the Syndics agreed that in the event of Burges's election, the annual profits from the printing house should be divided so that Archdeacon should receive four parts to Burges's five.

5 Ian Maxted, *The British book trade, 1710–1777; an index of masters and apprentices recorded in the Inland Revenue registers at the Public Record Office* (Exeter, 1983), p. 2. He had been recorded as an inhabitant of St Botolph's parish since at least 1776: Bowes, 'Biographical notes on University Printers', *Cambridge Antiquarian Soc. Communications* 5, (1866), p. 321.

6 *Cambridge Intelligencer*, 19 September 1795; Bowes, 'Biographical notes', p. 321. Burges had passed a bill from Caslon for payment on 11 December 1789.

7 UA Pr. vouchers, 1797/3i; presumably this was the press approved (therefore retrospectively) by the Syndics the following October.

8 UA CUP 23/1.

9 Cf. Glenn Hueckel, 'War and the British economy, 1793–1815; a general equilibrium analysis', *Explorations in Economic History*, 10 (1973), pp. 365–96.

10 *Cambridge Chronicle*, 17 December 1785. Deighton was succeeded briefly at his Cambridge address by John Vowell, a stationer more than a bookseller, though he had some stock: see advertisements in the *Cambridge Chronicle*, 25 March 1786 (Isola). For Cater, see Nichols, *Literary anecdotes*, 3, pp. 634–5, and Maxted, *London book trades*.

11 *Cambridge Chronicle and Journal*, 4 October 1794.

12 A copy of the 1792 catalogue is in the Houghton Library, Harvard University. Deighton announced in it his recent removal from 274 to 325 Holborn.

13 *Love's labour's lost* (1598); *Much ado about nothing* (1600) and *The merchant of Venice* (1600). There is a copy of this catalogue in the John Rylands University Library.

14 *Cambridge Chronicle*, 6 January 1787, 13 October 1787, 17 December 1792, 4 February 1797 (removal to 332 Oxford Street, announced for 10 March). For a time after moving to London, he retained his old Cambridge premises as a warehouse, staffed part-time during term, but this was given up in 1799 (*Cambridge Chronicle*, 11 November 1797, 2 November 1799). The sale of his stock and of the lease of his shop in Oxford Street was announced in the *Cambridge Chronicle*, 23 February 1799; but Leigh and Sotheby sold his stock only in January 1802, the year in which he established a 'classical library' at 30 Soho Square (Maxted, *London book trades*, p. 143). In July 1813 he advertised unsuccessfully for a successor, but he was still at Soho Square when he died in summer 1815 (*Monthly Literary Advertiser*, July 1813, February and August ('the late Mr. Lunn') 1815).

15 James Lackington, *Memoirs of the forty-five first years of the life of James Lackington*, 9th edn (1794), pp. 210–12.

16 *Cambridge Chronicle*, 4 October 1794.

17 *Cambridge Chronicle*, 24 October 1801; Cooper, *Annals*, 4, p. 483; McKitterick, *Cambridge University Library*, p. 359.

18 *A guide through the University of Cambridge* (Cambridge [1803]), advertisement on cover.

19 *Cambridge Chronicle*, 1 November 1794.

20 *Cambridge Chronicle*, 20 August 1796.

21 Gee took over this business from W. Cowper in July 1794: *Cambridge Chronicle*, 2 August 1794.

22 *The new Cambridge guide* (Cambridge, 1804), p. 98.

23 A. B. Gray, 'John Bowtell: bookbinder of Cambridge (1753–1813)', *Cambridge Antiquarian Soc. Proceedings*, 11 (1907), pp. 346–84; *Cambridge Chronicle*, 21 March 1789; McKitterick, *Cambridge University Library*, pp. 310, 312–14.

24 George Pryme, *Autobiographic recollections* (Cambridge, 1870), p. 92.

25 A list of Deighton's publications was bound up with *A guide through the University of Cambridge* [1803].

26 Michael J. Murphy, *Cambridge newspapers and opinion, 1780–1850* (Cambridge, 1977), pp. 24–42.

27 *Monthly Review*, 2nd ser. 8 (1792), pp. 270–85; B. C. Nangle, *The Monthly Review; second series, 1790–1815; index of contributors and articles* (Oxford, 1955), p. 52.

28 *An account of the proceedings in the University of Cambridge, against William Frend* (Cambridge: printed by Benjamin Flower, 1793); John Beverley, *The trial of William Frend* (Cambridge [1793]); John Beverley, *The proceedings in the Court of Delegates on the appeal of Wm. Frend* (Cambridge [1793]); Cooper, *Annals*, 4, pp. 447–50; Frida Knight, *University rebel; the life of William Frend (1757–1841)* (1971). Glimpses of Frend's later life are in a book by his daughter, Sophia Elizabeth de Morgan, *Memoir of Augustus de Morgan* (1882).

29 In Bridge Street, near Holy Trinity Church: *Cambridge Chronicle and Journal*, 31 May 1800.

30 Coleridge to Thomas Poole, 26 December 1796: *Collected letters*, ed. F. L. Griggs, 6 vols. (Oxford, 1956–71), I, pp. 166–7. See also Nicholas Roe, *Wordsworth and Coleridge: the radical years* (Oxford, 1988).

31 *Annual register*, 1793, pp. 34*, 48*.

32 See the following chapter.

33 T. F. Dibdin, *An introduction to the knowledge of rare and valuable editions of the Greek and Roman classics* (Glocester, 1802), pp. v–vi.

34 Now in the British Library, 11707.dd.14. A further leaf on vellum survives in one of the copies in Trinity College, Cambridge: see H. R. Luard, 'Porson', *Cambridge essays* (1857), pp. 125–71, at p. 161. Luard draws attention (p.165) to the Grenville Homer, published at Oxford in 1801, while Porson was

at work on Euripides: copies were issued on large and ordinary paper, and twenty-five of the large paper copies were supplemented by twenty-two additional leaves containing 'a few extra various readings': for payment to Porson in this, see Percy Simpson, *Proof-reading in the sixteenth, seventeenth and eighteenth centuries* (Oxford, 1935), p. 217.

35 Luard, 'Porson', p. 153; Philip Gaskell, *A bibliography of the Foulis Press*, 2nd edn (Winchester, 1986), pp. 386–7.

36 Peter Isaac, *William Bulmer, the fine printer in context, 1750–1830* (Biddenden, 1993).

37 See below, pp. 270–1.

38 T. F. Dibdin, *The bibliomania; or book-madness* (1809), pp. 54–68.

39 UA Pr. vouchers, 1794/15i.

40 UA Pr.v.2, Syndicate minutes, 28 October 1795. Edmund Fry had shown his new diamond type, 'the smallest letter in the world', in his specimen of 1785, but it was hardly practicable for printing the Bible with the presses currently available, and prolonged reading would have imposed intolerable strain on readers.

41 UA Pr. vouchers, 1796/10i; 1797/5. The price of Grosvenor & Chater's wove may be compared with the cost of the more ordinary royal paper supplied from Thetford in 1798–9, charged at 16s.6d. and 17s.9d. a ream (UA Pr. vouchers, 1799/10i).

42 UA Pr.v.2, Syndicate minutes, 24 February 1796. It was supplied by William Bulmer: 'To an Iron Screw Hotpress, with brass box, complete, & iron pulling Pin, packing &c. – To an Hotpress oven, with fitting up doors, & 15 Iron Press Plates complete, To 11 Gross of glazed Pasteboards, freighted & cartage, & 2¼ dozen of pasteboard Fences. &c &c – £103.18.0'.

43 *Cambridge Intelligencer*, 14 June 1794. By 1796, Lunn was offering the superior edition of the Rowley poems at 9s. (*Cambridge Chronicle and Journal*, 5 March 1796).

44 *Cambridge Chronicle and Journal*, 25 April 1795. It was advertised by W. H. Lunn and John Deighton.

45 A copy of the Syndics' notice is in King's College Library, MS Lib.12, p. 75. The project foundered with the first volume.

46 Grosvenor & Chater to Burges, 13 January 1797: UA Pr. vouchers, 1797/4.

47 See, for example, the advertisements for John Holloway, *Principles of animal magnetism* (*Cambridge Chronicle and Journal*, 20 November 1790), Rollin's edition of Quintilian (*ibid.*, 3 March 1792).

48 Prices for 1796 are taken from the Syndics' minutes, 7 June 1796. For Baskerville, see Gaskell, *John Baskerville*, pp. 30–3: Baskerville's octavo prayer books, set in great primer and English, had the prices printed on the title-pages, ranging from 6s.6d. to 8s.6d.

49 UA Pr.v.2, Syndicate minutes, 2 November 1798, 1 March, 22 June 1799, 1 November 1800; CUR 33.1(44).

50 UA Pr.v.2, Syndicate minutes, 21 May, 29 June 1798.

51 The Thetford paper-maker was R. Pawson: UA Pr. vouchers, 1798/24, 1799/10 etc., listing consignments from August 1798 onwards, for the privileged books. See Shorter, *Paper mills*, p. 219. Thetford and Cambridge are linked by the Little Ouse, which joins the River Cam about three miles north of Littleport.

52 Bible and prayer book stock book, UA CUP 35/1; Pr.v.2, Syndicate minutes, 15 November 1800.

53 *Report from the Committee on the booksellers and printers petition* (Parliamentary papers, 1801–2, ii, pp. 89–129, p. 14 (internal numbering). Cf. Lee Erickson, *The economy of literary form* (Baltimore, 1996), p. 20n.

54 Coleman records that in Whatman's ledger for 1780–7, the amount paid in excise duty in 1781 was approximately 4 per cent of total production expenditure, and in 1785 it was 22 per cent. Between 1770 and 1800, in the country as a whole, 'the output of paper rather less than doubled, whilst the yield of the duty multiplied just over eleven-fold'. (*British paper industry*, pp. 140–2.)

55 Timperley, *Encyclopaedia of literary and typographical anecdote* (1842), 2, pp. 790–1; Herbert, *Historical catalogue*, 1377.

56 Herbert, *Historical catalogue*, 1390 (1795), 1411 (1796). Timperley (*Encyclopaedia*, pp. 790–1) considered Ritchie 'the father of English fine printing'.

57 UA Pr.v.2, Syndicate minutes, 13 May 1795. Joseph Jowett was a great-uncle of Benjamin Jowett: see Evelyn Abbott and Lewis Campbell, *The life and letters of Benjamin Jowett*, 2 vols. (1897), 1, pp. 7–8.

58 The complete list of prices is in UA Pr.v.2, Syndicate minutes, 22 February 1800; they may be compared with the similar list, 7 June 1796.

59 UA Pr.v.2, Syndicate minutes, 1 November 1800.

60 See, for example, the annotated Bible printed by J. W. Pasham in London in 1776 (Herbert 1249): Herbert includes other similar examples of 1790 (T. Rickaby, London, no. 1346), 1792 (Darton and Harvey, London, no. 1371), 1796 (R. Bowyer, London, no. 1405), 1800 (C. Corrall, London, no. 1447) and 1803 (John Fenley, Bristol, no. 1467): see also the ingenuous and disarming remarks on the 'pretence of notes . . . placed there merely as a cover to the piracy of printing' included in the Bible printed for Reeves in 1802 (Herbert no. 1457).

61 UA Pr.v.2, Syndicate minutes, 1 November 1800, 10 December 1801, 5 February 1802, 12 February 1803.

62 Coleman, *British paper industry*, p. 127.

63 Details are set out in Appendix 1, below.

64 UA Pr.v.2, Syndicate minutes, 26 December 1792. The heads of agreement concerning compositors' pay, reached by the London master-printers in 1785, were copied into the minute book. See also Howe, *London compositor*, pp. 72–4 and Appendix 1, below.

65 Bible and prayer book stock book, UA CUP 35/1; CUP 23/1. Yet for some reason the duodecimo brevier New Testament, printed in editions of 20,000 in most years during the 1790s, was still printed three times in the same sized edition in 1802, 1803 and 1804.

66 UA Pr.v.2, Syndicate minutes, 22 November 1799. For Dilly's business at 22 Poultry, see Maxted, *London book trades*, p. 66. The Syndics appointed Deighton on 15 May 1801.

67 Apart from advertisements in his books, Mawman's full-page advertisements in the *Monthly Literary Advertiser*, October 1815 and October 1817, provide a useful introduction to his list. For Clarke, see William Otter, *The life and remains of Edward Daniel Clarke*, 2 vols. (1825).

68 All these figures are taken from UA CUP 23/1.

69 J. A. Venn, *Oxford and Cambridge matriculations (1544–1906)* (Cambridge, 1908).

70 UA CUP 23/1.

13 *Richard Watts and the beginning of stereotyping*

1 The standard biography remains that by his niece, Mary Milner, *The life of Isaac Milner, D. D., F. R. S. . . .* (1842). Gunning, *Reminiscences*, 1, pp. 257–76, remarks his despotic behaviour as President of Queens'. For an unsympathetic summary, see John Twigg, *A history of Queens' College, Cambridge, 1448–1986* (Woodbridge, 1987), pp. 181–3. For his evangelical leanings, see Ford K. Brown, *Fathers of the Victorians; the age of Wilberforce* (Cambridge, 1961), pp. 289–92.

2 He was buried at St Botolph's, the parish church.

3 Details of Milner's search are taken from UA Pr.v.27.

4 *Report from the Committee on the booksellers and printers petition* (1802) Parliamentary papers 1801–2, ii, pp. 89–129; Giles Barber, 'J. J. Tourneisen of Basle and the publication of English books on the Continent *c.* 1800', *The Library*, 3rd ser. 15 (1960), pp. 193–200.

5 UA Grace Book Λ, p. 413 (Deighton appointment), p. 425 (Watts). Pr.v.2, Syndicate minutes, 1 May 1802 (appointment of Eadson and Smith).

6 UA Pr.v.2, Syndicate minutes, 1 May 1802.

7 For the third Earl Stanhope more generally, see especially Aubrey Newman, *The Stanhopes of Chevening; a family biography* (1969).

8 Wilson to the Vice-Chancellor (Joseph Procter), 27 October 1802: UA Pr. vouchers, 1802/20. Wilson charged 20 guineas for his expenses in connection with this survey (UA Pr. vouchers, 1802/21A).

9 See above, p. 245.

10 UA Pr. vouchers, 1798/25.

11 UA CUP 23/1: the changes date from 1 January 1803.

12 UA Pr. vouchers, 1803/15, 1803/25.

13 'To a New Crown Press with best Ribs & Cramps . . . with one Pull', UA Pr. vouchers, 1803/29, 1803/29i; 1797/3 (describing it merely as 'large').

14 McKitterick, *Cambridge University Press*, 1, pp. 313, 316.

15 Willis and Clark 3, p. 133.

16 University accounts, 1785–6; Willis and Clark, 3, p. 134.

17 UA Pr. vouchers, 1797/28, 1799/29.

18 Details of names from UA CUP 23/1. There is not space here for the kind of detailed analysis that this volume permits concerning the composition and printing of each book, on a scale comparable with McKenzie's account of the first years of the Press.

19 UA Pr. vouchers, 1798/8.

20 Details, again, from UA CUP 23/1.

21 Copy in Trinity College library, T.10.18(2).

22 UA CUP 23/1.

23 Howe, *London compositor*, pp. 69–83 (London compositors' scales, 1785–1805) and 95–109 (pressmen's scales, 1794–1816).

24 *Patents for inventions; abridgements of the specifications relating to printing* (1859), pp. 97–100, 101–2. See also p. 244.

25 John Feather, 'John Walter and the Logographic Press', *Publishing History*, 1 (1977), pp. 92–134. In October 1780 Henry Johnson took out a patent for casting words or parts of words, 'whereby every species of printing may be executed in one fourth of the time in which they have been usually executed, and consequently at much less expense' (*Patents for inventions*, p. 91).

26 *Monthly Review*, 70 (1784), p. 221.

27 Baron van Westreenen van Tiellandt, *Verslag der naspooringen, omtrent de oorspronkelijke uitvinding en het vroegste gebruik der stereotypische drukwijze* ('s Gravenhage, 1833), trans. with other accounts of the same subject in George A. Kubler, *Historical treatises, abstracts & papers on stereotyping* (New York, 1936).

28 Edward Rowe Mores, *A dissertation upon English typographical founders and founderies* (Oxford, 1961), p. 55.

29 *Patents for inventions*, pp. 93–5.

30 Jean Lafaure, *Les assignats et les papier-monnaies émis par l'état au XVIIIe siècle* (Paris, 1981); A. G. Camus, *Histoire et procédés du polytypage et du stéréotypage* (Paris, 1802).

31 Lort's copy of Henry Johnson, *An introduction to logography* (1783), bound up with the *Biographical memoirs of William Ged* (1781), a broadside by Walter (December 1788), various other cuttings relating to Walter and Richard Cumberland, and a copy of the 1730s Cambridge broadside relating to Fenner, was sold by E. P. Goldschmidt to *The Times* (Goldschmidt catalogue 100, no. 75), but cannot now be traced.

32 UA Pr.v.27.

33 *Report from the Committee on the booksellers and printers petition*, Parliamentary papers, 1801–2, ii, pp. 89–129, at p. 4 (internal pagination).

34 For much of the following, see Michael Turner, 'Andrew Wilson: Lord Stanhope's stereotype printer; a preliminary report', *JPHS*, 9 (1973–4), pp. 22–65.

35 Quoted in Turner, 'Andrew Wilson', p. 32, from a draft in Stanhope's papers. In the absence of any finished copy known to have been sent out to the trade, it must remain an open question whether it was in fact circulated as Wilson seems to have intended. The first book to be printed by Wilson from stereotype plates was J. A. Freylinghausen, *Abstract of the whole doctrine of the Christian religion*, printed for Edmund Harding and sold by Cadell and Davies, 1804.

36 The history of the Stanhope press is authoritatively summarised in Horace Hart, *Charles Earl Stanhope and the Oxford University Press*, repr. with notes by James Mosley (1966). Bulmer was later

said to have acquired his press as early as 1800 (p. xxiii). Hart's paper was originally published in the Oxford Historical Soc. *Collectanea*, 3rd ser. (1896), pp. 365–412.

37 See above, p. 261.

38 Hansard, *Typographia*, pp. 815–6. Stereotype printing from plaster moulds is described in some detail by Hansard, pp. 815–87, and in George Dodd, *Days at the factories* (1843), pp. 342–6 – describing Clowes's printing house.

39 UA Pr.v.4, Syndicate minutes, 20 April 1804, quoted in Turner, 'Andrew Wilson', pp. 39–40.

40 François Callet, *Tables portatives de logarithmes* (Paris, 1795), 'Avertissement' by Firmin Didot.

41 Matters came to a head in 1811, with the establishment of a Bible Society Auxiliary (that is, local branch) at Cambridge: see Cooper, *Annals*, 4, p. 501, Gunning, *Reminiscences*, 2, pp. 278–80, and Ford K. Brown, *Fathers of the Victorians; the age of Wilberforce* (Cambridge, 1961), pp. 295–316. For some of the associated literature, see for example Christopher Wordsworth, *Reasons for declining to become a subscriber to the British and Foreign Bible Society* (1810) and *A letter to the Right Hon, Lord Teignmouth, President of the British and Foreign Bible Society* (1810); Herbert Marsh, *An inquiry into the consequences of neglecting to give the prayer book with the Bible* (Cambridge, 1812) and *An address to the Senate of the University of Cambridge, occasioned by the proposal to introduce in that place an auxiliary Bible Society* (1812); Isaac Milner, *Strictures on some of the publications of the Rev. Herbert Marsh, D. D. intended as a reply to his objections against the British and Foreign Bible Society* (1813). The early history of the Bible Society, and its thorny relationship with the committed high churchmanship of the SPCK, are documented in Roger H. Martin, *Evangelicals united: ecumenical stirrings in pre-Victorian Britain, 1795–1830* (Metuchen, N.J., 1983), pp. 80–122.

42 Bible Society, Sub-Committee minutes, 14 May 1804.

43 UA Pr. vouchers, 1804/13, 1805/5, 7, 12, 17, 1806/3.

44 UA Pr. vouchers, 1806/37, 1807/2,9.

45 UA Pr. vouchers, 1806/8.

46 Hart, *Stanhope*, pp. xix–xxv. The press is described in detail in C. Stower, *The printer's grammar* (1808), pp. 499–511: by this date several modifications had been made to the design, and the price had been reduced from that originally charged by Walker.

47 The first stereotype plate to be cast at Cambridge was interred with due ceremony under the foundation stone of Downing College on 18 May 1807: see Willis and Clark, 3, pp. 763–4.

48 *Arbitration between the University of Cambridge and Andrew Wilson; Mr. Wilson's case* (1806), p. 42.

49 Bible Society Sub-committee, 6 August 1804. See also Leslie Howsam, *Cheap Bibles; nineteenth-century publishing and the British and Foreign Bible Society* (Cambridge, 1991), pp. 79–80.

50 Sub-committee, 3 September 1804. For demand for the Welsh Bible see John Owen, *The history of the origin and first ten years of the British and Foreign Bible Society*, 2 vols. (1816), 1, pp. 2–16, and William Canton, *A history of the British and Foreign Bible Society*, 5 vols. (1904–10), 1, pp. 5–7.

51 On 1 November 1804 the Syndics agreed to 1,000 octavo bourgeois Bibles, 2,000 duodecimo minion Bibles, 3,000 duodecimo nonpareil Bibles, 5,000 duodecimo brevier New Testaments, 20,000 duodecimo nonpareil Bibles in Welsh, and 5,000 duodecimo brevier New Testaments in Welsh.

52 Details again taken from the Bible Society Sub-committee minutes, 3 April, 13 May 1805.

53 Details of composition and presswork are recorded in UA CUP 35/2. The early editions of the stereotype New Testament were dated by the month, and even to the day, the date apparently recording the completion of making the stereotype plates, not of printing or publication. For the Welsh New Testament, see p. 275 below.

54 Owen to Lord Teignmouth, 5 July 1806; D. E. Jenkins, *The life of the Rev. Thomas Charles of Bala*, 3 vols. (Denbigh, 1908), 3, p. 57.

55 Cf. the remarks of Watts concerning the first Welsh work: 'Perhaps it will be better to strike off *1000 Copies of the Welsh Test.* in the first instance, for an early supply.' Watts to Joseph Tarn, 18 June 1806: Jenkins, *Thomas Charles*, 3, p. 54.

56 On 18 May 1805, the University entailed charges 'To 3¼ Doz^n. of small boxes to pack the Stereotype

plates of a Testament in at Mr Wilsons office – 3.10.0. To 3 strong boxes to Carry the above small boxes & plates in to Cambridge – 1.7.0' (UA Pr. vouchers, 1806/3).

57 For the following, see Hart, *Stanhope*.

58 Minutes of the Delegates, Oxford University Press: Hart, *Stanhope*, pp. 389–90.

59 Mary Milner, *The life of Isaac Milner, D. D., F. R. S.* (1842), pp. 324–5.

60 Portions of Milner's notes on the stereotype process are printed in Roberts, *Cambridge University Press*, pp. 125–6. In December 1806, he explained 'the whole stereotype business' to a full meeting of the Syndicate.

61 Sub-Committee minutes, 21 July 1806.

62 Figures from UA CUP 35/1, CUP 35/2 and *Arbitration between the University of Cambridge and Andrew Wilson; Mr. Wilson's case* (1806), p. 25. The success of the Bible was a distraction from the prayer book, of which Wilson only records stereotype editions between 1805 and 1809 in duodecimo set in minion (1805), long primer and brevier, and octavo in pica.

63 The Welsh New Testament printed at Oxford in 1800 seems to have been intended principally for this society: see Darlow and Moule, no. 9609.

64 John Owen to Lord Teignmouth, 5 July 1806: Jenkins, *Life of the Rev. Thomas Charles of Bala*, 3, p. 58.

65 UA CUP 35/2.

66 *Ibid.*

67 Darlow and Moule, no. 9608 (1799). See Martin, *Evangelicals united*, pp. 99–103.

68 BFBS sub-committee minutes, 3 September 1804.

69 Jenkins, *Thomas Charles*, 3, pp. 68–9. The dates on the earliest Welsh New Testaments, 6 and 7 May 1806 (see Darlow and Moule, nos. 9612 and 9613), were the dates of the making of the stereotype plates by Wilson in London, not of printing in Cambridge, and still less of publication. See Watts to Tarn, 18 June 1806, Bible Society, Home correspondence inwards, box 10.

70 UA CUP 35/2. Darlow and Moule, no. 9611, with the imprint of John Smith, Cambridge, 1806, must have been printed after Smith's appointment as University Printer in 1809.

71 *Arbitration between the University of Cambridge and Andrew Wilson; Mr. Wilson's case* (1806). This document is also printed in George A. Kubler, *The era of Charles Mahon, third Earl of Stanhope, stereotyper, 1750–1825* (New York, 1938).

72 *Arbitration between the University of Cambridge and Andrew Wilson* (1806), pp. 10–11.

73 UA CUR 33.7(26).

74 UA CUR Pr.v.50.

75 Turner, 'Andrew Wilson', pp. 48–64.

76 Andrew Wilson, *Arbitration*, p. 29.

77 UA CUP 35/2.

78 BFBS sub-committee minutes, 4 November 1805.

79 BFBS sub-committee minutes, 14 March 1808; the request applied in the first instance to an order for 10,000 copies of the small pica Bible, but it was also directed at every other edition.

80 Howsam, *Cheap Bibles*, pp. 125–9. In 1812 a binding specification was laid down under ten heads.

81 On 17 June 1805, that is, before any stereotype edition of any kind had appeared from Cambridge, the BFBS sub-committee agreed on wording for the Society's title-pages: 'London: printed for the British and Foreign Bible Society, instituted in the Year 1804'.

82 See also below, p. 308.

83 Dard Hunter, *Papermaking; the history and technique of an ancient craft*, 2nd edn (1947), pp. 522–5; Horst Kunze, 'Matthias Koops und die Erfindung des Strohpapiers', *Gutenberg Jahrbuch* 1941, pp. 30–45.

84 BFBS sub-committee minutes, 21 and 28 December 1807.

85 For binders' complaints of paper that was too thick (albeit not in a book printed at Cambridge), see BFBS sub-committee minutes 14 March 1808. Problems with paper are further discussed by Howsam, *Cheap Bibles*, pp. 95–9.

86 UA CUP 35/2.

87 *Ibid.*

88 Watts to Joseph Tarn, 12 December 1806: Bible Society, Home correspondence inwards, box 10; Jenkins, *Thomas Charles,* 3, pp. 77–8.

89 Watts to Tarn, 22 October 1807: Jenkins, *Thomas Charles,* 3, p. 94.

90 Darlow and Moule, no. 9614. Watts discussed these in his letter to Tarn on 22 October (see previous note).

91 John Owen to Lord Teignmouth, 5 July 1806: Jenkins, *Thomas Charles,* 3, p. 57.

92 Jenkins, *Thomas Charles,* 3, p. 83.

93 *Christian Observer,* July 1810, summarised in Jenkins, *Thomas Charles,* 3, pp. 68–9.

94 Thomas Charles to Thomas Smith, 13 October 1806: Jenkins, *Thomas Charles,* 3, pp. 72, 74.

95 Jenkins, *Thomas Charles,* 3, pp. 91–2.

96 BFBS Third annual report, 'Donations in money or books'.

97 James Twitchett to the Vice-Chancellor and Syndics, 19 October 1836: UA Pr.B.3.1(2).

98 Clay was apprenticed in 1803: see James Moran, *Clays of Bungay* (Bungay, 1978), pp. 14–15, with a reproduction of his indenture signed by Watts. See also below, p. 284.

99 UA CUP 23/1, pp. 309, 312.

100 At Oxford: see Andrew Wilson, *Arbitration,* p. 15. In 1854, the jubilee volume of the Bible Society remarked in its account of Bible printing by the Queen's Printers that many editions were printed from type rather than from stereotypes, partly on account of cost, and partly because type metal was much harder. (L. N. R., *The Book and its story* (1853), p. 208.)

101 UA CUR 33.7(24).

102 *Monthly Magazine,* 23, p. 264, 1 April 1807.

103 *Monthly Magazine,* 23, p. 373, 1 May 1807.

104 Turner, 'Andrew Wilson', prints part of the sale catalogue.

105 J. Johnson, *Typographia, or, the printer's instructor,* 2 vols. (1824), 2, pp. 658–9.

106 Stower, *The printer's grammar,* p. 485. But Stower still dedicated his book to Stanhope.

107 UA CUP 23/1. 1,500 copies were printed. For Buchanan, see Clark, *Endowments,* pp. 380–1 and McKitterick, *Cambridge University Library,* pp. 378–84. The poem was advertised in the *Cambridge Chronicle,* 9 February 1805.

108 UA Pr.v.4, Syndicate minutes, 16 June 1808; Watts had tendered his resignation on 13 June.

109 *Facts and observations relating to the state of the University Press* [Cambridge, 1809]. Watts's printed letter of resignation (UA U. Papers 1, no. 235) is dated 30 October 1809.

110 He also became printer to the East India College (Haileybury), and there and subsequently in London gained a considerable reputation as printer of oriental languages. See James Moran, *Stephen Austin's of Hertford* (Hertford, 1968), pp. 24, 25–6.

111 *Facts and observations,* p. 15.

112 UA U. Ac.2(4).

113 UA CUP 23/1, p. 307.

114 See below, p. 289.

14 Hellenism and John Smith

1 J. C. T. Oates, 'Cambridge University and the reform of the Copyright Act, 1805–1813', *The Library,* 5th ser. 27 (1972), pp. 275–92; McKitterick, *Cambridge University Library,* pp. 402–3.

2 A collection of printed notices and testimonials is in UA U. Papers 1 (Webb collection).

3 According to his memorial in St Botolph's church he was born on 12 September 1777. His annual stipend as University Printer was £400.

4 UA Pr.v.4, Syndicate minutes, 26 June 1810; UP2(59).

5 John Smith, 'Observations relating to the affairs of the Press', 16 March 1829: UA CUR 33.1(46).

6 UA CUP 14/3, p. 232.

7 The literature is substantial. See in particular William St Clair, *Lord Elgin and the marbles* (1967); David Watkin, *Thomas Hope, 1769–1831, and the neo-classical idea* (1968); R. W. Liscombe, *William Wilkins, 1778–1839* (Cambridge, 1980). For Clarke, see W. Otter, *The life and remains of Edward Daniel Clarke*, 2 vols. (1825) and McKitterick, *Cambridge University Library*, pp. 362–74. For Tweddell, see R. Tweddell, *Remains of John Tweddell*, 2nd edn (1816).

8 Syndicate minutes, 6 July 1782.

9 Trinity College, MS O.3.9; Syndicate minutes, 2 November 1782, 16 May 1795.

10 UA Pr.v.2, Syndicate minutes, 1 July 1795; see below, p. 291.

11 UA Pr.v.2, Syndicate minutes, 12 February 1803. For the fire and its aftermath, see Luard, 'Porson', *Cambridge essays* (1857), p. 158, and J. S. Watson, *The life of Richard Porson* (1861), pp. 129–31. But Porson's edition was published only in 1822, under the care of P. P. Dobree. For Porson, see more recently C. O. Brink, *English classical scholarship* (Cambridge, 1985), ch. 6.

12 'Being the first book in which the name of Edward Clarke had appeared in the title-page (all his former publications having been anonymous), it was otherwise got up with great care, and at no inconsiderable cost. But this over-nursing was in one respect injurious to it. The subject, though excellent for a pamphlet, was neither popular nor comprehensive enough for the expensive form in which it was thus obliged to appear (the price was eighteen shillings) . . .' Otter, *Edward Daniel Clarke*, 2, p. 218. For the inscriptional Greek, see J. H. Bowman, *Greek printing types in Britain in the nineteenth century: a catalogue* (Oxford Bibliographical Soc., 1992), p. 62.

13 Apart from Clarke's works, and those mentioned by Bowman, *Greek printing types*, p. 62, see also, for example, early uses in *Museum Criticum*, 1, no. 4 (1814), P. P. Dobree, *Greek inscriptions from the marbles in the library of Trinity College, Cambridge* [Cambridge, 1825] and the (later) F used in Richard Dawes, *Miscellanea critica*, ed. Thomas Kidd (Cambridge, 1828).

14 Figgins to Watts, 21 March 1807 (UA Pr. vouchers, 1807/18).

15 UA Pr. vouchers, 1808/11. See James Mosley, 'Porson's Greek types', *The Penrose Annual*, 54 (1960), pp. 36–40, with a valuable collection of reproductions including several of Porson's Greek hand. Evidence that the scrap of paper now Trinity College, MS B.13.27, fo. 92 was that provided to Austin as a model seems slight.

16 Austin to Watts, 9 March 1809 (UA Pr. vouchers, 1809/5).

17 Bowman, *Greek printing types*, p. 2.

18 UA Pr.v.4, Syndicate minutes, 29 May 1805.

19 *Quarterly Review*, 5 (1811), p. 228; Hill Shine and H. C. Shine, *The Quarterly Review under Gifford; identification of contributors, 1809–1824* (Chapel Hill, 1949).

20 *Classical Journal*, 4 (1811), p. 252.

21 Dyer, *Privileges*, 2, 'The rise and progress of printing at Cambridge', pp. 32–3. repr. in the *Classical Journal*, 32 (1825), pp. 12–15).

22 [E. V. Blomfield], 'Account of the present state of classical literature in Germany', *Museum Criticum*, 1 (1814), pp. 273–8, at p. 276.

23 George Huntingford to his nephew, Henry Huntingford, Winchester College, 30 March 1813: Hofmann and Freeman catalogue 26, no. 86.

24 *Museum Criticum*, 1 (1814), p. 118.

25 Bowman, *Greek printing types*, pp. 23, 29 etc.

26 Some of the work of Porson's disciples is discussed briefly in Brink, *English classical scholarship*, pp. 111–13.

27 For the programme to publish Porson's unpublished work, see D. McKitterick, 'Books and other collections', in D. McKitterick (ed.), *The making of the Wren Library* (Cambridge, 1995), pp. 90–3.

28 Maltby's annotated copy is in the British Library, 12923.g.7. A second edition was published at London in 1824.

29 *Museum Criticum*, 1 (1813), pp. 138–9.

30 *Ibid.*, p. 129; McKitterick, *Cambridge University Library*, pp. 370–4, with further references.

31 Dobree published little in his lifetime, and bequeathed his annotated books to the University Library:

an edition of his *Adversaria*, edited by Scholefield, was published in 1831–3. More than anyone else, he was associated with Porson's legacy: see for example the remarks by Julius Hare in the *Philological Museum*, 1 (1832), pp. 204–8.

32 *Life, letters, and journals of George Ticknor*, 2nd edn, 2 vols. (1876), 1, p. 224. Some aspects of the reforming influence of Trinity College more generally in this are described in Winstanley, *Early Victorian Cambridge*; Robert O. Preyer, 'The romantic tide reaches Trinity: notes on the transmission and diffusion of new approaches to traditional studies at Cambridge, 1820–1840', in J. Paradis and T. Postlewait (eds.), *Victorian science and Victorian values: literary perspectives* (New York, 1981), pp. 39–68; and M. M. Garland, *Cambridge before Darwin* (Cambridge, 1980).

33 In 1809–12, C. J. Blomfield played a prominent part in reviewing classical Greek literature for the *Edinburgh Review*; see *Wellesley Index*, 1, pp. 446–9: among other contributions, he was reponsible for the notices of Butler's edition of Stanley's Aeschylus. His own edition of the *Prometheus Vinctus* (1810) was reviewed by Peter Elmsley (*Edinburgh Review*, 17 (November 1810), pp. 211–42) and by J. H. Monk (*Quarterly Review*, 5 (1811), pp. 203–9: see above, note 19.

34 Macaulay to Zachary Macaulay, 14 May 1816: Macaulay, *Letters*, ed. T. Pinney, 6 vols. (Cambridge, 1974), 1, p. 77.

35 Macaulay to Zachary Macaulay, [20? October 1817], *Letters* 1, p. 87.

36 *Classical Journal*, 1 (1810), pp. 16–30.

37 *Ibid.*, p. 173.

38 *Jenaische Allgemeine Literatur-Zeitung*, 105 (June 1816), col. 362.

39 Summarised in the *Classical Journal*, 4 (September 1811), pp. 139–40.

40 *Museum Criticum*, 1 (1814), p. 417; *Monthly Literary Advertiser*, March 1814.

41 The English version was taken up by the Boston publishers Cummings, Hilliard & Co. in the year of publication.

42 Charles Babbage, *Passages from the life of a philosopher* (1864), pp. 26–7.

43 See, for example, the advertisement of W. H. Lunn in the *Monthly Literary Advertiser*, February 1815.

44 Gregorius Corinthius etc., *De dialectis linguae Graecae* (Leipzig, J. A. G. Weigel, (1811)). A pre-liminary leaf to this book lists Mackinlay and Lunn (London), Luchtmans (Leiden), Remondini (Venice), M. de Romanis (Rome), Piatti (Florence), Schaumburg (Vienna), Bohn (Hamburg) and De Bure, Schoell and Renouard (all in Paris).

45 E. Werdet, *De la librairie française* (Paris, 1860). For the German background to some of these firms, see F. Barbier, 'Entre la France et l'Allemagne: les pratiques bibliographiques au XIXᵉ siècle', *Revue de Synthèse*, 4th ser. 1–2 (1992), pp. 41–53, and, more generally, F. Barbier, *L'empire du livre; le livre imprimé et la construction de l'Allemagne contemporaine (1815–1914)* (Paris, 1995), especially pp. 257–82. For German immigrants to the Paris trade in the early nineteenth century, see Helga Jeanblanc, *Des Allemands dans l'industrie et le commerce du livre à Paris (1811–1870)* (Paris, 1994). For London booksellers, see for example *The picture of London*, 22nd edn (1824), p. 315.

46 J.-M. Chatelain, 'Bilan et enjeux culturels du commerce international du librairie entre la France et l'Allemagne au XIXᵉ siècle', *Revue de Synthèse*, 4th ser. 1–2 (1992), pp. 85–97.

47 For the development of the trade in Germany of books published in England (especially English literature) during the eighteenth century, see Bernhard Fabian, 'English books and their eighteenth-century German readers' in P. Korshin (ed.), *The widening circle; essays on the circulation of literature in eighteenth-century Europe* (Philadelphia, 1976), pp. 117–96, esp. pp. 138–54. Bernhard Fabian, 'Die erste englische Buchhandlung auf dem Kontinent' in B. Fabian (ed.), *Festschrift für Reiner Gruenter* (Heidelberg, 1978), pp. 122–44, and Bernhard Fabian, *The English book in eighteenth-century Germany* (1992).

48 'Account of the present state of classical literature in Germany', *Museum Criticum*, 1 (1814), pp. 273–8. For Wolf in this context, see Sandys, *A History of classical scholarship*, 3 vols. (Cambridge, 1903–8), 3, pp. 59–60.

49 See pp. 269, 301, 459.

50 *Göttingische Gelehrte Anzeigen*, 1816, p. 1094, 1817, pp. 1137–49.

51 Giles Barber, 'Galignani's and the publication of English books in France from 1800 to 1852', *The Library*, 5th ser. 16 (1961), pp. 267–86.

52 The German book trade at this period may be most conveniently studied in C. G. Kayser, *Vollständiges Bücher-Lexicon*, 4 vols. (Leipzig, 1834–8).

53 *Museum Criticum*, 2 (1826), pp. 324, 326–7.

54 Ticknor to Edward T. Channing, Leipzig, 17 September 1816: *Life, letters, and journals of George Ticknor*, 2nd edn, 2 vols. (1876), 1, p. 90.

55 *Jenaische Literatur-Zeitung*, 105 (June 1816).

56 In 1828 he was translated to London. For a summary of his literary work, see H. R. Luard, 'Memoir', in the *Journal of Classical and Sacred Philology*, 4 (1858–9), pp. 196–200 and 348–9.

57 *Historical register*, pp. 353, 602; Garland, *Cambridge before Darwin*, pp. 118–19.

58 J. H. Monk, *A sermon preached in the chapel of Trinity College, Cambridge, on Dec. 16, 1817* (Cambridge [1818]), pp. 10–11.

59 *Philological Museum*, 1 (1832), p. 209.

60 'Appendix to the Cambridge edition of Aeschylus', *Quarterly Journal of Education*, 9 (1835), pp. 110–17, at p. 111.

15 John Smith

1 Leonard Jenyns, *Memoir of the Rev. John Stevens Henslow* (1862), pp. 16–19; J. W. Clark, 'The foundation and early years of the Society', *Proc. Cambridge Philosophical Soc.*, 7 (1891), pp. i–l; J. W. Clark and T. McK. Hughes, *The life and letters of Adam Sedgwick*, 2 vols. (Cambridge, 1892), 1, pp. 205–9; A. Rupert Hall, *The Cambridge Philosophical Society; a history, 1819–1969* (Cambridge, 1969), pp. 4–7.

2 Syndicate minutes, 14 December 1820.

3 William Whewell to his aunt, Cambridge, 28 March 1821: Mrs Stair Douglas, *The life and selections from the correspondence of William Whewell, D.D.* (1881), p. 63.

4 Syndicate minutes, 21 February 1823.

5 The title-page announced that it was volume 1; but Whewell changed his plans, and no further suggestion was made of any incompleteness in the several revised editions that followed. See I. Todhunter, *William Whewell, D.D. An account of his writings*, 2 vols. (1876), 1, pp. 13–19. For Whewell's mathematical work, see especially Harvey W. Becher, 'William Whewell and Cambridge mathematics', *Historical Studies in the Physical Sciences*, 11 (1980), pp. 1–48.

6 Richard Jones to William Whewell [1 October 1819], Trinity College, MS Add. c.52(1).

7 *Ibid.*

8 Charles Babbage, *Passages from the life of a philosopher* (1864), pp. 28–9. For the following, see also W. W. Rouse Ball, *A history of the study of mathematics at Cambridge* (Cambridge, 1889), pp. 120–7, and M. M. Garland, *Cambridge before Darwin* (Cambridge, 1980), pp. 29–30.

9 Babbage, *Passages from the life of a philosopher*, pp. 38–9.

10 *Ibid.*, pp. 39–40.

11 'Cambridge differential notation', *Quarterly Journal of Education*, 8 (1834), pp. 100–10, at p. 110.

12 UA CUP 29/5.

13 *Ibid.*

14 'I do not know the actual day of publication of my first small volume of Cambridge Observations, 1828, and of circulation. The date of the preface is Apr. 27 1829 . . . The system which I endeavoured to introduce into printed astronomical observations was partially introduced into this volume, and was steadily improved in subsequent volumes. I think that I am justified, by letters and other remarks, in believing that this introduction of an orderly system of exhibition, not merely of observations, but of the steps for bringing them to a practical result – quite a novelty in astronomical publications – had a markedly good effect on European astronomy in general.' (G. B. Airy, *Autobiography* (Cambridge, 1896), p. 86.)

15 Hare had stressed the importance of Niebuhr to Thomas Arnold a few years previously. 'It was in

1825 that, through the recommendation of Archdeacon Hare, he first became acquainted with Niebuhr's History of Rome. In the study of this work, which was the first German book he ever read, and for the sake of reading which he had learned that language, a new intellectual world dawned upon him, not only in the subject to which it related, but in the disclosure to him of the depth and research of German literature, which from that moment he learned more and more to appreciate, and, as far as his own occupations would allow him, to emulate.' (A. P. Stanley, *The life and correspondence of Thomas Arnold*, 7th edn (1852), pp. 33–4.)

16 'The Syndics paid the expenses of the book & then Rose sold it to Murray.' Whewell to Richard Jones, 10 January 1828: Trinity College, MS Add. c.51(46).

17 Claudius Buchanan, *Christian researches in Asia*, 3rd edn (Edinburgh, 1812), pp. 134–5; McKitterick, *Cambridge University Library*, pp. 377–84, with further references.

18 Buchanan to Browne, 6 December 1811 and following: UA CUR 33.7(29, 30, 31). For the Leiden edition, and for disputes over the system of pointing in the Luchtmans-Muller edition of 1708, see Darlow and Moule, no. 8969.

19 Darlow and Moule, no. 8977.

20 UA Grace Book N, p. 127; Pr. vouchers, 1827/14 (shipping note). In 1826 the University also agreed to give books to the new St David's College at Lampeter: UA Grace Book N, p. 149.

21 UA Pr.v.5, Syndicate minutes, 10 May 1839 (Sidney: list of books in Pr.v.7, 17 June 1839 etc.), 25 October 1839 (Athens: list in Pr.v.7, 4 February 1840), 4 February 1840 (Nova Scotia), 27 November 1840 (Jamaica: list in Pr.v.7, 11 December 1840); Grace Book Ξ, pp. 96 (Sydney), 117 (Athens), 174 (Jamaica).

22 UA Pr.v.5, Syndicate minutes, 21 May 1833. For the attempt by W. L. Mackenzie (bookseller and printer in Toronto) to use imported Bible plates from New York, see George L. Parker, *The beginnings of the book trade in Canada* (Toronto, 1985), pp. 151, 285.

23 Tim Chilcott, *A publisher and his circle; the life and work of John Taylor, Keats's publisher* (1972), pp. 170–5; R. H. Super, *The publication of Landor's works* (Bibliographical Soc., 1954), pp. 31–40.

24 'The publishers find the sale so slow that they fear a considerable loss on the two volumes now completed, and will not venture to go on at their own risk. The prospect of a continuation seems to depend on the disposition there may be in the directors of our University press to bear a part of the expenses.' (Connop Thirlwall to Bunsen, 10 October 1833: Connop Thirlwall, *Letters literary and theological*, ed. J. J. Stewart Perowne and Louis Stokes (1881), p. 109.)

25 The following is taken from UA CUR 33.4(10,12).

26 *The devotional diamond pocket Bible* (J. Jones, Lambeth, 1816: Herbert, *Historical catalogue*, 1621).

27 Adam Clarke, 'Introduction' to *The holy bible* (Liverpool, 1813).

28 T. S. R. Boase, 'Macklin and Bowyer', *JWCI*, 26 (1963), pp. 169–76. For the part-issue Bibles printed by Brightly and Childs at Bungay, see Tony Copsey and Henry Hallam, *Book distribution and printing in Suffolk, 1534–1850* (Ipswich, 1994), pp. 135–7.

29 *Morning Chronicle*, 23 January 1819.

30 *Morning Chronicle*, 29 January 1819.

31 Herbert, *Historical catalogue*, 1658, dating it 1817 (as on the title-page of the BFBS copy) rather than by the dates of the parts; the plates are dated between January 1814 and September 1816.

32 Charles Rivington to Smith, 3 July 1816: UA Pr.v.50.

33 Syndicate minutes, 10 May 1819: 5,000 copies were to be printed, in eighteen parts, at £370 for each part, the price to be altered if the price of paper changed.

34 Not all of the edition was provided with illustrations. Steel-facing of copper engravings, allowing many more copies to be taken, was not introduced until the 1850s. Steel engravings were developed in the 1820s: see Luke Hermann, *Turner prints; the engraved work of J. M. W. Turner* (Oxford, 1990) and Basil Hunnissett, *Steel-engraved illustration in England* (1980), pp. 197–8.

35 Details of the production are taken from UA Pr. vouchers, 1821, 1822, 1823, 1824, 1825. For Bird, see Leslie Howsam, *Cheap Bibles* (Cambridge, 1991), pp. 124–5, and Ellic Howe, *A list of London bookbinders, 1648–1815* (Bibliographical Soc., 1950), p. 12.

36 Syndicate minutes, 15 July 1820.

37 John Smith, 'Observations relating to the affairs of the Press', 16 March 1829: UA CUR 33.1(46).

38 Syndicate minutes, 5 and 19 July 1827, 13 March 1836 (Pr.v.5); CUP 14/3, pp. 187–8 (paper supplied by Dickinson) and 262 (binding of 1,500 copies). Wootton's premises, in Pembroke Street, were the closest to the Pitt Press.

39 Joseph Tarn to Smith, 23 December 1817: Bible Society correspondence book 9.

40 Syndicate minutes, 17 March, 23 October 1819, 7 June 1820.

41 UA VC Corr.1.1(28)iv.

42 Hansard also challenged the benefits of stereotyping on grounds of accuracy and improvement, drawing on his experience of a book printed in London:

> In five editions of the work in thirteen years, the routine of wear and tear gave the advantage of progressive improvement in type to each edition; and that not to a work requiring any particular display of elegance or good printing; and I may further add, and can *prove*, that, without any more than proper attention in the reading department, the correctness of the editions has been improving also. Now, what would have been the case, if the work had been stereotyped in 1805? Instead of being put to press five times, it would probably have been so put thirteen times. Each movement of the plates and putting to press would have been attended with, at least, liability to accident; for every printer knows that the work of fixing the plates; the process of making-ready; working; taking-off; cleaning; and packing up again, must be attended with a great chance of batters; besides the mislaying or transposing a plate; wear, by frequent use of the lye-brush; and all the casualties which occur in a press-room. *The face of the type must have remained the same*; errors could not, as in the ordinary mode of work, have been corrected, because the work would never have been read for that purpose; batters must have multiplied; and the work would have been gradually sinking, instead of rising in appearance to met the improved state of modern printing. (*Typographia*, pp. 843–4.)

43 *Report from Select Committee in the King's Printer's patents*, 1832 (House of Commons papers 1831–2, xviii), paras. 1021–4; Childs worked in partnership with Charles Brightly, on whose pamphlet on stereotyping Abraham Rees drew extensively for his article on stereotyping in his *Encyclopaedia* (1819), vol. 34. Hansard remarked that Brightly 'carried on business to a great extent, and, from various circumstances, being enabled to do his work *very cheaply*, obtained a great deal of the London Booksellers' work, at a time when printing in London was in a state of considerable depression. He executed his business chiefly by *females!*' T. C. Hansard, *Typographia* (1825), p. 837. For Brightly and Childs, see Copsey and Hallam, *Book distribution and printing in Suffolk*, pp. 31–2, 36–7. In 1840, Childs protested vigorously at the description in *The Times* of his business as 'a cheap establishment of women and children', and rejoined, 'I suppose it is customary in all printing offices to employ women for some parts of the warehouse work, and boys for errands; but it happens that only two women, and but one person, male or female, so young as sixteen years, is employed in my office.' (John Childs, *The Bible monopoly* (Bungay [1840]): copy in Trinity College library, MS O.14.27.)

44 *Report from the Select Committee on King's Printer's patents*, para. 1518.

45 *Gentleman's Magazine*, 93.2 (1823), pp. 21–2 (letter by J. Murray), 453; *Annals of Philosophy*, n.s. 6 (1823), p. 68 (remarks by W. T. Brande). Cf. the remarks in Rees's *Cyclopaedia* (1819), vol. 26, art. 'Paper', sig. Y1r:

> The bleaching process has given rise to great complaints from the printers, as many printing papers are now made from cotton rags. The oxygenated muriatic acid being applied for the purpose of obtaining dispatch and delicacy of colour, produces a paper of a good appearance from inferior staple. Nothing can be more perplexing to a printer, nor more detrimental to his labours, than this kind of bleached paper; for although it may be thick, and seem strong in the ream, no sooner does the water penetrate through it, than it loses its adhesive quality, and becomes so loose and soft as scarcely to bear handling, and in working under the press sinks down into the cavities of the letters, leaving a part of the substance behind, after every impression, until it so clogs the type, that the work is rendered scarcely legible. Nor is it less exceptionable in point of durability, as it must moulder away in a little time, with the common use that popular books generally undergo.

46 UA U. Ac.2(4), 1809–10, 1810–11, 1813–14, 1814–15.

47 Joan Evans, *The endless web; John Dickinson & Co. Ltd, 1804–1954* (1955), pp. 20–1. Some idea of the

importance of the paper trade in and near Rickmansworth is conveyed by the fact that in about 1840 six mills in the parish employed almost 600 people (male and female) between them: see A. H. Shorter, *Paper making in the British Isles; an historical and geographical study* (Newton Abbot, 1971), p. 122.

48 See their letters to Smith, 3 July, 20 September 1813; Smith to Martindale, 25 July 1814: UA Pr.v.50. For steam drying, see Richard L. Hills, *Paper-making in Britain, 1488–1988; a short history* (1988), p. 115. Longman and Dickinson became the principal suppliers, though the Press continued to buy occasionally from others such as Matthew Towgood at St Neots, Robert Hawkes of Taverham, near Norwich, and another branch of the Towgood family at Dartford, Kent (UA CUP 14/1: 1816–18, and CUP 14/2: 1825–6). For the transition in paper-making in an American context, and from the point of view of its manufacture (with its social consequences), see Judith A. McGaw, *Most wonderful machine; mechanization and social change in Berkshire paper making, 1801–1885* (Princeton, 1987).

49 Although the supply of imported rags became easier after 1814, the introduction of machinery, increases in production, a lack of definition of paper sizes for machine-made papers (leading to waste and misunderstandings between suppliers and printers – one source of the Press's dispute with Martindale) and modifications in the chemical constituents of paper in a search for cheaper products all added their own complications. See also Coleman, *British paper industry*, pp. 212–17.

50 Syndicate minutes, 28 February 1814. This machine is described in Abraham Rees, *Cyclopaedia*, 28 (1819), art. 'Printing', with an illustration in *Plates* 4 (1820), 'Printing', pl. 3.

51 UA Pr.v.5, Syndicate minutes, 13 July 1832.

52 The annual bills for printing ink in 1813–16 were between £238 and £283 (UA Pr. vouchers, 1814/24, 1816/5, 1816/49). Grafton, Baker & Biggs (cf. Pr. vouchers, 1822/25) do not, according to C. H. Bloy (*A history of printing ink, balls and rollers, 1440–1850* (1967)) figure in the London printing ink trade.

53 T. C. Hansard, *Typographia*, pp. 632–4; C. H. Bloy, *A history of printing ink*, pp. 56–9.

54 UA Pr. vouchers, 1821/8 (treacle from William Cory), 1821/11 (cloth remnants from Lunn & Co.), 1821/15 (kersey etc. from John Haslop), 1823/24 (fabrics from E. B. Ind, Market Hill), 1821/7 (pearl ash, liquorice juice and Venice turpentine from Thomas Watson), 1824/12, 1825/6 (candles from Michael Headly).

55 Letter by Whewell, 17 October 1824: Todhunter, *William Whewell*, 2, pp. 53–4. 'Our new court' is New Court, in Trinity College, known at first as the King's Court. The matter of Caius had been on the agenda for some months; on 24 May 1824 the University Improvement Syndicate agreed 'that the Master of Caius be requested to ascertain from his Society the practicability of removing their College', and on 31 May the same syndicate learned that the college had signified its willingness to move. The principal suggestion was that it should move to land belonging to Peterhouse. (UA Min.vi.1) For further details and ideas, see R. W. Liscombe, *William Wilkins, 1778–1839* (Cambridge, 1980), pp. 134–8.

56 The beginning of the prolonged debate in the 1820s and 1830s on university improvement is described in Willis and Clark, 3, pp. 101–6.

57 *VCH Oxfordshire*, 3 (1954), pp. 56–7; Charles Batey, 'The Oxford partners; some notes on the administration of the University Press, 1780–1881', *JPHS*, 3 (1967), pp. 51–65, at pp. 61–2.

58 Now in Hanover Square.

59 Camden's letters to the Vice-Chancellor are printed in Willis and Clark, 3, pp. 136–9: I have usually only summarised Willis and Clark's account of these events where they relate to the architecture: however, as they do not deal with how the buildings were to be used, I have added details in the following.

60 Willis and Clark, 3, p. 135.

61 By December 1828 Whewell could speak of these old buildings as empty (Willis and Clark 3, p. 100).

62 Camden to the Vice-Chancellor, 5 April 1829: Willis and Clark, 3, p. 139.

63 Willis and Clark, 3, pp. 142–4; E. A. Crutchley, *A history and description of the Pitt Press* (Cambridge, 1938).

64 In its first years, the building was used to store a collection of minerals, and (the Fitzwilliam Museum not yet being completed) the Mesman bequest of works of art. Later on, rooms were used for lectures.

The University Registrary was based there for a century from the 1830s. See Cooper, *Annals*, 4, p. 706; Crutchley, *History and description of the Pitt Press*, pp. 25–31; Basil Herbertson, 'The Mesman Museum, Cambridge, 1834–1848', *Journal of the History of Collections*, 5 (1993), pp. 217–22.

65 For one early example, see Adam Sedgwick, *A discourse on the studies of the University* (Cambridge, 1833). The vignette was approved on 21 May 1833: UA Pr.v.5. Publication of Sedgwick's book was shared between Parker, Deighton and Stevenson. This vignette itself took on a measure of authority: a copy was used in Valletta in 1840 on the title-page of a translation of the prayer book. (I am grateful to D. N. Griffiths for drawing my attention to this book in the library of the SPCK.)

66 Hansard, *Typographia*, p. 806. For details of a London printing house built at this period, see Iain Bain, 'James Moyes and his Temple Printing Office', *JPHS*, 4 (1968), 1–10.

67 Hansard, *Typographia*, p. 807.

68 Details from UA plans P.XL.1, working plans by J. Arding & Son, builders, Fleet Street.

69 UA CUP 14/3.

70 'Observations relating to the affairs of the University Press, submitted to the Syndics', 1829, UA CUR 33.1(46).

71 James Twitchett to the Vice-Chancellor and Syndics, 19 October 1836: UA Pr.B.3.1(2).

72 UA CUP 14/1, fos. 99, 101.

73 Smith to Longman and Dickinson, 24 May 1813: UA Pr.v.50.

74 James Moran, *Printing presses* (1973), pp. 59–69.

75 UA CUP 14/3, pp. 184–5 etc.; see also Pr.v.5, 23 April 1833, 11 February 1834.

76 The University paid Bacon and Donkin £125 in part payment for 'a Printing Machine' in February 1814 (UA Pr. vouchers, 1814/4). The machine was specifically for demy octavo stereotype plates (Syndics minutes, 28 February 1814); further costs were recorded separately: 'To an Apparatus fitted up for equalizing the Stereotype Plates comprising a cast iron block turned true on the face with carriages, levers, screws, & a mahogany Block planed up', £39.14s.7d.; 'a cast iron plane fitted up with staple and screws & 4 cast steel cutters fitted to do. for Stereotype plat', £4.8s.6d.; '4 inking Cylinders fitted complete with copper tubes, brass ends, wrought iron collar, spindles cast Iron wheels, and Brass pinions', £30.9s.2d. (UA Pr.v.50). For further costs, see UA Pr. vouchers, 1817/20. For Bacon and Donkin's machine, see *Patents for inventions; abridgements of the specifications relating to printing* (1859), pp. 128–9, Rees, *Cyclopaedia*, vol. 28, art. 'Printing', and Moran, *Printing presses*, pp. 175–6. For a sheet printed on one side only (sheet S, in an octavo New Testament, 1816, for the BFBS: 560 × 440mm.), dated in manuscript 26 April 1817, see Cambridge University Library, Broadsides B.1817. See also below, p. 335.

77 T. C. Hansard, *Typographia*, p. 701.

78 T. C. Hansard to the Vice-Chancellor, 7 June 1824: UA VC Corr.1.1(4).

79 T. C. Hansard to the Vice-Chancellor, 26 February 1825: UA VC Corr.1.1(6).

80 T. C. Hansard to Syndics, 27 February 1829: UA CUR 33.7(68); Pr.B.24.8.

81 For these firms, see Michael Twyman, *Lithography, 1800–1850* (Oxford, 1970).

82 Several of Dodd's commissions are listed in UA CUP 28/1.

83 T. C. Hansard to William Webb, 30 June 1828: UA VC Corr.1.1(13). Thomas Davison was a printer in Lombard Street, Whitefriars.

84 T. C. Hansard to William Webb, 19 March 1830: UA VC Corr.1.1(15). Despite his disappointment, Hansard maintained cordial relations with Webb, Master of Clare College, sending him a bundle of asparagus plants 'of a most outstanding large-growing species' in 1830.

85 See, for example, Henry Pearson, *A syllabus of plane trigonometry* (1830; 2nd edn, 1832).

86 Thomas Constable, *Archibald Constable and his literary correspondents*, 3 vols. (Edinburgh, 1873), 3, pp. 366–447, 477–86; John Sutherland, 'The British book trade and the crash of 1826', *The Library*, 6th ser. 9 (1987), pp. 148–61.

87 Charles Knight, *Passages of a working life during half a century*, 3 vols. (1864), 2, pp. 42–4.

88 UA Pr.v.5, 27 February 1827.

89 Much of the following is drawn from a catalogue bound up with a copy of *Timaei Sophistae lexicon*

vocum Platonicarum (London: R. Priestley, 1824): it was quite normal for booksellers to insert their own catalogues into others' publications at this period.

90 UA CUP 29/5.

91 UA U. Ac.2(4,5); Pr. vouchers, 1825/16.

92 UA CUR 33.7(56).

93 Clowes to Webb, 28 February 1829: UA CUR 33.7(68). For a brief account of Parker (1792–1870), see the *DNB*.

94 Newman to R. F. Wilson, Oriel College, 31 March 1834: J. H. Newman, *Letters and diaries*, ed. Ian Ker and Thomas Gornall, 4 (Oxford, 1980), p. 227.

95 Newman to John William Bowden, Oriel College, 1 April 1834: Newman, *Letters and diaries*, 4, p. 228.

96 Newman to Bowden, Oriel College, 10 August 1834: Newman, *Letters and diaries*, 4, p. 321.

97 UA Pr.v.5, 15 November 1831; W. K. Lowther Clarke, *A history of the S.P.C.K.* (1959), pp. 188–9. Newman viewed the separation of Rivington and the SPCK with considerable self-interest. 'As to Rivington's ceasing to be the SPCK Bookseller, it may work *us* good. It has struck me, whether his taking our Tracts in hand has anything to do with this prospect. He might also set up by our means a Tract Library himself, as he has (and perhaps with better success than he has) set up a Theological Library. His connexions are extensive. We would write and get written all sorts of popular Tracts, if there was so good an opening for them.' (Newman to John William Bowden, Oriel College, 5 June 1834, Newman, *Letters and diaries*, 4, p. 264.) Mark Pattison recorded that Rivington took up the Oxford *Tracts for the times* at about the time of his separation from the SPCK (Mark Pattison, *Memoirs* (1885), p. 191), but in fact he agreed with Newman some months before that to circulate them, in April 1834: Newman, *Letters and diaries*, 4, p. 235.

98 UA Pr.v.5, 19 June, 13 July 1832 (with copy of the agreement).

99 Lowther Clarke, *A history of the S.P.C.K.*, p. 182; Newman, *Letters and diaries*, 4, p. 265.

100 UA Lett.17(20); Thomas Curtis, *The existing monopoly an inadequate protection of the Authorized Version of Scripture* (1833); Thomas Turton (Regius Professor of Divinity at Cambridge), *The text of the English Bible* (Cambridge, 1833; 2nd edn, corrected and greatly enlarged, 1833); Edward Cardwell, *Oxford Bibles* (Oxford, 1833); Scrivener, *Authorized edition*, pp. 35–6. But cf. also the issues raised in James Scholefield (Regius Professor of Greek at Cambridge), *Hints for an improved translation of the New Testament* (Cambridge, 1832; 2nd edn, with additions, 1836).

101 William Whewell had his copy of Turton's pamphlet bound up with several others on the position of dissenters in Oxford and Cambridge (Trinity College Library, 289.c.80.92). For some of the contemporary debate about dissenters, see Winstanley, *Early Victorian Cambridge*, pp. 85–94.

102 UA CUR 33.7(36–42).

103 *Report from the Select Committee on the King's Printer's patent, 1832*, Parliamentary papers 1831–2, xviii, appendix D, nos. 8, 9, 10a, 10d.

104 'Observations relating to the affairs of the University Press, submitted to the Syndics', 1829, UA CUR 33.1(46).

105 UA Pr.v.5, Syndicate minutes, 28 May 1824.

106 For Sumner, later Bishop of Winchester, and for Walker's unhappy career, see the *DNB*. Walker later confessed,

> The truth is, that I have been guilty of great and unwarrantable liberties with regard to the translation of Milton. I understood it to be his [Sumner's] wish that I should make no alterations, except such as were approved of by him; and with this wish I conformed for a short time, except some minute encroachments *after the sheet was returned from Windsor*; but as I went on, so many instances occurred to me in which, so I thought, the translation might be bettered, that at last I dropped all remorse and altered without compunction. The truth was, that although the translation would in any case have been quite as good as is generally thought proper to bestow on modern works, written in foreign languages – so that the public would not have complained, – I could not be satisfied, unless it were something better. (Quoted by Knight, *Passages of a working life*, 2, p. 31.)

107 UA CUP 14/2, pp. 171, 173. The vellum copies were charged to the Government Annuity Fund.

108 Knight, *Passages of a working life*, 2, p. 30.

109 UA Pr.v.5, Syndicate minutes, 25 October 1836.

110 UA Pr.v.5, Syndicate minutes, 20 November 1824. Fridays were settled on in November 1836 (Syndicate minutes, 22 November 1836).

111 These figures have been drawn from the Unversity's audited accounts (UA U.Ac.2(4,5)), and Smith's own slightly different summary in his 'Observations relating to the affairs of the Press', 16 March 1829: CUR 33.1(46).

112 UA U.Ac.2(5).

113 G[eorge] P[eacock], *Observations on the plans for the new Library, &c., by a member of the first syndicate* (Cambridge, 1831), p. 56. See also, for the Library and for the financial crisis of the early 1830s, McKitterick, *Cambridge University Library*, pp. 475–86.

114 Darlow and Moule, nos. 1455, 1456, 1458 etc.; for Bagster's understanding of the crucial importance to his business of his stereotype plates, see S. Bagster, *Samuel Bagster of London, 1772–1851; an auto-biography* (1972), pp. 175–6.

115 *Philological Museum*, 1 (1832), Preface. Connop Thirlwall, who edited later numbers of the same journal, expressed himself similarly when writing to Bunsen in 1833: 'I cannot help thinking that we are in great danger of sinking into that state of general confirmed indifference to this branch of knowledge which the revolution and the system of Napoleon have produced in France, where, I believe, a taste for it is generally considered as a kind of fancy not much more respectable than that of a bibliomaniac, and an indication of a somewhat weak head.' (*Letters literary and theological of Connop Thirlwall*, ed. J. J. Stewart Perowne and Louis Stokes (1881), pp. 109–10.)

16 John Parker: London publisher and Cambridge printer

1 *Report from Select Committee on the King's Printer's patents, 1832* (Parliamentary papers, 1831–2, xviii, para. 1524.)

2 J. E. Norton, *A bibliography of the works of Edward Gibbon* (Oxford, 1940), pp. 98–103, 114–18.

3 Samuel Smiles, *A publisher and his friends; memoir and correspondence of the late John Murray*, 2 vols. (1891); Geoffrey Keynes, *William Pickering, publisher; a memoir and a check-list of his publications*, revised edn (1969).

4 For one example, cf. the second edition of Thomas Turton, *The text of the English Bible*, with the imprint: 'Cambridge: Printed, at the Pitt Press, by John Smith, Printer to the University. London: John W. Parker, Cambridge Depository, West Strand. Sold also by Rivingtons, St Paul's Church-yard; Deightons, and Stevenson, Cambridge; and Parker, Oxford. M. DCCC. XXXIII.'

5 Parker to ?the Vice-Chancellor, 16 May 1834: UA Pr.B.3.II(1).

6 UA Pr.v.5, Syndicate minutes, 6 July 1836.

7 Parker to ?the Vice-Chancellor, 6 October 1836: UA Pr.B.3.II(3).

8 *Ibid.*

9 James Twitchett to the Vice-Chancellor and Syndics, 19 October 1836: UA Pr.B.3.I(2). Twitchett, said to have been with the Press for fifty-five years, was (unusually) awarded an annual pension of £65 in 1849: Pr.v.8, Syndicate minutes, 18 May 1849.

10 UA Grace Book Ξ, p. 7; UP 11(244); CUR 33.1(49).

11 Advertisement in *The Publishers' Circular*, July 1843.

12 See, for example, his advertisement in *The Publishers' Circular*, 15 June 1838.

13 See, for example, his advertisement in *The Publishers' Circular*, 16 February 1846. Both Grant and Hall advertised regularly in the *Cambridge University calendar*. For Paley's lasting presence in the under-graduate curriculum see M. M. Garland, *Cambridge before Darwin; the ideal of a liberal education 1800–1860* (Cambridge, 1980), ch. 4.

14 Parker to Whewell, 7 December 1842: Trinity College, MS Add. a.65(29); italics as in the original.

15 Although the account of a proof-reader's room, grimy with cobwebs, the plaster falling off the walls, poorly lit and even more poorly furnished, given by Charles Manby Smith in 1857, is not modelled

on provision at the Pitt Press, his well-known account of the reading boy who assisted him offers a hint of the manner of proceeding. Thus, the boy read his text, interspersing it with instructions as to lay-out etc.:

> "This *ruling passion* two ital par the most enduring of all the passions which obtain a mastery over the mind close is described in Pope's eps thus turns odious in woollen 'twould a saint provoke close were the last words that poor narcissa spoke turns no let a charming chintz and Brussels lace wrap my cold limbs and shade my lifeless face one need not sure be frightful though one's dead and Betty." (Here the reader dips his pen in the ink, and the boy takes the opportunity to blow like a young grampus for a few seconds, and then resumes.) "Give my cheek a little red close turns again I give and I devise close old Euclio said and sighed turns my lands and tenements to Ned close turns again your money sir close turns again my money sir what all why if I must close then wept turns again I give it Paul close turns again the manor sir close turns again the manor hold close he cried turns again not that I cannot part with that close and died pop ep one oct ed p two five three." (*The working man's way in the world* (1857), pp. 288–9.)

In the University Press, further attention than is described here must have been paid on such occasions to details of punctuation and capitalisation. A description of conditions found in readers' closets in London – small, ill-lit and badly ventilated – is given in the sixth report on public health (Parliamentary papers 1864.xxviii, pp. 391–2: evidence drawn from the premises of Hansard, Bradbury, Smith & Elder, Savill, Spottiswoode, H. M. Printers, Kelly, Gilbert, Clay and Cox & Wyman).

16 UA Plans P.xl.1.

17 For the weekly cash accounts, 1837–9 (but with very few employees named) see UA CUP 1/4. CUP 23/9 consists of printed forms, with the names of overseers, 1843–4: the compositors in the charge of Messrs Twitchett and Collings; the machine room in the charge of Collins; and the pressmen in the charge of Purser. A branch of the London Union of Compositors was established at Cambridge by 1836: see Howe, *London compositor*, p. 242.

18 Notes by Thomas George Malcom, deputy printer, UA Pr.B.ix(3).

19 Hansard to ?the Vice-Chancellor, 7 June 1824: UA VC Corr.1.1(4).

20 UA Pr.B.3.ii(3).

21 UA Pr.v.5, Syndicate minutes, 10 March 1837.

22 UA CUP 1/4, 12 July 1839; J. J. Smith, *The Cambridge portfolio*, 2 vols. (1840), 2, p. 478.

23 UA Pr.v.5, Syndicate minutes, 19 February 1841.

24 J. Moran, *Printing presses; history and development from the fifteenth century to modern times* (1973), pp. 116–7.

25 UA Pr.v.8, Syndicate minutes, 7 April 1843, 17 January 1845.

26 In November 1846, the overseers' names were Burrell, Day, Lewis, Mills, Nichols, Pinner, Roschone and Wheaton. At least Burrell, Day, Mills and Wheaton remained in 1854 (UA CUP 27/8).

27 Hansard, *Typographia*, p. 712.

28 Smith, *The Cambridge portfolio* 2, p. 478.

29 Cf. John Murray to Horace Twiss, 11 May 1842: 'The publishing of books at this time involves nothing but loss . . . I have found it absolutely necessary to withdraw from the printers every work that I had in the press.' (Smiles, *A publisher and his friends*, 2, p. 494.) See also Royal A. Gettmann, *A Victorian publisher; a study of the Bentley papers* (Cambridge, 1960), p. 23. For the American depression of 1837–43, and the background to the Copyright Act, 1842, see James J. Barnes, *Authors, publishers and politicians; the quest for an Anglo-American copyright agreement, 1815–1854* (1974).

30 Printed report to the Syndics, dated 23 November 1844.

31 UA Pr.v.8, Syndicate minutes, 6 December 1844, 12 and 15 May 1849.

32 Details of production are taken from UA CUP 27/8, the Machine Room record book, November 1846–July 1854: all production figures are translated into reams here for the sake of clarity, though at the time both reams (i.e. paper used) and impressions (on one side of a sheet) were recorded.

33 The pressmen's scale of 1810 provided for machining of smaller type to be paid at a higher rate: see William Savage, *A dictionary of the art of printing* (1841), pp. 740–2.

34 Hansard, *Typographia*, p. 714.

35 UA Pr.v.8, Syndicate minutes, 2 April 1844.

36 UA Pr.v.8, Syndicate minutes, 13 November 1846, 10 November 1848.

37 *Bibles, Testaments, Books of Common Prayer, and proper lessons, printed at the Cambridge University Press, by John William Parker* (Cambridge, October 1839). A copy of D'Oyly and Mant's edition of the New Testament, marked with corrections authorised by Thomas Turton (then Regius Professor of Divinity and Dean of Peterborough) and others in the 1830s survives in Cambridge University Library, Cam.b.825.2.

38 See also below, p. 343; David Keir, *The house of Collins* (1952), pp. 165–7.

39 The phrase is that of John Childs, in a letter to *The Times*; see his handbill, *The Bible monopoly* (Bungay [1840]), copy in Trinity College, MS O.14.27.

40 Cambridge University Commission, *Report* (1852), Evidence, p. 21.

41 See, for example, the evidence and opinions presented to the committee of enquiry into the King's Printer's patent in Scotland: *Report from the Select Committee to inquire into the nature and extent of the King's Printers' patent (Scotland)*, Parliamentary papers 1837.xiii.

42 A catalogue of Bagster's Bibles and biblical works is printed conveniently at the back of the *London catalogue of books . . . 1831–1855* (1855): apart from publishers' series, his is the only separate publisher's list in this much used trade reference book.

43 Hall also ran a circulating library. For weekly summary accounts of his printing, 1846–9, see Bodleian Library, MS Johnson e.18. Apart from textbooks for a local market, his printers were employed mostly on ephemeral printing for societies, the local parishes, and local government. He seems usually to have employed four men. Pix graduated as 32nd wrangler in 1843, from Emmanuel College, and later became a schoolmaster.

44 UA CUP 17/1*. The artists of the lithographs were A. and H. Schranz.

45 *DNB*, art 'Pashley'.

46 Michael Twyman, 'A directory of London lithographic printers, 1800–1850', *Journal of the Printing Historical Society*, 10 (1974–5), pp. 1–55, at pp. 29–30, with further references. Day and Haghe were paid £82.6s. for the lithographs to Pashley's book (UA CUP 17/1*).

47 *Salopia antiqua, or, an enquiry from personal survey into the 'Druidical', military and other early remains in Shropshire and the north Welsh borders; with observations upon the names of places, and a glossary of words used in the county of Salop* (London: John W. Parker, 1841). The most recent account of Hartshorne is Arnold Hunt, 'A study in bibliomania; Charles Henry Hartshorne and Richard Heber', *The Book Collector*, 42 (1993), pp. 25–43, 185–212.

48 Keynes, *William Pickering*; Ruari McLean, *Victorian book design and colour printing*, revised edn (1972).

49 The Syndics agreed to print the publications of the Parker Society on 29 January 1841: UA Pr.v.5.

50 For Stokes (d. 1847), see William Jones, *The jubilee memorial of the Religious Tract Society* (1850), especially pp. 95–104. Successive prospectuses of the Parker Society are in Trinity College, MSS O.14.26 (24 August 1840) and O.14.27 (31 December 1840; February 1841). The original proposal was that members should subscribe £1 per annum, a thousand such subscriptions being sufficient to provide three volumes, totalling 1,100–1,200 pages a year. In fact, the Society quickly grew to a much larger body.

51 Cf. Peter Sutcliffe, *The Oxford University Press; an informal history* (Oxford, 1978), pp. 8–9.

52 *Ibid.*, p. 9.

53 UA Pr.v.8, Syndics' Minutes, 26 May 1843.

54 Parker Society annual reports, printed at the back of the society's publications.

55 Thirteenth and final report, prefixed to Henry Gough, *A general index to the publications of the Parker Society* (1855).

56 Mark Pattison, *Memoirs* (1885), p. 212.

57 *Ibid.*, pp. 236–7.

58 UA CUP 20/4.

59 'The establishment which they superintend, must necessarily be conducted, to a great extent, on the ordinary principles of trade, and the same reasons which deter a person engaged in business from making public minute details concerning it, seem to the Syndics to show that such a course of proceeding would also be detrimental to the interests of the University Press.' (Richard Okes, Vice-Chancellor, to the Bishop of Chester, 5 March 1852: Evidence, p. 19.)

60 In 1839, none of the largest London printers employed this many journeymen and apprentices. Bradbury & Co. employed a total of 62; Clowes (at two sites), 186; Clay, 40; Gilbert & Co., 86; and Hansard, 100 at their old and new houses, with a further 28 in Paternoster Row: Howe, *London compositor*, pp. 298–302.

61 Cambridge University Commission, *Report* (1852), Evidence, p. 21.

62 Report, p. 36. For the background to the establishment of the Commission, and steps taken to ensure that its members would be sympathetic if critical in their work, see J. W. Clark and T. McK. Hughes, *The life and letters of Adam Sedgwick*, 2 vols. (Cambridge, 1890), 2, pp. 167–87.

63 These figures are taken from the machine room book, UA CUP 27/8.

64 UA U.Ac.2(5).

65 George Peacock, *Observations on the statutes of the University of Cambridge* (1841), p. 139.

66 *Ibid.*, pp. 137–8.

67 *Ibid.*, p. 144.

68 *Report from the Select Committee to inquire into the nature and extent of the King's Printers' patent (Scotland)*, Parliamentary papers 1837.xiii; *Report from Select Committee on Queen's Printer's patents (Scotland)*, Parliamentary papers 1837–8.xxiii.

69 UA Lett.17(22); Roberts, *History*, pp. 136–7. This edition, in a special binding, was exhibited at the Great Exhibition in 1851: see fig. 31.

70 Report by Parker to the Syndics, November 1849: UA Pr.B.3.11(11).

71 Parker to the Syndics, 18 May 1849: UA Pr.B.3.11(8).

72 UA CUR 33.7(79), Report of Syndics; Pr.B.3.11(9), Parker's list of reductions in staff.

73 Francis Bashforth, *Observations on some recent university buildings, together with remarks on the management of the Public Library and Pitt Press* (Cambridge, 1853), p. 32.

74 Robert Potts, *A few brief remarks on the scheme proposed for the future management of the University Press, Cambridge* ([Cambridge], 1854); Sutcliffe, *Oxford University Press*, pp. 6–7; W. R. Ward, *Victorian Oxford* (1965), pp. 151–2.

75 Catalogue at the end of *Euclid's Elements of geometry*, ed. Robert Potts, school edn (1850).

76 *The Bookseller*, 26 February 1860, p. 99.

77 In Cambridge, he relied most on Sibley, whose salary was increased in 1844 to £250 on Parker's recommendation (UA Pr.v.8, Syndicate minutes, 2 April 1844).

78 Parker to Whewell, 6 February 1843: Trinity College, MS Add. a.210(91). But for a list of books published jointly by Parker and Deighton, well after this date, see the advertisements attached to Adam Sedgwick's *Discourse on the studies of the University of Cambridge*, 5th edn (1850).

79 Parker's son, likewise John William Parker, who joined his father in 1843, died in 1860. The business was sold to Longman's in 1863, and Parker himself died on 18 May 1870 (Bowes, 'Biographical notes', p. 331). An obituary of Parker is printed in *The Bookseller*, 1 June 1870.

80 James J. Barnes, *Free trade in books; a study of the London book trade since 1800* (Oxford, 1964), chs. 2–8.

81 Cambridge University Commission, *Report* (1852), Report, pp. 136, 137.

82 Bashforth, *Observations*, p. 32.

83 *Ibid.*, p. 33.

84 UA Pr.v.8, Syndicate minutes, 3 February, 29 March 1854; Pr.B.3.v(32); Syndics' report, 26 May 1854: CUR 33.1(50); Grace Book O, pp. 525, 531; Deeds of partnership: Pr.B.2.10.

85 UA Pr.v.8, Syndicate minutes, 24 July 1854.

86 *The Publishers' Circular*, November 1853.

87 For the scale of 1810, see Savage, *Dictionary*, pp. 736–50.

88 John Murray, *Practical remarks on modern paper* (Edinburgh, 1829), p. 77. The connected problems of demand, shortage of traditional raw materials, and technical shortcomings of paper-making machinery in the face of alternative materials, are examined in a French context in Louis André, *Machines à papier; innovation et transformations de l'industrie papetière en France, 1798–1860* (Paris, 1996), especially ch. 6.

89 W. Whewell to J. Cartmell, 3 August 1854: UA Pr.B.4.1(128).

90 Howe, *London compositor*, pp. 305–6.

91 C. J. Clay to J. Cartmell, 7 October 1854: UA Pr.B.4.1(129).

92 W. W. Bourn (for Parker) to C. J. Clay, 8 August 1854: UA Pr.B.4.1(130).

93 UA Pr.B.3.IV(3).

94 UA CUR 17/1.

95 Damp paper, combined with soft packing on the tympan, and a heavy impression, were common until the end of the century: Howe, *London compositor*, p. 296, who also mentions the experiments of T. L. de Vinne in America, using dry paper in the 1870s. Dry working was desirable on the smoother paper surfaces introduced in the later nineteenth century, but Joseph Gould's much used *The letter-press printer* also spoke of the increasing use of dry paper 'on account of the hurry with which much of the work is wanted and executed not allowing sufficient time for damping' (4th edn, 1888, p. 144).

96 House of Commons, *Report from the Select Committee on the Queen's Printer's patent* (1860), para. 864.

97 Richard Clay to James Cartmell, 16 September 1854: UA Pr.B.3.IV(2).

98 UA Pr.B.3.VII(4,5). His debts amounted to about three times the estimated value of his estate. The business was taken over by George Bell, and became Deighton, Bell & Co.

99 J. C. Hare to Daniel Macmillan, 1 June 1844: T. Hughes, *Memoir of Daniel Macmillan* (1882), p. 161.

100 J. W. Parker to J. Cartmell, 15 November 1854: UA Pr.B.3.II(19).

101 UA Pr.B.3.XIII(1).

102 Sir James Stephen, *Lectures on the history of France*, 2 vols. (1852), I, p. vii.

103 *Ibid.*, p. viii.

17 Enterprise, authors and learning

1 See above, pp. 231–4.

2 Sir G. B. Airy, *Autobiography* (Cambridge, 1896), p. 67.

3 Reading University Library, Parker paper and print ledger 1833–62. The following details of payments by Parker are all taken from this ledger.

4 Some of these are discussed in J. A. Sutherland, *Victorian novelists and publishers* (1976) and Lee Erickson, *The economy of literary form; English literature and the industrialization of publishing, 1800–1850* (Baltimore, 1996).

5 Sutherland, *Victorian novelists and publishers*, pp. 122–4.

6 Reading University Library, Parker paper and print ledger, 1833–62. The third edition (1868) was published by Deighton, Bell.

7 Alexander Macmillan to James MacLehose, 23 June 1860: Alexander Macmillan, *Letters*, ed. George A. Macmillan (1908), p. 53, quoted (without comment) in Charles L. Graves, *Life and letters of Alexander Macmillan* (1910), p. 156.

8 *The Publishers' Circular*, 15 January 1838; a combined catalogue of the more elementary works, and editions of classical authors, was printed in the issue for 15 October 1838, and a more comprehensive list on 15 January 1839.

9 *The Publishers' Circular*, 15 December 1837, p. 93.

10 *Wellesley index*, 2, pp. 303–521.

11 UA CUP 20/4, November and December 1844. Unfortunately, James Foster's invaluable (if slightly incomplete) *Bibliographical catalogue of Macmillan and Co.'s publications from 1843 to 1889* (1891) does not list printers systematically, and provides no details of edition sizes.

12 Parker to the Syndics, 18 May 1849: UA Pr.B.3.II(8).

13 Report by Parker to the Syndics, November 1849: UA Pr.B.3.11(11).

14 *The Publishers' Circular*, 1 February 1847.

15 J. W. Parker to ?the Vice-Chancellor, Richard Okes, Provost of King's, 27 January 1852: UA Pr.B.4.1(47).

16 J. W. Parker to ?the Vice-Chancellor, 17 February 1852: UA Pr.B.4.1(49).

17 *The Publishers' Circular*, 1 February 1853. Parker was J. H. Parker, the Oxford bookseller and publisher.

18 William B. Todd and Ann Bowden, *Tauchnitz international editions in English, 1841–1955; a bibliographical history* (New York, 1988); Simon Nowell-Smith, *International copyright and the publisher in the reign of Queen Victoria* (Oxford, 1968), pp. 41–63.

19 Hansard, 10 April 1845.

20 Hansard, 27 April 1854. Both Goulburn and Horsman were members of Trinity College.

21 J. W. Donaldson, *Classical scholarship and classical learning* (Cambridge: Deighton Bell, 1856), especially pp. 128–47. Donaldson quotes a different version of Horsman's speech.

22 UA Grace Book O, p. 216; McKitterick, *Cambridge University Library*, pp. 543–52.

23 UA Pr.v.8, Syndicate minutes, 26 November, 10 December 1852. A list of works under consideration in 1853, with their current status, is in Pr.B.4.1(112).

24 UA Pr.B.4.1(44): Parker (47) had assumed a fee of £50, but this seems to have been reduced by the Syndics.

25 UA Pr.B.4.1(118).

26 UA Pr.B.4.1(1, 20–42, 109, 110).

27 UA Pr.v.8, Syndicate minutes, 26 October, 9 November 1849.

28 He proposed it in October 1852: UA Pr.B.4.1(107).

29 F. H. Scrivener to the Syndics, 26 April 1852: UA Pr.B.4.1(105).

30 Details from the *Historical register*. Boase, *Modern English biography*, and the *DNB*, record him as 25th wrangler. For his interest in the affairs of the University Press, see below, pp. 362–3.

31 UA CUP 20/4, November 1845.

32 A New York edition of the Euclid was published by Trow in 1876, and the book was still authorised for schools in Canada in the 1880s: a Toronto edition was published by Gage in 1881.

33 UA CUP 27/8, 1850.

34 *Sammlung geometrischer Aufgaben und Lehrsätze*, trans. Hans H. v. Haller (Hannover: Hah'sche Hofbuchhandlung, 1860).

35 William Paley, *A view of the evidences of Christianity, and the Horae Paulinae*, ed. Robert Potts (Cambridge, 1849), p. v. The Previous Examination was the first of two that undergraduates were required to sit before obtaining a degree. In 1849 the hours for the examination were increased from six to fifteen.

36 UA CUP 27/8.

37 Details from *Works by Robert Potts, M. A.*, a handbill inserted in Trinity College, 7.c.85.36.

38 H. A. Holden to J. W. Parker, jr, 24 June 1846: Cambridge University Library, MS Add. 8201.

39 H. Byerly Thomson, *The choice of a profession* (1857), p. 322. This may be compared with a starting salary at this time of £300 for graduate entrants into the Indian Civil Service (W. J. Reader, *Professional men; the rise of professional classes in nineteenth-century England* (1966), p. 92) and an average doctor's income of £500 (Byerley Thomson, p. 169).

40 Stopford Brooke to Alexander Macmillan, 27 September 1871: Simon Nowell-Smith (ed.), *Letters to Macmillan* (1967), pp. 119–20.

41 UA Pr.B.3.XI(4).

42 UA Pr.v.15 (1869–70, 1870–1, 1871–2); Pr.v.8, 15 December 1871.

43 UA Pr.v.15 (1871–2).

44 The detailed costs set out in Charles Babbage, *On the economy of machinery and manufactures* (1832), pp. 166–7, 261–3, for printing, binding etc. of that book indicate a proportion of 1 to 3, excluding advertising.

45 UA Pr.v.6.

46 UA CUP 17/1; Cambridge University Press, *Catalogue* (1952).

47 Matthew Robinson, *Autobiography*, ed. J. E. B. Mayor (Cambridge, 1856), pp. xix–xx.

18 Partnership

1 Cambridge University Commission, 1852, *Report*, p. 136.

2 Sutcliffe, *Oxford University Press*, pp. xxvi, 28; Charles Batey, 'The Oxford partners; some notes on the administration of the University Press, 1780–1881', *JPHS*, 3 (1967), pp. 51–65.

3 Robert Potts, *A few brief remarks on the scheme proposed for the future management of the University Press* (Cambridge, 1854).

4 R. Potts to C. J. Clay, 5 June 1854: UA Pr.B.3.v(38).

5 *The Bookseller*, 26 January 1860, p. 65.

6 UA Pr.B.3.XIII(8). Potts's obstreperous attitude contrasted notably with that of those involved in the Ecclesiastical History Society (not to be confused with the modern society of that name), for which the Press had printed some volumes before it collapsed in 1856, leaving the burden of debt the personal responsibility of the Revd Robert Eden, Vicar of Wymondham. Eden undertook to pay the Society's bill, and to take out a life insurance policy so as to ensure that this would be done. (Pr.B.3.XIII(7).)

7 C. J. Clay to J. Cartmell, 19 October 1857: UA CUR 33.7(91).

8 *The Bookseller*, 26 January 1861, p. 2; an obituary by J. A. Froude appeared in the *Gentleman's Magazine*, n.s. 10 (1861), pp. 221–4.

9 James Moran, *Clays of Bungay* (Bungay, 1978).

10 Richard Clay to John Evans, 15 April 1854: UA Pr.B.3.v(12b).

11 These figures are taken from the *Cambridge University calendar*, 1854. A fuller account, slightly before this time, is in the Cambridge University Commission, *Report*, pp. 71–3. For J. R. Seeley's efforts to supplement his income from the chair of modern history, by lecturing in Scotland and the large towns of northern England, see G. W. Prothero, *art.* 'Seeley', in the *DNB*. The stipend for this chair had declined since earlier in the century.

12 UA CUR 33.1(61); Pr.B.2.10.

13 West House, in West Road. In 1900 his next-door neighbour was the physicist J. J. Thomson. Details from successive local directories.

14 Jennifer Sherwood and Nikolaus Pevsner, *Oxfordshire* (Harmondsworth, 1974), pp. 289–90, 305.

15 Batey, 'The Oxford partners', at pp. 56–7.

16 Report by C. J. Clay, February 1856: UA Pr.B.3.v(66).

17 The cylinder presses were presumably the Middleton double cylinder and the Napier single cylinder identified in the inventory of equipment in 1868. At that time the Press also possessed seven Napier double platens, besides two Brown, two Hopkinson, one Long and one Brooks: UA CUP 33/1. See also Pr.v.8 (Syndicate minutes), Pr.v.9, 24 July 1854, 30 October 1862, 13 October 1863.

18 UA Pr.v.8, Syndicate minutes, 13 October 1863.

19 Report by Sub-syndicate, 23 November 1855: UA Pr.B.3.v(58); CUP 17/1. Large, for Cambridge, as some of these figures were, they were tiny when compared with the extraordinary statistics associated with Cassell's *Illustrated family Bible*, published in parts and by May 1860 reported to be selling 250,000 copies of each part. The numerous wood engravings made it especially appealing, but the secret of its success lay principally in its being sold as a periodical, rather than a book. (*The Bookseller*, 26 May 1860, p. 280.)

20 *Report from the Select Committee on the Queen's Printer's patent* (1860), para. 543.

21 *Ibid.*, para. 554.

22 *Ibid.*, para. 613.

23 UA Pr.v.15 (annual summaries of accounts). Because the headings used in these summaries changed sometimes year by year, it is difficult to discover many consistent comparisons year on year for the Press's printing profits.

24 UA CUP 17/4, pp. 11, 82.

25 UA CUP 18/4, July 1871, February 1872.

26 See, for example, the *American Publishers' Circular and Literary Gazette*, 15 November 1867. When Alexander Macmillan opened a branch in New York in 1869 (see below, p. 398), he promoted Oxford University Press books, since he was by then University Printer.

27 UA Pr.B.3.v(58).

28 Details of printers are based on E. R. Kelly, *The Post Office directory of Cambridgeshire* (1869).

29 T. D. Rogers (ed.), *Sir Frederic Madden at Cambridge* (Cambridge Bibliographical Soc., 1980), pp. 10–11. Madden's printed street ballads are now in Cambridge University Library: most of those printed at Cambridge are in volume nineteen of the collection. See also Philip Ward, *Cambridge street literature* (Cambridge, 1978), pp. 26–9. There were two printers in Cambridge named Sharman in 1838. By 1869, George Sharman had established himself as printer in March (Kelly, *Post Office directory*, p. 174).

30 UA CUP 18/2, May 1861. For some comparable examples in America of books printed from stereotype plates, but naming the wrong printer, cf. Warren S. Tryon and William Charvat (eds.), *The cost books of Ticknor and Fields* (Bibliographical Soc. of America, 1949), p. xxxvi.

31 UA CUP 18/3, October 1865; CUP 17/3, p. 64: the cost was £53.11s.6d.

32 UA CUP 18/3, February 1866; CUP 17/3, p. 97.

33 UA CUP 18/4, 7 December 1870. 2,000 copies were printed of *Tom Brown's schooldays*, 1,500 of *Bible teachings* and 1,500 of Creasy (CUP 17/4, pp. 71, 73, 74).

34 UA CUP 18/4, April 1871: the impressions were of 2,000 and 4,000 respectively.

35 UA CUP 17/4, p. 140; CUP 18/4, November 1871: the impression was of 2,000.

36 UA CUP 17/4, p. 140; CUP 18/4, December 1871: the impression was of 3,000.

37 UA CUP 17/4, p. 79. Hales was editor of Bishop Percy's folio manuscript, and taught English literature and classical composition at King's College School, in the Strand. The beginning of the notes, set at Cambridge, falls midway through a sheet. The first edition, published in 1870, had been designated 'part i', a distinction that the 1872 edition suppressed.

38 *Children's Employment Commission (1862), fifth report* (Parliamentary papers 1866.xxiv), evidence by C. J. Clay, p. 36.

39 UA Pr.B.vi(5); Pr.v.45, 20 July 1858.

40 UA Pr.v.8, Syndicate minutes, 31 October 1868; Pr.v.15, 1867–8.

41 UA Pr.v.8, Syndicate minutes, 25 March 1870, 7 February 1872. Collings had lived virtually on the premises, in the printer's house in Mill Lane.

42 *Census of England and Wales, 1861; population tables* 2 (1863), pp. 221ff. The total population of Cambridge at this time was 26,361.

43 Howe, *London compositor*, p. 310.

44 *Children's Employment Commission (1862), fifth report* (Parliamentary papers 1866.xxiv), evidence by C. J. Clay, p. 36.

45 *Report from the Select Committee on the Queen's Printer's patent* (1860), para. 860.

46 UA Pr.v.45. Glimpses of Clay's life in the rifle volunteers are afforded in Enid Porter, *Victorian Cambridge; Joseph Chater's diaries, 1844–1884* (1975) and in George Scurfield, *A stickful of nonpareil* (Cambridge, 1956).

47 UA CUP 17/3, p. 92. See further below, p. 395.

48 'Yes please read the Shakespeare as you do your bible. We understand that it must be paid somewhat extra.' (Alexander Macmillan to C. J. Clay, 22 June 1864: British Library, MS Add. 55383(1).)

49 The tale of Tischendorf's discovery and subsequent negotiations has been told many times. See, for example, C. von Tischendorf, *Notitia editionis codicis Bibliorum Sinaitici* (Leipzig, 1860), and F. H. Scrivener, *A full collation of the Codex Sinaiticus with the received text of the New Testament* (Cambridge, 1864). Scrivener summarises the gradual discovery and piecing together of the manuscript. See also Bruce M. Metzger, *The text of the New Testament; its transmission, corruption and restoration*, 2nd edn (Oxford, 1968), pp. 42–5.

50 G. W. Prothero, *A memoir of Henry Bradshaw* (1888), pp. 92–9.

51 F. H. Scrivener, *A plain introduction to the criticism of the New Testament* (Cambridge, 1861), advertisement. The Bishop Phillpotts library (founded by Henry Phillpotts, Bishop of Exeter, d. 1869) opened in nearby Truro only in 1871: see Elizabeth B. Bentley and G. E. Bentley jr, 'Bishop Phillpotts Library, the Franke Parker bequest and its extra-illustrated Macklin Bible, 1800', *The Book Collector*, 29 (1980), pp. 363–94.

52 Some of Hort's opinions and dealings with Scrivener are alluded to in A. F. Hort, *Life and letters of Fenton John Anthony Hort*, 2 vols. (1896).

53 Arthur Westcott, *Life and letters of Brooke Foss Westcott*, 2 vols. (1903), I, p. 399.

54 F. H. Scrivener, *A full and exact collation of about twenty Greek manuscripts of the Holy Gospels* (Cambridge, 1853). See Bruce M. Metzger, *The text of the New Testament; its transmission, corruption and restoration* 2nd edn (Oxford, 1968), p. 137.

55 F. H. Scrivener to W. Whewell, 12 September 1853: Trinity College, MS Add. a.212(53).

56 *Ibid.*

57 F. H. Scrivener to the Master and Seniors, Trinity College, 27 September 1856: Trinity College, MS Add. a.212(55).

58 G. W. Kitchin, *Edward Harold Browne, D.D.; a memoir* (1895), p. 167. Browne was incumbent of Kenwyn, just outside Truro.

59 F. H. Scrivener to W. Whewell, 11 October 1856: Trinity College, MS Add. a.212(56).

60 William Kingsley to Joseph Edleston, [October 1856]: Trinity College, MS Add. a.212(61).

61 F. H. Scrivener to W. Whewell, 25 October 1856: Trinity College, MS Add. a.212(58).

62 F. H. Scrivener to W. Whewell, 17 February 1857: Trinity College, MS Add. a.212(59).

63 UA CUP 17/1, p. 150; CUP 17/2, opening 47.

64 F. J. A. H[ort], Review in the *Journal of Classical and Sacred Philology*, 4 (1859), pp. 373–84. For a summary of the scholarly context, see Metzger, *The text of the New Testament*, especially pp. 124–8.

65 Scrivener's annotated copy of the 1864 printing is in Cambridge University Library, Adv.b.94.42.

66 *Codex Bezae Cantabrigiensis*, ed. F. H. Scrivener (Cambridge, 1864). 750 copies were printed: UA CUP 17/2, opening 249.

67 F. H. Scrivener, *A full and exact collation of about twenty Greek manuscripts of the Holy Gospels* (Cambridge, 1853), Introduction.

68 *Notes and Queries*, 1st ser. 8 (1853), pp. 456, 501; 9 (1854), p. 83; 2nd ser. 1 (1856), pp. 37, 104, 160. Helmut Gernsheim, *Incunabula of British photographic literature, 1839–1875* (1984) offers a candidly partial summary of the subject.

69 *Photographic facsimile of the remains of the Epistles of Clement of Rome made from the unique copy preserved in the Codex Alexandrinus*, intro. F. Madden (British Museum, 1856).

70 *Report from the Select Committee on the Queen's Printer's patent* (1860), para. 906.

71 UA Pr.v.8, Syndicate minutes, 15 December 1871; Prothero, *Henry Bradshaw*, pp. 179–80.

72 G. Seeley to ?the Vice-Chancellor, 25 November 1854: UA Pr.B.4.1(119).

73 G. Seeley to C. J. Clay, 29 August 1855; notice of withdrawal, 3 January 1856: UA Pr.B.3.v(50, 64).

74 Hamilton, Adams & Co. to Charles Clay, 19 May, 9 June 1857: UA Pr.B.3.vii(13, 14).

75 UA Pr.v.8, Syndicate minutes, 20 October 1857; *The Bookseller*, 23 March 1858.

76 UA CUR 33.7(100). For details of the Rivingtons, see Septimus Rivington, *The publishing family of Rivington* (1919). They advertised their new position in *The Bookseller*, 30 September 1862.

77 The Bible, prayer book and binding department formerly in Stationers' Hall Court was removed to 3 Waterloo Place: *The Bookseller*, 3 January 1873.

78 *The Bookseller*, 26 January 1860. The difference wrought by the introduction of Scottish editions could be remarkable, and on 26 May 1860 *The Bookseller* remarked (p. 280):

> Messrs. Barritt, who appear to be the Routledges of the Bible trade, and to sell whatever is cheap, and profitable to themselves, and saleable to their customers, send us what, a few years ago, we should have considered a family Bible fit for an earl, but which, in these levelling days, is brought within reach of a journeyman carpenter. It is a demy quarto, printed in Scotland, in good type and on good paper, with references,

family register, and other apparatus, bound in French morocco, with gilt tooling, gilt edges, and protected with massy gilt rims and clasp, the selling price of which is 42s.

79 Advertisement in *The Bookseller*, 1 October 1868.

80 *The Bookseller*, 26 May 1860, p. 280.

81 *Chambers's encyclopaedia*, 10 vols. (1860–8), art. 'Book-trade'.

82 The Cambridge shop was at 19 Trinity Street, between the Blue Boar inn and Matthews the grocers opposite Trinity College.

83 Macmillan inserted a notice in *The Bookseller*, 31 August 1863, announcing that the new arrangements with Oxford would commence on 1 October.

84 *The Bookseller*, 25 July 1859, p. 1073.

85 *The Bookseller*, 31 December 1862, p. 963. The Bible and Learned sides merged in 1906. (Sutcliffe, *Oxford University Press*, p. 117.)

86 *The Bookseller*, 31 July 1863, p. 463.

87 *The Bookseller*, 31 May 1866, p. 475. James Catnach, ballad printer in Seven Dials, London, depended for his very considerable success on the poor and cheap quality of his products.

88 *The Bookseller*, 29 September 1866, p. 783. The name of Baskerville was invoked on other occasions as a means of praise: a report on recent Oxford prayer books in *The Bookseller*, 31 December 1867, remarked on 'a specimen of the Baskerville edition – one of the handsomest volumes yet printed' (p. 1253).

89 *The Bookseller*, 23 April 1858, p. 146.

90 *Correspondence reprinted from* The Times *regarding the new arrangement of the church services* (Cambridge, 1876); *The Bookseller*, 12 December 1871.

91 The early years of public examinations are usefully portrayed in T. D. Acland, *Some account of the origin and objects of the new Oxford examinations*, 2nd edn (1858); see also John Roach, *Public examinations in England, 1850–1900* (Cambridge, 1971).

92 UA Synd. VII.2.

93 Rivington's catalogue, *Books for schools and colleges* (February 1870).

94 See for example the advertisement inserted in the educational number of *The Bookseller*, 1 February 1869, p. 171.

95 *The Boookseller*, 26 January 1860, p. 31.

96 John Seeley, 'Liberal education in universities', in F. W. Farrar (ed.), *Essays on a liberal education* (1867), pp. 145–78, at pp. 146–7; repr. in his *Lectures and essays* (1895), pp. 200–37. See also Deborah Wormell, *Sir John Seeley & the uses of history* (Cambridge, 1980), especially pp. 48–55.

97 He succeeded Charles Kingsley in the chair of Modern History at Cambridge in 1869.

98 Seeley, 'Liberal education in universities', p. 147.

99 Seeley, *Lectures and essays*, p. 200.

100 Wormell, *Sir John Seeley*, p. 52.

101 Henry Sidgwick to H. G. Dakyns, 25 September 1867, quoted in A. S[idgwick] and E. M. S[idgwick], *Henry Sidgwick; a memoir* (1906), p. 170.

102 C. J. Clay to the Vice-Chancellor, 30 January 1866: UA Pr.B.3.v(83).

103 UA Pr.v.8, Syndicate minutes, 21 November 1863.

104 *The Bookseller*, 29 November 1858, p. 547. The last copy of Wilkins's book was sold from stock in 1907. ([R. W. Chapman], *Some account of the Oxford University Press, 1468–1921* (Oxford, 1922), p. 61.)

105 John Chapman, 'The commerce of literature', *Westminster Review*, n.s. 1 (1852), pp. 511–54; John Chapman, *The bookselling system* (1852); John W. Parker (ed.), *The opinions of certain authors on the bookselling question* (1852); *Additional letters on the bookselling question, 1852* (1852); R. D. Altick, *The English common reader* (Chicago, 1963), pp. 304–5; J. J. Barnes, *Free trade in books* (Oxford, 1964), pp. 24–8, 182–7.

106 Hansard, 12 May 1852, adjourned debate on paper duty.

107 *Chambers's encyclopaedia*, art. 'Book-trade', signed by W. C.

108 UA Pr.v.8, Syndicate minutes, 1 July 1870.

109 UA Pr.v.8, Syndicate minutes, 30 October 1862, 12 June 1863 (report to Senate), 30 November 1863, 27 July 1872; CUR 33.7 (105–9); Willis and Clark, 3, p. 144.

110 UA Pr.v.8, Syndicate minutes, 27 July 1872.

111 UA Pr.v.8, Syndicate minutes, 30 November 1863.

112 Cambridge University Commission, *Evidence*, p. 452.

113 *Report*, p. 136.

114 UA Pr.v.8, Syndicate minutes, 1 May, 15 May, 29 June, 9 October 1860.

115 *The Bookseller*, 24 February 1860, p. 100.

116 UA Pr.v.9, 6 November 1854, 16 November 1858.

117 UA Pr.v.45 (Clay's notes), 17 November 1858.

19 Macmillan

1 The following is drawn principally from Thomas Hughes, *Memoir of Daniel Macmillan* (1882) and from Charles Morgan, *The house of Macmillan (1843–1943)* (1943).

2 N. Merrill Distad, *Guessing at truth; the life of Julius Charles Hare (1795–1855)* (Shepherdstown, 1979). A memoir of the two brothers Augustus William and Julius Charles was prefixed to the edition of *Guesses at truth* published by Macmillan in 1866.

3 Daniel Macmillan to J. C. Hare, 7 March 1843: Hughes, *Daniel Macmillan*, p. 146.

4 Daniel Macmillan to J. C. Hare, 24 August 1843: Hughes, *Daniel Macmillan*, p. 148.

5 *The Publishers' Circular*, 16 March 1840.

6 W. H. Smith Ltd. archives, Bowes and Bowes papers 3 (cash account book, October 1843–September 1846). They paid £704.17s.6d. for Newby's business.

7 Hughes, *Daniel Macmillan*, pp. 220–1; Morgan, *House of Macmillan*, p. 29. Stevenson's executors were paid £1,611.5s.7d., plus bills at six, twelve and fifteen months (Bowes and Bowes papers 3).

8 Hughes, *Daniel Macmillan*, p. 221.

9 [James Foster], *A bibliographical catalogue of Macmillan and Co.'s publications from 1843 to 1889* (1891). Although there are some omissions in this list, I have left totals as they are recorded here.

10 J. C. Hare to Daniel Macmillan, 8 March, 1 June 1844: Hughes, *Daniel Macmillan*, pp. 158, 163. For Lumley, see most recently Wallace Kirsop, *Books for colonial readers – the nineteenth-century Australian experience* (Melbourne, 1995), ch. 3.

11 J. C. Hare to Whewell, 21 October 1843: Trinity College, MS Add. a.77(135).

12 Daniel Macmillan to J. C. Hare, 21 June 1844: Hughes, *Daniel Macmillan*, pp. 163–5.

13 *Ibid.* For the local political background, see Michael J. Murphy, *Cambridge newspapers and opinion, 1780–1850* (Cambridge, 1977), pp. 102–5.

14 J. C. Hare to Whewell, 3 December 1841: Trinity College, MS Add.77(131).

15 *Bibliographical catalogue of Macmillan and Co.'s publications from 1843 to 1889*, pp. 102–4.

16 F. D. Maurice to J. C. Hare, 30 September 1840: Frederick Maurice, *The life of Frederick Denison Maurice*, 2 vols. (1884), 1, p. 290; F. D. Maurice, 'Introductory lecture', by the Professor of English Literature and Modern History, King's College, London, *Educational Magazine*, n.s. 2 (1840), pp. 273–88. See also Alan Bacon, 'English literature becomes a university subject: King's College, London as pioneer', *Victorian Studies* (1986), pp. 591–612.

17 Thomas Lund, *An exposure of a recent attempt at book-making in the University of Cambridge* (1858). Lund had a personal interest in Wood's book, since he had revised it in 1845; the fifteenth edition had appeared in 1857.

18 Production figures are taken from UA CUP17/3, 17/4.

19 Advertisement inserted in I. Todhunter, *Spherical trigonometry* (Cambridge, 1859).

20 Morgan, *The house of Macmillan*, p. 30.

21 See, again, the advertisement in Todhunter, *Spherical trigonometry*.

22 Bowes and Bowes papers 2, letters from Macmillan to McQueen. Iain Bain, 'Thomas Ross & Son: copper and steel-plate printers since 1833', *JPHS*, 2 (1966), pp. 3–22; Anthony Dyson, *Pictures to print* (1984). For the few large paper copies printed, pulls on thin paper were pasted onto the title-pages.

23 *The Athenaeum*, 31 January 1852; *Notes and emendations to the text of Shakespeare's plays* (1852); Dewey Ganzel, *Fortune in men's eyes; the career of John Payne Collier* (Oxford, 1982) generally takes a charitable view of Collier. For the Shakespeare Society, founded in 1840, see H. R. Steeves, *Learned societies and English literary scholarship in Great Britain and the United States* (New York, 1913), pp. 144–8.

24 *The Athenaeum*, 21 May 1864, p. 721.

25 See above, p. 372.

26 Annotated proofs of this specimen, and of the Cambridge Shakespeare, are in Trinity College library. Unfortunately, proofs of the Globe Shakespeare seem not to have survived.

27 Alexander Macmillan to James MacLehose, 23 June 1860: Alexander Macmillan, *Letters*, ed. George A. Macmillan (1908), pp. 52–3.

28 UA CUP 17/2, p. 178.

29 Alexander Macmillan to James MacLehose, 28 July 1860: Macmillan, *Letters*, p. 60.

30 Robert Sinker, *Biographical notes on the librarians of Trinity College* (Cambridge Antiquarian Soc., 1897), pp. 75–6.

31 Macmillan & Co. to George Robertson, 15 November 1862: Bowes and Bowes papers 2.

32 UA CUP 18/2, 20 November–3 December 1862.

33 UA CUP 18/2, 3 January 1863.

34 Macmillan & Co. to MacLehose, 15 December 1862: Bowes and Bowes papers 2.

35 *The Bookseller*, 6 December 1862, p. 928.

36 Macmillan & Co. to Burn, 14 March 1863: Bowes and Bowes papers 2.

37 A planned lithograph edition of Blake's *Book of Job*, to have been printed by Vincent Brooks, also figured at this time, but was abandoned (Correspondence with Brooks: Bowes and Bowes papers 2).

38 W. W. Greg, *Catalogue of the books presented by Edward Capell to the library of Trinity College in Cambridge* (Cambridge, 1903).

39 Dyce's rival edition, also in nine volumes, was published by Chapman and Hall in 1863–7: cf. Marvin Spevack, 'James Orchard Halliwell and friends. II. Alexander Dyce. III. Thomas Keightley', *The Library*, 6th ser. 18 (1996), pp. 230–45, at p. 236.

40 *The Bookseller*, 30 September 1864, p. 623.

41 George Gissing, *The private papers of Henry Ryecroft*, Spring, section xii.

42 Gary Taylor, 'General introduction', in Stanley Wells, Gary Taylor, John Jowett and William Montgomery, *William Shakespeare; a textual companion* (Oxford, 1987), at pp. 56–7. Notwithstanding assumptions and allegations to the contrary, the Globe and the Cambridge texts differ – not surprisingly, given the circumstances of editing and publication.

43 Alexander Macmillan to W. A. Wright, 1 June 1864: British Library, MS Add. 55383(1). For the general assumption in the nineteenth-century trade, shared by authors, publishers and printers alike, that proofs were an opportunity not just for correction, but for major alteration and rewriting, see Allan C. Dooley, *Author and printer in Victorian England* (Charlottesville, 1992), ch. 2.

44 Alexander Macmillan to C. J. Clay, 22 June 1864: British Library, MS Add. 55383(1).

45 Alexander Macmillan to W. A. Wright, 25 July 1864: British Library, MS Add. 55383(1). Macmillan's emphasis.

46 Alexander Macmillan to James MacLehose, 24 May 1864: Macmillan, *Letters*, pp. 171–2.

47 Others were cheaper still: John Dicks, the mass-market publisher, offered an edition in 1861 for a shilling: by 1868 this was reported to have sold almost a million copies. (*The Bookseller*, 1 July 1868; William Jaggard, *Shakespeare bibliography* (Stratford-upon-Avon, 1911), p. 535.)

48 Alexander Macmillan to C. J. Clay, 16 October 1864: British Library, MS Add. 55383(2).

49 They were sent on 26 October: British Library, MS Add. 55383(2).

50 Macmillan & Co. to C. J. Clay, 22 October, 12 November 1864: British Library, MS Add. 55383(2).

51 UA CUP 17/3, p. 92.

52 Macmillan & Co. to C. J. Clay, 2 December 1864: British Library, MS Add. 55383(2).

53 UA CUP 17/3, pp. 92, 95, 96, 122, CUP 18/3, 18/4. A duplicate set of plates was prepared in December 1866–January 1867, so that Richard Clay could print a shilling edition, in London (CUP 17/3, p.142).

54 Macmillan & Co. to C. J. Clay, 22 July 1864: British Library, MS Add. 55383(1).

55 The figures are taken from Altick, *The English common reader*, pp. 384–9.

56 UA CUP 15/3, 1864.

57 UA CUP 15/3, 15/4.

58 UA Pr.v.15, 1855–6, 1863–4.

59 UA CUP 18/3, 18 December 1865.

60 UA CUP 18/2, 27 August 1860.

61 UA CUP 18/2, 17 and 21 October 1861.

62 UA CUP 18/2, 16 June, 11 and 20 October, 10 and 22 November 1862.

63 UA CUP 18/4, 15–20 and 31 January 1872.

64 J. R. Seeley, 'The teaching of politics', *Lectures and essays* (1895), p. 319.

65 *Macmillan's Magazine*, 21 (1870), pp. 433–44, repr. in his *Lectures and essays* (1895), pp. 318–48; D. Wormell, *Sir John Seeley and the uses of history* (Cambridge, 1980), pp. 43–7.

66 UA CUP 18/3, 28 June 1865 (Boston), 25 January 1866 (packing cases for Lippincott). In 1865, Roberts Brothers, formerly bookbinders, were building their list: later on they were to publish Louisa M. Alcott (*Little men*; *Little women*) and Susan Coolidge (*What Katy did*). Macmillan's choice of American publisher may have been affected by the presence of Shakespeare in lists of other publishers. Certainly at this time there was no regular connection with an American house, and in 1862 Palgrave's *Golden treasury* had been published in Cambridge (Mass.) by Sever and Francis. The Globe Shakespeare was advertised by Roberts Bros in the *American Literary Gazette and Publishers' Circular*, 15 August 1865 and subsequently at prices from $2.50 to $7.00 depending on the binding. For Roberts Bros see Raymond L. Kilgour, *Messrs Roberts Brothers, publishers* (Ann Arbor, 1952), John Tebbel, *A history of publishing in the United States*, 4 vols. (New York, 1972–81), 2, pp. 429–32 and 3, pp. 277–82, and the house history of Little, Brown and Company, *One hundred and fifty years of publishing, 1837–1987* (Boston, 1987), pp. 57–65.

67 Alexander Macmillan to James Fraser, 29 July 1867: Macmillan, *Letters*, p. 230.

68 Macmillan to R. C. Trench, 29 October 1867, to W. E. Mullins, 30 October 1867, to David Masson, 18 November 1867: Macmillan, *Letters*, pp. 231–3.

69 Macmillan to Goldwin Smith, 30 November 1869: Macmillan, *Letters*, pp. 256–7. For Goldwin Smith, see Elisabeth Wallace, *Goldwin Smith, Victorian liberal* (Toronto, 1957).

70 Cassell had opened in 1860: *The Bookseller*, 26 May 1860, p. 276.

71 *American Literary Gazette and Publishers' Circular*, 1865 (advertisements of British publishers), 16 October 1865 ('English publishers in the American market'), 1 July 1869 (appointment of Brett). Obituaries of Brett were printed in the *Publishers' Weekly*, 14 June 1890, p. 798, and 26 July 1890, p. 135, the latter reprinted from *The Bookseller*. Brett had joined Macmillan only in 1868. He was succeeded at Macmillan's by his son, George P. Brett.

72 *Chambers's encyclopaedia*, 10 vols. (1860–8), art. 'Book-trade'.

73 Bowes and Bowes papers 1; W. J. de Kock and D. W. Krüger (ed.), *Dictionary of South African biography*, 2 (Cape Town, 1972), pp. 352–3; F. Rossouw, *South African printers and publishers, 1795–1925* (Cape Town, 1987), pp. 86–9, both with further references.

74 A. Macmillan to W. P. Wilson, 21 July 1867: Macmillan, *Letters*, p. 228.

75 Macmillan and Co. to George Robertson, 17 May 1860: Bowes and Bowes papers 1.

76 See, for example, letters from Macmillan and Co., 12 July, 15 August etc. 1862: Bowes and Bowes papers 1. For McCoy and his differences with the University of Melbourne, see B. Nairn, G. Serle and R. Ward (ed.), *Australian dictionary of biography*, 5 (Melbourne, 1974), pp. 134–6.

77 Bowes and Bowes papers 1.

78 A. Macmillan to C. B. Clarke, 16 December 1869: Macmillan, *Letters*, p. 258.

79 C. W. Dilke, *Greater Britain; a record of travel in English-speaking countries* (1868), preface.

80 These heads were also to be set on the cases designed for the bound volumes: Macmillan & Co. to George Simpson (Bread Street Hill): Bowes and Bowes papers 1.

81 Newton, Clark and E. Percival Wright, from Dublin, retired almost immediately, and the journal was then edited by Humphry and by William Turner, of Edinburgh.

82 A. Macmillan to the Revd Peter Holmes, Plymouth, 5 June 1860: Bowes and Bowes papers 1.

83 A. Macmillan to James MacLehose, 1867: Charles Graves, *Life and letters of Alexander Macmillan* (1910), p. 275.

84 A. Macmillan to Bartholomew Price, 30 October 1863: Macmillan, *Letters*, p. 158; Sutcliffe, *Oxford University Press*, p. 19.

85 Sutcliffe, *Oxford University Press*, pp. 22–3.

20 Opening in London

1 UA CUR 33.7(112).

2 The work on, and publication of, the Revised Version will be discussed in the next volume. Meanwhile cf. Luther A. Weigle and C. F. D. Moule, 'English versions since 1611', in S. L. Greenslade (ed.), *The Cambridge history of the Bible; the west from the Reformation to the present day* (Cambridge, 1963), pp. 361–82, especially pp. 371–3.

3 See, for example, William Marsh's untitled pamphlet 'For the members of the Studies Syndicate', 1 December 1853.

4 *Historical register*, pp. 703, 737.

5 W. H. Drosier, *The duties of a professor of zoology and comparative anatomy* (Cambridge, 1866); George Cowell, *Life and letters of Edward Byles Cowell* (1904); UA CUR 39.28, CUR 39.29.

6 UA CUR 39.30 (international law), CUR 39.32, O.xiv.7 (fine art), CUR 39.33 (experimental physics).

7 He became the first Professor of Physiology in 1883: see Gerald Geison, *Michael Foster and the Cambridge school of physiology* (Princeton, 1978).

8 H. Latham, *On the establishment in Cambridge of a school of practical science* (Cambridge [1859]); W. J. Beamont, *Fine art as a branch of academic study* (Cambridge, 1863) and *Opinions on fine art as a branch of liberal education and of academic study* (Cambridge, 1864); Henry Yates Thompson, *An Englishman in the American civil war*, ed. Sir C. Chancellor (1971); McKitterick, *Cambridge University Library*, pp. 646–7; H. R. Luard, *Suggestions on . . . the establishment of a historical tripos* (Cambridge, 1866); Jean O. McLachan, 'The origin and early development of the Cambridge historical tripos', *Cambridge Historical Journal*, 9 (1947).

9 *Historical register*, p. 102. The choice of the first Slade professor took a practical turn, in Sir Matthew Digby Wyatt, architect of the recently completed front of the new Addenbrooke's Hospital: see N. Pevsner, *Matthew Digby Wyatt, the first Cambridge Slade Professor of Fine Art* (Cambridge, 1950).

10 Henry Sidgwick to his mother, 21 October 1866: *Henry Sidgwick; a memoir*, p. 153. Cf. S. Rothblatt, *The revolution of the dons; Cambridge and society in Victorian England* (Cambridge, 1981), pp. 152, 169–72.

11 Winstanley, *Later Victorian Cambridge*, pp. 240–3.

12 There were many earlier exceptions to this rule, major and minor, most pervasively in Gonville and Caius College and Trinity Hall: see C. N. L. Brooke, *A history of the University of Cambridge. 4. 1870–1970* (Cambridge, 1993), pp. 104–5. But even in Caius, the prize was still a living, and (until 1860) an end to celibacy: C. N. L. Brooke, *A history of Gonville and Caius College* (Woodbridge, 1985), pp. 160–1, 223–7.

13 The prolonged attempts by Trinity College to be allowed to revise its statutes so as to provide a permanent professional career are discussed in Winstanley, *Later Victorian Cambridge*, pp. 256–61.

INDEX